CZECHOSLOVAKIA

MARY HEIMANN

CZECHOSLOVAKIA
THE STATE THAT FAILED

YALE UNIVERSITY PRESS | NEW HAVEN AND LONDON

For information about this and other Yale University Press publications, please contact:
U.S. Office: sales.press@yale.edu   www.yalebooks.com
Europe Office: sales@yaleup.co.uk   www.yalebooks.co.uk

Set in TT Garamond by IDSUK (DataConnection) Ltd.
Printed in Great Britain by the MPG Books Group

Library of Congress Cataloging-in-Publication Data

Heimann, Mary.
  Czechoslovakia : the state that failed / Mary Heimann.
    p. cm.
  Includes bibliographical references and index.
  ISBN 978-0-300-14147-4 (ci : alk. paper)
1. Czechoslovakia—History—20th century. 2. Czechoslovakia—Politics and government—20th century. 3. Czechoslovakia—History—Autonomy and independence movements.
4. Ethnic relations—Czechoslovakia—History—20th century. 5. Nationalism—Czechoslovakia—History—20th century. I. Title.
  DD901.B78.H465 2009
  943.703 2—dc22

                                                                      2009021977

A catalogue record for this book is available from the British Library.
10 9 8 7 6 5 4 3 2 1

For my son Michael and in memory of my father, John P. Heimann

CONTENTS

ILLUSTRATIONS AND MAPS

Picture section

1. Edvard Beneš at Versailles, 7 May 1919 (reproduced from F.X. Šalda, *Dr. Edvard Beneš ve fotografii*, 1947)
2. President T.G. Masaryk and Foreign Minister Edvard Beneš in the 1920s (Semencov/reproduced from J. Hořec & K. Čapek, *Masaryk ve fotografii*, 1932)
3. Hitler at Prague Castle, 16 March 1939 (De Agostini/Superstock Images)
4. South view of Hodonín labour camp in Moravia, 1942 (Oldřich Kučera/reproduced from C. Nečas, *The Holocaust of Czech Roma*, 1999)
5. Germans waiting to be deported from Prague, May 1945 (Česká tisková kancelář)
6. Hlinka Guard assembling Jews in Michalovce for deportation from Slovakia, (reproduced from E. Mannová (ed.), *A Concise History of Slovakia*, 2000)
7. President Edvard Beneš signing a decree to nationalize industry, 24 October 1945 (reproduced from *Československý státník Klement Gottwald*, 1947)
8. Czechoslovak Communist Party leader Klement Gottwald speaking at the Old Town Square in Prague, 21 February 1948 (reproduced from V. Kopecký, *Klement Gottwald*, 1954)
9. Anniversary of the Slovak National Uprising being celebrated in Zvolen, 29 August 1949 (reproduced from V. Kopecký, *Klement Gottwald*, 1954)
10. Arrested members of the Jozef Tiso government being taken to Bratislava, 29 October 1945 (Jozef Teslík/Tlačová agentúra Slovenskej republiky)
11. Premonstratensian abbot Augustin Machalka testifying at the Czechoslovak State Court in Prague, 31 March 1950 (Česká tisková kancelář)
12. Memorial to President Klement Gottwald in Gottwald Square, Bratislava, 13 October 1982 (Peter Šimončík/Tlačová agentúra Slovenskej republiky)

Maps

ACKNOWLEDGEMENTS

I would like to express my grateful thanks to Hsi-Huey Liang of Vassar College, who first sparked my interest in the history of Czechoslovakia; to the history students at the University of Strathclyde whose enthusiasm and curiosity helped to sustain it; and to Tony Morris, who first suggested a book on the subject.

I am deeply grateful to John Bossy, David Goodall and Robert Pynsent, who read the entire manuscript at various stages and gave me the benefit of extremely detailed and helpful criticisms, often at very short notice; and to Dinos Aristidou, David Green and James Simpson, who offered encouragement and advice at some crucial moments.

I am indebted to the Leverhulme Trust, whose generosity enabled me to spend two years, based in the Czech Republic, researching and writing the first draft of this book; and to the Arts and Humanities Research Council, whose Research Leave scheme enabled me to complete it. My thanks also to Phoebe Clapham, Josh Houston, Candida Brazil and Robert Shore at Yale University Press for their courteous professionalism; and to Peter Biller, Pavla Červená, the Goodall family, Denise Guthrie, Desmond McGhee, David McKee, Josef Švéda, Helena Trnková and Iva Voráčková for various kinds of help, direct and indirect, along the way.

Josef Fronek welcomed me to the Department of Slavonic Languages and Literatures at the University of Glasgow, where I was able to learn Czech from scratch, almost entirely due to the gifted and dedicated teaching of Ilona Klemm (*née* Bílková), who taught me for three consecutive years. My thanks also to the Czech government for awarding me scholarships to Czech-language summer schools run by Charles University in Poděbrady (1999) and in Prague (2000); and by Masaryk University in Brno (2001).

A number of people were generous enough to share their knowledge of Czechoslovak history with me. Robert Pynsent helped me to untangle the Czech and Slovak national revivals; Kirsty Wallace put her collection of sources on the postwar transfer of the Sudeten Germans at my disposal; Scott Skinner gave me permission to use his unpublished interview on the 1989 revolution; Elaine Galway gave me a copy of her MA thesis on the restitution of Catholic church property in the Czech Republic, and Hannah Schling her undergraduate dissertation on anti-Semitic caricature in the Slánský trial. Colin Heaton left me copies of SOE military plans relating to Slovakia and the Protectorate of Bohemia and Moravia; Eva Benda (*née* Blochová) sent me unpublished reminiscences, including her impressions of Prague and wartime experiences as an inmate of Theresienstadt and Auschwitz; Mariana Hovorková (*née* Kloudová) gave me access to unpublished family papers concerning wartime anti-Semitic legislation and postwar political show trials; Květuše Bihellerová (*née* Prášilová) lent me a variety of unpublished family reminiscences of life under the Habsburgs, in the First Republic and under Communism; Petr Míkeš and Phyllis Burch gave me an entire series of *Zemědělské noviny* newspapers found in the attic of their Moravian *chata*; and David Green brought me back various ephemera, including maps and photographs, from Subcarpathian Ruthenia.

Ilona Bílková, Jan Čulík, Jiří Hovorka, Mariana Hovorková, Matúš Minárik, Vít Novotný and Marcela Reslová were kind enough to allow me to interview them formally and at length about their lives in the former Czechoslovakia. Lenka Kapsová and her *Kaktus* seminar group in Prague not only tolerated my rudeness about aspects of Czechoslovak history, but gave me aphorisms about their lives under Normalization and enriched my life by introducing me to that giant of Czech history, Jára Cimrman. Andrea Buchelová helped me with various aspects of specifically Slovak language and history, Eamonn Butler and Zsuzsanna Varga with Hungarian, Tanja Tkachuk (Táňa Tkačuk) and Olena Tonn with Ukrainian, and Jana Špirudová of the Slavonic Institute of the Czech Academy of Sciences (*Slovanský ústav AVČR*) with all sorts of Slavonic linguistic, historical and cultural queries.

A number of scholars and archivists went out of their way to help me with my research. Oldřich Tůma gave me a personal tour of the archives and library at the *Ústav pro soudobé dějiny* (Institute for Contemporary History) in Prague; Jan Kalous of the *Úřad dokumentace a vyšetřování zločinů komunismu* (Office for the Documentation and Investigation of Communist Crimes) introduced me to his colleagues at the Ministry of the Interior, arranged a visit to Pankrác prison and made me a gift of several feet of documents published by his office. Dalibor Státník, archivist at the Ministry of the Interior, was especially generous, uncovering reams of secret-police files as well as supplying me with endless cups of coffee during the eight months I spent working in the StB archives in Prague. I am also grateful to anonymous staff at the *Masarykův ústav* (Masaryk Institute) who helped me to find my way around the Beneš and Masaryk archives; and to those at the *Státní ústřední archiv* (State Central Archive) and National Library (Klementinum) in Prague, and at the *Slovenský národný archív* (Slovak National Archive) and *Univerzita*

Komenského (Comenius University) in Bratislava who helped me to locate a number of less obvious sources.

I owe special thanks to Vít Novotný for his responsiveness to my developing theories about Czechoslovak history, for helping to track down innumerable references, and for enduring my early attempts at speaking Czech; to the late Květuše Bihellerová for her insights, memories and warm hospitality; to Jana Špirudová for her kindness, solidarity and humour; and, above all, to Ewa Darda and Aleksandra Branicka, my first guides to the Czech Republic, for their friendship through thick and thin.

My father, who did not live to see this book published, has nevertheless been an important influence upon it. His fascination with politics and diplomacy helped to form my own; and his empathy and tolerance for humanity are values that – despite, or perhaps because of, its painful history – hold a special place in the Czechoslovak tradition. This book is dedicated to his memory, to the grandson he never met, and to the family and friends he left behind, with my love, gratitude and respect.

SPELLING, TRANSLATION
AND PLACE NAMES

The first problem that any historian of East Central Europe encounters is which language to use when referring to cities and geographical features in the region. This is no simple matter, since official place names have changed many times and remain politically sensitive, and yet English-speaking readers cannot automatically be expected to know that, for example, the Hungarian name Pozsony, the German Pressburg and the Slovak Bratislava all refer to the same place, the city that is now the capital of the Slovak Republic. The system that has been adopted in this book is a compromise between incompatible demands for consistency and historical accuracy; it is not intended to express judgements on the intrinsic value of any particular language or people.

Place names in Czechoslovakia are normally given in their current Czech or Slovak forms unless there already exists a widely used, standard spelling in English, in which case they are given in their common English form. Thus English forms are used for Bohemia (*Čechy, Böhmen*), Moravia (*Morava, Mähren*), Slovakia (*Slovensko*), Prague (*Praha, Prag*), Subcarpathian Ruthenia (*Karpats'ka Ykrajina* or *Ukraïna, Kárpátalja, Podkarpatská Rus*) and Silesia (*Slezsko, Śląsk, Schlesien*); whereas the Czech or Slovak form is preferred for places assumed to be less well known to English-speaking readers such as Hradec Králové (*Königgrätz*) in Bohemia, Turčiansky Svätý Martin (*Turócszentmárton, Sankt Martin*) in Slovakia and Mukačevo (*Mukachevo, Munkács, Munkatsch*) in Subcarpathian Ruthenia. In order to enable the reader easily to skip over alternative spellings of place names, these will be italicized and placed within parentheses.

German place names, where they are likely to be well known by English-speaking readers, are given in parentheses the first few times the less familiar Czech or Slovak name is used, as in the cases of Brno (*Brünn*), Těšín (*Teschen*) or Ústí nad Labem (*Aussig*). The same policy has been adopted for geographical features, as in the cases of the Labe (*Elbe*) and Vltava (*Moldau*) rivers.

When referring to places in Bohemia, Moravia, Silesia, Slovakia (*Felvidék*) or Subcarpathian Ruthenia before the creation of the Czechoslovak state, Czech, Slovak or English forms are given precedence for the sake of consistency; but the first reference to a place will be followed by its alternative Hungarian,

German, Polish or Ukrainian names, given in rough order of contemporary importance. Thus Košice in the Hungarian highlands (Felvidék or Upper Hungary, later renamed Slovakia) will be referred to throughout by its Slovak name, Košice; but the first reference will also include its contemporary Hungarian name, Kassa, and the German alternative, Kaschau; the regional capital of Subcarpathian Ruthenia will normally be referred to by its Czech and Slovak name, Užhorod, but alternative Ukrainian, Hungarian and Russian forms (*Uzhhorod, Ungvár, Uzhgorod*) will be given in parentheses the first time the city is referred to; the region of Silesia will normally be referred to by its familiar English name, but Polish (*Śląsk*), German (*Schlesien*) and Czech (*Slezsko*) forms will be given in italics in parentheses after the first citation, and so on.

Antiquated or alternative spellings of persons and places, when cited from sources, are always reproduced exactly as they appear in the original. In the author's own narrative, however, modern English forms are preferred.

People with Czech, Slovak, German, Ukrainian, Hungarian or Polish names will normally have their name presented in the relevant language, but where anglicized or German versions are so well known to English-speaking readers (as with St Wenceslas or Charles IV) that it would seem pretentious to present them in an unfamiliar form, the familiar English or German forms will be used. This policy will inevitably lead to some inconsistencies: *sv. Václav* and *Václavské náměstí* become, respectively, 'St Wenceslas' and 'Wenceslas Square', but Václav Havel, the former Czechoslovak and Czech president, does not become 'Wenceslas' Havel.

Anglicized forms of Czech and Slovak names, which omit diacritics, are always reproduced exactly as given in citations from, or bibliographical references to, sources and secondary works; otherwise, Czech and Slovak forms, with diacritics, are preferred. This will inevitably lead to inconsistencies, as in the case of Vojtěch Mastný, a Czech émigré who published in English, who will appear in the body of the text with diacritics, but, when listed in notes and the bibliography as a published, English-language author, as 'Vojtech Mastny', without diacritical marks.

Care is taken throughout to distinguish clearly between the terms 'Czech' (in other words, a speaker of the Czech language) and 'Bohemian' (an inhabitant of the region or, sometimes, the Kingdom, of Bohemia). This is not always straightforward, since the Czech and Slovak word *Čech* can mean either 'Czech' or 'Bohemian', and requires the word's meaning to be deduced from the immediate context. To the uninitiated, the distinction may seem pedantic: but to translate the term *Čech* as 'Czech' when it ought to be 'Bohemian' is a mistake equivalent to – and just as liable to cause offence as – describing a native English-speaker from Scotland or Wales as 'English' rather than 'Scottish', 'Welsh' or 'British'.

To the equally politically sensitive question of when, and when not, to include the hyphen in the nouns Czecho-Slovakia/Czechoslovakia and the adjectives Czecho-Slovak/Czechoslovak, the following policy has been adopted. When citing others, the terms are always reproduced exactly as given in the original source or secondary work; in all other cases where it is practical to apply the rule, the terms are given as legally correct during the period under discussion. Thus the hyphenated forms 'Czecho-Slovakia' and 'Czecho-Slovak' will normally be used for the period from 28–30 October 1918 (Czecho-Slovak independence) until 29 February 1920 (when the first full Czechoslovak constitution ruled that the hyphen be dropped); and again from 6 October 1938 (when Slovakia briefly became autonomous and the hyphen was reinserted) until 14 March 1939 (when Slovakia became a separate polity for the duration of the Second World War). At other periods of the state's history, the unhyphenated form 'Czechoslovakia' will usually take precedence.

During the so-called 'hyphen war', which lasted for three weeks (31 March 1990–20 April 1990), the state officially became the 'Czecho-Slovak' Federative Republic in Slovakia but the 'Czechoslovak' Federative Republic in the Lands of the Bohemian Crown (Bohemia, Moravia and Silesia) and abroad. It will not always be practical, when referring to this brief period, to cite the state's name in both variants. Between 20 April 1990 and the final dissolution of the state on 31 December 1992, the country's name formally became the 'Czech and Slovak Federative Republic'. On 1 January 1993, it was split into two independent states: the Czech Republic and the Republic of Slovakia.

In addition to the confusing period of the 'hyphen war', when the state's official name was different in Slovakia, there are two other periods when the correct use of the hyphen is genuinely unclear and discretion has to be used: from 1914 to 1918, before the state had come into existence, but when it was described variously in official documents that sought to establish a greater Czech/Slovak state; and again from 1939 to 1945, when the state – parts of which were incorporated into Hungary, Poland and Germany, some of which became the Protectorate of Bohemia and Moravia, and some the first independent Slovak Republic – did not legally exist. I have tended to favour 'Czecho-Slovakia' in the first case, since this is the spelling found in most official documents written between 28 October 1918 and 29 February 1920; and 'Czechoslovakia' in the second case, since the aim of those who eventually restored the state at the end of the Second World War was to re-create it as it had existed immediately prior to the signing of the Munich Agreement on 30 September 1938.

Subcarpathian Ruthenia (*Podkarpatská Rus, Karpats'ka Ykrajina* or *Ukraïna, Kárpátalja*), a territory that now belongs to the republic of Ukraine, formed

Czechoslovakia's easternmost province from 1920 until 1939, when it declared itself an independent republic, only to be taken over by Hungary within twenty-four hours. It was returned to Czechoslovakia in 1945, but transferred, within weeks, to the Soviet Union. Although terms that refer to the region's situation in the Carpathian mountain range – Podkarpatská, Karpats'ka, Carpathian and the like – are politically neutral, those that refer to the language/ethnicity of a majority of the local population – variously defined as Rusyn, Ukrainian or Russian – are politically loaded. In order to try to avoid prejudicing the reader in favour of one nationalist interpretation or another, the geographically descriptive term 'Subcarpathian Ruthenia' will be given preference over more overtly nationalist names for the region (such as Carpatho-Rus' or Carpatho-Ukraine). When it is necessary to distinguish between local inhabitants of the region (who also included Jews, Hungarians, Gypsies, Romanians and Germans) and speakers of the local Slavonic language or dialect (and who are variously known as Rusyns, Rusnaks, Huculs, Huzuls, Ukrainians or Little Russians), there is no wholly neutral option to choose. In this book, 'Ruthenian' will be used to mean 'inhabitants of Ruthenia', and 'Rusyn/Ukrainian' or 'Ruthene' to refer more specifically to inhabitants of the region who speak the local *patois* which some consider to be 'Ukrainian' and others 'Rusyn'.

After considerable thought and some consultation, it has been decided not to use the currently fashionable term 'Roma' in lieu of the more traditional 'Gypsy' to describe the darker-skinned people or peoples, thought to be of north Indian origin, who settled in the Habsburg territories in about the fourteenth century. Although many Gypsies living in the territories of Bohemia, Moravia, Silesia, Felvidék/Slovakia and Subcarpathian Ruthenia apparently spoke the Romany/Romani language and therefore may properly be described as Roma (as opposed to German-speaking Sinti or other distinct communities of Gypsies), many others appear to have spoken Slovak, Hungarian or Czech as their first or only language, yet were nevertheless classified as 'Gypsies' or *'Romové'* ('Roma'). Since the Gypsies of Central Europe (who have nothing to do with the so-called 'Travellers' of the British Isles) were not itinerant, but were nevertheless discriminated against under all Czecho-Slovak/Czechoslovak regimes, it seems that it was principally because of their physical appearance – not language or lifestyle – that they were set apart. Although the word 'Gypsy', thought by some to carry pejorative overtones, is not entirely satisfactory, at least it has the virtue of being a term that was used throughout the whole of the twentieth century and that hints appropriately at racial – rather than misleadingly at linguistic – difference.

It is assumed that most readers of this book do not speak Czech or Slovak. Wherever possible, readers are therefore referred to English-language translations of Czech or Slovak sources and will be alerted if an English translation appears to differ substantially from the original Czech or Slovak. In cases where no English-language version of a Czech or Slovak work exists in print – as in the case of most printed sources, many histories and virtually all archival materials – translations, unless otherwise indicated, are always the author's own.

GUIDE TO PRONUNCIATION

The diacritical marks (ˇ, ´, °) that make Czech and Slovak look so dauntingly foreign to the native English-speaker are there to enable Slavonic sounds to be expressed concisely in the Roman, rather than the Cyrillic, alphabet. First advocated at the turn of the fifteenth century by the Bohemian religious reformer Jan Hus (John Huss), they circumvent the problem, especially acute in that subset of Indo-European languages known as Slavonic, of having to use two or more Roman letters to convey a single sound. Thus the sound that is expressed in English by the two letters 'sh', or in Polish by the two letters 'sz' (which was also the older Czech spelling), requires only the single letter *š* in modern Czech or Slovak; while the sound represented in modern Polish by the two letters 'cz', or in English by the two letters 'ch', is represented by the single Czech or Slovak letter *č*. The one sound that is supposed, among European languages, to be unique to the Czech language, and is represented by the letter *ř* (as in Dvořák), is closely related to the Polish 'rz' and appears to have been preserved intact from the original Sanskrit.

Czech and Slovak spelling is usually phonetic, and therefore not especially difficult to pronounce, so long as it is understood that the most frequently used diacritical marks, known as the *háček* or 'little hook' (ˇ), the *čárka* ('little line') or acute accent (´) and the *kroužek* or 'little circle' (°), signal a different sound from the same letter without diacritical marks; and that the stress in both Czech and Slovak is almost always placed on the first syllable.

The *háček* (ˇ), like all other diacritical marks used in Czech and Slovak, changes the sound of the letter (or preceding letter) in question. Thus the plain letter 'c' is pronounced like the English 'ts' as in 'i*ts*', but the letter *č* like the English 'ch' as in '*ch*urch'; the letter *s* is pronounced like the English 's' as in '*s*tar', but the letter *š* is pronounced like the English 'sh' as in '*sh*out'; the letter *z* is pronounced like the English 'z' in '*z*ero', but the letter *ž* like 's' in the English pronunciation of 'plea*s*ure', 'mea*s*ure' or 'trea*s*ure'; the unadorned letter *r* is pronounced like a Scottish 'r', but the Czech letter *ř* (which does not exist in Slovak) is pronounced like an 'r' simultaneously trilled with a '*ž*', as in the name Dvořák; *n* is pronounced like the English 'n' as in '*n*ot', but *ň* like the first soft 'n' in 'o*n*ion'.

When used with the letters *d*, *t* and *l*, the *háček* (ˇ) takes on the appearance of a *čárka* (ʹ) and softens the sound. Thus, while *d* is pronounced like the hard 'd' in '*d*en' or '*d*ark', *ď* is pronounced like the soft English 'd' in '*d*ew' or '*d*uty'; *t* is pronounced like the hard 't' in 's*t*ill' or 's*t*ark', but *ť* is softened, as in the English pronunciation of 's*t*ew' or 's*t*eward'; *l* is pronounced like the 'l' in '*l*it' or '*l*ittle', but the Slovak *ľ* (which does not exist in Czech) is softened and pronounced as if immediately followed by the letter 'y', rather as in the pronunciation of the French word *lieu*.

When applied to vowels, the *čárka* (ʹ) and the *kroužek* (°) lengthen the sound. Thus *i* and *y* are both pronounced exactly like the English sound 'i' in '*l*i*t*', whereas *í* and *ý* are pronounced like 'ee' as in 's*ee*d', 'n*ee*d' or 'f*ee*d'. The plain letter *u* is pronounced like the English 'oo' as in 'l*oo*k', but *ů* as in 'l*oo*m' or 'd*oo*m'; *o* like the English 'o' in 'h*o*t' and *ó* like the English 'o' in 'm*o*re' or 'st*o*re'. In Slovak, though not in Czech, the acute accent or *čárka* is also used to change the sound of the consonants 'l' and 'r', lengthening the sound and creating a new syllable, as in the words '*hĺbka*' ('depth') and '*vŕba*' ('willow').

The umlaut (¨) and the circumflex (ˆ), which are used in Slovak but not in Czech, change the sound of vowels. The Slovak *ä* is pronounced just like the German *ä* as in 'M*ä*nner' (somewhere between the short English 'a' as in 'r*a*t' and the short English 'e' as in 'n*e*t'). The Slovak *ô*, a diphthong as in *dôvera* (in Czech, *důvěra*), is pronounced like a short 'u' immediately followed by a short 'o', not unlike the final sounds in the English pronunciation of 'd*uo*'.

In both Czech and Slovak, *ch* represents a single sound (and, indeed, is counted as a separate letter in the alphabet, one that falls between the letters *h* and *i*). It is pronounced exactly like the Scottish pronunciation of the final two letters in the word 'lo*ch*'.

INTRODUCTION

I first seized upon the history of Czechoslovakia as a teaching experiment, a way of getting students to develop their capacities for historical imagination and empathy. I encouraged them to identify themselves with the plight of a relatively obscure Central European country which had little influence in international affairs and had the misfortune to experience military, democratic, Fascist and Communist rule, all within the space of a single person's lifetime. My hope was that taking this angle to twentieth-century history would bring even the most familiar topics (the Versailles Treaty, the Munich Crisis, Nazism, Stalinism, the Cold War, the Prague Spring) to life, presenting them in a fresh way and enabling students to confront the Whiggishness of their own Western, Great Power assumptions.

The experiment proved so fascinating, if only to me, that it led me to put all my other writing and publishing commitments on hold, learn Czech and move to Prague. This book is the product of those years.

The attitudes that I have to Czechoslovak history have changed considerably since I first became gripped by T.G. Masaryk's *The Making of a State*, Jaroslav Hašek's *The Good Soldier Švejk* or Alexander Dubček's 'Socialism with a Human Face'. The Czechoslovakia I imagined when I could only read English-language accounts of it was a country with deeply rooted humane, liberal and democratic values that was twice betrayed: first, in 1938, by its Western allies and again, in 1968, by its eastern neighbours. Nazism and Communism were misfortunes that befell the state, like natural disasters. Czechoslovakia's enemies – most notably 'the Germans' but also 'the Magyars' and 'the Poles' – were shadowy, sinister figures, whose motives were never quite explained; 'the Slovaks' were simple peasants with an even simpler faith; and Ruthenians, Jews and Gypsies more or less invisible.

The present work tells a different story, one in which Czech and Slovak chauvinism is held to have been among the principal causes of the instability that led to the Munich Crisis in 1938; made the persecution of Jews and Gypsies not only possible but energetic; lost the country to Stalinist bigots; and turned it into one of the most hardline states of the Eastern bloc for all but the briefest interlude in the 1960s. Czech and Slovak nationalists, in short, turn out to have been no more immune from the temptations of authoritarianism, bigotry and cruelty than anyone else. The case of Czechoslovakia is not only fascinating in its own right: it shows how nationalism, even in a democratic country, could move seamlessly from democracy through Fascism to Socialism, Communism and back again. Above all, it offers a warning as to how easily a nationalist outlook – together with the perception of belonging to a victim country – can lead perfectly ordinary, decent people from liberal democracy to the police state.

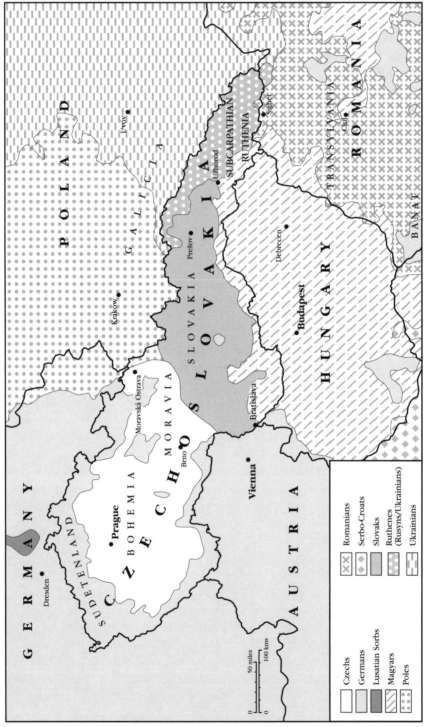

Central Europe: Dominant ethnolinguistic groups, c. 1930

GERMANY
Dresden •

POLAND
• Lvov

G A L I C I A
Kraków •

SUDETENLAND
C Z E C H
B O H E M I A
• Prague

Moravská Ostrava •
M O R A V I A
Brno •

S L O V A K I A
Prešov •
• Užhorod

SUBCARPATHIAN
RUTHENIA

• Sighet

TRANSYLVANIA
R O M A N I A
• Cluj

Bratislava •

Debrecen •

Vienna •
AUSTRIA

H U N G A R Y
• Budapest

BANAT

50 miles
100 kms
0

Czechs
Germans
Lusatian Sorbs
Magyars
Poles

Romanians
Serbo-Croats
Slovaks
Ruthenes
(Rusyns/Ukrainians)
Ukrainians

CHAPTER 1

BEFORE CZECHOSLOVAKIA

Czechoslovakia (*Československo*), a state whose name was occasionally – at times and for reasons that will be explained – spelled Czecho-Slovakia (*Česko-Slovensko*), lasted for just seventy-four years, the span of an average person's lifetime. In these years it was federalized, centralized, dissolved and reconstituted; and went through every kind of political regime, from military dictatorship to parliamentary democracy, and from Nazi colony to Soviet satellite. From its improbable creation at the end of the First World War until its unexpected collapse at the end of 1992, Czechoslovakia was caught up in the most dramatic political crises of the twentieth century. This was a place where it was not only possible, but normal, for a single person to have all the varied experiences of being born a subject of the Habsburg Empire; brought up with the ideals of Wilsonian democracy; come of age under Nazism; joined in the postwar quest for social equality; been indoctrinated with Stalinism; successively re-educated in the ways of reform and neo-conservative Communism; converted to free-market capitalism; and, all along, stubbornly clung to old-fashioned, Romantic nationalism.

Czecho-Slovakia was first declared independent on 28 October 1918, as the First World War was drawing to a close and the Austro-Hungarian Empire was falling apart. Its borders were approved, as part of a broader scheme to rebalance power in Central Europe, by the Victorious Powers who gathered at the Paris (Versailles) Peace Conference in 1919. Territory for the new state was found by joining together five regions of the old Habsburg (Austro-Hungarian) Empire: Bohemia (*Böhmen, Čechy*); Moravia (*Mähren, Morava*); Silesia (*Schlesien, Śląsk, Slezsko*); Subcarpathian Ruthenia (*Kárpátalja, Karpats'ka Ykrajina or Ukraïna, Podkarpatská Rus*); and Upper Hungary or the Hungarian highlands (*Felvidék*), officially renamed Slovakia (*Slovensko*) after the First World War. Of these five territories, three – Bohemia, Moravia and Silesia, collectively known as the 'Bohemian Crown Lands' (a term often mistranslated into English as the 'Czech' Lands)[1] – had been Austrian (Cisleithanian) possessions.[2] The other two territories – Felvidék or Upper Hungary (afterwards known as Slovakia) and Subcarpathian Ruthenia – had belonged to the Kingdom of Hungary.[3]

The creation of Czecho-Slovakia/Czechoslovakia did more than simply bring together five separate territories from two distinct political traditions. It altered the balance of power among the various ethnolinguistic groups or peoples ('nations' in Central European parlance) who had lived in the same place for generations, but unexpectedly found themselves in a new state that accorded them different status. Czecho-Slovakia was named for just two peoples – the Czechs of the Bohemian Crown Lands and the Slovaks of Upper Hungary – but could boast a good six nationalities (eight, if one includes Gypsies as a distinct category and counts Czechs and Slovaks – whose languages are mutually intelligible – separately rather than as members of a single 'Czechoslovak' nation). Although this was considerably fewer than the eleven 'nationalities' whose languages had been officially recognized in the old Austro-Hungarian Empire, it was quite enough distinct 'nations' or peoples to complicate matters for a state that claimed its right to exist partly on the grounds of 'national self-determination' for the 'Czecho-Slovaks' (but not the other 'nations') and partly on the historical rights of the Bohemian Crown Lands (which were nearly two-thirds Czech, a third German, and included a tiny Polish region). The problem of 'national' coexistence was further aggravated by the fact that members of the German, Hungarian, Polish and Rusyn/Ukrainian ethnolinguistic groups who found themselves classified as 'minorities' in the Czecho-Slovak/Czechoslovak state lived for the most part in relatively compact and well-defined areas, characteristically along a border dividing them from people who spoke the same language.

None of this need necessarily have mattered. Belgium, for all its internal tensions and the arbitrariness of its own borders, emerged from the twentieth century in one piece, albeit divided into mutually hostile German, as well as Walloon and Flemish, sections; Switzerland, with its mixed German, French and Italian populations, managed not only to hold together, but even to keep out of two world wars. Like these other peoples with historical experience of the Habsburg way of doing things, the Czechs, Germans and Poles of the Bohemian Crown Lands and the Slovaks, Magyars and Rusyns/Ukrainians of Upper Hungary might have learned to tolerate – if not necessarily to like – one other, acknowledging the benefits of bilingualism or trilingualism and embracing the richness of their multicultural heritage. Instead, intransigent nationalist polemic became so deeply entrenched on all sides that it came to seem perfectly natural to millions of ordinary Czechs, Slovaks, Germans, Magyars, Poles, Rusyns and Ukrainians not only to view their own ethnolinguistic group as an exclusive and mystical entity known as the 'nation', but also as the only 'nation' in the immediate vicinity to be deserving of the benefits of statehood.

Classic histories of what are misleadingly referred to as 'the Czech Lands' or 'Slovakia' (neither of which were familiar concepts before the nineteenth

century) invariably begin with fragments of pottery, coins and other archaeo-
logical remains that purport to trace the origins of the relevant 'nation' to the
primordial mud. The struggles of medieval monarchs to establish, extend or
keep their kingdoms are portrayed as the 'rise' of the nation's first state. The
Hussite rebellions of the fifteenth century, the Reformation of the sixteenth
century, and the Counter-Reformation of the seventeenth century, anachro-
nistically emptied of contemporary religious meaning, become stories about
the nation's 'struggle' to free itself from foreign domination and oppression.
The Czech-speaking Bohemian priest and activist Jan Hus (John Huss),
presented as a sort of Martin Luther, becomes the chief symbol of Czech
resoluteness and independence; while the Taborite (radical Hussite) Jan Žižka,
a kind of Oliver Cromwell figure, is cast in the role of proto-nationalist and
primitive socialist. Crucially, the defeat of the Bohemian estates at the Battle
of the White Mountain (*Bílá hora*) on 8 November 1620 – which resulted in
the flight of the Bohemian Protestant nobility, the re-Catholicization of the
Bohemian Crown Lands, and the loss of the Kingdom of Bohemia's rights as
a semi-independent state – is treated not as a Protestant, but rather a 'national',
defeat: the Czech Culloden.

After centuries of alternating between national triumph and national
calamity, the emancipation of the peasants – together with the integration
or expulsion of the Jews – in the late eighteenth century, and especially the
'rediscovery' of languages spoken by the common people, are presented
as offering new rays of hope. The final chapter, which takes place in the
nineteenth and twentieth centuries, unfolds as a narrative of the 'awakening'
of national consciousness and the flowering of national culture, followed by
'struggle' and finally 'emancipation'. The crowning achievement, an internationally recognized nation-state, comes last: but can be dated from 1918, 1939
or 1993, depending upon whether the first genuine state is considered to
have been post-Versailles Czechoslovakia, post-Munich Slovakia or the post-
Communist Czech and Slovak republics.

This deeply felt – and thoroughly politicized – understanding of the past,
which continues to be affirmed and reaffirmed in countless school textbooks,
political speeches, pamphlets, histories, television programmes, newspaper
articles and museum exhibitions, is no doubt reassuring and even inspiring to
many members of the 'nations' it seeks to exalt. Nor are its tone and message
exactly unfamiliar to those raised on accounts of the 'rise of democracy'
in the Anglo-Saxon tradition, although now long discredited in the West as
'Whiggish'. But whatever the power of modern national myths to create
or sustain a sense of communal worth and national destiny, they offer propaganda, not history. As a new generation of scholarship on the Bohemian
Crown Lands is beginning to make clear, there was never anything particularly natural or self-evident about how national identity in the region came

to be defined primarily through language.[4] Yet the late nineteenth-century convention – which only hardened throughout the course of the twentieth century – came not only to be widely accepted, but to be both resilient and self-perpetuating. Indeed, it persists in most popular and even scholarly accounts right up to the present day.

It was not language so much as religious difference that first marked out rival communities in the territories of the medieval kingdoms of Bohemia and Hungary. But although one stream of modern Czech nationalism – the one that happened to dominate Czechoslovak political discourse in the twentieth century – came to lampoon Catholicism as a tool of Habsburg oppression and liked to pretend that Czechs, as representatives of 'the nation of Hus', had always been innately 'Protestant' and 'progressive' in their instinctive egalitarianism and anticlericalism, this was not the only possible, let alone the most plausible, reading of Czech history.[5] While it made intuitive sense to French anticlericals, was easily adapted by Czech socialists and Communists, and fitted in neatly with parallel English and American foundation myths (Wycliff as the 'morning-star of the English Reformation', the Pilgrims as America's 'founding fathers'), it ignored such inconvenient facts as the active participation of Czechs on both sides of the Hussite wars (which in any case predated Protestantism) and the promotion – rather than suppression – of Czech national identity by a series of 'enlightened' Habsburg rulers. It thus failed to account for the (at least nominal) Catholicism of the overwhelming majority of Czech speakers – Bohemians and Silesians as well as more traditionalist Moravians – together with the loyalty that most showed to the Habsburg Empire right up to its dissolution.

The equivalent national 'awakeners' and 'defenders' of the Slav language eventually dubbed 'Slovak' were usually Lutherans conscious of their historic links with neighbouring Bohemian/Moravian Czech Protestant traditions. There also existed a rival, but less successful, Catholic Slovak nationalist strand, one which lost out to broadly Protestant or anticlerical conceptions of a 'Czecho-Slovak' nation for most (though not all) of the life of the Czechoslovak state. The number of 'nationally conscious' (in other words, anti-Hungarian) Slovaks on the scene before Czecho-Slovak independence, whether Protestant or Catholic, could in any case be counted on the fingers of one hand.[6] As even the most superficial knowledge of the region – with its ubiquitous Catholic Baroque architecture, overwhelmingly Catholic Czech majority, important Lutheran Slovak minority, distinctly Greek Catholic contingent and significant Czech, Hungarian, Slovak and German Jewish populations – makes clear, the political and religious history of both the Bohemian and Hungarian kingdoms was far more complicated than simplistic nationalist myths of the twentieth century – whether Czech, German, Slovak, Ruthenian, Ukrainian or Hungarian – would suggest.

According to the way in which 'nationality' was defined in the latter years of the Habsburg Empire and continued to be understood in Czecho-Slovakia/ Czechoslovakia, the largest 'nation' in the state was the 'Czech nation', made up of some six million Bohemians, Moravians and Silesians who, when required in census returns to identify themselves with just one language, claimed Czech rather than German to be their principal language ('language of daily use' or 'maternal language').[7] This put Czechs in a two-thirds majority in Bohemia and Moravia (and so in the Bohemian Crown Lands as a whole) but left them in the minority in Silesia, where the majority claimed Polish, a minority German and only a handful Czech as their main language.

The second largest 'national' group was made up of self-declared Germans (which included German-speaking Jews), roughly two and a half million of whom had for centuries been settled along the periphery of Bohemia and Moravia (in an area that – after the map of Europe was redrawn at Versailles in 1919 – bordered on Germany and Austria; this was the horseshoe-shaped territory that, in the 1930s, came to be widely known as the 'Sudetenland'). Several hundred thousand more German speakers could be found inland, scattered across the remainder of the state in so-called 'language islands', including in the city of Brünn/Brno (the provincial capital of Moravia) and the town of Pressburg/Prešporok (which, despite being populated mainly by German- and Hungarian-speakers, was in 1919 made the regional capital of Slovakia and given the Slavonic-sounding name of 'Bratislava'). Of the regional capitals, only Prague – which from 1918 doubled as the capital of the state as well as the regional capital of Bohemia – was overwhelmingly Czech. By far the largest city in the new state, it could also boast considerable political and administrative experience.

In third place in the state as a whole (but first in the newly created region of Slovakia) came the Slovak-speakers of the Hungarian highlands, approximately two and a half million of whom dominated what were now considered to form western, northern and central Slovakia. Eastern Slovakia, together with the whole length of the southern Slovak border with Hungary, was home to the next-largest nationality: more than half a million Hungarian-speakers (also known as Magyars), including Hungarian-speaking Jews. In the province of Subcarpathian Ruthenia, and spilling over the regional frontier into eastern Slovakia, lived some 120,000 speakers of a local dialect that was variously defined as Rusyn, Russian or Ukrainian, and whose Christian members were characteristically Greek Catholic (Uniate) in religion (although they might also be Roman Catholic or Russian Orthodox).[8] There were also perhaps as many as 100,000 people living in the territory who identified themselves primarily as Jews (mainly Hassidic or Orthodox, as opposed to the characteristically reform Jews of Bohemia and Moravia), who might speak Hebrew, Yiddish, Hungarian, German, Ruthenian/Ukrainian or

Slovak. The eastern, formerly Hungarian half of the state was also home to most of the 100,000 or more racially distinct Gypsies who lived in Czechoslovakia, only some of whom spoke Romany and can therefore accurately be described as *Roma*; the rest spoke local languages. Finally, about 100,000 Polish-speakers (or, more accurately, speakers of a dialect that was judged to fall somewhere between Czech and Polish) were concentrated in Czech Silesia and in northern Slovakia, along an especially hotly contested border with Poland.

Of the five regions that made up the twentieth-century Czecho-Slovak/Czechoslovak state, it was the three previously Austrian (Cisleithanian) territories of Bohemia, Moravia and Silesia – collectively known as the Bohemian Crown Lands – that had the strongest claims to be considered a discrete political and administrative – although not linguistically homogeneous – unit. Bohemia (*Čechy*) itself, an area of about 52,052 sq km (20,097 sq miles) that forms the western half of today's Czech Republic, had first emerged as a coherent political entity at the end of the tenth century, under the leadership of a dynasty of Czech-speaking princes or dukes known as the Přemyslids, who ruled from the early ninth century until the beginning of the fourteenth century. At the turn of the eleventh century, when Bohemian, Magyar, German and Polish lands across Central Europe were all solidifying into separate monarchies, each with its own distinctive dynastic house, core territory and patron saint, it was the Crown of Václav (St Wenceslas, mistakenly remembered as Good *King* Wenceslas in the Victorian Christmas carol) which was stamped on coins as the principal symbol of Bohemian statehood, just as the Crown of István (St Stephen) was being stamped on Hungarian ones.

In the eleventh century, the Czech Přemyslids, by then in possession of the whole of Bohemia, went on to conquer Moravia (*Morava*), an area of about 26,800 sq km (10,347 sq miles) immediately to the east of Bohemia, which was thereafter usually considered to form an indissoluble part of Bohemian dynastic territory. Moravia nevertheless remained a distinct political unit, a margravate, which was normally ruled by sons of the rulers of Bohemia. Silesia (*Slezsko*), a territory that is today divided between Poland and the Czech Republic, and whose Czech portion covers just 4,452 sq km (1,719 sq miles), became part of the Polish lands in the eleventh century, but was gradually absorbed into the lands of the Crown of St Wenceslas over the course of the fourteenth century. Most of the Silesian duchies were taken over by Prussia in 1741–42; the fragment that remained under Habsburg control (Austrian Silesia) continued to be included in the 'indissoluble' Bohemian Crown Lands and so eventually fell to Czecho-Slovakia.

In the fourteenth century, the Lands of the Bohemian Crown (the Crown of St Wenceslas) passed from the Czech Přemyslid to the German Luxembourg dynasty. This brought Bohemia, Moravia and Silesia into the Holy Roman

Empire, giving rise to later German nationalist claims that the territory belonged by right to the German Empire or Reich; but also – particularly after Prague was twice chosen to be the imperial capital – gave the Kingdom of Bohemia new importance and significance as a distinct entity. Especially under Holy Roman Emperor Charles IV (Karl IV) of Luxembourg – who was also king of Bohemia – a large number of foreigners were brought into Prague, where Czech and German, alongside Latin, were decreed to be official languages. Charles IV also established a university (1348), based on the model of Paris, at Prague and transformed the royal castle (*hrad*) into a seat of imperial splendour overlooking Prague's New Town, Old Town and Lesser Town. The *Hrad* (Castle), as the labyrinthine collection of Baroque palaces, offices, residential quarters and reception rooms that cover Hradčany (*Hradschin*) hill continues to be known, was to remain the official residence of all rulers of Bohemia – and, by extension, of all subsequent Czech and Czecho-Slovak/Czechoslovak states – right up to the present day.

Czechoslovakia's Hungarian territories had a separate formation and history from that of the Bohemian Crown Lands. The territory that was named 'Slovakia' (*Slovensko*) after the First World War, and that makes up today's Slovak Republic, consists of an area of about 49,000 sq km (18,920 sq miles) bounded by the River Morava to the west, the River Tisza to the east, the Tatra Mountains to the north, and the middle Danube to the south. In the ninth century, before the territory fell to a series of Magyar princes, its western part belonged to the Greater Moravian Empire, which was Christianized (in the Eastern rite) by two missionaries sent from Byzantium in about the year 863, SS. Cyril (Constantine) and Methodius, who developed a special alphabet – the ancestor of modern Cyrillic – in order to catechize the indigenous Slavs.[9]

Slovak nationalists in the late nineteenth and twentieth centuries liked to claim descent from the remote 'Slav' and 'Christian' state of Greater Moravia for two reasons. It enabled them rhetorically to treat the thousand years during which Slovak-speakers were ruled by Magyar or Hungarian princes as in effect a millennium of unwanted colonial rule; and it allowed Catholic, as well as Protestant, nationalists to insist that their Christian faith and Slav tongue were two sides of the same Slovak nationalist coin. Twentieth-century Slovak nationalist appeals to the ninth-century 'Kingdom of Samo' or the 'holy bishopric of Nitra' notwithstanding, from the late eleventh century until the creation of Czecho-Slovakia in the early twentieth century, the territory later known as 'Slovakia', although home to speakers of a Slav language with a close family resemblance to Czech, was neither politically nor geographically differentiated from the rest of the Kingdom of Hungary. It was simply Felvidék (Upper Hungary or the Hungarian highlands), an integral part of the Lands of the Crown of St Stephen or core of the Kingdom of Hungary (just as the Lands of the Crown of St Wenceslas were later claimed to constitute the core of the Kingdom of Bohemia).

Subcarpathian Ruthenia (*Podkarpatská Rus*), the other territory that the Czecho-Slovak/Czechoslovak state acquired from Hungary, consists of an area of about 12,694 sq km (4,900 sq miles) situated immediately to the east of Slovakia, on the south-western slopes of the Carpathian Mountains. The region, which today belongs to independent Ukraine, has variously – and confusingly – been called everything from 'Ruthenia', 'Rus' and 'Rusinia' to 'Transcarpathia', 'Transcarpathian Ukraine', 'Carpatho-Ukraine', 'Carpatho-Ruthenia', 'Carpatho-Russia', 'Subcarpathian Russia' and 'Subcarpathian Rus'. The variety of names reflects the inability of the region's nationalist leaders to have the Slavonic language spoken by locals decisively and permanently categorized as either a distinctly 'Rusyn' language or as a dialect of either Ukrainian or Russian, a fact that – as will be seen – was to have serious political consequences for people living in the territory, particularly since Rusyns/Ukrainians shared their land with significant communities (Jews, Magyars, Germans) who were not Slavs (i.e. speakers of a Slavonic language).

Over the course of the twelfth, thirteenth and fourteenth centuries, large numbers of German-speaking settlers were invited to both the Bohemian and Hungarian Crown Lands as skilled craftsmen and farmers, in special arrangements that accorded them substantial legal and economic autonomy, together with other privileges. This selective immigration policy led to the sprinkling of settled communities of German-speakers across all five regions of the future Czechoslovak state, leaving it vulnerable to further claims by German nationalists that it naturally belonged to a greater German sphere, and to arguments by Czech nationalists that, since 'the Germans' had come as 'colonists', they had no moral claim to the land. The other two notable groups to settle in the territory were religiously (and sometimes linguistically) distinct: Jews, first recorded as living in Prague in the tenth century and in the Kingdom of Hungary from the twelfth century, and the people now usually referred to as Roma (*Romové*, dark-skinned, originally Romany-speaking Gypsies), who are thought to have originated in northern India and to have come to Central Europe, probably in the fourteenth century, by way of the Middle East.[10]

The fates of the Bohemian and Hungarian kingdoms became intertwined after the Battle of Mohács (1526), at which Hungary was defeated by the Ottomans and Bohemia simultaneously lost its absentee king. The Hungarian kingdom was partitioned into three parts: the central Hungarian plain, which was placed under direct Ottoman rule; Transylvania, which was left for the time being as a semi-independent vassal state; and the western and northern areas, roughly coinciding with the territory of modern Slovakia, which fell, as the rump kingdom of 'Royal Hungary', to the Habsburg emperor Ferdinand

I. Since Buda had been captured by the Ottomans, the city of Pozsony (*Pressburg, Prešporok*) became, for the next 175 years, the temporary capital of 'Royal Hungary', the place where Hungarian kings were crowned and the principal government offices housed. It was this historical accident, together with its strategic position on the other side of the Danube from Vienna, which centuries later made the city (renamed 'Bratislava' in February 1919) seem an appropriate place to locate the regional (later, national) capital of Slovakia.

In exchange for promises of religious toleration, the Bohemian diet followed the Hungarian in electing Ferdinand I as its king. This linked the kingdoms of Bohemia (including its Moravian and Silesian possessions) and Royal Hungary (comprising most of the territory of the future Slovakia and Subcarpathian Ruthenia) under the rule of a single Habsburg monarch. The first decades of Habsburg rule were immediately complicated by the divisive effect of Reformation thought. It was Calvinism that attracted most Magyar nobles, and therefore made inroads into the Hungarian countryside (including among Slovak peasants), but Lutheranism that spread first to the predominantly German-speaking towns (and so to a proportion of Slovak, Czech and Magyar burghers).

After the Bohemian estates joined with German Protestants in the Schmalkaldic League in an abortive attempt to overthrow their king and emperor, Ferdinand I persecuted the Czech Protestant sect known as the Bohemian Brethren ('Unity of the Brethren' or *Unitas Fratrum*; in Czech, *Jednota bratrská*), who had been prominent in the uprising. Some fled to Moravia, where they published an official hymnbook (1561) and a six-volume edition of the Bible, with commentary, in the Czech vernacular, the Kralice Bible (*Kralická bible*, completed in 1588), which was to become the standard version known to Slav/Slovak-speaking Hungarian Protestants as well as to Czech-speaking Bohemian, Moravian and Silesian Protestants.[11] This preserved the closeness of Czech with today's Slovak, leaving the two languages, although distinct in certain aspects of grammar, syntax and vocabulary, so close as to be mutually intelligible. Ultimately, this was to pave the way for some nineteenth- and twentieth-century Slav nationalists to claim that 'Czecho-Slovaks' spoke a single language, and so formed a single people or 'nation'.

In 1707, the long partition of Hungary came to an end with the 'liberation' of Transylvania from the Ottomans. Instead of gratefully swearing fealty to the Habsburg emperor, the local Hungarian nobility made a bid for independence under the leadership of the Transylvanian prince Ferenc Rákóczi II. Since Rákóczi declared that peasants who supported his struggle for 'the Hungarian people' would be freed from many of their duties as serfs, his armies were largely made up of Slovak and Rusyn mercenaries. Hungarian nobles led by Sándor Károlyi eventually deserted Rákóczi in favour of the terms offered by the Habsburgs in the Peace of Szatmár (1711), which guaranteed the Kingdom of Hungary its traditional privileges and customs in exchange for recognition of the Habsburg monarch as king of Hungary. Rebel peasants were returned to serfdom; one of the most notorious, the bandit Juraj Jánošík (executed in 1713), afterwards became a Slovak folk hero, a kind of Robin Hood. Those Rusyn peasants who could escaped, emptying the region of its labourers. Later, peasants from Galicia – mostly Jews and Rusyns – were offered favourable terms to repopulate the region. This left rival Roman and Greek Catholic, Orthodox and Hassidic Jewish populations scattered across the territory of Subcarpathian Ruthenia.[12]

In the late eighteenth century, gentlemanly attachment to the province (what is called *zemský patriotismus* in Czech and *Landespatriotismus* in German, literally 'land patriotism') characteristically expressed itself in the Habsburg territories through the formation of learned societies whose aim was to accumulate systematic knowledge of the *patria*, recording and classifying all possible data relating to the territory, from its flora and fauna to its artefacts, manuscripts and architectural ruins. It was this impulse that led to the establishment of such institutions as Prague's Museum of the Bohemian Kingdom (1818–29), which was only much later provocatively recast as a 'national' museum.[13] Characteristically Enlightened attempts to chronicle, classify and chart regional dialects as local curiosities provided one impulse to codify peasant languages; another came from the Church's duty to ensure that catechetical and devotional works were accessible to everyone across a vast, multilingual empire.

A first attempt to come up with a standard, literary form of what was then usually still called the 'Slav' rather than the 'Slovak' language was put forward in Hungary in 1787 by Catholic priest Fr Anton Bernolák and further promoted in his *Grammatica Slavica* (1790) and Slav/Slovak-Czech-Latin-German-Hungarian dictionary (1825–27). This *bernoláčtina* or 'Bernolák-ese', based on a western dialect, was championed mainly by Catholic seminarians based at the Hungarian university in Trnava (*Nagyszombat, Tyrnau*) in today's western Slovakia. In Austria, Czech was given an equivalent boost by Catholic scholars such as Gelasius Dobner (1719–90) and Václav Fortunát Durych (1735–1802), the Pauline monk who was commissioned by Empress Maria Theresa to bring out a new Czech translation (1780) of the Bible. The Hungarian-born priest now known as Josef Dobrovský (but who then spelled himself Joseph Dobrowsky) built on the work of these scholars, pioneering what was to become the field of Slavonic (Slavic-language) studies by contributing *Geschichte der böhmischen Sprache und Literatur* (A History of Czech Language and Literature; 1791–92), *Ausführliches Lehrgebäude* (A Detailed Grammar of the Czech Language) and a two-volume Czech–German dictionary. When Dobrovský made the case to Leopold II (1791) for the establishment of a first chair of Czech Language and Literature at the

University of Prague, where German was replacing Latin as the language of instruction, he did so mainly on the pragmatic grounds that Enlightened gentlemen – whether priests or administrators – ought to be able to communicate in all languages that were spoken in the empire. The first professor of Czech, Franz/František Pelzel or Pelcl, was duly appointed in 1793.

The first wave of Romantic nationalism to affect the Habsburg Empire, conventionally dated from about 1790 to 1820, is remembered in the Czech and Slovak nationalist traditions as the 'National Awakening' (*národní obrození* in Czech and *národné obrodenie* in Slovak).[14] It began when a proportion of German-speakers living in the territories of what are now Germany, Austria, Hungary and the Czech and Slovak Republics, inspired by the French Revolution, first put forward the pan-German notion that speakers of German, regardless of which state they happened to belong to, were mystically united, through their shared language, as a single 'nation' or 'people'. In order to combat this dangerous notion, the Habsburg court in Vienna, although itself reliant on German as the empire's unofficial *lingua franca*, increasingly stressed the notion of the Habsburg Empire as 'Austrian', in other words a melting pot of various nationalities, languages and religions, rather than a branch of a greater German 'nation'. It was correspondingly eager not only to protect, but actively to promote, other languages spoken in the empire.

'Hungarian' identity, which had for nine centuries been based upon feudal ties to the Lands of the Crown of St Stephen, theoretically included not only Magyars (Hungarian-speakers), who dominated the aristocracy and therefore political institutions, but also speakers of the other languages spoken in the Kingdom of Hungary. Now scholarship, inspired by the latest political thinking, purported to demonstrate the coherence of a Magyar 'people' or 'nation' as evidenced through the antiquity of the Hungarian language. This matched German pretensions, but risked leaving those subjects of the Hungarian Kingdom whose language was not Hungarian – among others, speakers of German, Croat, Romanian, Slav/Slovak and Rusyn/Ukrainian – out in the cold. Promoters of the Slavonic languages soon joined in the competition. A new form of Czech/Slovak, based largely on biblical Czech or *bibličtina* (the sixteenth-century language of the Kralice Bible, which was still being used, barely modified, by Slovak Protestant communities), began to be promoted by two Slav/Slovak Lutherans from Upper Hungary who were later considered to be Czechoslovak heroes: Ján Kollár (1793–1852) and Pavol Šafárik (1795–1861).

Kollár, author of the quintessential allegory of Slav unity and reciprocity, *Slávy dcera* (Daughter of the Slavs), first published in Buda in 1824, was not content simply to chronicle what he called the 'Czechoslovak dialect' in isolation, but sought to place it within a grand narrative that presumed the existence of an ancient 'Slav' mother language to account for the marked similarities between such languages as Russian, Ukrainian, Polish, Slovak, Czech, Serb and Croat.[15] Šafárik followed with pioneering ethnographic research into an imagined community of ancient 'Slav' people, bringing out a work on what he called 'Slavonic antiquities' in 1836–37 and 'Slavonic ethnography' in 1842. Slav Romanticism in the Habsburg territories was beginning to compete with German and Magyar.

In the 1820s and 1830s, to publish in Czech or in Slav/Slovak (*bernoláčtina*) rather than in German, Latin or – at a pinch – Hungarian was to strike an attitude, to make a public statement. It was rather like donning peasant dress and flaunting it on the streets of Vienna: there was an implicit challenge, a provocation. It was 'artificial' in the same way that wearing a kilt or pointedly speaking Welsh or Gaelic in the House of Commons might be. Habsburg gentlemen who chose to present themselves as Czech or Slovak (or, for that matter, Serb or Croat) generally had to learn 'their' language from a pile of grammars and practise speaking with like-minded patriots in nationalist clubs and societies; they would have conversed or written much more easily in German, French or Latin. In Pest, a handful of intellectuals – Catholic and Protestant – began actively to promote the use of the Slav/Slovak language through reading groups such as the Slovak Readers' Society and the Society of the Lovers of the Slovak Language and Literature. In Prague, the Bohemian Museum Society – which was starting to get more narrowly Slav and less inclusively Bohemian – in 1827 launched the first scholarly journal ever to be published in the Czech language. A society dedicated to publishing scholarly works in Czech, the *Matice česká* (Czech Foundation), inspired by the Serb *Matica Srpska* of 1826, followed in 1831.[16] It took another generation for a *Matica slovenská* (Slovak Foundation) to be created, but one duly appeared in 1863, at the end of suitably rousing pro-Slav/Slovak celebrations to commemorate 'a thousand years' since the arrival of SS. Cyril and Methodius in the Greater Moravian Empire.

In the end, the form of literary language to be codified and officially adopted as standard Slovak was neither *biblíčtina* (a form of Old Czech used by Slovak Lutheran communities), nor *bernoláčtina* (which was associated with Catholic doctrinal and devotional writings), but rather *štúrovčina*, a dialect advocated by Ľudovít Štúr (1815–56), a founding member of the 'Czechoslav' Society and teacher at the Lutheran Lyceum in Pozsony in the 1830s. In self-conscious rivalry with the Hungarian *Pesti Hírlap* (The Pest Gazette), Štúr founded the first newspaper to be published in Slovak, *Slovenskij Národnje Novini* (Slovak National News) in 1845. In the next year, in response to an appeal circulating in Prague to find a 'single literary language for the Bohemians, Moravians and Slovaks', he brought out a pamphlet on 'The Slovak Dialect or the Need to Write in This Dialect'. It was this *štúrovčina* that became the standard Slovak dialect to be used by Slav nationalists on both sides of the Hungarian religious divide.[17]

The new political game, of defining identity primarily through language rather than territory, held the immediate attraction of being one that anyone could play, landless commoner as well as aristocrat; but it was not a game at which everyone could win. Just as Hungarian identity had traditionally been tied not to language but rather to the Crown of St Stephen, so Bohemian identity had been tied to the Crown of St Wenceslas. To suggest that the Bohemian Crown Lands might be innately 'German' or innately 'Czech', or even (in the case of Silesia) 'Polish', could hardly fail to be divisive. The new, more trenchant mood of what is usually termed the 'second phase' of the 'National Awakening' was epitomized (in Bohemia) by Josef Jungmann (1773–1847), who wrote almost exclusively in Czech, which he sought to revive as an intellectually and socially respectable literary language with translations of Chateaubriand, John Milton and Goethe, and with the publication of an exhaustive Czech–German dictionary (1835–39). But it was the 'father' of the Czech 'nation' and central figure of the Czech 'National Revival', František (Franz) Palacký (1798–1876), who was most influential in putting the case that speakers of Czech formed a distinct people or 'nation' with the implicit right to autonomy within the Habsburg Empire with his five-volume *History of the Czech Nation in Bohemia and Moravia* (1836–67).

The 1848 revolutions radicalized all of the peoples ('nations') of the Habsburg Empire. In Bohemia, the Liberals' bid for independence, fatally weakened by internal divisions, was easily crushed by Habsburg troops because Germans, Czechs and Jews proved as eager to attack one other as to stand together on the barricades. In Hungary, where the revolution was initially successful, the new Liberal regime in Budapest was betrayed by Slovaks, Ruthenes and others who preferred to conspire with the Habsburgs and Russians than to share in an independent Hungary dominated by Magyars. The first three volumes of Palacký's *History of the Czech Nation* (published between 1836 and 1842) had been written in German, not Czech. After his revolutionary experience, he wrote the remaining volumes directly in Czech; arranged for new editions of the earlier German-language volumes to be issued in Czech translation; and began to argue that the whole of Bohemian history, especially the Hussite wars, exemplified an 'age-old' struggle between what he now grandly termed 'Slavdom' and 'Germandom'. A Moravian Protestant, Palacký took a particular interest in rehabilitating the reputation of Jan Hus, whom he presented, in the first volume of his *History* to be written and published in Czech, as at once a proto-Protestant and a proto-nationalist martyr. This view was to have a profound influence upon – among others – the man who was eventually to found the first state ever to be named for the Czechs and the Slovaks: lapsed Catholic and fellow Moravian Tomáš Masaryk.

The question of nationality in the Bohemian Crown Lands in the second half of the nineteenth century was no longer restricted to grammarians, poets and historians, but increasingly aroused ordinary Czechs, determined to prove their cultural worth, to establish – or at least to support – specifically Czech institutions, usually created in direct imitation of rival German ones. From the 1860s, such projects were often funded – in whole or in part – by the state, as the Habsburgs sought to contain the growing threat of pan-Germanism, which was only slowly coming to be matched by the danger of pan-Slavism. *Národní listy* (National Mail, founded in 1860) became one of the best-known patriotic Czech newspapers, while perhaps the most important body to spread Czech nationalism was the pan-Slav gymnastic organization formed in 1862 in opposition to the German gymnastic society *Turnverein* and known as *Sokol* (The Falcon). Soon, Czech political parties also began to multiply.

To be a Czech or a Slovak patriot in the late nineteenth century and early decades of the twentieth century was still a political choice, not a fluke of birth. It meant adopting the posture of a Slav patriot: reading the right newspapers and books; donating to the right causes; supporting the right cultural events; joining the right university societies and belonging to the right kind of political party. One did not have to be born or raised in the right language group to do this. Konrad Henlein, the leader of the extreme German nationalist *Sudetendeutsche Partei* (afterwards *Heimatfront*) of the 1930s, had a Czech mother. Heinrich Fügner, the co-founder (with Miroslav Tyrš, formerly Tirsch) of the emphatically pan-Slav *Sokol*, was a German-speaker from the German Bohemian town of Leitmeritz/Litoměřice who never mastered the Czech language and had to change his name to 'Jindřich Fuegner' to be accepted by the (still mostly German-speaking) Czech nationalist élite in Prague.[18] Tomáš Masaryk/Masárik, born in 1850 to a German mother and a Moravian Slovak father, although educated entirely in German and scarcely literate in Czech when he began his university career, similarly 'converted' as a young man to the Slav cause, inserting the patriotic 'Vlastimil' ('Lover of the Fatherland') into his name as a sign of his allegiance.[19] Jozef Tiso, who rose to become leader of the Slovak People's Party and dictator of the extreme nationalist Slovak state of 1939–45, was at best 'silent' on the subject of his Slovak nationalism before Czecho-Slovakia and presumably as 'Magyarone' (assimilationist) as most other clergy in the prewar Hungarian Catholic Church.[20]

The political formula for would-be nationalists in the Habsburg Empire was becoming clear. Rather than follow the French model, in which 'the nation' was broadly defined as a people who lived on the same territory, were ruled by the same government and were subject to the same laws, in the Habsburg territories it was to be a variation on the German model, derived largely from Herder, in which 'the nation' was understood as a people linked predominantly through language and culture, that was to apply.[21] To be in a position to claim a national identity it was first necessary to codify a language.

Armed with grammars and lexicons, one could then proceed to demand recognition of one's 'nationality' and so gain political standing. With luck and perseverance, public subsidies, civil rights – perhaps even autonomy – would follow. It was along these lines of Romantic nationalist thinking that, on 6 June 1861, Slovak patriots from Upper Hungary met at Turčiansky Svätý Martin (*Turócszentmárton, Sankt Martin*) to declare, in a document later known as the 'Memorandum of the Slovak Nation', that 'we Slovaks are as much a nation as are the Magyars' and to demand 'the recognition of our nation, in the area which it actually occupies, as a coherent, undivided territory under the name of the Slovak Region of Upper Hungary'.[22]

In what appears practically to have been a one-man Ruthenian 'National Awakening', the Greek Catholic priest and 'father' of the Rusyn 'nation' Aleksander Duchnovyč (1803–65) tried his best to give local people – who sometimes referred to themselves as 'Rusnaks' – the requisite 'literature' to enable them to qualify as a 'nation' of 'Rusyns', Ruthenes or indigenous Ruthenians. Duchnovyč was the author of the first Rusyn play and the first history of the Rusyn people. He was also the founder of the Prešov Literary Circle, which published the first Rusyn almanac, one of whose poems, '*Podkarpatskij rusynŷ, ostavte hlubokŷ son*' ('Subcarpathian Rusyns! Arise from your deep slumber'), became the national anthem; another, which opened with the line '*Ja Rusyn bŷl, jesm i budu*' ('I was, am, and shall remain a Rusyn'), became a nationalist motto. But because Duchnovyč's attempts to codify the language brought it closer to Russian, he alienated both the local Greek Catholic clergy (who spoke Hungarian and continued to identify with the Hungarian state), and also the Habsburg government (which encouraged Ukrainian and Greek Catholic self-identity among the local people as preferable to Russian-sponsored Orthodoxy and pan-Slavism).[23] The Rusyns' attempted National Awakening, therefore, never quite took off in the same way as the Czechs' or the Slovaks'.

In 1867, the Habsburg Empire was reconstituted as the Dual Monarchy of Austria-Hungary. This meant that the Habsburg territories were reorganized as a confederation of two semi-independent states, Hungary and Austria (Cisleithania), which shared a common army, foreign policy and currency. The Bohemian Crown Lands (Bohemia, Moravia and Austrian Silesia), represented by the *Reichsrat* (parliament) in Vienna, fell under the authority of the Austrian half of the empire; while Upper Hungary and Subcarpathian Ruthenia, represented in the parliament in Buda (from 1873, Budapest), fell to Hungary. Czech as well as German nationalists, arguing that Bohemia's claim to political autonomy was every bit as good as Hungary's, were outraged. But since Czechs now completely outnumbered Germans in the bustling commercial and industrial centre of Prague, where there were reckoned to be about 125,000 Czechs to only 30,000 Germans in 1869,[24] and were rapidly outstripping the Germans economically and numerically, Czech patriots hijacked the debates and led protests in which Czech nationalism and Bohemian regionalism began to be fatally intertwined.

The Czech nationalist lobby made use of the new freedoms enshrined in civil rights legislation to show its anger by issuing a State Rights (*Staatsrecht*, *státní právo*) Declaration (1868); by formally presenting Emperor Franz Joseph I with 'Fundamental Articles' demanding constitutional recognition for the 'historic rights' of the Kingdom of Bohemia (1871); and by launching a high-minded, but ineffectual, ten-year boycott (often broken by Moravian Czechs) of the Vienna parliament. These were the years of growing Czech as well as German nationalism in Austria in which Austrian Slav Antonín Dvořák (1841–1904), who might otherwise have been condemned forever to playing polkas, mazurkas and marches in his village band, built his career by writing a mixture of Czech nationalist pieces, like the patriotic cantata for male voices *Hymnus: Dědicové Bílé hory* (Hymn: Heirs of the White Mountain), first performed in 1873, and pieces composed for state occasions, like his *Slavnostní pochod* (Festival March) for the silver wedding anniversary of Emperor Franz Joseph and Empress Elisabeth.[25] Even Bedřich Smetana (1824–84), the first thoroughly nationalist Czech composer who ended his career as a sort of Czech Wagner, did not have the confidence to compose anything so grandiose as the symphonic cycle *Má vlast* (My Fatherland) until 1876; by 1882, having won, with his *Libuše*, a competition for the ceremonial opening of the National Theatre in Prague, he had become such a national hero that, in order to satisfy demand, he had to repeat the 'one hundredth performance' of his *Prodaná nevěsta* (The Bartered Bride) with a second 'one hundredth performance'.[26] Since the Czech nationalist programme by now held that the historical territory of the Bohemian Kingdom, with its mixed German, Czech and Polish populations, was entitled to autonomy, but at the same time that collaboration between its various ethnic/language groups or 'nationalities' was impossible, it is not altogether surprising that the campaign was unsuccessful. The failure of successive cabinets to resolve the language question in Bohemia, blocked by the obstructionist tactics of both German and Czech deputies, led to complete political stalemate.[27]

While the Austrian half of the empire struggled with problems not altogether unfamiliar to the peoples of the British Isles, the Hungarian took an approach that more closely resembled the American idea of the 'melting pot'. In 1868, as a way of solving the nationalities problem, a new Hungarian law decreed that 'all citizens of Hungary constitute a single nation, the indivisible, unitary Hungarian nation [*Magyar nemzet*], of which every citizen, to whatever nationality [*nemzetiség*] he belongs, is equally a member'.[28] What made the enforcement of so-called 'Magyarization' politically explosive was the double blow of the relative economic and political weakness of the majority of non-Magyars living in Hungary, together with their increasing self-identification of language with their identity (whether as Slavs, Germans or Romanians). After the *Matica slovenská* was closed down by the government in 1874 as a hotbed of anti-state, pan-Slav activity, the two existing Slovak political parties, inspired by the Czech deputies' example, boycotted the Hungarian elections of 1878. But when, in 1881, they decided to change tactics, they were in any case unable to win a parliamentary seat.

Unable either to gain political representation in the Hungarian parliament or to block its legislation, Slovak nationalists expressed themselves in other ways. The Slovak *Narodný dom* (National House), a self-proclaimed literary and cultural centre, was founded in Turčiansky Sväty Martin in 1887, a Slovak National Museum opened in 1890 and a Slovak Museum Society was founded in 1893. By 1887, even something as apparently innocuous as an exhibition of Slovak embroidery was being claimed by Slovak nationalists as proving 'to the world' that 'a Slovak nation does exist' and that 'these artistic creations testify to its developed culture'.[29] In such a climate, it was inevitable that even a party of Christian values that was supposed to cut across linguistic and denominational divisions – the Hungarian People's Party (*Magyar Néppárt*, founded in 1894) – would fracture within a few years. First a Slovak Catholic newspaper, *L'udové noviny* (The People's News), was established in Turčiansky Sväty Martin in 1897. Then, in Prague, inspired by Prague professor T.G. Masaryk, three Slovak Lutherans – Vavro Šrobár, Pavol Blaho and Antonín Štefánek – started up a Protestant Slovak newspaper called *Hlas* (The Voice) which sought to promote the idea of a common 'Czecho-Slovak' identity and destiny. In 1905, a group of Slovak Catholic priests led by Fr Andrej Hlinka broke away from the Hungarian People's Party, which was not living up to its promise to support non-Hungarian-speakers on the language question, to create a separate, clerical wing of the movement. It was this exclusively Catholic, Slovak and clerical wing that, in 1913, became the 'Slovak People's Party'.

The last quarter of the nineteenth century was the quintessential era of ambitious and showy public projects throughout the Habsburg Empire as each 'nation' sought to prove its cultural and linguistic superiority and therefore its right to dominate the others. In Prague, Czech nationalists erected a grandiose National Theatre dripping with gold leaf (1868–81), which was proudly rebuilt by public subscription in 1883 after being destroyed by fire. Czech nationalists insisted upon the division of Prague's university into completely separate Czech and German sections (1882) and, in 1890, opened a massive neo-Renaissance palace at the top of Wenceslas Square to house what had once been an inclusively Bohemian – but was now a provocatively and exclusively Czech 'national' – museum. Political campaigns urged ordinary Czechs to buy only from Czech shops, rent only to Czech tenants, drink only Czech beer.[30] The defensive German terms 'language border' (*Sprachgrenze*) and 'language islands' (*Sprachinseln*) began to be widely used.[31] In Silesia, where rivalry existed not only between Czechs and Germans, but also Poles, each 'nation' had come to insist on not only its own schools, opera, libraries and theatres, but even its own fire brigades.[32]

By the 1890s, the mutual animosity between Czech and German workers in Bohemian cities like Brüx (*Most*) and Reichenberg (*Liberec*) had grown so extreme that a new party, *Deutschnationaler Arbeiterbund* (National German Workers' Federation), was established with the explicit purpose of combating the Czech menace. Although then only able to command about 5 per cent of the German Bohemian vote, this was the party – with its heady mix of socialist policy and pan-German mysticism – that was later to be acknowledged by the Nazis of the Third Reich as their inspiration and forerunner.[33] The Czech side was no less extreme in either its nationalism or its socialism: the Czech National Socialist Party, which was primarily interested in eradicating Germans, was just as militantly anti-Semitic as its opposite number; indeed, all the more so since it saw Jews, many of whom spoke Yiddish, as a sub-species of German.[34] When, in 1897, the Austrian prime minister, Count Badeni, ruled that all public officials in the Bohemian Crown Lands would have to prove a working knowledge of both German and Czech within three years or else lose their posts, the reform led to such widespread protests and violence that within a month Badeni had been forced to withdraw the decrees and resign his post.[35] These last, tense decades of the Habsburg Empire, marked by an atmosphere of increasingly chauvinistic competition, were to sow the seeds of the ethnic hatreds – German, Czech, Slovak, Jewish, Magyar and Polish – that were to bear such bitter fruit in the twentieth century.

Among the 'nations' of the Habsburg Empire who (unlike the Gypsies, long the deliberate target of state as well as popular discrimination) had a reasonable chance of being able to work the political system to their advantage, the Rusyns and Jews were lagging behind. When, in 1882, Adolf Dobrjans'kyj was expelled from Hungary for his political activities, the Rusyn nationalist movement seemed to have left with him. Polish Galicia became a prime place of refuge for Rusyn/Ukrainian-speakers, underlining their fragmentation across international frontiers; while those Ruthene nationalists who stayed behind split into 'Magyarone' (assimilationist) and 'Russophile' (pan-Slav) factions.[36] Jewish immigrants, encouraged to settle in the emptying region, continued to grow in number, so that by the 1930s they had come to represent half of the population of the city of Mukačevo, which, with its thirty synagogues, was being called 'the Jewish capital'. But even here, because of internal linguistic, religious, political and assimilationist/separatist differences, Jews could not unite under either the banner of religious orthodoxy or political Zionism, and so were similarly unable to keep pace with the strides being made by better-organized, and more militant, neighbouring nationalist movements.[37]

On the eve of the First World War, there was a great deal of talk of the 'nationalities problem' within the Austro-Hungarian Empire. There was even some pressure on the Habsburgs to seek a federal solution to the benefit of the Slav majority, thought by some Western liberals – mainly academics – to be unfairly treated by German and especially Magyar élites. But no one suggested that the empire could or would be replaced by a collection of independent states, among them a newfangled country named for two Slav peoples of whom scarcely anyone outside the empire had heard: the Czechs and the Slovaks.

Electoral reforms in Cisleithania, which came into force in 1907, dramatically increased Czech representation in the Vienna *Reichsrat*. But even when flexing their new political muscles in the last prewar elections (1911), the dozen or so Czech political parties – Socialist, National Socialist, Christian Democrat, Catholic and other – had abandoned the dream of one day restoring independence to the Bohemian Crown Lands, and were instead resolved to work within the structures of the Habsburg Empire to press for greater autonomy and more political rights. In the Hungarian half of the empire, where the vote was still denied to the vast majority of the population, there was no discernible threat to Magyar dominance from any other 'nation': certainly not from the Slovaks, who could barely scrape together three political parties, and about half a million of whom had already emigrated to the United States; let alone from the Rusyns/Ukrainians, some 100,000 of whom had also left, permanently, for the United States.[38] Absurd and implausible as the idea would have seemed to anyone in 1914, a remarkable reversal of fortune – in which Czech-, Slovak- and even a proportion of Rusyn/ Ukrainian-speakers would suddenly find themselves counted as the official peoples of an independent Slav state in which the Germans and Magyars were cast in the role of minorities – was less than five years away.

CHAPTER 2

THE INVENTION OF A STATE

The subjects of Austria–Hungary first learned that they were at war from an imperial proclamation, issued on 28 July 1914 in all the principal languages of the empire (German, Hungarian, Czech/Slovak, Polish, Ukrainian, Italian, Slovene, Serbian/Croat and Romanian), in which Emperor Franz Joseph expressed his sorrow at having to declare war on Serbia and appealed to all his 'nations' for their support. Official representatives of the Czech and Slovak 'nations' were among the first to respond. If, as was later put about – most memorably in Jaroslav Hašek's comic masterpiece of 1923, *The Good Soldier Švejk* – they felt ambivalent about being called up to fight against the Serbs and Russians, fellow Slavs, and alongside their resented German and Magyar fellow subjects, these were not views that were much expressed at the time.[1] Nationalists on all sides, used to competing with each other for imperial favour, sought rather to outdo one another in their expressions of loyalty to the Habsburgs in the hope that it would win them advantage in any postwar settlement of the nationality question.

The first signs of dissent from official Habsburg policy did not come from within Austria–Hungary, but rather from Czech and Slovak émigré groups in Russia, France and Britain, where Austro-Hungarian nationals suddenly found themselves classified as enemy aliens. In London, an impromptu 'Czech Committee' began issuing special identity cards to stop its members being deported; in Paris, an equivalent organization began recruiting for the French army and the Foreign Legion.[2] In Russia, where the largest concentration of émigrés was to be found and foreigners were already being rounded up, a delegation of Czechs and Slovaks living in Kiev went so far as to petition the tsar to bring what it referred to as 'the Czechoslovak nation' into an enlarged pan-Slav Russian empire so that the 'free and independent crown of St Wenceslas' might 'shine in that of the Romanovs'.[3] Other expatriate groups in Moscow and Petrograd came up with the idea of establishing a special Czech detachment of the Russian army, the *Družina* (brigade), to confuse and demoralize ethnic Czechs and Slovaks serving in the Austro-Hungarian army. In the United States, which was officially neutral in the war, but was home to about half a million Czech and Slovak émigrés living in defined communities in Texas, Ohio, New York, Illinois and Pennsylvania, most were loyal to the Old Country and so supported the Habsburg side. Two nationalist-minded Czech émigré groups that did not – one led by Ludvík Fischer in Chicago and another by Emil (Emanuel) Voska in New York – merged, in early 1915, to form what they called the 'Bohemian National Alliance' to lobby for Bohemian (not Slovak) independence from Austria–Hungary.

In Austria, nationalist-minded Czech deputies naturally began to debate whether loyalty to the government or clandestine support for Russia and Serbia – or both – offered the best hope of emerging from the war with political advantage. One of the very few Czech newspapers to speculate in print about what might happen to Bohemia if the other side won was *Čas* (Time), a journal run by a close-knit circle centred around Tomáš Garrigue Masaryk, by then quite a well-known figure on the Czech nationalist scene, who had been professor at the Czech section of the university in Prague since its creation in 1882. From August 1914, as *Čas* sailed increasingly close to the wind, copies were frequently confiscated, a fact that it began to announce in its own pages to boost its credentials as an independent liberal Czech voice.[4]

T.G. Masaryk (born Masárik), whose upbringing in Moravia and education in Vienna had given him little by way of an *entrée* into Prague society, was a free-thinker and anticlerical who had made a name for himself in the 1880s and 1890s through his public involvement in two *causes célèbres* which – although they made him temporarily reviled by extreme Czech nationalists in the empire – won him respect in rival German and Jewish nationalist circles, and even abroad. Ultimately, they gained him the helpful reputation of being an honest seeker after truth capable of rising above petty nationalist prejudice.[5] In 1900, together with other Czech liberal progressives, Masaryk founded the 'Czech Progressive' or 'Realist' Party, a tiny fringe party that (along with about a hundred Czech deputies representing a dozen more mainstream political parties, most notably the Agrarians, National Socialists and Social Democrats) sent a single representative – Masaryk – to the Vienna *Reichsrat*. The son of a freed Slovak serf and a German cook, Masaryk had got his start in life through the patronage of a (German-speaking) Austrian police chief, whose son, one of his classmates, Masaryk had tutored through *Gymnasium* (grammar school) in Brünn/Brno and university in Vienna in exchange for living as one of the family. Brought up in Moravia as a German and a Catholic, the youthful Masaryk first renounced his religion and then his nationality, reinventing himself in Vienna as a modern Slav moral philosopher and teacher of liberal, humane values. In 1883, he was made professor at the newly opened Czech section of the university in Prague; by 1914, he was an established figure on the Czech nationalist scene, with a reputation for fair play and a 'realistic' approach to the

Czech Question, which he claimed could only be solved within the framework of the Habsburg Empire.

In secret, Masaryk took his first, faltering steps in subversion on 2 September 1914, when he asked Czech émigré Emil Voska to pass on some economic and military secrets to Henry Wickham Steed, whom Masaryk had known in Vienna as correspondent for the London *Times*, in exchange for 'finding a way' to stop Russian troops from firing on predominantly Czech and Slovak regiments of the Austro-Hungarian army.[6] On 4 September 1914, the leader of the Czech National Socialist Party, Václav Klofáč, who had been indulging in similar acts of intrigue, was arrested and his party's newspaper suspended; he was to be held, without charge, for over two years.[7] The chorus of loyalist applause in the mainstream Czech press following Klofáč's arrest was the last straw which led a young socialist and Czech nationalist called Edvard Beneš, whose older brother was in Masaryk's 'Realist' Party, to approach their leader for advice.[8]

Edvard (born Eduard) Beneš (1884–1948) was a hard-working loner of thirty who had spent time in Germany and France (which he loved) and England (which he hated) while writing a doctoral dissertation on the Bohemian Question, ostensibly for Charles University in Prague, where Masaryk was a professor, but which he also tried (unsuccessfully) in 1908 to have accredited by the University of Dijon.[9] Although he did not keep terms or attend lectures, Beneš read and wrote voraciously. In addition to producing his formal dissertation (which agreed with Masaryk – and just about everyone else – that the Bohemian Question could be solved only within the framework of the Habsburg Empire), he also contributed about a hundred newspaper articles to Czech radical anticlerical and Marxist newspapers, including *Právo lidu*, the Social Democratic Party daily. After *Právo lidu* turned him down for a job as full-time correspondent, he set himself to writing a 'Concise Sketch of the History of Socialism' (in three volumes), which was published, with his brother Vojta's help, in 1911.[10] After war was declared, he avoided being recruited in the imperial army by simulating a limp.

According to nationalist legend, it was in the autumn of 1914, during a walk on Letná hill overlooking the centre of Prague, that Masaryk thrilled Beneš by confiding that he had 'already started' working against Austria–Hungary and suggesting that they 'work together'.[11] Beneš responded by providing the first of several instalments from his personal bank account. These earned him the further confidence that Masaryk had been talking about the possible political uses of the war, not only with his closest former students and fellow Realists,[12] but also with Josef Scheiner, chairman of the pan-Slav gymnastic organization *Sokol*; and that, having come into possession of some 'extremely valuable documents', Masaryk was planning a secret mission to Holland.[13] Having successfully persuaded the *Čas* circle to help him, Masaryk began to accumulate donations from the United States: some through his American wife's family connections; others through Charles Crane, the philanthropist who had helped to found Slavonic studies at the University of Chicago, where Masaryk had spoken as a guest lecturer. He also received funds from a variety of Czech émigré societies, including such curiosities as the 'John Hus League of Slav Free Masons' of Gary, Indiana.[14] Masaryk then met with a selection of Czech and German Austrian deputies to sound out their views on the political possibilities created by the war.

Masaryk's next move in subversion was to try to recommend himself to British intelligence as a Russian expert who, in exchange for providing secrets from the War Ministry in Vienna, would be allowed to influence the postwar settlement of Central Europe. In neutral Holland, away from the prying eyes of the Austrian police, Masaryk wrote to anyone he could think of – mostly academics and journalists – who knew or cared about the nationalities of Austria–Hungary. In addition to Henry Wickham Steed and Emil Voska, these included Robert Seton-Watson, who had published on the national minorities in Hungary and was sympathetic to the Slovak plight, and Ernest Denis of the Sorbonne, a French Calvinist and author of *La Bohême depuis la Montagne blanche* (Bohemia since the White Mountain) and *La fin de l'indépendence tchèque* (The End of Czech (*sic*) Independence), who was sympathetic to the Czech cause. In late September, having failed to meet his British contacts in Holland, Masaryk returned to his circle of fellow Realists and contributors to *Čas*, whom he persuaded – in part by showing them copies of the private correspondence of the governor of Bohemia with the Austrian minister of the interior and prime minister – to join in his campaign of subversion against the Habsburgs.[15] After receiving an official warning about *Čas*, Masaryk met with Franz Thun-Hohenstein, the governor of Bohemia, 'a decent fellow with whom one could talk pretty openly' (and the same man whose letters he had been illicitly reading), whom he tried to persuade to distance Austria from German foreign policy or else face what he predicted would be mass Czech anti-Semitic demonstrations on the streets of Prague, since Jews tended to be lumped together with Germans in Czech nationalist thinking.[16]

It was not Masaryk, who – although openly critical of the Habsburg *rapprochement* to Germany – was still assumed by everyone to be loyal to Austria, but Lev Sychrava, the leader of the State Rights Party, who first left Austria–Hungary to work for the cause of Bohemian independence abroad. While Sychrava established an émigré base in neutral Switzerland, Masaryk managed – at the end of October 1914 – to meet up with Seton-Watson in Rotterdam, where they stayed indoors by day but walked together 'for miles along the quays after it was dark'. On his return to London, Seton-Watson drew up an 'ultra-secret' memorandum summarizing Masaryk's ideas, not only about 'the internal situation in Bohemia and in Austria–Hungary', but also about 'the settlement which ought to follow the war, and the policy which the Allies should pursue'.[17]

From the official British point of view, any Czech nationalist pipe dreams about Bohemian independence can have been of academic interest only; Masaryk's usefulness would depend on the value of his insights into Russian affairs and the quality of the intelligence that he claimed to be able to provide about submarine warfare and other secret military plans. All the same, Seton-Watson passed copies of his memo to the British, Russian and French foreign ministries. All three governments were thus privy, at an early stage of the war, to Masaryk's arguments that 'without a decisive defeat of Germany there can be no independent Bohemia; but Germany once defeated, it can be created on maximum lines', in which case 'the proper course would be to restore the historical Bohemia-Moravia-Silesia, and add to this the Slovak districts of Hungary (*Slovensko*)'.[18] This much of Masaryk's dream, which combined traditional Bohemian state-rights arguments for the three historical provinces of the Bohemian Crown (Bohemia-Moravia-Silesia) with Czech nationalist (language-based) claims to Slovak-inhabited areas of Upper Hungary, did, astonishingly enough, come to pass. Other, equally adamant, assertions did not: that, for the scheme to succeed, it would be 'essential' that Russia 'directly border upon Bohemia'; or that the new state 'could only be a kingdom, not a republic', one for which the 'selection of a sovereign' would be 'of quite special importance, if the *historic* kingdom is to be restored; for there would then be an important minority of 3–4,000,000 Germans, who would accept a Danish, but never a Russian, prince'.[19]

In early 1915, it was not Britain, France or the United States, but rather the Romanov Empire that looked like the best hope for Czech nationalists who were also Bohemian autonomists, since the Russian imperial army seemed on the brink of entering Austria–Hungary as part of its expected triumphant march to Germany. From the Russian point of view, dangling the possibility of Bohemian autonomy was an excellent way to sow dissension within the Habsburg Empire. The Russian Ministry of War duly sent a Czech Muscovite to set up a 'National Council of Czech Colonies' in Paris; and, in Prague, a courier for the Russian Press Agency instructed Karel Kramář, the leader of the Young Czech Party, Edvard Beneš and a few other would-be Czech conspirators in the art of putting together 'a telegraphic code, a scheme for the sending of couriers, and the type of news, especially that of a military character' in which the Russians were interested.[20]

In March 1915, the little band centred around Masaryk's *Čas* formed itself into a secret organization, calling itself the *Maffie*, whose aims were to work 'against' Austria–Hungary and 'towards' Bohemian independence. Despite its impressive-sounding name, one that had been used before by the core staff of *Čas*,[21] the group as yet consisted of just five people: Přemysl Šámal (1897–1941), who took over from Masaryk as head of the Realist Party; Karel Kramář (1860–1937), leader of the Young Czech Party; Alois Rašín (1867–1923), a deputy for the Young Czech Party; Josef Scheiner (1861–1932), the chairman of *Sokol*; and Edvard Beneš (1884–1948), who took on the job of secretary. The leaders of the Old Czech and People's parties, airily dismissed as 'aristocrats' and 'clericals' by the *Maffie*, were deliberately left out, while the leaders of the two most important Czech parties – the Agrarians and the Social Democrats – ignored them as an eccentric band of political amateurs.[22]

In Russia, the Czech exile population could by this point be divided into three broad political groupings. The first consisted of Czechs organized into a 'League of Czech Clubs' led by a Czech-born Ukrainian, Václav Vondrák. The League, whose political outlook was tsarist, conservative and pan-Slav, was supported by the Czech 'colony' in Kiev, whose own mouthpiece was the newspaper *Čechoslovan* (Czechoslav). The second grouping was the Czech and Slovak 'colony' in Petrograd, led by Bohdan Pavlů, which was liberal, nationalist and generally supportive of Masaryk; it was this Petrograd grouping that, after long discussions held in March 1915, agreed to promote, through a rival newspaper called *Čechoslovák* (Czechoslovak), the cause of a joint Czech and Slovak state, albeit one that could be maintained 'only in complete agreement with the whole Slav world, and especially with its great protector, Russia'.[23] Finally, there were those Czechs and Slovaks who were either held in Russian prisoner-of-war camps or else serving in the special military unit known as the *Družina*, the nucleus of the future 'Czecho-Slovak' Legions. This last group was officially represented by the *Klub spolupracovníků Svazu* (Club of the Associates of the Union), which was supported by the Petrograd group.[24]

After hearing that Prague's entire 28th Infantry Regiment had surrendered to the Russians, possibly for pan-Slav reasons, Kramář, leader of the Young Czech Party and head of the *Maffie*, seized on what appeared to be a propitious moment (3 April 1915) to send a memorandum to the Entente outlining his vision of how a postwar, autonomous Bohemian state could be incorporated in a greater pan-Slav empire.[25] In the same month, Masaryk – who happened to have been called to London by Seton-Watson and Wickham Steed because they wanted to pick his brains on the Yugoslav Question – again set down his ideas for a postwar reconstruction of Austria–Hungary, this time in a long memorandum entitled 'Independent Bohemia', of which two hundred copies were printed and circulated in official British circles, and four smuggled back to the *Maffie* in Prague.[26]

Masaryk's notion of an 'Independent Bohemia' as articulated in April 1915 had changed since he had first talked about the idea with Seton-Watson in October 1914. It was also different from the plan that had been agreed by the *Maffie* and was simultaneously being proposed by Kramář. In late 1914, Masaryk had offered to cede the predominantly German-inhabited part of Silesia to Germany and Polish-inhabited part of Silesia to Poland; he had also sketched the border between what he called 'Slovakia' (*Slovensko*) and the rest of Hungary in such a way that relatively few Hungarian-speakers (Magyars) would be caught on the wrong side. Subcarpathian Ruthenia, which he had assumed would be taken by imperial Russia, had been left out of his plan altogether. Six months later, Masaryk was no longer willing to leave the Polish-speakers of Těšín (*Teschen, Cieszyn*) or the Magyars of Upper Hungary (Slovakia) out of his projected state, insisting that, without the territories they inhabited, the state would not be viable.[27]

Once the *Maffie* in Prague had worked out cipher codes and pseudonyms, and learned how to smuggle messages inside book covers, pencils, fountain pens and specially made keys,[28] the most pressing question that absorbed its attention was who should be sent abroad next. Scheiner, whose activities were known to the police, was refused a passport. Kramář, the politician with the most clout among Czech Bohemians, wanted to stay in Prague to welcome the Russian liberating troops, who were expected imminently. The *Maffie* therefore settled on a deputy from the Agrarian Party, Josef Dürich, who shared Kramář's vision of an autonomous Bohemia within an enlarged Russian Empire, on the grounds that he might be able to bring the powerful Agrarian Party 'on side'; spoke French and Russian; and, crucially, already had a passport.[29]

On 21 May 1915, Scheiner and Kramář were arrested in Prague. Scheiner was released a month later for lack of evidence; but Kramář was sent to prison to await trial for treason, a capital offence. The removal of the leader of the Young Czech Party and head of the *Maffie* had far-reaching consequences for the embryonic Bohemian independence movement. At home, it was an unqualified disaster, since it destroyed the *Maffie*'s credibility, frightened the Czech press and lost the Young Czech movement support. Abroad, however, Kramář's sudden removal from the political scene gave Masaryk, a less well-known figure whose position on the Habsburgs was not yet clear, the opportunity to seize the limelight and begin to build up an anti-Habsburg exile movement abroad. Safe in England (although worried that the Austrian police might poison him through his laundry),[30] Masaryk moved on to Geneva where, in Seton-Watson's words, he spent the summer of 1915 'gathering a small group of absolutely devoted followers round him'.[31]

On 6 July 1915, the public occasion of the five-hundredth anniversary of Jan Hus's death, when the enormous Art Nouveau statue of the martyr that dominates Prague's Old Town Square was unveiled to Czech nationalist acclaim, Masaryk came out in public as an opponent of the Habsburg regime.[32] Less than a week later, Alois Rašín, another Young Czech deputy and member of the *Maffie*, was arrested in Prague. Finally, in August 1915, Masaryk was indicted and *Čas* banned. Since Masaryk was out of danger in Switzerland at the time, the publicity did him nothing but good, advertising his importance and raising his credibility within Czech émigré circles. For the remaining members of the *Maffie*, whose cover was blown, it was more serious. Beneš, in imminent danger of arrest, fled to Switzerland to join Masaryk and Sychrava. About eighteen conspirators who were left behind – among them Beneš's wife, Hana, and Masaryk's daughter, Alice – were arrested and sent to prison, leaving just one original member of the *Maffie* – Přemysl Šámal – at liberty in Prague.

Unexpectedly landed with Beneš, Masaryk took an executive decision: he would return to London, which he would make into a base for lobbying the English-speaking world; Beneš would go to Paris to work for the cause in France; and Sychrava would hold the fort in Switzerland. Seton-Watson, helpful as ever, busied himself with procuring Masaryk a false passport and creating a special post for him at King's College, London, so that he could circumnavigate difficulties with British immigration. Masaryk's stay in London, which ended up lasting over a year and a half (from the end of September 1915 until the end of April 1917), was spent concentrating on what he called his 'propaganda' work. This involved 'placing' articles, through the help of journalist friends, in the British press; setting up a 'Czech Press Bureau';[33] and fitting up a shop window in Piccadilly Circus, prominently marked 'Kingdom of Bohemia' and 'Czech National Alliance', with displays of 'maps; information about us and about Central Europe; the latest news about ourselves and our enemies; denials of untrue reports; and various other kinds of publicity'.[34]

In the United States, it was the Slovak League of America, an exile group run by Albert Mamatey (Mamatej) from Cleveland, Ohio, that took the lead in lobbying for autonomy for 'Slovakia' (meaning the predominantly Slovak-speaking parts of the Hungarian highlands). On 22 October 1915, Voska's Bohemian Alliance of America and Mamatey's Slovak League joined forces by signing a document known as the Cleveland Agreement which committed both groups to work towards 'independence of the Czech [*sic*] Lands and Slovakia' and the uniting of 'the Czech and Slovak nations' in a federal structure in which Slovakia would have 'its own Diet, schools, administration and state language'.[35] At the time, this development – which Masaryk was able smoothly to integrate into his own propaganda – helped to establish his credentials as a spokesman for the Hungarian Slovak as well as the Czech Bohemian independence movements abroad; later, as will be seen, the Cleveland Agreement's apparently broken promises of Slovak autonomy came back to haunt both him and his political successors.

While Masaryk seemed to be making progress in the English-speaking world, Beneš, alone in Paris, was floundering. He tried to look up acquaintances from his earlier stays in Dijon, but found that everyone was either away fighting in the war or else had 'forgotten' him. He then tried to ingratiate himself with professors at the Sorbonne and French socialists.[36] Under pressure to set up an organization of Czech exiles in order that an anti-Habsburg manifesto that Masaryk was planning to release in concert with other Bohemian Czech 'centres' around the world could be signed locally, Beneš found that he was unable to get the Czech 'colonies' in Paris to agree to anything. Finally, in sheer exasperation, he simply declared a 'Czechoslovak Foreign Committee' (*Zahraniční výbor československý*) to exist.[37]

On 14 November 1915, Beneš's Czechoslovak Foreign Committee in Paris solemnly issued what it called a 'Declaration of War' on Austria–Hungary. Although, as the Declaration explained, Czech political parties had previously hoped to transform the Dual Monarchy into a 'federalist monarchy' with 'extended autonomy' and 'essential rights' for all its 'nations', the war had exposed this 'spurious solution' to be impossible. 'By forcing us to carry arms against other Slavs,' the Declaration insisted, 'the Habsburgs have broken the last link that tied us to them. What we demand henceforth is a COMPLETELY INDEPENDENT CZECHOSLAV [*sic*] STATE.'[38] Since the Czechoslovak Foreign Committee had no army, no formal authority to speak for the Czech and Slovak peoples, and, indeed, existed only on paper, its 'Declaration of War' was, in itself, laughable. Its real purpose was, of course, not military but political: to undercut the insistence of the three largest Czech political parties in Austria – the Agrarian, Social Democratic and Young Czech parties – that the Czech 'nation' wished to continue to live under Habsburg rule. As Masaryk had planned, the document was signed and simultaneously issued from as many different Czech 'centres' as possible, in order to give an impression of a groundswell of opinion against the Habsburgs.

In December 1915, Beneš was joined in Paris by Milan Rastislav Štefánik (1880–1919), a Slovak Protestant who had studied astronomy in Prague and Paris and who was serving in the French air force, having become a French national in 1912 and a knight of the Legion d'Honneur in 1914. Charming, well connected and at ease in French society, Štefánik was in a position to give Beneš some useful introductions as well as a crash course in diplomacy; for his own part, he wished to bring yet another possible solution to the Czech Question to Professor Masaryk's attention. Masaryk, whatever he may privately have thought of Štefánik's scheme, was in no position to turn down his offer of a private meeting with Aristide Briand, the French minister of foreign affairs, for which he hurried over to Paris on 28 January 1916 so that there would be time to call on the Russian ambassador first. On 3 February 1916, Masaryk met with Briand, to whom he explained that it would be necessary to 'limit' Germany by replacing Austria–Hungary with a series of small states which, by their 'very existence', would be the 'natural aid of France'.[39] In a memorandum called '*L'Europe centrale pangermanique ou une Bohême indépendente?*' (A Pan-German Central Europe or an Independent Bohemia?), written expressly for the French Foreign Ministry, Masaryk expounded at length his developing thesis that the creation of an independent Bohemia, in concert with other friendly states, would be the best means of preventing the French bogey of a 'pan-German' postwar Europe.

Štefánik, left in charge in Paris when Masaryk returned to London, upgraded Beneš's Czechoslovak Foreign Committee to a *Conseil national de pays tchèques* (National Council of Czech [*sic*] Lands, hereafter referred to as the National Council in Paris), to be jointly headed by two Czech deputies in exile: Masaryk (Realist Party) and Dürich (Agrarian Party), who moved to Paris in February 1916. Beneš, at Masaryk's insistence, was made secretary-general.[40] The last member to join the Paris team was Sychrava, who was expelled from Switzerland in April 1916 for compromising Swiss neutrality with his anti-Habsburg propaganda and whose broadsheet, *Československá samostatnost* (Czechoslovak Independence), became the Paris National Council's first official newspaper. According to Beneš's memoirs, even the Slovak-born Štefánik agreed to restrict the Council's remit to '*les pays tchèques*' on the grounds that, given the Allies' 'complete ignorance of Slavonic affairs', introducing 'the Slovak question' could only 'complicate' the 'political struggle' for independence.[41]

While things seemed to be picking up in Paris, they had slowed down in London. Having observed that British audiences had a weakness for the underdog, Masaryk searched hard for examples of oppression and barbarism to put Austria on the same propaganda footing as Germany and win for the Czechs the kind of sympathy that was being shown to the Belgians. The trials, which concluded on 3 June 1916, of the Czech National Socialist Party deputies accused of having met with Masaryk on 1 October 1914, and especially the sentences of death by hanging for Young Czech deputies Kramář and Rašín, came as a propaganda gift. Masaryk's London and Paris teams whipped up as much publicity as possible, ensuring that Austria-Hungary's oppression of 'its own people' was picked up by the press in all the Entente countries, since, as Masaryk drily observed, 'martyrdom, and especially blood, win sympathy'.[42] Members of the special Czech regiment in the Russian army, the *Družina*, finally allowed to go into battle, were instructed to cry out: 'For Kramář! For Rašín!'

It was still from Russia, not the West, that 'liberation' was expected to come. But it was also in Russia that the substantial Czech population was most politicized and divided, and where Masaryk had, as yet, the least political influence. In the summer of 1916, two people ostensibly representing the 'Czecho-Slovak' nation were sent out to Russian prison-of-war camps to recruit ethnic Czech and Slovak volunteers to fight on the Entente side with Russia, Britain and France against Austro-Hungary. The first was Dürich, an Agrarian deputy and the *Maffie*'s official representative, who left Paris for Russia on 23 June 1916, and whose mission was to forward the cause of an autonomous Bohemian kingdom within a Russian-dominated federation of

Slav nations. The second envoy was Štefánik, who was sent out on 28 July 1916 by the French government, but with Masaryk's backing, since he shared Masaryk's vision of a postwar Europe in which a chain of independent kingdoms – Polish, Bohemian, Serbian and Hungarian – would encircle the German-speaking nations and prevent the creation of a Greater Germany. Unlike Masaryk's projected state, however, Štefánik's Bohemia was to exclude Slovakia, have a joint border with Serbia and be ruled by a French (as opposed to a Danish or British) monarch.[43] Explicitly in order to 'counterbalance' what it saw as the 'growing influence' of Masaryk and the London-backed Kiev Committee, the Russian government decided to cultivate Dürich rather than Štefánik, even going so far as to help Dürich establish, in Petrograd, a rival National Council to the one based in Paris.[44]

In November 1916, Emperor Franz Joseph, who had been on the Habsburg throne since 1848, died. His heir, the young Charles (Karl), one of whose first political acts as emperor was to commute Kramář's and Rašín's death sentences into prison terms, made clear from the first his sympathy for the empire's minority 'nations' (ethnolinguistic groups). Through the intermediary of Prince Sixtus of Parma, he also initiated secret negotiations with the French government over the possibility of coming to a separate peace agreement in order to end the ghastly war more quickly. These overtures, which were supposed to be kept strictly confidential, were made public at just about the same time that President Woodrow Wilson of the United States (which did not declare war on Austria-Hungary until 4 December 1917) requested each side in the conflict clearly to state its war aims. To the complete astonishment of the Czechs and Slovaks, the Entente's formal reply to Wilson (10 January 1917) included, as one of its war aims, 'the liberation of Italians, of Slavs, of Roumanians, and of Czecho-Slovaks from foreign dominations'.

Although members of the Masaryk team were at a loss to explain the explicit reference to the 'Czecho-Slovaks', they naturally liked to think of it as a fruit of their propaganda work. Czech politicians in Austria reacted more soberly. Unable to believe that the Entente powers, even should they prove victorious in the end, could seriously intend to abolish the Habsburg Empire, and seeing in the new emperor hope of greater autonomy, the Czech Association and National Committee in Prague took full part in Charles I's coronation on 30 December 1916. Worse still, from the point of view of the National Council in Paris, on 24 January 1917 the Association of Czech Deputies explicitly rejected what it referred to as Wilson's 'insinuation', declaring that 'as always in the past, so too at the present time and also in the future, the Czech nation envisages the conditions of its development only beneath the sceptre of the Habsburgs'.[45] For Masaryk and his fellow conspirators, this formal 'disavowal' was a complete disaster, since it publicly destroyed their credibility as spokesmen for the Czech 'nation' and broad-cast to all the world that the Austrian Czechs, although they wished for more autonomy within the Austro-Hungarian Empire, were firmly opposed to Bohemian independence.

It was the Russian Revolution of 1917 that unexpectedly altered the Masaryk team's luck. The fall of the tsarist government in March (February according to the old calendar) immediately changed the political scene so that the League of Czech Clubs in Kiev, which had until then been the most influ-ential of the Czech exile groupings, lost out to the smaller groups in Petrograd, Kiev and Moscow that Masaryk had been cultivating. Quick to show support for the revolution, which he welcomed as a victory of 'democ-racy' over 'theocracy', Masaryk telegraphed his congratulations to the Duma (the Russian parliament) as soon as he heard the news; and got his old friend Pavel Miliukov, now well placed as the new Russian foreign minister, to state at a press conference on 3 March 1917 that the 'solution' to the 'Czecho-Slovak question' lay in 'the creation of an independent Czecho-Slovakian [*sic*] state that will act as a barrier against the advance of the Germans towards countries with a non-Slavic population'.[46]

The sudden fall of the Russian government also meant that Masaryk could rid himself of his chief political rival. Dürich was expelled from the Paris-based National Council even before he was repudiated by the new Russian govern-ment. After Dürich's expulsion, the National Council in Paris consisted of just three members: Masaryk, its president, who was now the only elected Czech deputy on the committee and *de facto* leader of the whole exile movement; Štefánik, its vice-president; and Beneš, its secretary. These were the three men who were afterwards to become celebrated as Czechoslovakia's founding fathers, the *trojka* (triumvirate) whose triple portrait was to replace the crucifix on the walls of formerly imperial Austrian and Hungarian schoolrooms.

Masaryk arrived in Petrograd on 16 May 1917, travelling on a British pass-port in the name of Thomas George Marsden.[47] His travel plans were compli-cated, first by the 'May Crisis' of the provisional Russian government and then by the outbreak of the Bolshevik ('October') Revolution in November 1917, so that he ended up staying in Russia just short of a year. During this time, Masaryk worked above all to win political control of the Czech and Slovak deserters and prisoners of war who were fighting for the Russians on the Entente side in the successor to the *Družina*, which in April 1916 became the 'Czecho-Slovak Rifle Brigade'. After a Czecho-Slovak unit distinguished itself at the Battle of Zborów (in Czech, Zborov) (2 July 1917), Beneš and Štefánik set to work to persuade first the French and then the Italians that such units could be of use to their own armies. Eventually, this led to the formation of special 'Czecho-Slovak' or 'Czechoslovak' units (known variously after the war as the Czech, Czecho-Slovak or Czechoslovak 'Legions') in the French and Italian, as well as the Russian, armies. Despite the many heroic legends that grew up around these soldiers, both during and after the war, their primary purpose was propagandist, rather than military: to demoralize the overwhelming majority of Czech, Slovak and other Slav soldiers who were continuing obediently to fight for the Habsburgs; and to give the National Council in Paris evidence to back up its repeated assertions that the 'Czecho-Slovaks', despite all appearances to the contrary, were actually on the Allied side in the war.

Masaryk, by now the acknowledged leader of the liberation movement abroad, still lacked weight with Czech politicians in Bohemia. This was again made clear when, in response to Emperor Charles I's announcement that he would be convening parliament on 29 May 1917 (for the first time since 1914), Masaryk and Beneš alternately ordered and begged the Czech deputies to boycott the event. The dramatic absence of Czech deputies at the grand opening of the *Reichsrat* was supposed to back up the Masaryk team's propaganda by showing the world that any appearances of Austrian liberalism were a sham; and that the Czechs, terrorized and oppressed, held no genuine allegiance to the Habsburg dynasty. Instead, the Czech deputies not only attended the opening of the Vienna parliament, but formally requested that Austria be restructured along ethnic lines into a new confederation of states, one in which the Slovak-inhabited districts of Upper Hungary would be joined in a single entity with Czech-inhabited parts of the Lands of the Bohemian Crown. Although the Czech deputies had come on board to the extent of agreeing that 'Slovakia' should somehow be joined to the Bohemian Crown Lands, by working through the *Reichsrat* and continuing to campaign for autonomy rather than independence they again undercut Masaryk, Beneš and Štefánik's pretensions to have the right to speak for either the Czechs or the Slovaks. Soon afterwards, the emperor released deputies Kramář and Rašín from prison and deputy Klofáč from custody; Masaryk and Dürich, meanwhile, because they had broken parliamentary rules by neither attending nor formally excusing themselves from the session, lost their right to sit in the *Reichsrat*.[48]

When President Woodrow Wilson presented his Fourteen Points to the US Senate on 8 January 1918, he was quite careful, in Point 10, to limit US support for 'the peoples of Austria-Hungary' by stating that they should be accorded not independence, but rather 'the freest opportunity of autonomous development'.[49] It was only with the gravest hesitation and misgivings that the Allies began, from early 1918, deliberately to incite rebellion within Austria–Hungary as a means of hastening an end to the war. Many thought the policy shift – to support what amounted to treason – not only morally repugnant but dangerous, since it risked provoking copycat actions within British, French, Italian and American spheres of interest.[50] Furthermore, as professional diplomats like the United States' own Robert Lansing could see clearly enough, Wilson's calls for 'self-determination' were hopelessly open to interpretation. 'When the President talks of "self-determination",' Lansing pondered on 20 December 1918, 'what unit does he have in mind? Does he mean a race, a territorial area or a community?'[51] By 30 December, after the phrase had been taken up by various national groups and delegations, he had grown even more concerned: 'The phrase is simply loaded with dynamite. . . . What a calamity the phrase was ever uttered! What misery it will cause!'[52]

In 1918, despite the obvious risks, the Allies finally decided to abandon the Austro-Hungarian Empire to the mercy of its disgruntled minorities. Public scandal over the Sixtus letters had removed the possibility of reopening secret negotiations towards a separate peace with the Habsburgs. Widespread, sympathetic reporting of a Congress of Oppressed Nationalities of the Austro-Hungarian Empire (held in Rome on 8–10 April), in which Masaryk's team took a prominent part, had also aroused popular sympathy in the West for the causes of the Poles, Czechs, Slovaks and 'Yugo-Slavs', and put pressure on their governments to help these 'oppressed nations' to break free of the Habsburg 'yoke'. At this point, the Slovak National Party jumped on board, holding a meeting at Turčiansky Svätý Martin (*Turócszentmárton*) on 24 May 1918 to decide whether or not the party thought it would be more advantageous to stay with Hungary or else to support the 'Czecho-Slovak' cause. Fr Andrej Hlinka, the fiery and charismatic leader of the Slovak People's Party, spoke in favour of adopting the 'Czecho-Slovak orientation'.[53]

At the end of May 1918, President Wilson finally agreed to abandon hopes of a separate peace with the Habsburg Empire and to take 'the other way – the way which he disliked most intensely – of setting the Austrian people against their own Government by plots and intrigues', and therefore to 'support the Czechs, Poles and Yugoslavs'. The change in US policy, signalled by a declaration of 'sympathy' for 'the nationalistic aspirations of the Czecho-Slovaks and Yugo-Slavs for freedom' (29 May 1918), was immediately echoed in equivalent statements by the French, Italians and British.[54] On 31 May 1918, three émigré organizations in the United States (the Slovak League, Bohemian National Alliance and the Federation of Czech Catholics) issued a statement, later known as the Pittsburgh Agreement, which approved plans to unify the Czechs and Slovaks in an 'independent state consisting of the Lands of the Bohemian Crown and Slovakia'. The agreement, which was written in Slovak, was prominently signed by T.G. Masaryk for the Czech side and Albert Mamatey for the Slovak, although not by anyone actually living in the Habsburg Empire. The document, whose implementation was later to form the main platform of the Slovak People's

Party under the leadership of Andrej Hlinka, followed the earlier Cleveland Agreement in explicitly guaranteeing that Slovak would be the official language of 'Slovakia' (*Slovensko*), which would also have its own judiciary, administration and diet.[55]

Political spokesmen for the Ruthenes of Hungary, considered by some to be 'Ukrainian' and by others to be 'Rusyn' or 'Russian' in nationality, had not been included in the National Council's propaganda or represented among the signatories of the Cleveland or Pittsburgh Agreements. On 29 June 1918, encouraged by Lansing's statement that 'all branches of the Slav race should be completely freed from German and Austrian rule', an organization calling itself the Ukrainian Federation of the United States, and which claimed to represent 'more than 700,000 Ruthenians and Ukrainians', sent President Wilson a request that he endorse the efforts of their 'mother countries' to 'free' themselves from the Habsburgs and Romanovs.[56] At a meeting held on 23 July 1918 at Homestead, Pennsylvania, a coalition of Greek Catholic societies, calling itself the American National Council of Hungarian-Ruthenes (*Amerikans'ka Narodna Rada Uhro-Rusinov*) and proclaiming itself to be the only legitimate representative of the Hungarian Ruthenes, asked that Ruthenians be granted some form of autonomy and that their 'nationality' be respected by allowing them to unite with neighbouring Greek Catholic Ruthenes in Galicia and the Bukovina.[57]

In the months following the signing of the Treaty of Brest-Litovsk (3 March 1918), as the twists and turns of the Russian Revolution were unfolding before an astonished world, a unit of the Czecho-Slovak Rifle Brigade in Siberia refused to obey Bolshevik orders to surrender to the Germans, instead beginning slowly to fight its way back from Siberia to Vladivostok. The fact that these soldiers were in a place where the Allies had no troops, and that they were defying the Bolsheviks, put their story on the front page of Western newspapers and meant that they came to acquire an importance out of all proportion to their actual military strength. Beneš and Masaryk, although they had repeatedly and explicitly instructed the soldiers to remain scrupulously neutral in internal Russian affairs, and who were not above exaggerating the number of men they had at their disposal, realized from the world's sudden interest in Siberia that they had a bargaining counter.

With the help of his old patron Charles Crane, Masaryk got himself included in a lunch held at the White House to discuss whether or not the US should intervene in Siberia; this won him a private interview with President Wilson on 19 June 1918, which he was able to follow with a letter to the American secretary of state in which he hinted heavily that he ought to be granted political recognition as leader of the 'Czecho-Slovaks' since, 'although he had at his disposal three armies, fighting in Russia, France and Italy' and was 'the master of Siberia and half Russia', yet he was still 'in the United States formally a private man'.[58] Beneš, meanwhile, asked by the British to leave the troops in Siberia, was told that HM Government would be prepared to recognize the Czecho-Slovaks as Allies; French prime minister Georges Clemenceau went further, promising that his government would go 'all the way' in return for getting the soldiers to the Western Front. Beneš, sensing French desperation, pressed his advantage, asking for a range of statements and declarations, including that 'the Czecho-Slovaks were independent for long centuries' and an explicit promise that 'the Slovaks would be united with the Czechs in a Czecho-Slovak state' to be 'composed of the four [sic] historic provinces of Bohemia, Moravia, Austrian Silesia and Slovakia' (Slovakia was not, of course, one of the historic Lands of the Bohemian Crown).[59]

On 29 June 1918, Czechoslovak troops captured Vladivostok from the Bolsheviks, causing a splash in the world press. The French foreign minister reacted immediately, sending Beneš every formulation and statement that he had requested (including the bogus reference to Slovakia as one of 'the four historic provinces'). By now bombarded with press cuttings about the plucky and gallant Czechs, the Supreme War Council declared to President Wilson that an Allied intervention, making use of the Czech troops in Siberia, had become 'an urgent and imperative necessity'.[60]

The widespread and sympathetic Allied publicity which was given to the Legions, together with the French commitment to some form of Czecho-Slovak independence, were the first clear signs that the Czech deputies at home had seen to indicate that Masaryk's grandiose hopes for an enlarged, independent postwar Bohemian kingdom were becoming politically possible. On 13 July 1918, Kramář revived the National Committee (Národní výbor) in Prague, a group of thirty-eight Czech deputies led by himself, Václav Klofáč, Antonín Švehla and František Soukup, the leaders of the Young Czech, National Socialist, Agrarian and Social Democratic parties. For the first time, Austrian Czech political opinion – as formally represented by elected deputies acting through the Czechs' National Committee – showed itself willing to back the Masaryk–Beneš team by declaring itself in favour of the creation of an 'independent Czechoslovak state with its own administration within its own domain and under its own sovereignty'.[61]

Although he had promised the French that the Legions would be sent to the Western Front, given their sudden political importance to the British, Beneš could see no reason – when he discussed the matter with Prime Minister Balfour in early August 1918 – why they could not 'temporarily' be left in Siberia. Since, as he put it, formal recognition of the National Council in Paris as the government of a future Czecho-Slovak state would greatly improve 'the fighting morale of the troops', he added his hope that the British would feel able to follow the French in granting such recognition.[62] In no time Beneš had his desired statements: that 'the Czecho-Slovaks' were 'an Allied nation'; the 'three Czecho-Slovak Armies' an 'Allied and belligerent Army'; and the Czecho-Slovak National Council in Paris 'the present trustee of the future Czecho-Slovak Government'.[63]

Now the US was under pressure to follow the French and British. Having been persuaded only with misgivings to help the 'Checho-Slovaks' [*sic*] at all, Wilson reluctantly agreed, on 2 September 1918, to go so far as to recognize the National Council as the '*de facto* belligerent government' of the 'Czecho-Slovaks'; but only so long as it continued to wage war 'against the common enemy'.[64] Wilson's cautious approach, which he reckoned had 'just about' managed to preserve the 'general policy of keeping ourselves free for the peace treaty', was promptly undermined by his allies. The French, rightly suspecting that the British were trying to remove the Czecho-Slovak Legions from their influence, did indeed go 'all the way'. In early September 1918 – in exchange for being allowed to direct the Czecho-Slovak troops as they pleased – the French pledged to help the 'Czechoslovak [*sic*] nation' to 'recon-stitute' (*sic*) an 'independent Czechoslovak state' composed of Bohemia, Moravia, Austrian Silesia and 'Slovakia' (*Slovaquie*). They even agreed, at Beneš's insistence, that Czecho-Slovakia would have the 'right' to be repre-sented at all inter-Allied conferences that touched upon its interests.[65]

By the autumn of 1918, Austria-Hungary was on the brink of total collapse. In a last-ditch appeal to President Wilson, on 7 October the Habsburg government asked to reopen negotiations based on the Fourteen Points – in other words on the basis of 'autonomy' rather than independence – for its 'nations'. A week later, on 14 October 1918, Beneš announced from Paris that the leaders of the National Council had formed a Provisional Czecho-Slovak Government; one that he took care to have rapidly recog-nized by as many Allies as possible.[66] On 16 October, perhaps only a couple of days too late, Emperor Charles released an 'Imperial Manifesto' that granted 'autonomy' to the 'nations' (as represented by self-proclaimed National Councils) within the Austrian half of the empire. Even at this late hour, there were some grounds for hope that the offer might be accepted. It did, after all, fulfil the criteria of Wilson's Point 10; was precisely what the Czech deputies in Prague had formally requested in May 1917 (and, indeed, had been demanding at regular intervals since 1848); and could have saved the Allies the difficulty of having to try to find an alternative scheme to manage Central Europe.

Thrown into a panic, the Provisional Czecho-Slovak Government did all it could to make a compromise between the Allies and the Habsburg govern-ment impossible; or, as Masaryk put it in his memoirs, to 'checkmate' the emperor's manifesto. Forced to give up his vague promises to the British about a Danish or British monarch, and having just about managed to persuade Štefánik to abandon his own hopes of a French king for the

Bohemian throne, Masaryk – who was still in Washington, D.C. – dropped everything to rush out a republican 'Declaration of Independence' so fast (18 October 1918) that there was not even time to issue a Czech translation.[67] As things turned out, the Provisional Government need not have panicked. Wilson had already drafted a reply to explain that, since he had already recognized that 'a state of belligerency exists between the Czecho-Slovaks and the German and Austro-Hungarian Empires' and that 'the Czecho-Slovak National Council is a *de facto* belligerent Government', he was 'no longer at liberty to accept the mere "autonomy" of these peoples as a basis of peace'.[68]

On 21 October 1918, the day that Wilson's reply appeared in the Austrian press, German deputies reacted by withdrawing from the Vienna *Reichsrat*, declaring themselves to be the Provisional National Assembly of an independent German-Austrian (*Deutsch-Österreich*) state.[69] Even Victor Adler, the Marxist leader of the Social Democrats and one of the staunchest ethnic German opponents of nationalism, accepted the inevitable, offering 'fraternal greetings' to his 'Slavic and Latin comrades', whose rights to 'self-determination' he recognized 'without reservation and without limitation', but which he demanded 'also for our German people'.[70] While the government desperately cast around for a suitable reaction, the Habsburg army, from which Croat and Hungarian troops were rapidly deserting, collapsed.[71] In Prague, the Czech Socialist Council began circulating pro-republican leaflets; and there were hurried discussions as to how to begin drafting a constitution. On 25 October, a delegation of senior deputies from the National Committee, led by Kramář and Klofáč, left Prague for Geneva, where they were to meet up with Beneš, now secretary of the Provisional Czecho-Slovak Government, at the Hôtel Beau Rivage. This left younger, less experienced deputies – Švehla, Rašín, Stříbrný and Soukup – who remained in Prague, to be improbably cast in the role of revolutionaries.[72]

Masaryk, who had been circulating his latest propagandist tract (a pamphlet entitled *The New Europe: The Slav Standpoint* which ran to seventy-four pages and was presumptuously signed 'Thomas G. Masaryk, President of the Czecho-Slovak Republic'), was in Philadelphia on 26 October 1918 to sign a 'Declaration of Common Aims of the Mid-European Nations'. It was here that he first sounded out Gregorij Žatkovič (Gregory Žatkovyč), leader of the American National Council of Hungarian-Ruthenes, about the possibility of including 'Carpatho-Ruthenia' in the Czecho-Slovak state in return for granting it 'national autonomy'. He was also approached by Nicholas Pačuta of the American Russian National Defence about a scheme to unite 'all' of the 'Carpathian Russians' in a single autonomous region.[73]

After revolutions broke out in Vienna and Budapest, the Habsburgs abandoned all pretence of trying to hold the empire together, focusing instead on trying to prevent a Bolshevik coup. It was in this climate that, in the late hours of 27 October and the early hours of 28 October 1918, special editions of the Prague newspapers announced that the Austro-Hungarian foreign minister, Count Gyula Andrássy, had accepted President Wilson's peace conditions. To the people of Prague, including those members of the National Committee who had yet to leave for Geneva, this was the signal that Austria-Hungary, defeated in all but name, was ripe for the taking. On Monday, 28 October 1918, the day afterwards commemorated as Czechoslovak Independence Day (and still kept as a state holiday in the Czech Republic, though not in Slovakia), Antonín Švehla, the leader of the Czech Agrarian Party, and František Soukup, the leader of the Social Democratic Party, declared themselves, 'in the name of the National Committee', to be in control of the Corn Institute (*Obilní ústav*) in Prague, the local administrative headquarters housed just off Wenceslas Square.[74] There was no resistance to their announcement: it had already been agreed between the Vienna and Prague military commands that they would 'work together', and Vienna had specifically asked the National Committee to distribute food rations.[75] Czech soldiers were therefore told to 'remain obedient' to their Austrian superiors while Hungarian soldiers, posted around the city to keep order, allowed themselves to be draped in the tricolour as Praguers – having just read or heard the news of Andrássy's note – gathered to celebrate at the Jan Hus memorial in the Old Town Square or in front of the equestrian statue of St Wenceslas at the top of the long boulevard known as Wenceslas Square. Here the crowd was treated to speeches – punctuated by effusive thanks to the absent Masaryk, Wilson and the Legions – by the National Committee; *Sokol*; the Workers' Physical Training Association; the Union of Czech Students; and a number of other Czech nationalist organizations. The emotive '*Kde domov můj?*' ('Where is my home?'), originally written for a Czech operetta and soon to become the first verse of the Czechoslovak national anthem, was sung.[76]

At noon on 28 October 1918, the Agrarian, Young Czech and Social Democratic deputies Švehla, Rašín and Soukup – now joined by National Socialist deputy Jiří Stříbrný – called at the governor of Bohemia's residence in Prague to ask that administrative control be handed over to the National Committee. Since Governor Coudenhove was away in Vienna, they had to wait until he phoned Prague that afternoon to get the chance to speak to him. By about six o'clock in the evening, the National Committee felt confident enough to declare that 'an independent Czechoslovak [*sic*] state had come into being', hastening to add that its 'precise form' would be decided later, by 'the National Assembly in conjunction with the National Council'. In the meantime, 'all imperial and provincial laws' would continue to remain in force.[77] Because he happened to have arrived in Prague that morning, Vavro Šrobár, the founding editor of the pro-Masaryk newspaper *Hlas*, was quickly brought on board. By adding his signature to the proclamation of independence, Šrobár became the fifth – and the only ethnic Slovak – member of the 'revolutionaries' afterwards known as the 'Men of 28 October'.

When Governor Coudenhove arrived in Prague on the morning of 29 October, he was escorted from the station by members of *Sokol*, now playing the role of revolutionary guard.[78] Coudenhove duly agreed to recognize the National Committee as the 'executive organ of the nation's sovereignty' and to acknowledge its 'joint management of the public administration'. Declining an offer to join the Committee himself, he formally tended his resignation as governor of Bohemia. At intervals during the day, the police headquarters, provincial high court and public prosecutor's office in Prague were all declared to be under the control of the National Committee. As members of the Habsburg Supreme Military Command canvassed opinion among their troops as to 'whether they favoured a republic or the dynasty', the War Office in Vienna authorized the military commands in Prague, Brünn (*Brno*) and elsewhere to respect the authority of the National Committee and to follow its instructions.

Technically, the revolution was over. Not a shot had been fired; and cooperation, rather than resistance, had been offered by the Habsburg government.[79] A few signs in German had been torn down; and the porticos of some government buildings in Prague and in Brünn were damaged by the removal of the double-headed eagle, emblem of the Habsburg Empire. It was not until a week later, on 4 November 1918, that the column of the Virgin Mary which had stood in the Old Town Square since the seventeenth century was toppled by a crowd of Czech socialists on their return from a rally at the site of the Battle of the White Mountain (*Bílá hora*), apparently in the mistaken belief that it had been put up in 1620 to mark the Habsburg victory over the Bohemian estates. News of this impious vandalism sent the first of several shockwaves about Czech socialism and anticlericalism through observant Catholic circles across Central Europe, including in Slovakia, and began speculation in conservative Czech Catholic circles in Moravia and Bohemia as to whose version of Czech nationalism would prevail in the new state.

Beneš, hours after arriving at the Hôtel Beau Rivage in Geneva on 28 October 1918, was far from pleased to be brought the news that a coup had just taken place in Prague, since he and Masaryk had been planning a formal transfer of power to take place on the more evocative date of 8 November, anniversary of the defeat at the White Mountain. Caught off guard by their compatriots in Prague and Brünn, and determined to impress upon the deputies gathered at Geneva the magnitude of their diplomatic achievements abroad, the exile leaders began to issue a series of hurried statements claiming joint authority for the day's events and making explicit their right to decide the country's political future.

After being persuaded by Beneš that the Czechs were so favoured by the Allies that they would be able to choose whatever frontiers they liked at the forthcoming peace conference, the National Committee took care to coordinate its movements with those of Masaryk's Provisional Government, and to endorse and approve all its statements and proclamations. As Kramář reported excitedly from the Geneva consultations: 'If you saw our Dr. Beneš, and his mastery of all global questions ... you would take off your hat and say it was truly marvellous!' Klofáč went even further. 'Wilson or anyone else would never say anything that Masaryk or Beneš did not underwrite,' he declared; 'the authority of these people is simply unbelievable.'[80] On 31 October 1918, the last day of the Geneva meetings and in the same party atmosphere, the posts of prime minister (Kramář), president (Masaryk), foreign minister (Beneš) and minister of war (Štefánik), together with the rest of a first, 'revolutionary' cabinet, were parcelled out.

The Czechs were not the only subjects of the rapidly disintegrating Austro-Hungarian atmosphere to seize the moment. In the confusion that followed the release of Emperor Charles's manifesto, hundreds of self-proclaimed National Councils sprang into existence across Habsburg territory. The Cisleithanian territories were fracturing along Czech-German lines (in Bohemia and Moravia) and Czech-German-Polish lines (in Silesia); in Upper Hungary, which was rapidly descending into anarchy, rival Slovak, Magyar, Jewish and Romanian National Councils formed, as did violent rival gangs – Slovak, Jewish and Magyar – who began to terrorize each other's populations. Out of the bewildering number of claims and counter-claims to surface, the most alarming to the self-proclaimed 'Revolutionary Cabinet' in Prague were those made by the four German 'Provisional Governments', which announced their existence on 29 October 1918, the day after the Czech National Committee in Prague had announced the creation of a new 'Czechoslovak' [sic] state. The Germans' four rival 'Governments' to the 'Czecho-Slovak Government' proclaimed by the Czechs were named for four regions in the Bohemian Crown Lands in which German-speakers formed a majority: Deutschböhmen (in northern Bohemia, along the German frontier); Sudetenland (in Silesia and northern Moravia, adjoining Germany); Böhmerwaldgau (in south-western Bohemia, facing Bavaria); and Deutschsüdmähren (in southern Moravia, adjoining Austria). The Provisional Government of Deutschböhmen, based at Liberec (*Reichenberg*) and led by Rudolph Lodgman von Auen, was the first to request inclusion in the newly proclaimed state of 'German Austria', which it was granted by the Austrian National Provincial Assembly on 30 October 1918. The Provisional Government of the Sudetenland, which was based at Opava (*Troppau*), followed suit the next day.

Two days after the Czechs and a day after the Germans, the Slovaks also reacted. On 30 October 1918, a group representing the Slovak National Party, the Slovak People's Party and the Slovak Social Democratic Party assembled a 'Slovak National Council' at Turčiansky Svätý Martin (*Turócszentmárton*) which declared, in what came to be known as the Martin Declaration (30 October 1918), that 'the Slovak nation, linguistically, culturally and historically, is a part of one Czecho-Slovak Nation'.[81] This Slovak National Council, the most important out of about 344 different ones that emerged throughout Upper Hungary to promote Slovak (as opposed to Magyar or Jewish) 'national' interests, afterwards came to be presented as having given the assent of 'the Slovak nation' to union with the Lands of the Bohemian Crown in a unitary Czecho-Slovak or Czechoslovak state. At the time, however, it was merely one – albeit the most politically significant – of a cacophony of Slovak voices to express hopes for the verdict of the forthcoming peace conference. Furthermore, because the original text of the Martin Declaration went missing and thus its precise wording and spelling cannot be checked, it is not possible to establish with certainty whether the state was envisaged at the time by the principal Slovak political parties as unitary or federative.[82]

On 1 November 1918, Hungary formally seceded from the Austro-Hungarian Empire as an independent state led by the Károlyi government. The National Committee in Prague decided that the territory it called 'Slovakia' (a sizeable chunk of Hungary's historic kingdom) should be occupied immediately, without waiting for permission from the Allies. This led to Prague's first military campaign against Hungary, which lasted for just under three months – from early November 1918 until the end of January 1919. The French government, meanwhile, called for an inter-Allied conference, to be held on 4 November, to discuss the Hungarian crisis. On the morning of 2 November, having heard that there was to be a meeting to which representatives of the newly declared Czecho-Slovak state had not been invited, the intrepid Beneš went over to the French Foreign Ministry to remind the French of their promises that the Czecho-Slovak National Council would be entitled to attend Allied meetings that touched upon its interests. By agreeing that he could come, the French established a precedent for the Provisional Czecho-Slovak Government to be represented at the Peace Conference when it opened in Versailles a few months later, despite Wilson's view that to admit the 'inchoate nationalities' would be 'most undesirable'.[83]

Beneš, who was all of thirty-four years old at the time, could 'scarcely believe in the reality of what was happening' when, for the first time, on 4 November 1918, he stepped into 'a motor-car decorated with our flag, and drove through Paris via St Cloud and Sèvres to Versailles' to take his place among 'the mighty of this world . . . mighty especially at that moment when they were settling the destiny of three Empires in Europe and Asia'.[84] On the same day that, in Paris, Beneš was basking in the glory of being addressed as 'foreign minister', in Prague the National Committee decided to start tidying up the mess in Upper Hungary by appointing an unelected 'Slovak Government' consisting of Šrobár and four hand-picked ministers. On 5 November 1918, accompanied by about seventy Czech gendarmes, the five 'Czecho-Slovak' ministers crossed the Moravian-Hungarian border to declare the existence of the 'Czecho-Slovak Republic' and set up temporary administrative headquarters in the town of Skalica (*Szakolca, Skalica, Skalitz*). Many Slovaks, hoping to be protected from further raids and rioting, seemed glad to see them.

In Teschen in Silesia, rival Czech and Polish National Councils agreed provisionally to divide the territory along roughly ethnic lines while they awaited the arrival of Allied troops, which was thought to be imminent. Subcarpathian Ruthenia was the last, as well as the easternmost, of the future Czechoslovak territories to be claimed. On 8 November 1918, at Stará Ľubovňa (*Lubló*), Greek Catholic priest Emiljan Nevyćkyj declared an Hungarian Ruthene National Council to have come into existence (one that, although not enthusiastic about remaining in Hungary, was divided over the question as to whether uniting with Ukraine or Czecho-Slovakia would represent the better option). The next day, after a rival group met in Užhorod (*Ungvár, Uzhgorod*) to declare its loyalty to Hungary, the Council reconvened in Prešov (*Eperjes*), under the leadership of Antonij Beskyd, to call for 'self-determination' and 'national freedom'.[85]

On 11 November 1918, Germany surrendered and Emperor Charles abdicated. The war was over. Instead of being invaded, the former territories of the Habsburg Empire were unexpectedly left to reorganize themselves on what Wickham Steed had helplessly warned would be the principle of '*J'y suis, j'y reste*'. Beneš, quick to realize that as much territory as possible needed to be seized before the peace conference had a chance to convene, repeatedly emphasized that this must be done quietly, so that the Czechs could be presented to the Allies as a force for order and stability in the region.[86]

It did not look as if this was going to be easy. In the formerly Austrian territories, Silesia was divided uneasily between Polish and Czech National Councils. In Bohemia and Moravia, four German Provisional Governments repudiated the authority of the Czechs' Provisional Czecho-Slovak Government; German Bohemian and Moravian socialists also banded together in national militias – *Volkswehren* or *Volksheere* – to organize strikes and obstruct the Czecho-Slovak authorities' attempts to control the railways.[87]

On 13 November, France nearly lost Slovakia for the Prague regime by absent-mindedly concluding a provisional peace treaty with Hungary that guaranteed the integrity of the historic Lands of the Crown of St Stephen. Panicked into immediate action, the National Committee in Prague assembled itself, the very same day, as a 'National Assembly' made up of 219 Czech deputies apportioned in the ratio of their political parties' results in the 1911 elections to the Vienna *Reichsrat*. On 14 November 1918, the National Assembly formally took power, giving all rival Czech National Councils until mid-December to dissolve themselves. It also issued a 'provisional' or 'temporary' constitution, thrown together by the Czech Social Democrat Alfréd Meissner, which outlined the rights of a 256-strong National Assembly to nominate a president, appoint a seventeen-member cabinet and pass emergency legislation. Masaryk, who was still in the United States, was 'unanimously' confirmed as president and Kramář as prime minister.

In Upper Hungary, things remained more confused. Slovak National Councils were closed only in those counties where a sheriff (*župan*) had already been appointed, and were given until 23 January 1919 to dissolve; some nevertheless continued to function until March. Šrobár was at first coopted into the National Assembly in Prague, leaving another *Hlasist*, Pavol Blaho, in Skalica as head of the Provisional Czecho-Slovak Government in Slovakia. The latter was replaced, first by a department, and then by a special ministry, for Slovakia.[88] Šrobár was then given *carte blanche* simply to appoint forty Slovak deputies to the National Assembly. On 15 November, Hungarian troops broke up the Slovak National Council at Turčiansky Svätý Martin, arrested its chairman and pushed Šrobár's gendarmes back to the border with Moravia.[89] In Bohemia, meanwhile, there was machine-gun fire on the streets of Brüx (*Most*) as local *Volkswehr* (national militiamen) tried to prevent the Czecho-Slovak authorities from occupying the overwhelmingly German city.[90]

Until Hungarian borders were finally settled by the Treaty of Trianon (4 June 1920), the question of where Slovakia ended and Hungary began remained a matter of political opinion and changing military circumstances. Things were complicated by the change of régime in Budapest, since Hungary's new Liberal government under Mihály Károlyi not only expressed a willingness to conclude a peace treaty with the Allied powers, but also boasted a minister for nationalities, Oszkár Jászi, who seemed quite genuine about allowing autonomous development for Hungary's minorities in the spirit of Wilson's Fourteen Points. Alarmed by the possibility that the Allies might simply leave the issue of the disputed territories under Hungarian control to be settled at the forthcoming peace conference, Beneš insisted that it was time to act. Using the same tactics that had proved so successful over the past year, the Beneš-Masaryk team exploited Allied fears of Bolshevism and played one Ally off against another to press for formal recognition of territories that had been – or were just about to be – seized by Czecho-Slovak troops. Again it was France that was particularly susceptible to arguments that a strong Czecho-Slovakia could prevent Austria and Germany from uniting as a 'pan-German' force in the middle of Europe; Britain and then Italy followed

France; the US took the longest to be persuaded, in this case coming on board just weeks before the peace conference opened in January 1919.

Things began to get messy when the Hungarian government refused to obey French orders to evacuate 'Slovakia' (*Slovensko*), on the grounds that no territory of that name appeared on its maps. Slovak deputy Milan Hodža, in independent negotiations with the Hungarian minister of defence, then came to an agreement for the evacuation of only some of the territory that Beneš claimed. Then, on 6 December 1918, Viktor Dvorčák (Dvortsak) declared the existence of an independent 'East Slovak Republic' on the grounds that 'eastern Slovaks' formed a different nationality from the rest. In the general free-for-all, the Ruthenes of eastern Ruthenia also set up a short-lived republic at Jasina, complete with miniature cabinet and parliament, but this fell as soon as Romanian troops invaded in May 1919.[91] Even the tiny village of Terchová, birthplace of Jánošík, the legendary eighteenth-century Slovak bandit, is said to have expressed the wish to have a 'small autonomous state' of its own.[92]

Šrobár placed the territory that he was calling Slovakia under martial law, but most Czecho-Slovak Legions were still out of reach, in Russia and Italy, and so could not come to his aid, while the rest of Hungary, together with Ruthenia, had already gone Bolshevik. Beneš therefore had to badger the French to go beyond the Allies' carefully worded promises and statements and the Prague government to dissociate itself from Hodža's negotiations to get troops to the Bohumín–Košice railway line in eastern Slovakia. The troops' arrival in Košice on 30 December 1918 caused the fall of the East Slovak Republic, while another column occupied Pozsony (*Pressburg, Prešporok*; soon to be renamed Wilsonovo, then Bratislava) on 1–2 January 1919. Plans were then made to occupy Teschen in Silesia.

While the Czecho-Slovak authorities were busy consolidating their territories in Bohemia, Moravia and Slovakia by a combination of diplomacy and military force, rival groups of Rusyn/Ukrainian nationalists were still discussing among themselves how best, in the present confusion, to achieve the greatest possible autonomy for Subcarpathian Ruthenia. Meetings held in Bardejov, Svidník, Stropkov, Medzilaborce and Humenné in late November and early December 1918 reiterated calls for the peace conference to settle Rusyn claims to self-determination; rival councils held at Svaljava and Maramarosh called for union with Ukraine.[93] On 21 December, Beskyd's group joined with the Lemko National Council from Galicia to form a new Carpatho-Russian National Council which, at Prešov (in Ukrainian, *Prjashiv*) on 7 January 1919, announced its wish that Subcarpathian Ruthenia be united with Czecho-Slovakia. This resulted in Beskyd being called to Prague, where it was agreed that he be sent to the peace conference as part of the Czecho-Slovak delegation. In the meantime, Czech troops took Užhorod. It was only a fortnight later that news came from the United States, where Masaryk had been busy negotiating, that the Ruthene-Americans had voted for Subcarpathian Ruthenia's inclusion in a new Czecho-Slovak state.

There remained only Silesia to be settled before the Czecho-Slovak government in Prague could present the Paris peacemakers with the *fait accompli* of an apparently united territory under its political control. Here the main problem was the Duchy of Teschen which, although theoretically Czecho-Slovak already, was three-quarters Polish-speaking, occupied by Polish troops and being run by a Polish National Council. Teschen mattered economically, because of the Bohumín–Košice railway and the coal-rich Karviná district; but also politically, because should the 'principle' of the 'indissolubility' of the Bohemian Crown Lands be undermined, there would be no plausible grounds for retaining, against their will, the Germans of Bohemia and Moravia. The Prague government, in clear defiance of Allied orders, therefore began to mass troops along the Silesian border.[94]

By 20 January 1919, just two days after the Peace Conference opened at Versailles, the Czecho-Slovak government in Prague had Bohemia and Moravia completely under its control, was poised to take over Silesia (which it occupied just three days later) and had the territory that it called Slovakia (*Slovensko*) and the Hungarians Felvidék under martial law. Subcarpathian Ruthenia, although still in chaos, could at least be shown on paper to have 'requested' inclusion as an autonomous part of the new state. Thanks to the willingness of the French government to act independently of its allies, and of the British, Italian and United States governments to deviate from their own policy statements under immediate political pressure, the provisional Czecho-Slovak government – as represented by Prime Minister Kramář and Foreign Minister Beneš – was able to enter the peace talks in a uniquely privileged position. Not only was it – alone of all the Austro-Hungarian successor states – formally represented at the armistice talks that preceded the conference, but most of the territory that it claimed by right was already under its military and political control.

At the beginning of the First World War, the notion that the Czechs and Slovaks might one day live in their own sovereign state, separated from other countries by international borders, had not been seriously contemplated by anyone. Nevertheless, a new republic, named for the Czech and Slovak peoples, and bordering on Germany, Austria, Hungary, Poland and Romania, was about to take its place at the centre of a freshly redrawn map of Europe. Those who were primarily responsible for setting up the new Europe – representatives of the victorious powers who met together at Versailles – concluded and drafted maps in 1919 as if they had already forgotten that most Austrian and Hungarian Slavs, as obedient Habsburg subjects, had been their enemies right up to the empire's end in the autumn of 1918. Czechs and Slovaks, who were to replace Germans and Magyars as the dominant groups in the new multinational state, had as much reason as anyone to feel surprise at their change of fortune. Although the two main Czech-speaking parties in prewar Austria – the Christian Socialists and the National Catholics – were now taunted for having been 'monarchist' and 'pro-Austrian', at the time of the last prewar Austrian elections (1911) every eligible Czech political party (the Agrarians, Social Democrats, National Socialists, Young Czechs [Liberals] and State Rightists) had agreed that, while greater autonomy for the Bohemian Crown Lands might one day be possible, a magical return to Bohemian independence – given the size of its German population – was unthinkable. This had also been the platform of the tiny 'Realist' Party, a fringe political organization noteworthy only with the benefit of hindsight, because its founder and sole representative in the *Reichsrat*, Tomáš Garrigue Masaryk, had just been unanimously elected Czecho-Slovakia's first president.

The Slovaks, who were brought on board for Czecho-Slovak independence even later than the Czechs, had even more reason to be astonished. Whereas the Austrian Czechs – who outnumbered German-speakers in the Bohemian Crown Lands – had had more than a hundred deputies representing a dozen political parties in the Vienna parliament and wielded considerable political power in Austria (enough to block legislation or bring down cabinets), the Hungarian Slovaks – who had managed to return only three deputies to the Budapest parliament in the last prewar elections (1910) and had just about managed to scrape together three political parties (the Slovak Nationalist Party, the Slovak Social Democratic Party and the Slovak Populist Party) – had hardly been more than a political nuisance. As for the Slavs of Subcarpathian Ruthenia, whose self-appointed spokesmen in the United States were persuaded, in exchange for promises of autonomy, to join the new state at the last minute: their traditional dilemma had been to decide whether to define themselves as Ukrainian, Rusyn or Hungarian, not whether or not to align themselves with the Czechs or Slovaks.

Subsequent nationalist propaganda notwithstanding, there was nothing inevitable about the 'rise' of a Czecho-Slovak or Czechoslovak 'nation', let alone the creation, in the second decade of the twentieth century, of an internationally recognized, independent state made up of the old Austrian provinces of Bohemia, Moravia and Silesia together with large chunks of the Hungarian highlands (*Felvidék*) and Ruthenia. The leaders of the Czecho-Slovak independence movement, above all Masaryk and Beneš, had achieved a remarkable victory against the odds. In the process, they had ridden roughshod over the stated wishes of many of their new citizens, most notably German-, Hungarian- and Polish-speakers, and had spoken on behalf of their Slovak, Ruthenian and Silesian populations without proper authority to do so.

They had also, with the possible exception of Romania, seriously alienated every one of their new neighbours: Germany, Austria, Hungary and Poland. The victorious Allies, who had helped to make all this possible by pursuing what they perceived at the time to be their own interests, later came to regret the part they had played in demolishing the Habsburg Empire and establishing what soon turned out to be a contentious and unstable state at the heart of Europe. Lloyd George, writing in 1939, faced with the very war the peace conference had so earnestly hoped to prevent, could not disguise his bitterness. 'The Czechs,' he wrote, 'were specially favoured by the Allies' since they had 'rendered considerable service to the Allied cause by starting the rot in the Austrian Army which hastened that process of disintegration that destroyed its value as a fighting machine.' The result, he continued, 'was the recognition of the polyglot and incoherent State of Czechoslovakia, and the incorporation in that State of hundreds of thousands of protesting Magyars and some millions of angry Germans'. Founding the new state had proved astonishingly easy; keeping it was to prove much more difficult.

CHAPTER 3

A TROUBLED DEMOCRACY

The First Czechoslovak Republic, traditionally dated from Independence Day (28 October 1918) until the signing of the Munich Agreement (30 September 1938), is usually treated as the pinnacle of Czechoslovak achievement, the gold standard by which all subsequent regimes are to be measured. These were the years in which the Czechs' supposedly innate tendency towards democracy – as proven by centuries of Bohemian independence and the righteousness of the Czech Hussite tradition – finally found political expression: in an independent, humane and liberal republic in which even women were given the vote, the Communist Party was allowed to take part in elections and minority rights were protected better than anywhere else in Central Europe.

People had never had it so good. Czechoslovakia ranked tenth in the world industrial league. It was famous for world-class enterprises like the Bat'a shoe empire at Zlín and the Škoda automobile works at Mladá Boleslav, and for its light industry, from glass ornaments and textiles to Prague ham and Pilsner beer. Culture flourished. The Barrandov studios on the outskirts of Prague churned out scores, perhaps hundreds, of Czech-language films which spanned every genre from comedy and tragedy to farce and horror. Opera and concerts were of the highest standard. Villas, factories and municipal buildings were built in as boldly Cubist, Constructivist or Functionalist a style as any to be found in Berlin, Vienna or Budapest (or, for that matter, Paris, Brussels or New York). Czech writers Karel Čapek (whose disturbing science-fiction play *R.U.R.* introduced the word 'robot' into the English language) and Jaroslav Hašek (whose hilarious *The Good Soldier Švejk* became an international bestseller) became household names. T.G. Masaryk, Czechoslovakia's Liberator-President, was the subject of half a dozen admiring biographies published in the English language alone. Czechoslovakia, in short, was a mature and progressive nation that was innately suited to democracy. The republic was worthy to take its place beside France and Britain as one of the democratic and morally advanced countries of the modern world.

There were at least two serious problems with this glowing account of the interwar First Czechoslovak Republic. The first was that it put forward an exclusively Czech nationalist, rather than an inclusively Czechoslovak multinational, point of view. There was no heroic Hussite past in the Slovak or Ruthenian nationalist traditions, let alone in official German, Polish or Magyar historical memory; even perfectly patriotic Czechs, but who took their Catholicism seriously, minded the Masaryk circle's vigorous promotion of a heretic as the prime symbol of Czech/Czechoslovak nationalism, and sought to replace him with an orthodox medieval martyr, St Jan of Nepomuk.[1] The second problem, largely concealed until Czech nationalists were finally given the opportunity to create a state in their own image, arose from the many overlapping, and sometimes conflicting, meanings that had attached to the word 'democracy' in different Czech nationalist circles. As Melissa Feinberg points out, in prewar Czech political discourse, 'democracy' could mean a 'liberal state with republican government', an 'egalitarian community of citizens', a 'state dedicated to social justice and equality of economic opportunity' or 'something else entirely'. Even after the establishment of the republic, the term 'democracy' was deliberately left hazy, since any attempt to pin it down definitively would have risked shattering 'the political community that had constituted itself around the idea of a Czech democracy'.[2] The coexistence of a variety of uses of the term left it flexible, ultimately allowing the Czech electorate to continue to conceive of itself as 'democratic' even when it was marching quite far down the authoritarian road, willingly accepting such dubious forms of government as 'limited democracy' and 'people's democracy' in order to protect an abstraction called 'the nation' (as opposed to individual citizens) from danger, disorder or merely defamation.[3]

The same state that was brought into being at the end of the First World War by the skilful exploitation of a favourable international climate was lost, twenty years later, through less astute handling of an unfavourable one. Between the declaration of Czecho-Slovak independence in October 1918 and the loss of the 'Sudetenland' (together with control over Slovakia and Ruthenia) in October 1938, the state had just two decades in which to establish its political conventions, gain an international reputation and learn a few conditioned reflexes. Seventy years after the Munich Crisis, it is still standard to present the interwar First Czechoslovak Republic (1918–38) as an 'island' of democracy in a stormy Central European 'sea' of radical authoritarian alternatives, whether Fascist or Communist. But Czechoslovakia's brief period of democracy, however good it may look when compared with German Nazism or Italian Fascism, was seriously flawed from the first.

In the classic narratives of interwar Czechoslovakia written during the Cold War, usually by Czech exiles living in the West, the subject of Czechoslovak democracy is invariably handled with kid gloves. In chapters with titles such as 'Years of Progress, Years of Trial', the obvious constitutional parallels with the

French and American republican systems are invariably drawn and emphasis placed on the width of the franchise, the fairness of elections, the justice of proportional representation, the explicit protections for minorities and the statesmanlike qualities of President Masaryk.[4] What is not made explicit to the innocent outsider is that in contemporary Central European thought, democracy was popularly considered to be as much about equal standing for the 'nation', i.e. for the ethnolinguistic group, as about voting or other rights for the individual. Czechs could legitimately assure their Western friends that any citizen, regardless of nationality, was free to participate in Czechoslovak elections; they did not usually add that – regardless of the election results – the same five Czech political parties would club together, across the usual Left-Right political divisions, to keep the other nationalities out of government. Similarly, while pointing to the constitutional rights accorded to minorities, they did not readily volunteer the information that the German 'minority' was substantially larger than the Slovak population and so was not really a minority at all. Nor did they make plain that official 'nationality' figures could be massaged to suit political exigencies; or explain why and how testimony given to the Allies at Versailles was deliberately controlled, and partially falsified, by an ethnically Czech 'Czecho-Slovak' delegation which did not hesitate to have those who disagreed with it locked up.

The First Czechoslovak Republic began (1918–20) and ended (1938–39) with brief periods of military dictatorship. From the spring of 1935 to the autumn of 1938, it was in a period of prolonged domestic and international crisis. But even during the fifteen years (1920–35) when the country's borders appeared settled and the state's official minorities seemed more or less reconciled to their inclusion in the state, a number of highly questionable practices were used to ensure that political control was centred in Prague and that the overwhelming majority of non-Czechs were excluded from power. Czechoslovakia did indeed retain its own, increasingly idiosyncratic version of parliamentary democracy for longer than its European neighbours; but it did so against the clearly expressed wishes of a majority of its non-Czech citizens. Had the First Czechoslovak Republic been less Czech-chauvinist and less Prague-centred, it would have gone authoritarian, and even Fascist, at about the same time as its neighbours. As things turned out, this happened anyway: but not until just after the international community – represented by Germany, Italy, France and Britain – had intervened at Munich to break Czech domination of the multinational state. Czechoslovakia's disintegration into its constituent ethnic parts followed within the week.

When the Austro-Hungarian Empire fell apart at the end of the First World War, it did so largely because its enemies had managed successfully to exploit the jealousies, suspicions and rivalries that existed among its various 'nationalities' or peoples, not least among its Czech, German, Polish, Jewish,

Slovak, Rusyn and Magyar populations. Instead of trying to glue the territory of the Habsburg Empire back together, the victorious Allied powers chose to replace it with a series of modern, liberal, democratic states of roughly equal size. This was supposed to ensure stability in the region by curbing German and Magyar influence, appeasing the nationalist aspirations of the Slav majority and aligning Central Europe with the Entente powers, especially France. The newfangled entity called Czecho-Slovakia took the industrial heartlands of Austria (Cisleithania) in the shape of the Bohemian Crown Lands (Bohemia, Moravia and Austrian Silesia) and the entire highland district (Felvidék or Upper Hungary) of the Lands of the Crown of St Stephen, the historic Hungarian kingdom. Poland was reconstituted mainly at the expense of Prussia; while Croatia, Slovenia, Serbia and the formerly Habsburg part of Serbia were combined to form a second newly invented state, this time named for the southern Slavs ('Yugo-Slavs'), as distinct from western Slavs like the Poles or 'Czecho-Slovaks' of Austria-Hungary.

Although the Austro-Hungarian Empire was not revived, it continued to cast long shadows over all of the successor states that were set up to replace it. As even the most casual visitor to the country could not fail to notice, Czechoslovakia's food, architecture and culture remained exuberantly and irrepressibly Habsburg. So did most of its legal, bureaucratic and political instincts and practices, including those chillingly evoked by the German-speaking Bohemian Jew Franz Kafka in his *The Trial* and *The Castle*; or more light-heartedly satirized by Jaroslav Hašek, the Czech-speaking Bohemian author of *The Good Soldier Švejk* and founder of a mock-political party rejoicing in the name of 'The Party of Moderate Progress within the Bounds of the Law' (*Strana mírného pokroku v mezích zákona*).[5]

Old imbalances that had existed between the two halves of the prewar Austro-Hungarian Empire were hardly likely to disappear with the creation of a state whose western half was made up of the prosperous, relatively urbanized and heavily industrialized Bohemian Crown Lands (where the dominant culture was Austrian petty bourgeois), but whose eastern half, consisting largely of impoverished Hungarian highlands and emptying Ruthenian forests, held traditional country values as shaped by Magyar aristocrats and Slav peasants. It felt fifty years away from Prague's smart shops, cafés, theatres, concert halls, cinemas, museums, opera houses and nightclubs – or, for that matter, from the factories, housing estates and brew-eries of Ostrava in Silesia – to the sleepy provincial Slovak capital of Bratislava (formerly Pressburg). And it felt more like a hundred from the rustic world of the eastern Slovak peasant and the outer reaches of Subcarpathian Ruthenia, where visitors, who refused to drink the water, found it difficult to decide which ethnic group was the more miserably destitute and oppressed: the Rusyns, the Gypsies or the Jews.[6]

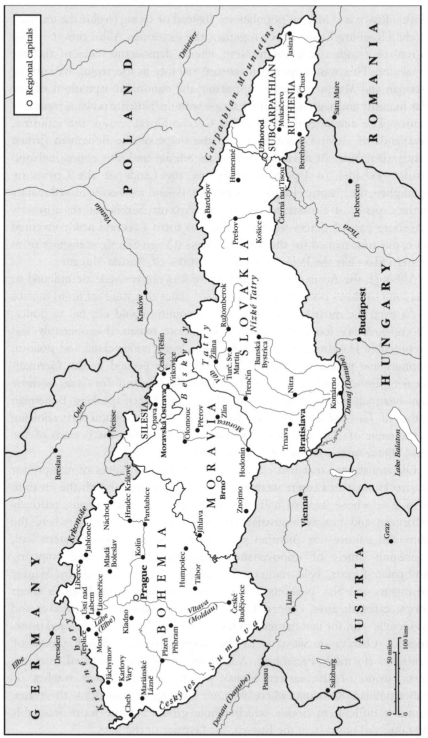

The First Czechoslovak Republic, 1920–38

In addition to their many other obvious advantages, citizens of the new Czecho-Slovak republic living in the formerly Austrian regions of Bohemia, Moravia or Silesia found themselves within easy reach of Prague, suddenly turned capital city, and already *au fait* with the state's legal, political and fiscal conventions, which remained Austrian in all but name. People living in the eastern, formerly Hungarian, regions of Slovakia and Subcarpathian Ruthenia, on the other hand, were not only remote from the centre, but had to learn the new rules from scratch while simultaneously struggling with disrupted trade routes, inadequate infrastructure and a series of military invasions as their land was fought over by rival powers. While bands of ethnic Slovak, Jewish, Magyar and Ruthene mercenaries turned Czecho-Slovakia's eastern provinces into bandit country for the first months – even years – of the state's official existence, at the same time that Czechoslovak, Romanian and Hungarian armies were fighting over them, things were relatively quiet in the western regions where Austrian Czechs slipped easily into the place of Austrian Germans, issuing a steady stream of decrees, directives, regulations, laws and bye-laws – this time from Prague rather than Vienna or Budapest – for the instruction and control of those living in the provinces.

The most far-reaching aspect of *fin-de-siècle* Austro-Hungarian thought to be retained by the Czechoslovak republic was its way of conceiving of 'nationhood' or 'nationality'. Although 'nationality' (not to be confused with 'citizenship') was defined primarily through language, the term was used in much the same way as 'ethnicity' or 'race' in the English-speaking world. Everyone who had grown up in the empire, in addition to being counted as a subject, had become used to being categorized – through mandatory participation in official government censuses – as belonging to a single 'nationality'. But although every household was legally required to provide a census return, it was ultimately up to the person being questioned to declare his or her principal language, which in turn decided ethnolinguistic affiliation. Despite being subjective, these 'nationality' figures were afterwards treated as if they were at once objective and meaningful. At their most innocent, these were the figures that were used to calculate the number of state-subsidized schools, libraries, theatres and other such language-specific institutions to be supplied to each 'nation' (ethnolinguistic group). They were also the statistics that were left, unchallenged, to politicians, sociologists, historians and others with an interest in making generalizations about the supposed progress, treatment, plight or attainment of each 'nation', whether under the old Habsburg or successive Czechoslovak/Czecho-Slovak administrations. Crucially, they were the figures that determined which 'nation' or 'nations' were to be treated as the official state-forming people or peoples and which classified as mere 'minorities'. Ultimately, they were to determine who was to be allowed to remain in or be forcibly removed from the state.

Census figures, coloured maps, school textbooks and nationalist histories notwithstanding, the dozen or so peoples who had inhabited the Habsburg Empire for centuries, and now made up the bulk of the population of Czecho-Slovakia/Czechoslovakia, did not live apart from each other in a state of chemical purity, but were hopelessly intermixed. It could hardly have been otherwise. People from different language groups could and did intermarry and bring up their children bilingual or even trilingual. They frequently spoke one language at home and another at work. Some chose – whether for pragmatic, political or romantic reasons – to identify themselves with a 'national' group whose language they could barely speak. They could be persuaded, bribed or bullied by census-takers into identifying themselves, if only on paper, with one group rather than another. Finally, they could always switch back and forth between (or among) nationalities, as expediency seemed to dictate. As multilingual, multiethnic (in Central European parlance, 'multinational') states, Austria and Hungary had somehow had to try to accommodate the rival claims of a dozen mutually suspicious peoples or 'nations' without destroying the fabric of the state. Although they did not manage this with conspicuous success – one of the reasons for the empire's downfall – the successor states, which, over the course of the twentieth century, ended up resorting to such extremes as attempted genocide, wholesale expulsions and forced exchanges of populations, were to manage even less well.

What mattered most in the First Czechoslovak Republic was not political affiliation, but ethnicity or 'nationality'. It was not only the explicitly nationalist and fascist parties that were strictly divided along ethnolinguistic lines; so were the liberal, conservative, Christian and socialist parties. This was a country in which even the Communists – usually renowned for the strictness of their party discipline – had to be badgered by Moscow for a full five months before reluctantly agreeing, in October 1921, to form a single Czechoslovak Communist Party (*Komunistická strana Československa* or *KSČ*), which thereafter held the honour of being the only political party in the state in which all language groups were represented. Not for nothing did Mussolini quip that 'Czecho-Slovakia' should instead have been named 'Czecho-Germano-Polono-Magyaro-Rutheno-Rumono-Slovakia'.[7]

When the Czechoslovak Republic first came into being at the end of October 1918, it was a Czech state in which there was also some token Slovak representation. Proclamations and declarations issued from Paris, Prague and Washington, D.C. in the last days of the war had spoken grandly of a 'Czecho-Slovak' state for a 'Czecho-Slovak' nation, but had been conceived with the much more narrowly Czech nationalist objective of promoting Czech Bohemian – as against German Bohemian – interests. Since Upper Hungary was in a state of chaos, Silesia was being claimed by Poland, and Ruthenia was as yet undecided as to which of its new neighbours would be most likely to grant it autonomy, the self-proclaimed Czecho-Slovak government in Prague was for the time being in control of just two regions – Bohemia and Moravia – which were in turn inhabited by two main groups: the Germans, who had excluded themselves as well as having been excluded from power; and the Czechs, who were running things. It was during this first, chaotic chapter of the state's history – which lasted from the end of the European war in November 1918 until March 1920, when the first full Czechoslovak constitution came into effect – that the country's territory, and therefore its ethnolinguistic composition, was decided.

The provisional Czecho-Slovak government in Prague, which at first had no control over the highlands of Hungary, simply decreed Hungarian law no longer valid in 'Slovakia', a territory that it declared would henceforward be administered in the Slovak language. The Prague government further asserted its right to 'issue decrees' and do whatever it deemed 'necessary' to 'consolidate the situation' and keep 'order' in Slovakia until the state could begin to function 'properly'.[8] In order to police the region, purge the state sector of Magyars (Hungarian-speakers) and impose its own administration, Slovakia's first dictator, Vavro Šrobár, was in December 1918 appointed head of an institution that was to survive until 1927: the *Ministerstvo s plnou mocou pre správu Slovenska* (Ministry with Power of Attorney for the Administration of Slovakia, hereafter cited as the Ministry for Slovakia). Initially based at the mainly Slovak-speaking town of Žilina (*Sillein*), it was soon moved to the city that was to become Slovakia's regional capital: the predominantly German- and Hungarian-speaking town of Pressburg/Pozsony (*Prešporok/Prešpurk*), which – after toying briefly with the name *Wilsonovo* (Wilsonville) – was on 15 February 1919 given the misleadingly Slavonic-sounding name of Bratislava.[9]

With the imposition of Czecho-Slovak rule came a distinct anticlericalism. It seems rational to assume that, in a country in which about 80 per cent of the population were baptized Catholics, the signs must have been disturbing to millions of citizens – of whatever nationality – who took their formal membership in the Catholic Church at more than face value. On 3 November 1918, a Czech National Socialist crowd on its way back from a rally held at Bílá hora (the site of the Bohemian Protestant defeat at the Battle of the White Mountain) pulled down the seventeenth-century column of the Virgin Mary which since 1915 had shared Prague's Old Town Square with an enormous Art Nouveau statue of Jan Hus. Czech nationalists attacked Catholic statues throughout the Bohemian Crown Lands, insisted on the removal of crucifixes from schools and were suspicious or contemptuous of observant Catholics, who were pilloried as 'superstitious' and 'reactionary' peasants or else treated as crypto-imperialists who might be working secretly towards a Habsburg restoration.[10] Masaryk, who had formally renounced his own Catholic faith in favour of an idiosyncratic blend of Protestantism, Catholicism and Czech nationalism, represented a stream of thought that blended easily with modern Liberal thought; others rejected God and organized religion altogether in favour of socialism or Marxism; still others considered 'Czechoslovak' nationality to derive from shared Czech and Slovak non-conformist traditions. Within days of its assumption of power in Slovakia, the Šrobár regime had deeply alienated Slovak Catholic opinion with its obvious favouritism towards Slovak Lutherans, together with its undisguised contempt for Catholicism. This prompted Fr Andrej Hlinka, the Slovak nationalist who had won international sympathy in the late nineteenth century for his maltreatment – including imprisonment – by the Hungarians, to re-establish the Slovak branch of the People's Party as a vehicle to lobby for Catholic interests, together with the right of Slovak-speakers (as opposed to Czechs, Magyars or Jews) to administer affairs in Slovakia.

While Slovakia was being dealt with in the manner of a conquered, rather than a liberated, territory, the regions of Bohemia and Moravia were being treated to a series of measures, at once socialist and nationalist, designed to transfer political and economic power from the old German and Magyar to the new Czecho-Slovak élites. Aristocratic titles, most of which had been held by Germans or Magyars, were abolished overnight; unemployment benefit was set up and an eight-hour working day established.[11] The 'revolutionary' Kramář government further promised to work towards the nationalization of the coalmines and the redistribution of large landed estates, most of which had previously been held in German and Magyar hands.[12] The sudden transition from empire to nation-state was, as Eagle Glassheim has put it, particularly traumatic for German-speaking aristocrats, whose 'national' identity, as they had defined it, 'simply disappeared, replaced by a middle-class nation-state that treated both Germans and nobles as national antagonists'.[13] Poor and middle-class German speakers were also hit after finance minister Alois Rašín drastically reduced the supply of Austrian crowns in circulation from February 1919;[14] later claimed to have spared Czechoslovakia hyperinflation, its most obvious effect at the time was substantially to increase postwar misery in the German-inhabited border areas of Bohemia and Moravia, where the export market collapsed and severe unemployment followed.

Since no one could be certain that the borders that the Masaryk-Beneš-Štefánik team had proposed in the last year of the war would actually be accepted by the postwar peace conference, the Prague government – working closely with President Masaryk and Foreign Minister Beneš – did all it could to enforce compliance in advance of Versailles. First, Czech troops put down the self-proclaimed 'capitals' of Deutschböhmen and Sudetenland and took control of Bohemia. At his formal inauguration as President of the

Republic at the Castle (*Hrad*) at Hradčany in Prague on 21 December 1918, Masaryk bluntly informed his German compatriots that they had no hope of being attached to German Austria. Within the month, there were new laws to prevent Austrian Germans from visiting relatives and former neighbours in what were now classed as 'Czecho-Slovak' villages unless they carried formal travel documents; the penalty for noncompliance was set at a fine of a thousand crowns or a month in prison.[15]

In his first address to the National Assembly (22 December 1918), President Masaryk again spelled out the message: the Germans would not be allowed to leave the state, but the state belonged morally to the Czechs. '*We* have created this State,' he told his fellow Czechs in Parliament, 'and this determines the constitutional position of our Germans who originally entered the country as immigrants and colonists.'[16] The implication, that German-speakers – who, like the Magyars and Poles, as yet had no representatives in parliament – had less right than Czech-speakers to a share of power in their common homeland, was hardly calculated to reassure German Bohemians, already anxious enough to find themselves trapped in a state dominated by their old Czech rivals. In his New Year speech on 1 January 1919, President Masaryk made explicit his view that there was 'an obvious difference' between the two nations in the possible applications of the right to self-determination since 'with the exception of a few small frontier minorities we Czechs and Slovaks are a homogeneous nation', whereas 'our Germans ... do not represent their whole nation but [are] only its colonising avant-garde'.[17] None of this did anything to soften the already legendary pan-German nationalism of the Bohemian Germans, who had just lost more men, proportionately, in the war than any other ethnic German group in Europe and who were being lectured by a man who had himself grown up a German and made his career by switching sides. Hoping against hope to be allowed to express their own 'right' to 'national self-determination' and to join in the new Austrian state, where they would belong to the majority nationality, rather than become a despised minority in a Slav-dominated enlarged Bohemian state, the Germans of the Bohemian Crown Lands – like every other self-consciously 'national' group in Central Europe – now pinned their hopes on the forthcoming peace settlement.

The long-awaited peace conference opened at Versailles, near Paris, on 18 January 1919. It was to conclude its business with Austria with the signing of the Treaty of St Germain-en-Laye on 10 September 1919 and with Hungary when the Treaty of Trianon was finally signed on 4 June 1920. On 5 February 1919, the Czecho-Slovak delegation was granted the special privilege of being allowed to put its case directly to the Council of Ten, the collective name given to the premiers and foreign ministers of the five principal Allied countries (the USA, Britain, France, Italy and Japan), which was gradually reconfigured as Councils of Five, Four and, eventually, Three.[18]

Despite being officially headed by Prime Minister Kramář, it was Czecho-Slovakia's foreign minister, Beneš, who held forth most memorably about the indissolubility of the Lands of the Bohemian Crown (now, audaciously, claimed to have formed a single state since the sixth century) and the right to 'self-determination' of the Slovak-speakers of Upper Hungary. After being subjected to hours of the foreign ministers of Czecho-Slovakia and Poland expounding on their rival claims to the economically and strategically impor-tant district of Teschen (*Těšín, Cieszyn*) in Silesia, historically part of the Bohemian Crown Lands but overwhelmingly Polish in ethnicity, President Wilson was not alone among the members of the Council of Ten in feeling exasperated by 'the futility of listening day after day to complicated claims' whose merits he did not feel in a position to judge competently.[19] Isaiah Bowman, another member of the US team, similarly recalled how when the Polish representative 'related the claims of Poland, he began at eleven o'clock in the morning and in the fourteenth century, and could only reach 1919 and the pressing problems of the moment only as late as four o'clock in the afternoon', while Beneš, 'who followed immediately afterwards with the counter-claims of Czechoslovakia . . . began a century earlier and finished an hour later'.[20]

In the end, the Council handed over the whole complex of problems of the successor states to special commissions of 'experts'. These turned out to be less well informed than had been blandly assumed. As a youthful Harold Nicolson, one of the 'experts', later recalled, 'I had myself specialized for ten years upon the problems of the Balkans and South-Eastern Europe. Yet I was appointed to the committee on Czecho-Slovak frontiers, a subject for which I was totally ill-equipped.'[21] He later found, to his horror, that decisions he had taken on aspects of Czecho-Slovakia's borders, which he had assumed would be checked by a higher and more competent authority, were simply left to stand unchallenged.

The Commission on Czecho-Slovak Affairs sat from 28 February until 12 March 1919, when it presented its recommendations regarding the new state's frontiers. Thanks mainly to French backing, on 4 April 1919 the new state's proposed borders with Germany were nodded through. There was not even discussion of the possible need to protect the German-speaking minority (estimated in Austrian statistics to number about two and a half million and by the Czecho-Slovak delegation to number 'approximately 800,000'). Only on 1 May 1919, after it occurred to someone to question the wisdom of including quite such a large German minority, was the matter referred to a subcommittee. In order to forestall the inevitable objections, on 20 May 1919 Beneš submitted a special 'Note on the Régime of Nationalities in the Czecho-Slovak Republic' in which he declared it to be his government's intention to 'make of the Czecho-Slovak Republic a sort of Switzerland, taking into consideration, of course, the special conditions in Bohemia'. Although never stating in so many words that Czechoslovakia would replicate the Swiss canton system exactly, this was – not unnaturally – what his listeners assumed. He further specified that, although 'Czech' (*sic*) would become the official state language, German would be used 'on an equal footing with Czech' in matters of administration, before the courts and in parliament; that all public offices would be open to all nationalities; that the voting system would ensure proportional representation for all nationalities; that state-funded schools in all relevant languages would be supplied according to the needs of local children; and that local administration would be conducted 'in the language of the majority of the population'. All this, Beneš reiterated, would make Czecho-Slovakia an 'extremely liberal' state that would 'very much resemble that of Switzerland'.[22]

Lloyd George, one of the many veterans of the peace conference later to conclude that he had been deceived by the smaller nations, remembered with particular clarity how Beneš had 'larded' his speech with phrases that positively 'reeked with professions of sympathy for the exalted ideals proclaimed by the Allies', and with what 'skill and craft' the Czecho-Slovak case had been presented at Versailles.[23] Another eyewitness noted that the youthful Beneš possessed the 'rare gift' of 'identifying his country's aspirations with the postulates of a settled peace', and wryly observed how he would begin 'by detaching himself from all national interests' and, 'starting from general assumptions recognised by the Olympians' would 'lead his hearers by easy stages to the conclusions which he wished them to draw from their own premisses'.[24] At the end of May 1919, the Peace Conference approved Czecho-Slovakia's proposed borders with Germany. At a stroke, this granted Czech nationalists the dream that they had been harbouring for sixty years or more: the restoration of an independent Bohemian state, but this time ruled and dominated by the Czechs. The pair who had achieved the impossible were flushed with success. Beneš wrote to his old professor that the Allies insisted that he was 'the only person who has credit here and who at the conference can achieve everything'; Masaryk confided back his own view that, if the Ententemen 'had any sense', they would make him, Masaryk, a member of the Council of Four.[25]

The Council of Ten's members, together with their teams of 'experts', may have been ignorant of the intricacies of Central European geography, history and ethnic conflict, but they were not stupid. They could hardly fail to notice the central contradiction in the Czecho-Slovak delegation's argument, which relied on the principle of 'historic right' to claim the German-speaking parts of Bohemia and Moravia and the Polish-speaking parts of Silesia, but abandoned the principle when it came to Hungary's corresponding rights to the historic Lands of the Crown of St Stephen, suddenly turning to pragmatic arguments (for the economic and strategic viability of the new state) or emotive appeals to 'self-determination' (for Slovaks and Ruthenes, but not Magyars, Jews, Romanians or Germans). In part because 'Czecho-Slovakia' had already been accorded the status of a friendly, Allied state; in part because all of the Austro-Hungarian successor states were distorting their national histories and population figures; but above all because the existence of a Slav state bang in the middle of ethnic German territory was central to the Franco-British vision of how postwar Central Europe should be reorganized, everyone was at first willing to overlook the contradictions. Successive councils not only indulged the Czecho-Slovak delegation's improbable statistics, but also a number of its equally dubious assertions, among others that the Czechs and Slovaks, although 'separated for a thousand years', nevertheless formed a single 'nation', and that the Bohemian Germans 'themselves realized' that they 'must remain' in Bohemia or else face economic ruin.[26]

The Czecho-Slovaks had raised eyebrows when, at the very start of the conference, they invaded Teschen. Now, as weeks and then months passed in endless committee meetings, the number of anomalies brought to the Allies' attention began to mount up. In February, news reached France of demonstrations in Bratislava at which eight demonstrators had been killed and another forty injured by Czecho-Slovak legionnaires. On 4 March, during Bohemian German demonstrations against being prevented from participating in Austrian elections, fifty-three mostly unarmed Germans were killed and a further eighty wounded by Czech gendarmes in response to such provocations as the raising of a German flag over the central market square in the German-speaking Bohemian town of Kaaden/Kadaň and the singing of the German nationalist song '*Die Wacht am Rhein*'.[27] At the end of March, a 'petition in boots', 'smelling like a sheep pen', actually turned up at Versailles, a delegation having come all the way from the Spiš and Orava districts of northern Hungary to beg President Wilson to have their 'little mountain pocket' attached to Poland rather than to Czecho-Slovakia.[28] None of this put either the Prague government or the Czecho-Slovak delegation in Paris in a good light; behind his back at the peace conference, Beneš was already being called 'the little fox'.[29]

On 4 May 1919, Štefánik left Italy for what was meant to be a triumphal return to his native Slovakia; he was killed when his plane crashed in a field outside Bratislava. As it happened, for some months Beneš had been sending confidential reports to Masaryk and to French officials, warning that Štefánik was plotting to sideline the French in favour of the Italians, and even to place an Italian prince on the Bohemian throne.[30] Once Štefánik was dead, Beneš joined in the general chorus of his praise,[31] but this did not prevent unconfirmed rumours from spreading in some Slovak circles that the Czecho-Slovak military had deliberately shot down his plane.[32] Since no one knew what Štefánik would have done next, Lutherans and Catholics, centralists and autonomists, were all able to claim his mantle, making him one of the most uncontroversial and – as things turned out – enduring of Slovak national heroes. A vast mausoleum to house his earthly remains was built at Bradlo, north-east of Brezová pod Bradlom, where it stands to this day, dominating a hill overlooking the village of his birth. The same familiar photograph of him in uniform is routinely reproduced in school textbooks, histories and documentaries about the founding of the state.

On 8 May 1919, Gregory Žatkovyč (Gregorij Žatković), leader of the American Ruthenes' 'Central Rusyn National Council' based at Homestead, Pennsylvania, with whom Masaryk had been negotiating in Scranton, Pennsylvania, was named as ruler (later governor) of Subcarpathian Ruthenia. In a similar arrangement to that which prevailed in Šrobár's Slovakia, Žatkovyč – together with four ministers – was initially granted dictatorial powers and given instructions to prevent a Bolshevik revolution, enforce Czecho-Slovak law and 'de-Magyarize' (i.e. purge) the region. The territory's 'temporary' borders (which later turned out to be permanent) left about one-fifth of the total Rusyn/Ukrainian speaking population in the Prešov/Prjashiv region of eastern Slovakia.[33]

After the Communist coup in Budapest on 21 March 1919, conflict again broke out between the Czecho-Slovak and Hungarian armies. On 15 June 1919, the Hungarian Communist regime led by Béla Kun signalled its willing-ness to retreat behind the demarcation line set by the peace conference; the following day, 16 June 1919, a Slovak Soviet Republic was declared in Prešov (*Eperjes*); and on 20 June, a Council of People's Commissars was set up by the Hungarians in nearby Košice, in what is now eastern Slovakia. Béla Kun's Bolshevik regime, known in the region as 'Jewish-Bolshevik' because of the prominent number of Jews – including Kun – in the Revolutionary Governing Council, collapsed in August 1919.[34] Hungary again declared itself to be a monarchy, thus unexpectedly reopening the possibility of a Slovak-Hungarian *rapprochement*, perhaps even the restoration of a federated Habsburg Empire.[35]

Andrej Hlinka, one of original signatories of the Martin Declaration (30 October 1918) which had proclaimed Slovakia's desire to unite with the Czechs in a joint Czecho-Slovak state, had already felt it necessary to revive the Slovak People's Party to protect Slovak Catholic interests as against those of Slovak Protestants like Šrobár's Hlasists. In August 1919, he found out about the existence of the Pittsburgh Agreement, the declaration that Masaryk had signed with Slovak and Czech émigré groups in Pittsburgh, Pennsylvania on 30 May 1918, but which had not been known about in Slovakia. Incensed by what he saw as the broken promises that Slovakia would have its own administration, courts and diet, and that 'Slovak' (rather than 'Czecho-Slovak') would be the official language of schools and in public affairs, in mid-September 1919 Hlinka travelled surreptitiously to France, on Polish travel documents and accompanied by a Hungarian (Magyarone or assimilationist) Slovak priest, František Jehlička, to request that the peace conference grant 'Slovakia' autonomy and 'the Slovaks' (not Czecho-Slovaks) minority protection. 'We are neither Czechs nor Czechoslovaks,' declared the memo that Hlinka and Jehlička carried with them; 'we are just simply Slovaks.'[36] Though Hlinka never managed to meet with the representatives of the Great Powers, Beneš had him arrested for treason as soon as he returned from Versailles; he was kept in prison, safely out of the way, until April 1920.

On 4 June 1920, Hungary agreed to the Slovak-Hungarian demarcation line as set out in the Treaty of Trianon, but only on the explicit understanding that the treaty represented a stopgap measure open to the possibility of later, negotiated revision. Later, when it became apparent that the provisional 'demarcation line' had hardened into a firm, internationally recognized border, Hungary – which lost a staggering two-thirds of its former territory (without Croatia) and roughly 60 per cent of its population – came to resent the whole postwar settlement as a deceitful trick played on it by a Franco-Czech conspiracy and did all it could to tempt Slovakia and Ruthenia back. The new arrangements were not welcomed by all Slovaks, either. The sudden appearance of an international border to separate Felvidék/Slovakia from what remained of Hungary was especially hard on agricultural labourers, who had been used to being able to travel freely to the Hungarian plain for seasonal work, and also on local industries, which had previously been protected by Hungarian subsidies but now had to face competition from the Bohemian Crown Lands. Just as the local Slovak economy seemed to be collapsing, the Prague government tactlessly imposed considerably higher taxes than in the Bohemian Crown Lands; worse still, it broke with Hungarian conventions by insisting upon enforcing their collection.[37] Small wonder that figures for ethnic Ruthene and Slovak emigration, already terrible before the war, actually worsened in the first years of the Czecho-Slovak dictatorship. As Hlinka put it – with characteristic melodrama – the Slovaks, in their 'brief association with the Czechs', had already 'suffered more' from them than they had 'from the Magyars in a thousand years'.[38]

Rusyn nationalist leaders, who had specified inclusion of 'all the original Uhro-Ruthenian counties'[39] in an autonomous Ruthenian territory, and who had been assured that the notional boundaries of Subcarpathian Ruthenia described in the treaties of 28 June 1919 and 10 September 1919 were subject to further discussion and revision, were similarly crestfallen to find that the Ruthenes of the Spiš, Šariš and Zemplín counties (the Prešov district) of Slovakia were to be left out. Eventually, in March 1921, Governor Žatkovyč resigned over the issue, and a Russian National Party (*Rosiys'ka Narodna*

Partija), which continued the campaign, was set up in Prešov by Antonij Beskyd. Not until he was appointed second governor of the province, in 1923, did Beskyd begin to tone down his anti-Prague polemic,[40] thus earning the contempt of a rival, Ukrainophile faction, which took over the job. What even an apologist for the Czechoslovak government in 1921 could not describe as a satisfactory situation in the destitute and repressed region was blamed on 'the Magyar Government' for having left Ruthenia in 'a state of intellectual and economic bankruptcy', on local 'Jewish masters' to whom the Ruthenians were 'mere slaves', and on local 'officials' who 'also exploit the Ruthenian peasantry'.[41]

In order to prevent the possibility of Slovak or Ruthenian territory being returned to Hungary, Beneš approached Yugoslavia and Romania, which had also received large portions of formerly Hungarian land, with a scheme, later known as the 'Little Entente', to prevent any revision of the Trianon settlement. Beneš had the first treaty ready in time to be signed by all three beneficiaries on 14 August 1920. In the meantime, the question of Teschen had become so emotive – on both sides of the Polish–Czechoslovak border – that it was considered too explosive to hold a plebiscite and left to the Peace Conference to take an executive decision. On 28 July 1920, it was decided that Poland could have the city of Teschen and the territory to the north, but that Czecho-Slovakia would get the economically and strategically vital railways and coalfields. The settlement, which satisfied no one, left Silesia uneasily divided. Since the conference's decision came at the same time as the Soviet advance on Warsaw, the Poles blamed the Czechs for what they saw as their taking advantage of them at a moment of national danger.[42]

Czecho-Slovakia emerged from the peace conference with virtually all of its territorial demands satisfied. Only Masaryk's wilder fantasies that special treatment be accorded to the Sorb minority in Lusatia or a special corridor be created to guarantee Czecho-Slovak access to the Adriatic Sea were dismissed, in the first case as 'mere rubbish' and in the second as 'completely unjustified'.[43] Masaryk's wartime dream had come true. Never mind that there were half a million more Germans than Slovaks living in the country; that the city of Bratislava was overwhelmingly German and Hungarian; that only a handful of Slovaks shared the bright vision of a progressive Czecho-Slovakia; or that most Ruthenians seemed to be in the thrall of Bolsheviks, Jews or Greek Catholic 'clericals'. Much of this could be expected to improve over time, providing the central government in Prague took seriously its primary tasks of promoting Czech interests, encouraging the growth of a resolutely Czecho-Slovak nation and insisting upon loyalty to the state. Over the course of the second half of the nineteenth century, Czechs had moved from the periphery of Bohemian life to its economic, cultural, social and even political centre with remarkable speed, outstripping the Germans in almost every aspect of public life. Masaryk and Beneš were confident that success would continue to breed success and that firm political leadership, combined with 'natural demographic change', would make the problem of Czechoslovakia's nationalities melt away. Since it could safely be assumed that ambitious Germans and Magyars would master whatever language they needed to get ahead, just as Czechs and Slovaks had, there would be an inbuilt tendency for Czech- and Slovak-speaking populations to increase at a rate to outstrip German and Magyar growth, resulting, within a few decades, in what Beneš confidently predicted would be a 'fifteen-million nation' which could neither 'disappear or be denationalised'.[44]

The first, crucial step in making Czecho-Slovakia into a 'national' state of Czecho-Slovaks (Czechs and Slovaks) was to alter the way in which census information was gathered. This would give the nation a head start by ensuring that the maximum possible number of 'Czechoslovaks' and minimum number of 'Germans' and 'Magyars' were recorded. The last census (1910) to be carried out by the Austro-Hungarian government had asked respondents to give their 'nationality' according to their 'language of daily use' (*Umgangsprache/obcovací řeč*). This formulation, as Czech and Slovak nationalists were quick to point out, had solicited artificially high numbers of Germans and Magyars (Hungarian-speakers), since it was a practical necessity for any ambitious Czech to conduct at least some of his business in German and impossible for an ambitious speaker of Slovak or Rusyn/Ukrainian to get very far without Hungarian.

In 1921, when the first Czechoslovak census was taken, the offending question was replaced with one that asked for the respondent's 'mother tongue' (*mateřský jazyk*), a question that was kept in the following census (1930), last to be taken before the Second World War. While the formulation 'mother tongue' rid the census of one sort of bias, it did so only to replace it with another. By failing to take account of people who ceased to speak Czech or Slovak when they left the nursery, who were raised in bilingual or even trilingual homes, or who normally used German or Hungarian at school, university or work, the new phrasing was calculated to inflate the number of speakers of 'Czechoslovak'. Hence the sharp discrepancies between the 1910 and 1921 census results for 'nationalities' living in the territories of Czechoslovakia, which in the first case gave the number of 'Germans' as 3,750,327, but in the second – despite overall population increases – as only 3,123,568, while the number of people officially categorized as 'Magyars' similarly fell from 1,070,854 to 745,451.[45]

It was easy to inflate the number of 'Czechoslovaks' further by suggesting to Ruthenes living in Slovakia that, since the local term 'Rusnak' had a primarily religious meaning, they should consider themselves to be 'Slovaks of the Greek Catholic faith' and put themselves down as 'Czechoslovaks'. This appears to be the reason that a preliminary census taken in Slovakia in 1919 found that the number of people claiming to be Rusyn (93,411) had dropped by 17,869 from the number recorded in the last Hungarian census, of 1910. The figure fell even lower in the first Czechoslovak census of 1921, to 85,628.[46] In addition to inflating the figures for 'Czechoslovaks', those for 'Germans' and 'Magyars' could be further reduced in census returns by encouraging German-, Yiddish- and Hungarian-speaking Jews to opt for the new category of Jewish 'nationality' (as opposed to religion). In the city of Prague, for example, which had been overwhelmingly Czech-speaking since the late nineteenth century, the Jewish population had been more or less evenly divided between German- and Czech-speakers (the 1900 census had recorded that, out of a total Jewish population of about 25,000, 14,145 considered Czech and 11,346 German to be their 'language of daily use'). But in the first Czechoslovak census of 1921, although the Jewish population had risen to about 30,000, because some 5,900 opted for the new category of 'Jewish nationality', only 7,406 Jews were recorded as 'Germans', the remaining 16,342 being classified as 'Czechs'.[47]

Czechoslovak censuses avoided taking separate figures for Czech- and Slovak-speakers, who were disingenuously classified as 'Czechoslovaks'. To lump Czechs and Slovaks (not to speak of the occasional Rusyn) together into this single category served at least two politically useful ends. First, it papered over the inconvenient fact that German-speakers outnumbered Slovak-speakers. Second, it endorsed the official government line that Czechs and Slovaks were really separate branches of a single 'nation', which, thus defined, could be said to form a healthy majority 'nationality' of some 65 per cent of the total population. It was as 'Czechoslovaks', not as 'Czechs' or 'Slovaks', that native speakers of Czech or Slovak were granted the special status of belonging to the 'state-forming people' (*státotvorný národ* or *Staatsvolk*), the official constituent 'nation' of the state, as distinct from mere 'minorities', which was how Germans, as well as Magyars (Hungarian-speakers), and Poles and Ruthenians who did not opt to be counted as Czechoslovaks, were classified. Two groups did not quite fit the scheme and were weakened politically as a consequence: Jews, who were entitled to claim Jewish 'nationality' (and therefore minority status), but only if willing to put their 'religious affiliation' ahead of their 'maternal language'; and Gypsies (*Roma*), who were left out of the equation altogether by not being given the option to claim either race or the Romany language as their primary 'national' identifier.

When, in October 1918, Czechs cheered for a 'democratic' Czecho-Slovak republic, they did so, as Melissa Feinberg reminds us, at least as much because they believed it to be 'the form of government that would best enable the Czech nation to flourish' as because it could help create 'a just system of governance for all'.[48] The double message – that the state was to be strictly democratic in giving citizens the franchise and the right to participate in politics, but nevertheless would privilege the Czech (technically, the 'Czecho-Slovak') nation above the others – was clear as soon as the state ceased to be ruled by decree and controlled by the military. The first full Czechoslovak constitution, adopted on 29 February 1920, certainly looked liberal – at times even radically egalitarian – on paper. The state was declared to be a democratic republic, headed by an elected president, with legislative power in the hands of a National Assembly composed, along French lines, of a three hundred-strong Chamber of Deputies (a lower house for which the voting age was twenty-one) and a smaller Senate (an upper house of 150, for which the voting age was twenty-six). Freedom of the press, of assembly, the right to privacy of private correspondence and freedom from censorship, 'except as specified by law', were guaranteed.[49] Presidents were to be elected for a maximum of two terms of seven years each; women given the vote on the same terms as men; aristocratic titles abolished; equality guaranteed to all nationals 'without distinction of origin, nationality, language, race or religion' and 'privileges of sex, birth or occupation' to go unrecognized.[50]

In practice, the constitution favoured one ethnic group above the others: those who had won the state from Germans, Hungarians and Poles and felt it to be theirs by right of revolution. First, the hyphen went out of the state's name, enabling it to appear not as a voluntary union of two equal but separate Czech and Slovak nations, but rather as a nation-state of the 'Czechoslovaks', implicitly one people who could be represented interchangeably by speakers of either dialect of their common language. Presidents were to serve for a maximum of two terms, but a special exception was made for 'the first President of the Czechoslovak Republic',[51] even though Masaryk was detested by the Germans and suspected by the other nationalities as an unprincipled Czech chauvinist. All political parties and nationalities could compete in elections; but a constitutional clause that explicitly guaranteed the right of parties to 'group together'[52] meant that Slovak parties could be forced into a single 'Slovak Club' dominated by pro-Czech Hlasists and the main Czech parties, by clubbing together in parliament, could keep out the German parties, regardless of how many votes they won. Giving women the vote sounded emancipated: it also doubled Czech voting strength. Abolishing aristocratic titles and redistributing the nobility's great landed estates sounded quintessentially egalitarian, progressive and modern: it transferred wealth and power from Germans and Magyars to Czechs and Slovaks at the same time as transferring aristocratic and Church property to the state.

Religion, which – like Marxism – tended to cut across ethnic divisions, proved more complicated. A concession to conservative Christian feeling was made through a clause in the constitution that stated that 'marriage, the family and motherhood' would be 'under the special protection of the law',[53] and that private schools, including Church schools, could be established. A proviso that 'ultimate responsibility' for education would rest with the state left room, however, for the secularization to come.[54] Freedom of religion and of conscience were guaranteed; but the tone of the state was to be firmly agnostic, since all oaths to be taken by president, ministers, deputies and judges, like those to be sworn by all other government employees (including railway and postal workers), were secular;[55] elections were to be held on Sundays; public instruction was to be conducted so as 'not to be in conflict with scientific research'; and the government reserved the right to prohibit 'certain religious practices' should they be found to be 'contrary to public order or to morality'.

Masaryk wanted a complete separation of Church and state to undermine the traditional Catholic parties, further diminish the power of the Hungarians and Germans and quash any talk of Slovak autonomy; but he was blocked by the combined efforts of the Slovak, Moravian and Bohemian branches of the People's (Catholic) Party, supported – for different reasons – by conservative Agrarian and progressive Socialist factions.[56] Masaryk then sought to counter the hold that he was convinced the Catholic Church retained over a majority of his fellow citizens – or, as he put it, to 'de-Austrianize' them – by establishing a new 'Czechoslovak Church' (*Československá církev*), made up of surviving Hussite groups and constituted along Presbyterian lines, but with four elected (not consecrated) bishops. The newfangled Church, which rejected traditional Catholic doctrines concerning original sin, purgatory and the veneration of saints, was refused recognition by the Vatican (which was becoming concerned about the anticlerical tone of the new state) but was granted formal state recognition in a law passed on 15 September 1920.[57] Masaryk evidently hoped that the new Church, with its characteristically Czech mix of elements of Catholicism, nationalism and Protestantism, would gradually take on a role like that of the established Church of England in Great Britain. In the first flush of patriotic fervour, a large number of baptized Catholic Czech-speakers did indeed join up; but by the mid-1920s the bubble had burst, and the Czechoslovak Church never managed to win over more than about 5 per cent of the population.

Busts and photographs of the President-Liberator were distributed, free of charge, to schools, post offices, government buildings and other public places. Masaryk not only behaved, but was also supported and promoted, much in the manner of a Habsburg emperor. Not only did the full machinery of state propaganda advertise his image as President-Liberator, Philosopher-Statesman and Humanist-Democrat; he also had the support of the vast imperial police network that Czechoslovakia inherited from the Habsburgs, including the traditional 'state security' units which existed in every branch of the police and intelligence services in the Ministries of Defence and Foreign

Affairs. In addition, the president maintained a special intelligence service of his own whose primary purpose was to keep tabs on party-political activity.[58]

To the most acute problem facing the new state – how to balance the perceived need for Czech primacy and a strong central government with democracy and protection for minority rights – the response was mixed. On the one hand, all citizens were entitled to 'freely use any language whatsoever',[59] 'forcible denationalization' was made a criminal offence,[60] and minority schools in towns and districts where a 'considerable proportion' (in practice, 20 per cent) of Czechoslovak citizens belonged to 'a minority as regards race, religion or language' were to be funded by the state.[61] On the other hand, the state reserved the right to make instruction in the 'Czechoslovak' language compulsory;[62] to restrict the participation of 'foreigners' in 'political associations';[63] and to revoke minority rights in cases of disruption to 'public order, the safety of the State, or effective supervision by the State'.[64] Crucially, there was no mention of anything resembling the Swiss canton system and no promise of autonomy for any region except Subcarpathian Ruthenia, despite the clear expectations of German-, Polish-, Slovak- and Rusyn/Ukrainian-speakers living in compact communities in the other regions of the state.

The Slovak Question was dealt with elliptically, through references to a mysterious entity called the 'Czechoslovak language'[65] which was described in a special Language Law published separately from the constitution. This declared the state language to be 'Czechoslovak', of which there were said to be two 'branches', one 'Czech' and the other 'Slovak'. This legal fiction, enabling Czech- and Slovak-speakers to be defined as 'Czechoslovaks', was obviously intended to ensure that 'Czechoslovaks' would form an overall majority within the state. The law came to be increasingly resented, not only by the Germans and Magyars whom it was intended to exclude from power, but also by many Slovaks who, in addition to minding the absence of any reference to Slovak autonomy, saw in the legal creation of a 'Czechoslovak' language and nationality – together with tactless predictions that over time the two dialects would merge into one – an insidious means, akin to Magyarization, of denying their distinctively Slovak national identity.

The Czech-dominated and Prague-centred government's choice of national symbols reinforced the double message of democratic freedoms for the individual but supremacy for the Czechoslovak 'nation', giving the *coup de grâce* to any hopes that the state would be inclusively multinational. A state flag, selected from a possible twenty designs in red, white and blue, was passed into law on 29 February 1920. By adding blue to the red and white of the Bohemian flag, the national colours were given kinship with the French Tricoleur, the United States' Old Glory, the British Union Jack and the *Sokol* banner.[66] The national anthem joined together the plaintive Czech '*Kde domov můj?'* ('Where is my home?') with the rousing Slovak '*Nad Tatrou sa blýska*' ('Lightning is flashing over the Tatras'), following the by-now established protocol of Czech first, Slovak second (there was no third, German stanza). From mid-March 1920, it became legal to alter German and Hungarian names of towns, regions and streets to Czech or Slovak ones.[67] The new names – sometimes completely unrecognizable to local inhabitants – changed not only on maps and road signs, but were also called out at tram, train and bus stops. The Hussite motto *Pravda vítězí* ('Truth will prevail') was chosen to decorate the presidential standard and also the largest official state crest, which prominently displayed the double-tailed Bohemian lion, surrounded by the Slovak double cross, the Moravian and Silesian eagles, and the Ruthenian bear.[68]

Postage stamps were issued, including one featuring a famous portrait of T.G. Masaryk by Max Švabinský on one side and an image of the republic – portrayed as a woman breaking free of her chains – on the other.[69] The first Czechoslovak coins, designed by Otakar Španiel and featuring the Bohemian lion on one side and a sheaf of wheat on the other, were minted in 1921.[70] Whereas Czechoslovak banknotes followed Austro-Hungarian convention in being written in all official minority as well as state languages, Czechoslovak passports were issued in Czech and French only. Postage stamps, which were never written in any language but Czech and which appear at first to have featured only Bohemian landscapes, *Sokol* events and other scenes of purely Czech nationalist interest, can hardly have helped to make non-Czechs feel included. The first postage stamp even to notice another region of the country appears to have been a stamp of the Tatra Mountains which was issued in 1926; this was followed, a couple of years later, by some Moravian scenes, dreamed up to commemorate ten years of independence.[71] It was not until 1935, when President Masaryk finally retired and German and Slovak calls for autonomy had grown so strident as to be unavoidable, that some attempt finally seems to have been made to rectify the regional – though still not the ethnic or linguistic – imbalances in state-wide postage stamps. Similarly, it was not until 1935 that the Slovak member of the wartime Paris National Council, Milan Štefánik, was prominently added to the nationalist pantheon, his handsome, uniformed portrait being made into an inseparable part of the legend of the *trojka* or triumvirate of founding fathers: Masaryk-Beneš-Štefánik (who conveniently doubled as representatives, respectively, of Moravia-Silesia, Bohemia and Slovakia, leaving only Subcarpathian Ruthenia without an official founding father).[72]

The degree of influence wielded by President Masaryk and his intimate circle of friends and advisors, among them unelected persons such as Foreign Minister Beneš and the writer Karel Čapek, known after the presidential residence as the *Hrad* or Castle group, presented another set of problems for democracy in the new state. Masaryk made use of every means at his disposal to influence the development of Czechoslovak society as he thought best: through anonymous articles in the press; in lectures to the Chamber of Deputies, cabinets and individual politicians; through private audiences with influential individuals; and at the regular salons held at Čapek's house. As the single most important figure behind the creation of the state, and its only well-known politician abroad, Masaryk commanded more influence than was healthy for a democratic republic. Masaryk, and Masaryk alone, appeared as the dignified face of Czechoslovak statehood, a statesman who seemed to rise above the political fray and quickly became the prime symbol of Czech standing in the world. This was in part a consequence of his gentlemanly bearing, good connections and professorial gravitas; but also of his political savvy, use of the secret police and wartime training in the arts of subterfuge and propaganda.

In 1920, the year in which a rigidly centralist and Czech-dominated Czechoslovak polity was being created, conditions looked ripe for a Bolshevik coup on the pattern of those that had taken place in Hungary, Germany and Slovakia the year before. During the state-wide General Strike led in December 1920 by the Communists, there were widespread demonstrations against President Masaryk, and the seizure of public buildings, churches and factories by rioting workers. The situation became so explosive that martial law was declared in parts of Bohemia, Slovakia and Subcarpathian Ruthenia, a total of about three thousand people were arrested and tried, and a dozen or more people – the great majority ethnic Germans – were killed by ethnically Czech Czechoslovak authorities. A Law against Terror, with particularly severe penalties for the use of political violence, followed.[73] Marxist belief, like Catholic faith, ought, in theory, to have cut across the ethnolinguistic barriers and petty nationalist divisions of Central Europe. Instead, it too was hopelessly entangled, and often compromised, in conflicting nationalist interpretations of events as Austro-Marxism gave way to national Marxist movements – Jewish, German, Czech, Hungarian, Slovak – at the same time that the political Left was also splintering over the question of whether to favour an evolutionary or revolutionary path to power.[74] In Czechoslovakia, ideological, nationalist and ethnic tensions on the political Left, culminating in the formation of the Czechoslovak Communist Party in 1921, split what had been the strongest political force in the country into two, correspondingly weakened, parties, in much the same way that the Catholic vote was fractured along ethnic and nationalist, as well as traditionalist and progressivist, lines. Disarray on both the political Left and Right enabled Švehla's Agrarian Party to rise to prominence as the single most popular political party in the country, so that from October 1922 right up to the Munich Crisis in September 1938, with only one brief exception, every prime minister of Czechoslovakia was an Agrarian.[75]

In the summer of 1921, Vojtech Tuka, a 'Magyarone' Slovak who lost his position at the university in Bratislava during the anti-Hungarian purges of 1919, presented Andrej Hlinka with a draft proposal for Slovak autonomy which suggested that Czechoslovakia be reorganized into a federation of two sovereign states, one 'Czech' and the other 'Slovak', which would be bound to one another only in matters of peace and war. Although his draft proposal bore no relation to the proposal that was actually presented to parliament by the Slovak People's Party on 27 January 1922, Hlinka was impressed enough with Tuka to make him editor of *Slovák*, the Slovak People's Party newspaper. Tuka proceeded to make a name for himself by having an inflammatory appeal, entitled 'The Voice of the Slovak Nation, Condemned to Death, to the Civilized World', adopted by the Slovak People's Party as the so-called Žilina Memorandum of 3 August 1923 and even took it – in French, English, German and Italian translation – to the League of Nations in Geneva and the Council of Ambassadors in Paris.[76] Increased disaffection with the Prague regime and the beginnings of political radicalism in Slovakia could also be felt through the emergence, under Tuka's guidance, of a uniformed Slovak Youth organization known as the *Rodobrana* (originally a breakaway movement from the Catholic *Orol* youth movement), whose members, known as *rodobranci*, turned up at Slovak People's Party rallies, ostensibly to protect speakers from being harassed by Communists or police. *Rodobranci*, who swore loyalty to 'the Slovak nation' and to a 'Slovak and Christian heritage', like emerging Fascist paramilitary groups elsewhere, wore black shirts with an armband (in this case decorated with a crown of thorns over the Slovak double-barred cross) and were organized into cells or 'wings' which covered the whole of Slovakia.

After the assassination of the finance minister, Alois Rašín, in 1923, a law modelled on legislation that had followed the murder of Walter Rathenau in the Weimar Republic was passed by a shocked National Assembly (although opposed by the Communist Party, the Slovak People's Party and every minority party). This was the Law for the Protection of the Republic, which severely restricted the right to disseminate political propaganda, protected the President of the Republic from libel, and included special protection 'for the democratic opinion of ordinary citizens' and 'democratic symbols'.[77] The *Rodobrana*, although banned by the Ministry of the Interior from the end of August 1923 as a violation of the Law for the Defence of the Republic, encouraged by radical separatists like Vojtech Tuka and Alexander Mach, continued, albeit sporadically, to function right up to 1928. By 1925, Tuka was a member of the Presidium of the Slovak People's Party as well as a deputy in parliament. In the same year, in tacit recognition of the 'Leader' principle that had become so fashionable in Fascist circles abroad, the Slovak People's Party was formally renamed *Hlinkova slovenská ľudová strana* (Hlinka's Slovak People's Party).[78] Increasingly, Ruthenians came to resent the Prague government's delays in implementing measures that were supposed to lead to the promised full regional autonomy, while ethnic Rusyns/Ukrainians living in Slovakia's Prešov region complained of Slovak discrimination in the allocation of schools and other Rusyn- or Ukrainian-language institutions. Even after the first Ruthenian deputy joined the National Assembly in 1924, continued Ruthene disaffection with the state, born of poverty as much as thwarted nationalism, showed itself through overwhelming support for the Communist Party which, with the single exception of the 1929 elections, remained the strongest single party in Subcarpathian Ruthenia.[79]

The First Czechoslovak Republic was characterized by a series of coalition governments in which the Agrarians and Social Democrats remained the strongest political forces and the same five political parties – the Agrarians, Social Democrats, National Democrats, Czechoslovak People's Party and National Socialists – dominated all governments, with the single exception of the period October 1926 to December 1929. In order to ensure that Czech interests remained paramount, whatever the election results, the phenomenon known as the *Pětka* developed. The *Pětka*, or 'Five', referred to the habit of the leaders of the five main Czech political parties of meeting together to reach cross-party gentlemen's agreements as to how ministers would be appointed and public policy conducted. There was just one brief period, of about three years, when the *Pětka* did not control the Czechoslovak government: from October 1926 to December 1929, the German branches of the Christian Socialist and Agrarian parties briefly replaced the Czech Social Democrats and National Socialists in government; and from January 1927 to December 1929, the Slovak People's Party (including Jozef Tiso, who was made minister of health) agreed to participate. It was a deepening sense that the central government was really a government for the Czechs, or for Czech interests, that led minority-language Hungarian, Polish and German parties, whose prewar progenitors had been divided along the usual class, religious and ideological lines, increasingly to group together under purely nationalist banners, and for Hlinka's Slovak People's Party, which campaigned for Slovak autonomy along the lines of the Pittsburgh Agreement, to move within a decade from being on the political margins to becoming Slovakia's single most important political party.[80]

By participating in government, the Slovak autonomists were able to win two concessions. The first was an agreement with the Vatican (20 January 1928) that removed the Catholic Church in Slovakia from the jurisdiction of Hungary's archbishop of Esztergom, brought the papal nuncio to Prague and increased state-funded salaries for priests. The second was the replacement of the old county (*župný*) system, which had divided Slovakia into six counties (each unit headed by an official approved by the central government), with a provincial system in which Slovakia and Ruthenia each counted as single units, the other provinces being Bohemia and Moravia-Silesia. The reorganization of the country into four provinces, which Hlinka welcomed as 'a glint of autonomy' since it for the first time recognized Slovakia as a discrete administrative unit, resonated differently among Ruthenian autonomists, who concluded that there was little point in continuing to fight what was obviously a losing battle to unite the Rusyns of Subcarpathian Ruthenia with those living across the provincial border in the Prešov district of Slovakia. Although it managed to wring a couple of concessions from Prague by finally participating in government, the Hlinka's Slovak People's Party leadership was punished so badly by the Slovak electorate for having failed to deliver full Slovak autonomy, as outlined in the Pittsburgh Agreement, that it refused to collaborate again.

The *coup de grâce* came with the political furore that surrounded the trial of Tuka. This began with an editorial, published in the first edition of *Slovák* to appear in 1928, which claimed that a secret clause attached to the (by then missing) Martin Declaration of 30 October 1918 allowed Slovakia to reconsider, after a period of ten years, its decision to join the Czechoslovak state. According to Tuka, this meant that, on 30 October 1928, Czechoslovak laws would become invalid in Slovakia. Tuka, accused of treason, was stripped of his parliamentary immunity and tried, in a blaze of publicity, for ten weeks. Convicted of treason and plotting, together with the *Rodobranci*, to destroy the republic by separating Slovakia from it, he was sentenced to fifteen years in Prague's Pankrác prison. Officially in protest at the Tuka trial, but more plausibly because Slovak voters refused to allow Hlinka's Slovak People's Party to compromise on autonomy, the party thereafter refused point-blank to join Czech-dominated coalition governments, thus becoming a party in permanent opposition.[81]

The Foreign Ministry, where Masaryk's protégé Beneš remained as foreign minister until December 1935 (when he finally took over from Masaryk as Czechoslovakia's second president), included not a single ethnic German or Hungarian; even Jan Masaryk, the president's son, was counted as a 'Slovak' to make up the numbers.[82] Beneš's continued deference to Masaryk ensured that the president exercised considerable, if unofficial, control over the shaping of Czechoslovak foreign policy. Until 1932, when the Foreign Ministry moved to the enormous Czernin Palace, it was housed in the Castle complex. Even after Kamil Krofta formally took over as foreign minister, Beneš, who was incapable of delegating, continued to dictate.[83] This makes it less surprising that the state's official foreign policy should so strongly have reflected the duo's wartime vision of what Bohemia/Czechoslovakia's role in Europe should be, as well as promoting measures designed to defend the grounds upon which they had succeeded in establishing the state in the first place.

The first element of this policy was to prevent the possibility of a Habsburg restoration, together with any revision to Hungarian borders, which was how common Yugoslav, Romanian and Czechoslovak interests came to be enshrined in the Little Entente. As late as 1934, Beneš dumbfounded Elizabeth Wiskemann, the foreign correspondent for *The Statesman*, by declaring that he would 'prefer the *Anschluss* of Austria with Germany to a Habsburg restoration'.[84] František Moravec, who took over as head of military intelligence in the same year, remembered how the Czechoslovak secret service was so fixated on the bogey of a Habsburg restoration that its reports 'about the private life and love affairs of former archdukes and other monarchists' read 'like a Lehar operetta'. General Sergej Ingr apparently also complained that he had 'no idea of the battle order of even the peacetime German divisions' but the reports 'tell me which Austrian archduke has slept with whom, and what Zita had for lunch. I think our intelligence service must be the worst in the world.'[85]

It took until 1932 for the Great Depression to reach its peak in Czechoslovakia, with unemployment at the sharpest highs and exports the worst lows. As well as further alienating Germans and Magyars, the economic crisis gave a new edge to Slovak and Rusyn complaints that Czechs took their jobs, while a Czech-dominated government in Prague deliberately exploited and overtaxed them, keeping them in rural poverty. The sense of a growing crisis in the state's eastern regions resulted in a flurry of political speeches on the Slovak Question, together with the establishment of a Department for Slovak Personnel in the prime minister's office in Prague.[86] The leadership of Hlinka's Slovak People's Party, unable to succeed with its electorate if it took part in government, began to perfect the arts of demagoguery. After successfully taking control of the *Matica slovenská* (Slovak cultural centre) in Turčiansky Svätý Martin in 1931, in August 1933 Hlinka's party invited a showdown when it made spectacular use of official state celebrations held at Nitra to mark the anniversary of the arrival of Christianity by staging a huge show of support for Hlinka, who – although he had not been invited to speak – was propelled to the rostrum. Upon reaching the platform, Hlinka seized the moment – in front of an audience of about 150,000 people, including distinguished foreign guests – to demand autonomy, within the framework of existing Czechoslovak borders, for Slovakia.[87] About 150 people were immediately arrested.

The Slovak and Ruthenian problems, together with the ever-present risk of their exploitation by Hungarian irredentist propaganda, probably still seemed remote to most ordinary Czechs: something for politicians, the Ministry of the Interior and perhaps the Foreign Office to worry about. Although official expressions of disaffection with the centralized state were growing steadily more vocal in two out of four of the state's regions, from 1933 they were overshadowed by a problem that was at once much closer to home and much more immediate: the German problem. By 1930, there are estimated to have been about 3,218,000 Germans, 7,447,000 Czechs and 2,309,000 Slovaks living in Czechoslovakia, together with about 720,000 Magyars, 569,000 Ruthenes, 100,000 Poles and 266,000 'others' (including some 100,000 Jews and 100,000 Gypsies).[88] This meant that there was still nearly one German to every two Czechs. Nazi successes in neighbouring Germany, combined with the disproportionate economic hardship endured by ethnic Germans living in the border areas of Bohemia and Moravia in what was widely coming to be known as the 'Sudetenland' (although it covered a much larger area than the territory of the same name which had been declared on 29 October 1918), popularized the radical German nationalist parties, including the local branch of the Nazi Party.

Prague reacted to fears of German radicalism by passing Law 201 (25 October 1933) 'concerning suspension of activities and dissolution of political parties', which ruled that any organization could be dissolved or suspended by the government if it 'gravely endangered' the 'independence, the constitutional unity, the integrity, the democratic-republican form, or the security of the Czechoslovak Republic'.[89] The local Nazi Party and the German nationalist Sudeten German Party (*SdP*) were immediately suppressed. Included in the carefully considered provisions of Law 201 were prohibitions on canvassing for supporters or funds; the wearing of uniforms or exhibiting of emblems belonging to banned organizations; and any gathering of the same people, under whatever pretext. Members of outlawed political parties were denied the right to privacy of correspondence, could be kept under police surveillance and could even be confined to or expelled from specific locations for unspecified periods.[90]

Konrad Henlein, leader of the German gymnastics society *Turnverband* (the German equivalent of *Sokol*), immediately filled the gap left by the outlawed Sudeten German and Nazi parties by setting up a new party, the Sudeten German *Heimatsfront*, to defend Czechoslovak ('Sudeten') German interests. Although usually treated as indistinguishable from the Nazi Party, the *Heimatsfront*'s base in the Völkisch *Kameradschaftsbund* meant that it followed the Catholic Fascist teachings of Viennese professor Othmar Spann rather than the neo-paganism of the Nazis. Although its ultimate dream was to create a Catholic corporatist utopia uniting ethnic Germans across Central Europe, in the short term it sought increased German political unity, and ultimately autonomy, within Czechoslovakia.[91] By now, levels of unemployment in the German border regions of Bohemia-Moravia and Silesia were twice as high as those in the Czech interior.[92]

With hindsight, 15 March 1935 looks as if it was probably the last day on which changes in Czechoslovakia's domestic or foreign policy might conceivably have averted the long, drawn-out catastrophe that was to follow. After 16 March 1935, when Germany publicly announced that it was rearming, the

European situation became increasingly tense, since the announcement gave the impression that Germany was further along the path of rearmament than it really was while at the same time making clear that, whatever the Great Powers or the League of Nations said officially, revision of at least some of the terms of the Versailles peace settlement would be tolerated in practice. Supported at home by the Communists and Social Democrats, the Czechoslovak government followed the example of the French (2 May 1935) in concluding a treaty of mutual assistance (16 May 1935) with the Soviet Union. Despite prudently ensuring that Soviet assistance could only be set into motion if France became involved first, the signing of the treaty further alienated the Sudeten German, Slovak Populist and Agrarian parties at home while exacerbating the hostility of Germany, Poland and Hungary abroad.

The results of the May 1935 elections came as a rude shock to the central government in Prague, since they revealed the sudden importance of the *Heimatsfront/Sudetendeutsche Partei* (which had friendly links, not only with the ruling Nazi Party in Germany, but also with conservative circles in the West, especially Britain), while simultaneously demonstrating a sharp rise in the popularity of movements for national autonomy. The most alarming result for the Czechs was to find that the *SdP*, which was participating in parliamentary elections for the first time, had won the largest number of votes (1,249,530, or 15.2 per cent), even more than the Agrarian and Social Democratic parties, which followed with 1,176,593 (14.3 per cent of the vote) and 1,034,774 (12.6 per cent of the vote), respectively. After the Communists, who came next with 849,509 (or 10.3 per cent of the vote), followed a whole raft of autonomist parties, dominated by Hlinka's Slovak People's Party, but also joined by the (traditionally Protestant) Slovak National Party, the Ruthenian Autonomy Party and the Polish Party. Despite the overwhelmingly anti-centralist, anti-Czech and anti-socialist message sent by the electorate, when the new government coalition took over on 4 June 1935 under the premiership of Jan Malypetr, it represented the same grouping of political parties as the one it immediately succeeded (Agrarians, Social Democrats, National Socialists, German Social Democrats, Czechoslovak People's Party), leaving the increasingly intransigent German and Slovak autonomist blocs out in the cold. The only token concession was the appointment, on 5 November, of a Slovak Agrarian, Milan Hodža, to replace Malypetr as prime minister.

On 21 November 1935, aged eighty-five and suffering badly from senility, T.G. Masaryk was persuaded to step down as president of Czechoslovakia. In the midst of all the intrigue and politicking that followed, and faced with the distinct possibility that he might not be chosen to succeed him, Edvard Beneš – who got nowhere when he tried discreetly to sound out Henlein's party, though he fared well with the Communists – ended up relying on the support of Esterházy, leader of a bloc of Hungarian nation-alist parties, to whom he promised various concessions, and especially Hlinka, to whom he went so far as to promise to try to decentralize the state.[93] On 18 December 1935, Beneš was elected as Czechoslovakia's second president. To those who were already disaffected with Prague – the vast majority of the country – Beneš's appointment can only have underlined the sense that, whatever people did and however they voted, the same old gang would remain in charge.

In the fifteen years since Versailles the tide of opinion in Europe had turned and the critics and would-be revisionists of the postwar European settlement were clearly in the ascendant. The war in Abyssinia, in which Mussolini's Italy seemed to be given a free hand, soon overshadowed all other international news. The Hoare-Laval agreement of December 1935, intended to return Italy to the League of Nations by confirming Italy's possession of the colony, only reinforced the message that military might was what counted and that the League of Nations could be bypassed. By 1936, when it was clear that Beneš, blocked by his coalition partners, would be unable to deliver on Slovak autonomy, Slovakia sought to bring its grievances to international attention. At the Slovak People's Party's Seventh Congress, held at Piešt'any in September 1936, Karol Sidor and Ferdinand Ďurčanský ensured that representatives of the French Fascist and German Nazi parties were there to witness Hlinka read out a declaration that asserted Slovakia's right to autonomy within a federal Czechoslovak state and went on to condemn its own government's 'coopera-tion with the international representatives of a materialistic ideology and a Judeo-Bolshevik anarchy' and to claim its rightful place 'in the anti-Communist front' alongside 'the nations that are guided by Christian princi-ples'.[94] In November 1937, roused by political speeches given by senators Sokol and Sidor, university students in Bratislava took to the streets, many wearing party badges with the motto 'Slovak in Slovakia' and chanting the song 'We Were Born Slovak', which included such lines as 'Slovaks, come with us to Bratislava/Armed with your hatchets to defend the Slovak language'.[95]

When, in March 1936, Germany reoccupied the demilitarized zone in the Rhineland, it openly defied the border guarantees given at Versailles and reiterated in the Locarno treaties of 1925; the crisis incidentally exposed Britain as either unwilling or unable to come to the aid of France. The Czechoslovak government began to make provisions so that it would be able, at a moment's notice, to suspend the 1920 constitution in favour of a new one that would invest the government with dictatorial powers as determined by a Supreme Defence Council. Should the integrity of the state, the consti-tution, public order, peace or the republican-democratic form of the state be endangered, the government could invoke a 'state of military preparedness in case of war', militarizing all 'border districts' within 25 km (16 miles) of the border, expelling all politically unreliable persons and ensuring that the police stations in these areas were all manned by Czechs.[96] What the Czechs saw as defensive, ethnic Germans regarded as aggressive. According to one *SdP* spokesman writing in 1936:

> The Germans have about 44,000 state posts too few. Almost in every German town a Czech has been appointed Postmaster, Stationmaster, President of the Court or Customs or Finance Director: and many other German officials have been replaced by Czechs. This systematic reduction of Germans to a lower political and cultural level, on the part of the state, is the one expression of the prevailing Czechoslovak state policy.[97]

Then came German and Italian intervention in the Spanish Civil War, the German-Japanese Anti-Comintern Pact and, in July 1937, the Japanese attack on China, to which no action was taken in response, though the 'aggressors' were rebuked by the League of Nations.

On 20 February 1938, Hitler declared that the Reich had a mission to protect 'ten million' Germans. The Austrian crisis, ending with the union or *Anschluss* of Austria and Germany – which had been expressly forbidden at Versailles – followed on 13 March 1938. This suddenly brought Czechoslovakia's Sudeten German problem, which had been receiving only mild interest abroad, centre stage. In a speech given at Karlovy Vary (*Karlsbad*) on 24 April 1938, Konrad Henlein put forward radical political demands, which combined the vague rights to 'profess' and 'disseminate' the Nazi world view and have 'injustices' imposed since 1918 'removed' with demands for specific protections and rights for all ethnic German citizens of Czechoslovakia, as well as for full administrative and legal autonomy for the territory of the so-called 'Sudetenland' (in other words, the horseshoe-shaped border areas of Bohemia and Moravia in which declared German-speakers overwhelmingly outnumbered declared Czech-speakers but whose precise boundaries were not entirely clear).[98] Within the week, the *SdP* showed its confidence by establishing a paramilitary organization, the *Freiwilliger Schützkorps*, and the British and French were prevailing upon the Prague government to meet the Sudeten German demands in the interests of preserving the peace in Europe. Instead of heeding their advice, Beneš – acting on what turned out to be incorrect Czechoslovak intelligence reports that a German invasion was imminent – on 21 May, less than three weeks later, ordered partial mobilization of the Czechoslovak army, bringing the whole of Europe to the brink of war.

The so-called 'May Crisis' of 1938, which turned out to have been caused by Czechoslovakia's unjustified military provocation, exasperated and infuriated all of the Great Powers, not least France (which warned Prague that it would not go to war on Czechoslovakia's account), Britain (which was in any case showing increasing sympathy for the Sudeten Germans' grievances) and Germany (which was indignant at what it saw as a devious provocation and which it claimed publicly as further evidence that Beneš was a warmonger). Local elections at the end of the month showed a landslide victory for the *SdP*, which drew somewhere between 87 and 90 per cent of the Czechoslovak German vote. From July, the plight of the Sudeten Germans was being raised in the British House of Commons; by August, an editorial in *The Times* could refer to the idea that 'the condition of the Sudeten ought to have been improved many years ago' as 'common ground'.[99] In response to popular pressure, but without an invitation from the Czechoslovak government, British prime minister Neville Chamberlain sent a former Liberal MP and cabinet minister, Lord Walter Runciman, to mediate between the Czechoslovak government and the Sudeten Germans. Runciman's subsequent report to the prime minister concluded that the Czechs were prone to 'petty intolerance and discrimination' and that the predominantly German-inhabited areas of Czechoslovakia ought to be ceded to Germany. Even in areas 'where the German minority is not so important', his devastating report recommended that 'an effort be made to find a basis for local autonomy within the frontiers of the Czechoslovak Republic'.[100]

The long-anticipated crisis finally came after Beneš unwittingly set the ball rolling by announcing, on 5 September 1938, his 'Fourth Plan', an arrangement that accepted almost all of the points put forward in Henlein's Karlsbad programme. In response to the arrest, perhaps staged, of two Sudeten German deputies in Moravská Ostrava, the *Heimatsfront* broke off negotiations. On 12 September, at the annual Nazi Nürnberg (Nuremberg) rally, Hitler declared his support for Czechoslovakia's Germans, whom he vowed to protect. After what appears to have been an attempted Sudeten German coup was put down by the Czechoslovak army, on 15 September Henlein fled to Germany. Two days earlier, in response to the gauntlet that Hitler seemed to have thrown down, Neville Chamberlain requested an audience, for which he flew to Berchtesgaden to meet with Hitler. The result of their talks on 15 September, during which Hitler claimed to feel strongly enough about the Sudeten Germans to risk war, was for Chamberlain to agree in principle to the transfer of the Sudeten German population to Germany. Upon his return to London, Chamberlain was easily able to persuade the cabinet that it was the only realistic option. Even the French, who came to London for talks on 18 September, agreed, although they stipulated that the remainder of Czechoslovakia – after the transfer of the 'Sudetenland' to Germany – be guaranteed against any further demands. On 19 September, the proposal was put to the Czechoslovak government, which – in the absence of British or French support – had no real option but to accept.

There could hardly have been a worse possible failure, in the eyes of the Czech-dominated Czechoslovak administration, whose very *raison d'être*, in classic Central European thinking, was to advance the interests of its people or 'nation' against those of its rivals, than voluntarily to break up the 'indissoluble' Bohemian Crown Lands in order to cede large chunks of territory to the Czechs' traditional enemy. For Beneš, it would mean national disgrace as well as political suicide. He therefore all but begged that 'the most extreme Franco-British pressure' be brought to bear to give him at least a fig leaf of national respectability. His allies took pity on him to the extent of letting him have a statement to the effect that 'if the refusal were maintained France and Britain would leave the Czechs to their fate'.[101]

Chamberlain met again with Hitler, this time at Godesberg on 22 September, to tell him the good news: that agreement over the 'Sudetenland' had been reached. Hitler now insisted that this was no longer enough, maintaining that Czech 'terror' against ethnic Germans justified the immediate occupation of the territory by German troops; and that, in addition to the question of the transfer of German-inhabited land to Germany, there was the further question of Slovak autonomy, together with Hungarian and Polish grievances, to be settled. General mobilization began. Chamberlain caught the mood when he observed, in a radio broadcast to the nation, 'How horrible, fantastic, incredible it is that we should be digging trenches and trying on gas masks because of a quarrel in a far away country between a people of whom we know nothing.'[102] Not only Chamberlain, but also Roosevelt, Mussolini and many other world leaders begged that a peaceful solution to the German-Czechoslovak crisis be given one last chance. On 28 September, Hitler agreed that a conference between four powers – France, Italy, Germany and Britain (but not Czechoslovakia) – might be held in Munich. Its outcome, given the alternative to an immediate settlement, was not in much doubt.

On the morning of 29 September 1938, the final act of the Czechoslovak tragedy was played out, as the heads of government and foreign ministers of Italy, France and Britain, each with its separate entourage, converged on the city of Munich, where Hitler and his delegation had arrived from Berlin the day before. Vojtěch Mastný, Czechoslovak ambassador to Germany, and Hubert Masařík, a member of the Czechoslovak Press Bureau, were flown in later that afternoon, but as 'observers' rather than participants. Eyewitness accounts of the proceedings of the Munich Conference, of which there are many, are confused and contradictory, but all convey an atmosphere of stressful disorientation for the British and French ministers. There was no agenda, seating plan or notepaper; instead of being seated at a long table, the participants were scattered in armchairs or sofas around the room. The meeting opened with a statement from Hitler that the German occupation of the 'Sudetenland' must begin without delay, the presumption being that the participants had been brought together to decide how, not whether, the task was to be accomplished.[103]

In the small hours of 30 September 1938, the text of the Munich Agreement was read out to the Czechoslovak observers in the hall outside the conference room, where British and French officials remained on hand to answer questions. The agreement, together with its five annexes (one of which was a map), was then signed by Chamberlain, Daladier, Hitler and Mussolini in separate English, French, German and Italian (but not Czech) versions. The document stated that 'the Sudeten German territory' was to be ceded to Germany; that the evacuation of the area was to be carried out between 1 and 10 October 1938; and that the Czechoslovak government would be held responsible for any damage to military installations on the territory, which were to be handed over intact. Four zones, marked on the accompanying map, were to be occupied by German troops in short stages between 1 and 7 October; the area of a fifth zone, described as 'the remaining territory of preponderantly German character', was to be decided by an 'international commission' and handed over by 10 October at the latest.[104]

Together with the main text of the agreement came several addenda. The first stated that the French and British governments stood by their offer to guarantee the new boundaries of the state against 'unprovoked aggression', but that the German and Italian governments would only add their own guarantees once 'the question of the Polish and Hungarian minorities in Czechoslovakia' had been 'settled'. The second stated that, if the Polish and Hungarian questions had not been settled within three months, they would be decided by the same four powers; the third that all questions arising from the transfer of territory would be referred to an international commission; and the fourth that this commission would be composed of the German foreign secretary, the British, French and Italian ambassadors in Berlin, and 'a representative to be nominated by the Government of Czechoslovakia'.[105]

What all of this meant in practice – quite apart from the public humiliation and blow to Czech national feeling – was the end of Czechoslovakia's security as an independent state. The so-called 'Sudetenland' included not only Czechoslovakia's natural mountain defences, but also the Maginot-style line of border fortifications, intended to protect the state against military attack from Germany (which, since the *Anschluss* with Austria six months earlier, surrounded the state on three sides). The territories also contained some of Czechoslovakia's most important industries, including armaments factories. The ominously vague references to the necessity of 'settling' the Polish and Hungarian minority problems to the four powers' satisfaction hinted that the eastern part of Silesia, the area around Teschen, as yet unclaimed by the Germans, would perhaps be awarded to Poland, and southern Slovakia or Subcarpathian Ruthenia, or both, would be awarded to Hungary. The references to an as yet unspecified 'fifth zone' held the further risk that even inland territories with a substantial German-speaking population, such as the cities of

Bratislava, Brno and Jihlava, might be deemed – by a commission in which the Czechoslovaks were to have at best only one vote to the other powers' four – to belong to Germany. When Masařík and Mastný asked how soon a reply would be needed from the Prague government, they were told that an answer was not expected since the plan was regarded as settled. The Prague government would need to send someone to Berlin by 5 p.m., since a Czechoslovak representative would be required to help with the details of the evacuation of the first zone, which was supposed to begin the very next day, 1 October.[106] No wonder Mastný's immediate reaction was to dissolve into tears.[107]

Kamil Krofta, the Czechoslovak foreign minister, was woken in Prague at 6.20 a.m. by the German *chargé d'affaires*, who handed him the text of the Munich Agreement. When Krofta asked to see the accompanying map, he was told that no spare copy was available, but that he could probably get one from the British legation.[108] Beneš was brought the news by his private secretary at about seven in the morning, while he was having his bath. 'It's a betrayal that will be its own punishment,' he declared. 'It is unbelievable. They think that they will save themselves from war or revolution at our expense. They are mistaken.'[109] He then phoned the Soviet minister in Prague to ask for his government's views as to the respective merits of 'further struggle' or 'capitulation'.[110] Since the minister was unable to get through to Moscow by phone, he sent a telegram before setting off for Hradčany.

As the results were broadcast on the radio, including over public loud-speakers in Wenceslas Square, people wept openly in the streets. For Beneš, the morning was taken up with consultations with the cabinet, army officers and the leaders of the political parties. Klement Gottwald called, on behalf of the Communist Party, to ask that the government reject the Munich Agreement and prepare to fight; a group of deputies meeting in the editorial offices of *Lidové noviny*, a Brno-based newspaper that had begun issuing a separate Prague edition from 23 September to cover the crisis, sent the president the same message.[111] The president then had to face his coalition partners and fellow Czech nationalists. Military leaders, flown in from Vyškov to give their expert advice, underlined the general sense that it was twenty years of Beneš's wasted diplomacy that were primarily to blame for Czechoslovakia being left in the terrible predicament of being surrounded by enemies, abandoned by allies, and defenceless in the face of German aggression. Jan Syrový, who was minister of defence as well as prime minister, reminded his despondent listeners that many military fortifications on the border with Germany were not yet complete, and that, even if the Soviet Union were to decide to send troops, the country could not be held long enough to enable them to arrive safely. The chief of the general staff, Ludvík Krejčí, agreed, saying that, even if the Soviet Union decided to act, it would take about six weeks to get troops to Moravia, by which time it would in any case be too late. The situation, he added pointedly, would have been different if Poland had been on Czechoslovakia's side. General Husárek pointed out that military plans had been based on the assumptions that should Germany attack Czechoslovakia, it would simultaneously have to fight France and probably Poland; that Hungary would be facing an onslaught by all three members of the Little Entente; that the southern border with what had been Austria would not need defending; and that Poland and Romania would be able and willing to allow Soviet troops a quick and safe passage through their territories. Since not one of these assumptions still held, only one general – General Vojcechovski – insisted that, despite everything, Czechoslovakia should refuse the terms of the Munich Agreement and fight to keep its territorial integrity.[112]

By noon, the government had reached its dismal consensus. There was no realistic option but to accept the Munich Agreement. When, moments later, Soviet Ambassador Alexandrovskii arrived at the Castle, he was informed by Beneš's secretary that the government of Czechoslovakia no longer required an answer.[113] The lack of a formal response from the Soviet Union later enabled the Czechoslovak Communist Party to claim that the USSR would have intervened if it had been asked to do so. As Zeman and Klímek describe, there was still the Council for the Defence of the Republic to tell. Pale, red-eyed and at first incoherent, Beneš eventually calmed down enough to say that 'History has no parallel for dealing with a sovereign state in such a manner. . . . We are deserted and betrayed.' In the discussion that followed, Gottwald, the head of the Communist Party, argued that even 'barefooted Ethiopians found courage to resist the armed might of Italy'. But Beneš had made up his mind. 'We were not defeated by Hitler,' he insisted to his fellow politicians, 'but by our friends.'[114]

On 1 October 1938, the first evacuations of Zone 1 began. Daladier, Chamberlain, Mussolini and Hitler were rapturously applauded in their home countries for having averted war. The League of Nations in Geneva proposed 'the people of Czechoslovakia and Edvard Beneš' for the Nobel Peace Prize. The Polish foreign minister, having already demanded the territory surrounding Teschen, now presented the Czechoslovak government with an ultimatum that it was in no position to refuse. Beneš pulled himself together enough to try to get French backing for a proposal that only districts in Zone 5 that were 75 per cent, rather than – as the Germans suggested – 51 per cent, German according to the last Habsburg census be handed over. He also fought to avoid the possibility of plebiscites being held in German enclaves such as Brno and Jihlava, just as the German side worked to prevent plebiscites in the overwhelmingly Czech or Polish regions that lay between the Svitavy enclave and Silesia.[115] A British diplomat, reporting from the

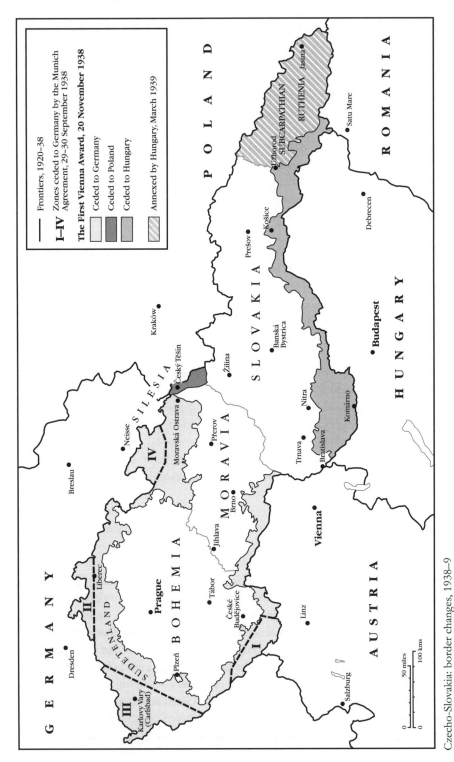

Czecho-Slovakia: border changes, 1938–9

International Commission in Berlin, found the negotiations impossible since 'it was not uncommon for four or five Sudeten Germans and the Czech representatives all to be shouting at once', while the chairman proved 'quite incapable of maintaining order'.[116]

Between 2 and 12 October, Polish troops occupied the Teschen region; by 10 October, they had also helped themselves to a few additional Polish-inhabited territories to the west. Hungary, meanwhile, announced its own claim to a long strip of territory along the Slovak–Hungarian border, and to the whole of Subcarpathian Ruthenia. Within days of the international crisis, the foreign press corps, which had initially swarmed over the streets of the Czechoslovak capital, had gone. The city of Prague, its streets cleared of traffic by the army and its windows blacked out in case of air raids, took on the appearance of a baroque shell as people stayed indoors, tensely waiting to see what would happen next.[117] On 3 October, the Slovak minister Matúš Černák threatened to resign from the cabinet if Slovakia were not granted autonomy within twenty-four hours. The next day, Slovak autonomy having not yet been granted, Černák did resign, causing the fall of the government. Only now could Beneš – with whom Hitler refused point-blank to negotiate over the composition of Zone 5 – be persuaded to resign as president, Czechoslovakia having been denied even the limited input to the negotiations that it had been promised, Germany been awarded even more territory than Hitler had originally envisaged, and Beneš's impotence, if possible, under-lined even further.

The final blow came from the executive of Hlinka's Slovak People's Party, which announced that, as a consequence of the crisis, it would be holding a meeting at Žilina (*Sillein*) the following day in order to make a public 'declara-tion' concerning the 'right of self-determination for the Slovak nation'. On the evening of 5 October 1938, Beneš broadcast his farewell to the nation. It was a masterly speech in which he managed to blame the road to Munich on vague, impersonal forces such as 'the whole system of the balance of power in Europe', 'influences from abroad' and 'the whole course of European development', and simultaneously on the 'four Great Powers' who had 'met and agreed among themselves' as to the 'sacrifices which they asked from us in the name of world peace'. Although claiming not to wish 'to criticize' or 'to utter a single word of recrimination', he nevertheless insisted that 'the sacrifices which we were asked to accept and which were then forced upon us are out of all proportion and unjust'.[118] Warning his listeners that 'the home of the Czechs and Slovaks is in real danger' and urging all to 'give way to one another whenever necessary',[119] he could not prevent himself from brightening at the prospect of what it would mean no longer to have to share the state with the Germans. 'We shall have,' he considered, 'a national State as in one sense the development of the principle of nationality indicates.

Herein will lie the great strength of our State and Nation. . . . We are still strong enough, numerous enough. Let us therefore look hopefully towards our national future.'[120] Or again: 'The stem of the tree of our homeland has had some branches lopped from it but the roots of the Nation are still firm in the earth. Let us go back to our roots. Let us concentrate all the old strength of our race in them as we have done so often in our history, and after a while the stem will again put forth new shoots.'[121] With the assurance that he was not 'leaving the ship because there is a gale' and that he would not forget his 'duty to continue working as a citizen and a patriot', he bade the 'Republic' and the 'Nation' farewell.[122]

Beneš and his wife, Hana, moved out of the Castle the same evening, arriving at their country house at Sezimovo Ústí on the morning of 6 October, where Beneš promptly took to his bed, ill and exhausted. Presidential functions were taken over by the prime minister, General Jan Syrový, who simultaneously became head of a caretaker central government based in Prague and backed by the army. Jozef Tiso, the leader of the Hlinka's Slovak People's Party since Andrej Hlinka's death a couple of months earlier, was made 'minister for the administration of Slovakia' (*pre správu Slovenska*), with the power to appoint a further four ministers.[123] At Žilina later the same day, he triumphantly told assembled journalists and Slovak politicians: 'The moment has come when the Slovaks as a sovereign and independent nation start to write their own history.'[124] So began the period known as the Second Czecho-Slovak Republic during which the state's name reverted to its original, hyphenated form as a mark of Slovakia's autonomous status, and every part of the newly federated republic, thoroughly disillusioned with democracy, began moving towards its own, idiosyncratic variant of Fascism.

CHAPTER 4

THE FASCIST APPEAL

The Second Czecho-Slovak Republic, which lasted from 6 October 1938 until 13 March 1939, is usually skipped over in history books in a sentence or two. After the Munich Crisis and the loss of the Sudetenland, we are told, Hungary and Poland cynically helped themselves to further chunks of Czechoslovak territory. The final destruction of the state by Nazi Germany was completed on 15 March 1939, with the occupation of Prague and the takeover of what remained of Bohemia and Moravia. Within another six months, Europe was at war, unmasking Hitler's real intentions and showing the policy of 'appeasement' to have been morally bankrupt. Czechoslovakia had been proved right and the rest of the world wrong.

Even though the Second Republic lasted for only half a year, it should not be relegated to a footnote; nor should it be conceived of simply as a postscript to the Munich Crisis or prelude to the Second World War. It was a crucially important period in turning Czechoslovakia from an imperfectly democratic to a frankly authoritarian state, one whose central and autonomous governments ruled by decree, promoted racism, neutralized political opponents, rigged elections, set up forced-labour camps and persecuted Jews and Gypsies, all before any of this could plausibly be blamed on Nazi Germany. However brief, this disturbing chapter in the state's history went well beyond what is usually described euphemistically as Czechoslovakia's post-Munich 'disillusionment' with 'democracy' and 'the West'. The Second Republic shows us what Slovak, Ruthenian and Czech variations on the contemporary European themes of anti-Semitism and Fascism looked like at the time and hints at how they might have developed had Germany and the Second World War not intervened. It also introduces us to a number of totalitarian tricks and techniques – mainly Slovak, but also Czech – that were later to be perfected and used state-wide by the postwar Czechoslovak Communist Party.

It all began on 6 October 1938, the day after Beneš's resignation as president, when the promised 'Manifesto of the Slovak People's Party' was read aloud from the balcony of the *Katolícky dom* (Catholic House) at Žilina to cheers and prolonged applause from the crowd below. 'We Slovaks,' the manifesto began, 'as an independent nation which has inhabited the territory of Slovakia since antiquity, hereby put into effect our right to self-determination.' In the hope of being able to contribute to 'a Christian disposition of affairs in Central Europe' and vowing to remain 'at the side' of 'all nations fighting against Jewish Marxism', the Žilina manifesto demanded that 'legislative and executive powers' be granted 'to Slovaks in Slovakia'. It ended with the rousing slogans 'Long live the freedom of the Slovak nation!' and 'Long live the Slovak Government in Slovakia!'[1] The manifesto, widely understood to represent the fulfilment of the promises of Slovak autonomy made in the Pittsburgh Agreement, was immediately endorsed by all Slovak political parties that were represented at the meeting (but not by the Communist, Social Democratic and Jewish parties, whose leaders had deliberately been kept in the dark).

The Czechoslovak prime minister, Syrový, gave in to the demagoguery without protest. When, on 10 October, Jozef Tiso (as minister plenipotentiary of Slovakia) met for the first time with his fellow ministers, he was able to announce that authority for Slovak affairs would be taken immediately, ahead of any formal alterations to the constitution, and ministerial portfolios could simply be parcelled out. Hlinka's Slovak People's Party naturally took the top prizes, Tiso declaring himself prime minister and minister of the interior, while Ferdinand Ďurčanský became deputy prime minister and minister of justice, social welfare and public health, and Alexander Mach was made the first chief of the Office of Propaganda. Matúš Černák, who had yet to join the party but had been instrumental in bringing down the Czechoslovak government, was made minister for education.[2]

Prime Minister Syrový, who had evidently hoped to shelve the Slovak problem by offering Tiso a cabinet post, together with a free hand in Slovakia as minister plenipotentiary, had presumably hoped to be able to make the Ruthenian Question disappear in the same way by having Ivan Párkányi, the president's secretary for Ruthenian affairs, appointed to the newly created post of 'minister' (in effect, governor) of Subcarpathian Ruthenia. He was outmanoeuvred on 8 October 1938, when, at a copycat meeting called by the First Ukrainian Central National Council in Užhorod (*Uzhhorod*), it was 'unanimously decided' to 'demand the same rights' for Subcarpathian Ruthenia 'as have been or will be granted to Slovakia'.[3] After a couple of days' negotiations in Prague, it was agreed that the newly autonomous government of Subcarpathian Ruthenia would be led by Andrei Brodii (Andrej Bródy/Andrij Brody) in a cabinet made up of one fellow Russophile (Stepan Fentsik/Fentsyk) and four Ukrainophiles (Edmund Bachinskii/Bachynsky, Ivan P'eshchak/Pieshchak, Iuliian Revai/Yulian Revay and Avhustyn Voloshyn).[4] Syrový accepted the Ruthenian demands with the same weary resignation he had shown in accepting the Slovak autonomists' and, on

11 October, dismissed Minister Párkányi so that the Bródy cabinet could take over the administration of Subcarpathian Ruthenia.

Slovak and Ruthenian autonomy were thus seized within ten days of the signing of the Munich Agreement, although only passed into law retrospectively, through separate bills which went through the Czecho-Slovak parliament on 22 November 1938.[5] According to the new constitutional arrangements, the central government in Prague continued to be responsible for foreign affairs, defence, customs, foreign trade and state loans (as well as taxation relating to any of these purposes); but Slovakia and Ruthenia were responsible for everything else within their own *krajina* ('land' or 'region').[6] Since Slovakia and Subcarpathian Ruthenia now had their own diets (the Slovak *Snem* and the Ruthenian *Soim*), whereas Bohemia and Moravia continued to be governed by the central Czecho-Slovak government in Prague, it was not – as George Kennan, the new US *chargé d'affaires*, put it – entirely 'facetious to say that in Czechoslovakia [*sic*] everyone now has autonomy except the Czechs'.[7]

The first political party to be suppressed by the new leadership of autonomous Slovakia was the Carpathian German Party led by Franz Karmasin, the Slovak equivalent of the Bohemian and Moravian *Heimatsfront*, which was abolished on 5 October 1938. Presumably because someone pointed out that the international climate was not propitious to indulging too publicly in anti-German feeling, the party was reinstated within the week, renamed the *Deutsche Partei* (German Party). As if to make amends, Karmasin was also put in charge of a new 'State Secretariat for German National Minority Matters in Slovakia', which was allowed to form its own *Deutsche Jugend* (German Youth) and paramilitary *Freiwillige Schutzstaffel* (Voluntary Protective Brigade) organizations.[8] The extreme right-wing Carpathian German Party (*Deutsche Partei*) was to prove loyal to the equally extreme right-wing Slovak state, often taking its side in misunderstandings or disputes with the German Reich.

On 9 October, the activities of the Communist Party in Slovakia were suspended, but this time as a prelude to the party's actual dissolution, which was ordered by the Slovak Ministry of the Interior on 23 January 1939, when the Jewish and Social Democratic parties were also axed. At a stroke, this removed the entire left wing from Slovak politics. It was not until May 1939 that a secret underground organization, whose goals included the establishment of 'an independent, Soviet Socialist Slovakia', created an illegal Communist Party of Slovakia (*Komunistická strana Slovenska* or *KSS*), to be considered of equal standing to all other national Communist parties affiliated with the Communist International.[9]

On 8 November 1938, the Slovak branches of the Czechoslovak People's Party, Czechoslovak National Socialist Party, Agrarian Party, National Democratic Party, Tradesmen's Party and the National Community of Fascists merged into a single political party, the awkwardly named 'Hlinka's Slovak

People's Party – the Party of Slovak National Unity' (hereafter referred to simply as 'Slovak National Unity'). Only *Národná strana*, the (traditionally Protestant) Slovak National Party, initially refused to come on board, preferring to dissolve itself on 23 November; but most of its members merged with Slovak National Unity on 15 December 1938.[10] This left autonomous Slovakia with just three permitted political parties: Jozef Tiso's Slovak National Unity, now the only 'party' for Slovak-speakers; Franz Karmasin's *Deutsche Partei* for German-speakers; and János Esterházy's *Egyesült Magyar Párt* (United Hungarian Party) for Hungarian-speakers. Slovakia's Ruthene, Jewish, Czech and Gypsy minorities were left without even the pretence of political representation.

The merging of all centrist and right-wing Slovak-speaking political parties into a single mass political organization called Slovak National Unity corresponded well to the Fascistic outlook of the new Slovak leadership, with its high-minded disdain for compromise and politicking, its self-image as a repository of Christian culture and Christian values, and its notion of politics, not as a means of resolving conflict, but rather as a vehicle through which to express the united 'will' of the 'nation'. Quite what former deputies of the Slovak People's Party, suddenly catapulted into power as the leaders of Slovak National Unity, were actually supposed to do all day was not so obvious, since there were no longer any political parties with which to compete and their own party's objectives – which for years had consisted of the single issue of implementing the terms of the Pittsburgh Agreement – had just been satisfied. Small wonder that the Tiso leadership floundered, issuing decrees, making proclamations, setting up new departments and running up debts as it tried to carve out a separate Slovak – and, increasingly, Fascist – identity for itself.

One of the new Slovak diet's first acts was to establish a 'Hlinka Youth' movement, modelled on the *Hitler Jugend*; and it could think of no better way to mark 28 October 1938, Czecho-Slovak Independence Day, than to order the dissolution of all associations and organizations (most notably *Sokol, Orol, Sedliacka Jazda* and the Workers' Gymnastic Union) whose head offices were to be found outside Slovakia. It then drew on the *Rodobrana* to form the nucleus of its very own SA-style paramilitary organization, the Hlinka Guard (which was subdivided into various branches, such as the Hlinka Transport Guards, the Hlinka University Guards, the Academic Hlinka Guard and so forth) to be the 'moral auxiliary organ' of 'all government offices'.[11] Under the leadership of Karol Sidor and, from 4 December 1938, his deputy Alexander (Šaňo) Mach, the Hlinka Guard steadily broadened its remit. Although unsuccessful in trying to make membership in the Hlinka Youth compulsory for all Slovak boys aged 6 to 18 and in the Hlinka Guard for Slovak men aged between 18 and 60, from 1 December 1939 the Hlinka Guard was re-established as a 'corps' within 'the framework of Hlinka's

Slovak People's Party'. Explicitly organized according to 'military principles', and with the legal right to bear arms and to wear uniforms, it had duties that were defined as providing 'pre-military training', submitting 'appropriate reports and proposals' to the 'authorities', helping to maintain 'public order' and 'public security', and defending 'the state'.[12] Within three weeks, the same protections and privileges had been extended to the *Freiwillige Schutzstaffel* and *Deutsche Jugend*, the German minority's equivalent organizations. Sidor's other big project – to replace politically lukewarm municipal boards with fiery pro-autonomist organizations called 'National Committees' (*národné výbory*) – did not take off in the short term;[13] but his idea of resurrecting National Committees succeeded spectacularly after 1945 – only, this time, to the benefit of the extreme Left rather than the extreme Right.

In the other newly autonomous Czecho-Slovak province, Subcarpathian Ruthenia, the political transition was less smooth. Prime Minister Bródy and Minister Fentsyk, in addition to complaining about an overabundance of Czech schools and personnel, called loudly for all Carpathian Rusyns, from the Poprad to the Tisza rivers (in other words, from eastern Slovakia as well as Subcarpathian Ruthenia), to join together in a 'unitary, free state'.[14] The provocation might have been overlooked by the central government in Prague had it not been for the fact that the new leaders of autonomous Ruthenia appeared to be trying to engineer plebiscites to return Ruthenia – together with the eastern Slovak region of Prešov – to Hungary, this time as an autonomous 'Rusyn' province. Since the central Czecho-Slovak government was just about to enter into the negotiations with Hungary and Poland required by the Munich Agreement, the very last thing it needed was to have further chunks of its territory being loudly offered, by groups of its own citizens, to a hostile power. On 26 October 1938, Czecho-Slovak prime minister Syrový met with the Ruthenian ministers in Prague, where he had Bródy arrested for treason; Fentsyk apparently escaped to Hungary by way of the Polish Embassy.[15] The first autonomous Ruthenian, and pro-Rusyn, government, which had lasted a fortnight, was replaced by a new, pro-Ukrainian government led by Mgsr Avhustyn Voloshyn, supported by local Ukrainian Blackshirts (*Chornorubashechnyky*), and with Iuliian Revai/Yulian Revay and Edmund Bachinskii/Bachynsky – both Ukrainophiles – kept on as ministers. It was all so sudden that Voloshyn apparently had to be appointed – and even sworn in – as prime minister in telephone calls between Užhorod and Prague.[16] Subcarpathian Ruthenia (*Podkarpatská Rus*) was immediately renamed Carpatho-Ukraine (*Karpats'ka Ukrajina*) and Ukrainian made the official language for all administrative and educational purposes. All Czech inscriptions in Chust/Khust were ordered to be changed to Ukrainian by 10 December.[17] The new Carpatho-Ukrainian government even got a reluctant central government to agree that all laws and decrees that pertained to the territory would henceforward appear, in the official

Sbírka zákonů a nařízení (Bulletin of Laws and Decrees) published in Prague, in Ukrainian rather than Czech.[18]

In the immediate aftermath of the Munich Crisis, Slovak and Ruthenian political leaders had sought to save their territories from Hungary by distancing themselves from the Prague government on the assumption that this would win them preferential treatment in negotiations with Nazi Germany. Instead, in what looked alarmingly like a prelude to the occupation of Bratislava, Germany immediately helped itself to two small, but strategically important, territories on the outskirts of Slovakia's regional capital: Petržalka (*Engerau*), opposite Bratislava on the right bank of the Danube; and Devín (*Theben*), a sacred place in Slovak national myth because of its associations with the Greater Moravian Empire, but of interest to the Reich for its situation at the confluence of the Morava and Danube rivers. Not only the German consul, but also the leader of the Carpathian German Party urged the Reich authorities to leave the ruins of Devín castle alone since, as Karmasin explained to Göring, 'All Slovak history books would have to be burnt if the Slovaks were to lose the castle.'[19] On 10 November, in response to formal Slovak protests, Germany informed the central Czecho-Slovak government (rather than the Slovak diet) that there was no question of the territories being returned; indeed, it had additional claims to make in Slovakia. These turned out to represent about 43 sq km (16.6 sq miles) of Slovak territory, inhabited by some 15,566 people, which ended up being directly annexed by Germany.[20]

On 1 November 1938, the day after the Munich Agreement was signed, the governments of Czecho-Slovakia and Poland exchanged diplomatic notes on changes to their common border. This time, the Silesian coalmining areas of Karviná and (Moravská) Ostrava and the railway junction at Bohumín, which had been assigned to Czecho-Slovakia at Versailles, went to Poland. The Slovaks' turn came the next day, with the First Vienna Arbitration Award (2 November 1938), which, although supposed in theory to settle disputed territories with Hungary by means of an 'international commission', was in fact left to Germany to decide.[21] To the horror of the Slovaks, who had assumed that only the Czechs would lose large chunks of their territory, Germany decided to award Hungary the entire strip of predominantly Magyar-inhabited territory that ran along its border with Hungary, representing a further 10,390 sq km (4,011 sq miles) of territory, inhabited by 854,217 people, of whom some 270,000 were claimed as Slovak.[22] Even Poland then took a few villages beyond its southern borders.[23] Tiso, appalled, went on radio to complain 'that a terrible injustice has been committed against the Slovak nation', but also to make explicit that 'all responsibility falls upon those politicians who have been deciding our fate without us, and against our will, for the past twenty years'.[24]

Official Slovak propaganda had blamed the Czechs for the Munich disaster. Now it sought to blame the unexpectedly heavy losses of Slovak territory to Hungary on Jews, giving the green light to the first in a series of semi-official Slovak pogroms and expulsions launched by the Hlinka Guard with the slogan 'With Sidor and against the Jews!'[25] For Leopold Löwy, a German-speaking Jew living on Schanzstrasse in Bratislava, whose father had never bothered to take out Czechoslovak nationality, the knock on the door came on 4 November 1938, when a Slovak and a German policeman informed him that he and his family had ten minutes to prepare themselves to leave Czecho-Slovakia; buses were waiting outside to deport them, together with other Jewish families, to Hungary, where they were presumed 'to belong'.[26] Jews, dragged out of their homes, 'usually at night', were informed that they could take with them no more than 60 kg (132 lb) of personal luggage and 500 crowns in cash. They were then shoved into trucks and dumped across the border, only to be sent back to find that the Hlinka Guard had taken possession of their businesses, workshops, houses and flats. The Hlinka Guard fell with equal enthusiasm upon Czech employees, who were evicted from their homes and deported to the Slovak-Moravian frontier, where, after being robbed of their valuables, they were pushed across the border.[27]

Subcarpathian Ruthenia, though no one seemed to notice or care, came out of the Vienna Arbitration even worse than Slovakia, losing the whole of its south-western corner to Hungary, including the important cities of Mukačevo/ Mukachevo and Berehovo and even the provincial capital, Užhorod, which the autonomous government was given just one week to vacate. After the loss of Užhorod, the regional capital was moved eastwards, to Khust (formerly *Chust*), a backwater of eighteen thousand inhabitants that could boast a 'decent' Government House, airfield, prison, a few churches and a synagogue, and a block or two of modern flats, but whose streets were mostly unpaved and overrun with chickens and geese.[28] Only because Germany had decided to support pan-Ukrainianism as a means of dividing and weakening the Soviet Union, judged American diplomat George Kennan, was it willing, for the time being, to leave the pro-Ukrainian Voloshyn government in power and the truncated province of Ruthenia in Czecho-Slovakia. The Voloshyn government, however, seems actually to have believed that, in the fullness of time, the Third Reich would see fit to organize and fund the unification of fifty million Ukrainians into an independent state that would stretch from the Carpathian Mountains to the Sea of Azov. It therefore eagerly signed agreements with the German Foreign Ministry to develop Ruthenia's infrastructure, preserve its forests, export its raw materials and concentrate German capital in the country.[29] The Prague government helped to sustain the local dream of a bright pan-Ukrainian future to the extent that, in order to prevent any further incursions by

Hungary (or, indeed, Romania) into what was still Czecho-Slovak territory, it gave permission to the Ukrainian National Defence to turn itself into yet another SA-style uniformed, paramilitary organization on Czecho-Slovak soil: Dmyto Klempush's Carpathian *Sich* (Owl).

In total, Czecho-Slovakia's territorial losses in the weeks after Munich added up to 41,098 sq km (15,868 sq miles) and about 4,879,000 people, of whom about 1,250,000 were said to be Czech or Slovak. This left Czecho-Slovakia with a territory of just 99,395 sq km (38,376 sq miles) and a population of about ten million. Just as territorial losses exacerbated pre-existing anti-Hungarian, anti-Czech and anti-Jewish feeling in Slovakia and Ruthenia, so they also intensified traditional anti-German sentiment – which had always included a distinctly anti-Semitic element – in Bohemia-Moravia, where local xenophobia was intensified by the arrival of unwanted Jewish-German refugees from the Sudetenland, the former Austria, and elsewhere. In order to 'solve' the 'problem' of refugees from the Third Reich, the Prague and Berlin governments agreed (20 November 1938) that Czecho-Slovak law should be changed in such a way as to remove the protection of Czecho-Slovak citizenship from all refugees from Nazi Germany or post-*Anschluss* Austria: in other words, primarily German Jews, together with German-speaking political opponents of the Nazi regime.[30] The extradition of political refugees to imprisonment in the Reich was undertaken not only with punctilious thoroughness but also, according to at least one eyewitness, with malicious satisfaction. Kurt Weisskopf, a left-wing, German-speaking Jew from Prague, remembered watching incredulously as a unit of Sudeten German Social Democrats, who happened to be passing through Prague, were rounded up by Czech guards in Masaryk railway station, loaded onto trucks and sent by armed train to Germany, where they could expect to be taken into German concentration camps. When he tried to protest, the Czech official he got on the phone called him a 'stinking Jew' and a 'Red pig' before slamming down the receiver.[31] While the central and regional governments sought to contain unemployment by transferring some 41,000 Czech, Slovak and Ruthenian workers to paid work in Germany, a law against vagrancy (passed on 2 March 1939) insisted that all unemployed men over the age of eighteen be sent to forced-labour camps set up and run by the Czecho-Slovak authorities.[32]

From his sick bed at Sezimovo Ústí, Beneš kept a dignified official silence over the rapid disintegration of the state that he had done so much to establish and to shape. He was not so discreet with friends and visitors, in whose company he was liable to explode with impotent rage at what he saw as the treachery of allies and neighbours alike. 'Poland will be the first to be hit,' he prophesied with malicious satisfaction; 'France will suffer terribly for having betrayed us, wait for that. . . . Chamberlain will live to see the consequences of his appeasement. . . . Hitler will attack them all.'[33] On 22 October 1938, ex-President Beneš – together with his wife and a small entourage – left Czecho-Slovakia. After a brief stay with Jan Masaryk in London, the Benešes moved on to Chicago, where Edvard was welcomed as 'Europe's most distinguished democrat' and given the post of professor of sociology.[34]

Czechoslovak Communist leaders (including Party Chairman Klement Gottwald), although not in too much danger from the regime so long as the Soviet–German Pact held, nevertheless thought it prudent to leave for Moscow, where in November 1938 they established a Presidium in exile which included leading Czech Communists such as Rudolf Slánský, KSČ General Secretary, as well as prominent ethnic German Communists such as Rudolf Appelt and Robert Korb.[35] The prevailing public mood in Prague, where students at the arts faculty of Charles University overturned a statue of T.G. Masaryk, portraits of Masaryk and Beneš were being removed from schools, government buildings, post offices and other public places, and the names of both Czechoslovak presidents were being 'execrated and dragged in the mud', was scathing about democracy, the West and the First Republic.[36] Ministers and right-wing newspapers called for a public enquiry to be held into the causes of the 'national catastrophe'.[37] People were especially bitter about Beneš, whose misguided foreign policy was taken to have lost the state not only large chunks of its territory and millions of its citizens, but also its security, independence and international standing.[38] George Kennan, who had taken up his post as US *chargé d'affaires* on the day the Munich Agreement was signed, was shocked by the atmosphere. 'Every feature of liberalism and democracy', he confided in early December 1938, is 'hopelessly and irretrievably discredited.' During weekend visits in the country,

> the guests did nothing but toss down brandy after brandy in an atmosphere of total gloom and repeat countless times: 'How was it possible that any people could allow itself to be led for twenty years by such a *Sauhund* – such an international, democratic *Sauhund* as Beneš? Such a people doesn't deserve to exist. It ought to be annihilated,' etc.

The climate, he noted, seemed ominously reminiscent of that of the Schuschnigg regime in Austria in 1935: 'There is the same disapproval of democracy, the same distrust and alienation of the labour element, the same Catholic piety, the same moderate and decorous anti-Semitism.'[39]

Czech Fascist and extreme right-wing movements, although not popular enough with the electorate to form a government in their own right, proliferated, putting the semi-military caretaker government under pressure to become more radical. The most important Czech Fascist groups were Radola Gajda's *Národní obec fašistická* (National Fascist Community) and the *Národní liga* (National League) led by Jiří Stříbrný, one of the 'Men of 28 October';

those closest to the contemporary Nazi model were Josef Rys-Rozsévač's *Vlajka* (The Banner) and *ANO* (*Akce národní obrody* or Action for National Restoration), an anti-Semitic pressure group linked to the *Hnutí mladých advokátů a lékařů* (Movement of Young Lawyers and Doctors).[40]

Amid general agreement that government needed to become more authoritarian and the old party system radically simplified, Rudolf Beran, the leader of the Agrarian Party, capitalized on the public mood by suggesting that the Czechs form a mass 'national' party of their own to promote an 'authoritarian and disciplined democracy, free from corruption and putting the service of the State before party interests'.[41] On 18 November 1938, just ten days after the creation in Slovakia of the mass 'Hlinka Slovak People's Party – The Party of Slovak National Unity', the main centrist and right-wing Czech parties of Bohemia and Moravia (the National Socialist Party, Traders' Party, National Alliance Party, Czechoslovak People's Party and the National League) merged with the Agrarian Party into a single right-wing block, the Czechs' very own 'Party of National Unity' (*Národní jednota*).[42]

Ten days later, on 30 November 1938, a former president of the Supreme Administrative Court, Emil Hácha, was elected Czecho-Slovakia's third president. General Syrový stepped down as prime minister and interim head of state, resuming his place in the cabinet as minister of defence. Rudolf Beran, formerly head of the Agrarian Party and now leader of Czech 'National Unity', took over as prime minister while Karol Sidor, the Slovak leader of the Hlinka Guard, became deputy prime minister. At the same time, Slovakia and Ruthenia set up 'representative offices' of their respective autonomous governments in Prague – the first headed by Karol Sidor and the second by Vincent Shandor – to facilitate official business with the central government.[43] Beneš, who immediately telegraphed his congratulations to President Hácha, gave no hint at the time that he considered the new, far-right Czecho-Slovak government to be illegitimate; it was not until some months later that he began to argue that his own resignation as president of Czechoslovakia had been 'forced', making it as 'invalid' as the Munich *diktat* that preceded it. At the new central Czecho-Slovak government's first meeting, held on 2 December 1938, Hácha cautioned members of the Czech cabinet that they should take the Bohemian duke and saint Wenceslas – who had 'fought for German-Czech understanding, although initially he did not find understanding with his own people' – as their model.[44] The new president, an observant Catholic, broadcast the message more widely by kissing the saint's bones in St Vitus Cathedral on Hradčany, a gesture simultaneously intended to signal the desirability of increased cooperation with Germany and a shift from the old anticlericalism to official approval of Catholicism.[45] František Chvalkovský, the new foreign minister, made it equally plain, in an article published on 16 December, that Czecho-Slovak foreign policy would

henceforward consist of 'friendly cooperation' with its neighbours, a euphemism that everyone understood to mean Germany.[46] He is remembered in
Czech nationalist folklore as having behaved like a complete sycophant when
he first met Ribbentrop, the German foreign minister, on 14 October, saying,
'And in foreign policy we shall lean on you, *Herr Reichsminister* [sic], if you
allow us.'[47]

On 15 December 1938, having already introduced pre-publication censorship, the central parliament in Prague passed a special Enabling Act, reminiscent of Hitler's, which entitled the government to alter the constitution, amend
constitutional laws and, in case of 'emergency', rule by decree. Because the
central government needed the support of the ministers for Slovakia to get
the act passed by the National Assembly, it agreed that all members of the
autonomous Slovak government would automatically also become members of
the state-wide Czecho-Slovak Council of Ministers; as a further concession to
Slovak nationalist feeling, the text of the law appeared in Slovak rather than in
Czech.[48] On 23 December, the central government again followed the Slovak
example by outlawing the Czechoslovak Communist Party (*KSČ*), which meant
that within a few days it had also been banned in Carpatho-Ukraine (formerly
Subcarpathian Ruthenia). About one thousand ethnic German Communists
are estimated to have left for Britain at this point;[49] a month later, Czecho-
Slovak and Reich police agreed to work together to provide cross-border
assistance to suppress any undercover Communist activity.[50]

According to the constitutional amendment that had established Slovak
autonomy, elections to the first Slovak diet had to be held according to the
same parliamentary procedures that had prevailed in the First Czechoslovak
Republic. Slovak prime minister Tiso neatly circumvented the problem by
announcing forthcoming elections and inviting candidates to register in the
usual way; but too late for any candidates (apart from the few his party had
forewarned) to register in time to be eligible to stand.[51] On 18 December
1938, the farce of 'elections' to the autonomous Slovak *Snem* took place.
Voters, instead of being able to select individuals, were presented with a
single slate of candidates, chosen by the leadership of Slovak National Unity;
those on the list were regarded as elected if the voter assented to 'a free, new
Slovakia'. At the polling booths, where uniformed Hlinka Guards officiated,
voters were theoretically at liberty to reply that they did not want 'a free, new
Slovakia' and to reject the entire list, but were hardly likely to do so when
discouraged from pulling the curtain for privacy or asked to hand over their
ballot papers directly to the officiating officer.

As a result of these simple tactics, Hlinka's Slovak People's Party –
The Party of Slovak National Unity won an overwhelming 97.5 per cent of
the Slovak vote.[52] Although rigged, the first 'elections' to the autonomous
Slovak diet gave the excuse for tremendous pageantry and speechifying and

created a magnificent backdrop for displays of Slovak, Nazi and papal flags, together with ranks of Hlinka Guards whose official greeting, George Kennan noted, seemed, symbolically enough, a kind of 'halfhearted compromise between a friendly wave and a full-fledged fascist salute'.[53] Both the Slovak and the Ruthenian political leaders, he judged, were 'making awful fools of themselves; dressing up in magnificent fascist uniforms, flying to and fro in airplanes, drilling comic-opera S.A. units and dreaming of the future grandeur of the Slovak or Ukrainian nations'.[54]

The central government in Prague, which by now effectively controlled only Bohemia and Moravia, did not follow the example of the autonomous regions of Slovakia and Ruthenia in immediately instituting strict one-party rule. Instead, it decided to permit a single, tame opposition party on the political Left to exist alongside the overwhelmingly dominant 'National Unity' on the political Right. This was *Národní strana práce* (National Labour Party), a merger of the socialist parties (but excluding the recently outlawed Communist Party). Bohemia and Moravia, unlike the other regions of the country, thus retained for the time being a veneer of electoral choice. Even so, for the central Czecho-Slovak government to limit and regulate parliamentary democracy to this extent was to sail dangerously close to Fascism, particularly since Czech National Unity's own youth organization, *Mladá národní jednota* or Young National Unity, had a uniformed paramilitary force that voiced extreme anti-Semitic views akin to those of the Hlinka Guard in Slovakia and the *Sich* in Ruthenia. By late February 1939, there were increasingly insistent calls from the right-wing Czech press for the political system in Bohemia and Moravia to be further 'simplified', and the Czech Party of National Unity formally recommended the reorganization of 'public life' in accordance with the 'corporate' model.[55] It can only have been a matter of weeks before Bohemia-Moravia would have followed the Slovak and Ruthenian examples and gone completely Fascist.

In all parts of the federal Czecho-Slovak Republic, one of the most pressing questions on the political agenda was how to make the dominant 'nation' – whether Czech, Slovak or Ukrainian/Rusyn – attain 'national purity' (hegemony) within its claimed territory. The Czechs, albeit unwillingly, had already lost the bulk of their German population with the transfer of their borderlands to the German Reich and their Polish population with the loss of Silesia; Slovaks and Ruthenians had lost the majority of their Magyar minority as a consequence of the Vienna Arbitration. This seemed to open up the possibility of making each region of the federated Czecho-Slovak state nationally homogeneous: Czech, Slovak or Ukrainian. Over the question of the resented – but sometimes needed – qualified Czechs living in Slovakia, many of whom had already been chased out of the region, the Slovak autonomous and central Czecho-Slovak governments came to a formal agreement, on 12 December 1938, that about nine thousand Czech state employees, from teachers to administrators, should be removed so that they could be replaced with Slovaks. This still left extreme nationalists, racists and Fascists with two unsolved 'problems': how to rid the Czecho-Slovak republic of its Jews and Gypsies.

In Prague, where fresh bouts of anti-Semitism were stimulated after each wave of Jewish and political refugees arrived from the Reich (first from Germany proper, then from post-*Anschluss* Austria, and finally from the annexed Sudetenland), from October Czecho-Slovak officials were lobbying the British to use their influence with Berlin to stop the German authorities from 'dumping these unwanted Jews' in Bohemia and Moravia,[56] and complaining that the British government seemed to show 'interest and practical sympathy' to 'the Jews and the German Social Democrats' at the expense of 'the Czechs and the Slovaks'.[57] By mid-November, Foreign Minister Chvalkovský was saying in private that, although the Germans were 'pressing' for 'action to be taken against the Jews', there must be 'no pogroms before January or February', since bad publicity might jeopardize the Czecho-Slovak government's chances of another big Anglo-French loan. In the meantime, he hinted darkly, 'all the Jews in the country' might spontaneously 'decide' to emigrate.[58]

Pressure was certainly being brought to bear on Czech Jews, although not yet too directly or obviously by the central government. It was *Sokol*, the Czech patriotic organization so beloved of T.G. Masaryk, that passed a resolution on 23 October to urge all Jews who had arrived after 1914 to 'return' to their 'original homes'; and the youth wing of National Unity that issued a pamphlet explaining that the Jews, a 'foreign' minority, would soon have their legal position 'regulated' so that they could be 'removed' from state employment and prevented from 'influencing education' and 'dominating' in other fields 'out of proportion to their numbers'. By Christmas 1938, rumours in the Czech press – presumably deliberately leaked by the government – were rife, some suggesting that Jewish university professors, civil servants and teachers would all be pensioned off on 1 January 1939, others warning that all Jewish schoolteachers would be dismissed on that day.[59]

In the end, Czecho-Slovak Decrees 14 and 15 were not issued by the central government until 27 January 1939; and they did not mention the word 'Jew' once. They simply announced that persons who had been naturalized as Czechoslovak citizens at any point between 1918 and 1938, unless they could be readily identified as 'Czech', 'Slovak' or 'Carpatho-Rusyn', would have their citizenship removed and be deported from Czecho-Slovakia. Although the law did not specify who would be affected, it was obvious in the general climate that – as the British minister in Prague had no difficulty in understanding – it was designed to be 'against the Jews'.[60] Not to be outdone, the autonomous government in Slovakia, while welcoming the central government's move as a partial solution, promised to go further and, on 23 January 1939, set up a parliamentary subcommittee, including names as eminent as those of Sidor and Ďurčanský, to look into possible solutions to the 'Jewish Question'. Tiso, meanwhile, declared Jews in Slovakia to be entitled only to those 'rights' that were 'appropriate' to a people who held a 'disproportionate' share of the country's wealth. He further claimed it to be a mark of the Slovak nation's 'maturity' that it would take a 'legal approach' to this 'problem'.[61] The 'problem of Jews', the Ruthenian prime minister declared in a published interview in late January, 'is an all-state matter. Therefore, we Ukrainians embrace the same attitude as that of the Central Government.'[62] In Ruthenia, Vincent Shandor later claimed, Prime Minister Voloshyn revealed to him 'in confidence' that '150 [sic] Austrian Jews' were living in Carpatho-Ukraine 'whom we ought to transfer to a safe country [sic] whence they could proceed to Palestine', an action that, he added, needed to be carried out 'in utmost secrecy'. Shandor promised to help.[63]

It is often claimed that the Czechs, unlike the Slovaks and the Germans, had no deep-rooted tradition of anti-Semitism and therefore had to be forced by the Nazis to persecute the Jews of Bohemia and Moravia. It would be more accurate to say that Czech anti-Semitism, whose roots were as deep as those anywhere else in Europe,[64] initially had a different flavour from other contemporary Central European varieties in that it was primarily conceived as a matter of ethnolinguistic prejudice, a variant of anti-German feeling rather than a hatred justified on religious grounds (as in the Slovak case) or racial ones (as in the German).[65] Otto Grünfeld, for example, who grew up in Náchod and Ústí nad Orlicí in north-eastern Bohemia, remembered how he was simultaneously mocked by German fellow pupils for being Jewish, and by Czech schoolteachers for having a German-sounding surname.[66] Similarly, Eric Stein, the only Jewish boy in his class in Hradec Králové, remembered taking turns with a Slovak boy to be the butt of teasing and bullying by his Czech classmates.[67] After Grünfeld's father was forced, in early 1939, to give up his job as head of the textile firm Henrych and Son, the family moved to Prague, where many Czech-speaking Jews continued to feel safe on the grounds that they had long been classified in censuses as being of Czech (rather than Jewish) 'nationality', were partly or wholly secularized, and felt themselves to be as much a part of Czech society as the nominally Catholic majority.

At a time when German-speaking Jews were being publicly sacked from businesses, theatres, newspapers and places of higher education throughout Bohemia and Moravia (including the German section of Charles University in Prague), Czech professional organizations, such as those that forbade Czech Jews from practising medicine or law, tried to keep pace with anti-Semitic racism of the German variety, but more discreetly, characteristically through internally published changes of administrative practices or hiring procedures rather than – as yet – government decrees or published laws. Even the Czecho-Slovak central government's decision to rid itself of all employees whose parents were Jewish did not require a change of law, but only an internal announcement.[68] Increasingly placed on the defensive, the Union of Czech Jews in the Czecho-Slovak Republic (*Svaz Čechů židů v Česko-Slovenské republice*) did what it could to provide counter-intelligence to the avalanche of anti-Semitic propaganda that was coming from all sides. The Union argued that Czech Jews had no influence in the world of big business or international capital; that they formed less than 1 per cent of the population of Bohemia and Moravia (as opposed to the 11 per cent of Jews to be found in some eastern Slovak provinces and in Ruthenia); and that anti-Semitism was not a traditional part of Czech culture.[69] Sadly, the Nazi historian Wolfgang von Wolmar was probably closer to the mark when he lamented the inability of German and Czech National Socialists to work together – despite sharing 'so many goals, including anti-Semitism' – because of their mutual national antagonism.[70]

Anti-Gypsy prejudice, which attracted less interest internationally than anti-Semitism, could for the same reason be more easily translated into direct action by the central Czecho-Slovak government.[71] On 2 March 1939, a new law was passed to set up two forced-labour camps for so-called 'nomads': one at Lety in southern Bohemia, and another at Hodonín in central Moravia. This was the beginning of the infamous Czech Gypsy camps from which just 5 per cent of all Czech Gypsies (mainly Romany-speakers, i.e. Roma) were to return after 1945, a majority of those who survived the Czech-run camps having been transported, in 1943 and 1944, to be gassed at the German-run Gypsy Camp at Auschwitz.[72]

At the same time that ethnic tensions among Czechs, Jews, Gypsies, Germans and Slovaks were becoming strained almost beyond the point of endurance, relations between the central government in Prague and the autonomous regions further deteriorated. In January 1939, according to George Kennan, two incidents finally decided the central Czecho-Slovak government in Prague to try to claim back political control of Carpatho-Ukraine, which it was continuing to fund from central resources. The first was that money sent to the Khust government from Prague, which it said had been earmarked for road building, turned out to have been spent on propaganda, much of it anti-Czech. The second, and more important, incident was that irregular Ruthenian soldiers had launched an abortive attempt to recapture the city of Mukačevo from Hungary, leading to a border fracas in which there were several casualties, damage to property and a potentially harmful breach between the Prague and Budapest governments.[73]

On 17 January 1939, the central Czecho-Slovak government appointed Lev Prchala, a former member of the Czechoslovak Legion in Russia and general in the Czecho-Slovak army, as minister of the interior and finance in the regional Ruthenian government. What Shandor recalled, nearly sixty years later, as 'a gross political mistake' on the part of those who 'could not understand that they were no longer masters in Carpatho-Ukraine', inevitably led to macho posturing by the *Sich* guard and to loud complaints by the Khust government that Prague was trampling on its right to run its own affairs.[74] The incident might easily have provided an excuse for Germany to intervene in Czecho-Slovakia's internal affairs. Instead, the Prague government got away with it, despite provoking a fresh wave of anti-Czech demonstrations in Ruthenia; and the Voloshyn government, which was entirely financially dependent on the central Czecho-Slovak government, had to content itself with focusing on its upcoming (purely cosmetic) 'elections' to the autonomous Ruthenian *Soim* on 12 February 1939, at which the thirty-two candidates from the Ukrainian National Union, the only permitted political party (who again appeared on a single list) were duly 'elected' as deputies with 93 per cent of the vote.[75]

That Prague was able to intervene in Ruthenia's political affairs without provoking a reaction from Germany emboldened the central government to try to curb Slovakia. When, in mid-February, members of the Slovak autonomous government came to Prague with requests, not only for more money, but also to arm the Hlinka Guard and to put Slovak commanders in charge of all regiments of the Czecho-Slovak army stationed on Slovak soil, they were curtly informed that if they wished to continue to receive substantial financial support from Prague they would have 'to stop their "double-faced policy" '.[76] On 21 February, in a long speech to the Slovak diet to launch his new 'policy of reconstruction', Tiso – although he explicitly rejected rumours that Slovakia was about to go independent – nevertheless strongly implied that the day was coming. 'The Slovak nation,' as he put it in characteristically confusing and mystical language, 'is building its State, creating its new State, building its own Slovak State. . . . Slovak national consciousness is working, is organizing its State services so that it can prove that it wants to live characteristically according to this principle, which today is the world motto: nationality.'[77] A week later, it was further noted in Prague that ministers of the autonomous Slovak government – who had drawn their own conclusions from the Ruthenian incident – had bypassed Prague and gone directly to Berlin to negotiate economic assistance.[78]

By early March 1939, Czech–Slovak tensions were almost at breaking point. In Bratislava, as in Khust, there were public demonstrations against both Czechs and Jews, and a jubilant sense of national ascendancy. Alexander (Šaňo) Mach, the head of Slovak propaganda and *éminence grise* of the Hlinka Guard, went on the record as saying that it would be a 'national catastrophe' not to 'construct' a 'Slovak state'.[79] Travelling east from Prague, a French foreign correspondent was taken aback to find such a striking contrast between what he saw as the gloom and tension in the state capital and the 'atmosphere of juvenile exuberance and total jauntiness' prevailing in Slovakia.[80] The Prague government, suspicious of the Slovak leadership's intentions and faced with the prospect of having to cover Slovakia's budget deficit, demanded that the Slovak autonomous government immediately proclaim its loyalty to the Czecho-Slovak state, dismiss Mach as chief of propaganda, and abandon attempts to build an independent Slovak army, which was how it interpreted the requests for Slovak generals and support for the Hlinka Guard.[81]

The autonomous Slovak administration and leadership of the Hlinka Guard, sensing the sudden change of mood in Prague, concluded that a plot to reassert Czech dominance over Slovakia was being hatched. They therefore flew to Berlin for consultations, and began to hint that they could always secede from Czecho-Slovakia altogether. This further escalated the already serious tensions, which the Slovak cabinet attempted to calm on 6 March 1939 with a formal assurance that, whatever happened, Slovakia would – as had been declared at Žilina on 6 October 1938 – remain within the framework of a Czecho-Slovak state. By this point the atmosphere of mutual mistrust had reached such a low – in part because *Slovák*, the Slovak National Unity daily newspaper, was continuing to write about building a 'new independent home in a free Slovakia' – that even this announcement only aroused suspicion in Prague that the Slovaks were planning to replace the central Czecho-Slovak government with a Czech diet, so that the Slovaks, Ukrainians/Ruthenians and Czechs would be represented in mathematically exact proportions.[82]

Rather than wait for any further diminution of its power, the Prague government decided to strike. On 6 March 1939, President Hácha dismissed the Ukrainian-oriented members of the autonomous government in Ruthenia. The Presidium of the Slovak National Unity Party, shocked that the central Czecho-Slovak government could disregard its own law on Ruthenian autonomy so blithely, concluded that the only realistic long-term option for autonomous Slovakia was full independence, but also that this would have to wait until the region had the financial backing and personnel to go it alone. Local Nazi authorities in Vienna, who were quicker than the central German government in Berlin to see the potential benefits to the Third Reich of playing off the Czechs against the Slovaks, began to urge Tiso and Sidor to follow the advice of their own radicals, cut the apron strings that tied them to Prague and take the leap to full independence. When, three days after it had sacked the Carpatho-Ukrainian government in Ruthenia, there was still no reaction from Germany, the Prague government decided to strike again, this time in Slovakia.

On 9 March 1939, President Hácha dismissed all members of the autonomous Slovak government (with the single exception of Pavol Teplanský), announced a new government led by Jozef Sivák and declared martial law.[83]

When Tiso protested at being deprived of his office by presidential decree, he was briefly locked up in a monastery. About 250 Slovaks from the radical wing that supported the cause of immediate Slovak independence – among them Vojtech Tuka, Alexander Mach and Matúš Černák – were arrested and sent to prison in Moravia. Deputy Prime Minister Ďurčanský and Karol Murgaš, the official head of the Hlinka Guard, fled to Vienna, where, in cooperation with local Nazis, they began to broadcast pro-independence and anti-Czech propaganda in Slovak.[84]

It was Sivák, away in Rome at the time, who put a spanner in the works of Prague's plans by refusing to accept the post of prime minister. In a special radio announcement on 10 March, the Slovak people were exhorted to stay calm and informed that 'anyone who tells you that the German Empire wants to separate Slovakia from the Czecho-Slovak state is a lying adventurer'.[85] Another Slovak government was named, this time headed by Karol Sidor and excluding Teplanský, leaving rival Slovak groups in Bratislava and Vienna to argue over the airwaves as to which of them was the real 'traitor' to the 'Slovak nation'. Behind the scenes, meanwhile, rival German groups in Berlin and Vienna debated whether or not to support the Slovak separatists. In Slovakia itself, Karmasin's Carpathian German *Deutsche Partei* urged a 'common front of Slovaks and Germans' to defend what it referred to as a 'free Slovak state'.[86]

The constitutional crisis that Prague provoked in March 1939 was intended to enable the central government to strengthen Czecho-Slovak unity and save Czecho-Slovak resources while Germany, which had no reason to be interested, looked the other way. Instead, by breaking its own laws, the Prague government gave the Third Reich its first pretext since Munich openly to intervene in Czecho-Slovakia's internal affairs. The British ambassador to Germany, Sir Neville Henderson, who could see that Prague was 'playing Hitler's game for him', remembered how, on 11 March 1939, it was suddenly announced in Berlin that Tiso (not Sidor, who had just been named head of the Slovak autonomous government) had appealed to the German government for protection. The German press, 'which up till then' had devoted 'little space' to the Czecho-Slovak constitutional dispute, suddenly and ominously adopted 'a violently pro-Slovak attitude'.[87] By the next day, 12 March, it was full of 'wild tales of Czech atrocities' and of 'Germans flying for refuge', racial incidents having been reported in Brno, Jihlava and Olomouc, where there were large German populations. In Prague, a few prescient souls began to display the swastika in their windows.[88]

On the same day, 12 March 1939, Hitler phoned Döme Sztójay, the Hungarian minister to Germany, to inform him that he had decided to withdraw his protection from Czecho-Slovakia and to recognize the independence of Slovakia. Out of 'friendship' to Hungary, however, he said that he would 'hold up for 24 hours the decision whether to grant similar recognition to Ruthenia'.[89] Hitler then invited Jozef Tiso, who had just suffered the twin shocks of being deposed as leader of autonomous Slovakia and imprisoned, to meet him in Berlin. The leadership of Slovak National Unity gathered hurriedly in the basement of the *Slovák* offices in Bratislava to decide what to do. They agreed that Tiso should certainly go to the meeting with Hitler, but should not enter into any binding agreements without first consulting them.[90]

Tiso, who had just lost his position as prime minister to his rival Sidor, and who might just as easily have ended up being tried for treason in a Prague courtroom, was naturally delighted, upon his arrival in Berlin on 13 March 1939, to find that he was accorded all the honours usually reserved for a head of state. Accounts of the famous meeting between Tiso and Hitler that followed are in broad agreement about what was said, but differ, sometimes sharply, over whether the Slovak delegation was bullied or only tempted into declaring independence. Even Tiso later told two versions of the story: in one, the Führer had generously warned him that the Slovaks would have to act quickly if they wished to decide their own destiny; in the other, Slovakia would never have opted for independence had it not been for the pressure under which it had been placed by Hitler.[91] In a sense, both versions of the story were true. Hitler could indeed have dispensed with Slovakia as carelessly as he had just disposed of Carpatho-Ukraine (Subcarpathian Ruthenia); on the other hand, Prague had just forced Tiso to face the uncomfortable fact that, however much Slovakia might like the idea of independence, it could not yet afford to finance it. Tiso neglected, in published recollections, to mention any more personal motives; but it can hardly have escaped his notice that, in agreeing to declare Slovak independence, he was also being given the chance to displace his rival, Karol Sidor, and to rise from being merely a provincial leader to the head of an independent state. Years later, Jozef Kirschbaum, sometime commander of the university wing of the Hlinka Guard, still insisted that 'the hour of decision in regard to Slovakia's independence had arrived' and that Hitler had offered the nation 'one of the historical opportunities which numerically small, dominated people cannot bypass without paying heavy penalties'.[92]

According to most accounts, Hitler opened the meeting with a diatribe against the Czechs, but then surprised the Slovak delegation by informing them that Bohemia and Moravia were about to be occupied by German troops. He stressed that Slovakia's immediate choice was either to opt for independence, in which case Germany would willingly guarantee its new borders, or else to reject German assistance, in which case he would 'no longer be responsible' for events. It was immaterial which way the Slovaks chose, since German interests did not extend east of the Carpathians, but if they wanted to make a bid for independence they would need to come to a 'very rapid' (*blitzschnell*) decision. There was little reason for Tiso not to be persuaded by Hitler's characteristic bullying mixture of apparently friendly advice, *Realpolitik* and threats. He expressed his deep gratitude to the Führer, together with assurances that 'the Slovak nation' would give him no reason to regret what he had done on its behalf.[93] The meeting had lasted thirty-five minutes. At about midnight on the same night, 13–14 March 1939, Fr Voloshyn sent a telegram to Hitler, via the German consul in Khust, to request that Carpatho-Ukraine be taken under German protection.[94]

From the meeting with Hitler, Tiso went to the Czecho-Slovak legation to phone Sidor, whom he asked to arrange an emergency session of the Slovak diet for the following day. Sidor passed on the request to President Hácha, who in turn consulted Prime Minister Beran. Permission was granted. Sidor then went on Bratislava radio to urge all Slovak deputies to turn up for an 'historic' session of the Slovak National Assembly the next day. When, on the morning of 14 March 1939, the Slovak diet went into emergency session – with Tiso in attendance – there was little doubt as to what it must mean. Sure enough, when the first bulletin appeared at lunchtime, it was to announce that the Slovak parliament – no longer a mere diet – had unanimously brought into being an independent Slovak state. Tiso was restored as prime minister, Sidor made minister of the interior and Vojtech Tuka brought in as minister without portfolio. The first Slovak parliament's next acts were to rush through land and pension reforms and to begin to set down on paper the exact terms of its economic relationship with the German Reich.[95] After a decent interval of a few weeks, Sidor was sent off to be envoy to the Vatican, leaving Tiso as the unchallenged dictator of Slovakia.

Voloshyn's autonomous Carpatho-Ukrainian government in Khust found out about Slovak independence from the one o'clock news. Since it had still received no reply to its telegram to Hitler, the Council of Ministers went into an emergency session for the rest of the afternoon. At about 6.30 p.m., a slightly reshuffled cabinet – of which Fr Voloshyn remained leader – emerged from Government House. A Proclamation of Carpatho-Ukrainian Independence was read out to the small crowd that had gathered to find out what was going on. The next morning, the blue and yellow flag was flying from Government House and *Sich* guards, just released from prison, were marching down the streets of Khust, terrifying local Jews and encouraging any remaining Czechs to pack up their things and leave at once.[96]

President Hácha and Foreign Minister Chvalkovský, whose country was breaking into pieces, requested and were immediately granted an audience with Hitler in Berlin. Contrary to the impression given in most accounts that the meeting was intended solely to belittle and humiliate Hácha (rather as if he had been a second Beneš, instead of an already compliant ally of Nazi Germany), the president was received with full honours. Even Hácha's daughter, who accompanied him on the trip, was presented with a bouquet of flowers from Ribbentrop and with a box of chocolates from Hitler.[97]

Czecho-Slovakia's president and foreign minister nevertheless had to endure hours of suspense while Hitler and his entourage watched a film; such contradictions were, as Ian Kershaw has taught us, entirely characteristic of Hitler's unorthodox behaviour.[98] The Czecho-Slovak delegation was finally admitted into the Führer's presence at about midnight.

According to anecdotal accounts of the interview, Hitler – who later claimed to have been taken aback by Hácha's submissiveness – pressed his advantage, announcing that within six hours German forces would enter Czecho-Slovakia from three sides and ruthlessly crush any attempt at resistance. Göring backed up Hitler's threats, insisting that the German air force would reduce Prague to rubble if the slightest resistance were shown. Since the president looked as if he might faint, Hitler's private physician, Dr Morell, gave him an injection. Hitler later enjoyed telling his inner circle how, if Hácha had called his bluff, he would have 'irredeemably lost face' because 'at the hour mentioned fog was so thick over our airfields that none of our aircraft could have made its sortie'.[99] The story, which has the false ring of one of Hitler's boasts, was presumably exaggerated and oversimplified through its telling and retelling by the Führer and his many flatterers. It scarcely matters. What does matter is that Hácha signed a declaration that stated that, in order to 'achieve ultimate pacification', the president of Czecho-Slovakia 'confidently placed the fate of the Czech people and country in the hands of the Führer of the German Reich' in order to guarantee the Czechs 'autonomous development of their ethnic life as suited to their character'.[100] The meeting was over by 3.00 a.m., Hitler having been promised an orderly and peaceful occupation, and Hácha assured that the Czechs of Bohemia and Moravia would retain some sort of national autonomy.

News of the German occupation came over the radio in stages. At 4.30 a.m., Radio Prague announced that German troops would begin to occupy the country at 6.00 a.m. At 5.00 a.m., Berlin radio broadcast a special announcement from Goebbels, who read out Hitler's 'Proclamation to the German People', justifying the impending invasion on the grounds of Czech maltreatment of its minorities, of Slovakia's secession of the day before, and of the Lands of the Bohemian Crown having belonged to the 'Reich' for 'over a thousand years'. From 6.00 a.m., the text of Hácha's declaration was added to the broadcast in further justification.[101] Operation Green (as a contingency plan for the occupation of Bohemia and Moravia had been known to the German military since 1937) did not proceed completely smoothly. In Bohemia, there were embarrassing breakdowns of German army vehicles in the unusually cold and snowy weather. In Moravia, bilingual posters that German soldiers began to plaster on billboards to announce an eight o'clock evening curfew had to be replaced after it was pointed out that they had been printed in German and Romanian, rather than in German and Czech.[102] Despite these and other slight hiccoughs, German troops entered

Prague at about nine o'clock in the morning, just as most people were on their way to work, following their government's instructions to go about their ordinary business.

As mostly silent onlookers began to line the streets to watch the mechanized vehicles proceed through the city centre, some wept or shook their fists, while others gave the Nazi salute or simply looked on impassively. Some eyewitness reports stress the hostility of the German army's reception; others judge it to have been relatively friendly. Contemporary photographs can be found to support both versions of events. The whole of the country was occupied by the afternoon, the source of some bitterly self-deprecating Czech jokes. Ethnic German leaders organized scenes of rejoicing and thanksgiving to welcome the German occupation of Bohemia and Moravia. General Radola Gajda, the leader of the Czech Fascist Community, seeing a golden opportunity to seize power, entered the parliament building in Prague to proclaim his own group – together with members of the pro-Nazi *Vlajka* and anti-Semitic *ANO* movements – as forming a new 'Czech National Committee'.

On 15 March, Hungarian troops captured Khust, putting an end to the independent republic of Carpatho-Ukraine, which had only been in existence for a day. By 27 March, the whole of Carpatho-Ukraine had been forcibly annexed to Hungary. As things were to turn out, this was almost the end of the region's association with Czecho-Slovakia/Czechoslovakia, since it was to be annexed to Ukraine, a part of the USSR, less than a month after being liberated from Hungary at the end of the Second World War and with the Prague government's formal permission.

It is often pointed out that Britain, France, Germany and Italy were bound, by the terms of the Munich Agreement, to defend Czecho-Slovakia's post-Munich borders in the event of 'unprovoked aggression'. It was not immediately clear at the time whether or not such an act had occurred. After all, Slovakia and Ruthenia had voluntarily seceded from the state, while President Hácha had requested, in writing, that Bohemia and Moravia be placed in the 'care' of the Third Reich. The Czecho-Slovak army had not been mobilized, nor had there been any spontaneous show of resistance to the German troops. British and French officials expressed sympathy for the Czecho-Slovak plight, but generally took the same line as Chamberlain, who assured the archbishop of Canterbury that 'some day' the Czechs would see 'that what we did was to save them for a happier future'.[103] Their consulates and legations – just like those of the United States – suddenly besieged with Jews, Social Democrats, refugees from Germany, and others with good cause to fear the Nazis – turned the terrified asylum-seekers away.[104]

Hitler, perhaps caught off guard by the speed and success of the occupation of Bohemia and Moravia, appears at first to have had no clear notion of what to do with the new territory in his possession. To the considerable alarm of his immediate entourage, he suddenly announced his desire to make an unscheduled visit to Prague, which he had never seen. Apparently having been duped by his own country's propaganda, he insisted upon taking elaborate security precautions to cross the frontier and seemed surprised to find that there were no victims of anti-German 'terror' for him to visit in hospital.[105] Arriving in Prague at about eight o'clock in the evening, just after the streets had been cleared for the curfew, Hitler, Ribbentrop and other high Nazi officials – together with Konrad Henlein, the former leader of the Sudeten German Party – slipped into the Castle so unobtrusively that Hácha and the Czecho-Slovak cabinet, who were meeting in another part of the complex, were not even aware that they were there.[106]

On 16 March 1939, executive power over Bohemia and Moravia passed to the commander in chief of the German army. *Lidové noviny* led with the announcement of the occupation, together with assurances that the 'Czech nation' had been guaranteed 'autonomous development' and 'national distinctiveness' (*národní svébytnost*).[107] General Johannes Blaskowitz was named as the military commander with responsibility for Bohemia, and General Sigmund List for Moravia. Military tribunals were set up; radios and firearms began to be collected. The territory's new status, as the 'Protectorate of Bohemia and Moravia', was passed into Reich law and the 'Protectorate Decree' read over the radio by Ribbentrop.

The term 'protectorate', whose meaning was not quite clear but which had distinctly colonial overtones, echoed the sense of Hácha's declaration of the night before that the territories of Bohemia and Moravia were in some sense being taken into the 'care' of the Reich; but also suggested that a degree of Czech autonomy would be retained.[108] The understanding appeared to be that German military rule was only a temporary, stopgap measure until suitable arrangements could be made for a *Reichsprotektor* – a sort of governor or viceroy – to take over. Hitler received the mayor of Prague, President Hácha and Minister of Defence Syrový, confirming the impression that the current Czech administration was somehow to continue under the new regime. He deigned to appear at a window of the Castle to acknowledge the rapturous cheering of a group of local Germans below, and, in the Castle courtyard, to inspect a band of local Nazis who claimed to have been wounded in clashes with the Czechs. Having shown his face and allowed himself to be photographed looking in command, Hitler left Prague on 16 March, going on to Silesia (where he spent the night) and then to Brno and Olomouc, before leaving for Vienna on the 17th. Hitler's visit to Prague, which was never to be repeated, was commemorated in one of the first postage stamps to be issued in the Protectorate of Bohemia and Moravia.

In the wake of the Munich disaster, Czechoslovakia had been left vulnerable to attack from all sides. The central government in Prague, finally forced to give away long-disputed territories to Germany, Hungary and Poland and to grant Slovakia and Ruthenia autonomy, had tried to appease its neighbours, especially Germany, while simultaneously keeping control of its citizens and protecting the state from any further border revisions. After the proclamation of Slovak independence on 13–14 March, the German occupation of Bohemia and Moravia-Silesia on 14–15 March and the forcible Hungarian annexation of Carpatho-Ukraine (Subcarpathian Ruthenia) on 15–27 March, there no longer existed a Czecho-Slovak state to protect. Czechoslovakia/ Czecho-Slovakia, which had been in existence for less than twenty years, had been destroyed by a combination of internal discontent – led by its own German, Slovak and Ruthenian autonomists – and external pressure – applied mostly by Germany, but to which Italy, Hungary, Poland, Britain and France had each contributed a share. There was no reason to suppose that the state, a failed experiment in multinationalism, would ever be restored.

CHAPTER 5

A REPUBLIC AND A PROTECTORATE

Czecho-Slovakia disappeared from the map of Europe twenty years after it had first appeared there and six months before the start of the Second World War. Its most hotly contested border areas having been transferred (in accordance with the Munich Agreement of 30 September 1938) to Germany, Poland and Hungary, from the middle of March 1939 until early May 1945 the bulk of the former state consisted of two entirely separate entities: the Protectorate of Bohemia and Moravia (*Protektorat Böhmen und Mähren* or *Protektorát Čechy a Morava*), a satellite of Nazi Germany; and the Slovak 'state' or 'republic' (*Slovenský štát* or *Slovenská republika*), an independent state. Despite the fact that both polities were closely allied to Nazi Germany, at the war's end Czechoslovakia was not only resurrected, but counted on the side of the victorious Allies. To have pulled off such a stunt for the second time within a generation was a remarkable achievement; but this Czechoslovak success, like that which had followed the First World War, came at a price.

The first independent Slovak Republic, a sovereign state with some 2,655,000 inhabitants and a surface area of 38,004 sq km (14,673 sq miles), ended up lasting just over six years (from March 1939 until April 1945). It is usually described by the rather unhelpful term 'puppet state', the implication being that it was directly controlled from Nazi Germany. The new state, which certainly proved to be one of Germany's most faithful allies, agreed from the first to the stationing of German troops on its soil (in a Protected Zone created along its western boundary), and even, in a bilateral treaty concluded with Germany ten days after independence, to align its defence and foreign policies with those of the Third Reich.[1] But although these arrangements made nonsense of Slovak 'independence' when it came to military or international affairs, it would be quite wrong to suppose that the country's authoritarian and xenophobic domestic policies, whose origins lay in the Second Czecho-Slovak Republic (when Slovakia was autonomous but not yet independent), were somehow foreign and imposed rather than voluntary and Slovak.

Since it was in Germany's interests for Slovakia to be ruled by a stable regime with which it could do business, it was perfectly content for the new republic to keep its own brand of Fascism – the pseudo-Catholic, xeno-phobic and anti-Jewish variety of the kind favoured by Slovak National Unity under the leadership of prime minister (later, president) Jozef Tiso[2] – rather than to support the Hlinka Guard, whose radical racism and ideal of 'perma-nent revolution' more nearly approximated to the ideology of the German SS.[3] Leaving the Tiso regime to continue to manage Slovakia's domestic affairs not only saved Germany the bother, it also made out of the young Slav state a showcase – what the German consul in Bratislava called a 'display window' or 'visiting card' – to advertise 'how independently a small country can live that places itself under the protection of the Greater German Reich'.[4] In exchanging economic and military dependence upon Prague (the devil it knew) for Berlin (the devil it did not know), the Slovak government was taking a gamble. But it would have been far more risky not to have thrown in its lot with the only superpower in the region, especially since Germany showed no intention of standing in the way of Slovakia's transfor-mation into a more distinctively Slovak and Catholic, rather than German and Nazi, Fascist state.

On 16 March 1939, Prime Minister Tiso announced that, since the Slovak state was not born out of 'hate', but rather arose from the Slovak people's 'great love' for their 'own kin' and their 'own state', it would be necessary to remove the Czechs; but this would be done in 'a Christian way', without 'cruelty' or 'hatred'. As for the Jews: they would be dealt with separately, in a forthcoming government bill.[5] Eight days later, the Ministry of the Interior was instructed to set up a camp to hold those whom it had 'reason to fear' would 'create an obstacle' to the 'building of the Slovak state'.[6] Independent Slovakia's first concentration camp, at Ilava near Trenčín, was open for busi-ness within the month, its inmates sent there, without benefit of trial, at the command of the Ministry of the Interior. In April, the ministry set up a special secret police organization, the *Ústredňa štátnej bezpečnosti* (State Security Headquarters) or *ÚŠB*, to monitor, punish or eliminate 'enemies of the state' (e.g. real or imagined opponents of the current regime, which included, by definition, all 'Jews', 'Czechs' and 'Bolsheviks'). Among those to be routinely monitored, rather than imprisoned or deported, were local Germans and Hungarians; the members of all legal and illegal Slovak political parties; and university students. Slovaks living abroad were also, wherever possible, to be kept under surveillance. As if in anticipation of the postwar Czechoslovak Communist regime's own 'state security' (the secret police known in Czech as the *StB* and in Slovak as the *ŠtB*), the Slovak *ÚŠB* censored letters, intercepted parcels and tapped telephones. It also used informers and undercover agents and ran its own network of concentration camps and prisons: Patrónka (near Bratislava), Sered', Nováky, Žilina and Poprad were soon added to the first concentration camp at Ilava. Even when released, ex-prisoners from camps run by the *ÚŠB* were kept in a state that fell somewhere between parole and house arrest, since they were not allowed radios; were refused access to public places; were denied permission to travel without a special pass; and were required to submit their private correspondence to be censored.[7]

Independent Slovakia's first full constitution (21 July 1939), which was passed unanimously by the Slovak parliament, did little more than set down on paper political conventions that had already been established during the six months of autonomy under the Second Czecho-Slovak Republic. The Slovak state, although described as a 'republic' headed by an 'elected president' and ruled by an elected 'parliament', did not permit its citizens to make actual political choices. Instead, Slovak National Unity (now explicitly stated in the constitution to be the sole means through which the 'Slovak nation' participated in 'state power') continued to hold purely cosmetic 'elections' in which voters were presented with a single list of candidates chosen by the leadership from the three symbolic 'parties' (one apiece for the ethnic Slovaks, Hungarians and Germans). Slovakia's 'nationalities problem' was dealt with in a similarly disingenuous way to that of its 'political life'. According to the Slovak constitution, minorities were to be guaranteed only those rights that were accorded to Slovak-speakers living in the so-called 'mother country' of the group in question. This left the two officially recognized minorities (Germans and Magyars) hostages to the actions of foreign governments that they were powerless to influence, and the position of Jews and Gypsies, who had no nominal 'homeland' to which to appeal, ominously unclear.[8]

The first coins issued by the new Slovak Republic (and which appeared in Slovak only) featured President Tiso, in clerical dress, on one side, and the episcopal double cross of the Slovak crest on the other. The mottos read '*za Boha život*' ('One's life for God') and '*za národ slobodu*' ('Freedom for the nation').[9] One of the principal ways in which the Slovak government sought to demonstrate its competence to manage its own affairs and its independence from the contemporary German model was by taking its own, distinctively Slovak approach to 'solving' the Jewish 'problem'. In keeping with its declared aspiration to be a 'Christian' state, and to distinguish its own, unique authoritarian contribution to what Fr Tiso preferred not to call 'Fascism', anti-Semitic legislation dreamed up by the Slovak parliament differed from Germany's Nürnberg Laws of 1935 chiefly in that its definition of what constituted a 'Jew' was more confessional and less racial.[10] In Slovakia, conversions to Christianity, providing that they had taken place before 30 October 1918 (in other words, before the creation of the Czecho-Slovak state), were initially upheld as valid; whereas anyone who remained married to a Jew, or to the child of Jewish parents, was thereby also considered in law to be Jewish.[11] As with all such legislation, there were anomalies and contradictions. A person who was entirely nonreligious, for example, might nevertheless be classified as a Jew and thus be subject to state discrimination; but the child of two Jewish parents, providing he or she had converted to Christianity before 30 October 1918, would be defined in law as Christian and so be immune from anti-Semitic legislation.[12]

The first overtly anti-Semitic law to appear on the Slovak (as opposed to the earlier Czecho-Slovak) statute books, which forbade Jews from involvement in the manufacture or sale of Catholic liturgical and devotional objects (such as crucifixes, rosaries or liturgical candles), was passed on 30 March 1939.[13] This peculiarly conceived ban, with its implicit appeal to traditional fears about the 'misuse' by Jews of Christian symbols, sent out two important signals: the legal term 'Jew' was to have a predominantly confessional, rather than a racial, meaning; and Jews were regarded by the state as suspect. The combination enabled the Slovak government to appear to follow Vatican guidelines regarding the need to uphold Christian baptisms while simultaneously pandering to popular anti-Semitism. This made it easy for Slovak nationalists to argue that their path was essentially different from that of the 'pagan' Nazis and to leave room for Christian consciences to accept the increasingly severe forms of exclusion that were to follow. On 18 April 1939, the Slovak government forbade Jews from holding the post of notary public, editing non-Jewish periodicals or representing non-Jews in court. A week later, it followed the central Czecho-Slovak government's example by dismissing Jews from all state employment. Restrictions on Jews in pharmacy, medicine and the army followed over the summer, together with the first laws concerning the registration of Jewish property.[14] A similar strategy of encouraging prejudice through legislation appears to have been adopted to soften up public opinion to accept increasing cruelty towards the Gypsies, who were initially (23 June 1939) banned from 'trading in horses' in the region of Bratislava, and then, just three months later (25 September 1939), stripped of their rights in constitutional law.[15]

The influence of Catholic social teaching, particularly as interpreted by the Austrian Catholic Fascist Othmar Spann, could be seen principally in the independent Slovak regime's plan, never fully realized, to put into place a corporatist conception of the state as a kind of Christian Socialist alternative to secular Marxism. In the utopia that this new corporatist order was supposed to bring about, class antagonisms were to be healed through a medieval conception of society as a single body in which everyone's work was sanctified because it contributed to the organic whole. Work was therefore made obligatory, but also 'protected' by the state, while employers became legally required to take 'family circumstances' into account in setting wage levels.[16] Freedom of 'religion' was guaranteed, but only in so far as it did not conflict with 'the law', 'public order' or 'Christian morals'. The teaching of religion in school, by 'qualified Church members' only, was made compulsory.[17]

Corporations (*stavy*), to which every citizen was legally required to belong (but from which Jews had already been explicitly barred in a separate law), seem to have been envisaged as neo-medieval guilds, crosses between the (by then abolished) trade unions and professional associations. Had they been fully realized, they would also have provided convenient administrative structures through which the government could make its will known to the population, section by section, in the seemingly organized and logical way beloved of authoritarian and bureaucratic states. In theory, corporations were supposed to look after the economic, social and 'cultural' interests of their members, balancing the needs of producers with those of consumers, harmonizing labour relations and regulating working conditions throughout the seven sectors into which the economy was divided: the state sector; agriculture; industry; trade and commerce; finance and insurance; information and propaganda; and the professions (law, medicine and the Church).[18]

While the Tiso regime in Slovakia was developing its own, distinctive mix of authoritarianism, anti-Semitism and political Catholicism, new political arrangements were also being tried out in the neighbouring Protectorate of Bohemia and Moravia. Journalists, and even historians, sometimes write of the establishment of the Protectorate of Bohemia and Moravia, which was formally passed into German law on 16 March 1939 and into Czech law on 17 March 1939, as if it meant exactly the same thing as incorporation into the Third Reich. But although the so-called 'Sudetenland' (the border regions of Bohemia and Moravia and those parts of Silesia that did not go to Poland) had indeed been so incorporated, the legal status of the Protectorate was different. Had Germany wished to do so, it could have dismissed the right-wing and autocratic Czech president, prime minister and cabinet and replaced them with a permanent military dictatorship, a cabinet made up of local 'Sudeten' Germans, perhaps headed by Konrad Henlein, or else a puppet government made up of Czech Fascists, who had already made clear their eagerness to serve. To everyone's surprise, Germany chose none of these options, setting in place a considerably more complicated and confusing – but ultimately successful – arrangement.

According to the 'Führer Decree' of 16 March 1939 that established the Protectorate, the territories of Bohemia and Moravia, officially taken into the 'care' of the Reich at a time of emergency, were placed under German administration only temporarily.[19] German-speakers who had belonged to the former Sudeten German Party automatically became citizens (*Staatsangehörige* and *Reichsbürger*) of the Reich; other German-speakers – including German-speaking Jews and *Sinti* Gypsies, Social Democrats, Communists, homosexuals, Jehovah's Witnesses and others deemed undesirable – were entitled to apply for (though they would not necessarily be awarded) Reich citizenship.[20]

All other inhabitants of Bohemia and Moravia became subjects or citizens (*Staatsangehörige*) of the Protectorate.

President Hácha, given the new title of State President of the Protectorate of Bohemia and Moravia, thus lost authority over most – but not all – Germans; but he continued to be responsible for everyone else, including those officially classified as Jews; Gypsies or *Roma* (whether Slovak-, Czech- or Romany-speaking); and the whole of the Czech 'nation' (i.e. all those who had been classified as Czech-speakers in the last Habsburg, not Czechoslovak, census). The State President retained the right to appoint cabinet ministers, although his choices had now to be confirmed by the *Reichsprotektor*; he was even allowed to head a modest Czech militia. Bohemian and Moravian Germans, meanwhile, became answerable to an entirely separate, German administration headed by the *Reichsprotektor*, a citizen of the Reich appointed from Berlin. To add to the confusion, although the Protectorate had its own capital (Prague) and was legally defined as both 'autonomous' and 'self-governing', it was nevertheless obliged to 'align' its political, military and economic policies with the 'needs' of the Reich. Germany further reserved the right to station troops in the Protectorate, whether to defend its borders or simply 'in the interests of safety and order'; to alter its internal transportation, postal and telecommunication arrangements; and – just like the Hácha Protectorate regime – to decree laws that it deemed to be 'in the public interest'.[21]

Despite the reasonable expectations of local, home-grown Fascists that they would stand to gain from the dissolution of the federal Czecho-Slovak state and its replacement with a new political entity, the Berlin authorities immediately and explicitly prohibited 'interference' in the Protectorate by anyone who did not belong either to the Protectorate government or to the military occupation regime. This excluded from power not only the Czech Fascist group that had tried to stage a putsch on the morning of 15 March 1939, but also, more surprisingly, prominent Bohemian and Moravian German Fascists, who found that – with the exception of the post of 'state secretary of the Protectorate' (which was given to a rabidly anti-Czech Sudeten German, Karl Hermann Frank) – virtually all positions of power that were not given to ethnic Czechs were awarded to Reich, rather than to Bohemian and Moravian, Germans.

Since the German military leadership needed Czech cooperation in order to administer the new territory, it took care not to overturn harmless Czech customs and institutions and to show formal marks of respect for Czech national feeling, such as ensuring that the Czech flag was always flown alongside the swastika and giving the military salute to the Tomb of the Unknown Soldier. The Protectorate's first *Reichsprotektor* was also chosen with tact: Konstantin von Neurath was no Nazi sycophant, but a traditional career diplomat who had been dismissed as German foreign minister in 1938 for voicing disapproval of Hitler's expansionist policies. Having calculated that it would be counter-productive to humiliate the Czechs or outrage international opinion any more than was necessary, Reich Germans appeared to be granting the Czechs, who resented them as conquerors, only very slightly less autonomy than the Slovaks, who hailed them as liberators. This was not what Sudeten German nationalists, who had been storing up resentment against the Czechs for decades, had wanted or expected.

Scarcely had supporters of the bitterly anti-Czech Sudeten German Party stopped cheering for Hitler than they found themselves, as citizens of the Reich, eligible for military duty, while their Czech neighbours were free to stay at home with their families, making money and enjoying themselves. Bohemian and Moravian Germans were also expected, as members of the greater German *Volk*, to contribute generously to Nazi causes, however hard they might be hit by Czech boycotts of their shops and businesses. As Chad Bryant has discovered, German-speakers who lived in so-called language 'islands' (relatively isolated communities surrounded by Czech-speakers) found themselves subjected not only to snubs and jeers from their Czech neighbours, who they said intimidated German customers and shunned German businesses, but also to slights and condescension from Reich Germans, who made fun of the local German patois and treated them as country bumpkins. Reich Germans failed adequately to sympathize with the poverty, 'terror' and 'Czechization' policies to which local Germans claimed to have been subjected by the Czechs for decades; their tactless observations that the Czechs 'weren't so bad once you got to know them' or that Czechs could sometimes seem 'more German' than the 'Sudeten Germans' cut local Germans to the quick, making them feel that they were being treated as 'second-class Germans'.[22]

On 21 March 1939, a week after he had formally requested German protection, President Hácha dissolved the old Czecho-Slovak parliament. Amid calls for more state control over the economy, less Jewish influence and closer ties with the Nazi Party, the two political parties for Czech-speakers that had been permitted in Bohemia and Moravia during the Second Czecho-Slovak Republic were reduced to just one: a mass 'party' along the lines of Slovak 'National Unity' calling itself the Czech 'National Alliance' (*Národní součenství*), which not only excluded Jews from membership, but also began the laborious job of registering all Jewish property.[23] After a campaign to encourage as many 'Aryan' Czech men as possible (women were not eligible to join) to show Czech unity and solidarity by joining the National Alliance, astonishing results – of between 98 and 120 per cent – were reported. The Reich Ministry of the Interior, desperate to raise the number of 'Germans', responded by declaring that 'whoever professes himself to be a member of the German nation is a member of the German nation' and explicitly stated that 'even someone who is partly or completely of another race [*Stamm*] – Czech, Slovak, Ukrainian, Hungarian, or Polish, for example – can be considered a German'.[24]

The overwhelming support shown to the National Alliance by the ethnic Czech population of Bohemia and Moravia was interpreted by some foreign observers at the time, and by many historians since, as a grand gesture of Švejkian defiance to make the regime's attempt to win Czechs to the cause of Fascism look ridiculous. Although this interpretation would be inspiring if it were true, the apparently widespread popularity of authoritarianism, anti-Semitism and Czech chauvinism throughout the Second Republic makes it unlikely. Bryant's recent study of Czech–German relations during the Protectorate offers a more plausible, if less heroic, explanation: that a substantial number of German-speakers – whether because they disagreed with the Nazis, were intimidated by their Czech neighbours or simply sought to avoid military service – wished to be counted officially as 'Czech' rather than as 'German' and so volunteered for the National Alliance. Later, when it became more advantageous in the Protectorate to be counted as 'German' rather than as 'Czech', the nationality tables swung back the other way.[25]

With the end of the interim German military regime; the arrival of a *Reichsprotektor* with a reputation for gentlemanly conduct; the retention of President Hácha and most of his cabinet; and the knowledge that Czechs vastly outnumbered Germans throughout post-Munich Bohemia and Moravia, there was a sense that things were returning to something like normal. It was just that 'normal' no longer meant things as they had been in the short-lived Czechoslovak/Czecho-Slovak republic, but rather a return to the old Habsburg game of nationality politics, a game at which the Czechs had played with the best of them, excelling at organizing boycotts, massaging statistics, constructing tit-for-tat national symbols and obstructing 'the Germans' whenever they did not get their way in parliament.

Underground Czech resistance groups which formed in the Protectorate, although they bore grand-sounding names like *Obrana národa* (Defence of the Nation), *Politické ústředí* (Political Centre) and *Petiční výbor Věrni zůstaneme* ('We Shall Remain Faithful' Petition Committee),[26] were small and weak. Gestures designed to assert a Czech national spirit, yet which prudently kept within the letter of the law, were more characteristic. Bouquets of flowers began to appear: first (and irreproachably) at the Tomb of the Unknown Soldier; then, more daringly, at the Hus monument in the Old Town Square; finally, and provocatively, at the Woodrow Wilson monument at the main railway station. There were other signs of Czech resentment. Official celebrations of Hitler's birthday, despite elaborate preparations, turned out to be a damp squib because unexpectedly large numbers of Czechs preferred to pay a small fine and stay at home rather than take part. When the remains of the nineteenth-century poet Karel Hynek Mácha were transferred from their burial place in the Sudetenland to the Vyšehrad cemetery in Prague, where most Czech heroes were buried, tens of thousands of Czechs turned out to show their respect, bouquets were heaped on the poet's grave and Czech flags were flown in visibly greater numbers than for occasions, such as the welcoming of the *Reichsprotektor* and Hitler's birthday, when they had been legally required. At a concert of Smetana's patriotic song-cycle *Má vlast* (My Fatherland), held in the National Theatre in Prague, itself a temple to Czech nationalism, the ovation lasted for a quarter of an hour, ending only after the conductor dramatically kissed the score, to even wilder applause.[27]

Although Bohemian and Moravian Germans were all too familiar with these traditional Czech methods of nationality-baiting, Reich Germans stationed in the Protectorate were perplexed. It was Hitler, the Austrian German who had served in the Habsburg army in the First World War and observed politics in Vienna, who seemed to veer between the immediate demands of *Realpolitik* and an apparently deeply held desire to punish Czechs, as well as Jews, for having weakened the nineteenth-century pan-German movement to the point that the Austrian Empire collapsed.[28] When pressure was first brought to bear upon the Hácha regime to become more radically anti-Semitic, Fascist and pro-German, it did not come from Berlin, or even Vienna. Instead, it came from Moravia, where there was still a substantial German minority and a correspondingly high level of tension between official Czech and German communities, making it an obvious target for disaffected local Fascists, whether Czech- or German-speaking. On 20 May 1939, Gajda, the disappointed leader of the (Czech) National Fascist Community, sparked a political crisis by resigning from the National Alliance to protest against its failure either to include more Fascists in the government or to implement the Nürnberg race laws. This led to clashes and agitations in Brno and Olomouc, where local German Fascists joined with Czech Fascists in fighting the (Czech) Protectorate police. By the end of the month, the number of people arrested since the establishment of the Protectorate had risen to 4,639;[29] in Moravia, the atmosphere had grown so tense that an entire class at a Prague secondary school were arrested on their way back from a field trip to the Baťa works at Zlín for jokingly replying to the greeting '*Heil Hitler!*' with the facetious '*Heil Moskau!*'[30]

At the end of May 1939, Hácha responded to the pressure by appointing a further seven radical Fascists to the National Alliance. The first overtly racist laws to be put in place by the Czech Protectorate (as opposed to the previously Czecho-Slovak) administration followed immediately. On 31 May 1939, several weeks ahead of the Slovak government, a first, cautiously worded anti-Gypsy decree bound the Protectorate authorities to 'pay special attention' to the 'life and behaviour' of the Roma and to see that they 'refrain from living or camping in groups larger than the immediate family or clan'.[31] Since 'wandering Gypsies' over the age of fourteen had, since 1927, been required to carry a special identity card and register with the local authorities upon arriving in a new place, this was little more than a continuation of the traditional Czechoslovak (and, indeed, Habsburg) practice of treating Gypsies with suspicion.

On 4 June 1939, another government decree was issued, this time to 'restrict' the participation of Jews in 'public life'. In this refinement of the Czecho-Slovak law of a few months earlier (which had sought to abolish the civil rights of those who were euphemistically described as 'non-Czechs'),[32] this time Jews were explicitly named and defined, but in a way that broadly followed the same political conception of earlier legislation while adding a newly racial element (anyone with three or more Jewish grandparents was defined as Jewish) and changing the cut-off date for being classified as a 'foreigner' from 28 October 1918 (Czechoslovak Independence Day) to 16 September 1935.[33] Since the Nürnberg race laws (which had led to a wave of German-speaking refugees arriving in Czechoslovakia) had been passed on 15 September 1935, it is evident that the unspoken intention of this second piece of anti-Semitic legislation was to protect well-assimilated Czech-speaking Jews (i.e. former Czechoslovak citizens with fewer than three Jewish grandparents) while simultaneously ensuring the entrapment of the largest possible number of German and Austrian Jews (i.e. anyone who had arrived in the country after 15 September 1935). Although it is often claimed that the Czechs, unlike the Slovaks, were not anti-Semitic and so had to be forced by the German authorities to implement the Nürnberg laws, a comparison of contemporary Czech, Slovak and German anti-Semitic laws, made in a shared climate of anti-Semitic opinion, reveals this to be a red herring. Czech nationalism, just like Slovak nationalism, had a long tradition of anti-Semitism; it was just that the Czech variant was more about language and the Slovak more about religious confession. The *Reichsprotektor* did take the matter out of the Czech authorities' hands, decreeing on 20 June 1939 that he alone held full power to transfer Jewish property. This seems not to have been because he found the Czechs lacking in anti-Semitic feeling, but rather because he saw through the anti-German dimension of Czech anti-Semitic legislation and did not want ethnic Czechs, as opposed to Germans, to profit from Aryanization.[34]

Since Germans and Czechs in the Protectorate were bound by different laws and responsible to different administrations, imposing any sort of coherent anti-Semitic policy was not likely to be straightforward. Jews, who could be found on either side of the language divide and yet were somehow supposed to be foreign to both nationalities, were in any case defined differently in Czech/Protectorate and German/Reich law. Confusion among politicians and bureaucrats across a wide range of central, district, regional and municipal authorities – German and Czech – appears to have led to rivalry among them as to who was best able to 'solve' the Jewish 'problem', a competence that – through the expropriation of Jewish property and a brisk trade in bribes – also meant considerable financial rewards. This seems to offer the most plausible explanation as to why anti-Semitic legislation tended constantly to escalate, while at the same time being characterized by nonsensical contradictions, anomalies and overlaps, so that Jews in the Protectorate were, for example, from July 1939 banned from 'setting foot' in theatres, and then, from February 1940, forbidden from 'visiting' theatres or cinemas. From the point of view of those labelled as 'Jews', the target of dozens – eventually hundreds – of prohibitions, bans, decrees and laws that were posted on notice boards, printed in local newspapers, or published in periodic issues of the official *Sbírka zákonů a nařízení* (Bulletin of Laws and Decrees), anti-Semitic legislation, wearying and bewildering in its scale even to the modern historian, must have come so fast and furious as to seem like a blur.[35]

It was not just over the question of who should be allowed to profit from the Jews that Czechs and Germans squabbled. The Reich authorities not only found that they were unable to enforce a decree to make German the sole language of official communication in the Protectorate: even when they tried to enforce equal status for the two languages, they were resisted and blocked at every turn. They were then drawn into increasingly acrimonious disputes with the Czechs over forced labour, the Protectorate government – which used forced labour itself – not objecting to the principle, but rather insisting that conscripted workers be kept within the territory of the Protectorate rather than sent to the Reich.[36] After local German authorities reacted to the murder of an ethnic German policeman in the Czech working-class district (and Communist stronghold) of Kladno by treating all local Czechs as suspects, things got even worse.[37] Working badly for Germans, cheating them, taking bribes from them: all began to be whispered to be 'patriotic' Czech acts. By the late summer of 1939, Czech–German relations had reached such a low that even Edvard Beneš, thought to have been discredited beyond any possibility of redemption, was beginning to recover 'a superficial boulevard popularity'.[38] This was not an opportunity that the former president, who had been anxiously following developments in the Protectorate from his new home in Chicago, was likely to pass up.

Beneš, who had kept a low political profile since his resignation on 5 October 1938, sprang back into public view as soon as the Nazis marched into Bohemia and Moravia on 15 March 1939. The former president declared, with curious logic, that, because Britain and France had failed to defend the country's post-Munich borders, this retrospectively invalidated the Munich Agreement of September 1938 and all that had come after it: Slovak and Ruthenian autonomy; the Vienna Arbitration Awards; even his own resignation as head of state. On 28 May 1939, American president Franklin D. Roosevelt – who had been ignoring the specious logic contained in Beneš's telegrams – nevertheless made the friendly gesture of inviting him to lunch. Beneš can scarcely have risen from the table before he began rattling off cables to Czech and Slovak missions all over the world to claim, unverifiably, that Roosevelt had told him: 'about the eventual recognition of the government in case of war: we have done it once, we can do it again. I still consider you to be the president, though I don't say so in public.'[39] (After the war, Beneš embellished the story still further, claiming that, after welcoming him 'as the President of the Republic' to Hyde Park, his home in upstate New York, Roosevelt 'added that, as far as he was concerned, Munich did not exist and I was still President'.)[40]

In July 1939, in feverish anticipation of the war that alone might offer him a second chance to reconstruct the Czechoslovak state and resurrect his own political career, Beneš moved to London, where Moravec's military intelligence network, unusual among Czechoslovak émigré groups in supporting the former president, was based, together with several thousand Sudeten German political refugees, mostly Sudeten German Communists and Social Democrats. Initially inclined to include the ethnic German and Slovak, as well as Czech, exiles in his movement, Beneš found, when he first met in London with Wenzel Jaksch, the leader of the Sudeten German Social Democrats, that – unlike German socialists from the Reich, who recognized Czechoslovakia's pre-Munich frontiers – Czechoslovakia's Germans considered federalization, roughly along the lines of Beneš's 'Fourth Plan' of 1938, to be the best long-term solution to the country's ethnic problems.[41] Similarly, the Slovak exiles, even when represented by as committed a Czechoslovakist as Milan Hodža, the Agrarian politician and former Czechoslovak prime minister, agreed that it would not be politically possible to go back to the old Prague centralism. But Beneš, true to his nineteenth-century Czech national socialist roots, refused to budge.

Since Moravec's only valuable spy, 'A-54', who was highly placed in the German intelligence network, had recently resumed contact with London, the British were willing to listen to what Beneš had to say. Being included in a lunch held by Winston Churchill, at which Harold Nicolson and T.G. Masaryk's old contacts Robert Seton-Watson and Henry Wickham Steed were also present, gave Beneš hope that the British and French might one day make amends for their earlier betrayals in the only manner that he found acceptable: by repeating what they had done towards the end of the First World War to establish the state; and by recognizing his own authority to lead a reunited postwar Czechoslovakia. On 23 August, the day that the Molotov–Ribbentrop pact was signed, Beneš happened to have an appointment with Ivan Maisky, the Soviet ambassador in London. Convinced by this meeting that the Soviet Union, rather than France or Germany, would emerge from the next war as the dominant force in Central Europe, Beneš was especially anxious to ensure that Czechoslovakia be counted among Stalin's closest allies. As Zeman and Klímek have found, Maisky's notes, although not those of the more cautious Beneš, even record Beneš's apparent agreement that, at the war's end, a direct frontier should be created between Czechoslovakia and the Soviet Union by having Subcarpathian Ruthenia incorporated into the Soviet Union.[42]

On 1 September 1939, the German army – cheered on by the Czech Protectorate authorities and accompanied by units of the Slovak army and Hlinka Guard – attacked Poland from the west, while the Soviet Union invaded the country from the east. Britain and France declared war on Germany on 3 September and took the trouble to break off diplomatic relations with Slovakia; but then stood aside while Poland was conquered, with particular brutality, from both sides. Within three weeks, Poland was divided into three parts: a western, German-controlled sector; an eastern, Soviet-controlled territory; and, in the middle, the so-called General Government of Poland, a dumping ground for Jews, intellectuals and other enemies of the two conquering totalitarian regimes, which became the site of the largest and most infamous of the SS-run European concentration and extermination camps, including the Auschwitz-Birkenau complex.[43] Slovak Communists, who had established an illegal underground party during the period of autonomy, stayed where they were, as did most members of the exile Czechoslovak Communist Presidium (including party president Klement Gottwald) who were already in Moscow. But Rudolf Slánský, the secretary-general of the *KSČ*, went to Paris to join prominent Slovak Communist Vlado Clementis and Czech Communist Jan Šverma; another group of Communist exiles, including the youthful Eduard Goldstücker, further complicated Beneš' life in London.[44] This left a number of experienced Czech and Slovak Communist leaders scattered abroad as well as at home, for the time being rendered impotent in the cause of underground resistance by the Soviet–German Pact.

As soon as war was declared, Beneš knew exactly what to do. First, he rattled off cables of sympathy and solidarity to the premiers and foreign secretaries of Britain, France and Poland. Then he sent the government in Prague a series of instructions. A Czechoslovak army abroad, he informed them, should be set up immediately, based in France. The disbanded army at home should begin planning intelligence and propaganda work, together with 'inconspicuous acts of sabotage', until the moment became ripe for revolution. While the precise timing of this revolution could be left to the local military authorities, Beneš should be informed, preferably six days in advance, of any planned uprising. Should the war fail to end in a German defeat, he warned, it would be necessary to organize 'mass demonstrations for the renewal of the state' and present the postwar peace conference with a *fait accompli*. Beneš would organize a provisional government in exile, with himself at its head (combining the functions of president and prime minister) for the duration of the war. Hácha's Protectorate government should remain in place, but be prepared to resign at short notice should 'foreign policy objectives' require a clear show of Czech defiance. The whole territory of the former Czechoslovakia, he assured the Hácha government, would be occupied by the end of the war, so enabling Slovakia to be 'brought back' into the 'unitary state'.[45]

While Beneš was dreaming of revolution, liberation and reunification, at home in Bohemia-Moravia permanent structures were being put in place to ensure the smooth running of the Protectorate to the benefit of the Third Reich. The end of the interim German military regime was signalled by the abolition of military courts (7 September 1939) and the replacement (18 September 1939) of the old Czechoslovak flag with a new Protectorate flag consisting of a simple tricolour of three horizontal bands in red, white and blue. The old Czechoslovak crest was simultaneously updated by having the Slovak double cross, Ruthenian bear and Silesian eagle removed, so that the only remaining heraldic forms were the Bohemian lion and the Moravian eagle.[46] On 27 September 1939, the Highway Code was brought into line with that of the surrounding territories of the Reich by making it the rule to drive on the right (rather than, as had previously been the case in Czechoslovakia, on the left). This change incidentally enabled a new stipulation to sneak through: that all information on road signs (including all place names) be given in German first, and only afterwards in Czech.[47]

As the war got going, Communists, Social Democrats, Jewish leaders, Catholic priests and prominent Czech intellectuals started being rounded up, and newspaper editors were called in for weekly 'press briefings' to make clear what should, and should not, be printed. A carefully balanced mix of repressive measures and material incentives was set up to ensure that the Protectorate economy, especially its armaments and other war-related industries, would run smoothly. Rationing coupons for meats, fats, sugar, milk and bread were issued in quick succession, especially generous rations being set aside for 'hard manual workers' and 'very hard manual workers'.[48] A Czech militiaman tried to explain to an English journalist friend why – in the absence of obligatory military service and despite the relatively good standard of living – it was nevertheless horrible for a Czech to live under the new regime:

> You must see the names in your village written up in German, hear the names of the tram-stops shouted out in German. . . . You are permanently living in

anxiety, permanently afraid of what the next day will bring. . . . You cannot get proper food. It is not the rationing itself, which brings discomfort in every country, but rather the way your food is rationed and why. . . . Your restriction is not a necessary sacrifice which you are making for the sake of your country, your army, your struggle. You are starving in order that the men you hate should be well fed.[49]

It was not long before Czechs in the Protectorate began to protest that Germany's promises of autonomy were not being honoured in full. After Slovakia was rewarded for its part in the Polish campaign by being given back the Spiš and Orava districts, Hácha raised with von Neurath – who in turn raised it with Hitler – the possibility of having the Teschen and Opava districts of Silesia, now in German-occupied Poland, similarly returned to the Protectorate.[50] Official celebrations on 28 September to honour the conveniently ambivalent St Wenceslas – officially supported by the Hácha regime as a symbol of Czech–German friendship, yet open to use as a symbol of Czech national identity – led to acts of provocation in Prague, Brno, Olomouc and elsewhere, where police reported the public singing of the Czech national anthem, the tearing down of *Reichsprotektor* decrees and raucous ovations during the patriotic passages of the Czech operatic classic *Libuše*.

On 30 September 1939, the first anniversary of the Munich Agreement, there was an effective Czech boycott of all public transportation in Prague, followed by a flurry of leaflets and handbills suggesting ways to protest peacefully against German rule on the most emotive date in the political calendar, Czechoslovak Independence Day (28 October). Preparations for a mass demonstration to be held in Wenceslas Square on that day brought to a head inevitable tensions among three groups, each of which ostensibly had authority for the Protectorate: the Czech administration under Hácha; the German Protectorate authorities under von Neurath; and the increasingly influential political and secret police under the combined authority of Secretary of State Frank in the Protectorate and Himmler, together with his ambitious protégé and second-in-command, Reinhard Heydrich, in Berlin.[51] The result, despite Jan Masaryk's urgent pleas in BBC broadcasts to 'the nation' that no risks be taken or provocations offered,[52] was that scuffles between Frank's security forces and demonstrators ended in the wounding of some policemen, the death of a Czech worker and the injury – fatal, as it turned out – of a Czech medical student called Jan Opletal.

Jan Opletal's funeral, which was held on 15 November 1939, although attended by about three thousand students, watched by some ten thousand onlookers and closely monitored by the security police, was peaceful. It was only afterwards, when students had dispersed into small groups to sing patriotic songs or chant provocative slogans, that the fateful incident occurred in which Secretary of State Frank's car was overturned and his driver beaten up. This gave Frank the pretext he needed to persuade Hitler that the Czechs should be treated with a firmer hand. On the night of 16 November 1939, the Gestapo raided a committee meeting of the Students' Union in Prague, arresting several students on the spot; others were taken from their homes. Student dormitories in Brno, where there had been no incident, were also attacked, and a total of 1,200 students arrested and sent to concentration camps to be 'taught a lesson'. At dawn the next day, 17 November 1939, nine Students' Union representatives – eight of whom, ironically enough, owed their positions to the fact that they had pledged themselves 'to work for Czech–German understanding' – were taken out and shot. The Czech universities and institutes were declared closed for three years (in fact they were to remain closed for the rest of the war), and the Czech section of Charles University in Prague was handed over to the German section. The closure affected some 18,998 students and 1,223 university teachers.[53]

In the terror that followed the sudden brutality of this action, Czech mothers refused to allow their children to be given routine inoculations, there were rumours that cigarettes were being poisoned to give Czechs tuberculosis and German customers complained that they were unable to get service in Czech shops. By the start of the new year, a Serb living in Prague was complaining that the economy was in such a mess that it was no longer possible to buy 'shoes, or a handkerchief, or even thread, or nails, or a shovel, or coal'. Just one week's stay in the capital, he concluded, would be enough for anyone to be 'cured for life' of 'admiration for German efficiency and German capacity'.[54] Since it now began to look to the three non-Communist Czech resistance groups (because of the Soviet–German Pact, Communists were officially supposed to be on friendly terms with the Nazi regime) as though they might finally be able to recruit some Czechs to the anti-German cause, in early 1940 *Obrana národa, Politické ústředí* and *Věrni zůstaneme* joined forces in a loose organization calling itself *ÚVOD* (*Ústřední výbor odboje domácího* or the Central Committee of Home Resistance).[55] *Reichsprotektor* von Neurath, who could see that the situation was impossible, was able to convince Hitler that the German authorities should return to the policy of avoiding provocations likely to lead to 'mass actions'. Hitler agreed, but only on condition that 'any Czech defiance' be 'crushed with the harshest means'.[56] The Czechs, with their first shocking lesson in terror still fresh in their minds, hardly needed to be warned. Although *ÚVOD* agreed with Beneš that 'the Czech nation also needs its Lebensraum (as Nazi terminology would have it)' and that the native Germans of the Bohemian Crown Lands were 'wholly alien, something that must be removed', Czechs living in the Protectorate were not to attempt another mass act of protest until Hitler was safely dead and victory, in the shape of liberating troops, was within clear sight.[57]

On 18 January 1940, as part of a new law passed on military service, the Slovak government excluded Jews and Gypsies from the draft, forcing them instead to take part in 'obligatory labour'. A week later, a special office was set up under the direction of Augustin Morávek to handle the next stage in the Slovak 'solution' to the Jewish 'problem': the seizure and redistribution of Jewish property. From March 1940, the state was empowered to seize all Jewish farms and smallholdings; from April, Jews were forbidden to sell property, start new businesses or sell shares without permission from the state. The same law also stipulated that all shops or businesses owned by Jews must display a sign announcing them to be 'Jewish' and declared them automatically eligible for 'Aryanization', in other words forced seizure or purchase by the state.[58]

At the end of May, more forced-labour camps were opened, ostensibly to enable Jewish and Gypsy men, who were not allowed to serve in the army, to fulfil their civic duty; a special decree reinforced the point by defining 'Gypsy' as meaning 'a nomadic vagabond who avoids work'.[59] Like Jews, who turned out not to be so easily defined in law, Gypsies who were sent to the camps were in practice selected according to a confused set of criteria – mainly racial or linguistic – so that they included children as well as fully employed and settled adults. It was their slave labour, at camps like the Dubnica nad Váhom Gypsy Detention Centre in western Slovakia and Ústie nad Oravou in central Slovakia, that built roads, railways and reservoirs for the state, including the largest reservoir in Slovakia (Oravská priehrada).[60]

While the inhabitants of Slovakia and the Protectorate were resigning themselves to the new political realities, Beneš's big plan – to consolidate a government-in-exile with himself at its head – seemed to be going nowhere. None of the Allies was at first willing to agree to what seemed an absurd notion: that the Munich Agreement could simply be declared null and void, and treated as if it had never existed as an historical and legal fact. The French, who had by then had a bellyful of Beneš, refused even to meet him, explaining that they were not authorized to enter into negotiations with 'a private individual' on behalf of 'the Czecho-Slovaks', but would continue to liaise with the formally accredited Czecho-Slovak minister in France, Štefan Osuský. But when Osuský then managed to get the French to agree to the establishment on their soil of a 'Czecho-Slovak army' (to serve under either French or joint Allied command), and even to recognize a Czecho-Slovak government-in-exile (providing that it excluded the discredited Beneš), Beneš won over enough potential ministers to scupper the scheme. On 17 November 1939, Beneš established – instead of a fully fledged 'Government-in-Exile' – a 'Czechoslovak National Council'. The National Council had no authority to speak for the Czechs and Slovaks at home and was granted no diplomatic privileges, despite Jan Masaryk's misleading words – broadcast by the BBC a month later – that the Allies had made an 'independent Czechoslovakia' one of their war aims, and that Beneš's National Council, with an army of its own and the right to conduct the nation's military and political affairs, 'genuinely' represented 'the Czechoslovak people'.[61] In a speech to the British Royal Society a couple of months later, Beneš dropped his first public hint that postwar 'transfers of population' would need to be considered.[62] According to Kirsty Wallace, his next public allusion to the policy did not come until May 1941, when he announced, in a speech at the University of Oxford, that he was considering 'the exchange of populations' to 'make possible the radical settlement of minority questions'.[63]

As the Third Reich went from military triumph to military triumph over the course of 1940, Hermann Göring, the leading architect of Germany's Four-Year Plan, set about turning the whole of Central Europe into a *Großraumwirtschaft*, a region whose *raison d'être* would be to serve Germany's economic requirements and make possible the realization of its grandiose colonial plans. Poland, already conquered and divided into German and Soviet sections, was to be used for slave labour; once emptied of its millions of racially, politically or physically unsuitable people, it would provide *Lebensraum* for ethnic Germans from all over Europe, while south-eastern Europe would provide the Reich with raw materials and foodstuffs. A central, industrialized core, which was to include both the Protectorate and Slovakia, was to be integrated economically into the Reich: in the Protectorate, this was sometimes stated explicitly, as when the *Reichsprotektor*'s office celebrated the final lifting of customs barriers between the Reich and the Protectorate as an historic 'milestone' on the way to the eventual 'incorporation' of the Protectorate of Bohemia and Moravia into the Greater German Reich.[64] By keeping Reich citizens sheltered from food shortages and blockades, and Reich armies well supplied for war, this crucial sector would become the engine of German expansion to the east. Ultimately, according to the plan, the whole of the continent would fall under Nazi control while Britain and the United States looked the other way. German pride and standing would be restored, and Bolshevism and European Jewry eliminated forever.[65]

Although even von Neurath agreed that, in theory, the 'most perfect solution' to the ethnic problem in the Protectorate would be 'the complete expulsion of all Czechs from the country and its settlement by Germans', in practice he argued that to do so would be 'impossible' because 'there are not enough Germans for the immediate occupation of the territories which belong in the foreseeable future to the Greater German area'.[66] For the time being, as the former Czechoslovak correspondent for the *Observer* and first editor of the Czech section of the BBC's European Service Shiela Grant Duff could see, only the country – not its population – was to become German, while what had been Czech would be turned into 'a picturesque feature of the countryside, a curiosity for tourists to come and look at, a quaint show-piece in the great and powerful German Reich'. The Czechs, she predicted

> were to be a folk, the culture permitted to them would be folklore. And when the war was over, they would be able to dance and sing very prettily for rich Americans. They could sell their brightly coloured pottery and their needlework. . . . So long as the Czechs could understand and obey German orders, that was all the germanisation which needed to take place. The Czechs could remain as Czech as they liked, and the more narrowly, blindly, provincially Czech they were, the better.[67]

After the Fall of Paris (14 June 1940) and the subsequent division of France into occupied and collaborationist halves, Göring's dream looked on the point of realization. Germany already controlled Central Europe; had no cause to fear Britain; was still allied with the Soviet Union; and was not yet at war with the United States. This meant that Nazi plans for Central Europe could move ahead more swiftly and with less concern for international opinion, and also that it could count on the help of many more willing collaborators. In the Protectorate, the Gestapo – which had previously had to send its enemies to the Reich or else make do with local, Czech-run prison camps – now set up a special prison for political opponents (mainly Communists and Social Democrats) at the Small Fortress in the old Habsburg garrison town of Theresienstadt (*Terezín* in Czech).

As in the Protectorate, the only remedies for Slovakia's economic ills tied it ever closer to the Reich. Unemployment was gradually tackled through the recruitment of workers to the Reich; and economic recovery stimulated by German demand for Slovak cannon, munitions and weapon parts as well as for Czech tanks, armoured vehicles and poison gas. Otherwise, there was money to be made out of Jews. On 3 September 1940, Slovak Constitutional Law 210 stipulated that all remaining property in Jewish hands be transferred into 'Christian' ownership and that Jews be 'removed' from Slovak 'economic' and 'social' life; on 18 October, Decree 271 ordered all Jewish bank accounts in Slovakia to be frozen.[68] By the end of 1940, it was becoming clear that, for all the talk of Czech autonomy and Slovak independence, the finances of both the Protectorate and the Republic were being steadily absorbed by the Reich. This did nothing to improve Czech–German relations in the Protectorate, where the two communities continued to lead parallel existences, refusing to mix even socially. George Kennan, who was still reporting from Prague as American *chargé d'affaires*, had nothing but sympathy for the Hácha regime, which he saw as trying its best to stem the steady erosion of Czech businesses, employment opportunities and administrative control.

Meanwhile, every statement uttered by a Czech official, whatever its message, was instantly 'greeted sympathetically' by the population 'as a statement extorted from the Germans' and deserving only of 'the invariable search for the double meaning, the existence of which no good Czech would ever doubt'.[69] Noting the 'distressing resemblance' of Czech complaints in late 1940 to those expressed by 'the more reasonable Sudeten Germans' four or five years earlier, Kennan realized, to his horror, that 'much of what [was] going on' was only 'a chronic expression of the national rivalries of the area' which would 'probably continue to go on for many years to come, either in one direction or another, depending on what shoe the foot is on'.[70]

Not only Czechs, but Slovaks, too, grumbled that shortages of consumer goods – especially bacon and sausages – were not due to the war as such, but rather to German greed. Inflation and the scarcity of consumer goods were already becoming so bad that the Slovak army was brought in to quell demonstrators – ethnic German as well as Slovak – during a particularly acrimonious miners' strike at Handlová. Locals were also increasingly concerned at German interference in Slovakia's domestic affairs. In late July 1940, Tiso was summoned to Salzburg for talks with Hitler and Ribbentrop; these ended with the dismissal of his own choice, Ferdinand Ďurčanský, as foreign minister and minister of the interior, in favour of his chief rivals, who were evidently preferred by Berlin: Alexander Mach, who was made minister of the interior; and Vojtech Tuka, who was given the Foreign Ministry as well as retaining the office of prime minister. This sent a strong signal to the leadership of Slovak National Unity that it was expected to become even more acquiescent, and gave Slovaks the impression that even their leaders could be dictated to by Germany. Mach, who as minister of propaganda had already shown himself enough of a sycophant to refer to Hitler as 'the finger of God pointing the way and showing what had to be done',[71] now competed fiercely with Tiso and Tuka to win the Führer's favour. Legislation expected to find approval with Germany escalated accordingly. In November 1940, Slovakia formally acceded to the Berlin–Rome–Tokyo Axis; and in February 1941, Tuka launched what his supporters hailed as a full Slovak 'National Socialist' revolution akin to the Nazis' own, with the publication of a fourteen-point Slovak National Socialist Programme to match that of the German Nazi Party.[72]

The years of supreme German confidence (1940–43) were a period in which Czech humiliations and German snubs to national feeling were not only felt but stored as resentments. They were also years in which one illegal Communist organization after another was uncovered and liquidated by the Gestapo,[73] often with the help of Czech informers, while the great bulk of the Czech population – farmers, administrators, civil servants, businessmen, factory workers, labourers and others – worked reliably and productively, sometimes to their own enrichment as well as to the benefit of the Reich. Among the hundreds of thousands of cases that were to come before postwar retribution courts in Bohemia and Moravia, there were untold numbers of defendants who, according to the Legal Commission of the Communist Party Central Committee, 'acted like patriots' among Czechs but 'simultaneously collaborated with the Germans'.[74]

Jews, whom it had previously been state policy to encourage to leave the country, were over the course of 1940–41 deliberately concentrated in the capital, Prague, so that they might be more efficiently stripped of their property, income, savings and investments. In November 1941, the population of Terezín/Theresienstadt was evacuated so that, from early 1942, the entire town could be turned into a vast concentration camp, this time specifically for Jews, and known as the Main Fortress (the Small Fortress continued to be run separately by the Gestapo, mainly for political prisoners). Whereas in 1939 German-speakers had tried to jump onto the bandwagon of the Czech National Alliance in order to get themselves classified as 'Czechs', after the Fall of Paris in June 1940 roles were reversed, with applications for German citizenship rising steeply, including absurdly large numbers from applicants with Czech surnames who could barely speak German.[75] Membership of Slovak National Unity rose equally dramatically over the same period, so that from an initial take-up of about 50,000 in 1938, it reached a high point of about 300,000 members in 1943.[76]

For Beneš, the Fall of Paris brought a windfall: the relocation of the centre of the Czechoslovak émigré movement – consisting of an embryonic army and a large number of Czech and Slovak émigré politicians – to London. Immediately alive to the possibility of raising his standing with the British Secret Intelligence Service (SIS) and, through it, with the British government, Beneš feverishly exploited the military intelligence being provided by František Moravec's mysterious agent A-54, stifling his recurrent doubts that A-54 might turn out to be a Nazi plant.[77] The British were in any case ready to clutch at any straw. Beneš, who wildly exaggerated the importance of the Czechoslovak army, Moravec's intelligence service and the strength of the organized underground resistance (ÚVOD) at home, was invited to lunch, first with Churchill, and then with the king.[78] In September 1940, a new communications centre for the use of Czech operators was set up by the SIS in Surrey, and in October a large Victorian villa near Leamington Spa was put at the disposal of the Czech brigade under General Miroslav. Moravec's spy team was then put in touch with a second British intelligence organization, the Special Operations Executive (SOE), which had been set up to help organize sabotage, riots, boycotts and acts of terror in the German-occupied territories.

The German attack on the Soviet Union (22 June 1941) finally brought the Soviet Union into the war. The violent end to the Soviet–German alliance also enabled Communists to become involved on the Allied side. On 24 June 1941, Slovakia declared war on the Soviet Union. The Protectorate was not at liberty to declare war, but President Hácha publicly welcomed the German crusade 'against Bolshevism' and urged his Czech compatriots to work harder than ever for a Nazi victory. Beneš, alarmed, sent President Hácha and Prime Minister Eliáš word that they ought to be prepared to resign rather than give comfort and aid to 'the enemy'. Not only, he warned, would the Soviet Union probably have a large say in Czechoslovakia's postwar borders, but Czech and Slovak Communists, if left to resist the German occupiers alone, would be given a 'pretext to take over power on the basis of the justified reproach that we helped Hitler'.[79] It was all very well for Beneš to lecture. Unlike Beneš, Hácha lived with the knowledge that he could at any time be dismissed from office, arrested or even executed. Nor was he in a position to discount the possibility – at that stage, probability – that Germany would win the Second World War, or, even in the event of an Allied victory, that Bohemia and Moravia would remain a part of postwar Germany. Beneš, although he had so far managed to persuade the British that any 'premature' action undertaken by the Czechs would only lead to the destruction of the underground resistance, was under quite different pressures. As British and Soviet casualties continued to mount, and the inhabitants of other Nazi-occupied territories to suffer in earnest, the argument that Czech lives should not be risked began to wear thin.

On 18 July 1941, the Soviet Union showed that it was backing Beneš as the Czech political leader with whom it felt it could do business by offering him all that he craved: full recognition of the London-based provisional government; guarantees of non-interference in any future Czechoslovakia's internal affairs; the right of the Czechoslovaks to establish an independent army on Soviet territory; and, crucially, a declaration that, as far as the Soviets were concerned, the Munich Agreement did not exist. Beneš was able to capitalize on the Soviet offer so quickly – warning his Western allies that unless they quickly followed suit they would be leaving postwar Czechoslovakia to an anti-Western Communist regime – that he had his first results within hours. Also on 18 July, the British Foreign Office agreed that the Czechoslovak National Council in London should be given the same status as the other governments-in-exile (although it prudently held back from mentioning either postwar borders or the status of the Munich Agreement). The United States, more cautious still, confined its own recognition to that of a 'provisional' government and explicitly pointed out that this did not constitute acknowledgement of Czechoslovakia's future borders or of Beneš's status as president.[80]

Soviet support came at a price. Beneš not only granted the Soviet authorities the right to veto any commander appointed to Czechoslovak units in the USSR, but also agreed, in a subsequent joint military convention of 27 September 1941, that all salaries, pensions, provisions and supplies should conform to the regulations governing the Soviet armed forces.[81] As Soviet casualties continued to increase, Moscow, not known for its sentimentality about the value of human life, appealed to the Czechs by radio to help by sabotaging petrol reserves, aircraft factories and railways in the Protectorate. The Soviet government also began to put pressure on Beneš to see that the Nazi campaign was at the very least slowed down by Czech acts of defiance. Since the only visible acts of resistance and sabotage in the Protectorate, in the shape of interfering with railway links and cutting military telephone wires, had been undertaken by Czech Communists in response to instructions from Moscow to protest the attack on the Soviet Union, Beneš had good grounds to fear that his own claims to lead the so-called 'democratic' national Czech resistance (*ÚVOD*) would be upstaged by the Communists unless he acted quickly. To increasing Soviet pressure was added British, since the British government was contemplating sending Sudeten German refugees – who refused to recognize Beneš's authority – to the Protectorate as saboteurs and spies. Moravec's intelligence service, under pressure from British SIS colleagues, added to the refrain, commenting drily that, at a time when Britain was fighting for its life, 'placing violets at the grave of the unknown soldier' was simply not good enough.[82]

On 9 September 1941, just a few days after the Protectorate had issued its latest round of anti-Semitic legislation, a new Slovak directive 'on the legal position of Jews', so thick that it had to be published as a separate bulletin, was passed into Slovak law as government decree number 198. This 'Jewish Code', as it came to be known, which ran to 270 articles, replaced the confessional approach of previous Slovak anti-Semitic legislation with a frankly racial one, along the lines of the German Nürnberg laws. As in the Protectorate, Jews in Slovakia were now forbidden to own cars, radios or cameras; to use parks, cinemas, swimming pools, cafés, restaurants, shops and public transportation; and to move freely in towns except during certain specified periods. They were required by law to wear the yellow Star of David, with which they were also obliged to mark any letters they wished to send. In a move that went beyond the anti-Semitic legislation in Nazi Germany, Jews in Slovakia were further forbidden to possess flags or state emblems of any kind.[83]

At the end of September 1941, it was announced that von Neurath was to be replaced as *Reichsprotektor* of Bohemia and Moravia by an infinitely more sinister figure: Reinhard Heydrich. Heydrich, who had been head of Reich Central Security since 1939 and an energetic member of the SS since 1931, was considered ruthless even by Nazi standards; and it was to him that Göring entrusted the administration of the 'final solution' to the 'Jewish Question' at just the time that the first experimental mass gassings of prisoners were being carried out at the Auschwitz-Birkenau concentration camp in the General Government of Poland. Emphasizing the strategic, economic and military importance of the Protectorate to the Reich, Heydrich proposed to continue and extend the policy of granting workers and farmers preferential treatment, since giving the workers their 'fodder' (*Fressen*) would keep the economy strong while simultaneously dividing Czech society, making it unable or unwilling to resist. Short, carefully controlled doses of terror, accompanied by positive incentives to collaborate, would break any organized resistance while simultaneously preventing the Czechs from being driven to rebellion on the grounds that they had nothing to lose.[84]

Since, according to Heydrich, 'Slavs' tended to bow to pressure, only to spring back once the pressure had been removed, he decided first to break their spirit with a short burst of terror.[85] On 27 September 1941, Prime Minister Eliáš, known to be in communication with London via Moravec's intelligence service, was arrested by the Gestapo and sent to stand trial in Berlin. Martial law was declared, and special summary courts set up throughout the Protectorate; red posters giving the names and fates of those brought before the courts – always death or transportation to a concentration camp – were then prominently posted on billboards all over the Protectorate.[86] Josef Bílý and Hugo Vojta, generals of the 'home' army who had been in contact with London, were shot; other members of *ÚVOD* were tortured at Pankrác prison in Prague before also being shot, at Kobylisy on the outskirts of the capital.[87]

The cabinet, informed that its failure to report the prime minister's links with London made its members complicit in his crimes, immediately gave Heydrich promises of full obedience. On 1 October 1941, as part of a speech that he read out at his show trial in Berlin, Eliáš claimed that he would 'willingly accept' punishment if his 'sacrifice' led the Czechs to 'sincere and loyal' collaboration with the Germans.[88] The plea did not save him from the death sentence, but it indefinitely postponed the date of his execution, leaving him a hostage to Czech good behaviour. By 5 October 1941, lines of communication between London and *ÚVOD* had been cut, the latter's secret codes compromised, last transmitters seized and remaining members rounded up.[89] Since A-54's most recent communication to London had also been found, it was not much longer before the Gestapo discovered his identity: Paul Thümmel, a senior officer in the German intelligence-gathering agency known as *Abwehr* ('defence').

Having ensured compliance on the part of the Protectorate government within weeks of taking up his new post, Heydrich turned his attention to implementing his racial plans, which included evacuating all Gypsies and imprisoning all Jews. Adolf Eichmann's Central Office for Jewish Emigration in Prague – which had fallen under the jurisdiction of the Security Office,

Heydrich's previous area of responsibility – had already begun the painstaking process of re-registering every Jew living in the Protectorate. The bureaucratic feat, which encouraged denunciations and drew upon the assistance of the secret police, successfully tracked down many 'Jews' who had up to that point managed to avoid being categorized as such.[90]

Theresienstadt, which opened for business in December 1941, was officially termed a Jewish 'town' or 'ghetto' rather than a concentration camp, and its inmates were allowed to live in much better conditions than Jews held in other SS camps. Inmates held concerts, plays and sporting events, and there was even a temporary school; all of these were available to prisoners until it came time for them to be 'resettled in the east', a euphemism that nearly always meant being gassed at Auschwitz, although it could sometimes mean being gassed, shot or worked to death at a different camp. Theresienstadt – with its picturesque Habsburg architecture, parks and especially photogenic kindergarten – was ideal to use for propaganda purposes, to stifle rumours about what was happening to the rapidly disappearing Jews of Central Europe. As the first mass exterminations got under way in 1942, the town-sized camp was used to 'showcase' famous Jews who might otherwise have been missed. Later, it was chosen as the setting for an SS film – directed by Kurt Gerron, the famous German-Jewish actor and director (and inmate) – which portrayed Theresienstadt as a utopian experiment in Jewish self-administration. In order to create the illusion of something not unlike a postwar kibbutz, transports to the east were temporarily halted, children given slices of bread and butter in front of the cameras, the town park and gardens briefly opened to inmates; to sustain the illusion of a holiday camp, a swimming pool was even dug. The resulting propaganda film was able to cover up and falsify the reality of the camp; but even a director as talented as Gerron could not, as he confided to a fellow inmate, 'erase the horror' from people's eyes. As soon as filming was complete, Gerron, together with most of those who had taken part in the film (including all of the children), were transported to Auschwitz to be killed.[91]

On 23 June 1944, a couple of months after two Slovak Jews who had escaped from Auschwitz made public a credible and immensely detailed exposé of how the death camp functioned,[92] Theresienstadt was used for its last, and most successful, propaganda purpose: to stage a visit by the Red Cross, whose youthful inspector – apparently completely taken in by the elaborate charade – gave the camp a favourable report. By the end of the war, roughly 140,000 Jews had passed through Theresienstadt, of whom about 90,000 had been transported east: the last transport to Auschwitz took place on Czechoslovak Independence Day (28 October) 1944. When the camp was finally liberated in May 1945, it was revealed that just 6,875 Jews from the Protectorate, together with a further 240 from the Sudetenland, were still alive.

At the same time that Czech Jews were being concentrated in Theresienstadt, Slovak Jews were being organized in a similarly complicated operation, administered by a new Jewish Central Office run by Department 14 at the Ministry of the Interior and ultimately responsible to the minister of the interior, Alexander Mach, who was by then also commander-in-chief of the Hlinka Guard.[93] As in the Protectorate, local Jewish organizations were given the administrative tasks of drawing up lists of transports to the extermination camps and considering applications for exemptions; but in Slovakia it was the Hlinka Guard – rather than the German police – who took Jews to the Slovak camps at Patrónka, near Bratislava; and also at Sered', Nováky, Žilina and Poprad, which – in the days before Auschwitz-Birkenau was set up to receive Jews from abroad – were where most Slovak Jews were kept prisoner.[94]

It was not until 1942, the first year of organized mass killings of Jews throughout Europe, that Slovak Law 68 was passed to enable the mass transportation of Slovak Jews to Poland. Altogether, there were nineteen transports, arranged by the German authorities and paid for by the Slovak state, in which a total of 18,586 people were taken to be exterminated at Auschwitz; the Slovak Ministry of Transport and Public Works arranged for a further 39,006 to be taken in thirty-eight transports to Nałęczów in Lublin.[95] For just over a year, from October 1942 until 1944, the Slovak transports were halted. Although sometimes claimed to have been due to President Tiso's Christian charity, given his record this hiatus is more likely to have been due to an attempt to make money, since Jews kept in Slovak camps were expected to help bolster the economy with their slave labour, and continuing to pay Germany to take Slovak Jews away to Auschwitz and other camps was proving an expensive business.

As Nazi radicals became increasingly keen to implement their racial theories across German-occupied Europe, the question of how to make the Protectorate more 'German' and less 'Czech' began to be reconsidered from a racial, rather than a linguistic or cultural, angle. Racial experts, brought in from the Reich to reconsider all recent cases of applications to be German, were able – with the help of medical examinations, family trees and questionnaires – to 'catch out' many spouses of Jews or children of 'mixed' marriages, together with many other people who had not previously been classified as Jewish.[96] From the spring of 1942, the German Protectorate authorities also launched a covert campaign – by means of questions about family background in application forms for identity cards and through X-ray photographs taken by mobile units claimed to be screening schoolchildren for tuberculosis – to reassess the suitability of ethnic Czechs for 'Germanization' from the points of view of physical traits and ancestry rather than simply language, politics and culture. As Jeremy King, Chad Bryant and others have pointed out, this shift in the primary understanding of 'nationality' in the region from a mainly linguistic and cultural to a primarily physical or racial definition not only meant that national categories began to be assigned to individuals by the state, but that such categories, once assigned, could no longer easily be reversed. Although the 'national' categories of 'German', 'Czech' and 'Jew' remained as blurred and overlapping as they had always been, the state bureaucracy now began to treat them as if they were objectively verifiable and set in stone.[97]

From the end of 1941, after the launch of a Soviet counter-attack on the Germans outside Moscow and the entry of the United States into the war after Pearl Harbor, it seemed for the first time possible that the Allies might eventually win the war. In London, where the underground resistance in occupied countries was measured according to how much damage it had succeeded in causing the Nazis, the Protectorate was almost always at the bottom of the list.[98] Under increasing pressure from all sides, Beneš and Moravec began to seek a single, spectacular act that would demonstrate Czechoslovak solidarity with the Allies, remove the stigma of collaboration and show Beneš's National Council – rather than rival Sudeten German and Slovak groups in London or the Communist exile leadership in Moscow – to be in command of effective Czechoslovak resistance. This political imperative led to one of the most spectacular SOE actions of the entire war: Operation Anthropoid, the assassination of *Reichsprotektor* Reinhard Heydrich, by Czech and Slovak assassins trained in Britain and parachuted into the Protectorate by the Royal Air Force. The operation, which is described in minute and thrilling detail in a careful historical reconstruction pieced together by Callum MacDonald, was supposed to take place on 28 October 1941 (Czechoslovak Independence Day), when a Moravian Czech called Jan Kubiš and a Slovak from Žilina called Jozef Gabčík would shoot Heydrich as his car rounded a hairpin bend on his daily route to work. For security reasons, the plan was to be kept secret even from *ÚVOD* and other Czechoslovak agents based in London.[99] After a series of blunders and security leaks, on 12 May, *ÚVOD*, which already knew details of the planned assassination, pleaded with London to call off the attack on the grounds that, while it might very slightly advance the cause of the Allies, it would be certain to lead to appalling reprisals and to the wholesale destruction of the domestic resistance movement.[100] It would be far better, it suggested, to target a prominent Czech Quisling such as Emanuel Moravec, a Czech hero in the First World War but who actively promoted collaboration with the Nazis after Munich.

The assassination of *Reichsprotektor* Heydrich nevertheless took place, on 27 May 1942 rather than on 28 October 1941 because of a series of organizational problems and unforeseen delays, and by grenade because one of the assassins' guns jammed. Although initially still able to pull out a pistol and try to kill his attackers, Heydrich then collapsed, was taken to hospital and eventually died of his injuries eight days later, on 4 June 1942.[101] Beneš, who vigorously denied all involvement in what turned out to be a rather messy assassination, was nevertheless anxious to ensure that Czechs, rather than the Germans, got the credit for it. František Moravec claims in his memoirs that Beneš 'ordered' him to carry out the assassination (a view echoed in secondary works) and that he did so with the help of MI6, the British intelligence service. A recently published collection of documents, photographs and other materials concerning Heydrich, together with an official exhibition, on permanent display in the crypt of the Orthodox church of SS Cyril and Methodius in Prague, gives the most likely explanation, however: that Beneš and František Moravec planned Operation Anthropoid together, with assistance from the SOE.[102]

From the evening of the attack, Frank, the Sudeten German secretary of state, declared a state of emergency and a mass campaign got under way in the Protectorate to find the assassins. All routes to and from the capital were sealed off; and all Czechs over the age of fifteen were required to register with the police, the penalty for failing to appear to have one's identity card stamped being death by firing squad.[103] The first family groups were executed on 31 May; by the time Heydrich died, 157 people had already been shot.[104] Evidence taken from the scene of the crime was displayed in the window of the massive Bat'a department store on Wenceslas Square and a staggering reward of 5 million crowns was offered by the German Protectorate authorities for information leading to the capture of the assassins. Whole areas of the city were randomly cordoned off and searched. On 30 May, Hácha doubled the German offer, prominently advertising a reward of 10 million crowns for the capture of the culprits, while Emanuel Moravec, by then minister for propaganda in the Protectorate government, widely broadcast the message that 'the nation must not be destroyed for the sake of Beneš's mercenary gang and its British paymasters'.[105] The exile Czechoslovak government in London responded with a statement describing the attack on 'the monster Heydrich' as a symbol of the 'unyielding resistance of the Czech people' and urged the local population to hide the 'unknown heroes', warning that 'just punishment' would be meted out to anyone who betrayed them.[106]

After Heydrich died, on 4 June 1942, his body was taken to Hradčany, where it lay in state, under an enormous SS flag and surrounded by armed guards and burning urns, for two days. On 7 June, his coffin was loaded onto a gun carriage and solemnly led through the streets of Prague, following the route of T.G. Masaryk's funeral just five years before. Hácha and his ministers accompanied the coffin to Berlin, where an elaborate state funeral was held on 9 June. On 10 June, following inaccurate Gestapo reports that linked one of the assassins to the village of Lidice, 32 km (20 miles) north of Prague, the entire village was cordoned off. 173 men were shot on the spot and 196 women sent to Ravensbrück concentration camp. Out of 95 children, 7 considered eligible for Germanization were sent to be brought up in German homes, and the remaining 88 were gassed in Chełmno. German radio then triumphantly announced that the entire village had been razed to the ground.[107]

Tensions in the Protectorate continued to mount. After Frank declared an amnesty for anyone who could give information leading to the arrest of the assassins, over two thousand statements were submitted.[108] One came from Karel Čurda, a disillusioned Czech agent from a different SOE operation, who proved able to identify Gabčík's briefcase out of twenty similar cases, name a number of parachutists of whom the Gestapo had photographs, and betray several safe houses, including the flat where Kubiš had found refuge after throwing the grenade into Heydrich's car. After the safe houses were visited and their inmates tortured, one prisoner mentioned the catacombs of the church of SS Cyril and Methodius in Prague. Acting on the hint, lorry-loads of Waffen SS in full battle dress stormed the church from all directions on the night of 17–18 June 1942, where, with the help of the Prague fire service, they flushed out a dying Jan Kubiš, who had taken poison, together with the corpses of a number of other parachutist suicides from London. On 24 June 1942, the inhabitants of Ležáky, a second village – this time accurately linked by the Gestapo with the parachutists who had carried out the assassination – were shot and the buildings burnt to the ground.[109] On 3 July 1942, the state of emergency was lifted. An estimated 1,357 Czechs, excluding the victims of Lidice and Ležáky, had been executed and a further 3,188 arrested during the terror.[110] As the handsome young Communist journalist Julius Fučík (whose surreptitiously written prison notes were smuggled out and later published, making him a Communist icon) recorded, at Pankrác prison in Prague there was suddenly a steady stream of detainees making their 'daily Calvary' from Gestapo headquarters.[111]

For Czechs living in the Protectorate, *Heydrichiáda*, as the month-long terror and reprisals came to be known, represented the most horrifying chapter of the war since the brutal assault on the Czech universities at its beginning. Worse, because it resulted in the liquidation of the underground resistance, it represented the loss of the bravest and the most steadfast patriots, the flower of the Czech nation. By holding the entire Czech 'nation' to ransom for the actions of a few Czech exiles whom locals were powerless to influence, the Protectorate and Reich authorities can only have deepened many Protectorate Czechs' already pronounced tendency to hate 'the Germans' as their national enemy. But to the politically savvy Beneš, the Heydrich assassination – and especially the reprisals that followed – gave him precisely what his propaganda machine so desperately needed: an unequivocal example of Czech martyrdom and German evil, one white and the other black. Lidice, which the London team worked hard to make one of the best-known symbols of Nazi barbarity throughout the whole of the Allied world, finally won for the Protectorate the badge of suffering that it so badly needed: a martyrdom to enable it to be classed with other victim countries, such as Belgium or Poland, rather than alongside murky, semi-collaborationist states such as Austria.

The turning point in the war came in 1943. Barring accidents, as Norman Davies has put it, it now seemed clear that the 'Red Army was going to overrun Eastern Europe. The Western armies were going to drive through France and the Low Countries, and possibly over the Alps from Italy. And they were all going to meet in Germany, where the final showdown would occur.'[112] Even in Germany, Goebbels's propaganda had to admit the possibility of a German defeat, and began to appeal to a widespread terror of Bolshevism and fear of postwar retribution to rouse people who might otherwise find themselves on the losing side of what he now insisted must be 'total war', a fight to the finish. As Germany was being steadily turned to rubble by concentrated Allied bombing raids, the economies and weapons industries of both the Protectorate and Slovakia became even more important to the Reich. Accordingly, the Bat'a complex at Zlín was refitted to make rockets and tyres for the German army, while the Škoda car factory was put to use making tanks and airplane engines.[113]

As far as the Czechoslovak government-in-exile was concerned, the most pressing matters were how to deal after the war with collaborators and traitors and how to get approval from the Allies for the immediate postwar transfer of the entire German population from the former Czechoslovakia to Germany, a country where they had never lived. Czech and Slovak political leaders – whether Communist or non-Communist, and based in London or in Moscow – readily agreed with Beneš that the notion of collective guilt should be applied to 'the Germans', correctly gambling that in the immediate aftermath of war none of the victorious powers would be too particular about distinguishing Protectorate from Reich Germans. Beneš did, however, remind his colleagues that 'under no circumstances' should Czechoslovak anti-German legislation be allowed to 'appear like retribution solely against the Germans'; which was a good reason for adding Hungarians, Fascists and collaborators to the list of undesirables.[114] Although most exile Czech and Slovak politicians instinctively saw collective guilt and the need for national vengeance in a broadly similar light, they differed over the more delicate question of how far to target Czech and Slovak 'economic' and 'political' collaborators – in other words, their own co-nationals in the collaborationist Czech Protectorate and Slovak Fascist regimes.

Understanding that both Slovakia and the Protectorate would almost certainly be liberated by the Soviet Union, and in any case fall into the Soviet sphere of influence, Beneš hurried to Moscow to prevent his government-in-exile from simply being replaced, like that of the London Poles, and to lay the groundwork for what he saw as postwar Czechoslovak security. The result of these negotiations was a 'Treaty of Friendship, Mutual Aid and Post-War Co-operation between the Czechoslovak Republic and the Union of Soviet Socialist Republics', which was signed by Molotov and by Zdeněk Fierlinger, a former Czechoslovak ambassador to Moscow with Social Democratic sympathies, in the presence of Beneš and Stalin on 12 December 1943. Beneš evidently envisaged the document principally as a correction to the Czechoslovak–Soviet mutual aid treaty of 16 May 1935 which had failed to prevent Munich: a means of ensuring that the Soviet Union would immediately come to the assistance of Czechoslovakia in the event of any future attempt by Germany to encroach upon its territory. But although Beneš initially proposed that the treaty be ratified by parliament in Prague at the end of the war and run for five years in the first instance, he accepted without comment changes to the draft that set it to run for an initial period of twenty years and left out any need for parliament to approve it.[115] As Jan Masaryk, his foreign minister in exile, put it, 'We know that without Russia's friendship none of her small neighbours can revert to independent national life.' Klement Gottwald, the exile leader of the Czechoslovak Communist Party, concurred; speaking to the nation on Radio Moscow, he called the Soviet–Czechoslovak Treaty of Friendship 'vital', not just for the present, but 'also for all future generations to come'.[116]

Whereas the governments of Hungary and Romania could jump ship, changing from the Axis to the Allied side, the Tiso regime had bound itself so closely to Hitler that it had no option but to carry on, stemming the sudden rash of Slovak deserters from the army as best it could and trying to keep up Slovak Catholic and nationalist morale. It was therefore left to three spokesmen for the illegal Slovak Communist underground – Karol Šmidke, Gustáv Husák and Ladislav Novomeský – to join with three deputies of the banned Agrarian and Slovak Nationalist parties – Jozef Lettrich, Ján Ursíny and Matej Josko – to agree, on Christmas Day 1943, to create a Slovak National Council whose purpose would be to seize power from the Tiso regime as soon as a suitable opportunity presented itself.[117] The agreement further stated its wish that 'the Slovak and Czech Nations, as the most closely related Slav nations', shape their 'destinies in the Czechoslovak Republic, in a common state of the Czechs and Slovaks built upon the principle of national equality'; that the Czechoslovak Republic maintain 'close cooperation with all Slav countries and nations, especially with the USSR'; and that it 'lean on the USSR in the military and international fields'.[118]

The impetus for the insurrection that came to be known, somewhat misleadingly (since Slovakia came under German occupation only after the defeat of the rebellion), as the Slovak National Uprising was supposed to be provided by the arrival of Red Army troops in the Carpathian Mountains. The plan was that a few officers in the Slovak army – including Colonel Ján Golián, who was in command of troops at Banská Bystrica, and General Rudolf Viest – would work together with the Slovak National Council and in concert with the Beneš group in London. At the critical moment, the Slovak army, instead of attacking the Red Army, would unexpectedly open the front, enabling the Soviets to make their way rapidly across Slovak territory to Vienna. Before the Soviet troops' planned arrival in Subcarpathian Ruthenia, however, Soviet commanders began sending parachutists into Slovakia with the aim of starting a partisan war. Thousands of Slovak civilians and army deserters joined the agitators, leading to a chaotic situation in which the Slovak government was the target of terrorist attacks and in some cases whole villages were taken over by the partisans. The Tiso regime, whose police and army proved unable to control the situation, first declared martial law (11 August) but then had to call for help from German reinforcements, which began to arrive on 29 August 1944.

On 1 September 1944, the Slovak National Council, forced to act prematurely, declared itself 'the supreme representative of Slovak resistance on the home front', the 'only authorized spokesman of the Slovak nation' and the bearer of 'legislative and executive power throughout Slovakia' until such time as 'the Slovak Nation has, by democratic methods, appointed its legitimate representatives'.[119] It further declared 'the Slovak Nation' to have had 'nothing to do with the alliance with Hitlerite Germany'; to have been 'on the side of the allies, in all its ideals and convictions', all along; and to reject 'with indignation the Tiso-Tuka betrayal committed against Slavdom by the Populist regime which forced the Slovak Nation into the fight against the brotherly Russian Nation and other Slav nations'.[120]

The result was two months of struggle during which parts of Slovak territory were controlled by the Slovak National Council and its executive body, the *Zbor poverenikov* (Board of Commissioners). Although the whole point of the exercise was supposed to be to give the Soviets an easy passage to Vienna, the promised Soviet aid failed to materialize. Even when the first detachment of the 'Czechoslovak brigade', together with some fighter aircraft, finally arrived from the Soviet Union, General Golián found they were 'not a great deal of use' since they came 'without proper oil and petrol'. Claiming to have fifteen thousand men under his command, but whom he was unable to arm, he was understandably bitter about 'paper deliveries' promised, but not actually delivered, by the Soviet Union.[121] After nearly two months of fighting, Banská Bystrica, the centre of the insurrection, fell on 27 October 1944. Having done no more than delay the German advance for about six weeks, Generals Golián and Viest, like most of the other Slovak fighters, paid with their lives. Instead of ending the war in Europe in the autumn of 1944 (rather than the spring of 1945), the failed uprising resulted in a wave of Slovak purges; the introduction of the death penalty for 'acts of sabotage'; a stiffening of penalties for a further group of crimes (including the crime of 'activities inimical to the state'); and the establishment of a special court in Bratislava – a people's court in all but name, since it consisted of one trained judge and four lay judges – to review all sentences since 1 September 1944. The immediate result was forty-eight executions, the pronouncement of the death sentence on virtually all leaders of the rebellion and widespread terror.[122]

Although it decimated the Slovak resistance and Slovak Communist Party, and failed to achieve its stated war aims, the anti-Tiso and anti-German Slovak National Uprising was to prove politically crucial. Not only did it give Slovakia some desperately needed 'anti-Fascist' credentials, it also gave a genuinely Slovak political body – the Slovak National Council and its executive, the Board of Commissioners – the moral authority to upstage both the Beneš government-in-exile and the Czechoslovak Communist Party leadership's claims to speak for the Slovak as well as the Czech 'nation'.[123] Presumably with an eye to undermining Slovakia's chances of retaining too much postwar autonomy, in December 1944 Beneš decreed that a new form of local administration, to be called National Committees (*národní výbory*) and staffed exclusively by 'Slavs', should take over the governing of all liberated Czecho-Slovak territory until such time as the central government could resume power.[124]

The first Soviet troops finally crossed the Carpathians in September 1944, but although streams of German refugees, fleeing from the east, were already starting to clog the main roads across Slovakia and the Protectorate, it was not until 6 October 1944 that the first soldier from the Czechoslovak army corps arrived in Slovakia from the USSR. The battle for Dukla Pass, by far the longest and bloodiest engagement in which Czecho-Slovak units took part, became the stuff of heroic nationalist legend, taking on the propaganda role for the Second World War that Zborov (Zborów) had held after the First World War. From mid-January 1945, confidential memos from Khust/Chust in liberated Carpatho-Ukraine/Subcarpathian Ruthenia reported that Soviets were refusing to return liberated Czechoslovak territory to Czechoslovak administrators, as stipulated in the Soviet-Czechoslovak Treaty of Friendship of 1943, on the pretext that Soviet control was still needed to safeguard territory to the rear of the Red Army. Veiled warnings followed to the effect that Moscow considered it 'impossible' to prevent the 'fulfilment of a strong desire of the Carpatho-Ukrainians to become a part of the U.S.S.R.' and that since the area was 'ethnically Ukrainian and all logic pointed towards its inclusion into a greater Ukraine', Czechoslovak policy should begin to take 'this fact into account'.[125]

With the end of the war in sight and the might of the Soviet Union behind them, Czech and Slovak Communists who had spent the war in Moscow were in a position to dictate terms. As it happened, they did not have to. The government programme that Klement Gottwald, the head of the Czechoslovak Communist Party, had ready by 21 March 1945 was adopted, virtually unaltered, after a week of discussions held in Moscow (22–29 March 1945) by representatives of the Czech political parties, the Slovak National Council and Beneš, but from which anti-Fascist Sudeten German representatives and other ethnic minorities were excluded. A close comparison of the draft and final versions of the government proposals later known as the Košice Programme might be expected to reveal a struggle, or at the very least some differences of opinion, between Communists and non-Communists over such matters as the proposed nationalization of banks, insurance companies and major industries; the setting-up of extraordinary people's courts to try war criminals; the establishment of National Committees to administer the liberated territories; or the decision to model the Czechoslovak army on the Red Army. The non-Communist contingent, which let all of this pass without a murmur, was in fact preoccupied with two quite different matters: the punishment of 'traitors' to the Czech and Slovak 'nations'; and the degree of autonomy to be retained by Slovakia. Its only other contributions of any importance were to add, to the clause concerning the imminent transfer of Carpatho-Ukraine (Subcarpathian Ruthenia) to the Soviet Union, that 'the people' would decide the territory's destiny; and to assert that the freedoms of speech and assembly, together with the right to privacy of correspondence and the 'freedom to teach', would be safeguarded.[126] The Slovak National Council, unable to win the promise of a return to federation as it had existed during the Second Czecho-Slovak Republic, had to content itself with recognition of Slovak distinctiveness, together with promises that constitutional arrangements in the restored postwar state would be resolved in the spirit of a partnership of 'equal with equal'.

Tiso and his government fled Slovakia, together with units of the German army, at the beginning of April 1945, just ahead of the arrival of Soviet troops. From Austria, Tiso broadcast back the message that 'in the face of the assault of the Bolshevik army' the government saw it as its highest duty to 'defend the idea of the state independence of Slovakia'. He further promised, in words that appear to have hit their mark: 'We will work – you at home and us abroad – for as long as world opinion does not look positively upon the natural striving of the Slovak nation for Slovaks to be the exclusive rulers of their home.'[127] Fatally for any hope that independent Slovakia's past might, in the spirit of fraternal nationalism, be treated leniently by Czech nationalist opinion, however, the Tiso government insisted to the very end (25 April) that its 'friendly relations with the German Reich were and are based on the support which our great neighbour gave us in our just fight for the freedom of our nation'.[128]

On 4 April, at Košice in eastern Slovakia, the unelected Czechoslovak government-to-be, led by Zdeněk Fierlinger, took the oath of office in the presence of the miraculously restored, and thoroughly unhyphenated, Czechoslovak president, Edvard Beneš. The next day, 5 April 1945, the Košice Programme of the new 'Czechoslovak Government of the National Front of Czechs and Slovaks', as hammered out in Moscow, was proclaimed. This made clear that the immediate postwar period was not going to be a time of forgiveness and reconciliation, but rather one of retributive justice, and that it was going to seize the historic opportunity to rid the state of both Slav nations' traditional competitors – the Germans and the Magyars – and so make Czechoslovakia into a national state of the Czechs and Slovaks. Sections 8 and 9, which dealt with war criminals, collaborators, traitors and (in the same breath) the German and Hungarian minorities, were blunt: all ethnic Germans and Hungarians living on Czechoslovak territory before the signing of the Munich Agreement (except for those who could prove that they had been actively engaged in 'anti-Nazi' and 'anti-Fascist' activity) were to have their Czechoslovak citizenship revoked. Those awaiting the death sentence could remain on Czechoslovak soil until their execution; all others would be expelled.[129] All ethnic Germans and Hungarians who had moved to Czechoslovakia after Munich, unless they could be shown to have 'worked on behalf of Czechoslovakia', were also to be either executed or expelled. German and Hungarian schools, universities and polytechnics were to be closed. Libraries, theatres and other places of culture were to be 'cleansed' of 'collaborationist' staff and 'Fascist' content. Journalists, filmmakers and broadcasters were also to be 'thoroughly purged'.[130]

Section 6, which dealt with the position of Slovakia, was read out by Klement Gottwald, who called it a 'Magna Carta of the Slovak Nation'.[131] Copies of a leaflet, also entitled the 'Magna Carta of the Slovak Nation', were distributed all over newly liberated Slovakia. Despite its grand title, the Slovak 'Magna Carta' was not really a constitution, or even a legal document. Rather, it was a hodgepodge of fine-sounding phrases or pledges taken either from section 6 of the Košice Programme or else soundbites from political speeches given by Gottwald, Beneš, Fierlinger and other leading Czech politicians. These included the vague statement that Slovaks had 'the right' to be 'masters in their own land', the equally meaningless promise that the republic would be 'renewed as a common state with equal rights for two nations – the Czech and the Slovak' – and the seemingly more concrete assurance that the Slovak National Council would be 'the legal representative of the independent Slovak Nation' and 'the representative of state power in the territory of Slovakia'.[132] Although it had already been agreed with Moscow that the

'Czechoslovak' army would be brought into line with that of the Soviet Union, Slovak units – together with Slovak officers and staff – were to be retained, at their current rank, in the Czechoslovak army, providing they were recommended by the Slovak National Council, had committed no offence against 'Slovak national honour' and were not liable to prosecution for 'past activities under the former traitorous regime'. The central Czechoslovak government also undertook to 'perform common state functions in close cooperation with the Slovak National Council and with the Board of Commissioners as an executive organ of the Slovak National Council'.[133] Finally, the 'Magna Carta' promised that the Slovak National Council would be incorporated into the constitution and that Slovaks would be 'adequately' represented in 'central state offices, institutions and economic agencies'. It was left to 'the legitimate representatives of the Czech and Slovak Nations' to decide precisely how governmental powers would be 'divided between the central and Slovak organs'.[134]

As had happened after the First World War, temporary rule by an unelected Czechoslovak government, composed exclusively of politicians who had been in exile during the war, was justified on the grounds of ensuring an orderly transition to peace until permanent institutions could be re-established and democratic elections held. The interim National Front government was composed of a provisional National Assembly and cabinet (this time with a special élite known as the Presidium). Local administration was left to the new National Committees (organizations like those of the same name that Karol Sidor had once suggested using to radicalize Slovak nationalist opinion), about half of whose members were already Communist. As previously agreed between the wartime London and Moscow Czechoslovak governments, the National Front government was allowed to represent just six political parties (five, as in the old days of the *Pětka*, if one counts the two Communist parties as one). In contrast to the radical 'simplification' of parties that had occurred during the Second Czecho-Slovak Republic, this time it was the parties on the political Right, rather than the Left, that were outlawed. In postwar Bohemia and Moravia-Silesia, the only permitted parties were the Czechoslovak Communist, Social Democratic, National Socialist and Czechoslovak People's parties; and, in postwar Slovakia, the Slovak Communist Party (which had merged with the Slovak Social Democratic Party in September 1944, at the end of the Slovak National Uprising) and a single non-Communist bloc called the Slovak 'Democratic Party'. (Later, for reasons that will be explained in the next chapter, two more Slovak parties – the Labour Party and the Freedom Party – were added.)[135]

From the outset, the Third Czechoslovak Republic was at best only semi-democratic. It also – for all the contemporary talk of Czechoslovakia acting as a 'bridge' between East and West – quite clearly placed the country within the Soviet sphere of influence. Although the six permitted political parties in the National Front of Czechs and Slovaks were not purely cosmetic (as had been the case during the Second Czecho-Slovak Republic), the two most popular prewar parties (the Czech Agrarian Party and the Slovak People's Party) were banned outright. A continuing sense that the state ought somehow to express the united will of 'the nation' meant there was little sympathy for the politicking of the more pluralist First Czechoslovak Republic, which – for all its faults – had at least permitted most political parties to exist, and sometimes even expected them to compete.

Out of the twenty-five ministers who made up the National Front government, eight were Communist Party members. Communists held some of the most important ministries, including Agriculture (which, in the absence of the outlawed Agrarian Party and in anticipation of land reform, was now particularly important); Information and Education (which controlled all press and propaganda); the Interior (which had at its disposal both the ordinary and the secret police); and Labour (with power over the trade unions). In addition, the Communist Party had influence with the minister for defence, Ludvík Svoboda, and the Slovak secretary of state, Vladimír Clementis, though both had yet to join the party. Prime minister Zdeněk Fierlinger, like the ministers of industry and of food, who were not yet card-carrying Communists either, was on the left wing of the other Marxist party, the Social Democratic.

From the spring of 1944, the Czechoslovak government-in-exile had called on Czechs in the Protectorate 'immediately' to 'remove from all public functions citizens of enemy states and individuals who betrayed the Czechoslovak Republic or who collaborated with the enemy' and to 'detain all these individuals so they do not escape'.[136] But it was not until Hitler was safely dead, Slovakia had been completely liberated by the Red Army and US troops were already crossing into Bohemia from the west that there was any sign of rebellion in the Protectorate. On May Day 1945, more than a year after London's call to arms, the first signs of organized rebellion against Nazi rule finally came in the shape of a strike at the Škoda plant, some clashes between Czechs and Germans, and the first approaches to the SOE for Allied assistance to overthrow the occupiers. On 3 May, the German authorities declared Prague a 'hospital city' and began evacuating troops, only for them to return, just two days later, to reinforce SS troops who were unexpectedly faced with the insurrection afterwards known as the Prague Uprising and turned into a heroic myth commemorated, to this day, with plaques and memorials all over the city.

The Prague Uprising began on 5 May 1945, when groups of Czechs occupied public buildings – including the radio station – and began hoisting national flags. There were scattered outbreaks of fighting across the city. By

6 May, the same day the US 16th Armored Division arrived in Plzeň, the Czech National Council took charge of the insurrection and ordered the building of barricades.[137] Initially secure in the knowledge that US troops were only 80 km (50 miles) away, Czech patriots in Prague broadcast increasingly urgent calls for help over the airwaves; but which met with no response. The lack of support from the Allies, who stood aside while an estimated 1,693 Czechs (and 935 Germans) were then needlessly killed in the street fighting and in SS-run prisons, has gone down in history as a shameful betrayal on the same pattern as the Warsaw Uprising. But there were at least two compelling reasons why the Allies refused to come to the aid of the ill-timed Czech rebellion. The first, most familiar, explanation, is that the 'Big Three' (the Soviet Union, United States and Britain) had already agreed that the Soviet Union would liberate virtually the whole of the country, leaving only the territory to the west of an imaginary Karlsbad–Pilsen–Budweis (*Karlovy Vary–Plzeň–České Budějovice*) line for Patton's troops to liberate. The other reason, if the head of the German Military Surrender Mission, General Jodl, is to believed, is that the Prague Uprising was preventing his troops from being able to surrender, since he needed the broadcasting equipment that the Czech rebels had taken to transmit orders to his troops to surrender by the agreed time of the armistice (midnight on 8 May 1945).[138] To complete the fiasco, the first troops to enter Prague – although Russian – were not from the Red Army, but rather from General Andrei Vlasov's (hitherto collaborationist) Russian Liberation Army.

The Protectorate of Bohemia and Moravia and the First Slovak Republic had had what was, by the grim standards of the day, an easy war. They had certainly not got off scot-free, like Switzerland or Ireland: quite apart from the horrors to which Jews and Gypsies had been subjected, even White Gentiles had had to live under two extremely unpleasant authoritarian regimes. But they had been spared the terror and destruction of bombing raids that had decimated large parts of Britain and Germany; largely escaped the unspeakable horrors to which Poland and the Soviet Union had been subjected; and had profited from the war for as long as Germany had profited from it. More horribly, both the Czech and Slovak 'nations' had succeeded in becoming more homogeneously Czech and Slovak through a dramatic reduction in their Gypsy and the near-extinction of their Jewish populations. The trend towards ethnic homogeneity was about to be reinforced through the reassignment of the vast majority of the state's prewar Rusyn/Ukrainian population to the Soviet Union, the wholesale expulsion of all but a tiny handful of its native Germans and the transfer, expulsion or forcible 'Slovakization' of the great majority of its ethnic Hungarians.

Czechoslovakia was back on the map: this time with almost all of the territory that it had initially been granted by the Western Powers at Versailles in

1919, but now without a politically significant number of minorities. Stalin had been shrewd to back Beneš, a narrowly Czech nationalist and socialist who was bursting to repay his ethnic and political enemies, rather than to support alternative leaders of the Czech and Slovak exile movements. Beneš's very name – like that of the new foreign minister, Jan Masaryk – symbolically linked the new, postwar era with T.G. Masaryk, democracy and the founding of the state, giving the world a false impression that the postwar restoration of Czechoslovakia represented the fulfilment of the First Republic's democratic promise. Instead, Czech and Slovak political leaders were about to use their recent education in ethnic cleansing, rule by decree and the methods of the police state to build a new kind of democracy: a 'people's democracy'.

CHAPTER 6

FROM NATIONAL CLEANSING TO COMMUNIST DICTATORSHIP

The Third Czechoslovak Republic came into being on 9 May 1945, the day after VE Day. It fell three years later when the cabinet crisis known to pro-Communists as 'Victorious February' and to anti-Communists as the 'February Coup' tipped the delicate political balance in the National Front government decisively in favour of the Czechoslovak Communist Party (*Komunistická strana Československa* or *KSČ*). On 9 May 1948, three years to the day after the official liberation of Prague by the Soviet army, the Czechoslovak Republic adopted the constitution that set the seal on the country's fate as a totalitarian police state. Czechoslovakia, the last country in Europe to fall behind the Iron Curtain, was to remain under the control of the *KSČ*, itself kept under the watchful eye of the Kremlin, for the next forty-one years. But unlike other Soviet satellites of Central and Eastern Europe, the Czechoslovak People's Democracy was neither forced to go Communist nor to ally itself with the Soviet Union. It did both voluntarily, acting in what looked to the political leadership of the day to be national self-interest.

The Third Republic may have been brief, but it was understood, even at the time, to be politically significant. Beneš was not alone in believing postwar Czechoslovakia to be at a crossroads, its faith in parliamentary democracy and Western alliances too shaken to be recovered, its ethnic hatreds too deep to be overcome. 'Czech leaders', as Jeremy King has put it, 'convinced that their "nation" had barely escaped annihilation', naturally 'ranked questions of Communism or capitalism, East or West lower than the question of how to protect Czechs against a renewed German onslaught in the future'.[1] The decision to remove Czechoslovakia's principal ethnic minorities from the country and to purge the body politic of its right wing had been taken by the Czechoslovak National Council in London and the exile Communist leadership in Moscow long before it was formally announced at Košice in April 1945. It only remained for the unelected government of the National Front of Czechs and Slovaks to decide how far and how quickly – not whether – to move in the only direction that was politically possible, given its own political outlook and the current political climate: towards strong

government, socialist economic planning and the closest possible alliance
with the Soviet Union.

In May 1945, although Soviet and Czechoslovak flags were being flown
side by side and portraits of Beneš and Stalin were on display everywhere,[2] it
was not yet possible to guess how ruthlessly the Czechoslovak (*KSČ*) and
Slovak (*KSS*) Communist parties would come to emulate the worst features
of the Soviet system, nor how high the price of Soviet protection from the
bogey of a resurgent Nazi Germany would turn out to be. In those first
heady days following the liberation and reunification of a state that might
so easily have been left divided, it was easy to be swept along by President
Beneš's rhetoric about Czechoslovakia being historically determined to mediate
between East and West and follow its own, evolutionary path to a utopia that
was at once socialist and Czech nationalist. Some even imagined that the
renewal of the state at the war's end might mean a magical return to the
democratic, multinational state that had existed before the Munich Crisis. But
although Czechoslovakia had recovered most of its pre-Munich territory and
went back to its pre-Munich name, its ethnic composition, international
alliances and political structures, to say nothing of its public mood, were not
the same. The Third Republic, so often portrayed as a time of national liberation and democratic revival whose promise was only spoiled by the Communist
putsch of February 1948, was in reality a brutal and brutalizing time, one
whose ruthlessness was driven as much by resurgent Czech nationalism as by
specifically Communist ambition.

By the time that Czechoslovakia was back on the map, most of its Jewish
citizens were dead.[3] As survivors slowly made their way back across a
dislocated and chaotic Central Europe, the first horror to greet them was
discovering how few Jewish family members, friends and acquaintances
had survived. Eva Blochová, who had got through her teenage years at
Theresienstadt, Oederan and Auschwitz by telling herself that, once the war
was over, she would go back to Prague and her old lifestyle, quickly discovered
that 'the prewar city, with its lively Jewish community, did not exist any longer.
In this respect, Hitler had succeeded: Prague was *Judenrein* [free of Jews].'[4]
Shocking in a different way was to find out how many neighbours, friends and
acquaintances to whom Jewish families had entrusted their belongings before
being called up for deportation now denied that they had anything to return
or complained at having to give them back.[5] Nor was it easy for Jews who had
lived through the hell of the SS camps to listen to Czechs, who had been able
to stay in their own homes, complain of having had to live in fear of the
Gestapo, let alone of having been unable to send their children to university
or forced to endure the names of tram stops being called out in German.
Before the war, Blochová later mused, 'I hardly knew who among my
girlfriends was Jewish. Now the chasm, due to our very different wartime

experiences, seemed unbridgeable.'[6] Some Jewish survivors were as mistrustful of the new nationalism as they had been of the old; others sought refuge in the Communist Party, which claimed to despise anti-Semitism and oppose Fascism, and immediately had existing anti-Jewish legislation reversed.

Gypsies, like Jews, had been treated by the Czech and Slovak, as well as the German, authorities as a 'problem' to be 'solved' by means of forced labour, imprisonment, deportation and, ultimately, extermination. It was the German authorities who organized the systematic killing of Gypsies for which the special Gypsy Camp at Auschwitz became infamous; but it was Czech and Slovak officials who sent them there. Only a tiny fraction – estimated at between 5 and 12 per cent – of Bohemian and Moravian Gypsies, whether Czech- or Romany-speaking, survived the systematic attempt to destroy them. By contrast, the vast majority of Slovak Roma and other Gypsies survived the war, not because the Tiso regime was any more humane than that which prevailed in the Protectorate, but rather because the Slovak Ministry of the Interior came to the view that it was more efficient to keep Jews and Gypsies at home for slave labour than to continue to pay the German authorities to 'resettle' them in the east.[7]

Communists of all backgrounds, including two future *KSČ* general secretaries and presidents of the republic, had suffered in their tens of thousands as prisoners of Czech, Slovak or German authorities.[8] Out of a prewar Communist membership of about 100,000, more than half had spent the war in concentration camps, where about a quarter perished.[9] Just 28,485 prewar members of the Czechoslovak Communist Party (*KSČ*) and about 12,000 from the Slovak Communist Party (*KSS*) survived the war; only because 20,000 Social Democrats were added to the *KSS* by the forced merger of September 1944 was there a postwar Slovak Communist party big enough to be worth mentioning.[10] With its postwar membership so badly depleted, the Communist Party could not afford to be choosy about who joined its ranks, and on 12 May 1945, the *KSČ* officially declared its intention to 'open the doors of the party wide' and to welcome 'workers in the factories, working peasants and the intelligentsia'.[11] Although supposed in theory to be made up 'primarily' of those who had 'already proved themselves' in the 'heroic struggle against bestial fascism', in practice neither the Czech nor the Slovak branches of the Communist Party could afford to throw away the energy of the young, the ambition of careerists or the expertise of former members of the Gestapo, Hlinka Guard and *ÚŠB*.[12]

In addition to countless numbers of 'opportunists' – including peasants and workers eager for confiscated German and Magyar property in the former Sudetenland and in southern Slovakia – the Communist Party was able to recruit from the first generation of Czechoslovak citizens to be able to vote from the age of eighteen, many of whom were already starry-eyed young converts to Stalinism.[13] These children of the war, who had no conscious experience of any other political system than authoritarian totalitarianism, were especially ripe for conversion and easily exploited by the more seasoned prewar Communist leadership. Zdeněk Mlynář, a Bohemian Czech who joined the Communist Party in the spring of 1946, when he was not quite sixteen, remembered his decision to become a Communist as akin to a conversion experience. With the 'leap of faith' to Communism, as he later put it,

> comes automatic knowledge. Your inner world is transformed; it takes on direction, and though in fact you still know nothing, you now feel in a position to pass judgement on everything. You know what is progressive and what is reactionary, what is good and what is bad for the future of mankind. And you also know what is and is not scientific without having to bother with any concrete scientific research.[14]

Within a year of the liberation, Communist Party membership in Czechoslovakia had risen to over a million, making it as large as all the other political parties put together, and one-sixth the size of the Communist Party of the Soviet Union. By the end of 1948, membership figures had risen to almost two and a half million out of a population of roughly eleven million, meaning that every third adult was a card-carrying member of the Communist Party. The Czechoslovak Communist Party, which had twice as many members as the Hungarian and almost four times as many as the Polish Communist parties, thus became, 'in proportion to the total national population', the largest Communist Party 'in the whole world and of all time'; it may, indeed, have 'reached a pinnacle', not only 'in the history of Communism', but in the history of political parties generally.[15]

Wartime policies had already done a great deal to pave the way for the rise of Communism in the Bohemian Crown Lands. By abolishing the universities, imprisoning intellectuals, deporting Czech Jews and cracking down on patriotic societies, extreme right-wing Czech and Nazi German authorities had effectively silenced the Czech middle class. The policy of favouring manual labourers with extra rations, pay bonuses, works outings and other team-building exercises had helped to foster worker solidarity and class confidence. One of the many terrible legacies of the Nazi policy of divide and rule in the Protectorate was that traditional areas of class, ethnic and national conflict had only been further exacerbated. Resentment by those who had been losers in the war towards those who appeared to have profited from it combined with new government directives, decrees and legislation to give postwar class and economic jealousies an extra edge. Heda Margolius, a Czech Jew who had managed to escape from Auschwitz but lost everything in the war, parodied better-off peasants and small farmers in the countryside (who were soon to be victimized as 'kulaks' and forced to collectivize) as having 'Oriental carpets' on their floors and 'original paintings' on their walls, and as eating sausages off 'silver platters' and drinking beer out of 'cut glass'.[16] 'Partisans,' she remembered with bitterness,

> who throughout the war had lived in the woods, widows of the executed who for years had slept on the floor of some basement, and ailing survivors of the concentration camps spent day after day waiting at the Housing Authority while butchers and grocers and other wartime profiteers walked in by the back door and were seen first.[17]

The wife of a Communist functionary, scrimping and saving to get by, similarly resented her cleaning lady for demanding a 'meat lunch, morning and afternoon snacks, plus 40 Crowns an hour', far more, she claimed, than her husband was earning.[18] At a time when so many had suffered, to varying degrees and in different ways, sympathy for others appears to have been in short supply.

Among the many dubious practices that the postwar Czech and Slovak authorities learned from the Nazis was how to pre-empt political dissent with the judicious use of rationing, populist slogans, wage and benefits policies, and the redistribution of confiscated property. The National Front government now put these skills to good use, launching a sweeping nationalization programme, together with a dramatic land reform one, both of which were explicitly socialist as well as pro-Slav nationalist. Between 14 May 1945, when finance minister Vavro Šrobár announced the abolition of the anti-Semitic property laws,[19] and 27 October 1945, when twenty-three presidential decrees were rushed through in a single day (in order to coincide with the first postwar meeting of the Provisional National Assembly, itself timed to coincide with the twenty-seventh anniversary of Czechoslovak independence, soon to be renamed 'Nationalization Day'),[20] ninety-one laws came directly from the office of the president, the remainder either from the cabinet Presidium or individual ministries.[21] In order to keep up with the sheer volume of new legislation, the government printing office had to work on Saturdays as well as weekdays.[22] Together, the policies put forward by the National Front of Czechs and Slovaks added up to a brutally nationalist and radically socialist revolution, not a return to either democracy or the free market as they had existed before Munich.

Liberation brought joy and relief; it also unleashed envy, resentment and hate. At the Small Fortress in Theresienstadt, where the Nazi authorities had killed more than 8,000 Czechs, revenge by former prisoners was immediate. A doctor gave 45 German prisoners – mainly SS and Gestapo – lethal injections;

in all, about 550 out of the 3,725 German postwar prisoners kept in the Small Fortress are estimated to have died, 70 directly at the hands of former prisoners and the rest as a result of the conditions in which they were kept.[23] Nikolaus Martin, a recent inmate of the Small Fortress, whose mother was Czech and whose father was German, applauded the execution of his former SS guards, but was shocked, upon his return to Prague, to come across a group of German-speaking civilians, stripped to the waist and with swastikas painted on their backs and foreheads, being forced to replace cobblestones in the street. He was even more disturbed by the sight of three electrocuted bodies, said by the surrounding mob to belong to Gestapo agents, hanging from a lamppost in a nearby square.[24] Rosemary Kavan, the English bride of a Czech Communist, was similarly horrified to come across a group of German women, tufts of their hair having already been torn out, being forced by the surrounding crowd to lick a huge swastika painted on the pavement. Only because her husband had taught her the Czech phrase *'nejsem Němka, jsem Angličanka'* ('I'm not a German, I'm an Englishwoman') did Kavan narrowly escape the same fate.[25]

No sooner had the president of the Republic and ministers of the National Front government arrived in liberated Prague than they began inciting Czechs and Slovaks to take advantage of the historic opportunity to rid themselves, forever, of their ethnic German and Hungarian rivals. It was the 'democratic' Czechoslovak president and political leadership who led the calls to 'cleanse' the state of millions of its German- and Hungarian-speaking citizens, although Czech and Slovak Communist leaders Klement Gottwald and Gustáv Husák were quick to see the potential benefits to the 'class struggle' and only too eager to add 'economic traitors' and 'bourgeois elements' to the already impressive list of proposed victims. Above all, it was Beneš, who had been campaigning hard throughout the war for a 'radical' solution to the problem of Czechoslovakia's minorities, who could see that the Great Powers needed to be presented with an ethnic conflict appalling enough to make 'orderly' mass expulsions seem the more 'humane' and 'civilized' option. (A similar technique, it will be remembered, had been tried by the Czech leadership seven years earlier to rid the Second Czecho-Slovak Republic of its Jewish, especially its German-Jewish, population; it had also been used by the Slovak authorities to rid the region of its Czechs, Jews and Gypsies.)[26]

On 16 May 1945, in his first public speech in Prague after his return from exile, President Beneš explicitly appealed to the masses gathered in the Old Town Square to seize the moment to 'liquidate out [*vylikvidovat*]' the Germans and Magyars in 'the interest of a united national state of Czechs and Slovaks'. Minister of justice Prokop Drtina, another Czech National Socialist, similarly called on Czechs to take matters into their own hands, emphasizing: 'We must begin immediately, this very moment, to expel the Germans from our lands. We must use all possible means – nothing can be allowed to cause us to stop or even to hesitate.' The Czech Communist contribution to the general chorus of urgency lay in its demands – publicized in newspapers and on the radio – that local authorities not only 'immediately' begin the 'severe' punishment of Germans, but also that ordinary people spontaneously 'uncover and seize' ethnic Czech collaborators, traitors and 'lackeys', and 'chase them' to swift judgement and punishment before a 'people's revolutionary court'.[27]

Those who were lumped together – in political speeches, newspaper articles, radio addresses, presidential decrees and official statute books – as 'Germans, Hungarians, Traitors and Collaborators' were from the first subject to random acts of violence and cruelty, and to being rounded up into prisons and concentration camps, or simply dumped across the border with Germany or Austria.[28] The politically calculated orgy of violence, vigilanteism and ethnic hatred that lasted through the spring and summer (May to August) of 1945 is rather disingenuously known in Czech as the *divoký odsun* ('Wild Removal' or 'Transfer'), to distinguish it from the more 'orderly' and 'legal' official *odsun* (transfer or expulsion) of a further 2.8 million ethnic Germans from their homeland which followed over the course of 1946.

The cruelty shown to millions of ordinary German-speakers was justified through their official description as 'traitors' and 'Fascists' (with the misleading implication that the contemporary Czech and Slovak regimes had somehow not been Fascist or collaborationist). The opportunity to turn the tables on 'the Germans', regardless of whether or not German-speaking individuals had actually been Nazi, Nazi sympathizers or even German nationalists, proved impossible for many Czechs to resist, particularly when spurred on by their own national politicians. In the German-Czech city of Brno, where combined police and paramilitary forces had incarcerated some 1,600 suspected collaborators and war criminals – including about a hundred Czechs – the local authorities begged Prague urgently to set up some sort of war crimes tribunal, since, as they explained, they were being forced to use machine guns to keep Czech lynch mobs at bay.[29] At Olomouc, also in Moravia, the local Communist-controlled National Committee put up red posters (just like the ones previously used by the Protectorate authorities) to urge citizens to turn in not only Nazis and war criminals, but also 'profiteers', 'opportunists', 'open or hidden fascists' and Czechs who had 'in any way transgressed against the Czech people and their national honour'.[30] On 12 May 1945, a concerned Prime Minister Fierlinger asked his ministerial colleagues to issue a radio appeal to ask Czechs to stop attacking innocent Germans. Since the primary purpose of inciting pogroms was to drive away as many Germans and Hungarians as possible, it is depressing, but not surprising, to find that the rest of the cabinet dismissed his request as 'unnecessary'.[31] Fierlinger, like every other prominent Czech politician of the day, in any case agreed with the principle of national cleansing; and announced, at the celebration to commemorate the 325th anniversary of the Battle of the White Mountain (*Bílá hora*), that 'the wrong inflicted upon us after White Mountain, which was again to have been repeated under the Nazi regime, will be completely rectifed . . . Czechs and Slovaks will again be the masters of their own land'.[32]

Although most of Subcarpathian Ruthenia's 725,357 inhabitants did not yet know it, they were about to be handed over to the Soviet Union, their province turned into 'Zakarpats'ka Ukrajina', the Transcarpathian *oblast'* (region) of Ukraine. In order to forestall objections that 'the people' of the region ought, as had been promised at Košice, to be consulted, Subcarpathian Ruthenia's forcible inclusion in the Soviet Union was justified on the strength of a rally held by delegates from the Communist-dominated National Committees based in the recently restored regional capital of Užhorod (*Uzhhorod*). The transfer of property was then formally agreed in a Soviet-Czechoslovak treaty signed on 29 June 1945, which was pointedly passed into Czechoslovak constitutional law on 22 November 1945, seven years to the day after the central government in Prague had been forced to grant Subcarpathian Ruthenia its extorted autonomy.[33] From the point of view of the Prague government, the change meant that a common border was created with the USSR; the central Czechoslovak government was freed from having to subsidize what had always been its poorest region; and the state was rid of a potential cause of constitutional instability, together with a large number of minorities: not only Rusyn/Ukrainians, but also a smattering of Magyars, Romanians, Gypsies and Jews.

On 15 May 1945, two months before the central government, the Slovak National Council brought out a retribution law in the shape of a decree 'Providing for the Punishment of Fascist Criminals, Foreign Oppressors, Traitors and Collaborationists, and for the Creation of a National Tribunal and of People's Courts' in the territory of Slovakia.[34] Some 26,296 prisoners, mostly Carpathian Germans, were soon being held in sixty-three forced-labour camps across Slovakia[35] (including the infamous Svätý Jur, Ústie na Orave, Krupina, Nováky and Ilava ones, where the lack of medical care made the mortality rates particularly high). In the Lands of the Bohemian Crown, where there were as yet no specific directives from the centre, anti-German measures began to escalate out of control as denunciation followed denunciation and local authorities, in the absence of any specific directives from the centre, dreamed up whatever measures they thought best. In what many people began to notice was turning into a tit-for-tat revenge, which simply inverted victim and oppressor, ration allowances for ethnic Germans were cut to the same inadequate level that had formerly been allotted to Jews.[36]

In some places, Germans were required to wear a white armband so that they could be easily identified.[37] From June, German schools were forcibly closed. Germans were allowed to shop only at certain hours, and were forbidden to visit places of public amusement, to use public means of communication or to change their place of residence.[38] Hundreds of concentration camps and other facilities were used to hold Germans and suspected collaborators; by mid-June, roughly twenty thousand people were being detained at thirty-seven different locations in Prague alone.[39] At two of the most infamous postwar Czech camps – the Hanke internment camp for Germans near Ostrava and the Kolín camp for suspected collaborators in eastern Bohemia – the torture, rape and murder of inmates apparently became institutionalized in much the same way as in wartime camps run by the SS.[40]

Beneš could have tried to dampen the flames of ethnic hatred. Instead, he stoked them by deliberately conflating Sudeten, Carpathian and Reich Germans as if all were the same and all were equally responsible for Hitler's crimes. Speaking at Tábor in mid-June 1945, for example, he reminded his audience how, during the May Crisis of 1938, he had asked 'the Germans' for 'tolerance' and 'forgiveness'. Since 'their' answer had come in the form of 'terror, treason, concentration camps for us Czechs', he declared, it should not 'surprise anybody in the whole world when we say that we are determined to get rid of these [sic] Germans forever'.[41] On 21 June 1945, a presidential decree promised to speed up the confiscation and redistribution of land formerly belonging to 'Germans, Hungarians, traitors and enemies of the Czech and Slovak nation'.[42] This only added the incentives of greed and envy to an already lethal cocktail of ethnic hatred and collective guilt, a righteous fury that was kept on the boil by frequent reports of alleged German sabotage in the pages of *Rudé právo*, the Czechoslovak Communist Party's daily and the most widely read Czech newspaper of the day.[43]

The most notorious incident to result from the atmosphere that rumours of continued German sabotage and Gestapo plots engendered occurred on 31 July 1945, at Krásné Březno just outside Ústí nad Labem (*Aussig*) in the former Sudetenland, when somewhere between eighty and four hundred Germans – men, women and children – were lynched, shot or drowned in the River Labe (*Elbe*) in response to rumours that an explosion in a nearby military depot, which had killed twenty-eight people and injured more, was the work of German terrorists.[44] This horrifying incident was then used by Beneš and other leading Czech politicians as the clinching argument to justify the transfer of the maximum possible number of Germans (and Hungarians) from the Czechoslovak territories. On 20 July 1945, arrangements were made for Czechs, Slovaks and 'other Slavs' to 'resettle' the lands and property that had belonged to ethnic 'Germans, Hungarians and other enemies of the state' in the rapidly emptying border regions.[45] Jan Šejna, a Czech peasant who got his start in life by taking over a farm confiscated from a Sudeten German family awaiting deportation, was an enthusiastic recruit to the Communist Party in 1946. He not only did his bit to 'indoctrinate local farmers' and 'discredit the bourgeois opposition'; when the time came, he prepared lists of 'bourgeois elements' to be arrested 'without a twinge of conscience' since he considered them to be 'enemies of the revolution'.[46] He rose to become chief of staff to the Czechoslovak minister of defence before eventually fleeing the country.

It was becoming clear that a top political priority was the creation of a police network large, flexible and politically reliable enough to cope with the enormous demands being placed upon it by everything from mass trials and summary executions to forced expulsions and exchanges of whole groups of people. In the summer of 1945, in the midst of the initial, 'wild' phase of the 'transfer', prewar policemen, partisans and armed trade unionists were brought together under the umbrella of an organization calling itself the *Sbor národní bezpečnosti* (*SNB*) or 'National Security Corps'. The *SNB*, an enormous, sprawling organization, was subdivided into various specialist police agencies. These included a uniformed police corps known as the *Veřejná bezpečnost* (*VB*) or Public Security, a criminal investigation branch and so-called emergency units. Three additional police agencies that were soon to become intimately associated with the Communist regime were the *StB* (*Státní bezpečnost* or State Security, spelt *Štátná bezpečnost* in Slovak), which was originally created by the National Front government as a specialist agency to seek out collaborators, and two less prominent agencies that were set up by the Communist minister of the interior: the intelligence and espionage service known as *ZS*, and the border guards who were later to become so important in patrolling the perimeter of the Iron Curtain.[47]

From 19 June 1945, those identified by the *StB* as 'Nazi criminals; traitors; and their helpers' were dealt with by 'extraordinary people's courts' which were hurriedly set up all over the country to cope with the need for the state to be seen to be punishing the enemy within.[48] Although outwardly legal forms of trial and punishment had returned, Benjamin Frommer has found Czech retribution courts to have been so brutal as to have been almost without parallel in bloodthirsty postwar Europe. Czech people's courts not only convicted an astonishing 97 per cent of those who were brought before them, but – thanks to extraordinary provisions decreed by President Beneš which insisted that death sentences be carried out within two or three hours of a verdict and that there be no right of appeal – sent more defendants *per capita* to their deaths than anywhere else in Europe apart from Stalinist Bulgaria.[49] In all, this initial, 'wild' stage of the transfer of ethnic Germans resulted in the forced expulsion of about 660,000 German-speakers from Czechoslovakia, the killing of anywhere between 19,000 and 30,000 more, and the premature death of untold others. Uncounted numbers of ethnic Czechs, said by informers, people's tribunals or simply the surrounding mob to have collaborated with the 'enemy' or to have betrayed or shamed the 'nation', also perished.[50] By December 1945, complaints to the Ministry of the Interior that Czech policemen were torturing suspects and witnesses to secure convictions had become so commonplace that a young National Socialist politician pleaded explicitly with the nation to 'de-Nazify' its 'state administration' and 'security forces' and do something about its 'police jails where ... utterly innocent people have suffered'.[51]

While the Czech authorities were expelling and interning ethnic Germans and denouncing as a traitor any Czech who showed the slightest sign of having sympathized or fraternized with or profited from ethnic Germans, Slovaks – who were not in the position of being able to blame Fascism on a rival ethnic group – proved much more reluctant to convict war criminals and collaborators, although equally quick to take advantage of the opportunity to rid their own territory of ethnic Germans and Hungarians. When, at the end of October 1945, the Allies handed over ex-president Jozef Tiso and his government, whom they had captured in Austria, to the Czechoslovak authorities, the Prague government apparently expected the Slovak population to rejoice and be grateful. Instead, even the chairman of the Democratic Party and head of the Slovak National Council, Josef Lettrich, showed suspicion at the sight of 'Tiso and his government' being brought 'back to Slovakia in chains' by 'the State Security organs which were under the orders of a Communist Minister of the Interior'. This, he later remembered, was 'the first thing' in postwar Czechoslovakia to cause 'much bad feeling' among the Slovak population.[52] An underground leaflet campaign was immediately launched in defence of the Tiso regime, together with 'Cross Action', through which sympathy for Tiso was expressed by wearing a crucifix pin on one's coat lapel.[53] The Slovak people's courts, which by 31 December 1947 had tried 20,561 defendants, convicted only 8,059 (as compared with about 168,000 tried, and 69,000 convicted, in the equivalent Czech courts).[54] Slovaks proved at the very least ambivalent about being expected by the Czechs – widely considered in Slovakia not only to be a separate, but also an aggressively domineering, rival nation – to regard Slovak Fascists and anti-Semites, but who were also Slovak patriots and observant Catholics, as simple criminals.

On 2 August 1945, in concert with similar legislation across Central Europe (but following a precedent set by the Prague government in August 1939, when it had wanted to deprive Jews and German refugees of their Czecho-Slovak citizenship), several million ethnic Germans and Hungarians had their Czechoslovak citizenship revoked through a special constitutional law decreed by President Beneš.[55] This marked the beginning of the official expulsions, known collectively in Czech as the 'Removal' or 'Transfer' (*odsun*), which the Prague government justified as being in accordance with the principle of mass transfers of population agreed at the Potsdam Conference on 3 August 1945 (somewhat disingenuously, since it had done everything possible to influence the Potsdam decision).[56]

According to the letter of the law, 'reliable comrades and anti-Fascists' – in practice a euphemism for Communists – were supposed to be spared, in line with the government's insistence that the German and Hungarian populations were not being expelled as detested ethnic groups, but rather as Fascists, traitors and war criminals. Since it was Slovaks, not Hungarians, who had established the anti-Czech, anti-Communist and anti-Semitic Tiso regime in Slovakia, this logic was specious, to say the least. As it happens, unpublished correspondence between President Beneš and Minister of the Interior Nosek held in a Prague archive reveals that even the tiny minority of ethnic Germans who met the stringent 'anti-Fascist' criteria were also deported to Germany, the only difference in their treatment being that the 88,614 'anti-Fascist Germans' that the Ministry of the Interior recorded as having been expelled by 29 October 1946 were allowed to keep their property and were transported separately from the rest.[57]

According to detailed guidelines put forward by the Ministry of the Interior, which was responsible for the 'selection' and 'assembly' of German-speakers into concentration camps, their forcible expulsion – by train, motor vehicle or on foot – was considered so 'politically important' as to take precedence over any economic considerations.[58] Registers of those to be transported were prepared by district National Committees, which were also responsible for appointing the armed *SNB* (State Security) or army guards to head transports and 'confiscate' valuables, together with any 'anti-state' or 'anti-Czech' materials, during luggage and body searches.[59] Germans awaiting deportation were permitted to take up to 30 kg (about 66lbs) of personal luggage, including food, and up to 1,000 Deutschmarks [*sic*] per family, but no cameras, valuable watches or Czechoslovak currency. They were required to bring their own blanket, cutlery and bowl with them to the concentration camps, to leave their vacated homes tidy and securely locked, and to pack all forbidden articles in parcels, each to be accompanied by a detailed list of contents.[60]

Reporting for the *Daily Mail* in August 1945, Rhona Churchill described the first wave of expulsions from Brno. When the *SNB* arrived:

> They marched through the streets calling on all German citizens to be standing outside their front doors at nine o'clock with one piece of hand luggage each ready to leave the town forever. Women had ten minutes in which to wake and dress their children, bundle a few possessions into their suitcases, and come out onto the pavement. . . . Then they were marched at gun-point towards the Austrian border.[61]

A characteristically complacent report, filed by the Czech police a year later, shows that the procedure remained unchanged and unquestioned. 'On 12 July 1946,' this particular report reads:

> 214 persons of German nationality were taken from Pardubice to the concentration camp at Ústí n[ad]. Orl[icí]. Organizational arrangements went smoothly, down to the last detail. More than 20 gold and silver objects (rings, earrings, watches, etc), some articles of clothing, 57 bank and savings books and cash to the value of 44,515.80 crowns were seized and retained after the documentation check.[62]

On 15 March 1946, the seventh anniversary of the establishment of the Protectorate of Bohemia and Moravia, Karl Hermann Frank, one of the few Sudeten Germans to have held a post of any importance in the Protectorate, went on trial in Prague.[63] Since Frank, a vicious anti-Czech, shared direct responsibility for some of the worst atrocities to have taken place in the Protectorate – including the repression of Czech students in the autumn of 1939 and the terror (including the destruction of Lidice) that followed the assassination of *Reichsprotektor* Heydrich – his widely publicized trial was immensely popular from the first. It ended on 22 May 1946 with the spectacle of his public hanging, in front of thousands of spectators, in the courtyard of Pankrác prison. The trial – which was broadcast on state radio and improperly preceded by the publication of incriminating testimony taken from his interrogations – was treated in both parliament and the Czech press as the trial, not merely of a single war criminal, but rather of what Benjamin Frommer has termed the 'collective criminality of the German minority in Czechoslovakia' in order to prove 'the collective guilt of an entire nation'.[64]

The notion that Bohemian, Moravian and Silesian German-speakers, the Czech-speakers' traditional rivals in the Bohemian Crown Lands, were collectively guilty and inherently criminal helps to explain the inhumanity with which German-speakers (many of whom, ironically enough, could just as easily have opted to register as Czechs) were treated. Some Germans were deported immediately, others were rounded up, their citizenship removed, property confiscated and homes sealed, only to be left indefinitely in labour or concentration camps: those classified as 'political prisoners' could end up being kept for years or even decades. Vojna prison camp near Příbram, originally built in 1947 to hold German prisoners, was by 1949 the largest forced-labour camp for political prisoners in all Czechoslovakia. Surrounded by watchtowers, barbed wire and minefields, its resemblance to an SS concentration camp was made explicit by the temporary placement, at its main gate, of a placard that read 'Work Makes You Free', this time in Czech rather than German.[65]

On 15 November 1946, Czechoslovak Minister of the Interior Nosek presented President Beneš with a special illuminated parchment to mark and celebrate their joint achievement: the 'victorious completion' of the Czechs' 'ancient struggle for national and political rights' and the 'culmination' of the 'liberation' of the Czechs and Slovaks which had 'begun' on 28 October 1918 but been 'consolidated' by the 'May 1945 revolution' in the shape of the complete elimination of Germans from the Bohemian Crown Lands. The certificate showed the Ministry of the Interior's sensitivity to Beneš's particular weaknesses by taking the trouble to proclaim the 'transfer' of the Germans to have been undertaken 'legally' and with the explicit 'approval of the three Great Powers'. It also made clear the scale of the *SNB/StB*'s technical achievement, boasting with characteristically bureaucratic indifference to human misery that 2,170,598 Germans had – between 24 January and 29 October 1946 – been removed permanently by means of 1,646 trains, 67,748 railway carriages, 4 hospital trains, 960 automobiles and 12 boats. A further 249,911 Germans, the document proclaimed, still remained on Czechoslovak soil; but only temporarily, since they had yet to be 'transferred' for either 'economic' or 'humanitarian' reasons.[66] (This turns out in practice to have meant that, as had been the case with the 9,000 or so Czechs who were not immediately expelled from autonomous/independent Slovakia in 1938–39, they had specialist skills that the state still required; or else, as had been the case with Jews and Gypsies temporarily left in the Slovak camps under Tiso, that their slave labour, such as at the uranium mines at Jáchymov, was still required.)

The Western powers, albeit with varying degrees of enthusiasm, had proved willing to go along with the principle of collective guilt in the case of 'the Germans' (even if this meant Germans who had never set foot in the Reich) since 'the Germans' were also hated at home. They were not willing to consent so easily to the wholesale transfer of Hungarian-speakers, who were not associated in the public mind with any particular atrocities and seemed to have been rather less 'collaborationist' than the majority of Czechs and Slovaks. The National Front's determination to rid Slovakia of its ethnic Hungarians (Magyars) had therefore to be handled differently. Instead of a straight expulsion – and in line with the same logic that had prevailed in Slovakia under the Tiso regime – 73,000 Slovaks were moved from Hungary to Slovakia in exchange for 74,000 Magyars, who were moved from Slovakia to Hungary. A further 44,000 ethnic Hungarians were forcibly resettled in the border regions of Bohemia and Moravia that had been vacated by expelled Germans; additional arrangements were made to 'repatriate' ethnic Slovaks living in Yugoslavia, Romania and Bulgaria.[67] The rest were to be dealt with by a special 'Re-Slovakization Commission' (*Reslovakizačná komisia*) established in Bratislava. A series of strong measures, it informed the central government in Prague – including the removal of Hungarian-speakers from a whole range of jobs and the confiscation of their property – would need to be taken in order adequately to 're-Slovakize' southern Slovakia, which, as a consequence of the Vienna Arbitration Award, had been in Hungary for the past six years. The Commission stressed the vital importance of what it called the 'absolute purification' of municipal and district National Committees, tax offices, financial offices, post offices, courts and the police, together with banks and insurance companies.[68] In addition to those Hungarian-speakers who lost their jobs, property or liberty in the supposed interests of 'state security', Slovak historian Elena Mannová reports that a further 326,697 Hungarian-speakers were 're-Slovakized' (in other words, prevented from being allowed to work or vote until they agreed to declare themselves 'Slovak' rather than 'Hungarian').[69] Eugen Steiner, a Jewish member of the Slovak Communist Party, was struck by how insistent the Slovak minister of foreign affairs, Vladimír Clementis – although supposed in theory to be free, as a Communist internationalist, of national chauvinism – was 'on the Hungarian issue' and how 'vehemently' he fought 'for the annexation of three Hungarian villages on the right bank of the Danube',[70] which led to the 're-Slovakization' even of 'purely Hungarian' towns and villages. These were then given provocatively Slovak nationalist names, so that Párkány, for example, became 'Štúrovo' and Gyalla was renamed 'Hurbanovo'.[71] Steiner also noticed how Gustáv Husák, the leader of the Slovak Communist Party (KSS), deliberately avoided following the Czechoslovak Communist Party's example of appointing Jews to high posts on the grounds that to do so would make the Slovak branch of the party 'appear to be Jew-ridden' and therefore 'an easy target for hostile allegations, such as those which had been made earlier by Hlinka Party propaganda'.[72]

Fifty years before the term 'ethnic cleansing' was coined, semi-democratic Czechoslovakia – through a combination of border changes, legal discrimination, imprisonment, forced transfers, exterminations and expulsions – had rid itself of so many ethnic minorities that its claim to be a 'national' state of the Czechs and the Slovaks became plausible for the first time since its creation in 1918–20. In the border regions, from which some 2.5 million Sudeten Germans had been forced out, without compensation, approximately 1,460,000 persons deemed to be ethnically suitable Slavs were moved in to claim their property, houses, farms and fields.[73] German schools, shops, hotels, sawmills, glass factories, businesses and farms could be made over to look Czech relatively easily; not so the region's characteristically German cottages, churches and graveyards – battered and faded perhaps, but still with their German plaques, inscriptions and headstones, which gave the area an eerily abandoned and empty feeling.[74]

In 1921, the proportion of 'Czechoslovaks' (a category that, as discussed in Chapter 3, had then included not only Czechs and Slovaks but also a fair number of Jews and Rusyns/Ukrainians) had officially been put at around 64 per cent; by 1950, the figure for Czechs and Slovaks alone had risen to an astounding 94 per cent.[75] For the first time in their history, Bohemia, Moravia and Austrian Silesia – the historic Lands of the Bohemian Crown – because they were left with only a tiny minority of ethnic Germans and Poles, could claim with accuracy to be overwhelmingly 'Czech' lands. Only in Slovakia, where most Gypsies (Roma and others) had survived the war and there were still compact communities of Rusyn/Ukrainian-speakers in the Prešov region and semi-Slovakized Magyars along the border with Hungary, were there any significant minority populations left. Even so, all ethnic minorities – Poles, Hungarians, Romanians and a remnant of Germans – were thereafter kept under routine surveillance by the *StB*, whose regional officers were expected to report to Prague, every month, on their activities, political outlook and the state of their morale.

Changing the ethnic composition of the state was not only about satisfying Czech and Slovak nationalist sentiment, although this is the aspect of the postwar reorganization that has traditionally tended to be ignored or downplayed. It was also supposed to prevent the kind of destabilization that had led to Munich and associated disasters and to ensure the continued political dominance of the Left. Just as postwar Czechoslovakia's close alliance with the Soviet Union was deemed necessary to prevent a recurrence of German aggression, so the removal of its ethnic Germans, Hungarians and Rusyns/ Ukrainians was supposed to make it impossible for the state's minorities ever again to be used as fifth columnists by hostile foreign powers. But there was an elephant in the room. The problem that – together with the Sudeten German problem – had led most directly to the collapse of the first Czechoslovak state, the ethnic problem that no one wanted to mention, was the Slovak problem.

The Czechoslovak Communist Party had originally calculated that the postwar swing to the political Left would be sharpest in Slovakia, where there had been a genuinely widespread and popular uprising against the Tiso regime in 1944, and where most peasants – now that the Agrarian and Slovak People's parties had been outlawed, and there was confiscated land to redistribute – might be expected to vote Communist. It was with this assumption in mind that the Communist Party appeared initially to show such concern for Slovak – as well as Czech – national feeling, insisting upon the inclusion of the Slovak National Council in the National Front government and the maintenance of a separate Slovak Communist Party (one largely created by the forced merger in 1944 with the Slovak Social Democratic Party), and resulting in the stress it put on the so-called 'Magna Carta of the Slovak Nation', with its commitment to re-establish Czech–Slovak relations on the basis of sincere 'brotherhood' and genuine 'equality'.

It soon became apparent that the Slovak peasant and Catholic vote was not, as anticipated, being transferred to the Slovak Communist Party, but rather to the conglomeration of centre-right parties known as the Democratic Party. The other parties in the National Front sought to weaken the Democratic Party's support by exploiting its internal tensions and inconsistencies, while simultaneously taking advantage of the anti-German and anti-Hungarian decrees to expel as many Catholic clergy and religious as possible. As Karel Kaplan has found, the Slovak Communist leadership even tried to set up a rival, nominally Christian Democratic (Catholic) Party; but after it presented the Catholic clergy with a political programme which was a mere copy of the Communists' own, the Catholic side withdrew.[76] For its own part, the Czech Social Democratic Party attempted to revive its old Slovak branch by setting up a third Slovak political party, the Party of Labour. In the weeks leading up to the general elections set for May 1946, a block of conservatives within the Democratic Party formed a breakaway party, originally called the Christian Republican Party, but then renamed – because of objections by the National Front government to its confessional and conservative overtones – the Freedom Party.[77] This left Slovakia with four political parties.

In April 1946, just before the state-wide elections, the leadership of the Democratic Party struck a deal with the right wing of the Freedom Party, taking them into its own membership in exchange for a promise of a fixed ratio of Catholics to non-Catholics to hold office in institutions controlled by the Democratic Party, guaranteed state funding for Church schools, and other issues close to the heart of the old Slovak People's Party. The Democratic Party apparently also promised either to prevent Jozef Tiso from being put on trial, or else to ensure that, like some of the Czech Protectorate authorities, he would be given a relatively light sentence.[78] Having failed either to split or to discredit the Democratic Party in Slovakia, the *KSS* and *KSČ* were unexpectedly left to face state-wide elections without an alternative strategy for Slovakia.[79]

Czechoslovakia's first postwar general elections were held on 26 May 1946. The Soviet Union, which had announced that it would be moving troops across the country on 22 May, responded to protests that this might prejudice the election results and – with nothing much to lose, since all important aspects of its relationship with the Czechoslovak People's Democratic Republic had been decided with Beneš during the war – tactfully agreed to wait. This seemed to give weight to Stalin's assurances that the Soviet Union had no intention of interfering in Czechoslovakia's internal affairs and to President Beneš's assertions that his country's 'new and transformed democracy' would be able to live 'side by side' with 'the Soviet Socialist system' until Czechoslovakia could be turned gradually into a socialist utopia by an 'evolutionary path, empirically and by scientific economic planning, without catastrophes and without violence, by agreement and co-operation'.[80]

The 1946 elections were genuinely free, but they can scarcely be called 'democratic', given that the two most popular prewar parties, the Czech branch of the Agrarian Party and the Slovak branch of the People's Party, were not allowed to stand and that millions of the state's former citizens – Germans, Hungarians and all others classified by the *StB* as 'traitors' and 'collaborators' – were barred from voting. On the strength of a platform that included demands for a new constitution, the launch of a two-year economic plan, a further stage of land reform and new agricultural and commercial taxes,[81] the Communists, with almost 38 per cent, won by far the largest share of the state-wide vote. The second most popular party, the National Socialists, took 18.29 per cent, the Czechoslovak People's Party 15.64 per cent, the Democrats 14.07 per cent and the Social Democrats 12.05 per cent (the votes for the Slovak Labour Party and Freedom Party were negligible).[82] Klement Gottwald, as chairman of the Czechoslovak Communist Party, the single largest party, replaced the Social Democrat Fierlinger as prime minister, receiving ovations so enthusiastic that Harry Pollitt, head of the British Communist Party, claimed never to have heard the like 'except the ovations given to Comrade Stalin in the Soviet Union'.[83]

The government interpreted the swing to the Communist Party as indicating broad support for its nationalization programme as set out at Košice, together with its 'solution' to the minorities 'problem' of expelling unwanted ethnic groups and redistributing their wealth among Czechs and Slovaks. The Communists could see that the strategy of being even more Czech nationalist than the traditionally Czech nationalist parties was working like a dream in Prague, and generally throughout Bohemia. Overall, the state-wide election results were so astonishingly good that the Communist Party decided to make 51 per cent of the vote its goal for the next elections, which were scheduled for May 1948.[84] This campaign was launched by Gottwald with the slogan 'For a majority of the nation' and repeated assurances that the Czechoslovak Communist Party would not import the Soviet system, but follow its 'own road to socialism', one that would work with the other political parties to bring about a genuinely new republic, one that would be 'truly democratic, truly national, truly ours'.

But although the *KSČ* had proved overwhelmingly popular in Bohemia, suggesting that its policies had succeeded in wooing voters who might, in the old days, have supported the Agrarians, in Moravia the vote was more or less evenly split between the Communists and the Catholics, while in Slovakia it was the Democratic Party – not the Slovak Communist Party (*KSS*) – that emerged as the clear winner, taking 62 per cent of the vote to the Communists' 30 per cent, resulting in 63 seats in the Slovak National

Council for the Democratic Party, 31 for the Communist Party, and just 6 for the Labour and Freedom parties combined. This meant that Jozef Lettrich, chairman of the Democratic Party, became the chairman of the Slovak National Council, while the Communist Gustáv Husák became chairman of its executive body, the Board of Commissioners.[85] This regional disparity meant, as Steiner afterwards recalled:

> When the Slovak Communists wished to curb the power and influence of their stronger partner in the Slovak national organs, they had in practice to look to the central government in Prague for support and understanding. This was the case not only in important matters of economic and social policy, but even in matters which would ultimately represent an obstacle to the autonomy of Slovakia, even though it was for such autonomy that the Communists had earlier fought. In the end, the decision of the central government and Czechoslovak National Front in Prague to limit the powers of the Slovak National Council and the Board of Commissioners was accepted by the Slovak Communists.[86]

On 8 July 1946, the National Front government, now led by Prime Minister Gottwald, launched its first two-year economic plan. The Communist Party then turned its attention to solving the Slovak problem. The first step intended to bring Slovakia into line with the broadly socialist and anticlerical consensus in the National Front government was for the Communist Party to launch a smear campaign against the Democratic Party. As Jozef Lettrich remembered, Democrats were suddenly accused everywhere of 'anti-Soviet attitudes, of anti-Communist agitation, of having misused the influence of the Roman Catholic hierarchy for their own ends, and of having rehabilitated the former members of the Slovak People's Party'.[87] The climate of suspicion created by the Communist-led campaign made it easy to justify sharply curtailing Slovakia's administrative and governmental powers, which was done in the so-called Third Prague Agreement, which insisted that Slovak political and administrative institutions be subordinated to the relevant central governmental ministries and that legislation passed by Slovak representatives be approved by the central government in Prague.[88] Finally, at a joint meeting of the Presidiums of the *KSČ* and *KSS*, it was decided that there should be a severe verdict in the forthcoming trial of Jozef Tiso, together with another two members of the former Slovak National Unity, since – as Viliam Široký, a rising star in the Slovak Communist Party, put it – the trial would serve to 'liquidate the whole reactionary Slovak past'.[89]

The growing confrontation between the *KSS* and the Democratic Party in Slovakia, overlapping awkwardly with increasing tension between Slovak autonomists and Prague centralists, turned the Tiso trial into the catalyst for a dramatic resurgence of mutual Czech–Slovak mistrust. Even Lettrich, the chairman of the Democratic Party, although the Tiso regime had sent him to a concentration camp, appealed to Minister of Justice Drtina not to allow the former president to be condemned to death, while the Vatican requested that Tiso, as a Catholic priest, be kept in a monastery rather than a prison and that, in the interests of the peace, his trial not be held in public. In January 1946, a group of Slovak bishops sent a letter to President Beneš claiming that Tiso had sought 'the lesser evil' and begging that his case not be handled 'with ruthless harshness'.[90] On the occasion of a Czech–Slovak football match held in Bratislava less than a week after the May elections, the crowd sang the independent Slovak republic's national anthem, called for Tiso's release and shouted anti-state and anti-Czech slogans until they were restrained by units of the *SNB*.[91]

The Communists retaliated by organizing demonstrations against Tiso, inundating the president, Czechoslovak government and Slovak National Council with thousands of telegrams and resolutions, and sending deputations of partisans, former political prisoners, participants in the 1944 Uprising and workers to the chairman of the Slovak National Council, Lettrich, 'in order to exert the maximum pressure upon him against procuring clemency for Tiso'.[92] Right up to February 1948, as Steiner later recalled in wonderment, the leadership of the Slovak Communist Party 'did not directly oppose the limitation of Slovak autonomous rights even those guaranteed in the Košice Programme, and the increased influence of the central bodies in Prague' because it seemed more important to them to ensure the confiscation of German, Hungarian and collaborators' property and 'stricter punishment of leaders of the former Slovak State'.[93]

The Tiso trial lasted from 2 December 1946 until 19 March 1947 (which happened to coincide with his name day), when there were demonstrations all over Slovakia, dominated by women demanding his release and singing a mixture of Catholic hymns and patriotic Slovak songs.[94] After deliberating for a month, on 15 April 1947 the National Court sentenced Tiso to death, whereupon both it and President Beneš were besieged with telegrams and petitions either to insist that the verdict be carried out or else to appeal to the president to exercise his right to grant clemency. Despite the firm expectation throughout Slovakia that his sentence would be commuted to a long term in prison, Tiso was hanged almost immediately, on 18 April. As if to underline what looked suspiciously like a double standard in the treatment of Czech and Slovak war criminals, the trial of Rudolf Beran, the former leader of Czech National Unity and the Protectorate government, which took place in Prague at the same time as the Tiso trial in Bratislava, ended in a twenty-year jail sentence rather than an execution. Tellingly, among the crimes of which Tiso was convicted was that of dividing the republic. As Brad Abrams has pointed out, even under the heading of Tiso's 'crimes against humanity', maltreatment of ethnic Czechs was given precedence over the deportation of Slovak Jews.[95] This political trial was as much about the Slovaks' 'betrayal' of the Czechs as about the crimes committed by a thoroughly repellent Slovak dictatorship against its own citizens.

The next stage in the attempt to bring Slovakia into line came directly from the Communist Party, working in tandem with the security services, and especially the increasingly influential and well-organized *StB*. In May 1947, the Communist Party instructed the minister of the interior to draw up a list of all former members of the Slovak People's Party who were in influential positions, and to push for their retirement. This was followed, in June, with the presentation of a report to the National Front government, written by high-ranking officers in the *StB*, the aim of which was to persuade the central government that the security situation in Slovakia was becoming critical and the need to purge former members of the Slovak People's Party urgent. At a rally held at Devín on 6 July 1947, Prime Minister Gottwald accused the Democrats of being reactionaries and of aiding and abetting anti-state elements; the same accusations were immediately repeated by Antonín Zápotocký on his own tour of Slovakia.[96]

On 14 September 1947, the Slovak minister of the interior announced that an 'anti-state conspiracy', directed from abroad by Sidor and Ďurčanský, had been 'discovered': it was claimed that some fifty officials of the Democratic Party – including its general secretary, Fedor Hodža, the commissioner for finance, Matej Josko, and Ján Ursíny, the deputy prime minister of the National Front government – were in secret contact with Slovak émigré communities and plotting to renew an independent Slovak state and assassinate President Beneš.[97] After about seven hundred people had been arrested in connection with the 'conspiracy', the widespread atmosphere of paranoia and suspicion provided an excuse for the Slovak Congress of Trade Unions and Employees Councils, convened in Bratislava on 30 October at the request of the Communists, to call on the Board of Commissioners to resign and be replaced with men who 'enjoy the confidence of the Slovak people' and who would ensure that Slovakia would be ruled 'in the spirit of the Slovak National Uprising' and 'the reconstruction programme of the Gottwald government'.[98] Although a majority on the Board of Commissioners, who were from the Slovak Democratic Party, knew better than to do it, six members, led by their Slovak Communist chairman Gustáv Husák, did indeed resign. After protests from the Communist Party and the intervention of the Communist prime minister, Gottwald, on 20 November 1947 Slovakia's Board of Commissioners was reconfigured in such a way as to ensure that – despite the Democratic Party's clear majority in the 1946 elections – no single party had a majority.[99] Although Deputy Prime Minister Ursíny resigned in protest, the results of this Communist coup in Slovakia went unchallenged.

As members of the non-Communist parties became increasingly critical – in cabinet, the National Assembly and the non-Communist press – of the irregularity of the methods used by the Communists, and especially of their steady infiltration into all branches of state security, more and more revelations about brutal police interrogations, improper procedures, mass intimidation campaigns and other 'Gestapo methods' were brought to light. These were immediately countered by almost hysterical-sounding resolutions, speeches, telegrams and articles from the Communists about reactionary plotters in the 'anti-state' democratic parties. In his New Year's speech on 1 January 1948, Prime Minister Gottwald assured the Czech and Slovak nations that 'the National Front, resolutely following the government program and the will of the people', would rid itself 'of the reactionary elements which are working against the program of the government, against the people, and in the interests of subversion'.[100]

From September 1947, when the purge began in Slovakia, there was a rapidly escalating sense of a Communist offensive in the Czech lands as well, as the Communist-controlled Ministry of the Interior appeared to uncover 'plots' and 'conspiracies' with increasing frequency and to resort to 'mobilizing the masses' through organized strikes, petitions, demonstrations and telegram campaigns every time one of its demands or proposals was blocked by members of the other parties in the National Front. And there were other worrying signs. Parcel bombs were sent to Petr Zenkl, Jan Masaryk and Prokop Drtina. The Czechoslovak government, having voted to accept Marshall Aid, immediately withdrew its request after it was made clear that the Soviet Union considered taking American money to be an unfriendly act. As the atmosphere of mutual hostility and suspicion afterwards known as the Cold War began to make itself felt in earnest, Communist parties all over Central and Eastern Europe were growing less tolerant of national deviations, less willing to countenance the idea that there might be a variety of different 'roads' to socialism.

From the moment they had returned to Czechoslovak soil in the spring of 1945, ministers in the National Front government had worked together – Communist and non-Communist alike – to incite mob vengeance, establish people's courts, abolish the right of appeal and carry out summary executions, often based on retrospectively defined crimes and usually with a clear presumption of guilt. They had solicited denunciations, criminalized inter-ethnic mixing, and countenanced legal discrimination against German- and Hungarian-speakers: at first, they had even turned a blind eye to mob lynchings and police torture. Millions of their fellow citizens, including children, had been deliberately degraded, imprisoned and forcibly expelled. Only now, too late, did the non-Communist ministers appear to begin to understand that, unless they put a stop to the Communists' willingness to move seamlessly from national cleansing and postwar retribution to purging the politically impure and rooting out the 'class enemy', the next victims would be themselves.

On 13 February 1948, cabinet members from the National Socialist, Democratic and Czechoslovak People's parties finally sought to put a stop to further Communist infiltration of the *SNB* by asking Václav Nosek, the Communist minister of the interior, to explain the suspension of eight non-Communist police commissioners and their proposed replacement with eight Communist Party members. Instead of replying, Nosek pleaded illness and excused himself from the relevant cabinet meeting. On 17 February, the dissenting ministers announced that they would refuse to take part in further cabinet meetings until the non-Communist police were returned to their posts. The Communist Party immediately proclaimed a state of emergency for all its members, and began organizing a People's Militia.[101] The next day, National Socialists Petr Zenkl and Hubert Ripka met with Beneš, whom they – like many others – appear to have assumed would not give in to Communist pressure but would staunchly defend the 'democratic' state that he had helped to establish.[102]

On 20 February 1948, twelve ministers from the non-Communist (National Socialist, Slovak Democratic and Catholic Populist) parties forced a showdown by sensationally announcing their resignations from the cabinet. The apparent intention was to cause the government to fall, so forcing fresh elections which would reveal to all the world that the Communists had lost popular support since 1946 and so enable their influence to be curtailed. According to the constitution, half of the cabinet's twenty-six ministers would have to resign in order to bring down the cabinet. Since the Social Democrats and unaffiliated ministers – foreign minister Jan Masaryk and minister of defence Ludvík Svoboda – did not resign, the anti-Communist lobby found itself one minister short, with the Communist bloc in a majority of one. All attention now turned to Beneš, who as president could choose either to refuse or to accept the twelve resignations. As at the time of the Munich Crisis ten years earlier, Beneš, who bore a good deal of personal responsibility for this new crisis, stalled for time, unsure how to react.

While Beneš hesitated, Gustáv Husák, the Slovak Communist chair of the Board of Commissioners in Bratislava, acted. On 21 February, he dismissed the non-Communist ministers in the Slovak government on the grounds that, since their colleagues in Prague had resigned, they no longer had a mandate to govern. Husák then reconfigured membership so that ten out of fourteen seats were held either by the Communist Party, with just a token two seats left for the Democratic Party and one apiece for the Freedom Party and the Social Democrats.[103] This caused the collapse of the Democratic Party in Slovakia and gave the two socialist parties an overall majority in the Czechoslovak state. Meanwhile, the Czechoslovak Communist Party rallied its supporters with appeals on state radio for mass demonstrations to condemn the actions of the twelve ministers, described as reactionaries who wanted to block 'progress' and the fulfilment of the socialist promises set out in the National Front government's political programme. In addition, Gottwald appealed for 'Action Committees' to form themselves and remove 'reactionary and subversive elements' from public life. In all, the Action Committees are said to have dismissed about twenty-eight thousand state and public employees and expelled some seven thousand university students statewide.[104]

On 21 February, there was an overwhelming response to the Communist Party's appeals: gatherings and demonstrations took place throughout the country, crowned by a huge rally in Prague's Old Town Square, where Prime Minister Gottwald warned a receptive crowd that an 'anti-populist, anti-democratic, anti-socialist bloc' was threatening to push Czechoslovakia towards 'a new Munich'. At the Castle, meanwhile, Beneš was inundated with telegrams and petitions from delegations of factory workers insisting that he accept the ministerial resignations. The Communist Party continued to make use of the state airwaves to call for workers in every village, city and workplace throughout the country to form themselves into Action Committees to keep up the pressure.[105] On 22 February, out of eight thousand trade-union delegates assembled in Prague at the request of old-time Czechoslovak Communist Antonín Zápotocký, only ten were said to have withheld their support from the Communists.[106] Meanwhile, a self-styled People's Militia, consisting of around fifteen thousand men, some of whom were even armed, also took to the streets in protest. With the population seemingly split roughly 50:50 for and against the Communist Party, Beneš – even if he had wanted to – could not have risked calling on either the police – some forty thousand-strong, but thoroughly infiltrated by Communists and responsible to a Communist minister of the interior – or the army, made up of about 140,000 troops, and responsible to the same minister of defence, Ludvík Svoboda, who had failed to support the non-Communist ministers in cabinet.

The *coup de grâce* came on 24 February, when over two million citizens, roughly one-sixth of the entire country's population, took part in a general strike organized by the Communist Party and the trade unions to demonstrate support for the Communist prime minister. In the face of such a massive and well-organized show of popular feeling in favour of the Communist Party, President Beneš bowed to the pressure. On 25 February 1948, in the speech that was to become the prime symbol of the 'bloodless coup' afterwards referred to by the Communist regime as 'Victorious February' (*Vítězný únor*), Prime Minister Gottwald announced that he had 'just returned from the Castle', where the president had accepted the twelve ministers' resignations and approved the Communist-majority government. This was the moment frozen in a photograph that was afterwards painted, reproduced on posters, shown in museum displays and schoolbooks, and even featured on a postage stamp, which was taken to represent the very moment of the Communist victory over 'reactionary' and 'bourgeois' elements. Never mind that Czechoslovakia had already been a People's Republic for three years; that one of Gottwald's closest comrades would soon have to be airbrushed out of the photograph; that Gottwald was obviously and audibly drunk; or that the photograph had actually been taken during a speech that had been given a few days earlier, and at a different location.[107] Political truth was already more important than the literal truth.

On 26 February 1948, the day after the Communists' victory in cabinet, the lead story in all the newspapers was the composition of the new Gottwald government. The very next story to appear on the front page of *Rudé právo*, the Czech Communist Party daily, was the beginning of proceedings against Zenkl, under the ominous headline 'The People Clean the Republic of Saboteurs, Traitors and Unreliable Elements'.[108] Jozef Lettrich resigned as chairman of the Slovak National Council and went into exile; his place was taken by the Slovak Communist Karol Šmidke. Eleven out of the fifteen people on the Board of Commissioners were now members of the Communist Party.[109]

President Beneš swore in the new ministers in Gottwald's National Front government on 27 February 1948, bolstering Communist claims that their rise to power had been perfectly legal. Of the twenty-three ministers in the National Front government, eleven were now Communist Party members and an additional four were Social Democrats who could be relied upon to support the Communist line. Two further ministers – Jan Masaryk and Ludvík Svoboda – although without party affiliation, had done nothing to prevent the anti-Communist ministers from being ousted. Just six ministers – too few to block any new government measures – were from the other political parties in the National Front: the Czechoslovak People's Party and National Socialist Party for the Czechs and the Democratic Party and Freedom Party for the Slovaks. Although the outward form of the political system had not changed, a single Communist Party made up of two branches – the Czechoslovak Communist Party or *KSČ*, and the Slovak Communist Party or *KSS* – could now be sure that, providing it maintained internal discipline, whatever legislation it liked would be passed by the cabinet and rubber-stamped by the National Assembly. This was the logic of the prewar 'National Unity' and the postwar 'National Front' taken to its ultimate conclusion.

Czechoslovaks abroad, unsure what was going on at home, had to decide which way to jump. One of the many Czechoslovak diplomats to choose to stay abroad was General Jan Ingr, who eventually joined Moravec's exile counter-intelligence group in the United States. At the Czechoslovak Embassy in London, Rosemary Kavan, the English wife of the Communist press secretary Pavel Kavan, remembered how eight non-Communist diplomats asked for asylum while 'the rest of us threw a party and sang old revolutionary favourites and new militant songs with inspiring words like "Now we've got what we wanted!" and "Hey rup! Roll up your sleeves and get down to work!" '[110] At home, where political opinion was similarly split down the middle, it was already felt to be dangerous to criticize the Communist Party or to speculate aloud about the legitimacy of 'Victorious February'. Some people left the country altogether, going on 'holidays' from which they were never to return or braved illegal border crossings to seek political asylum in Austria or Germany. Others, unable or unwilling to leave their homeland, began to complain that they had been liberated from one form of tyranny only to be cast into another, a refrain that began to be taken up by Western anti-Soviet propaganda abroad.

On 10 March 1948, just two weeks after the cabinet coup, foreign minister Jan Masaryk, son of the President-Liberator, was found dead on the pavement below his residence in the Czernin Palace, the Foreign Ministry building. Rumours, which have persisted ever since, began to circulate that he had been pushed, either by Soviet or Czechoslovak agents; but – just like Beneš – Masaryk had shown no public sign of opposing the Communists and Pavel Kavan, the last person to have seen him alive, like others who knew about his history of depression, believed in the official verdict of suicide.[111] The case was to be reopened in 1968, 1993 and 2002.[112]

Like every other public occasion of the day, Jan Masaryk's funeral was seized upon as an opportunity to parade national unity, political consensus and cross-party solidarity within the Communist-dominated National Front government. A lavish state funeral was held, with tens of thousands of mourners following the slow progress of the coffin from the Czernin Palace to the Pantheon of the National Museum, and special memorial issues of popular magazines were brought out to commemorate the event.[113] Another crowd waited just outside the manicured grounds of the presidential summer residence in the village of Lány, where Masaryk was buried alongside his father, in a simple family plot. Principal mourners included not only the surviving members of the Masaryk and Beneš families, together with Prime Minister Gottwald and his wife, Marta, but also mayors dressed in their municipal robes, uniformed Legionnaires from the First World War, soldiers, police officers and a whole variety of Communist dignitaries. The new foreign minister, Slovak Communist Vladimír Clementis, was much photographed speaking at the Masaryk family grave; but for all the sentimental associations which were made with the pre-Munich First Republic, his appointment meant that yet another important cabinet post had gone to the Communist Party.

The end of the Third Czechoslovak Republic is usually presented as a second Czechoslovak tragedy to follow the first great tragedy of Munich. According to one version, the democratic, tolerant and humane traditions of the First Czechoslovak Republic – almost mystically embodied in the persons of Edvard Beneš, T.G. Masaryk's spiritual son, and Jan Masaryk, his actual one – were restored to the Czechoslovak 'nation' only to be destroyed by the wiles and ruthlessness of the Communists. A second classic view suggests that Czechoslovak Communism, which would naturally have taken a moderate, evolutionary and distinctively Czech or Czechoslovak path, was instead forced to conform to an inappropriate, crude and ruthlessly Soviet pattern. The ubiquity of these two views, which seem to underpin virtually all writings on the topic, helps to explain why so much effort has been expended – sometimes in the teeth of the evidence – to portray Beneš as committed to democracy during the February Crisis and to find evidence to suggest that Communist agents – ideally Soviet ones – were responsible for Jan Masaryk's death.[114] The obvious alternative, to blame the rise of Czechoslovak Communism on the nationalist chauvinism and political opportunism of some misguided Czech political leaders, is clearly less palatable. The Third Czechoslovak Republic, together with the illusion that the state could remain both socialist and democratic, a compromise between the parliamentary democracies of the West and the people's democracies of the East, was over after February 1948. So was the chance of keeping even a limited and partial democracy. These opportunities were not lost primarily because of outside interference, but rather because a majority of politically active Czechs and Slovaks wanted something more urgently than they wanted democracy: an ethnically homogeneous nation–state under the protection of the Soviet Union.

BUILDING THE SOCIALIST STATE

After 'Victorious February', the Czechoslovak and Slovak Communist parties found themselves in a position not just to accelerate the National Front's national and socialist revolution, but to lead the country onwards to a fully fledged 'dictatorship of the proletariat'. Just twelve years later (fifteen years after liberation), Czechoslovakia declared itself the first country after the Soviet Union to have 'achieved' socialism, and so to merit a new constitution (1960) and a new name: *Československá socialistická republika*, the 'Czechoslovak Socialist Republic'. The millions of Czechoslovak citizens who had cheered for Stalin, Beneš and Gottwald in 1945, voted for the Communists in 1946, or supported the Communist campaign to dominate the other parties of the National Front in 1947, did not immediately have reason to feel much tension between their instinctive patriotism as Czechs or Slovaks and the international implications of their chosen system of beliefs, practices and alliances. Nor, in the first flush of victory over the 'reactionary forces' in February 1948, were most 'progressives' aware that they, too, might one day fall victim to political persecution. This state of political innocence could not be expected to last forever.

The 1950s in Czechoslovakia is remembered as the quintessentially 'Stalinist' decade of political show trials, bombastic propaganda and economic restructuring during which Czechoslovakia was turned into a fully command economy and a hardline authoritarian one-party police state. These were the years in which virtually all of the Communist Party's domestic enemies – and a good number of its friends – were eliminated in the course of grand political purges and witch-hunts; in which farms were forcibly collectivized and regions clumsily industrialized; in which Socialist Realism pushed out alternative forms of artistic expression; in which even the Leninist principle of collective leadership was sacrificed to the Stalinist notion of 'democratic centralism' and the cult of a single great leader – in Czechoslovakia's case, Klement Gottwald (or simply 'K.G.' as he was known on countless *KSČ* banners and placards, busts, portraits and on the covers of coffee-table books). But although the methods used to enforce change in Czechoslovakia gave it – as they gave other Communist states across Central and Eastern Europe – a strong family resemblance to the Soviet Union, it is misleading to think of them as having been imposed from abroad.

It was Czech and Slovak Communists, not Russians or Soviets, who turned post-February Czechoslovakia into the Stalinist hell that it rapidly became, even if they frequently invoked the Soviet example and often sought Soviet advice on how best to do so. No one forced Czech and Slovak Communists to hold up for emulation the Soviet example in everything, from how to thresh wheat and write poetry to how to force peasants to collectivize or interrogate political prisoners. The initiative usually came from the Czechoslovak side: partly because the Soviet Union seemed to represent the future; partly because its support seemed vital to national security; and partly because it was a useful way of proving one's political credentials, winning the argument or getting ahead in one's career. Appeals in political meetings to the superiority of 'Soviet methods' – particularly by those who had no actual familiarity with the Soviet Union – helped to make one look like a sound comrade. They also papered over an underlying sense of unease that many Czech and Slovak Communists were only just beginning to feel: the tension between their ethnolinguistic nationalism and socialist internationalism.

The Czechoslovak Communist Party had come to power on the back of Czech and, to a lesser extent, Slovak nationalism. In order to stay there, and retain at least an outward appearance of legitimacy, it needed to co-opt, neutralize or eliminate all actual or potential vehicles for the expression of Czech or Slovak national feeling that might conceivably rival its own claims to be the single legitimate voice of the Czechoslovak 'nation'. To do so, it drew more naturally upon Czechoslovak/Habsburg precedent than on Soviet example; but after a certain point the distinction began to blur, authoritarian police states all having a certain sameness about them. In the immediate aftermath of February 1948, the party's first priority was to secure and extend its hold on power. Since general elections were looming at the end of May 1948, the *KSČ* – drawing on the technique that had been introduced by the Tiso regime in Slovakia – made provision for those who were not already excluded from voting to be presented at polling booths with two slips of paper: one giving the single slate of candidates drawn up by the National Front government (which the electorate was expected patriotically to endorse); and the second a blank sheet of paper (through which dissent, although futile, could formally be expressed).[1] It then sought to reinforce its credentials as the authentic voice of the Czech and Slovak nations by following the first wave of postwar nationalization with a second wave, rushing bills through parliament to nationalize radio stations, the construction industry, private flats, and all businesses that employed more than fifty people.[2] Rather than follow the Soviet example of criminalizing small-time peasants, an important source of party support, it set the limit for private land ownership at the reassuring figure of 50 hectares (124 acres), the same cut-off point that the Czech Agrarian movement of the late nineteenth century had judged to correspond to the yeoman class that embodied 'the core of Czech rural values'.[3]

On 9 May 1948, the third anniversary of the official liberation of Prague, the National Assembly passed the new constitution that the Communists had promised in 1946. Rather than reproduce Stalin's 1936 constitution (which still applied in the Soviet Union), Czechoslovakia's own constitution of 1920 was updated and amended to include the political, social and constitutional changes that had occurred since May 1945, and to make explicit that it was now officially 'the will' of the Czech and Slovak peoples to 'build up' the 'liberated state' into a 'people's democracy' to guarantee a 'peaceful path to socialism' and defend the 'national and democratic revolution' against 'reaction', whether domestic or foreign, 'just as we defended it in February 1948'.[4]

The Ninth of May Constitution defined Czechoslovakia, like other newly Communist states in the region, as a 'People's Democratic Republic' in which all power resided in 'the people'; but also, in line with the promises that had been given at Košice, as a 'unitary state of two equal Slavonic nations, the Czechs and the Slovaks'.[5] As in all previous Czechoslovak/Czecho-Slovak republics, the president, who was elected by the National Assembly for a seven-year term, remained head of state, and the government, defined as the highest legal and governing authority, was declared answerable to the National Assembly.[6] As had been promised in the 'Slovak Magna Carta' of 1945, the Slovak National Council (*Slovenská národná rada/Slovenská národní rada*) and Board of Commissioners (*Zbor povereníkov/sbor pověřenců*) were defined as the 'bearers of power' in Slovakia and 'equality between Czechs and Slovaks' was guaranteed 'in the spirit of a people's democracy'.[7] Finally, again in keeping with what had been agreed during the war and confirmed at Košice, the 'bearers of state power' at the local, district and regional levels were declared to be the National Committees (the same organizations that Karol Sidor had once suggested using to spread support for Hlinka's Slovak People's Party, but which were now used to empower the *KSČ*).[8] Just as the prewar Tiso regime had made it possible to express Slovak patriotism only through the extreme right-wing Slovak National Unity, the new postwar regime now ensured that it could be expressed only through the extreme left-wing Communist-dominated National Front. To underline the point, post-February Czechoslovakia's first big political show trial – of the general secretaries and deputies of the Slovak Democratic Party – was held in Bratislava, ending with the conviction, on 15 May 1948, of all the accused.

General elections went ahead, as scheduled, on 30 May 1948, amid a strong campaign run by the Communist Party to persuade voters not to use the privacy of the polling booth to return a blank form, but rather to vote 'openly' for the Communist-dominated list of approved National Front candidates. There was even a special election jingle, set to the tune of a well-known nursery rhyme, suggesting that only a traitor would choose to vote against the National Front.[9] Having chosen to go behind the screen to use the blank ballot, Eva Blochová remembered her terror when, upon leaving the polling station, she was asked to place her unused ballot in a bin. 'Now they would know how I voted!' she suddenly realized.[10] When the election results were announced, giving an astonishingly high 87.12 per cent of Czech and 84.91 per cent of Slovak votes to the single list of Communist-dominated National Front candidates (meaning that only 9 per cent of voters in the Czech lands and 14 per cent in Slovakia had used the blank return), it was clear to everyone that the campaign of intimidation – combined with appeals to patriotism and national unity – had worked.[11]

On 7 June 1948, for the second time in his career, an outmanoeuvred, depressed and ill Edvard Beneš resigned as president, leaving it to the prime minister and chairman of the KSČ, Klement Gottwald, to step temporarily into his place. It was thus Gottwald, rather than Beneš, who signed the new constitution into law on 9 June 1948; but this was a mere technicality. Five days later, Gottwald was unanimously elected president of Czechoslovakia, retaining his place as party chairman. Antonín Zápotocký (the chairman of the Central Council of Trade Unions who had been Gottwald's right-hand man during the February Events) took over as the country's second 'worker' (i.e. Communist) prime minister, while the impeccably Stalinist Rudolf Slánský remained in his post as secretary-general of the KSČ. The inauguration of the first Czechoslovak Communist president was held, as usual, in St Vitus Cathedral at Hradčany and celebrated with a *Te Deum* presided over by the bishop of Prague, Josef Beran. Although the Gottwalds, obviously unused to Church ceremony, looked ill at ease and had to be discreetly steered by the bishop and officiating priests, the very fact that they appeared in church seemed to signal that distinctively Czechoslovak traditions would be preserved and to indicate that non-Communists might not have too much to fear from the new dictatorship.

Once the requisite measures had been taken to ensure that the Communist Party's domination of the National Assembly, cabinet and presidency could not be challenged through either the constitution or the ballot box, the KSČ concentrated on removing its own most obvious sources of weakness: the inclusion of too many card-carrying members to ensure strict obedience to the leadership's directives; and the existence of a separate, Slovak branch which held the potential to challenge Prague's authority to speak on behalf of both nations in the state. From 15 July, the KSČ launched a policy of selective recruitment for new members, who were no longer to be welcomed automatically, but rather screened first for appropriate political views and class origins. Special short courses were set up by the party to fast-track workers without university education into influential positions in the law courts, the secret police, the army, industrial management and every other sphere in which the middle classes had formerly been dominant. Everyone could feel the sudden emphasis on the 'importance of cadre': in other words, the purging of those said to be insufficiently politically committed or socially suspect and their replacement with irreproachably 'loyal' and zealous Communists, preferably of working-class background.[12]

The next matter to be tidied up was the role of the Slovak Communist Party. The formal expulsion of Yugoslavia (28 June 1948) from the recently formed Information Bureau of the Communist parties (Cominform), the obvious successor to the Comintern, gave the *KSČ* leadership in Prague the perfect excuse to blame its ruthless internal reordering on what was vaguely termed the 'international situation'. When the *KSČ* Presidium of the Central Committee met at the end of June to discuss the Soviet–Yugoslav split, it did not point the finger at President Gottwald, although his slogan, as the leader of the Communist Party throughout the Third Republic, had echoed Tito's in promising that Czechoslovakia would follow its own 'road to socialism'. Instead, as Slovak Communist Eugen Steiner remembered incredulously, it 'almost expressly stated' that the analogy to the Yugoslav problem was rather to be found in Slovakia's tendency to want to go its own way.[13] On 26–27 July 1948, the *KSČ* Presidium announced that 'the working class and the toiling masses of Czechoslovakia' required 'one political leadership in the form of a united Communist Party'.[14] The *KSS* was explicitly asked to make it clear that it was 'subordinate' to the *KSČ* and that the role of its Central Committee was merely to 'carry out' the policy directives given to it by the *KSČ*. At the next plenum, held on 27 September 1948, the *KSS* duly defined itself as 'a territorial organization' of the Communist Party of Czechoslovakia 'in Slovakia'. Its subordinate position was then formally cemented at the Ninth Party Congress, held in 1949.[15]

Having neutralized the *KSS*, the *KSČ* turned its attention to its remaining rivals: institutions that could conceivably claim to speak for 'the nation' in its stead. These, if at all possible, were to be persuaded to join in the 'unity' shown by the 'National Front': in other words, to obey the *KSČ*. Organizations that agreed to do so would be fêted and included as part of the 'nation' and the 'working class'; those that refused to cooperate would be neutralized or destroyed. The *KSČ* increasingly relied upon the Ministry of the Interior to remain 'vigilant' to 'secure' the 'gains' of February 1948 by staying alert to the risks presented by any gathering, anniversary or memorial that might conceivably seek to 'reverse' its 'achievements' by upstaging its own claims to speak for 'the working people' and 'the nation'. *Sokol*, the patriotic gymnastic organization that had done so much to spread Czech nationalism in the nineteenth century, that had been actively supported and promoted as part of Czechoslovak identity by T.G. Masaryk, and that had once again proved its nationalist credentials during the war, was just such an organization; and the first postwar *Sokol* jamboree (*slet*), scheduled for 5–6 July 1948, offered just such an opportunity. To make matters even worse, the current head of the state-wide *Sokol* organization, Antonín Hřebík, who had been interned by the Nazis in Theresienstadt, Auschwitz and the Gestapo prison at Benešov, was a member of the Czech National Socialist Party, the only political party to which President Beneš had ever belonged and the one with the longest Czech nationalist and socialist pedigree. But although Hřebík is now remembered as having been a brave opponent of the Communist regime, his files in the Ministry of the Interior tell another story.

When Hřebík was first called in for questioning in March 1948, he was no stranger to the secret police. The *StB* already had a thick file of reports that had been sent in regularly since 1946 by his secretary, František Beneš, that covered everything from his circle of acquaintance and the state of his marriage to his private vanities and other foibles of character.[16] Despite the viciousness of these reports, which were obviously intended to damage him as much as possible in the eyes of the Communist authorities, Hřebík's secret-police interrogators found that he had in fact behaved 'absolutely loyally' during the February Events, having immediately ordered all branches of *Sokol* to form Action Committees to 'come to the defence of the National Front'. As far as the *StB* officers could judge, Hřebík appeared sincerely to believe that Sokolists and Communists held certain core values in common – such as 'masculinity, openness and loyalty to their ideals'.[17] Since it became obvious during his interrogation that Hřebík, far from being a dangerous opponent, was prepared to help the regime there was no need to downplay or cancel the first postwar *Sokol* jamboree; instead, a special commemorative postage stamp was issued to celebrate this symbol of Czech liberty and unity after what were euphemistically described as the years of 'unfreedom'.[18]

By mid-June 1948, the *StB* had gathered information – including members' names, addresses, employment and political profiles – on every *Sokol* group throughout the whole of the country. They also knew, from a careless conversation in a public tram, that some Sokolists were opposed to the Communist takeover and determined 'to show Prague' what 'it means to be a *Sokol*'.[19] Although plans had already been drawn up for *SNB* and *StB* officers to be stationed at every point along the route of the *Sokol* march, the Ministry of the Interior issued further directives that anyone who 'took advantage' of the *slet* to call out 'provocative' or 'anti-state' slogans – such as 'Long live Beneš' or 'Long live Beneš and Masaryk's republic' – should immediately be placed under arrest and taken away.[20] Although the *slet* went off quietly in Prague, the *StB* was nevertheless able to report that it had arrested 230 'anti-state agitators' and heard a total of fifty-five provocative chants, including 'Let the world hear! Beneš must come back' and 'Every *Sokol* knows that truth alone will prevail'.[21] This gave the government the excuse to request that *Sokol*, like every other sporting organization, be merged into a single, unified Czechoslovak Sports Union, a move that Hřebík apparently supported.

The reorganization bore political fruit at the 1952 Olympic Games (the first in which the Soviet Union consented to participate, walking away with twenty-two gold medals), when Czech long-distance runner Emil Zátopek won three gold medals for the People's Republic of Czechoslovakia. This enabled the Party once again to blend Czech patriotism with propaganda about the superiority of socialist man, and gave it an excuse to launch a special government crusade to 'raise the political and athletic level of all sportsmen and gymnasts in Czechoslovakia'.[22] Even the fact that Zátopek's wife, Dana (herself an outstanding sportswoman who had taken part in the 1952 Olympics), was the niece of the 'traitor' General Jan Ingr was not allowed to stand in the way of the couple being used to promote the image of sport as simultaneously Czech nationalist and internationally socialist.[23] The all-*Sokol slet* of 1948 was the last to be held under the Communists. But *Sokol* itself – thanks largely to the 'sensible' views expressed by Hřebík – was not banned as 'bourgeois' or 'reactionary'. Instead, it was officially remembered as a 'patriotic' organization that had 'voluntarily' dissolved itself into the unified Sports Union, helping to underline the notion that Czech nationalism and Czech socialism were one, and that both were best represented by the National Front as led by the Czechoslovak Communist Party. The regime therefore felt perfectly able to bring out an official commemorative album of the 1948 *slet*, with warm introductory texts by Edvard Beneš, Klement Gottwald and the late Jan Masaryk;[24] and to retain an honourable place in the Communist history books for Miroslav Tyrš, one of *Sokol*'s two founders, who even had a sports medal named after him. In case anyone had missed the point, a special postage stamp, first issued in 1953, was circulated to proclaim the message (in Czech): '*Sokol* belongs to the working people.'[25] Only after a decent interval of seven years was an obvious socialist substitute, the mass gymnastic extravaganza known as *Spartakiáda*, introduced to take the corporatist place that the *Sokol slet* had held in the First Czechoslovak Republic.

The next challenge for the regime came with the death, on 3 September 1948, of Edvard Beneš. Although Beneš, a socialist and Czech nationalist who was determined above all to rid the postwar state of its German population and to place it under Soviet protection, had proved pliable to Communist wishes since as early as 1943, in death his much longer and more intimate association with T.G. Masaryk, the founding father of the state, and with the steering of foreign and state policy during the First Czechoslovak Republic was uppermost in everyone's mind, making him an obvious figurehead around which anti-Communist dissent could rally. A seventeen-year-old living in Humpolec in Bohemia, upon hearing the news on the radio, confided to his diary his fear that Czechoslovak liberty had died with its founder, and that Communist 'terror' would now prevail.[26] As shop and flat windows filled with flags, portraits, photographs and busts of the former president, there was a widespread sense that an era was ending.

Beneš's body was shown the same respect as Jan Masaryk's had been, and was laid in state at the mausoleum at Vítkov where, by evening, the queues of people wanting to pay their last respects had grown so long that it took one group of mourners four hours to advance just 400 m (437 yards). As midnight approached, when visits to the casket were supposed to end, *SNB* vehicles that turned up to disperse the crowd were met with angry chants such as 'You ought to be ashamed to be paid for this!' and 'We want to see President Beneš', as well as the singing of the National Anthem and other patriotic songs such as '*Hej Slované*', 'St Wenceslas' and the Czech folk song said to be T.G. Masaryk's favourite: '*Ach, synku, synku*' ('Ah, my little son'). The mood turned more defiant when about two thousand people gathered in the city's central boulevard, Wenceslas Square, where the appearance of *SNB* officers led to the singing (to the tune of 'Hey ho, hey ho, it's off to work we go') of the jeering '*Hey hou, trpaslíci jdou!*' ('Hey ho, here come the dwarves!'). The *SNB* dispersed the protestors with water cannon and tear gas. By the time that Beneš's state funeral ceremony was scheduled to begin, at 10 a.m. on the morning of 8 September 1948, People's Militia had been stationed throughout Prague city centre in such numbers that it seemed to the schoolboy Jan Zábrana that the Communists must have been expecting a full-blown counter-revolution.[27] To the consternation of the Ministry of the Interior, which took the trouble to solicit information from all twenty-four regions into which the Bohemian Crown Lands were now divided, *StB* officers reported sightings of posters and leaflets in cities as far afield as Opava, Tábor, Uherské Hradiště, Ostrava and Český Těšín that, among other crimes, accused the Communists of having murdered both Jan Masaryk and Edvard Beneš.[28]

With the death of the two prime symbols of continuity between the First (now officially 'bourgeois') Czechoslovak Republic and the postwar 'People's Democratic Republic', there was no longer any reason for the Communist Party to restrain itself from publicly discrediting the National Socialist Party, the party whose very existence challenged the *KSČ*'s claims to be the only genuine mouthpiece for values that were at once socialist and Czech nationalist. Josef Lesák, a National Socialist who had set up a youth organization to rival the Communist-dominated Union of Youth (*Svaz české mládeže* or *SČM*) and helped to organize the only notable anti-Communist demonstration to take place during the February crisis – a student march held on 25 February

1948 – was arrested while trying to flee the country, on 4 June 1948.[29] In private, his captors offered him his freedom in exchange for going on state radio to say that Petr Zenkl – who had by then sought political asylum in the USA – had, in league with other National Socialist politicians, plotted to overthrow the Communist regime. Because he refused, Lesák was to spend the next twenty years in a series of prison and labour camps.[30]

Even without Lesák's help, enough 'evidence' was gathered to prepare for the first great Czech political trial to follow that of the Slovak Democratic Party in May 1948. This was the show trial of a group of twelve politicians (mostly National Socialist, but also including one former Communist and some Social Democrats) who were supposed to have been led into treacherous, anti-state activities by Milada Horáková, their National Socialist 'ringleader', whose real crime had been to resign from parliament after the February Events. The trial, which opened on 31 May 1950, was covered in a blaze of publicity and featured sensational 'confessions', matched by public 'demands' by workers and peasants that the guilty be given the 'most severe sentences possible'. The trial ended on 8 June 1950, with all the defendants found guilty of anti-state activity in a judgement that ran to fifty typed pages.[31] The most sensational of the four death sentences was that of Milada Horáková herself. She was hanged at Pankrác prison, where she had already served time under the Nazis, on 27 June 1950. The Horáková case led to 35 copycat trials in the regions, in which a further 639 inconvenient politicians were condemned, 10 to death and a further 48 to life imprisonment.[32]

The Catholic Church, another obvious rival institution to the Communist Party, offered a particularly delicate problem for the regime, since – as Masaryk and Beneš had also found – the government could not afford to be seen to be oppressing religious believers too crudely in what was, after all, an overwhelmingly Catholic country: even most Communist officials were baptized Catholics, and hundreds of thousands of card-carrying Communists blithely continued to attend Mass, to have their children baptized and to get married in church.[33] Since the Communist Party was not primarily concerned with private belief or discreet religious practice but rather with political control, Gottwald was at first optimistic that the Church would see sense, consent to cut its links with the Vatican and quietly submit to state control.

The early signs looked promising. By presiding over the first Communist president's inauguration after Victorious February, Archbishop Beran appeared to have given the new regime the Church's blessing. The ecclesiastical hierarchy further accepted the imposition of a so-called 'Roman Catholic Committee' to regulate Church affairs and showed every indication of being willing to endorse government resolutions when required to do so. Slovak bishops met at Nitra in August to publish a Pastoral Letter that helpfully emphasized the scriptural text 'Give to Caesar what is Caesar's, and to God what is God's'.[34] The Ministry of the Interior identified about 180 'progressive priests' ready to take their instructions from the National Front government rather than their bishops, and to spout Marxist jargon as and when required, in order to help with the covert propaganda aim of drawing a sharp distinction in the public mind between the Vatican-appointed hierarchy and the 'patriotic masses' of the laity. So long as the Church authorities did not 'abuse' their positions, Gottwald assured the conference of bishops held in Prague on 14–15 December 1948, they would continue to be allowed to handle their own affairs.[35]

Communist–Catholic relations first soured, and then broke down altogether, over three main areas of conflict. The first was the promotion by the regime of 'nationalist' and 'politically engaged' (i.e. Marxist and pro-regime) priests to positions of political importance, and particularly the elevation of the especially aggressive Marxist Catholic priest Fr Josef Plojhar (who had already been made leader of the Czechoslovak People's Party) to the cabinet as minister for health.[36] The second area of conflict concerned whether or not a *Te Deum* ought to have been sung at Gottwald's inauguration as president, a number of Communists, as well as Catholics, having been repelled by the politico-religious combination. But the last, and most bitter, dispute began with the discovery, on 22 March 1949, that a Conference of Bishops was being bugged by the secret police. This was the final straw that led Archbishop Beran to send Gottwald an angry memo in which he declared that, in the circumstances, the Church could not declare its loyalty to the government.[37] Not content with rebuking the government in private, Beran then went public, declaring that the government's so-called Roman Catholic Committee was causing divisions among Catholics and instructing the clergy to ignore it.

The *KSČ* immediately struck back. When, the following week, Beran was supposed to deliver his next sermon at St Vitus Cathedral on Hradčany, hecklers from the People's Militia prevented him from speaking. Upon returning home, he was placed under house arrest, where he was to remain a prisoner for several years. On 26 June, Beran managed to smuggle out a Pastoral Letter that accused the government of persecuting the Church. The government responded by banning Pastoral Letters, together with any assembly of Catholic clergy that had not been given advance approval. On 3 July 1949, the government announced that Slovak peasants were resisting government legislation; this gave it the excuse, on 7 July 1949, to ban all religious communities except those already under explicit state control. When the Vatican stepped in, on 13 July, to excommunicate all members of the Communist Party, together with their sympathizers, it was open warfare.[38] Over the course of 1949, against the background of an anticlerical campaign that stressed the wartime atrocities of the Tiso regime, described the pope as 'Hitler's ally' and linked expressions of Slovak and Polish devotion to an international anti-socialist conspiracy,[39] the *KSČ* proceeded to ban religious publications, censor Catholic newspapers, outlaw any religious activity that took place out of doors and take control of all seminaries, monasteries and convents. These moves were then crowned by a new law, passed by the National Assembly on 14 October 1949, which declared all Church matters to be under the control of a special minister for Church affairs appointed by the president.[40] Although most obeyed the new law, some clergy and laity refused, continuing to practise their faith in a rival 'secret' or underground Church to the officially approved one.

An ambitious government campaign was then launched to discredit the Catholic Church with the general public by demonstrating its supposed links, through the Church hierarchy, with 'treasonous imperialism dressed up in Vatican propaganda'.[41] Perhaps the most astonishing *StB* contribution to the state's anticlerical crusade was the elaborate hoax, later made famous by its thinly disguised counterpart in Josef Škvorecký's novel *The Miracle Game*,[42] in which the *StB* faked a 'miracle' in rural Bohemia in order sensationally to 'unmask' the fraud and blame it on the Church. At the nine o'clock Mass held on 11 December 1949 at the parish church of Číhošť, the crucifix on the altar was seen to move at the precise moment when Fr Josef Toufar, the parish priest, uttered the words 'Our Saviour is here with us in this tabernacle'. As news of the strange occurrence spread, prompting pilgrims, journalists, *StB* agents and the papal nuncio to investigate, Fr Toufar was taken in for a month of particularly sadistic *StB* interrogations which successfully persuaded him to 'confess' to homosexual offences with boys under the age of consent and to having fraudulently staged the 'miracle' of the moving crucifix as 'an anti-Communist symbol, a symbol of the struggle against Marxism-Leninism'.[43]

The final stage of the secret-police farce was to force Toufar to take part in a 'reconstruction' of his crimes which was to be filmed so that it could be shown as 'evidence' in a forthcoming show trial whose purpose would be to link the Czechoslovak ecclesiastical hierarchy with treasonous attempts to overturn the Communist regime. Since Toufar inconveniently died, as a result of *StB* torture, at the end of February, the filming, which went ahead in March 1950, had to take place without his help.[44] The result was a crude piece of propaganda which showed the Číhošť crucifix spin with comic speed to the western point of the compass and in which the wires installed by the *StB* to move the crucifix were (as intended, since they were supposed to have been installed by Fr Toufar) clearly visible. A running commentary explained how the little village of Číhošť was just one small link in a chain that joined a vast network of Vatican agents to a den of capitalist conspirators based in Wall Street.[45] In a gaffe that might have been prevented had Toufar not died in police custody, the altar was covered in Easter flowers – despite the fact that the filming was purported to have taken place during Advent.

However much suppressed mirth the government's absurd propaganda film may have caused many Catholic viewers, the *StB*'s 'exposure' of the 'miracle' of Čihošt' served its political purpose. At the end of February 1950, Gottwald was able to inform the Central Committee of the *KSČ* that the Catholic clergy, in league with the Vatican, had organized an elaborate fraud to 'destroy the state'. This gave the government the necessary pretext to expel the papal nuncio, who left Czechoslovakia on 18 March 1950, and to begin rounding up members of the Church hierarchy and of religious orders.[46] In a complicated joint *SNB/StB* operation codenamed Operation K, 1,746 men and women from a variety of Czech religious orders in Ústí nad Labem, Liberec, Hradec Králové, Prague, České Budějovice, Plzeň, Karlovy Vary, Pardubice, Brno, Jihlava, Gottwaldov (formerly known as Zlín), Olomouc and Ostrava were seized from their monasteries or convents. They were arrested and placed in *StB* prisons, forced-labour camps or the special 'Concentration Cloister' set up at Želiv, where monastery buildings were turned into a mass prison camp. Ján Chryzostom Korec, then a young Jesuit living in Trnava in Slovakia, remembered how, on the night of 13 April 1950, men from the *SNB*, *StB* and militia, brandishing machine guns, stormed his monastery, loaded everyone onto buses and deported them to a deserted twelfth-century monastery in the remote town of Jasov. Since the police refused to say where they had gone, it was at first assumed by their families – tellingly enough – that they were being taken to the gas chambers.[47] Further follow-up police strikes in the summer and autumn of 1950 completed the operation, in which a total of some 6,000 monks and nuns were arrested and incarcerated.[48]

The final blow in the state's campaign to neutralize the Church as a possible centre of opposition to Communist rule came with a series of anti-clerical trials, the most sensational being the 'Trial of Vatican Agents in Czechoslovakia' which was held in Prague, amid a blaze of publicity, between 27 November and 2 December 1950. The trial, in which Bishop Stanislav Zela and a further eight defendants were sentenced to large fines and long terms in prison, featured demagogic haranguings by collaborator priests, most notably Fr Josef Plojhar, whose rantings as a witness in the open court-room were indistinguishable – both in style and in content – from those of secular Marxist prosecutors. The largest of the copycat trials that immediately followed in Slovakia – the show trial held in Bratislava between 10 and 15 January 1951 which included Archbishop Ján Vojtaššák and bishops Michal Buzalka and Pavol Gojdič – did not receive as much media attention, but resulted in harsher sentences, with fines of up to 500,000 crowns and life sentences for all members of the Slovak ecclesiastical hierarchy.[49] Even hard-ened Communist Party members who were not directly involved could not help noticing that there was something a little odd about the trials, privately finding it strange – though they did not raise their voices in public – that priests, nuns and bishops should 'promptly confess to every crime with which they were charged' and 'speak like lecturers on Marxism, formulating their testimony in the purest Party jargon'.[50]

At the *KSČ* Ninth Party Congress, which was held on 25–29 May 1949, chairman Klement Gottwald and secretary-general Rudolf Slánský summed up the party's principal tasks: to assume 'the cultural and spiritual leadership of the entire nation', overcome the 'survivals of bourgeois ideology' and restructure 'society according to socialist principles'. An ambitious Five-Year Economic Plan, to follow the National Front's Two-Year Plan, approved by the National Assembly in October 1948 and launched at the start of 1949, was to reorient trade from West to East, while simultaneously focusing on the industrialization of many rural areas.[51] In order to create a suitably 'socialist' culture, it was decided to adopt the arguments contained in A.A. Zhdanov's influential Soviet text of 1934, 'How to Be an Engineer of Human Souls', as official state policy on the role of art and culture in socialist society. This led to a new wave of highly fêted sculpture, painting, drama, opera, poetry and fiction, all in approved Socialist Realist style, whose purpose was avowedly political and explicitly intended to educate the public in Marxist-Leninist interpretations of the past as well as glimpses of the bright future that was supposed to lie ahead with the final realization of the utopia of 'Communism'. Even budding writers with the talent of a Milan Kundera got their start by composing paeans of praise to Gottwald or Stalin. Favourite subjects included heroic images of workers (especially coalminers, the 'aristocracy' of the working class); industrial landscapes (especially those featuring dams or electrical plants); portraits of Young Pioneers, People's Militia and other officially approved Socialist heroes; and idealized portraits of Communist martyrs, above all of Julius Fučík, the handsome young Czech journalist who had died at the hands of the Gestapo.[52] As for official portraits of Communist statesmen, above all Comrades Gottwald and Stalin, artists outdid themselves in their attempts adequately to elicit the politically correct responses of love, gratitude, trust and awe towards those who had freed them from bondage and were now leading them to the Promised Land. When Heda Margolius, the wife of an important Communist official, was careless enough to laugh at a new portrait of Stalin, complete with a violet tractor set against fluffy pink clouds, for its 'unbelievable *kitsch*', she was reported by a fellow worker. Only because the editor of the publishing house where she worked happened – despite twenty years in the Party – to be a 'rather sensible woman' was the matter not taken further.[53]

Ten-minute state-sponsored newsreels, which preceded every film shown in public cinemas from 1945 right up to 1989, kept up a steady barrage of 'good news': how the latest Soviet agricultural methods and industrial techniques were revolutionizing the economy; how new electrical plants were bringing light even to the most backward regions of Slovakia; how the 'revan-chist' plots of the West Germans, portrayed as warmongering Nazis, had yet again been uncovered and disarmed; how the peace-loving citizens of the People's Democratic Republic of Germany were enthusiastically 'building socialism'; how everything – from sporting triumphs and folklore festivals to art exhibitions and classical concerts (to say nothing of overtly political occasions such as the annual May Day, Victorious February and Great October Revolution celebrations) – demonstrated the superiority of the socialist system to that of the capitalist West.[54] While something like a million and a half books were taken off library shelves to be placed on a special index of prohibited books (whose titles can today be seen in the Klementinum Catalogue of Formerly Prohibited Literature), newly printed accounts of the past hammered home the lesson that, after centuries of human struggle to achieve socialism – as evidenced by the Hussite and French revolutions, together with every other historical movement that could conceivably be presented as radical, reformist or progressive – the first real breakthrough had been achieved by the Bolshevik Revolution of 1917. It was this uniquely successful experiment which, having triumphantly defeated Nazism along the way, had begun to spread its benefits to the rest of the world: to Eastern Europe, to North Korea, to China and to all the other countries that, one by one, were choosing to join the international family of socialist nations.

In the spring of 1950, when East–West tensions were reaching new heights with the Berlin blockade and the start of the Korean War, a huge anti-American campaign was launched. Posters and political cartoons featured Wall Street capitalists and US generals helping the West German 'Nazis' and imposing their will on the United Nations, while simultaneously torturing their own Black minority and ruthlessly exploiting labour at home.[55] Posters, newspaper articles, radio broadcasts and official weekly newsreels, together with the issuing of gasmasks and holding of frequent air-raid drills, helped to keep fear of the Western imperialists at fever pitch and to minimize complaints about continued rationing. One of the unexpected side effects created by anti-Western and anti-imperialist campaigns was the trouble caused to *SNB* and *StB* officers in the border regions, where they found them-selves repeatedly having to deal with attempts by citizens living along the frontiers with Austria, Poland or Hungary to flee inland out of fear that they would find themselves on the frontline when the imminently expected Third World War broke out. As early as September 1948, the problem was already so acute that the Ministry of the Interior realized that it would have to review the whole question of the security of the country's borders which, because of the increased number of fugitives from the regime, were simultaneously having to be reinforced with watchtowers, barbed wire, minefields and all the familiar paraphernalia associated with the building of the Iron Curtain.[56]

Encouraging Czechoslovak citizens to view the West with fear and hostility had obvious advantages in making citizens feel dependent for their safety on the state. It also made it possible to blame any economic misfortune – from a bad harvest to a village fire – not on mere accident or the short-sightedness of the Five-Year Plan, but rather on the evil cunning of imperialist agents who, if you believed the government propaganda, were lurking behind every bush. It was in this climate that a government campaign to blame ruined potato crops on the *mandelinka* or Colorado beetle (presumably a self-conscious revival of a similar scare of 1939) was launched in 1950, stimulating fears of pestilence at just about the same time that US planes were dropping anti-Communist leaflets in the border regions of the country.[57] The atmosphere of war hysteria, justifying the need for constant vigilance, was further maintained by the launching of a series of popular and well-made feature films, of which Josef Mach's *Akce B* (Operation B), a *Boy's Own*-style adventure story in which the *SNB* and Czechoslovak army triumphantly defeat a reactionary group of bandits (composed of an unsavoury blend of Vatican agents, international spies and *Banderovci* traitors) hiding out in the wilds of Slovakia is probably the best-known example.[58] Positive propaganda about the benefits of socialism and friendship with the Soviet Union was left to the enthusiastic messages on display in Communist Party glass-encased wooden notice boards which were to be found in every neighbourhood and village; to the constant emphasis on the peace-loving nature of the Slav and socialist worlds as opposed to West Germany and the warmongering West; and also to light comedy films such as *Bylo to v máji* (It Was in May), whose moral appeared to be that trusting 'politically engaged' (i.e. Communist) workers to lead society 'forwards' was the best guarantee of the nation's future security, happiness and fulfilment.[59]

Large industrial firms could be nationalized at the stroke of a pen, but the hoped-for collectivization of agriculture lagged far behind, small landowners, farmers and better-off peasants proving reluctant to join cooperative farms. Pressure therefore began to be applied systematically. At first, the government relied mostly on poster and newsreel campaigns to advertise the alleged benefits of cooperative farms, which were portrayed as infinitely more efficient and up-to-date than their 'capitalist' counterparts, while simultaneously presenting private ownership as greedy, selfish and inefficient. Since months of this approach passed without much discernible effect, and from 1 January 1949 there was the Five-Year Plan to think of, added muscle was lent to the cause. Tractors and farm machinery began to be requisitioned by the government on the slightest pretext and handed over to rival agricultural cooperatives in the same village; private farms were given quotas that were increasingly impossible to fulfil; the children of stubborn peasants were refused permission to attend *gymnázia* (prestigious high schools) or to go to university. Finally, farmers and peasants who continued to be uncooperative were branded in local newspapers as 'kulaks', a Russian term denoting 'tight-fisted' independent farmers, famously considered by Stalin the 'class enemy' of poorer peasants. They were then made the object of angry factory-floor discussions, charged with criminal acts of subversion, hauled before local courts and sentenced to terms in prison, after which their property could be confiscated by the state and parcelled out to the more politically reliable. Raimund Musil, whose father ran a medium-sized farm in Dědina that was already struggling to keep up with the quotas of milk, meat and poultry demanded by the government, finally gave the authorities an excuse to confiscate the family property altogether when he was found to be hiding some objectionable leaflets for his local branch of *Sokol*. The *StB* came after midnight, waking everyone up, and took him away for questioning. He was next seen in a courtroom in Brno as one of a large number of 'treasonous kulaks' to be tried against the usual background of local factory workers' petitions and resolutions that he be given 'the severest punishment' for his 'crimes' against the state. In the end, Musil's father was not sentenced to death, but to a large fine, the confiscation of his family's property, the removal of his rights as a citizen and sixteen years in prison. The conditions at Bory prison, on the outskirts of Plzeň, were so bad that he returned home after serving less than two years of his sentence: in a coffin. The whole family was forcibly moved out of the village around Christmas 1952.[60]

In the especially sensitive matter of the Czechoslovak army, although the officer class had been thoroughly purged by 1949 there were still the troops to consider. Since the army was largely made up of draftees called up for National Service, Communist Party, National Front and Union of Youth (*SČM*) organizations were enlisted to write political assessments of each recruit for scrutiny by the relevant local branch of the *StB*. With the beginning of the Korean War in 1950 and the consequent increase in Cold War tensions, the importance of a politically reliable army came to seem paramount. Ludvík Svoboda, a wartime hero, was relieved of his duties as minister of defence in March 1950 and put in charge of sport instead; at the end of 1951 he was again removed from his post, this time to spend a few months in prison before being sent to work on a collective farm. The new minister of defence was Alexej Čepička, Gottwald's son-in-law and an ardent prewar Communist who had survived Nazi concentration camps to be appointed minister of domestic trade in 1947 and minister of justice in 1948. Under Čepička, whose brief was to reform the army in line with the wartime Soviet-Czechoslovak agreements signed by Beneš, it was decided in September 1950 to create a special new category, 'Category E', for army recruits deemed 'politically unreliable', who were automatically to be placed in special units called *pomocné technické prapory* (auxiliary technical battalions).

These were the infamous *pétépáci* (PTPs) or 'Black Barons', recruits who were not allowed to take part in weapons training or to mix with other soldiers, but who were instead isolated in special camps and used for hard labour.[61] From 1 October 1950, each of the ninety thousand recruits called up for National Service had to fill out a detailed questionnaire whose answers were checked according to a revised list of eleven criteria for identifying the 'politically unreliable'. All those who had previously been tried for anti-state offences (whether under the 1923 or the 1948 laws for the Defence of the Republic) were automatically to be placed in Category E. So were factory owners, employers with more than ten employees, anyone who earned more than 10,000 crowns per month from property or other investments, peasants who owned more than 30 hectares (74 acres) of arable land, people who in the past had been removed from public positions by Action Committees, and students who had been expelled either from school or from university.[62] Although the number of Category E soldiers was at first too low to enable the army to fulfil its coal-mining and road-building obligation to the Five-Year Plan, by the end of 1950 army officers were taking their 'political duties' seriously enough so that, out of an intake of 83,000 fresh recruits to the army, 5,102 were assigned to the PTP and a further 1,900 marked down for further investigation; by making up numbers with priests, monks and seminarians, who were placed in a special road construction unit, the PTP finally consisted of 9,990 men, of whom the vast majority, some 8,000, were Category E prisoners, exactly the number estimated to be necessary by the army to carry out its required projects.[63]

PTP units were scattered around the country, mostly in Bohemia and the border regions. In theory, the men were supposed to have some free time, tolerable living conditions, and to attend 're-education' courses in Marxism-Leninism so that they could be rehabilitated and eventually reintegrated into society. In practice, it was common for prisoners to be worked well over the regulation daily eight hours, following night duty with a day shift; to be housed in makeshift tents or primitive barracks without hot water or even glass in the windows; or to find that their 'leisure' time consisted solely of being made to perform callisthenics or sing socialist songs.[64] Formal re-education classes turned out to be a joke, consisting of parroting answers in unison for the benefit of teachers who, according to legend, were in some cases themselves so poorly educated that one mysteriously persisted in calling Lenin 'the fifth of January', apparently under the delusion that that was what the initials 'V.I.' stood for in Vladimir Ilyich Lenin's name.[65]

From September 1949, even those Communist Party members who had zealously denounced and reported others began to feel at risk. This time, the initial pressure came not from the *KSČ* leadership so much as from 'fraternal' Communist parties in the neighbouring People's Democratic Republics, which were following the first major postwar trial in a Central European state of a Communist Party official: the trial in Budapest of László Rajk, the Hungarian foreign minister, for being a 'Titoist agent'. Although there was an initial reluctance on the part of the KSČ to seek the 'enemy within', the publicity given to the Rajk trial, together with 'evidence' read out in court that pointed the finger at Czechoslovakia, meant that it became increasingly difficult for the KSČ to ignore. Most of the evidence concerning Czechoslovak Communists, many of whom were explicitly named in the trial proceedings, came from the testimony of Noel Field, a US national who, although cast in the role of CIA agent, had in fact worked for the NKVD (the People's Commissariat for Internal Affairs, the USSR's public and secret police organization). Other members of his family also had links either with Czechoslovak or German Communists, Soviet intelligence or both.[66] In the spring and summer of 1949, as secret preparations for the Rajk trial were being made, the Fields, one by one, disappeared. Noel Field was last seen leaving the Palace Hotel in Prague with two men in May, though the bill for his vacant hotel room continued mysteriously to be paid; his brother, Hermann Field, disappeared on a flight from Warsaw to Prague in August; Herta Field, who had gone out to Prague to look for her missing husband and brother-in-law, herself disappeared from the Palace Hotel a few days later. Even Erika Glaser, a girl the Fields had helped to escape from postwar Germany and whom they referred to as their 'adopted daughter', vanished without trace after boarding the subway between West and East Berlin a year later, in August 1950.[67]

From the autumn of 1949, when their testimonies began to be heard in the Budapest courtroom, part of the Field family mystery started to be solved. The Fields, it turned out, had been arrested in Prague on the recommendation of the Hungarian secret service, which was in turn being helped by Soviet advisors. Also on trial in Budapest was Gejza Pavlík, a prominent Czech Communist who had worked with Noel Field in Switzerland and afterwards become head of the Czechoslovak Travel Bureau, Čedok, and whom the Hungarian authorities were claiming as the link between Field and a Hungarian Trotskyist group.[68] Among those named in depositions by Noel Field, Gejza Pavlík and others, all of whom were held in Hungarian secret-police cells, were some sixty prominent Czechoslovak Communists, including Otto Šling, the regional party secretary in Brno; Vladimír Clementis, minister of foreign affairs and a leading Slovak Communist; Vilém Nový, the editor of the Communist Party daily Rudé právo; Václav Nosek, minister of the interior since 1945; Richard Slánský, a diplomat and the brother of KSČ secretary-general Rudolf Slánský; and Evžen Löbl, deputy minister for foreign trade.[69]

As Evžen Löbl (Eugene Loebl) later recalled, one day in September 1949 he was summoned before the KSČ Central Committee. He was told that he was to be questioned, and that his future would depend upon his cooperation in telling the 'unadulterated truth without reservations'. As an obedient Communist, he scrupulously completed his résumé in a spirit of self-criticism which 'made no secret' of his mistakes and, if anything, presented his own actions and motives 'in too bad, rather than too good a light'. That same evening, Löbl was transferred to an improvised cell in the Central Committee building to complete his task. The next day, his interrogators took note of the fact that he 'was not of working class family' and that he had spent time in the West and had dealings with Western journalists, politicians and economists. To his surprise, he was then informed that the party was releasing him so that he could continue in his duties at the Foreign Office, but that he was not to leave Prague or to inform anyone about what had happened, on pain of expulsion from the party and immediate arrest.[70]

Löbl claims to have kept his mouth firmly shut, but a couple of months later a plainclothes *StB* officer entered his flat and delivered a summons from Minister of the Interior Nosek. Instead of being taken to Nosek (who was by then himself under suspicion), he was driven in the direction of Prague's Ruzyně airport and led to a large building where a uniformed *StB* officer arrested him. He was put in prison clothes and left entirely alone for four days. On the fifth day, he was interrogated by *StB* officers Vladimír Kohoutek and Bohumil Doubek. Since Löbl initially failed either to admit to any wrongdoing or to implicate others, he was subjected to 'hard treatment'. This meant being interrogated on average fourteen times a day; dragged out of sleep thirty or forty times a night; kept in continual hunger; and not allowed to sit down, even when eating or using the toilet. Often he was forced to spend the whole day standing with his face to the wall. The physical effects of not being able to sit down included such painful swelling to his feet 'that washing became torture and every step hurt'. To these physical sufferings was added the psychological distress of being kept in a constant state of tension, shouted at, threatened, insulted and kept within earshot of the interrogation room, where the cries and weeping of other prisoners, together with the bellowing of interrogators, could be plainly heard. Several times he was woken and led, blindfolded, to a basement room where he was made to listen to telephone discussions of what turned out to be bogus plans for his execution on the grounds that feeding him had become too great an expense, or that his interrogators' time was being wasted. Careful measures, he noticed, had been taken to prevent the possibility of suicide: the 'handkerchiefs' issued were of only 13 sq cm (2 sq inches) and glass windows were situated well beyond the reach of prisoners.[71]

After several months of this treatment, Löbl willingly 'confessed to every conceivable crime' without so much as toying with the idea of later retracting his statements in an open courtroom. From the point when he made his full 'confession' (to crimes that he had not committed), he was permitted to read and to accept parcels from his wife, and found that Kohoutek, his principal tormentor, suddenly became 'friendly and chatty' with him. Thanks to what was officially termed Löbl's 'responsible' attitude towards 'helping' his interrogators, the original list of suspects, as initially identified by Noel Field in similar circumstances in Hungary, was considerably enlarged.[72]

Accounts left by Party members who survived the ordeals of arrest, imprisonment and trial in 1950s Czechoslovakia (or by the widows of those who did not) have a depressing predictability and sameness about them. Suspects first became aware that they were being followed; then that their homes were bugged and their telephones tapped; then that they were in some indefinable way being held at arm's length and watched by their colleagues and superiors with suspicion. Next they were demoted or unexpectedly moved from influential positions. Only then did the *StB* come to take them away. Victims typically responded to being arrested with incredulity and indignation, demanding to be allowed to speak to President Gottwald, Secretary-General Slánský or to other powerful people in the party. When this response got them nowhere, they clung to the belief that there had been some terrible mistake which the party, in its wisdom, would eventually clear up. Left alone in solitary confinement for hours, days or even weeks, they discovered the prison rules and conventions by being shouted at. They were not to use their names, but only their prison numbers; the dazzling light in their cells would never be turned off; they could not place their hands under their blanket, however cold the weather; nothing could be kept in their cell except a tiny scrap of material, a dozen centimetres or a few inches square, officially called a 'handkerchief'; even combs and toothbrushes had to be specially requested and returned immediately after use. Prisoners were watched, day and night, by a series of *StB* prison staff through the peephole that was to be found at eye level in each cell door.

For most prisoners, the first interrogation, to which they were always brought blindfolded and disoriented, gave a ray of false hope. After solitary confinement, it was a relief simply to speak with another human being and to be in the comparatively normal environment of a prison office, with desk, chairs, carpet, typewriter and reassuringly familiar portraits of Stalin and Gottwald. Most looked forward to the opportunity to explain their innocence, while the first questions asked – name, occupation, place of birth – were soothing in their very banality. Only once prisoners found – with a nasty shock – that the questions would be repeated, and the interrogations continue, until the answers finally conformed to those the interrogators wished to hear, did they begin to realize the complete hopelessness of their position.[73]

The immediate impulse for the *KSČ* to hold what turned out to be the most extensive and elaborate Communist show trial outside the Soviet Union came from the first secretary of the Hungarian Workers' Party, who warned Gottwald at the beginning of September 1949 that when the forthcoming Rajk trial opened, it would include dozens of Czechoslovak names. Gottwald, who had already helped to ensure that the Field brothers were extradited to Hungary, again responded helpfully, by ensuring that some seventeen suspects, including Löbl, were immediately arrested and that veterans from the Spanish Civil War, Yugoslav Partisans, Communists who had spent the war in London and other 'anti-Party elements' were placed under surveillance. President Gottwald and KSČ secretary-general Slánský, eager to curry favour with Moscow and anxious not to put a foot wrong, further requested that the Soviet Union send 'advisors' to coach them on how to proceed.[74]

Although all seventeen initial Communist Party suspects either committed suicide or were brought to trial, the main political purpose for which the secret-police apparatus was being expanded – to uncover evidence of a conspiracy in the highest echelons of the party – had not yet been achieved. This failure on the part of the KSČ leadership seemed all the more suspect given Czechoslovakia's history. Not only had Czechoslovakia been created in the image of its 'bourgeois' and 'imperialist' allies, France, Britain and the United States; but a good proportion of the Communist Party leadership had spent the war in Britain, where they had worked closely with the Beneš government. After the war, the KSČ had preached the 'Titoist' notion of a distinct 'Czechoslovak road to socialism'; had voted to accept Marshall Aid before being rebuked for so doing by Moscow; and had been one of the first states to follow the Soviet Union in recognizing Israel, which by 1949 had disappointed Soviet hopes by allying itself instead with the United States. To Stalinists everywhere, it was simply inconceivable that Czechoslovakia could be immune from Titoist intrigue and Western infiltration when even countries that had been thoroughly purged during occupation by the Red Army were proving compromised.

Among the first in the Czechoslovak Communist Party to see the need for radical action was the secretary-general of the KSČ, Rudolf Slánský. Slánský had little to fear from his own past since – unlike his closest comrade, Klement Gottwald, who had repeatedly promised that Czechoslovakia would follow its 'own road' to socialism – he had long been renowned for his disciplined Stalinism and unquestioned loyalty to the Soviet Union. After a Comintern meeting in November 1949 characterized by an atmosphere of near-hysterical hate and fear and at which a second condemnation of the Communist Party of Yugoslavia was passed, it was becoming clear that any Communist parties that did not join in the wholehearted condemnation of even the slightest deviation from current Stalinist orthodoxy would themselves be suspect. At a speech to KSČ activists held in Prague on 7 December 1949, Slánský insisted that enemy agents must also have infiltrated their own ranks and called on the party faithful to show the utmost vigilance to 'unmask' the 'enemies in our own ranks, for they are the most dangerous enemies'.[75] Impatient with the Ministry of the Interior's apparent slowness in coming up with evidence of a conspiracy large and important enough to satisfy the rest of the socialist bloc, from mid-1949, Slánský began routinely to go over Nosek's head, giving instructions to StB agents directly from party headquarters. Not to be out-manoeuvred, in 1950 Gottwald insisted on taking direct responsibility for national security.

Just as wartime anti-Semitic and postwar anti-German legislation, parcelled out to rival, and sometimes overlapping, regional, district and national authorities in the late 1930s and early 1940s, had tended constantly to escalate in volume and intensity, so the confusion of party and state competencies in the late 1940s and early 1950s began to spiral out of control. The group that had taken charge of Löbl, for example, was made up of a mixture of StB officers from the Ministry of the Interior and officials from Party Central Office, renamed Sector IIa and organized into special sections to deal with 'Trotskyites', members of International Brigades and 'bourgeois nationalists' (i.e. Slovak Communists). In Slovakia itself, an equivalent depart-ment was established by the Ministry of the Interior, but supervised by KSS secretary-general Štefan Baštovanský and party chairman Viliam Široký, whose first task was to collect information on leading Slovak Communists. In May 1950, the StB broke away from the Ministry of the Interior to form its own, independent Ministry of National Security. Meanwhile, staff at the Party Control Commission, equally eager to find 'the Czechoslovak Rajk', began to make use of confidential reports at their disposal to find further suspects, whom they then took it upon themselves to interrogate or place under surveillance. Before long, the Commission had set up its own plants in the StB to see whether the National Security office itself might not be covering up for enemies within the party. Even regional and district party committees began to set up their own committees of investigation, reminis-cent of the immediate postwar people's tribunals and known in the districts as the 'threes', because they were made up of the district party security secre-tary and district SNB and StB chiefs, and in the regions, where they were joined by the regional public prosecutor and another official, as the 'fives'.[76]

In 1950, therefore, the same year that army reforms, together with the Milada Horáková, 'Vatican Agent' and thousands of less high-profile polit-ical show trials were spreading terror throughout Czechoslovak society, an equally fervent hunt was simultaneously being carried out within the Ministry of the Interior, the Department of National Security and the various police forces, as well as in all of the KSČ and KSS national, district and regional committees to find and expose the 'enemy within' the Communist Party. As each new prisoner was interrogated, more names were added to the list of suspects; as each interrogation group competed with the others to 'unmask' the plot (whose existence no one appears any longer to have doubted), suspicion fell not only on those who had already been arrested or placed under surveillance, but also on those working in rival departments, leading to a spiral of denunciations, arrests and confessions. But no matter how many Communists had already been forced to 'confess', the very logic of the search meant that the witch-hunt within the Communist Party could not be brought to a close until the 'Czechoslovak Rajk' had been found, condemned and executed. Only then could the socialist world be satisfied that Czechoslovakia had been 'purged' in the same way as the other People's Democracies.

The first likely candidate to provide a convenient scapegoat, and whose name had helpfully been suggested by Hungarian security, was the prominent Slovak Communist Vladimír Clementis. Since Clementis had disapproved publicly of the Soviet-German Pact of 1939, he could be presented as anti-Soviet; since he was Slovak, he could be accused of 'bourgeois nationalism'; because he was minister of foreign affairs and of Jewish background, he could be seen to resemble Rajk and be suspected of 'cosmopolitanism'. Unlike Gustáv Husák, who was more vulnerable to the charge of 'Slovak bourgeois nationalism' but who actually refused, while in the custody of the secret police, to 'help the Party' by confessing, Clementis proved pliable. As a Slovak Jew, he could also be tried alongside Czech Jews rather than non-Jewish Slovaks, making it harder for Slovak Communists to protest that they were being victimized by Prague.[77] Foreign Minister Clementis was arrested on 27 January 1951 in a special operation, codenamed 'Operation Stones', in which an entire replica of the border with West Germany was set up within a few kilometres of the actual border, complete with barbed wire, huts and *StB* agents impersonating border guards, so that – in a touch that was said to have appealed to Gottwald's sense of humour – the foreign minister could appear to have been caught in the act of attempting to defect to the West.[78]

Another possible scapegoat was Otto Šling, chief secretary of the Regional Committee of the *KSČ* in Brno, who had already been arrested on 6 October 1950, sparked by the sudden discovery by the security services of a letter purported to have been sent to Šling by Emanuel Voska, the head of a Czechoslovak spy ring based in the United States. The next month, the case was discussed by the Regional Party Committee in Brno, under the watchful eye of delegates from Prague, who agreed to expel Šling from the party and to enforce a radical change in the district party leadership. Within hours of the resolution, the *StB* had made its first arrests and launched an extensive hunt throughout Moravia for the rest of 'the Šling leadership'. By January 1951, some six hundred personal dossiers had been examined and twenty or more arrests made, mostly of Communists in the Brno region. By February, the number of arrests had risen to about fifty, and included a Slovak group, party officials from other regions who (like Šling) were of Jewish background and even top security men like deputy minister of national defence Bedřich Reicin and deputy minister of national security Karel Šváb. A special prison had to be set up at Koloděj House near Prague to deal with the sudden intake of prisoners. Interrogations at Koloděj, which were more sadistic and less controlled than those that had become routine at Ruzyně and Pankrác, also brought about the required results: Václav Kopecký was able to report to the *KSČ* Central Committee the following month that Šling, probably in league with Clementis, had conspired to depose *KSČ* secretary-general Slánský and assassinate President Gottwald; other prisoners further suggested that he had wanted to oust Antonín Novotný from his position as party secretary in Prague. The sensational 'revelations' became so widely publicized that a new term entered the language: 'Šlingism', meaning a combination of espionage, sabotage and treachery.[79]

As the security services worked overtime to extract the requisite 'detailed confessions' to manufacture a case against a band of conspirators centred around Šling, *StB* interrogators claimed to be struck by how often the name of *KSČ* secretary-general Rudolf Slánský – another Stalinist of Jewish background – came up during questioning. They began to toy with an idea so bold that, if realized, could give the secretary-general a taste of his own medicine and simultaneously prevent Czechoslovakia from ever again being accused of being 'soft' on its own party leadership. Since even the most brutal interrogation methods of scores of prisoners – from former *StB* officers to the highest party officials – had yet to produce concrete evidence of an actual conspiracy, the *StB* – and, through it, the party leadership – came to the conclusion that the real evil genius must be someone even higher up in the party hierarchy.[80] Slánský, although he had recently been awarded the highest honour in the land – the Order of Klement Gottwald for the Building of Socialism – was therefore, on 6 September 1951, removed from his post as secretary-general of the *KSČ*. Three days later, the security services informed President Gottwald that they had intercepted a letter – again presumed to have been sent by the Voska group – that warned someone referred to only as 'the Great Crossing Sweeper' that he was in imminent danger of arrest, but could be helped to defect. By 23 November 1951, Gottwald was apparently persuaded that the letter must have been intended for Slánský (it now appears that it was a provocation by the CIA).[81] The Slánskýs were arrested the same night on their way home from a dinner party thrown by the Zápotockýs, who obediently phoned the *StB* at the moment their distinguished guests left the party. Slánský, who endured the usual 'hard treatment' at Ruzyně for nearly two months, proved a hard nut to crack. But at the end of January 1952, after he had unsuccessfully tried to commit suicide by hanging himself with the alarm cord attached to his window, he confessed to the existence of a conspiratorial 'centre' and, thereafter, to anything else that was required of him.[82]

The next stage of the proceedings was for all the testimonies that had been so painstakingly extracted from hundreds of 'witnesses' and 'culprits' over the course of two years to be readjusted and realigned to fit the new political requirements: that it was no longer Clementis or Šling, but rather Slánský, who had been 'unmasked' as the 'real' Rajk. Whereas the Slovak Clementis and the Moravian Šling had been vulnerable to accusations of 'bourgeois nationalism' of a 'Titoist' kind, Slánský – although a Bohemian Czech – was of Jewish background. This opened the way for accusations of 'Zionism' and 'cosmopolitanism' to be added to the usual crimes of sabotage, espionage, Titoism and Trotskyism. Judaism could also provide the thread to link a large number of the 'conspirators' together, win favour in Moscow, advertise the 'correct' attitude to be adopted towards the state of Israel, and, relying on the strength of popular anti-Semitism, ensure that the members of the 'conspiratorial centre' would elicit no pity. Finally, focusing on the Jewish backgrounds of those who were now to be cast as the eleven leading members of a 'conspiratorial centre' led by Rudolf Slánský helped to deflect attention from the impeccably Bohemian Czech and Aryan, but politically compromised, Gottwald, who took care to ensure that the further accusation – that Slánský had propagated 'a Czechoslovak road to socialism' – was deleted from the final text of the indictment.[83] As Hannah Schling has found, in Gottwald's speech to the Central Committee conference of September 1951, which was afterwards sent to all party members in pamphlet form, he referred to the conspirators as largely made up of those who 'did not grow from the roots of our country and our Party, of whom the majority belonged to a different type, which at the January conference of the Central Committee of the Party I called cosmopolitans'.[84] Like many other Communists, Rudolf and Heda Margolius initially felt only relief when they heard of Slánský's arrest, assuming that the purge which Slánský had helped to launch would now be brought to an end. Instead, the arrests escalated, focusing on Jews. One of those to be arrested in this next purge of high Communist officials was the deputy minister of foreign trade: Margolius himself.[85] Although unable to protect the KSČ from having to go through the same terrible ordeal as the other People's Democracies, Gottwald was able to spare his own kith and kin – Bohemian Czech Communists – by offering Slovak, Moravian and Jewish Communists in their stead.

On 20 November 1952, the 'Trial of the Leadership of the Anti-State Conspiratorial Centre headed by Rudolf Slánský' opened as a grand piece of political theatre at the State Court in Prague. Fourteen leading Communists (Slánský, Löbl, Šling, Clementis, Margolius, London, Reicin, Šváb, Hajdů, Fischl, Geminder, Frejka, Frank and Simon), eleven of whom were explicitly described as being 'of Jewish origin', were accused of being 'Trotskyite-Titoist, Zionist and bourgeois nationalist traitors' and 'enemies of the Czechoslovak people', who – in the pay of 'the US imperialists' and under 'the direction of Western espionage agencies' – had conspired to create 'an anti-state conspiratorial centre' to 'undermine the people's democratic regime, frustrate the building of socialism, damage the national economy, carry out espionage activity' and 'weaken the unity of the Czechoslovak people and the Republic's defensive capacity' in order to 'tear the country away from its close alliance and friendship with the Soviet Union, liquidate the Czechoslovak people's democratic regime, restore capitalism and return the Republic to the imperialist camp and destroy its national sovereignty and independence'.[86] Only Clementis, the Slovak Jew, confessed to taking part in a 'subversive group of Slovak bourgeois nationalists' that had tried 'to separate the development of Slovakia from the development of the state as a whole, thus strengthening reaction and hindering the progress of socialism and the development of the people's democratic order'.[87]

The courtroom was packed with ministers, factory delegates and plain-clothes *StB* officers; the families of the accused – some of whom might not have shown proper satisfaction at the 'unmasking' of the traitors[88] – had to find out the verdicts from radio and newspaper reports. Not only the defendants and witnesses, who had learned their testimony word for word, but even the lawyers and the public prosecutor, Josef Urválek, had their lines written for them by the *StB*, who drafted and redrafted the script until it met with the full approval of the party leadership. The trial, which lasted a week, was held in a blaze of publicity, backed by a strongly anti-Semitic campaign which featured Slánský as a Judas, a rat or an anti-Semitic caricature.[89] The campaign inspired thousands of vindictive letters and angry resolutions from factory workers, groups of schoolchildren Pioneers (a sort of Communist equivalent of Boy and Girl Scouts) and agricultural cooperatives, in addition to the inevitable regional and district party resolutions. Gottwald was widely praised for his manliness, discipline and honour in not sparing even his closest associate and friend, while the nation was treated to the daily sensation of new 'revelations' in the press, together with live broadcasts of the entire proceedings, blared out over the loudspeaker systems on factory floors and in public places around the country. Inevitably, all fourteen defendants were found guilty of multiple charges of high treason, espionage, sabotage and military treason. Three – Evžen Löbl, Artur London and Vavro Hajdů – were sentenced to life imprisonment; the remaining eleven were sentenced to death on 27 November and executed at Pankrác prison on 3 December 1952. The entire transcript of the trial was then edited by the Ministry of Justice and published by Orbis, the state publisher, as a fat brown paperback which could be bought by anyone for 45 crowns.[90]

1 Edvard Beneš, a Czech nationalist, representing Czecho-Slovak interests at Versailles in 1919.

2 President-Liberator T.G. Masaryk and Foreign Minister Edvard Beneš in the 1920s. Beneš succeeded Masaryk as Czechoslovakia's second President in 1935.

3 Hitler stepping in to 'protect' Bohemia-Moravia after the collapse of Czecho-Slovakia in mid-March 1939. Slovakia and Ruthenia sparked the crisis by declaring independence.

4 Hodonín forced-labour camp in Moravia (1942). Czech Gypsies were interned here by the Czech Protectorate authorities from 1939.

5 German speakers, stripped of their rights as Czechoslovak citizens, awaiting deportation from Prague in May 1945.

6 Hlinka Guard assembling Jews for deportation during the Second World War. The Tiso regime prided itself on its 'independent' approach to solving Slovakia's Jewish 'problem'.

7 President Beneš signing the nationalization decrees which launched postwar Czechoslovakia's distinctly socialist and nationalist revolution

8 Klement Gottwald's balcony speech was made into the prime symbol of the Communist takeover of February 1948.

9 A celebration in Zvolen in 1949 to mark the fifth anniversary of the Slovak National Uprising. The Communists, like the Fascists, skilfully exploited Czech and Slovak national feeling.

10 Slovak Fascist leader Jozef Tiso being handed over to the Czechoslovak authorities in October 1945. The publication of this photograph sparked a campaign in his defence.

11 The trial of so-called 'Vatican agents' held in Prague in 1950. Political show trials were used to discredit rival organizations to the Communist Party.

12 This concrete monument to the Czech Communist leader Klement Gottwald overshadowed a central square in Bratislava until 1990.

13 On the night of 20–21 August 1968, the armies of five Warsaw Pact countries entered Czechoslovak territory. They claimed to be offering 'fraternal assistance' to prevent 'counter-revolution' in a fellow socialist state.

14 The Moscow Protocol, signed on 26 August 1968 by the Soviet and Czechoslovak Communist leaderships, pledged to reverse all the Prague Spring reforms except federalization.

15 Alexander Dubček breaking the bad news to the nation that a 'temporary' return to censorship would be needed to 'normalize' the situation (27 August 1968). With this speech, he won the necessary support to undo the Prague Spring reforms.

16 Gustáv Husák taking charge at an extraordinary permanent session of the Communist Party begun on the night of 28 August 1968. Husák presided over 'Normalization' and remained in power until 1987.

17 President Václav Havel being heckled during a speech in Slovakia in 1991. After it proved impossible to reconcile Czech and Slovak national grievances, Czechoslovakia was dissolved and replaced by independent Czech and Slovak republics from 1 January 1993.

18 An approved student demonstration, held in Prague on 17 November 1989, was unexpectedly met by a wall of riot police. The rumour that a student had been killed galvanized public opinion and quickly led to revolution.

The Slánský and related show trials of the early 1950s were not of a funda-
mentally different kind from the tens of thousands of other, far more obscure
Czechoslovak political trials – of National Socialists, Slovak Democrats, priests,
nuns, monks, scout leaders, members of *Sokol*, army recruits, 'kulaks' and
countless other 'class enemies', to say nothing of hundreds of thousands of
alleged 'traitors', wartime 'collaborators', 'saboteurs' and 'black marketeers' –
that preceded or accompanied this most sensational of trials. But there were
two important differences. Unlike the other trials, which were a purely
Czechoslovak affair, the quest for 'the Czechoslovak Rajk' was prompted by
'fraternal' pressure from other socialist countries, particularly Hungary, and
included some direct Soviet involvement. Pressure and advice were not,
however, the same thing as compulsion; and while contemporary Hungarian
and East German political trials bore an uncanny resemblance to the
Czechoslovak ones, the Polish Communist Party appears to have managed
successfully to ignore the hints and requests from Moscow to conform.

In later years, the Slánský trial and related purges and denunciations were
taken by Czechoslovak Communists themselves as a matter for 'self-criticism'
and explained away as a symptom of the 'personality cult' that a mistaken
reliance upon Stalin was supposed to have provoked. Upon closer inspection,
this turns out not to have been so much a 'self-criticism' as an avoidance of
the main point and a passing of the buck to other Communists – whether
rivals within the party or safely distant foreign comrades – who were held
individually responsible for the torture, forced confessions and fabrications
of evidence that had characterized the trials. At no point were the many thousands of other show trials publicly explained or regretted. For the first time
since February 1948, substantial numbers of Communist Party members
were included among the aggrieved and discontented with the regime at
home. By blaming the obvious miscarriages of justice on the Soviet authorities, they were able to leave their underlying faith in the righteousness of
Czechoslovak socialism intact.

On 5 March 1953, Stalin died. In Prague, Wenceslas Square filled to
capacity with mourners dressed in black for a special commemorative ceremony, with a podium set up outside the National Museum and an enormous
banner showing Stalin's face. Since Gottwald was in Moscow to attend Stalin's
funeral, the main speeches were given by Zápotocký (in Czech) followed by
Široký (in Slovak). According to the 'revolutionary' style in vogue at the time,
the speeches were declaimed rather than spoken, and were virtually indistinguishable from one another. The first half of each Communist leader's
speech expressed gratitude to the 'Great Stalin' as the 'Defender of Peace',
'Champion of Working People Everywhere' and Czechoslovakia's 'Teacher,
Liberator and Friend'; the second half, less traditionally for a funeral oration,
furiously lambasted 'capitalists', 'criminals', 'Fascists', 'traitors' and other

vaguely defined enemies. Široký, a short and slightly absurd figure, became so hysterical during the latter part of his speech that his voice cracked; but no one laughed. The speeches concluded, in a manner highly reminiscent of Nazi rallies, with the crowd asked to take a public oath to 'defend socialism'. The ceremony was then rounded off with a gun salute and the singing of 'The Internationale'.[91]

Within a fortnight, the entire performance had to be repeated, this time to mark the death of President Gottwald, who died on 14 March 1953, officially of a cold caught while attending Stalin's funeral, but presumably in fact because of his rampant alcoholism. Gottwald's body, like Stalin's, was embalmed and placed on public view in a glass coffin. Wrapped in the Czechoslovak flag and flanked by soldiers, the corpse of 'K.G.', the first 'Worker-President', was solemnly carried on a gun barrel from the Castle, past Letná plain, across the River Vltava to Republic Square, up to the National Museum at the top of Wenceslas Square, and then to its final resting place in a special tomb, reminiscent of Lenin's tomb in Moscow, at Vítkov. Despite frantic *KSČ* directives to keep numbers down, a crowd of 200,000 filled Wenceslas Square to capacity to hear his funeral oration. This time, they were treated to an even fiercer speech by Zápotocký, which climaxed with a public oath in which everyone present swore to continue to 'build socialism' and never to turn their backs on 'the Soviet Union', 'Lenin', 'Stalin' and 'progress'. On May Day 1953, which was marked by the launch of Czechoslovak television's first regular broadcast, the same message of 'no change' was again strongly signalled. The leadership had little choice but to continue on the same path. Not only was it in the middle of preparations for yet more political trials, to thoroughly purge the *KSS*, but the Czechoslovak economy – which had faithfully followed the Stalinist model of promoting grand symbols of heavy industry at the expense of consumer needs – was approaching collapse. A drastic devaluation of the Czechoslovak crown by a factor of ten, which was later remembered as the 'Great Swindle', was already scheduled for 1 June 1953.[92] As things turned out, the monetary reform was to lead to demonstrations and even riots so widespread and severe that they could only be put down by making the fullest, most brutal use of police powers, giving those who took part in the demonstrations another reason to resent and hate the regime under which they lived.

In Moscow, where Nikita Khrushchev took over as first secretary of the Communist Party of the Soviet Union, there were immediately signs that some sort of power struggle was taking place in the Kremlin. Luckily for Antonín Zápotocký, who as prime minister had betrayed Slánský to the *StB*, too many people were implicated in the recent party purges for his own neck to be at risk, and he was unanimously elected Czechoslovakia's second 'Worker-President' by the National Assembly on 21 May 1953. Antonín Novotný, who had been specially commended for his help in 'unmasking' Slánský and other 'traitors', took over as first secretary of the *KSČ*, while Viliam Široký, the rising Slovak Communist star who was hard at work rooting out 'Slovak bourgeois nationalism' in the *KSS*, was made deputy prime minister. Zápotocký made his first presidential appearance on the same balcony at the Castle where Hitler had received crowds of Sudeten Germans in March 1939. This time, a Czech crowd chanted 'Long live Comrade President!'[93]

No sooner had Stalin died than *Pravda*, the Soviet equivalent of the *KSČ*'s *Rudé právo*, suddenly stopped printing stories about a supposed plot hatched by Jewish doctors to take Comrade Stalin's life. Within six months, Beria, the chief of the Soviet secret police, had himself been accused, put on trial, sentenced and executed. As Zdeněk Mlynář, a promising young Czech Stalinist who had been sent to study at the Higher Political School in Moscow, later recalled, throughout 1954 and 1955 criticism of Stalinist terror was voiced more and more openly, while even party-controlled newspapers began to criticize aspects of Soviet bureaucracy and to write about the need for 'collective leadership' in the party, campaigns against 'cosmopolitanism' gradually died out and the atmosphere of suspicion relaxed. As a young Slovak Communist named Alexander Dubček who was brought up in the Soviet Union later recalled, the most extraordinary symbol of the changing times came at the end of 1955, when Khrushchev flew to Belgrade and addressed Tito – who until recently had been called an 'agent of imperialism', 'executioner' and 'imperialist lackey', and caricatured as a vulture-faced figure in Nazi uniform with a blood-soaked axe in his hand – as 'Dear Comrade'.[94]

Oblivious to the signs of change that those living in Moscow were beginning to notice, on May Day 1955 (ten years after the idea had first been mooted, six years after the foundation stone had been laid and two years after Stalin and Gottwald's deaths), a colossal statue of Comrade Stalin leading a vanguard of peasants and workers was solemnly unveiled on Letná plain, on the very spot that T.G. Masaryk had once selected as the national *Sokol* exercise ground.[95] The monument, the subject of 'voluntary' drives and 'enthusiastic' national campaigns, measured a full 30 m (32.8 yards) in height and weighed 14,000 metric tonnes (13,779 tons).[96] In the same year, a specifically Czechoslovak symbol of national and socialist unity was also launched: enormous sporting pageants, reminiscent of the *Sokol slets* of years gone by, in which masses of amateur gymnasts demonstrated their ability to move in perfect synchronization: the *Spartakiáda*. The *Spartakiáda*, which was designed – like economic plans – to recur every five years, and which continued right up to the year 1990, drew on the patriotic associations of gymnastics that *Sokol* had spread, but also sent out the subliminal message that each individual had a place in the great socialist collective, in which the whole was greater than the sum of its parts.[97]

Khrushchev's 'secret speech' on Stalin's crimes as delivered to the Twentieth Communist Party Congress at the beginning of 1956 dropped a bombshell to hardline Communists the world over, not least in Czechoslovakia. Mlynář, stunned, was particularly struck by the 'concrete details' of the 'torture and forced confessions in political trials', which, as he could see only too well, had 'direct implications for Czechoslovakia.' Dubček, who did not feel 'ready' to hear 'much of what they were saying', later recalled being 'shocked when they stated bluntly that Stalin had been a murderer'. The revelations were simply 'too sudden' and 'too momentous' to grasp.[98] In the People's Republic of Czechoslovakia, where everything possible had been done to elevate Gottwald to the status of a second Stalin, the currency reform of 1953 had led to widespread economic misery, and the political show trials had rivalled those of the Soviet Union in their scope, cynicism and brutality, the about-turn in Soviet policy came as a particularly nasty shock to the KSČ leadership. Since those members of the Communist Party who had survived the purges justified their part in creating terror on the grounds of faithfully following Soviet orders, they now found themselves in a dilemma. To admit their own guilt in creating and perpetuating what were suddenly being called Stalinist 'deformities' might end up costing them their necks; yet to continue to defend the status quo would make them vulnerable to the charge of 'deviating from the Soviet model', the very crime for which they had persecuted their former colleagues. Unsurprisingly, the party leadership tried to walk a tightrope between these two equally unpalatable alternatives, making a few noises of token approval of Comrade Khrushchev's new departure while at the same time doing everything possible to prevent any real reform from taking place within the KSČ or the KSS.[99] The first cautious criticisms of the Stalinist model were therefore raised, not by the top leadership, but in the lower ranks of the party and in university departments of Marxism-Leninism, and were then aired at the Second Writers' Congress held on 22–29 April 1956.

It was at a meeting of students from Charles University held on 26 April in the School of Chemistry in the Albertov district of Prague that pressure on the party leadership grew more trenchant in tone. Students suggested an end 'to mere copying of the USSR' on the grounds that 'mechanically adopting the Soviet experience' had 'done great harm to our educational system and, in particular, to our economic system'.[100] Since, as some claimed, 'further harm' had been done 'by playing the Soviet national anthem at the end of every broadcast day [sic] and the displaying of Soviet flags at all occasions', they also requested that 'the Soviet national anthem and Soviet flag be present only on occasions which directly involve the Soviet Union, e.g. the November 7 and May 9 celebrations'. The meeting turned into a heated debate, lasting five hours, which ended in the adoption of a formal resolution asking for 'a public review of the Slánský and other political trials' together with 'a guarantee of rightful political punishment for persons who tolerated illegal procedures during interrogations and for those who directly carried out these procedures'. It also requested an 'amnesty for convicted persons similar to the amnesty recently declared in the Polish People's Republic', and stated that it did 'not consider correct the view of Mr. Novotný' that 'The Central Committee ... decides and must decide the most important questions of the Party and state' since this ignored 'the principle that workers must be governed according to their own convictions' and 'distorts the real content and leading role of the Party'.[101] *Mladá fronta*, the official newspaper of the Communist-controlled Czechoslovak Union of Youth, which might have ignored or condemned the students, instead suggested that, like 'all honest people today', the students cared 'only about eliminating the insufficiencies and mistakes in our life as soon as possible'.[102] After a deputation of students in Prague solemnly called on the minister of education on 4 May with a resolution demanding change, copy-cat student resolutions began to appear all over the country: first at Comenius University in Bratislava and, by 15 May, at universities and colleges all over the country, including at Brno, Ostrava, Plzeň, Košice, Banská Bystrica and Nitra.[103] The student protest movement peaked on 20 May, when it made use of the traditional student carnival known as *Majáles*, reinstated for the first time since 1948, to demand reform.

Luckily for the KSČ leadership, any desire for reform by high Communist officials was for the time being dampened by the sight of the fraternal Communist Party in Poland having to be rescued by the Soviet Union in October 1956, and above all of the fraternal Communist Party in Hungary, where civil war had broken out and prominent Communists were lynched before the Soviet army came in to 'normalize' the situation and restore its preferred Communist leadership to power. This was just as well, since the Barák Commission, when it completed its investigations into the Czechoslovak political trials, found that too many men in the current Presidium – not least First Secretary Novotný – were so hopelessly implicated that it had little option but to conclude that the trials had been conducted in strict accordance with the law and to uphold all the guilty verdicts. In such a politically dangerous situation, Novotný, on Zápotocký's death on 13 November 1957, simply took over the presidency of the republic in addition to retaining his position as first secretary of the KSČ, blocking the way to any would-be rivals for power.

By 1960, the Communist regime in Czechoslovakia was proud of what it had achieved. In less than fifteen years, the nationalization of industry and collectivization of agriculture had been realized; the Church effectively silenced; the army purged; rival political parties rendered powerless; and the economy reoriented from wartime dependence on Germany to postwar dependence on the Soviet Union and the rest of the Eastern bloc. A vast network of prisons and forced-labour camps had been built or adapted to contain opposition and

The Czechoslovak Socialist Republic, 1960–68

to silence dissent. Many of the inspiring and revolutionary aims for which the older generation of Communists had been prepared to serve prison sentences in the First Czechoslovak Republic, or to risk their lives under Fascism, had been achieved, at however high a price. As Communists saw things, there were no longer private capitalists or the old divisions based on social class; officially at least, there was no unemployment and no homelessness. Free medical care, old-age pensions and education were available to everyone. The average standard of living, though by no means 'affluent', was 'decent' and believed to be rising. Even the housing crisis, clearly 'the most sensitive spot' in the matter of living standards, seemed to be 'soluble in time by stepping up housing construction, which the Stalinist emphasis on developing heavy industry had eclipsed'.[104] The *KSČ* and *KSS* had, in short, 'achieved' the primary aims of 'socialism' and so felt able to declare the People's Republic of Czechoslovakia a fully fledged Socialist Republic.

On 9 April 1960, the regime took the precaution of readjusting the regional boundaries of the state in such a way as to prevent any resurgence of Slovak 'bourgeois' nationalism and ensure a firm centralization of the state. This came in the shape of a new law that divided the country into ten regions: seven in the Bohemian Crown Lands and three in Slovakia (the western, central and eastern Slovak regions). On 5–7 July, a state-wide congress of the Communist Party of Czechoslovakia announced that socialism had been victorious in Czechoslovakia, and discussed a draft of a new constitution to acknowledge the fact. Article 1 of the constitution adopted on 11 July 1960 declared the 'unitary state of two fraternal nations possessing equal rights, the Czechs and the Slovaks', to be a 'socialist state founded on the firm alliance of the workers, peasants and intelligentsia, with the working class at its head', and to be 'part of the world socialist system'.[105] Although the Slovak National Council was preserved, it was specifically restricted to working 'under the direction of the Communist Party of Czechoslovakia' to ensure 'a uniform execution of state power and administration' together with 'the general development of the economy and culture in Slovakia'.[106] The body that was supposed to administer state policies in Slovakia, the Board of Commissioners, was abolished, as were several Slovak branches of central institutions.

Article 4 of the constitution made explicit that 'the guiding force in society and in the state is the vanguard of the working class, the Communist Party of Czechoslovakia', which was defined as 'a voluntary militant alliance of the most active and most politically conscious citizens from the ranks of the workers, peasants and intelligentsia'.[107] The 'entire national economy' was to be 'directed by the state plan for the development of the national economy', a plan that was 'usually to be worked out for a period of five years' and, together with the annual state budget, promulgated by law.[108] The place of ideology was assured in Article 16, which stated that the 'entire cultural policy of Czechoslovakia, the development of all forms of education, schooling and instruction' were to be 'directed in the spirit of the scientific world outlook, Marxism-Leninism, and closely linked to the work of the people'. The state and the 'people's organisations' were further instructed 'systematically [to] endeavour to free the minds of the people from the surviving influences of a society based on exploitation'.[109] As part of the constitution's stated aim of securing 'the full development of socialist society' and creating 'the conditions for the gradual transition to communism', particular attention was to be paid to 'eliminating the substantial differences between physical and mental labour and between town and country'.[110] In the latter aim, the 'fraternal co-operation between the Czechoslovak Socialist Republic and the Union of Soviet Socialist Republics and other countries of the world socialist system' was singled out for attention, and promises were made to 'systematically develop and strengthen this co-operation, which is based on mutual assistance and the international socialist division of labour'.[111]

With the power of the Communist Party secure at home, and protected internationally by the support of the Warsaw Pact and *de facto* Western acceptance of the Soviet sphere of influence, the Czechoslovak government and *KSČ* could afford to relax a little. Since a combination of fear, the desire to do right by one's family and the less lovely human characteristics of greed, envy and ambition appeared to be enough to keep most people in check most of the time, outright terror was no longer necessary. The subtext of the 1960 constitution was clear: although the most embarrassingly kitsch aspects of the personality cult would no longer be insisted upon, and although mass political show trials were no longer considered necessary to teach the population at large the value of at least outward conformity, the party would continue to monitor and control all aspects of citizens' lives, its ideology would remain firmly Stalinist, and its partnership with the Soviet Union would continue, in the words of a favourite motto of the day, forever.

CHAPTER 8

THE BRATISLAVA AND PRAGUE SPRINGS

The 'Prague Spring', as Czechoslovakia's 1960s experiment in reform socialism is usually known, became so famous that it is easy to forget that it represented merely one, relatively brief episode in four long decades of Communist Party rule. The selective freedom from censorship that the *KSS* decided to permit in Slovakia from 1963, and which was adopted by the *KSČ* as state policy in 1968, created an exhilarating atmosphere which those who experienced it were never to forget. It also won the Communist Party in Czechoslovakia a level of domestic support and enthusiasm that it had not enjoyed since the Communists' cabinet coup of February 1948. The Prague Spring, which opened the country up to the scrutiny of tourists and journalists, rehabilitated Czechoslovakia in the eyes of the Western world, turning its image from one of an exceptionally brutal Soviet satellite into that of the democratically inclined home of humane socialism. It would be nice to believe that members of the Communist Party leadership, their consciences awakened by the horrors of the 1950s, undertook the Prague Spring reforms for their own sake; but, in a political system that routinely disgraced and punished anyone who stepped out of line with current policy directives, there was not a lot of scope for independent initiative – let alone idealism – in either the Slovak or the Czechoslovak Communist parties. Nor, in a system in which the only way for the politically ambitious to get ahead was to oust those who stood in their way, can the labels 'reformist' or 'orthodox' be taken at face value.

Traditional political histories are often, and quite rightly, criticized for focusing too narrowly on political élites at the expense of ordinary people. In the case of 1960s Czechoslovakia, the risk is rather of making the opposite mistake. The Communist reforms that were tentatively launched in Bratislava in 1963, but became internationally known only after they were adopted in Prague in 1968, had more to do with political machinations within the *KSS* and *KSČ* leaderships than with big ideas. The notion that it was 'the people' of Czechoslovakia who brought about 'democratic change' to return the Czech and Slovak nations to their humane, socialist and democratic 'roots' was little more than party propaganda, this time espoused by so-called 'reformists' within the *KSS* and *KSČ* to rally support and discredit their opposite numbers. The new party line, obediently echoed by the party faithful and publicized by journalists, was uncritically adopted by émigré communities and spread throughout the West, where it flourished because it could be taken by the political Left to demonstrate the innate goodness of socialism, and by the political Right to show the universal appeal of liberalism.

That the new party line proved popular among many Czech and Slovak Communists is not surprising. It managed to square the circle by flattering idealized Czech and Slovak national self-portraits while simultaneously strengthening the notion of the Communist Party as the 'vanguard' of socialist society. However briefly, the Bratislava Spring managed to convince a majority in Slovakia that Slovak national interests were best protected by the *KSS*, just as the Prague Spring managed briefly to restore the sense – which had first triumphed during the Third Republic of 1945–48 – that an innately Czech nationalist and socialist identity was best expressed by the *KSČ*.

At the beginning of the 1960s, there was nothing to suggest that hardline Czechoslovakia would become the home of a Communist reform movement significant enough to divide socialist opinion for two decades. In 1960, fifteen years since the end of the Second World War and the year in which Czechoslovakia formally became a Socialist Republic, the ruling Czechoslovak Communist Party was still one of the most authoritarian and uncompromising in Europe. It was also one of the loudest in expressing its adulation of the Soviet Union and friendship with the other socialist states of the Warsaw Pact. In newsreels and bulletins, television and radio programmes, newspaper and magazine articles – to say nothing of the heavily stylized political speeches given at Communist Party plenums and congresses and at 'elections' – 'the Soviet example', 'Soviet experience' and 'Soviet teaching' were tirelessly held up to Czechs and Slovaks for admiration and emulation. State television and radio ended their daily broadcasts by playing the Czechoslovak and Soviet national anthems. Soviet flags were twinned with Czechoslovak flags not only on the 7 November and 9 May holidays, when this would have made logical sense, but even on holidays of purely Czechoslovak significance, such as 28 October (once known as Independence Day, but since the latest regime change rebranded as 'Nationalization Day'). Schoolchildren were taught Soviet, as well as Czech and Slovak, socialist anthems and traditional folk songs, and brought up on inspiring tales of socialist achievement, often translated from the original Russian or German. When they became Pioneers, the Soviet-inspired equivalent of the Boy and Girl Scouts, they vowed to 'defend socialism' and wore the same uniform as their Polish, East German, Hungarian, Bulgarian, Soviet and other Communist counterparts. Although travel to the Soviet Union and contact with real people from the USSR were virtually unknown for ordinary people, an élite within the Communist Party characteristically made use of Soviet advisors to resolve problems within large organizations of importance to the party, such as the army, judiciary and secret police; and promising young members of the Communist Party – the sorts of people who would later become candidate members of the Presidium of the Central Committee of the *KSČ* – were sent to the special party political school in Moscow for intensive study and training.

Reminders of the debt of gratitude supposed to be owed by the Czech and Slovak peoples to their Soviet liberators from Nazism were to be found in every part of the country, including in Slovakia, which had not been occupied by the Germans until 1944, and where the Slovak National Uprising – officially held up as a Communist and Bolshevik achievement – was still privately muttered to have been sabotaged by the Soviets. In Prague, some of the more prominent memorials to the Soviet Union included 'Soviet Tank Drivers' Square' (complete with the actual tank, Soviet Tank Number 23, said to have been the first to enter the city in May 1945), the vast cemetery for fallen Soviet soldiers at Olšany, and *Brotherhood*, the well-known statue depicting a Red Army and a Czechoslovak soldier clasped in a warm embrace.[1] All over the country, the pattern was the same: ideologically correct names, the most obvious of which were Lenin, Stalin and Gottwald, had been given to streets, squares, tram stops and factories as part of a heavy-handed political and didactic campaign to re-educate the nation. Prague's Reiger and Masaryk embankments along the River Vltava had been renamed the Gottwald and Marx and Engels embankments. The Škoda plant in Plzeň and Vítkovice ironworks had become the 'Lenin' and the 'Klement Gottwald' works. Even the Moravian city of Zlín, home to the Bat'a shoe empire, had been renamed 'Gottwaldov' ('Gottwaldville').[2]

From all important vantage points in Prague city centre – the Old Town Square, the top of Wenceslas Square, the middle of Charles Bridge – could be seen, on the crest of Letná hill, the colossal granite statue of the 'Generalissimo of the World Proletariat', the largest such representation of Comrade Stalin to be found anywhere in the world. On Vítkov, another of Prague's seven hills, an equally grotesquely oversized statue – that of the equestrian Hussite warrior Žižka – marked the place where Masaryk's monument to the Czechoslovak Legions had been turned into a mausoleum for Communist dignitaries and decorated with a suitable mixture of proletarian, Hussite and explicitly Communist themes. Inside, Gottwald's corpse, which had already been visited by over a million people, was carefully measured every day for humidity by a team of Soviet-trained embalming experts. At the far end of the monument, a chapel-like space had been turned into a special hall to honour the Red Army, complete with Socialist Realist mosaics of Soviet soldiers and – in the place where a holy water stoup would be found in a church – a stand containing a few grains of soil from the socialist motherland. In Bratislava, where Slovak National Uprising (*SNP*) Square had been graced by a prominent statue of Stalin since 1949, an obelisk to honour seven thousand Soviet soldiers lost in the battle for Bratislava was solemnly unveiled at the cemetery on the top of Slavín hill; the monument was so huge that it could be seen from virtually every street corner in the city. Another Bratislava Square (today's *námestie Slobody* or 'Freedom Square'), which in the First Republic had been presided over by a statue of Štefánik, had been turned into 'Gottwald Square' through the placement of a grotesquely over-sized statue of the first Czechoslovak, and Czech, Worker-President.

Although Czechoslovakia still retained the shell of the multiparty National Front coalition as created in 1945, together with the outward appearance of a parliament and president, the real power in the land was the Czechoslovak Communist Party (*KSČ*), whose first secretary – because he simultaneously held the office of President of the Republic – resided at the Castle on Hradčany in Prague. The Slovak Communist Party (*KSS*) was tightly controlled along the same lines as the *KSČ* and looked like the latter's mirror image, since it had its own Central Committee, secretariat, Presidium, first secretary and apparatus, and was kept busy issuing directives and holding meetings and congresses. In fact, however, since 1949 it had had no function other than to implement policy decisions as previously worked out by the *KSČ*.

Despite the air of fossil-like permanence that prevailed throughout the Socialist Republic, there was growing disaffection within the Communist Party, and especially in the *KSS*, since the powers that Slovakia had been promised in the Košice Programme, already compromised in 1949, had just been further watered down in the 1960 constitution and by the reorganization of the country into regions that undermined Slovakia's integrity as a coherent territorial entity and placed it under the competency of the Ministry of the Interior in Prague.[3] And there were also other, less tangible signs of Czech dominance. However much Hussite iconography and the cult of Klement Gottwald, the first Czech Worker-President, might resonate among Czech Communists, there seemed less and less room within the Communist Party even for politically engaged expressions of Slovak patriotism. While the most high-profile victims of the 1950s' show trials within the Czechoslovak Communist Party had been Jews accused of 'Zionist' as well as 'Titoist' crimes, in Slovakia most had been Slovaks accused directly of 'Slovak bourgeois nationalism'.

Many Czech Communists, especially those who had been accused, purged, demoted or imprisoned during the 1950s, were also disgruntled. A whole generation of committed Stalinists – mainly Czech, but also Slovak – who had joined the Communist Party just after the Second World War, typically when they were in their twenties or thirties, were on the brink of middle age and the most influential part of their careers. Many of those who, as promising young candidates, had been sent up for special training in Moscow at just the time that Khrushchev's reforms were taking hold in the Soviet Union found the Czechoslovakia to which they returned old-fashioned and excessively authoritarian. While they continued to justify the hardline Stalinism of their youth as having been necessary to uproot Czechoslovakia's 'bourgeois traditions', now that 'class warfare' had been officially declared to have ended with the 'victory of the working class', there no longer seemed any reason to prolong the mood of 'vigilance'.

As everyone was uneasily aware, the economy seemed to be in a chronic state of crisis, despite the constant trumpeting of the 'achievements of socialism' at Communist Party Congresses, on big Communist Party occasions like the annual May Day parades, in newsreels, and on television and radio, billboards and banners. Month after month, confidential situation reports from the *StB* diligently recorded the overheard complaints of housewives and others about the scarcity or poor quality of food and other staples. At politically sensitive times, such as just before elections, when such reports were brought to the direct attention of the first secretary of the *KSČ*, they were usually accompanied by clandestine public opinion surveys compiled by the *StB* from the private letters they steamed open, typically in batches of about seventeen thousand.

What was beginning to trouble economists in the party was the growing suspicion that five-year economic plans, which concentrated on heavy industry as political showpieces rather than as responses to demand, might be what was unbalancing the economy and leading to constant shortages of consumer goods. Now that the Soviet Union seemed more or less reconciled with Tito, the possibility of choosing the 'Yugoslav option' of introducing elements from the capitalist economic system to 'strengthen socialism' was no longer politically unthinkable. This seemed to so-called 'reform' economists one way in which Czechoslovakia might catch up with the increasingly embarrassing gap between the Stalinist-style command economies of the People's Democracies and the more consumer-oriented and technologically sophisticated capitalist countries of the West. Some of the more daring even began to suggest that it was the ideologically justified policy of 'wage equalization' that sapped the initiative from firms and agricultural cooperatives, just as pressure to fill the obligatory quotas led to indifference to quality, resulting in shoddy products that could not be traded on the world market for hard currency. A final matter of growing concern to the *KSČ* was the apparent indifference towards socialism on the part of the young, children of the revolution who, although too young to have imbibed the 'bourgeois' values of the First Republic, seemed unmoved by clarion calls to embrace socialism, declining to join the party or to take more than a token interest in political life. Some began to suggest that, rather than fall back on the traditional remedy for political laxity – to increase the pressure to 'engage' – a more 'positive' approach might be taken to strengthening the party's 'leading role' in the 'vanguard' of socialist society.

It was not so much Khrushchev's 'secret speech' of 1956, in which Stalin was first denounced to the party faithful, as the Soviet leader's addresses to the Twenty-Second Congress of the Soviet Communist Party, which was held in Moscow in October 1961, that first prompted change within the *KSČ* leadership. This time, Khrushchev not only renewed and extended his denunciations of Stalinism; he did so at a public meeting at which Antonín Novotný, first secretary of the *KSČ* (and, since 1957, simultaneously president of Czechoslovakia), was in attendance. The congress was immediately followed by the removal of Stalin's embalmed body from its resting place next to Lenin in the mausoleum in Red Square, in order to signal formal displeasure at the 'personality cult' of which he had become the prime symbol. This unambiguous sign from the Kremlin put Novotný in a tight corner. On the one hand, he could not afford simply to ignore Moscow's lead as the Chinese did, but must be seen to be liberalizing; on the other hand, he could not yet permit thoroughgoing Czechoslovak reforms, since any attempt to 'de-Stalinize' would inevitably lead to the pointing of accusing fingers at men who were still part of his Presidium – most notably Gottwald's remaining appointments, Viliam Široký, Karol Bacílek and Bruno Koehler – as well, perhaps, as himself.

In a political system in which one of the few ways for the ambitious to get ahead was to disgrace and oust the party leader, there was no shortage of political rivals willing to jump on the reformist bandwagon as a means of promoting their own careers. Alexander Dubček, who had been trained in Moscow and risen through the ranks of the *KSS* to be rewarded for fourteen years of loyal service by being appointed secretary for industry in the Central Committee of the state-wide *KSČ*, was among the first to sense the new possibilities. When, just after the Twenty-Second Soviet Communist Party Congress, the hitherto impeccably conformist Dubček was asked to accompany Novotný to an international congress of Communist Party leaders in Bucharest, nothing more was anticipated than the usual round of dull speeches. As it happened, however, the Chinese delegates' criticisms of Khrushchev's anti-Stalinist policies became so sharp that, in an unexpected departure from protocol, Khrushchev called an unscheduled meeting of all foreign delegates. Since there was no time to prepare a formal speech and have it translated into Russian, a language in which Novotný was not at home, Dubček, who had grown up in the Soviet Union and spoke perfect Russian, was suddenly given the floor. Quick as a flash, he used the occasion to defend Khrushchev's reforms, simultaneously ingratiating himself with the Soviet leadership and pushing Novotný into precisely the corner he had been so artfully managing to avoid since the first winds of change had begun to blow from the Kremlin in 1956. Small wonder that, as Dubček afterwards complained, Novotný systematically tried to 'cut him down', demoting him from his position as secretary in the state-wide *KSČ* to that of secretary in the regional *KSS*, and avoided taking him to further congresses.[4]

Novotný needed to buy time with further token gestures of Khrushchevization until his position within the Presidium could be sufficiently strengthened to allow him to introduce more sweeping economic reforms and, with them, some political changes. At a meeting held on 15 November 1961, he therefore laid what he described as two 'weighty' problems before his comrades in the Central Committee. The first was what to do about the Stalin monument at Letná, whose 'megalomania and bombast' and 'main figure' he now declared to be in conflict with the 'political convictions of our Party' as well as the 'purity' of the 'brotherly relationship' between the Czechoslovak and Soviet peoples. The second problem was what to do about Gottwald's embalmed body, whose symbolism, Novotný now proclaimed, 'hardly corresponds with the traditions and feelings of our people' and whose message was in any case not 'in harmony' with a properly 'Leninist understanding of the role of the personality and the collective nature of leadership'.[5]

Among the motions that the *KSČ* Central Committee adopted in late 1961 were therefore resolutions to remove Gottwald's body, cremate it and bury the ashes in the memorial hall at Vítkov, 'in the same way as was done with all other leading warriors of the Party'; to rename all factories and streets called after Stalin; and to appoint a 'politico-expert commission' to prepare 'plans for the best use of the site where the Stalin monument now stands', whose new subject might best stem from 'the revolutionary traditions of our people and of Prague, from May 1945 and February 1948'.[6] It was this resolution that led, in 1962, to a remarkable public spectacle: the destruction, on orders from the *KSČ* leadership, of the Stalin statue on Letná hill. Although Novotný's evident hope had been to deal with the matter quickly and without fuss, it took a full two months of jack-hammering, with crews working night and day, to reduce the monolith to rubble. Rumours quickly spread that the statue had cost as much as a hospital and a housing development combined; so did the joke that Stalin – who was shown in Napoleonic pose, with his hand on his heart – had been reaching inside his breast pocket for his wallet when, upon hearing how much the statue was to cost, he turned to stone.[7] Gottwald's remains were disposed of more discreetly: his corpse was cremated and the ashes buried at Vítkov in a private ceremony for no more than fifteen or twenty high Communist officials.[8] In Slovakia, where it was also necessary to show that the 'cult of personality' was officially discredited, the Stalin statue in Bratislava's SNP Square was duly removed, but the much more bombastic statue of Gottwald left in place.[9]

Making grand gestures to symbolize the 'abolition' of the 'cult of personality' in the Czechoslovak Socialist Republic, however much expectation they may have aroused among Czech Communists in particular, was relatively risk-free for the Novotný regime. A much more difficult problem was posed by the Soviet example of rehabilitating the victims of the Stalinist political trials and denouncing those held to have been responsible for extorting 'confessions' and fabricating 'crimes'. Czechoslovak minister of the interior and deputy prime minister Rudolf Barák appears to have been the first to plan to use the evidence that his commission had uncovered in 1955–57 to implicate most of the current leadership in the staging of the Czechoslovak show trials of the 1950s, including the Slánský trial, and thus to seize power for a rival group within the KSČ. Novotný swiftly had Barák removed from the Presidium and the KSČ and sentenced to fifteen years in prison on trumped-up charges of embezzlement. He even arranged, in classic 1950s style, for a special exhibition of the deputy prime minister's 'expensive suits and shirts', along with 'foreign banknotes, pictures and art objects', to be set up for the television cameras in order to discredit him with the public.[10] Having rid himself of his most immediate rival, Novotný concentrated on laying the ground for his future security by seizing the opportunities left by the deaths of Gottwald's immediate successor, Antonín Zápotocký (in 1957), and Václav Kopecký (in 1962), to staff the Presidium with three men – Jiří Hendrych, Drahomír Kolder and Michal Chudík – who were at once free of the taint of the political trials and personally indebted to him.[11]

At the KSČ's Twelfth Party Congress, which was held in late 1962, Novotný put forward draft proposals for a new version of the Communist Party statutes whose primary purpose appeared to be to cement his own position as leader of the party (as first secretary of the KSČ) and state (as President of the Republic). After these met with criticism, he circulated an ominous-looking appendix to the draft listing all the 'negative' points and opinions that had been raised during discussion.[12] By the beginning of 1963, Novotný had secured his position sufficiently to feel that he could not only risk Khrushchev-style reforms but, like Khrushchev himself, benefit from them. He therefore set up a new commission of enquiry into the Slánský and associated political show trials, under the direction of Drahomír Kolder, a regional party secretary in Ostrava who owed his position to Novotný's patronage. This time, the purpose of the investigation was to enable Novotný to claim the mantle of reform, simultaneously winning the approval of the current Soviet leadership and the loyalty of reform-minded members within his own Central Committee.

In February 1963, the Kolder Commission reported to the Presidium that the Slánský and associated political show trials of the 1950s had fabricated evidence, extorted confessions and in every way conformed to the pattern of the discredited Stalinist trials of the 1930s. The sensational revelations were passed on to the Central Committee in April 1963 and to the general public in late August. The Kolder Commission, of which Dubček was a member, although sweeping in its rehabilitation of the Czech Communists – who were absolved of any form of Titoist treason – was more reserved in the matter of the show trials of so-called 'Slovak bourgeois nationalists'. Vladimír Clementis, Gustáv Husák, Ladislav Novomeský and the other prominent Slovak Communists who had been victims in these trials, although granted civil rehabilitation, were not restored to full party membership on the grounds that Slovak 'bourgeois nationalism' genuinely represented a 'deviation' from properly 'proletarian internationalism'.[13] This gave Dubček – who replaced the former minister of security (Karol Bacílek) as first secretary of the *KSS* in May 1963 and knew that Novotný had reason to suspect him – the opportunity to play the Slovak card.

From the same time that Dubček, as a member of the Kolder Commission, received information that implicated Novotný as an outspoken supporter of the Slánský and other political trials of the 1950s, *Kultúrny život*, the weekly journal of the party-approved Union of Slovak Writers, was suddenly allowed to go beyond the bounds of censorship then permitted in the Czech-speaking regions of the country. In no time, even *Pravda*, the official mouthpiece of the *KSS* (not to be confused with the Soviet Communist Party's equivalent newspaper of the same name), began to press for a reinvestigation of the 'Slovak bourgeois nationalist' trials. At the Union of Slovak Writers' Congress in April, Ladislav Novomeský (who, together with Gustáv Husák, had been one of the most prominent victims of the 'Slovak bourgeois nationalist' trials) spoke critically of the power of the ruling élite surrounding Novotný in Prague, demanded 'truthful' and 'objective' interpretations of Slovak literary history, and was allowed to speak in defence of Clementis. At a congress of Slovak journalists, Miroslav Hysko went so far as to accuse Prime Minister Široký, known to be one of Novotný's closest allies, of having been the main instigator of the trumped-up charges.[14] Even when the accusation was printed in the Slovak *Pravda*, Dubček only commented that 'there can be no agreement with everything said by Comrade Hysko' who was dealt no worse punishment than to be moved from his position as director of the Slovak Research Institute for Journalism to a readership in journalism at Comenius University in Bratislava.[15] The *KSS* was turning on the *KSČ*; and *KSS* First Secretary Dubček – although he owed his position to *KSČ* First Secretary Novotný – was doing nothing to stop it.

When Novotný challenged Dubček to explain why the Slovak press was not being kept under tighter control, Dubček replied that 'the Party' felt that 'rehabilitation in Czechoslovakia' was 'going too slowly' in comparison with the Soviet Union, an argument that he knew Novotný 'could not openly reject'.[16] Dubček refused to go so far as to increase *Kultúrny život*'s paper allocation; but several hundred copies nevertheless reached Prague, where they began, astonishingly for an official Communist Party publication, to fetch black-market prices.[17] Although he was still keeping his cards close to his chest, Dubček appears to have been banking on widespread Slovak resentment of a whole range of issues, from the 'Slovak bourgeois nationalist' trials of the 1950s and curtailing of autonomy in the 1960 constitution to the widespread belief that the Czech-speaking regions received preferential economic treatment and that Novotný was personally insensitive to Slovak distinctiveness. Once Czech Communists had begun to notice and follow the Slovak Communist press, going so far as to reprint whole articles from *Kultúrny život* in *Literární noviny*, its Czech counterpart (the official weekly journal of the Czechoslovak Writers' Union), Novotný had little choice but to allow the three remaining Gottwald appointments whom he could no longer afford to save – Široký, Bacílek and Koehler – to be sacked, and to call for a new commission, known as the Barnabitky Commission, to reopen the files on the Slovak political trials.[18] The Presidium's disgraced members, all of whom had been Novotný supporters, were duly replaced by three men untainted by association with the Gottwald years: Jozef Lenárt, Martin Vaculík and Alexander Dubček.[19] The Bratislava Spring was spreading to Prague.

When, in 1963, the very first year of Czechoslovakia's third Five-Year Plan, GNP declined by 2 per cent, it was impossible to hide the discrepancy between the government's expectations and the actual workings of the economy. Faced with the prospect of economic collapse, the Novotný leadership was suddenly more open to the arguments of reform economists that some restrictions of the command economy should be removed and the Stalinist model of heavy industry partly reoriented towards consumer-friendly light industry.[20] The idea of reintroducing carefully circumscribed pockets where market forces would be allowed to determine supply and demand was most closely associated with the name of Ota Šik; but it was also supported by a variety of other economists, as well as by the newly appointed Presidium members Oldřich Černík and Lubomír Štrougal.[21] The 'New System of Economic Management' was therefore adopted as official party and state policy between 1964 and 1966. Novotný also began tentatively to loosen party controls in the arts. Although Socialist Realism remained the only style that was explicitly approved as a means of expressing and spreading the values of socialist society, when small theatres began to experiment with non-traditional themes such as Existentialism and human alienation (subjects that had previously been considered inappropriate, since alienation was officially impossible under socialism) they were neither censored nor closed down. Among the theatres in Prague that were to become most renowned for their vibrant experimentation were the Reduta, Na zábradlí and

Semafor theatres; but by the spring of 1963 there were so many that a special conference on 'small forms in theatre' was permitted to be held at Karlovy Vary.[22] Sensing increased freedom on the part of playwrights and literary critics, audiences – under cover of darkness – grew bolder. In 1964, when American folk singer Pete Seeger toured the country with his five-string banjo, he found to his astonishment that he had to remove the anti-Vietnam War songs from his repertoire because, although in harmony with the officially approved party line, such sentiments met with booing and jeering from concert audiences all over Czechoslovakia.[23]

From 1964 until 1967, Zdeněk Mlynář, a Soviet-trained lawyer who was tucked away in the Academy of Sciences, began to campaign for carefully controlled reforms with the aim of diffusing power within the Communist Party. Already the head of a legal commission, an advisor to various functionaries and a participant in a multitude of 'working groups', Mlynář steadily raised his profile by helping to write dozens of internal party brochures and giving hundreds of lectures to party archivists, regional and district functionaries, and also to 'workers' in 'the state apparatus' (including *StB* and army intelligence officers). In all these talks and pamphlets, he sought to persuade his comrades of two main points. The first was that for the party to determine 'what is or is not in the interests of the whole of socialist society', decisions must be made 'on the basis of qualified expertise', and 'society itself' must be given the 'opportunity to say what it thinks its own interests really are'.[24] Mlynář's second point concerned the 'leading role' of the Communist Party, which, he argued, was not 'ipso facto guaranteed for all time' but must be constantly re-earned if it were truly to represent the 'vanguard' of socialist society. The party, he explained, must itself enable people 'to express as well those needs and interests that the party does not consider relevant' and 'be ready to explain why it does not agree'.[25]

To those who felt that what they thought of as the progressive, humane and 'democratic' traditions of the Czech 'nation' ought to be allowed to re-infuse socialism, between 1964 and 1966 the magazine for young authors in the Czech Writers' Union, *Tvář* (The Face), was the exciting new periodical of choice. It had soon attracted non-Communist dramatists and novelists, among them a promising young playwright from a wealthy 'bourgeois' family, Václav Havel.[26] From early 1965, the magazine began to attract criticism from Jiří Hendrych, secretary for culture and information, as well as other Central Committee members, for printing 'militantly religious' and other 'scandalous' articles. Although rebukes of this kind had sufficed to control the press in the past, not only did the editor of *Tvář* now refuse to budge, but a number of young, hitherto impeccably Stalinist writers – among them Ivan Klíma, Pavel Kohout and Milan Kundera – unexpectedly came to its defence, blowing the issue up into an ideological battle over the limits of freedom of expression.[27] On 1 January 1966, the magazine ceased publication. As the more radical members of the Writers' Union considered continuing to print it anyway, the *StB* closely monitored their activities; among other options, it considered recruiting Václav Havel, then a candidate member for the Communist-dominated Writers' Union, as an *StB* agent.[28]

In October 1965, just as the reform movement in Czechoslovakia was beginning to gather a head of steam, Khrushchev was ousted from the leadership of the Communist Party of the Soviet Union and replaced by an unknown quantity, Leonid Brezhnev. It is an indication of the degree to which Novotný and the *KSČ* leadership had come to feel committed to the Khrushchev leadership that the *KSČ* Presidium responded to the news with the unheard-of step of sending a letter to the Soviet leadership to express 'surprise' at the 'sudden' changes in Moscow.[29] Novotný further signalled his preference for the reformist wing represented by the deposed Khrushchev by making friendly gestures towards Yugoslavia and Romania, by declining to engage in anti-Chinese polemics and by making tentative approaches to the West Germans.[30] One (albeit not very reliable) source goes so far as to claim that Novotný told Brezhnev that Khrushchev's recent visit to Prague 'had been a great success and there was a strong possibility of public demonstrations against the new First Secretary'.[31] Since it was unclear at the time how long Brezhnev would last, it is possible that Novotný's Presidium was simply backing the wrong horse; but its unusually bold gestures suggest that, at least in economic matters, it was genuinely persuaded of the need for Czechoslovakia to 'de-Stalinize'.

In Slovakia, Dubček took advantage of the controversy aroused by the findings of the Kolder Commission and the ongoing Barnabitky investigations by recommending that Slovak Communist Gustáv Husák be readmitted to the party, and by making sure that the suggestion was included in the Barnabitky report submitted to the *KSČ* Central Committee on 19 December 1963.[32] Husák, who was by then working in the history department of the Slovak Academy of Sciences, became a frequent contributor to *Kultúrny život*, where his main theme – his past conviction for 'bourgeois nationalism' notwithstanding – was the Slovak national question. As well as tacitly acknowledging injured Slovak nationalist feelings, and so boosting his popularity in Slovakia, Dubček's gesture indirectly challenged Novotný's reputation and authority, thus helping Dubček further to strengthen his own position. Armed with the damning indictments of the Barnabitky report, Dubček kept up the pressure on the central *KSČ* leadership by allowing a number of carefully selected Slovak grievances to be aired within *KSS* circles: that Ľudovít Štúr, traditionally dismissed as 'bourgeois' for not having taken part in the 1848 revolution, had nevertheless contributed to the Slovak National Awakening; that 'Stalinist' accounts of the Slovak Uprising of 1944, which suggested that only Communists and the Red Army had been involved, represented a 'dogmatic oversimplification'; even that Czech motives underlying the trials of 'Slovak bourgeois nationalists' might have been coloured by a 'nationalist deformation' of their own. In 1964, Dubček went so far as to allow a revisionist history of the Slovak National Uprising by Gustáv Husák to appear in print, although not actually to be sold. In Slovak Communist circles it was beginning to be said that President and KSČ First Secretary Novotný, who had gone on an official visit to Košice, was too scared to show his face in Bratislava.[33] Largely as a result of Dubček's tacit toleration of such views, by 1965 the sense of Slovak nationalist grievance had grown so strident that a conference held by Slovak historians in Banská Bystrica was permitted to take as its sole theme 'The Slovaks and their National Evolution'.[34]

Dubček, who had thus far not risked being seen to be committed to either side of the Slovak debate, made his first overt gesture of being on the side of the nationalists by taking part in celebrations, held at Uhrovec on 30 October 1965, to commemorate the 130th anniversary of Štúr's birth. He then made sure that the fact that he had been born in the same house as Štúr became widely known.[35] Even when Novotný came to Slovakia to put in an official appearance at celebrations in Martin to commemorate the establishment of the *Matica slovenská* (Slovak Foundation) he found himself outmanoeuvred. Dubček, who did not attend the event himself, was nevertheless able to make good capital out of Novotný's having supposedly behaved 'like a bull in a china shop' by declining to accept gifts of a fur coat and Slovak embroidery on behalf of his wife. Although the story could just as easily have been used to demonstrate Novotný's refusal to be bribed, it was presented as an example of his supposed contempt for Slovak national feeling, a rumour that Dubček then allowed to be blown up into a major political scandal.[36] Small wonder that Novotný, as Dubček later contemptuously expressed it, was 'convinced that someone somewhere in Slovakia was constantly conspiring against him' or, as the Ministry of the Interior archives reveal, began to keep a much closer eye on the KSS.[37]

At the Thirteenth Congress of the KSČ (31 May–4 June 1966), it was officially declared that since 'socialist social relations' in the Czechoslovak Socialist Republic had been 'characterized by the elimination of class antagonism', the future development of socialism in Czechoslovakia should be 'directly linked' to the 'spread of socialist democracy' and the 'participation of all working people in government management'.[38] The ensuing round of meetings and discussions gave Dubček the opportunity to advertise himself to the KSČ as the perfect compromise candidate to take over from the old guard in Prague. In a masterly speech, ostensibly simply a report on conditions in Slovakia, he managed to present himself as all things to all people.

Dubček supported his own constituency by pushing for further investment in Slovakia, showed how up-to-date he was by praising the new economic thinking, yet at the same time based his claims about recent Slovak economic successes in terms of the fulfilment of traditional five-year plans.[39] Insisting upon the implementation of 'full equality' between the 'fraternal' Czech and Slovak nations as promised in the Košice Programme of 1945, he spoke with equal resoluteness on the centrality of 'proletarian internationalism'. Even when Dubček applauded the Central Committee's admission of past 'mistakes' with regard to 'Slovak bourgeois nationalism' and the 1944 Slovak Uprising, he did so in 'practical fulfilment' of Gottwald's postwar promises of 'genuine brotherly unity' between the Czechs and the Slovaks. Similarly, although he hinted darkly at the 'misuse' of nationalism by 'past regimes', he spoke equally ominously of the current dangers presented by 'anti-socialist forces'.[40]

It was not so much what Dubček said that mattered, since his statements were vague, inconsistent and contradictory, but rather the way that he said it. Dubček's contributions, unlike those of most of his colleagues – and particularly the long-winded Novotný – were mercifully short, relatively free of clichés, and included some refreshing suggestions, such as that the Communist Party should stop launching campaigns 'against' particular evils but rather 'in favour' of positive 'good'.[41] Above all, Dubček hinted to the KSČ leadership (to whom he took the trouble to speak in Czech rather than in Slovak) that his own friendlier, more open style of leadership was already being tested, and shown to work, in Slovakia, where the economy was said to be improving and there was markedly more participation in political life by the young, ethnic minorities and other formerly disaffected groups. There was no reason to suppose, he hinted, that – given the right leader at the helm of the KSČ – the experiment could not work just as well throughout the rest of the republic.

Once official sanction had been given to reform by the KSČ leadership, a series of astonishingly critical, as well as brilliantly made, Czech films followed, all of which brought allegorical representations of the horrors of Stalinism to the general public. Among the most chilling were Jan Němec's *O slavnosti a hostech* (The Party and the Guests), Věra Chytilová's *Sedmikrásky* (Daisies) and Antonín Máša's *Hotel pro cizince* (Hotel for Foreigners). Although these films were ostensibly in line with the KSČ's own condemnations of the personality cult and the Stalinist 'deformations' of the 1950s, they were open to much more radical interpretations. In Němec's *O slavnosti a hostech*, for example, the host – who bears more than a passing resemblance to Lenin – wants nothing more than to hold a huge outdoor banquet for his guests; but there is an element of compulsion in how guests are brought to the party, and when one guest is discovered to have left the table, the atmosphere becomes terrifying.

The film ends with all but one of the guests joining in a huge search party, complete with rifles and Alsatian dogs, to track down the missing guest, whom even his wife has by then denounced. Chytilová's *Sedmikrásky*, a less obvious parable of socialism, presented an equally disturbing metaphor for the abuse of power. The two giggling anti-heroines of her film begin with acts that seem no more than girlish teasing and pranks, but end with ones of compulsive destruction and greed, devoid of any sense of conscience or restraint. However far these films could be defended as ideologically pure, they tacitly acknowledged and fed the sense of alienation that millions of people had evidently come to feel, not only for the 'Stalinist deformations' of the past, but also for the party-dominated present.

By 1967, as Dubček later phrased it, a 'direct clash' between Communist functionaries impatient for further reforms and those believed to be holding 'progress' back had become inevitable.[42] The confrontation finally came out into the open at the Fourth Writers' Congress, held in June 1967, at which speeches by former Stalinists like Milan Kundera, Pavel Kohout and Ivan Klíma publicly joined forces with those by non-party writers such as Václav Havel in opposing censorship, however discreet the techniques employed, and citing in their defence Aleksandr Solzhenitsyn's recent (and far more rebellious) letter to the Soviet Writers' Union's own Fourth Congress, parts of which were read aloud to the assembled gathering. Ludvík Vaculík, in a sweeping harangue that distinguished what he called Czechoslovakia's 'power system' from actual 'socialism', demanded to know why 'we can not live where we wish' and why a 'decent apology' had not yet been given to those who had been formally exonerated of political crimes. He rounded off his diatribe with the angry accusation that 'not one human problem' had been 'solved' during the previous twenty years:

> from such elementary needs as housing, schools and economic prosperity to the more subtle needs which the undemocratic systems of the world cannot provide: a feeling of one's full worth in society, a feeling that politics is subordinate to ethics, a belief in the meaning of humble work, the need for confidence among people, the advancement of education for the people.[43]

Unsurprisingly, the Presidium of the Central Committee of the *KSČ* found unacceptable such 'outright attacks and slanders' – not only against the 'socialist system', but also the 'domestic and foreign policies of our republic' and the Communist Party – and singled out Vaculík, Havel and others for special condemnation. In time-honoured fashion, the radicals were accused of being fed their lines by the CIA, this time via the exiled 'agent' Pavel Tigrid, editor of the radically reformist *Svědectví*, several hundred copies of which had recently been smuggled into Czechoslovakia from France. Because the leadership of the Writers' Union proved reluctant to discipline its own members, Novotný, Hendrych and others proposed at the September 1967 Central Committee plenum that the Union's weekly, *Literární noviny*, henceforward be edited by the minister of culture and information (Hendrych); that comrades Ivan Klíma and Ludvík Vaculík be expelled from the party; that Pavel Kohout be issued a warning; and that disciplinary proceedings be started against Milan Kundera.[44] Although Dubček later claimed to have 'opposed this step', the disciplinary measures – as Kieran Williams has pointed out – were endorsed by the whole of the Central Committee, Dubček and Černík distinguishing themselves from the others only in that they expressed the opinion that the 'causes' of the young writers' rebellion ought 'also' to be considered. The sanctions could, in any case, have been much more severe – including court cases and prison sentences – had the Novotný regime really been as authoritarian as its predecessors had been, or as Dubček afterwards liked to pretend it was.[45]

Novotný's next move was to reassert the Communist Party's authority by issuing a report, to be announced as a joint statement of the Central Committee, outlining the party's 'place in the political system'. In his opening speech, Novotný emphasized that 'only the Communist Party' and not 'just any group' could 'oversee and direct the social process, and where necessary set right shortcomings and mistakes which may arise during its development'.[46] Dubček, who was now emerging as one of the principal thorns in Novotný's side, proposed that the statement include elements of 'self-criticism' by the party leadership, that the line between government and party be stated more clearly, and that a new Action Programme be prepared. At the plenary session of the Central Committee that was supposed finally to approve the report, held on 30–31 October 1967, Dubček again took the opportunity publicly to criticize the report, calling for greater self-criticism on the part of the leadership, changes in how the party directed its affairs and greater autonomy for the *KSS*.[47]

To Novotný's astonishment, Dubček was soon being backed by Josef Smrkovský, a convinced Stalinist but who had been persecuted during the Slánský trial, as well as by two regional secretaries from Moravia (Oldřich Voleník and Josef Špaček), who may have held a grudge from the Moravian purges surrounding the Šling affair. František Kriegel, a doctor who had worked in the rabidly Marxist Fr Josef Plojhar's Ministry of Health from 1949, before being disgraced as a Jew during the Slánský years and finally rejoining the Central Committee in 1966, added his own indictments, claiming that in a third of party organizations in northern Moravia there was not a single member under the age of twenty-five, and that the Union of Youth (*Svaz československé mládeže* or *SČM*) and Pioneers were in crisis.[48]

On 31 October 1967, an incident occurred that added considerable heat to the already lively debates about the disenchantment of the young. At the university dormitories that had been opened to great fanfare two years before, at Strahov in Prague, leaders of the party-approved Union of Youth, led by Pavel Dvořák, having already made several appeals, were meeting to discuss how best to press the authorities to do something about the frequent power cuts that prevented them, as they complained, from being able to study.[49] When the electricity failed yet again, in the middle of their evening meeting, they decided to march, there and then, to the Castle to complain. When the regular ('Public Security') police (*Veřejná bezpečnost* or *VB*), already jumpy because of the expected arrival of a Soviet delegation,[50] were confronted with the sight of students marching in the streets holding lit candles and chanting 'We want light!' and 'We want to study!', they misinterpreted the slogans as politically subversive. At Neruda street, on the way to the Castle from the Old Town Square, the student march was met by a wall of police bearing riot shields and truncheons who, without stopping to ask questions, began to beat and arrest them.[51]

The brutal police reaction not only outraged the students, whose official youth organization, the *SČM*, demanded an inquiry, but also their parents, who were, of course, Communist Party members. News of the Strahov incident reached the *KSČ* Central Committee at about eight o'clock on the evening of 31 October 1967, just as its session was slowly drawing to a close. For the first time, a majority, taking quick advantage of the fiasco, criticized Novotný's draft statement as 'formulaic' and 'inadequate' and, in an unprecedented step, insisted that it be sent back for 'redrafting and fresh consideration' in December. As Dubček later recalled, there could have been 'no clearer signal' of Novotný's 'declining authority'. The Central Committee was 'itself surprised' by its 'sudden power. The crisis of leadership was now obvious to everyone.'[52] Seizing the moment, Dubček launched his first open attack on Novotný by suggesting that the tasks of 'central leadership' (in other words, the post of first secretary of the *KSČ*) and those of 'management' (in other words, the office of president of the Republic) be 'carefully separated'. Novotný, caught off guard by the attack, rejoined with a speech that was not only less temperate than Dubček's but that, fatally, reminded his listeners that the *KSS* was supposed to be subordinate to the *KSČ*.

By alienating a large part of the hitherto politically irreproachable student body from the police, the Novotný leadership gave those within the party who were pressing for change yet another means of discrediting the conservative wing. The magazine *Reportér* opened the battle with an article by Jiří Ruml with the provocative title 'More Light – and Not Just for Strahov'. Combined with the controversy that ensued from Dubček's speech and Novotný's rejoinder to it, the Strahov incident became so inflamed that even the National Assembly, which normally rubber-stamped whatever the party leadership recommended, spoke up to condemn the police action and demand an inquiry. Since the implication of such disobedience was that the *KSČ* party leadership was out of touch, not only with the regions, but also with the lower party echelons and even the government, Novotný, in serious need of reinforcement, disappeared to Moscow for several days.

Upon his return (10 November 1967), evidently having found some sympathy from Brezhnev, Novotný set up a five-man committee within the Presidium (composed of himself, Jiří Hendrych, Michal Chudík, Jozef Lenárt and Michal Sabolčík) to look into Dubček's 'national deviation'. Dubček, however, who was growing confident of his new influence within the Presidium, joined forces with Oldřich Černík, Jaromír Dolanský and Drahomír Kolder to press for a separation of the offices of president and first secretary. Although initially opposed by the remaining six voting members of the Presidium, Dubček managed to break Novotný's majority in the Presidium by hinting to Hendrych that, should the posts of president and first secretary be separated, Hendrych would stand to take over as first secretary. The bait evidently worked, since Dubček found that, when he was called in front of the commission to look into his 'nationalist deviation', Hendrych 'chose to remain entirely neutral', cleaning his glasses several times and taking a lot of notes, but not committing himself to disciplining Dubček. The Slovak Presidium, which could have taken the matter further, also declined to do so, only Chudík showing himself to be on Novotný's side by being prepared to persecute Dubček.[53]

By winter, the split within the Communist Party between a faction allied with *KSS* first secretary Dubček and another with *KSČ* first secretary Novotný had become such an open secret that it was beginning to cause a scandal throughout the socialist bloc. On 8 December 1967, Novotný invited Brezhnev to Prague, presumably to shore up his support once again. This time, in addition to Novotný, Brezhnev spoke to Dubček, Hendrych, Lenárt and Dolanský, which evidently persuaded him that Novotný was unable to control his party. Since this same Novotný had also shown himself capable of acting independently of Moscow, and had made clear in 1965 that his personal allegiance was to Khrushchev rather than to Brezhnev, there no longer seemed any good reason to save him. Although the often-repeated tale that Brezhnev declared *'Eto vashe delo'* ('It's your own affair') to the *KSČ* Presidium is almost certainly apocryphal, the effect of the Soviet leader's failure overtly to support Novotný, or to appear to care which of the grey men in the Presidium took over from him, came to much the same thing.[54] When, at the next Central Committee session (19–21 December), Dubček again raised the issue of separating the functions of president and first secretary, the discussion ended in a deadlock, those for and against the proposal remaining evenly split. Discussions resumed after the Christmas recess, during which time Miroslav Mamula, chief of the Central Committee's infamous Department VIII, and Jan Šejna, party chief of military security, had considered staging a putsch against the Dubček contingent but were evidently blocked by a rival, anti-Novotný contingent within the Ministry of Defence.[55] Finally, during meetings that lasted from 2 to 5 January 1968, the balance tipped against Novotný sufficiently for it to be suggested, first, that Dubček and Lenárt (both Slovaks) be proposed to take over from Novotný as first secretary of the KSČ, and, second, on the morning of 5 January, that Dubček alone be proposed. The Central Committee then passed a resolution that stated that, since the 'separation of the two highest posts' is a 'logical part' of the 'democratization process in the state and political spheres', it approved Comrade Antonín Novotný's 'personal request', as president of the Czechoslovak Socialist Republic, to be 'released' from the post of first secretary of the KSČ Central Committee.[56]

Although Dubček proved effective in uniting opinion against, and eventually ousting, Novotný as head of the state-wide party, this was not the same thing as having a secure position in the Presidium, let alone either the will or political backing to undertake reforms of the kind with which his name later came to be so closely associated. Just like Novotný before him, Dubček began by making a statement of the new leadership's intentions to right the wrongs of the past, while at the same time taking care to pledge nothing more concrete than what could be read into the usual political clichés. At a speech given at an agricultural congress on 1 February 1968, for example, he promised to 'develop a resolute approach to overcoming everything outdated' and to produce an Action Programme that would be 'linked with a purposeful approach to the detailed elaboration of the key problems of socialist progress' so as to 'enable us to do a good and prompt job of preparing the agenda of the Fourteenth Congress of our Communist Party of Czechoslovakia'.[57] As a contemporary was to observe, Novotný may have been 'defeated', but the 'system' that he represented certainly was not.[58]

It was not the canny Dubček but a few bolder members of his Presidium who began to put pressure on the KSČ Central Committee to spell out what the promised reforms might mean in practice. In an article published in Rudé právo on 9 February 1968, Josef Smrkovský stressed that one of the major problems to be resolved was 'the Slovak issue', which he described as a 'serious political problem' which had been brought about by the 'gradual narrowing of the "Košice" arrangement' and 'especially the last constitutional arrangement in 1960' with a resulting 'reinforcement of "Prague" centralism'. Stating baldly that 'passivity' and 'indifference' towards the Communist Party had become so widespread that it could no longer be concealed, Smrkovský further challenged Czechs and Slovaks to 'launch out courageously into unexplored territory' and search together for 'a Czechoslovak road to socialism', one that would strengthen 'unity' with 'the Soviet Union and with all socialist countries' while simultaneously leading to 'a type of socialism' that might 'even have something to offer the industrial countries in Europe'. The forthcoming Action Programme, he continued, if it were to make the party's 'leading role' more than a 'hollow phrase', would need to be addressed to 'all segments and groups of the population', each of which should find in it 'a reflection of their aspirations, requirements and demands'.[59]

Since Dubček's top priority, like that of Novotný before him, was to retain his hold on power, it is not surprising that he sought to do this in the same way as other Communist leaders: by surrounding himself with comrades who could be counted upon to remain loyal to him, while simultaneously attempting to rid himself of known enemies and rivals. What increasingly distinguished Dubček's methods from those of Novotný, Zápotocký and Gottwald before him, however, was his tendency to use rank-and-file party opinion, rather than the backing of the Moscow leadership, as the principal lever with which to enforce desired changes in the leadership of the *KSČ*. In his time as first secretary of the *KSS*, Dubček had learned that it was possible, simply by judiciously removing restrictions on censorship, to mobilize enough public and party opinion to topple even the first secretary of the *KSČ*. He now used the same methods to discredit his enemies and weaken the bloc in the Presidium that remained against him. Thus, within weeks of taking office, General Jan Šejna, who had plotted against Dubček, was exposed by the military prosecutor's office as a black marketeer. Instead of staging a show trial, Dubček left it to the media who were suddenly and unexpectedly given free rein to publish the news of Šejna's sensational escape to the West.[60] Journalists, completely unused to having to use their own judgement, were alarmed at not being told explicitly where the boundaries lay; but, as Kieran Williams has found, even when the editors of *Rudé právo*, the *KSČ* official daily, repeatedly invited Dubček to their offices to give them some guidance, he steadfastly refused to do so.[61] Before long, with the help of the Ministry of the Interior, they had traced Šejna's close connections with Novotný's son, which more than suited Dubček's purposes. A summary report of the case, running to sixty-seven typed pages, was then sent to the government by the minister of the interior, Josef Kudrna.[62]

On 4 March 1968, aware that Novotný had been thoroughly discredited, the Presidium began formally dismantling the system of censorship. The immediate result was that, on 8 March, the press for the first time printed demands that Novotný step down as president. Within weeks, there were further such calls from students, artists and other groups whose consciousness of the possibilities had been raised through 'mass meetings' held in Prague by 'cultural' and 'political' officials. Soon, there were additional calls to remove Michal Chudík, one of Dubček's oldest enemies, from his position as chairman of the Slovak National Council, to fire Prime Minister Lenárt, and to remove the leading officers of the Trade Union Council, the Union of Czechoslovak Youth (*SČM*) and the Union of Czechoslovak Journalists, together with 'sharp criticism' of the attorney general and of the ministers of defence and the interior; in other words, the same men who, in December 1967, had considered deposing the Dubček wing of the Presidium.[63]

In order to keep the spotlight firmly focused on the scandals of the past, by which the Novotný regime was thoroughly compromised, and to keep the grievances of those who had been purged in the 1950s at fever pitch, on 14 March the Presidium announced that it would speed up the rehabilitation of those who had been unjustly persecuted. On 15 March, it further accepted a demand from the Slovak National Council that Czech–Slovak relations be reorganized in accordance with the principles of federation. Censors at the Publication Board then published criticism of their own bosses, together with the minister of the interior, for not yet having 'responded' to 'the public criticism of censorship'. One of Dubček's most dangerous potential enemies, Jiří Hendrych, was singled out for special condemnation, being held personally responsible for having led them 'astray' on various occasions, most notably over the disciplining of *Literární noviny*.[64] Having allowed his principal rivals to be mauled by the press, Dubček took equal care to reward the generals at the Ministry of Defence who had resisted Novotný's attempts to remove him.[65]

Although Alexander Dubček, the very symbol of the Prague Spring, is usually portrayed as a deeply and sincerely convinced 'liberal', the pattern of his rise to power – first within the *KSS* and then within the *KSČ* – suggests that he used popular resentments to establish his own power base within the Presidium rather than adopting 'reformist' positions from conviction. As his half-admiring, half-contemptuous colleague Zdeněk Mlynář hinted, only such an analysis can make sense of why Ota Šik, a reformist who was associated with Novotný, was kept out of his Presidium, while notorious conservatives like Kolder and Štrougal, but who were unfriendly to Novotný, were retained.[66] Techniques that suited Dubček's means of consolidating power – first within the *KSS* and then within the *KSČ* – and that won for him the brief (and, as things were to turn out, only temporarily helpful) reputation of being a reformer, were not considered so benign by those neighbouring socialist regimes whose own leaders – in the more traditional Novotný mould – could just as easily have been toppled by the same methods. Only Brezhnev, who knew Dubček's past record of obedience and loyalty to the Soviet Union, remained, outwardly at least, confident of his political soundness and reliability, appearing to understand that Dubček needed to establish control over the Presidium before he could return things to normal.

By 18 March 1968, after censorship in Czechoslovakia had been all but abandoned and the press had started to fill with grievances and accusations directed at high Communist officials, even Brezhnev could not stop the East German authorities, afraid that their own party and population might follow suit, from banning travel to Czechoslovakia, together with any reporting of the situation there. Their fears were hardly likely to be assuaged by the almost immediate revival in Czechoslovakia of the non-Communist scouting organization *Junák*, the creation of a lobby group of 'former political prisoners' calling itself *K-231* (after the 'Law for the Defence of the People's Republic' of 1948 under which they had been sentenced),[67] and the establishment of a commission to look into the causes of Jan Masaryk's death.

On 21 March 1968, Novotný, by now blocked at every turn, announced his decision to step down as president. Ludvík Svoboda, the pro-Soviet war hero who had proved so helpful to the *KSČ* in February 1948 but afterwards had his own troubles during the Slánský trials, was put forward to replace him. To those reformists in the *KSČ* and *KSS* who had come to see Novotný as the symbol of all the evils and injustices of the 'Stalinist' era, his departure seemed almost too good to be true, a fairytale ending. Dubček's technique – of loosening contraints on public opinion sufficiently to purge his Presidium without having recourse to show trials – had worked once again. Whether he would be able to reunite a bitterly divided party and Presidium – let alone contain the reformist expectations being raised among the general population – remained to be seen.

On 23 March 1968, six members of the Warsaw Pact (the People's Republic of Bulgaria, the Hungarian People's Republic, the German Democratic Republic, the Polish People's Republic, the Union of Soviet Socialist Republics and the Czechoslovak Socialist Republic) met in Dresden (the two member states excluded from the meeting were Romania and Yugoslavia, once Czechoslovakia's partners in the interwar Little Entente, and more recently disgraced in the Kremlin for their deviation from Soviet norms). Although the official report of the Dresden meeting ended with the empty formula that the meeting had 'proceeded in a friendly atmosphere', this had been far from the case.[68] More than twenty years later, Dubček still remembered with indignation how the leaders of the five Warsaw Pact countries – Walter Ulbricht, Leonid Brezhnev, Władysław Gomułka, János Kádár and Todor Zhivkov, who had invited him to the meeting on the pretence that only the usual economic matters would be discussed, made recent political developments in Czechoslovakia the sole topic of discussion. Armed with thick file clippings from the Czech and Slovak press which were 'occasionally culled for a suitable quotation', the five socialist leaders 'with varying intensity' proceeded to attack the Czechoslovak delegation for 'losing control' and 'permitting a diversity of opinion' which bordered on 'counterrevolution' and opened the way to 'outside threats to the socialist camp'.[69] Dubček, on the defensive, had little choice but to resort to an uncomfortable mix of *Realpolitik* and the sorts of reformist arguments he had been hearing from Kriegel, Mlynář, Smrkovský and others: that the abolition of press censorship in Czechoslovakia would restore the 'leading role' of the party; that Josef Smrkovský and Jaroslav Pelikán, the head of Czechoslovak television, both of whom had been criticized by name, had impeccable socialist credentials; that no aspect of Czechoslovakia's external policy – from its Warsaw Pact defence to its Comecon trading commitments – would be in any way threatened; and, finally, that once the *KSČ* Central Committee published its forthcoming Action Programme the comrades would be in a position to see for themselves that there was no Czechoslovak threat to the socialist camp.[70] Within days of Dubček's return from Dresden, the Romanian press was protesting against its exclusion from the meeting, the East German press was blaming Smrkovský for giving encouragement to the West Germans, and Václav Havel was suggesting in the pages of *Literární listy* that a genuine opposition needed to be formed to keep the *KSČ* in check since, however sincere its intention to take opposing views on board, 'democracy is not a matter of faith but of *guarantees*' and 'government can be made to improve itself only when its existence is at stake, not just its good name'.[71]

On 5 April 1968, the Presidium approved the final draft of its long-awaited Action Programme, the manifesto of reforms whose stated aim was to bring about 'Socialism with a Human Face'. The document was divided into five broad sections which dealt in turn with the 'Czechoslovak Road to Socialism', the 'Development of Socialist Democracy', the 'National Economy and the Standard of Living', the 'Development of Science, Education and Culture' and the 'International Status and Foreign Policy of the Czechoslovak Socialist Republic'. Each section, written anonymously by a party working group, was further subdivided into sections with catchy titles such as 'The Leading Role of the Party – A Guarantee of Socialist Progress', 'Equality of the Czechs and the Slovaks – The Basis for the Strength of the Public', 'Division and Supervision of Power – Guarantee against High-Handedness', 'Socialism Cannot Do without Enterprising' and 'Problems of the Standard of Living – An Urgent Task of the Economic Policy'.[72] The section on the 'Czechoslovak Road to Socialism' served as the intellectual justification for what was coming to be seen as the party's central mission: the so-called 'democratization' of 'socialist society'. According to the historical analysis presented in the document, the 'national liberation struggle' of the Czechs and Slovaks which had led to 'the emergence of an independent state' in 1918–20 had collapsed because it had been unable to resolve 'onerous class antagonisms', 'ignored the individuality of the Slovak nation' and proved unable to cope with the 'extreme nationalism' of the state's minorities. Postwar Czechoslovakia's 'road to socialism' had contained many elements that could 'contribute towards achieving our present aim of democratizing the state', but, from February 1948, the party had taken a 'new road of socialist construction', which, complicated by 'problems' as well as 'progress' shared by the 'whole socialist camp', had turned out to be 'difficult'. 'Grave shortcomings, unsolved problems and deformations of socialist principles', otherwise known as 'the personality cult', had led to the 'mechanical acceptance' of 'ideas, customs and political conceptions' that were 'at variance with Czechoslovak conditions and traditions' and for which the 'leading bodies and institutes of the Party and State of that time' were 'fully responsible'. Since 1960, when Czechoslovakia had become a Socialist Republic, society had 'entered another stage of development' in which, since 'antagonistic classes' no longer existed, methods of 'direction and organization' of the economy had become 'outdated'. Since the 'next stage of historical development' would require that Czechoslovakia 'join in the scientific-technical revolution in the world', for which it would need to be able to compete internationally, 'broad scope' would be left for 'social initiative, frank exchange of views and democratization of the whole social and political system'.[73]

As followed from this analysis, all the current ills of socialist society were blamed squarely on the Novotný years, when 'an economic policy, enforced through the economic requirements and possibilities of the country', had led to 'exhaustion of its material and human resources'.[74] It was from this misguided economic policy that 'all of the difficulties with which the workers are still confronted daily' – including the 'slow increase in wages', 'stagnation of the living standard', the 'catastrophic state of housing', 'the precarious state of the transport system', 'poor quality goods and services', 'lack of cultural standard' and 'conditions in general which tangibly affect' the 'human factor, possibilities of developing human energy and the activity of man' which are 'decisive for a socialist society' – were claimed to have emanated.[75] All this, according to the Action Programme, was now going to change. Whereas in the past workers had 'not always' had 'the possibility of asserting their immediate and specific interests', the party now pledged to 'provide scope' for them to make use of 'all their political and social rights', and to strive for 'the humanization of work' and to improve 'the labour conditions of workers'.[76] Since the 'intelligentsia' had now become 'an intelligentsia of the people, a socialist intelligentsia', the former 'underestimation' of the 'role of the intelligentsia in this society' would be combated, together with 'everything that upsets relations between the intelligentsia and the workers'.[77] Czech–Slovak relations were henceforward to be understood according to 'the Leninist principle' that 'overlooking the interests of a smaller nation by the larger' is 'incompatible with socialist relations'. Each of the official national minorities – Hungarian, Polish, Ukrainian and German – was also to have the 'right' to 'its own national life'.[78] The young – students and workers alike – who were deemed especially sensitive to 'contradictions between words and deeds, lack of frankness, phrase mongering bureaucracy' and 'attempts to settle everything from a position of power', were to be borne especially in mind as the party strove to 'erase everything that evokes non-confidence towards socialism'.[79] Most risky for a socialist state, 'equalization' – in other words, wage-levelling – was to be abandoned in favour of the 'principle' of 'remuneration according to the quantity, quality and social usefulness of work', so that, while measures would be put in place to protect the weakest members of society, those who showed 'initiative' in 'advancing production, technical, cultural and social progress' would be 'respected' and 'rewarded'.[80]

The 'leading role' of the Communist Party was no longer to be understood as the 'instrument of the dictatorship of the proletariat' but rather as the prime vehicle for 'arousing socialist initiative', winning the confidence of workers, and 'satisfying the various interests' in society in such a way as to promote 'the interests of society as a whole' and to 'create new progressive interests'.[81] While the National Front would remain the only permitted institution to represent the 'many-sided interests' of society, the Communist Party would guarantee 'rights, freedoms and interests' and, conscious that Communists must over and over again 'strive for the voluntary support of the majority of the people for the Party line', be prepared to 'alter Party resolutions and directives if they fail to express correctly the needs and possibilities of the whole of society'.[82] In short, although the Communist Party was not to abandon its 'leading role', it was to make that phrase real by becoming more responsive to society as a whole and allowing power, which had formerly been concentrated at the top, to be diffused across the two national Communist parties as well as throughout their ranks.[83]

On the day after the Action Programme was released, 6 April 1968, the government resigned. Prime minister Oldřich Černík's new cabinet was agreed by 8 April, the day on which another reformer, František Kriegel, was elected chairman of the Central Committee of the National Front. Ten days later, Josef Smrkovský was elected chairman of parliament by the National Assembly. Dubček's hold on power – but also his reliance upon some of the more radically reformist members of the party – was now complete. On 1 June 1968, the *KSČ* Central Committee set the seal on its anti-Novotný coup by bringing forward the Fourteenth Congress, not due to be held until 1970, to 9 September 1968 so that it might 'settle the Party's political line for the months to come' and 'elect a new Central Committee' that would 'enjoy absolute confidence'.[84] This meant that Dubček – who must have counted on being able to curtail the more dangerous freedoms that, for tactical reasons, he had temporarily permitted – was in effect forced into the position of having to abide by the more radical views espoused by a narrow majority within his own Presidium, which were quickly made public through the publication of the Action Programme. He was therefore placed in a very delicate position: on the one hand, he needed somehow to contain any expression of opinion that might be interpreted as a threat to socialism, the interests of the Warsaw Pact and those of the Soviet Union, yet at the same time appear reformist enough to retain the allegiance of a majority within the *KSČ* Central Committee, revive the economy and avoid being discredited with the public as a breaker of promises.

The Prague Spring, as the experiment in 'Socialism with a Human Face' set out in the Action Programme of April 1968 came to be known, was doomed from the start. Things began to heat up almost immediately, as Brezhnev sent Dubček a letter, dated 11 April and handed to him by Chervonenko, the Soviet ambassador in Prague, on 14 April, that expressed his dissatisfaction at not having been consulted over the changes in the Presidium and at the Dubček leadership's failure to prevent opinions unfavourable to the Soviet Union from appearing in the Czechoslovak press. At about the same time, there was unexpectedly sharp criticism from some quarters at home that the proposed reforms were not going far enough. Among the most inflammatory was a speech given by Ivan Sviták at the arts faculty of Charles University, and subsequently published in *Student*, which complained that – in spite of three months of 'regeneration' – there had as yet been 'no structural changes in the mechanisms of totalitarian dictatorship' with the 'sole exception of the temporary non-existence of censorship'. This state of affairs, Sviták declared, was simply not good enough: what was wanted in the party was 'democracy, not democratization'.[85]

On 23 April 1968, the Warsaw Pact decided to bring forward to June military exercises that had originally been scheduled to be held in the Bohemian forest in September, since it was already clear to Brezhnev that Dubček needed a prod – or, more likely, a pretext – to begin to rein in his Presidium and party. But domestic pressure for the leadership to live up to popular expectations was also becoming more intense. Those who participated in the May Day celebrations of 1968, when the usual parades took place in front of the assembled Czechoslovak Communist leadership, remembered what a sharp contrast they presented with the staged demonstrations of support of previous years. Instead of appearing like regimented and disciplined troops, for the first time the population wore smiles that seemed genuine. 'This time,' as Dubček later recalled, 'people came on their own, carrying their own banners with their own slogans, some cheerful, some critical, some just humorous.'[86] Even permitted non-party organizations, newly created organizations such as *KAN* (*Klub angažovaných nestraníků* the Club of Engaged Non-Party People) and *K-231*, who carried slogans expressing support for

Dubček, took part, as did Legionnaires from the First World War and International Brigaders from the Spanish Civil War.[87] As Alois Indra, one of the narrowly outnumbered conservatives in the Presidium, noted with concern, not only had a T.G. Masaryk Association been founded in Prague, but even the media were starting to indulge in an 'unhealthy' exaltation of the President-Liberator.[88]

Completely unused to popularity, the Dubček leadership basked in the glory of being praised, taking it as a sign that its strategy for winning public opinion was working and that the KSČ had genuinely begun to take its place in the vanguard of a socialist society which – with all its diverse interests – accepted the party's 'leading role'. Soon, the reformers seem to have expected, both the party and the economy would be invigorated with new blood, work entered into cheerfully, and the party restored to its rightful place. On 2 May, buoyed up by the holiday spirit, *Literární listy* published an appeal that called on the National Assembly to abolish the People's Militia; the next day, some four thousand people gathered for an open-air meeting in the Old Town Square in Prague to demand the establishment of an opposition party and to show solidarity with students in Poland who, having already got into trouble in March, were again demonstrating against their own government under the provocative slogan 'Poland Is Waiting for Her Dubček'. Things were starting to get out of hand.

On 4–5 May, the Soviet and Czechoslovak leaderships met, and the Soviet Presidium made clear its view that the KSČ was losing control of the mass media and that its economic reforms might lead to a restoration of capitalism. As Kieran Williams has found, in the sessions that followed in the KSČ Presidium, Dubček, Černík and especially Smrkovský used increasingly hawkish language to warn of the dangers of rightist-opportunist plots and counter-revolution.[89] When, instead of acting on the hint, the minister of the interior, Josef Pavel, announced on 7 May that the jamming of Western radio stations had been halted, this prompted the five Warsaw Pact countries most alarmed by the situation – Poland, East Germany, Hungary, Bulgaria and the USSR – to call a meeting from which, this time, it was Czechoslovakia that was pointedly excluded. After Western newspapers unhelpfully applauded the Czechoslovak experiment and began to speculate that the 'Prague Spring' might represent the end of interference by the Soviet Union in the internal affairs of other socialist states, leading Soviet, Polish and East German newspapers hotly denied that Czechoslovakia's reforms were its own affair, insisting that they presented a threat to the whole socialist camp. Only Hungary, despite some provocative articles that appeared in the Czechoslovak press about the 1956 Hungarian Uprising, hesitated at first to add its own condemnations to those of the other four; but it was soon brought on board. The Soviet Union had to take what reassurance it could from the first signs of retreat within the *KSČ*, together with Ambassador Chervonenko's assurances to Moscow, sent by telegram on 12 June, that Dubček had promised to get rid of bolder reformers such as František Kriegel and Ota Šik.[90]

At the end of June, Ludvík Vaculík unwittingly provided hardliners in the *KSČ* and the Soviet leadership with evidence to confirm their growing sense that, unless they acted quickly, Czechoslovakia might be lost to the socialist camp altogether. This came in the form of a petition that invited Czechoslovak citizens – Communist and non-Communist alike – to take power into their own hands to rid the party of all remaining conservatives and put the reform movement on a more secure footing. Vaculík's petition, entitled '2,000 Words to Workers, Farmers, Scientists, Artists and Everyone', appeared simultaneously in four newspapers on 27 June 1968: *Literární listy*, *Práce*, *Zemědělské noviny* and *Mladá fronta*, although not in *Rudé právo*, the official *KSČ* daily.[91] While the petition cautioned that it would be 'unjust and unreasonable' to exclude the Communists from power, since it was the *KSČ*'s own liberal wing that had begun the 'revival process', it nevertheless urged citizens to 'demand' that the next Central Committee 'be better than the current one'; that factory workers and employees use their power to make their unions genuinely representative; that citizens set up their own commissions and committees to force the government to 'deal with questions which no one wants to know anything about'; and that official party newspapers be replaced with ones edited by representatives of the National Front or, if need be, started up by ordinary citizens. It also demanded that the many unenlightened apparatchiks who 'still hold instruments of power, especially in the districts and in the communities', be forced out of public life.

This inflammatory text, which implied that the Communist Party should follow citizens' demands rather than lead socialist society, claimed in effect to represent the conscience of the Czech nation. The seventy signatures on the public text included those of workers, doctors, artists, athletes, professors, singers, scientists, poets, composers and a few Central Committee members; household names like the Zátopeks, both of whom were Olympic champions, the poet Jaroslav Seifert, the film director Jiří Menzel, the playwright Josef Topol and the cabaret artist Jan Werich appeared among them. Within a fortnight, '2,000 Words' had been condemned in the Soviet press as a document whose authors 'speak on behalf of the rightist, antisocialist forces in the country' which are attacking the Communist Party and 'the working class'.[92]

By 15 July, the Warsaw Pact 'Five' had had enough. This time, the letter they sent – from a meeting held in Warsaw – was addressed directly 'to the Czechoslovak Communist Party Central Committee' and was reprinted in full in the Communist Party of the Soviet Union's *Pravda* (18 July 1968).[93] This text, usually known simply as 'the Warsaw Letter', stated the five 'fraternal nations' to be convinced that reactionaries, 'supported by imperialism', were threatening to push the Czechoslovak Socialist Republic 'off the path of socialism' and so to 'imperil' the 'interests of the entire socialist system'.[94] While the Five welcomed 'adjustment of the relations between Czechs and Slovaks' on the 'healthy foundations of fraternal cooperation within the framework of the Czechoslovak Socialist Republic', they could not tolerate the risk that Czechoslovakia might 'break away from the socialist commonwealth'.[95] Pointing out that warnings had already been given at Dresden, during several bilateral meetings and in letters sent to the Presidium, they argued that it was because the 'reactionaries' had met with 'no rebuff' that they had now appeared 'publicly before the whole country' through the publication of '2,000 Words', a document that contained an 'open appeal for struggle against the Communist Party and against constitutional rule, an appeal for strikes and disorders': in short, 'counterrevolution'. Emphasizing repeatedly that the situation in Czechoslovakia represented a risk to the security of the whole socialist bloc, the letter ended with a clear statement of what the Warsaw Pact Five expected from the *KSČ*: a 'resolute and bold offensive against rightist and antisocialist forces' drawing on 'all the means of defense created by the socialist state'; the banning of organizations that 'oppose socialism'; the party's reassertion of control over the media; and the 'steadfast observance' of the 'principles of democratic centralism'.[96]

The Presidium of the *KSČ* Central Committee formally replied to the Warsaw Letter on 18 July 1968.[97] It began peevishly, pointing out that the 'common cause of socialism' is 'not advanced' by the 'holding of conferences at which the policy and activity of one of the fraternal parties is judged without the presence of their representatives'.[98] It agreed that 'healthy socialist activities' in Czechoslovakia were accompanied by 'extremist tendencies' of concern to both the *KSČ* and its socialist allies and renewed its pledge to use 'all means' to crush any direct threat to 'the socialist system'. It disagreed, however, with the Warsaw Pact Five's view that such a danger already existed. Instead, it excused even the anti-party slogans that had been freely appearing in the press and elsewhere as the inevitable consequence of years of an 'antagonistic political situation' that could not be 'satisfactorily solved suddenly in a short time'. Hostility towards Communism was blamed on the 'distortions of the fifties' and the 'policy of their inconsistent removal by the leadership headed by A. Novotný'. The *KSČ* again sought to reassure the Warsaw Pact Five that Czechoslovakia's foreign policy was 'thoroughly socialist', that it remained fully committed to 'friendly relations with the Soviet Union and the other Socialist states', and that none of its treaties or alliances was under threat.[99] Any indication of a return to the old methods of overt party control would, it explained, 'evoke the resistance of the overwhelming majority of party members, the resistance of the working class, the workers, cooperative farmers and intelligentsia', while the 'overwhelming majority' of people 'of all classes and sectors of our society favour the abolition of censorship and are for freedom of expression'.[100] Although the KSČ agreed that '2,000 Words', which 'urges people to engage in anarchic acts' and to 'violate the constitutional character of our political reform', was unacceptable and pointed out that it had been condemned by the Presidium, government and National Front, it argued that the document, whose calls to action had not been acted upon, did not in fact 'threaten the party, the National Front and the socialist state'. Repeating several times that the solution to Czechoslovakia's idiosyncratic problems could only be solved if it were allowed 'to implement the tactical line of the May plenary meetings of the Central Committee' and 'to settle basic political questions at the extraordinary fourteenth congress in the spirit of the action program', it returned to the same argument: that the KSČ was 'trying to show' that it was 'capable of a different political leadership and management than the discredited bureaucratic-police methods'. Instead of resorting to crude force, the KSČ Central Committee insisted, it would win the confidence of the people on the strength of its 'Marxist-Leninist ideas' and its 'just policy supported by the majority of the people'.[101]

The next day, 19 July 1968, Dubček addressed a speech to a special KSČ Central Committee plenum, long excerpts from which were published in *Rudé právo* and *Svobodné slovo* the following morning.[102] He was clearly on the run, making feeble excuses as to why the Warsaw Pact Five were not even inviting Czechoslovak representatives to their meetings. His two main points were really appeals. The first, implicitly addressed to the rank and file of the KSČ, came in the form of a plea not to allow 'conservative, antisocialist forces' to 'abuse the letter of the five parties to cause a rupture in the party' and so frustrate the full implementation of the reformist May plenum. The second plea was addressed to the population at large, who were in effect promised that censorship would not be reimposed so long as they could be trusted not to go too far (i.e. indulge in 'anti-Soviet sentiments and hysteria'). Within two days, the Soviet *Pravda* had expressed its disapproval, stating that the KSČ had 'ignored the fundamental questions' raised in the Warsaw Letter and failed to recognize the 'dimensions of the threat to the socialist system in Czechoslovakia'.[103] On 27 July, president Ludvík Svoboda entered the fray with an indignant article in *Obrana lidu*, claiming that 'we ourselves have done nothing to cause the five allies to doubt our loyalty to proletarian internationalism' and complaining that the Warsaw Letter was 'nothing less' than a 'categorical imperative' for socialist Czechoslovakia to commit a 'moral suicide' which would one day 'rank next to the infamous Cominform resolution on Yugoslavia' as one of the 'darkest' moments in the entire 'history of the international workers' movement'.[104] Bilateral talks were turning into dialogues of the deaf.

By the end of July 1968, diplomatic relations between the Czechoslovak Socialist Republic and Union of Soviet Socialist Republics had reached such a low that the two states found it difficult even to agree on where to hold talks. In the end, they took place on the Czechoslovak–Soviet border, at Čierna nad Tisou, from 29 July to 1 August. The Soviets so little trusted the Czechoslovaks that they pulled their delegation back over the border each night, while the Czechoslovaks panicked about Soviet military manoeuvres and rumours that Soviet troops were moving towards Czechoslovakia from East Germany. Beyond the meaningless statements that the participants had 'exchanged detailed information' and that a 'broad, comradely exchange of opinions' had taken place, nothing official was reported in the Communist press, except that a further meeting of the Warsaw Pact Five, together with the Czechoslovaks, would take place in Bratislava on 3 August. This time, however, the communiqué read like a lesson in Marxist-Leninist theory, together with a brief synopsis of the Soviet view of world history and current affairs: an ominous sign.[105] Behind closed doors, Brezhnev made clear that he expected the Czechoslovaks immediately to reimpose censorship, outlaw *KAN* and *K-231*, and demote František Kriegel, Čestmír Císař (secretary of the Central Committee) and Jiří Pelikán (director-general of Czechoslovak television) as gestures of goodwill to form 'the basis' for further talks in Bratislava.[106]

The *KSČ* was finally frightened enough to rush through a new set of draft statutes to begin a return to 'democratic centralism', but with so many caveats and provisos that it seemed unlikely fully to satisfy either reformers or conservatives; nor was it likely sufficiently to reassure either the Soviet Union or the other members of the Warsaw Pact whose security was tied to Czechoslovakia's.[107] Dubček, desperate, sought what international socialist support he could, inviting Tito to Czechoslovakia where, at a press conference held on 9 August, he stressed the 'principle' of 'non-interference in another socialist state's internal affairs', and also Ceauşescu of Romania, who arrived on 15 August, and with whom he rapidly signed a 'Czechoslovak-Romanian Treaty of Friendship, Cooperation and Mutual Aid'. But it was too late. On 17 August 1968, in a decision that was to return to haunt subsequent Soviet administrations, the Central Committee of the Communist Party of the Soviet Union (Politburo) decided, by a narrow majority, directly and publicly to intervene in socialist Czechoslovakia's domestic affairs. On the night of 20–21 August 1968, ground troops from the Warsaw Pact Five crossed into Czechoslovakia as if in a ghastly re-enactment of the arrival of the German, Polish and Hungarian armies in 1939. The pro-Dubček faction in the Presidium, unable to keep control of either party or people, had not just lost credibility with the Soviet Union and the Warsaw Pact; it had shown its weakness to its own rivals for power within the *KSČ* and *KSS* leaderships.

CHAPTER 9

BACK TO NORMAL

The Action Programme of April 1968 could never have brought about the utopia that it promised: a world in which the Communist Party would be so finely attuned to the needs and desires of the people that it would be kept in power, forever, by popular acclaim, without the need ever again to resort to compulsion, censorship or even propaganda. Like anyone else with even a modicum of political savvy, Dubček, Smrkovský and Mlynář could see that wholly unrealistic expectations were being raised by the state-wide carnival atmosphere known as the Prague Spring. They could also see that the absence of censorship was leading to provocations to other socialist countries and that attacks on the Soviet Union and the Communist system were giving aid and comfort to the enemy. Everyone in the Central Committee – not just those traditionally singled out as traitors and Soviet lackeys – knew that the reforms would have to be reined in, the 'excesses' and 'provocations' associated with the Prague Spring brought to an end, the holes in state security repaired. The questions were: who should do so; when; and how.

The dispute between Prague and Moscow, a dispute that the whole world had been watching with mounting interest, finally climaxed on the night of 20–21 August 1968 when somewhere between a quarter and half a million Warsaw Pact troops – Soviet, Polish, East German, Hungarian and Bulgarian – began to cross into the territory of the Czechoslovak Socialist Republic with the stated aim of helping to prevent counter-revolution in a fraternal socialist state.[1] Although the 'invasion' was successfully presented to the outside world by the Czechoslovak Communist Party as if it had come as a complete bolt from the blue, Brezhnev was not lying when he said that he had received requests to intervene to prevent 'counter-revolution' in Czechoslovakia. These had been put to the Soviets not only by the other members of the Warsaw Pact Five, but also by some high Czechoslovak Communist officials, most notably Alois Indra, secretary for the economy in the Central Committee with responsibility for the forthcoming Fourteenth Party Congress and deputy leader of the KSČ, Vasil Bil'ak, first secretary of the KSS, Oldřich Švestka, the editor of Rudé právo, Central Committee member Drahomír Kolder, and Antonín Kapek, a candidate member of the *KSČ* Presidium.[2]

The arrival of Warsaw Pact troops placed Czechoslovakia at the centre of sustained world attention for the first time since the Munich Crisis. Thanks to the quick reactions of local cameramen and photographers across the country, images of mass demonstrations and civil disobedience against the occupiers were shown around the world within twenty-four hours and repeatedly broadcast during the whole of the following week. The invasion came as a gift to Western propaganda, which all but canonized Dubček as the latest victim in what it saw as a pattern of organized Soviet aggression in Central and Eastern Europe, and split the socialist world in two, dividing those who regarded the Soviet Union's action as justified from those who most emphatically did not. For all the emotion that the arrival of the troops aroused, for all the shocked and angry discussion that it was to promote, what followed in Czechoslovakia over the course of the following week was neither revolution nor counter-revolution. It was largely propaganda and political theatre.

According to the reconstruction of the events of the week of 20–27 August 1968 that was painstakingly pieced together at the time by Communist historians at the Czechoslovak Academy of Sciences,[3] the first signs that something was afoot came on the evening of Tuesday, 20 August 1968, when a couple of unscheduled Soviet flights landed at Ruzyně airport on the outskirts of Prague, discharged passengers in civilian dress, and then took off again. A few hours later, at about 10.45 p.m., a Soviet general from the Warsaw Pact joint command informed the Czechoslovak minister of defence, Martin Dzúr, that Warsaw Pact troops were about to arrive to offer 'fraternal assistance' to prevent 'counter-revolution'. Dzúr immediately got on the phone to Chervonenko, Brezhnev and Grechko to confirm the news; they, in turn, asked him to ensure that the Czechoslovak army remain in their barracks to avoid any risk of bloodshed, and assured him that his loyalty at this crucial moment would not be forgotten.[4] From about 11 p.m., the first ground troops from the USSR, People's Republic of Poland, People's Republic of Hungary, German Democratic Republic and People's Republic of Bulgaria began to cross Czechoslovak frontiers at more or less regular intervals. The Soviet ambassador in Prague, Stepan Chervonenko, then formally called on President Svoboda to notify him that the armies of the Warsaw Pact were entering the territory of the Czechoslovak Socialist Republic in response to a request from 'a majority' of members of the Presidium of the *KSČ* Central Committee to 'provide armed assistance' to 'the Czechoslovak people' to help them to 'resist counter-revolution'. He further informed Svoboda that comrades Dubček, Kriegel, Smrkovský and Císař were behaving 'dishonestly' and 'insincerely' and 'supporting the activities of the reactionary forces'.[5] Svoboda told the Soviet ambassador that he did not 'welcome' the arrival of the troops, but agreed not to 'act against the allied states' and added that he had known, when he accepted the post of president, that this would mean never cutting his 'ties' with the USSR.[6]

In the enormous Central Committee building on the banks of the River Vltava in Prague, a meeting of the *KSČ* Presidium was still in session when, at about twenty to midnight, prime minister Oldřich Černík was called away from the table to take a telephone call. When he came back, it was to inform the rest of the Presidium that Minister of Defence Dzúr had just told him that Warsaw Pact troops were crossing the country's borders. Zdeněk Mlynář, one of the most energetic promoters of the Prague Spring reforms, recalled later how hearing the news produced in him feelings very like those he had once had in a car accident: the actions and words of those around him took on an air of unreality, as if he were watching a film.[7] He vaguely remembered Dubček saying, 'So they did it after all – and to *me*!' and Vasil Bil'ak pacing nervously and saying to his fellow Presidium members, 'Alright lynch me! Why don't you kill me?'[8] Dubček, who later claimed to be unable to recall how he or the members of his divided Presidium first reacted to the news, is remembered by other witnesses as having suddenly pulled out a letter from Brezhnev, dated 17 August, whose contents he had not yet divulged to the rest of the Presidium.[9] The letter, which he now read aloud, contained nothing more that what Dubček later dismissed as 'the standard Moscow ranting' against the 'anti-Soviet and antisocialist material in *Literární listy* or *Reportér* and how this violated agreements made in Čierná and Bratislava'. His point seemed to be that, since nothing of substance had changed in the Soviet–Czechoslovak dialogue over the last few weeks, the sudden appearance of the Warsaw Pact armies was inexplicable. Having failed miserably, however one looked at it, to handle the situation, bewildered members of the Presidium launched into a confused discussion in which Mlynář and Dubček, among others, announced their resignations but were called back to earth by Svoboda, who reminded everyone that it would be foolish for elected Communist officials to initiate a purge by actually volunteering to be replaced. Someone, Mlynář later recalled, tried to turn the mood of the meeting against Dubček for having kept Brezhnev's letter to himself; but the majority were too shocked and depressed to be interested in apportioning blame.[10]

At midnight, while members of the *KSČ* Presidium were still trying to absorb the dramatic news, Dzúr issued an order to all army units to remain in their barracks, 'under no circumstances' to use their weapons, and to offer Soviet troops 'maximum all-round assistance'.[11] Shortly after midnight, two large planes with Soviet markings touched down at Ruzyně airport, the Czechoslovak air force having grounded its own planes to ensure a clear runway for unannounced landings. The several dozen Soviet soldiers who emerged from the flights immediately surrounded the main terminal building, evicted airport personnel and travellers from inside and, together with East German troops, took up positions on the airfield and surrounding roads. For the next half-hour, Soviet planes landed at intervals of about one per minute, after which women were allowed to return to the terminal-building waiting room to sit down, while men were kept outside. Those who found themselves trapped in the airport, including a number of hapless tourists, were eventually allowed to leave for town, on foot, at about 5.30 a.m. on the morning of 21 August.[12]

In the Presidium meeting, consensus was reached that the most pressing thing to do was to issue a statement in time for Czechoslovak radio to broadcast it before 2.00 a.m., when the station closed down for the night. The problem was whether formally to accept the offer of 'assistance', and to treat the arrival of the troops as officially welcome, which would put the Indra-Bil'ak wing of the Presidium in a good light and presumably lead to their elevation at the expense of the Kriegel-Smrkovský wing; or else to treat the action as a hostile act by a foreign power, thus maintaining the credibility and position of a narrow majority within the Presidium, but at the risk of seriously angering the Soviets and the other members of the Warsaw Pact. Arguments over the wording of the draft became so heated and long-winded that the Presidium barely managed to meet its deadline. The sentence for inclusion in the Presidium's proposed statement to the nation that aroused the sharpest conflict ran: 'The Presidium of the Central Committee of the KSČ considers this action to be contrary not only to the fundamental principles of relations between socialist states but also a denial of the basic norms of international law.'[13] Of those who had voting rights within the Presidium, Bil'ak, Kolder, Švestka and Rigo were against including the sentence; so were Alois Indra, Antonín Kapek and Miloš Jakeš, who as candidate members of the Presidium were entitled to take part in discussions, but not to vote. Smrkovský and Kriegel, calling those who opposed the sentence 'traitors', together with Špaček, Černík, Piller and Barbírek, formed a block of voting members who stood behind the draft resolution, and were supported, among those without voting rights, by Bohumil Šimon, Čestmír Císař, Václav Slavík, Štefan Sádovský and Zdeněk Mlynář. Dubček hesitated, but eventually came down in favour of the Smrkovský-Kriegel lobby.[14] In the end, the wording of the draft statement was passed by seven votes (Dubček, Smrkovský, Kriegel, Špaček, Černík, Piller and Barbírek) to four (Bil'ak, Kolder, Švestka and Rigo).[15] A narrow majority within the Presidium evidently gambled that they would be able to stand firm, protecting their own positions, the independence of their party and the sovereignty of the state, if only they could rally the party faithful and enough of the politically agnostic by appealing directly to their Czech and Slovak patriotism. It was a risky strategy, but the alternative option looked worse.

At about 1 a.m. on the night of 20–21 August 1968, Czechoslovak radio alerted listeners to stand by for an important announcement from the KSČ Central Committee. This was the first clue that most Czechoslovak citizens had that anything unusual was going on. But it was almost 2 a.m., by which time many could hear the sound of planes overhead or else an unusually heavy volume of military traffic on the roads, and just ten minutes before Czechoslovak radio was due to go off the air, before the proclamation passed by the Presidium of the Central Committee of the Czechoslovak Communist Party was finally read out to 'all the people of the Czechoslovak Socialist Republic'. The announcement, which effectively treated the arrival as a military invasion by foreign powers rather than as a rescue operation by international socialist friends, read as follows:

Yesterday, 20 August 1968, at about 11 p.m., the armies of the Soviet Union, the Polish People's Republic, the German Democratic Republic, the Hungarian People's Republic and the Bulgarian People's Republic crossed the state borders of the Czechoslovak Socialist Republic. This took place without the knowledge of the President of the Republic, the Presidium of the National Assembly, the Presidium of the government, and the first secretary of the Communist Party Central Committee. The Presidium of the Central Committee was in session, undertaking preparations for the Extraordinary Fourteenth Party Congress. The Presidium calls upon all citizens of the Republic to remain calm and not to resist the advancing armies, because the defence of our state borders is now impossible.

For this reason our army, the security forces, and the People's Militia were not given the order to defend the country. The Presidium of the Central Committee of the KSČ considers this action to be contrary not only to the fundamental principles of relations between socialist states but also a denial of the basic norms of international law.

All leading officials of the party and the National Front remain at their posts, to which they were elected as representatives of the people and members of their organizations according to the laws and regulations of the Czechoslovak Socialist Republic. The appropriate constitutional organs have called into session the National Assembly and the government of the Republic, and the Presidium of the Central Committee is convening the Party Central Committee in order to deal with the situation that has arisen.[16]

In getting its announcement on the air, the Presidium had two main aims: clearly to assert its authority; and to prevent the population from either resisting or collaborating with the incoming socialist armies, but rather to await instructions. As it happened, most people in the country heard only the first sentence of the broadcast before their radios went silent, Karel Hoffmann, the director of the Central Communications Administration, in cooperation with Miroslav Šulek of the Czechoslovak Press Agency and Viliam Šalgovič, deputy minister of the interior, having ordered the radio transmitters to be turned off.[17] Through an oversight, however, Prague radio was not affected, so that the message that the Presidium had not invited the armies – in direct contradiction of the claims being made in leaflets dropped by Warsaw Pact helicopters – got through to members of the National Assembly, the Presidential office, and Prague district and city committees, as well as to the general population of the capital.[18]

The meeting of the *KSČ* Presidium in Prague was adjourned as soon as the proclamation was broadcast. Prime Minister Černík went back to the Presidium offices; President Svoboda to the Castle; Bil'ak and Indra to the Soviet Embassy; and Oldřich Švestka, editor in chief of *Rudé právo*, the *KSČ* daily, to the newspaper's offices. The rest of the group retired to Dubček's office to plan what to do next. When, at about 3.20 a.m., Dubček phoned the prime minister's office, a government official informed him that Černík had been taken into custody by the Soviets.[19] A crowd of peaceful demonstrators, carrying the Czechoslovak flag and singing the national anthem and 'The Internationale', gathered outside the Central Committee building. From a window in Dubček's office, Smrkovský saw a young demonstrator get shot by a Soviet soldier. Incensed, he called Ambassador Chervonenko to tell him that he was holding him personally responsible for the young man's death.[20] Later, it was said that not just one but perhaps as many as fifteen protestors had been killed in the confusion.

At 4.30 a.m., Soviet armoured cars, led by an embassy limousine, arrived at the *KSČ* Central Committee building. Soviet paratroopers carrying automatic weapons jumped out while tanks and tight cordons of troops surrounded the building so that no one could leave.[21] At about the same time, Czechoslovak radio in Prague resumed broadcasting, showing which side it was on by repeatedly reading out the proclamation issued by the Presidium a few hours before. It was thus left to a new radio station, calling itself 'Radio Vltava', which was broadcast in both Czech and Slovak from East Germany, to announce, from about 5.30 a.m., the rival version of the events: that 'fraternal' Warsaw Pact armies had come to 'defend socialism' as requested by 'leading Party and state leaders who have remained faithful to socialism'.[22] At 6.00 a.m., a personal message from First Secretary Dubček, appealing to people to remain calm, go about their usual business and not resist the troops, was broadcast on Czechoslovak radio.[23]

From 7.00 a.m., Czechoslovak television, whose main transmitter on Petřín hill in Prague had by then been occupied, began to broadcast from another transmitter. It was therefore able to report that one of the Party district committee in Prague was demanding a city-wide *KSČ* conference, and that the Prague municipal committee was planning to hold a general strike and insisting that the Extraordinary Fourteenth Party Congress scheduled for 9 September should be brought forward and held immediately.[24] While continuing to call on citizens to show 'calm' and 'self-control', from 7.15 a.m. reporters from Czechoslovak radio were reporting that six tanks had been placed outside their studios, that shots had been fired and that they did not know how much longer they would be able to continue broadcasting. Explaining that people in Wenceslas Square were 'trying to stop vehicles of the occupation troops with their bodies', they pleaded with the population to 'try to engage the troops in conversation . . . our only weapon', and warned them not to pay attention to any unfamiliar voices that might later take over the broadcasts.[25]

The director of Czechoslovak television, Jiří Pelikán, and the director of Prague radio, Zdeněk Hejzlar, had made their loyalty to the Presidium clear. *Rudé právo*, however, whose editor-in-chief was Oldřich Švestka, initially backed the Warsaw Pact line and refused to include the Presidium statement in the morning edition of the all-important *KSČ* daily. Smrkovský, informed in time, had Švestka instantly replaced as editor by Jiří Sekera, forcing the newspaper into line with state radio and television.[26] Morning editions of *Mladá fronta*, *Zemědělské noviny*, *Práce*, *Večerní Praha* and *Lidová demokracie* then followed suit, printing the Presidium proclamation and supporting its main points: that the invasion was not justified; that the Dubček party leadership, Černík government and Svoboda presidency were the only legal representatives of the country; and that violent resistance should be avoided at all costs.[27]

By 8 a.m. on the morning of 21 August 1968, the Old Town Square in Prague was starting to fill with demonstrators who had heard the Presidium statement, seen the morning headlines or watched the tanks roll in with their own eyes. A group in Wenceslas Square was already holding up the dramatic symbol of a bloodstained Czechoslovak flag for the cameras;[28] and the radio and Central Committee buildings were surrounded not only by Soviet tanks and foreign soldiers, but also by angry Czech protestors. In Karlín, a traditional working-class district and Communist stronghold in Prague, there were further marches, with Czechoslovak flags held aloft, to express indignation at the arrival of the occupation forces. At 8.12, Czechoslovak radio broadcast a statement put together by the Presidium of the Czechoslovak Academy of Sciences which declared that it stood 'unanimously behind the Dubček leadership of the party, behind the legally elected President of the Republic, Ludvík Svoboda, and the Černík government', and condemned the 'occupation' by the armies of the Warsaw Pact as 'a flagrant transgression' of the 'principles of international law and state sovereignty' which 'damages the cause of socialism in the eyes of all the nations of the world'.[29]

Ludvík Svoboda, who as president was also commander-in-chief of the armed forces, had initially thought that the Czechoslovak army was following the will of a united Presidium in ensuring that maximum cooperation be offered to the Warsaw Pact troops. When he arrived at the Central Committee building to announce the good news that the Warsaw Pact had arrived, however, the smile froze on his face as he learned that Dubček had not said – as he had might well have done – that he had invited and welcomed the fraternal armies, but had instead denounced the action.[30] At 8.30 a.m., he, too, made sure that he got on the radio, to issue a very brief statement in which, without either applauding or condemning the action, he instructed the population to remain 'calm' and show 'discipline' and 'dignity'.[31] Within minutes of the broadcast, a battle for control of the Czechoslovak radio building broke out between staff inside and the Soviet troops surrounding it, during which seventeen people were afterwards said to have been shot and fifty-two taken to hospital.[32]

In Dubček's office, where about half the members of the Presidium, unable to leave the building, had spent an anxious and uncomfortable night, at about 9 a.m. on the morning of 21 August the doors suddenly 'flew open and about eight soldiers and low-ranking officers with machine guns rushed in, surrounded us from behind around a large table and aimed their weapons at the backs of our heads'. Two officers followed, one of whom was a colonel with medals displayed on his chest, pointed their guns at Dubček, Smrkovský, Kriegel and Špaček, and escorted them into Císař's nearby office, where they were met by a party of KGB and StB officers. As Dubček afterwards remembered with particular indignation, it was not a Soviet KGB officer but a plain-clothes StB man, one of the Czechoslovak state's own security officers, who announced to the four men that he was either taking them 'into custody' (or, more likely, 'under his protection').[33] In Dubček's office, where the others continued to wait, telephone links were cut and the windows closed, although noise from the crowd that had gathered below, including chants of 'Dubček!' and the singing of Czech patriotic and socialist songs, could still be plainly heard.[34] An emergency session of the National Assembly was convened at 10.07 a.m. which got out the message, at 10.20 a.m., that it demanded the 'immediate withdrawal' of all troops.[35] At about 11 a.m., Dubček was told to climb into a large, windowless armoured vehicle, in which he was later joined by Kriegel, and driven in the direction of Ruzyně. Despite his fear that he was being taken to the infamous StB prison, at about noon he and Kriegel were delivered to a private office in the nearby airport. Although the two men had no way of knowing it, Smrkovský and Šimon were also being held close by, in an adjoining office; eventually Černík was also brought in.[36]

At noon, a two-minute silence – with its obvious echoes of the Protectorate period – went ahead, as scheduled, in Prague. At 12.30, the news was broadcast that Presidium members Dubček, Smrkovský, Černík and Kriegel were being held in the Central Committee building, and that the chairman of the Czech National Council, Čestmír Císař, was in police custody in Bartolomějská Street.[37] Shortly after 2 p.m., there were reports that the four Presidium members had been taken by Soviet armoured personnel carrier to 'an unknown destination' and, by 5.10 p.m., that the Czech National Council considered the 'abduction' of Císař to be a 'crime' and was demanding his immediate release.[38] Over the course of the afternoon, foreign minister Jiří Hájek sent formal notes of protest to the governments of the five Warsaw Pact countries involved, declaring what they referred to as the 'armed occupation of Czechoslovakia' to be 'contrary to the Charter of the United Nations, the Warsaw Pact and the fundamental principles of international law'.[39] At about 7 p.m., the government issued a statement demanding the release of those held in custody and the withdrawal of all troops, together with further appeals to the population to maintain order.[40] At 10.30 p.m., President Svoboda again addressed the nation. This time, instead of remaining carefully neutral, he described the Action Programme as addressing 'the vital interests and the needs of all the people in our homeland' and called for 'unity' with the *KSČ*, the *KSS* and the National Front 'for the sake of a better life for our nations'.[41] This put him publicly on the side of the 'reform' lobby and the Dubček leadership. He did not yet judge it politic to reveal that he had made contact with Chervonenko and General Pavlovskii, the commander of the intervention forces, to ask that he be allowed to meet the Soviet leaders in Moscow.[42]

In Slovakia, where the *KSS* Presidium did not have the good luck to be in session when the news of the invasion first broke, its members were as divided as their counterparts in Prague, but with a slight majority on the opposite side. Since Dzúr had already let Gustáv Husák know that a new 'revolutionary' government might soon take charge and Vasil Biľak had phoned from the Soviet Embassy with the message that the *KSS* must under no circumstances condemn the invasion, it seemed that the official *KSČ* line was that the troops should be formally welcomed.[43] Miloslav Hruškovič rapidly convened an emergency session of the Slovak Presidium and secretariat at some point after 11 p.m., where his comrades were shown a letter of invitation to the troops which, although unsigned, he said had come from President Svoboda and the whole of the *KSČ* leadership, with the sole exceptions of František Kriegel and Josef Smrkovský. Ján Janík and three other *KSS* leaders duly expressed themselves in favour of the arrival of the Warsaw Pact troops, although others protested that the political situation in Slovakia did not warrant such drastic action. The result was that, out of ten members of the *KSS* Presidium, six initially voted to follow the line of the 'letter of invitation' while four (Faľtan, Daubner, Turček and Ťažký) voted against.[44] This showed the *KSS*, just like the *KSČ*, to be divided over the issue, with the *KSČ* voting narrowly against the occupation and the *KSS* narrowly in favour of it.

Not long after the ten members of the *KSS* had nailed their colours to the mast, a telegram arrived from Prague, informing them that the *KSČ* had not invited the armies in. Later that night, Gustáv Husák arrived, took over the meeting from Hruškovič and demanded that anyone who had been responsible for inviting the invaders publicly admit the fact. No one did. A majority at the meeting then insisted that some sort of public statement be issued. The ensuing *KSS* proclamation took a middle course: although it denied knowledge of any reason for the 'unjustified arrival' of the Warsaw Pact armies and refused to endorse anything 'undertaken beyond the legal, democratically elected Party and State leadership', it nevertheless stopped short of actually condemning the invasion. Stressing that the Slovak Communist Party and state organs had 'the situation' firmly in hand and remained loyal to Dubček, Černík and Svoboda, it called upon the Slovak people to 'work normally', not to 'provoke' the soldiers, and to maintain 'calm' and 'dignity'.[45]

From about 1.40 a.m. on the night of 20–21 August, Soviet tank divisions began to pour into Bratislava, Hungarian and Bulgarian troops having already crossed into Slovak territory at about 11 p.m. From 4.30 a.m., the *KSČ* Presidium's condemnation of the invasion was broadcast, Sarvaš having ignored Hoffmann's orders to stop. By dawn on 21 August, as tanks were swarming through the city centre, people tried to block off the main streets with barricades. By 9 a.m., no doubt encouraged by the *KSS* statement, a crowd had gathered outside the Soviet consulate and several thousand more in the city's central SNP Square to protest the invasion. Even after the main broadcasting station in Bratislava was seized by Soviet troops, regional stations continued broadcasting and a few makeshift stations were set up in the Slovak capital so that transmissions resumed on 22 August. By 23 August, Slovak technicians had also managed to restore radio links with Prague.[46]

At about 9 p.m. on the evening of 21 August, the six arrested *KSČ* leaders who had been taken from the Central Committee building in Prague to Ruzyně airport (Dubček, Smrkovský, Černík, Kriegel, Špaček and Šimon) were boarded first onto one plane, and then another, before finally taking off and flying for a couple of hours. They landed at what Dubček guessed must have been Uzhhorod (formerly Užhorod, capital of the Czechoslovak region of Subcarpathian Ruthenia) in the Ukrainian Republic of the Soviet Union. Dubček, Smrkovský, Černík and Šimon spent the night and the whole of the next day, 22 August, in separate rooms in a complex of government villas, without seeing any sign of the others. By then, it seemed to Dubček that something must have gone wrong with the Soviets' plans since they no longer seemed 'to know what to do' with him.[47] Smrkovský and Černík, surprised to be brought their first 'decent and civilized meal', complete with a bottle of wine, at lunchtime on 22 August, could also sense that there had been some sort of a change: instead of being handled like prisoners to be prepared for a revolutionary tribunal, they were once again being treated as statesmen.[48]

Dubček and the others were right to sense that something had gone wrong with the Soviets' plans. What had evidently been envisaged was a straightforward replacement of key members in the Presidium and government, not unlike the 'coup' that Dubček's own group within the Presidium had launched against the Novotný leadership in January 1968, but whose aim, this time, was to depose Dubček as first secretary of the KSČ and remove his coterie from power while simultaneously making it clear to the rank and file of the party that the Soviet Union and Warsaw Pact stood solidly behind the purge. The plan, which might so easily have worked, was that a majority of six out of the eleven voting members of the Presidium of the KSČ Central Committee (Indra, Kolder, Biľak, Piller, Barbírek and Rigo) would remove Dubček, Císař, Špaček, Kriegel and other objectionable 'rightists' from the KSČ leadership, while candidate members Lenárt and Kapek would also vote for the Indra group, supported by non-members Jakeš and perhaps Voleník, with only Císař, Sádovský, Slavík and Mlynář voting against.[49] A discussion of Brezhnev's latest letter to Dubček would then be forced, ending with a motion to request 'fraternal assistance' from Moscow to prevent 'counter-revolution'.[50] Šalgovič, the deputy minister of the interior, would take charge of preparing Ruzyně airport to receive Soviet planes as the first stage of the invasion, while Martin Dzúr and Ludvík Svoboda would ensure that the Czechoslovak army offered no resistance. As soon as the Warsaw Pact troops arrived, the StB would arrest the offending members of the Dubček leadership, who would be replaced by a Government of Workers' and Peasants led by the KSČ deputy party leader, Alois Indra. Svoboda would remain president; Černík, it was calculated, would immediately agree to continue as prime minister.[51]

After bringing Dubček and the other deviants before a 'revolutionary tribunal', the Indra government would make public the Presidium's appeal to the Soviet Union for Warsaw Pact troops to save Czechoslovakia from counter-revolution, while reliable cadres working in radio, television and the press agency would announce the takeover in politically correct terms. The KSS, National Assembly and district and regional committees would follow the lead of the KSČ, just as they always did. Once the new government had cemented its position, steps would be taken to ban all unauthorized political parties and organizations, reimpose censorship, and enforce the Bratislava and Čierná declarations: this would show the world a united socialist front and make clear to the governments of the West that the coup constituted no threat to their interests and no change in East–West relations. Since the Communist leadership, army, media and StB would all speak with one voice, backed by the presence of nearly half a million troops from five Warsaw Pact countries, the

Czechoslovak people would be presented with a *fait accompli*, to which they would submit just as they had submitted when Hácha had 'confidently placed' the Czech nation in Hitler's care in March 1939.

According to the script, the first act of the coup was to have begun on the afternoon of 20 August at the Presidium meeting, when Indra and Kolder were supposed to turn the first item on the agenda, an alarming situation report from the party's information department, into an attack on the 'rightist' elements within the *KSČ* leadership. As Kieran Williams has convincingly argued, this was supposed to draw a majority of the Presidium members into a condemnation of Dubček and the 'reformist' wing, which would lead in turn to a peaceful welcome to the 'fraternal' Warsaw Pact troops scheduled to arrive that same night and so ensure a smooth and orderly transfer of power, with the ultimate aim of returning the *KSČ* to internal and international policies favourable to the Soviet Union and the rest of the Warsaw Pact. The first surprise for the conspirators came when Dubček, who had evidently sensed that Indra and Kolder were planning in some way to obstruct the Presidium meeting, announced that, on procedural grounds, the first item on the agenda would be skipped over.[52] This meant that the long hours that were supposed to have been spent softening up the Presidium to accept the imminent invasion – or at least to keep its members out of harm's way – before the change in the *KSČ* leadership could be announced, were instead spent discussing what had originally been scheduled as the second item on the agenda, the draft of Dubček's keynote speech for the forthcoming Extraordinary Fourteenth Party Congress, to be held on 9 September.[53] Only once this matter had finally been dispensed with, by nightfall, did Indra and Kolder manage to force through their fifteen-page prepared statement on the Presidium, by which time Černík was already getting the first of several reports that the country was about to be occupied.[54]

Once Černík came away from his telephone conversation with Dzúr to drop the bombshell that troops had begun to cross into Czechoslovak territory, the conspirators within the Presidium, outvoted and with no clear instructions as to what to do next, panicked. Indra and Bil'ak went straight to the Soviet Embassy to report what had happened; Piller left for Kladno; Kapek for his *chata* (*dacha* or country cottage); and Kolder locked himself in his office.[55] The assumption that the media would immediately be placed under the control of 'loyal cadres' was perhaps the most serious aspect of the plan to go wrong. Although *StB* officers took over the main radio building in Prague at about 1.15 a.m., they overlooked one studio, which went ahead and broadcast the Presidium's condemnation of the invasion.[56]

Presented with contradictory orders from rival sections of a divided Presidium, the *StB* was thrown into confusion. A number of *StB* officers, told to stop radio broadcasts of the Presidium's condemnation of the invasion at

4.30 a.m., lost their nerve when they saw protesting mobs outside the radio station, and simply refused to obey orders.[57] Šalgovič, who had apparently believed Dubček to be behind the invitation to the Warsaw Pact armies, phoned Dubček at about 9 a.m. on 21 August, only to discover that it was actually Indra who had issued the directives to take over the media. He began to drink heavily, released Císař (whose arrest he had ordered just hours before), and anxiously told colleagues that 'terrible things are happening' and that he was caught between the Dubček and Indra factions. By evening, completely drunk, he joined the Indra group in the Soviet Embassy in a sorry state.[58]

The Prague Committee, by far the most reformist of the district and regional branches of the KSČ, managed to get the message through to most of its Czech (but not its Slovak) party delegates that the Extraordinary Fourteenth Party Congress would be brought forward from 9 September to 22 August, and held at a secret location, which turned out to be the ČKD factory works in Vysočany, an industrial quarter of Prague. Enough of the People's Militia responded to calls to ensure that the Vysočany site was guarded.[59] By about 11 a.m. on the morning of 22 August, word got back to the rump Presidium, led by Kolder in the Central Committee building, that the Vysočany congress had actually convened and begun its proceedings, with some thousand delegates, overwhelmingly Czech but representing nearly three-quarters of a full complement, in attendance.[60] Ludvík Vaculík, with his gift for rousing a crowd, was one of the first to speak, telling the congress that 'the absolutely unanimous reaction of our people' to the 'occupation of our country by the allied armies, a totally unjustified occupation', must be 'the single decisive guideline for the attitude which our Party ought to adopt . . . our attitude must be that we cannot reconcile ourselves to this reality, that we cannot accept it, that we must speak out unanimously against it'. When the 'prolonged, tumultuous' applause had died down sufficiently for him to be able to continue, he added significantly: 'If we wish to speak the language of our people, of our nations, we cannot speak any other way.'[61]

When Mlynář went back to the Central Committee building that same morning (22 August), he found that, although it was surrounded by soldiers and tanks, people with Central Committee passes were being let in, and there was no obvious military or secret-police presence inside.[62] A meeting of eleven members (Bil'ak, Indra, Kolder, Jakeš, Lenárt, Švestka, Piller, Barbírek, Rigo, Sádovský and Mlynář) out of a full contingent of the twenty-two strong party leadership was convened by Bil'ak, during which he emphasized that the only way forward was to negotiate with the Soviet army command and the Soviet Embassy, and that the group should declare itself 'competent to enter into negotiations "at the highest level" '.[63] In addition to the six missing members of the KSČ Presidium, there were also three people missing from the secretariat: Císař, Slavík and Erban.[64] After protests that the six arrested Presidium members – Dubček, Černík, Smrkovský, Kriegel, Špaček and Šimon – must be included in the discussions, and that the Presidium would negotiate only with the Soviet Embassy or party leadership collectively and as a whole, arrangements were made to bring the rump Presidium to the Soviet Embassy.[65]

While the eleven were left waiting in the Soviet Embassy for Ambassador Chervonenko to make an appearance, Mlynář made surreptitious use of one of the special phones in the building to send bulletins of the embassy negotiations directly to the Vysočany congress.[66] When Chervonenko finally arrived, it was to tell the assembled group that the Soviet Union favoured the formation of an exceptional organ of authority, a Revolutionary Government of Workers and Peasants, which would combine the functions of party and state leadership. Since the eleven members present enjoyed the full confidence of their Soviet comrades, he continued, they ought to decide whether or not to form such a body. As members of the group spent the next few hours squabbling among themselves – in some cases deliberately, to stall the proceedings – over who should be appointed to which post in the new body, the Vysočany group upstaged the Soviet Embassy group by declaring itself to be the official party congress with sole authority to elect a new Central Committee.[67]

The Vysočany congress went ahead, electing a new *KSČ* Presidium pointedly made up of precisely those members of the leadership who were known to be missing and understood to be in danger – Dubček, Černík, Smrkovský and Císař – together with those members of the government who had turned up at the congress. Also elected were people, among others Eduard Goldstücker and Marie Švermová, who had been publicly associated with support for the Prague Spring reforms or, like the secretaries of the Prague District and City Committees, had first protested against the 'occupation' and backed the Dubček party leadership. In order to give the congress an air of legitimacy, a further two delegates from each region of the country were also elected, most *in absentia*. Against Bil'ak's repeated advice, the Presidium of the *KSS* then decided to dispatch its own delegation to the Vysočany congress. In the meantime, the congress elected a new Central Committee of 144 people, and a Presidium made up of twenty-eight people, some fifteen of whom were not physically present. These included not only the 6 arrested leaders being held in Moscow, but also Gustáv Husák, who had by then flown out to Moscow; Ota Šik, who was in Yugoslavia; Čestmír Císař, who was hiding somewhere in Prague; and the whole of the Slovak delegation (including Colotka, Zrak, Ťažký and Pavlena) who were still stuck somewhere en route – in Břeclav or Bratislava; the chairman evidently thought it sufficient to rule that 'everything we decide will later be discussed with the Slovak delegates when a majority of them is present'.[68] The congress proclaimed Czechoslovakia to be 'a free and sovereign socialist State' whose 'sovereignty was infringed on 21 August 1968, when it was occupied by the armed forces of the Soviet Union, Poland, the German Democratic Republic, Bulgaria and Hungary'. It further declared that 'there was no counter-revolution in Czechoslovakia, nor was her socialist development threatened in any way. The people and the party were perfectly capable of resolving the problems that had arisen by themselves.'[69] It therefore 'categorically' demanded that 'normal conditions be created immediately for the work of Czechoslovak constitutional and political organs and that the arrested representatives be released without delay, so that they may return to their duties'.[70] In order to apply what pressure it could, it also issued appeals to socialists throughout the world and made known its plans to hold a general strike with the aim of ensuring the immediate removal of the troops.

By nightfall, an exasperated Ambassador Chervonenko therefore found that, instead of having a cooperative new Revolutionary Workers' and Peasants' Government, or even a prime minister, with whom to negotiate, he instead had a divided and suspicious contingent of squabbling Communists in the Soviet Embassy while a rival Communist group, at large in Vysočany, had resoundingly and publicly endorsed the very members of the leadership – Dubček, Černík, Kriegel, Špaček, Smrkovský and Šimon – who had been arrested and spirited out of the country precisely so that they would be out of the way.[71] At this point, a complete stalemate, President Svoboda unexpectedly stepped into the breach. It was Mlynář, still at the Soviet Embassy, who first remembered that it was constitutionally possible, in the event of a prime minister being unable to carry out his functions, for the President of the Republic to head the government in his stead. He and Sádovský therefore suggested that the group continue their talks at the Castle.[72]

According to Mlynář's recollections, President Svoboda rose to the occasion magnificently, refusing to Chervonenko's face to serve in a Revolutionary Workers' and Peasants' Government led by Indra and telling Piller that, were he to do so, 'the nation' would 'drive [him] out of this Castle like a mangy dog'.[73] Instead, he proposed to go to Moscow the very next morning to negotiate, directly with Brezhnev, for the return of Dubček, Černík, Smrkovský and the others. On the morning of 23 August, Svoboda again took to the airwaves to announce to the nation his intention to take part in 'direct talks with the highest representatives of the Soviet Union', from which he expected to return the same evening.[74] The *KSS* Presidium, meanwhile, by insisting that Husák rather than Bil'ak be sent to represent the Slovak side in the party that Svoboda was gathering to take to Moscow to negotiate, in effect removed Bil'ak as leader of the Slovak Communist Party and left the last shreds of the Indra group's credibility in tatters.[75] Although the president's gesture appeared to indicate that Svoboda, every inch the decisive general, was going to sort out the misunderstanding with the Warsaw Pact and bring home the Dubček-Černík leadership, he had in fact consulted the Soviets at every stage and all those whom he chose to accompany him to Moscow – the minister of defence, Martin Dzúr; deputy prime minister Gustáv Husák; justice minister Bohuslav Kučera, who was also chairman of the Socialist Party; and also Piller, Bil'ak and Indra – were already compromised, either by their initial association with 'the Revolutionary Workers and Peasants' Indra group or else by their failure to protest against the invasion. Significantly, there was no one from the anti-invasion group represented by the delegates of the Vysočany congress.[76] Presumably because rumours were circulating to the contrary, and there were echoes of Hácha's visit to Hitler, at 9.20 a.m. on 23 August Czechoslovak radio felt it necessary to assure listeners that the trip had been arranged on the president's own initiative and that he had not signed away the nation's sovereignty in return for being kept on in a collaborationist government.[77]

Moscow, having found that it could not easily replace what it saw as the bad apples in the *KSČ* leadership, now sought to put the whole leadership under pressure to reverse the Prague Spring reforms. On Friday, 23 August, Dubček was taken from his Ruthenian villa, given a pair of dark glasses to wear and driven to a regional committee of the Communist Party of the Soviet Union; at 11 p.m. Moscow time, he was delivered to the Kremlin where, without having had time to wash, he was set in front of four high Soviet officials: Brezhnev, Kosygin, Podgorny and Vornov. Brezhnev opened with a statement, addressed to Dubček in the familiar form (like the French *tu*), which stated the Soviet position. The aim of their talks, he began, was to find a 'solution' to the 'benefit of the Czechoslovak Communist Party' so that it might act 'normally and independently' along the lines laid down at the January and May plenary sessions, and as affirmed at the Bratislava meeting. (The April plenum, at which the Action Programme had been adopted and the new Presidium elected, was simply not mentioned.)[78] It could be 'stated flatly', Brezhnev continued, 'that the failure to carry out fixed obligations [had] impelled five countries to extreme and inevitable measures'. He said that 'right-wing' and 'anti-socialist' forces had prepared the 'illegal' Fourteenth Party Congress held at Vysočany and claimed that 'underground stations' and 'arms caches' had been found, suggesting an imminent risk of counter-revolution. The Soviet Union, Brezhnev stressed, had no wish or intention to make a 'further intervention' or to compromise the independence of the *KSČ*, but was holding these discussions in Moscow to enable the Soviet and Czechoslovak Communist parties to 'find a workable solution' together. Although under no illusion that 'everything' would suddenly be 'rosy', after a time 'material talks and contacts' would begin again, the bad smell would dissipate, and 'propaganda and ideology' would start to work 'normally'. In time, Brezhnev assured his Czechoslovak comrades, the 'working class' would come to understand that, 'behind the backs of the Central Committee and the government leadership', right-wingers had been preparing to transform Czechoslovakia from a 'socialist' into a 'bourgeois' republic.[79] Once the situation was 'normalized', talks on 'economic and other matters' could begin, and arrangements be made for the departure of troops.

> We have no *diktat*; let's look for another option together. . . . We consider you an honourable communist and socialist. In Cierna [*sic*] you were unlucky, and there was a breakdown. Let's cast everything that happened aside. If we start asking which of us was right, it will lead nowhere. But let's talk on the basis of what is, and under these conditions we must find a way out of the situation, what you're thinking and what we must do.[80]

Once Černík was brought into the meeting, the subject turned to the Vysočany congress, which was again described by the Soviets as the illegal action of right-wing elements within the *KSČ* whose ultimate aim was 'to separate Czechoslovakia from the socialist countries and create a bourgeois republic of the Masaryk type'.[81]

Dubček spent most of Saturday, 24 August in bed at the Kremlin, unwell. Just as Dubček had once been quick to capitalize on Novotný's political weakness, now Gustáv Husák promptly appeared to take charge, ensuring that the news got back to Czechoslovak radio that not only Dubček, Smrkovský and Černík, but also he himself, were taking part in high-level negotiations.[82] According to the Czechoslovak News Agency, which was continuing to release press statements, the 'occupiers' had thus far succeeded only in 'breaking Czechoslovak-Soviet friendship' and in 'turning world opinion against themselves'.[83] The rawer *Student* published a note to Brezhnev, to whom it referred as 'Judas Brezhnev': 'You were supposed to have been a worker once. Today you have lived to see the day when it can be written: "Brezhnev is Hitler." When did you cease to be an honourable person?'[84] When Dubček finally awoke, he asked the Soviets to arrange that Mlynář, Lenárt, Barbírek, Jakeš, Rigo and Švestka also be brought to Moscow, which was done.[85] Mlynář was thus able to tell Dubček about the widespread passive resistance at home, giving him an outline of what had been going on at the Vysočany congress, of the international support and sympathy being shown by Communist parties in the West, and of foreign minister Jiří Hájek bringing a protest about the invasion to the Security Council of the United Nations.[86] At home, meanwhile, Šalgovič had been dismissed as deputy minister of the interior (ironically enough by Štrougal, who was deputizing for Prime Minister Černík in his absence),[87] and Josef Rypl as head of the *StB*; the security services had been placed under the direct control of the reformist minister of the interior, Josef Pavel.[88]

What all of this meant, as Vladimír Kusín has pointed out, was that by 24 August 'the only open endorsement enjoyed by the occupiers came from their own propagandists. No Czechoslovak party, state or public organisation went on record to join them', while those who had been backing Moscow during the first hours and days of the invasion either 'felt it necessary, or were told' to 'proclaim publicly that they had not had a hand in the invasion'.[89] The apparently united front shown by *KSČ* and *KSS*, Czech and Slovak, made it impossible for a new government, led by Comrade Indra, to be imposed. It also opened the way for the return of the six leaders, whatever their stated platform, to be widely interpreted as a victory for Czechoslovak independence. As Kusín aptly points out, the Dubček men thus 'became symbols of liberalisation: with them, there would be freedom, without them, slavery'.[90]

The Czechoslovak–Soviet negotiations that took place in Moscow mainly consisted of discussions between the Soviet leadership on the one side, and Svoboda, Černík and Smrkovský on the other, the Soviets having tacitly recognized that Bil'ak, Indra and the others originally intended to form a new government needed to be dropped, since they had lost all credibility at home.[91] As it was no longer possible to maintain the fiction that 'fraternal assistance' had been requested by a united *KSČ* leadership in which there were only one or two bad apples, the Soviets' attention now focused on extracting concessions from those members of the party leadership and government who commanded authority at home. The concessions they needed to hear were that there had been a real danger of counter-revolution at home which had forced the Warsaw Pact to act; that the Fourteenth Party Congress at Vysočany had been convened illegally and its resolutions and elections were therefore null and void; and that the protest presented to the United Nations Security Council was a provocative act that did not represent the will of the *KSČ* leadership.[92] By Sunday, 25 August, when further members of the old party leadership – Mlynář, Lenárt, Barbírek, Rigo and Švestka – were flown out to Moscow to join the negotiations, it was already apparent that the façade of *KSČ* solidarity was cracking. Dubček was in bed, apparently in a state of nervous collapse; Indra was also said to be ill, and probably being held in a hospital somewhere outside the Kremlin; Kriegel, apparently singled out because he was a Jew, was being held separately and was nowhere to be found.[93] Those from the Czechoslovak delegation who were present were divided by mutual suspicion, hardly surprisingly since one faction, the pro-Indra group, had just been plotting to overthrow the other, pro-Dubček, contingent; and two members – Svoboda and Husák – seemed rather to be pushing themselves forward. Before the Czechoslovak side had so much as laid its draft proposal on the negotiating table, it had already made two major concessions to the Soviets: first, to annul the Vysočany congress, which Gustáv Husák insisted was illegitimate because it had not been attended by the delegates from Slovakia; and to withdraw discussion of the invasion from the UN Security Council, which everyone could see was a major provocation to the Soviets.[94]

After making these two crucial concessions, the Czechoslovak side presented its draft proposal of a resolution. This admitted that the KSČ had begun to lose control of the country, but rejected the notion that the situation had become counter-revolutionary; made the withdrawal of Warsaw Pact troops a priority; and insisted that the Action Programme continue to be the fundamental guide to KSČ policy. The Soviets returned the proposal, saying that it was an 'ultimatum' which the Czechoslovaks were in no position to make, and substituted a counter-proposal of their own. The Soviet draft differed from the 'Moscow Protocol' that was eventually signed by both sides in just three respects: it stated baldly that the invasion had been justified; made no commitment to withdraw troops at any time in the future; and failed to recognize any merit in the KSČ line.[95] In the heated discussions that followed on the Czechoslovak side, Ludvík Svoboda, who had promised the Czechoslovak people that he would return on the night of 23 August, insisted that a final decision must be reached quickly in order to prevent what he repeatedly stressed was the acute and imminent danger of thousands of civilian deaths while they pointlessly squabbled over semantic niceties.[96] Those who had been brought to Moscow by force, although they no longer felt themselves to be in immediate danger, were nevertheless aware that time was on the Soviets' side, since the Czechoslovak delegation could be kept in Moscow for as long as it took them to sign the Soviet draft proposal.[97]

On 25 August, Prime Minister Černík began to argue, like President Svoboda, that there was no real alternative but to sign. With the entire pro-Moscow contingent prepared to do so from the start, the only person of political significance who could conceivably have tipped the balance in the other direction was Dubček himself. Mlynář, Špaček, Smrkovský and Šimon all came to the conclusion that they should sign, justifying their decision to each other on the grounds that, by refusing, they would change nothing of substance, but only have the personal satisfaction of feeling heroic; whereas if they signed but remained faithful to one another, there might be a chance of salvaging at least something of the reforms that the Prague Spring had represented, and of retaining some influence within the KSČ. Dubček was also persuaded that it was the only realistic option, and that to leave the leadership in rival hands would only make things worse than they already were. Only František Kriegel, who was taken out of solitary confinement to join the rest of the Czechoslovak delegation at the last minute so that he could add his signature to the final version of the Moscow Protocol, steadfastly refused to do so. At Dubček's insistence, Kriegel was therefore not allowed to attend the final meeting that took place between the Czechoslovak and Soviet delegations.[98] It had taken the rest of the Czech and Slovak Communist leadership less than three days to crack.

The signing ceremony between the Soviet and Czechoslovak delegations took place on the afternoon of 26 August. At first Dubček was silent, Černík being left to make the opening remarks for the Czechoslovak side, in which he tried slyly to introduce some defence of the Action Programme and criticism of the invasion as not having been altogether in the interests of socialism. Dubček then spoke. Although at first stammering and slurring, he eventually blurted out a defence of the 'revival process' in Czechoslovakia, together with an indictment of the Soviet and Warsaw Pact invasion. This so provoked Brezhnev that he appears to have given a genuine response in turn, one that he did not bother to dress up in official phrases about the 'interests of socialism' or the threat of 'counter-revolutionary forces'. 'I believed in you,' Brezhnev told Dubček reproachfully; 'stood up for you against the others. . . . Our Sasha is a good comrade, I said. And you disappointed us all so terribly.' It was he, Brezhnev, who had allowed Dubček to replace Novotný, he reminded everyone; and it was he, Brezhnev, who had given Dubček every opportunity to seek his advice and support. But Dubček had neglected either to seek or to take Moscow's advice, and had concealed his true intentions. The result had been a predictable fiasco in which 'anti-socialist tendencies' had become rife; the press wrote whatever it liked, 'counter-revolutionary organizations' were formed, and the party leadership was continually forced to give ground to external pressure. If only Dubček had acted with Brezhnev's approval or advice, if only he had cut from his speeches the passages and words that Brezhnev had suggested, if only he had appointed the ministers and secretaries of whom Brezhnev approved, none of these horrors would have happened. The Soviet Union, Brezhnev continued to lecture everyone, had not won the Second World War at the cost of millions of Soviet lives and untold material and personal sacrifices only for one ungrateful little country to upset the entire balance of power in Europe as agreed by the Allies at Potsdam and Yalta and set down in treaties that even the United States government recognized as valid for at least the next fifty years. When Dubček again tried to argue with him, Brezhnev simply announced that the Soviet side was breaking off discussions. In a piece of pure theatre, he then marched his entire delegation out of the room, leaving the Czechoslovaks to fight it out among themselves.

Dubček, extremely upset, suddenly declared that he had changed his mind and would not sign the protocol. This then threw the others into a panic. The Czechoslovak delegation broke up into small groups, each retiring to a different anteroom to quibble over the precise wording of specific sentences or even points of punctuation. The sum total of these last-minute changes did not add up to much. There was a petty victory for the Soviet side, which insisted that the Action Programme adopted at the April plenary session of the *KSČ* should not be explicitly mentioned or approved, and a small victory for the Czechoslovak side in managing to get a clause inserted that guaranteed the departure of the Warsaw Pact troops once the situation in the country had been 'normalized'. By about midnight, Dubček having again been persuaded to give his assent, the final part of the ceremony – the signing of the Moscow Protocol by all members of both sides of the delegation (with the single exception of Kriegel) – was able to go ahead. Ten or more photographers suddenly burst into the room, their bulbs flashing not only at the moment of signing, but also at the moment when each Soviet member leaned across the long negotiating table to clasp his opposite Czechoslovak number in a warm embrace to show that Soviet–Czechoslovak friendship had been restored.[99] There were thus official photographs to accompany announcements of the fraternal agreement.

The final version of the agreement between the Czechoslovak and Soviet Socialist Republics, which was considered too provocative to be made available in published form in Czechoslovakia, amounted to a pledge to reverse virtually all of the Prague Spring reforms, with the notable exception of the federalization of the state into Czech and Slovak socialist republics. The document opened with the premise, which later crystallized into what came to be known as the 'Brezhnev doctrine', that it was the 'common international obligation' of all 'socialist countries' to defend 'socialism' in the 'implacable struggle with counterrevolutionary forces'.[100] It declared the 'so-called 14th Congress of the *KSČ*, opened August 22, 1968', to be invalid, and explained that it would be superseded by a 'special meeting' to be held 'after the situation has been normalized within the party and the country'.[101] Within ten days of the signing of the protocol, the Presidium was to 'review problems of the normalization of the situation within the country', and to 'discharge from their posts those individuals whose activities would not conform to the needs of consolidating the leading role of the working class and the Communist party'.[102] 'Top priority' was to be given to controlling the media and banning 'the activities of the anti-Marxist social democratic party'.[103] As soon as 'the threat to socialism in the ČSSR and to the security of the countries of the socialist community' had passed, the document promised that 'allied troops' would begin to be 'removed from the territory of the ČSSR in stages', but omitted to include a final date or any means of assessing when this moment would have arrived. Meanwhile, the Presidium of the *KSČ* Central Committee and the government were to ensure that 'conflicts between troops and citizens on ČSSR territory' did not occur.

Several 'personnel changes' in party and state 'organs and organizations' were to be carried out 'in the interest of ensuring complete consolidation within the party and the country'. Further measures were to be taken to 'consolidate the leadership' of the Ministry of the Interior. Dismissals of party members deemed to have 'struggled for the consolidation of socialist positions against antisocialist forces and for friendly relations with the USSR' would not be tolerated. All discussions between the Communist parties of the Soviet Union and of Czechoslovakia, including the details of the Moscow Protocol, were to be kept strictly confidential, and all efforts were to be made on both sides to 'intensify' the 'traditional friendship between the peoples of both countries and their fraternal friendship for time everlasting'.[104]

The principal members of the Czechoslovak delegation – First Secretary Dubček, Prime Minister Černík, President Svoboda, Josef Smrkovský, František Kriegel, Bohumil Šimon and Zdeněk Mlynář – were put on a plane bound for Prague at about 2 a.m. on the night of 26–27 August; Kriegel had only been allowed to return home, rather than continue to be detained in the Soviet Union, at the insistence of the Czechoslovak delegation that they would take full responsibility for his future actions. He was delivered independently to the plane to wait, in disgrace, until he was eventually joined by his compatriots who were being wined and dined at the Kremlin.[105]

The *KSČ* leadership's immediate task – to ensure prompt compliance with the terms of the Moscow Protocol, but without revealing the details of the agreement they had been persuaded to sign – was not going to be easy. They spent the first portion of the two-hour flight in depressed silence, aware, as Dubček put it, 'that this was no glorious return' and anxious, as Mlynář remembered, about 'how the people at home would react'.[106] Eventually, they roused themselves sufficiently to plan their new strategy on how to convey the bad news to party and country. Svoboda would be the first to make a public announcement, thus freeing Dubček to talk to the Vysočany Presidium, Černík to the cabinet and Smrkovský to parliament. Dubček would address the nation in the afternoon, in a speech that Mlynář and Šimon began writing for him on the plane; speeches by Černík and Smrkovský would follow over the next couple of days.[107] In order to prevent civil unrest, get the foreign troops out of the country, salvage what they could of the reforms and save their own necks, all were acutely aware that they would need to stay united and highly disciplined.

While the Czechoslovak Communist leadership had been away in Moscow, having the harsh reality of its position spelled out in words of one syllable, at home protests had turned into mass civil disobedience on a scale hitherto unknown. Buoyed up by the excitement and sense of solidarity that can suddenly bind people together in the face of adversity, the nation had never felt so purposeful, united or heroic. The return of the 'kidnapped leaders' to

Prague at about 8 a.m. Czechoslovak time on the morning of Tuesday, 27 August 1968 was therefore greeted with elation and high expectations. At the airport, Smrkovský refused to say more to waiting journalists than: 'It's hard for me to speak. By means of radio, I wish to pay my profound respects to this nation, which has accomplished so much. We have all come back, including Kriegel.' Reports of the meeting by Svoboda, Dubček, Černík and himself would, he assured the press, follow.[108]

In Bratislava, the *KSS* held its own Extraordinary Fourteenth Congress on 26–29 August, at which the now discredited 'traitor' Bil'ak was dismissed from his post as *KSS* first secretary and replaced by Gustáv Husák, known for the strength of his Slovak nationalism, for having suffered under Novotný and for being a Dubček appointment. All this gave Husák the credibility he needed to persuade his listeners that the only choices were either to back 'Dubček and the other leading comrades' in moving towards 'the normalization of our lives on the basis of the accord that has been concluded', or else 'to reject this concept' and resign from their functions. There was, Husák insisted, 'no third alternative', 'no third way'.[109] With these stark arguments, Husák was able, within hours of returning to Bratislava from Moscow, to persuade the *KSS* not to recognize the Vysočany congress on the grounds that it had not included enough Slovak delegates to be considered valid; this incidentally assured his own position, since it was at the *KSS* Extraordinary Fourteenth Congress in Bratislava – not the one held at Vysočany – that he had just been elected first secretary of the *KSS*. Having secured his own power base in the *KSS*, and simultaneously undercut Dubček's in the *KSČ* (in much the same way that *KSS* First Secretary Dubček had ousted *KSČ* First Secretary Novotný eight months before), he went on to persuade his Slovak Communist colleagues to give their 'full support' to the Dubček leadership, regardless of what it might actually propose.

In Prague, the first clear signal that all was not well with the reform programme came from press reports that Smrkovský's 'detailed report' on the 'negotiations in Moscow' had been given to the National Assembly in a 'sombre' voice and that the meeting had been immediately adjourned, without discussion, after his statement.[110] The text of the official communiqué on the Czechoslovak–Soviet negotiations, which was broadcast on Czechoslovak radio at 2.40 p.m., said very little, and what it did say was open to interpretation. While stating that agreement had been reached 'on measures aimed at the speediest normalization of the situation in the Czechoslovak Socialist Republic' and that 'effective measures' had been adopted in 'the interest of the socialist system, the leading role of the working class, and the Communist Party', as well as further to develop and strengthen 'friendly relations with the peoples of the Soviet Union and the entire socialist community', it also assured listeners that 'the troops of the allied countries that temporarily entered the territory of Czechoslovakia will not interfere in the internal affairs of the Czechoslovak Socialist Republic' and that agreement had been reached 'on the terms of the withdrawal of these troops . . . depending on the normalization of the situation in the Republic'. The press statement, far from supporting the Vysočany congress's clear statement of the illegality of the invasion, declined to mention the Fourteenth Congress at all, and baldly stated that the Czechoslovak government had not asked the UN Security Council to look into the legality of the 'so-called question of the situation in the Czechoslovak Socialist Republic'. On the other hand, it claimed Soviet support for the *KSČ*'s determination 'to proceed from the decisions adopted at the January and May [though, again, not April] plenary meetings of the Central Committee' in the 'interests of improving the methods of management of the society, developing socialist democracy, and strengthening the socialist system on the basis of Marxism-Leninism'.[111]

President Svoboda's personal broadcast to the nation at 2.50 p.m. echoed the same sense of hope mixed with retreat in his insistence that 'in the spirit of the January, April and May plenary sessions of the Central Committee of the Communist Party of Czechoslovakia, we want to continue to develop the socialist social system and strengthen its humanist, democratic character, as expressed in the Action Programme and the government's policy declaration'. Together with the whole National Front, he continued:

> We want to carry on building our country as the real homeland of working people. We shall not retreat a single step from these aims. We shall naturally not allow them to be misused by those to whom the interests of socialism are alien. To that end, all of us must purposefully and with determination direct our work.[112]

The first definite blow came with President Svoboda's brief communiqué which, instead of echoing the defiant resolutions of the Vysočany congress, shocked and angered both party and 'masses' alike by its avoidance of any explicit condemnation of the invasion and by stating that the foreign troops would leave only once 'calm' had been restored. This was immediately understood as an 'outright capitulation', the first sign that the government had not remained faithful to its promises or loyal to the efforts made by the nation.[113]

In the immediate wake of the first announcements by official Czechoslovak representatives in Moscow on 27 August, there was a flurry of indignant and uncomprehending resolutions, mainly circulated in pamphlet form. The *ČKS* branch of the Revolutionary Trade Union Movement (*ROH*) in Prague issued a defiant statement of unity, anti-Soviet sentiment and determination to continue on the road of 'democratic socialism'; workers at Czechoslovak airlines dismissed the results of the Moscow negotiations as having been extracted 'under duress' and proclaimed their adherence to the

'Extraordinary Fourteenth Party Congress and to the new Central Committee elected by it'; the Institute of History refused to accept what it called a 'diktat, accepted under unheard-of pressure'; while the Academy of Sciences declared that 'there is no reconciliation with the occupiers. A free people cannot live on its knees.' *Mladá fronta*, while declaring its faith in Dubček, went on to state that 'we recognize the Fourteenth [Vysočany] Congress as the only valid one, and we recognize only those party representatives who were duly elected to the Central Committee by the Fourteenth Congress'. *Literární listy* insisted that it would 'never again accept the "realistic" policy of filtered truths' since 'consistent development towards socialism' and censorship were incompatible. The faculty of journalism and information at Charles University insisted that 'basic civil liberties' must be preserved, and that while it would 'refrain from any expressions of shallow radicalism or despondency' it would 'not accept capitulation in any form'.[114]

A considerable volume of angry mail accusing the Dubček leadership of 'cowardice', 'treason' and 'selling out the nation', all of which was carefully passed on to the Ministry of the Interior, was received by the government and party offices from groups usually describing themselves simply as 'Communists', 'socialists' or 'working people'. One of the few groups brave enough to declare its name, the Czechoslovak Union of Partisans, also tried to reason with the *KSČ* leaders that, since they would in any case eventually be 'liquidated', they might as well follow 'T.G. Masaryk's dictum' that it is better to die than to live on one's knees.[115]

Had it not been for Dubček's own speech, broadcast late on the afternoon of 27 August 1968, trust between government and people might have irrevocably broken down and the course of 'Normalization' run considerably less smoothly. Dubček, however, with his rare ability to seem to speak straight from the heart, made a direct appeal:

We trust that you will assist us today in the same way you have supported us before – on the basis of a realistic assessment of the situation – with your continued confidence and active participation. We trust you will do this if we must carry out some temporary, exceptional measures restricting the degree of democracy and freedom of expression that we have achieved. I ask you to understand the kind of time we live in. The sooner we are able to achieve a normalization of the conditions in the country and the greater the support you can give us, the sooner we will be able to take further steps on our post-January course.[116]

More than his words, it was Dubček's delivery – punctuated by hesitations while he struggled to master his tears – that carried conviction. Because he was able to convey, without having to say so explicitly, that he shared the sorrow and anger of his listeners and that he was doing all that could conceivably be done, in the shadow of terrible potential threats, to save what little could be salvaged of the Prague Spring, his appeal for restraint from widespread demonstrations and provocations was taken on trust. 'With this speech,' Mlynář remembered, 'Dubček achieved what all of us, in the depths of our souls, feared was impossible: that the nation would believe once again that all was not lost, that there was still hope, and that Dubček was the man who could fulfil it.'[117]

On the next day, 28 August, *Rudé právo* showed its support for the Dubček leadership's cautious approach, and underlined the implicit promise that the clampdown on free expression would be only tactical and temporary by concluding its long list of thanks to the Vysočany workers, People's Militia, army, security corps, journalists and all citizens with the message: 'We are with you; be with us!' Editors of the non-Communist newspapers agreed temporarily not to publish in order to have time to 'reflect' on the government's appeals. The most provocative newspapers, *Literární listy* and *Student*, voluntarily disbanded; the Union of Journalists agreed that a new censorship office might be set up, but only on condition that it be shut after three months. The message in further government announcements – as given by Černík on 28 August and Smrkovský on 29 August – was the same. Once 'Normalization' had occurred – in other words, once censorship had been reimposed, provocation of foreign troops ceased, criticism of the Soviet Union been stamped out, and conformity to the behavioural norms of 'socialist society' resumed – the government would be in a position to continue, albeit more cautiously, on the course of reform to which it had pledged itself since January 1968. Foreign troops would then be removed and Czechoslovak sovereignty restored. To the often-repeated appeal for 'calm' and 'order' was also added the implicit threat that, should the Czechoslovak people not comply, worse would follow: either permanent military occupation by Warsaw Pact troops, or else the substitution of the current relatively benign leadership with a puppet government composed of the very 'traitors' who had invited the occupation forces in the first place. There was, the Dubček leadership continually stressed, no better alternative.[118]

The main aim of the widespread, Communist-led campaign that had sprung up in the immediate wake of the invasion of 21 August, and been maintained throughout the week-long absence of the leadership, had been to draw a black and white contrast between the treasonous villains ('collaborators' and 'traitors') in the Indra-Bil'ak-Kolder-Barbírek group and the heroes ('patriots' and 'reformers') in the Dubček-Smrkovský-Černík-Svoboda group, so that a puppet government could not be imposed over the heads of the 'legally elected' representatives of the Czechoslovak Socialist Republic.[119] The campaign was entirely successful in its immediate aims: to prevent the imposition of a Revolutionary Government of Workers and Peasants and ensure the safe return of all members of the Czechoslovak leadership. But by successfully persuading the vast majority of the public that certain individuals – above all Dubček, Smrkovský, Černík and Svoboda, but also Kriegel, Husák and others – were somehow innately on the side of good made 'Normalization' not only possible but easy. On the day that the delegation returned from Moscow, the week-long campaign of civil disobedience came to an abrupt end, showing an apparently united people led by a unified and disciplined Communist Party.

It was not long before factions within both the KSČ and the KSS reappeared. Since the Moscow Protocol had explicitly forbidden the purging of those Communists who had actively collaborated with the invaders or who were simply more orthodox in their notions of socialism, the Dubček leadership was left with a significant number of party members who were in a position to keep up the pressure to turn the clock back. Those – most notably Indra, Bil'ak, Piller and others who had reason to believe that they enjoyed Moscow's confidence but had just had the cup of power unexpectedly dashed from their lips – could be sent off to well-paid ambassadorial or provincial posts, but they could not actually be removed from the party in the usual way.

The reversal of the Dubček leadership's fortunes also gave hope to traditional Stalinists, those who had remained true to socialism as it was understood in the 1950s, who now came out of the woodwork.[120] On 9 October, several hundred of these ultra-conservatives, or 'ultras', met in Čechie Hall in Prague-Libeň and formed a Presidium (including one Central Committee secretary, Antonín Kapek), which declared its unswerving loyalty to Marxism-Leninism, explained the Prague Spring reforms as part of an imperialist plot and called for wide-ranging punitive measures to be taken against those deemed responsible, in particular a number of intellectuals, journalists and top party members. Members of this group were again present, booing and hissing, when Dubček laid a wreath at the Soviet cemetery on the anniversary of the 'Great October Revolution' (7 November); held a noisy pro-Soviet demonstration at Lucerna Hall on 10 November; and convened further meetings at Čechie Hall on 22 January 1969 and at the Military Academy on 17 March 1969.[121] Although the group, whatever its own expectations, had neither the popular clout nor the administrative competence to be considered seriously by the Soviets as a replacement government, its calls for extreme measures were nevertheless helpful to both the Soviets and the current leadership: to the first by keeping up the pressure on the existing leadership not to backslide; and to the second by showing the population at large that, however disappointed they might be at the Dubček leadership's 'capitulation' in Moscow, things might become much worse if they ceased to support the existing state and party leadership.

At first it looked as if 'Normalization' might mean little more than a tactical retreat by the KSČ leadership until the Warsaw Pact troops left the country and the 'post-January' course could be resumed. Although a few officials were immediately removed from office as unacceptable to Moscow, the number was remarkably small. František Kriegel, who had refused to sign the Moscow Protocol, and Jiří Hájek, the foreign minister who had registered a formal protest at the UN Security Council, naturally had to leave; so did Josef Pavel, the minister of the interior who had tried to realign the *StB*'s allegiances.[122] Others who had to go for being too visibly opposed to the occupation were Zdeněk Hejzlar, the director of Prague radio, and Jiří Pelikán, the director of Czechoslovak television. Čestmír Císař and Zdeněk Mlynář, although removed from their positions as party secretaries, were not yet sent out into the political cold.

The rehabilitation of some victims of the early political trials went ahead as scheduled, with new judges being sworn in on 17 September 1968. In Příbram on 12 December, a new trial of seven *StB* officers accused of having tortured and murdered political prisoners in 1949 was opened. On 13 September, the National Assembly passed a new law on the National Front, which at once clarified that outside organizations would not be tolerated, but nevertheless maintained the Prague Spring concept that the Communist Party would not simply be able to dictate to non-Communist Party members.[123] The bilateral treaty on the 'temporary presence of Soviet Forces on Czechoslovak Territory', which was signed on 16 October, agreed that 'some' Soviet troops would remain 'temporarily' with 'the aim of consolidating defenses against growing revanchist efforts by West German military forces', but stressed that they would be under Soviet command, respect Czechoslovakia's sovereignty and not interfere in its 'internal affairs'. Furthermore, the great bulk of the Soviet units, together with all East German, Polish, Hungarian and Bulgarian troops, would leave Czechoslovak territory immediately.[124]

Plans to federalize the country into Czech and Slovak halves also went ahead as planned. On 1 October 1968, the draft of the federalization bill was approved by the government; on 27 October, it was passed by the National Assembly; and finally, at Bratislava on 30 October 1968, the fiftieth anniversary of the Martin Declaration, it was signed into law by President Svoboda.[125] From 1 January 1969, the Czechoslovak Socialist Republic (*ČSSR*) became a federation of two republics: the Czech Socialist Republic (*ČSR*) and the Slovak Socialist Republic (*SSR*). This meant that the state now had three governments (Czech, Slovak and Czechoslovak), three parliaments (a bicameral Federal Assembly composed of the *sněmovna lidu*, or 'House of the People', and the *sněmovna národů*, or 'House of the Nations'), two National Councils (Czech and Slovak) and two Communist parties (the *KSČ* and the *KSS*).[126] Since the Czechoslovak and Slovak Communist parties were left unreformed, federalization represented a paper equality which lost the Communist authorities little or nothing in the way of Czech dominance, while simultaneously winning Slovak goodwill.[127]

For those who had eyes to see, there were more disturbing changes afoot. *KAN* and *K-231*, which Dubček now called 'frankly antisocialist', were banned on the grounds that their statutes had not been approved in advance by the Ministry of the Interior. The Social Democratic Party was also banned with the excuse that it had not officially requested approval of its statutes. On 13 September, the law that had discontinued censorship was rescinded, and editors were warned not to print criticisms of either the Warsaw Pact or socialist tenets. On 7 January 1969, the Presidium of the Central Committee formed a special Office for Press and Information to ensure that periodicals and news broadcasts would not deviate from the party line. This made it easier to ensure that the Extraordinary Fourteenth Party Congress held at Vysočany, which had not yet been condemned by the *KSČ* as it had been by the *KSS*, simply ceased to be mentioned officially.[128]

By mid-September, popular suspicion of the Communist leadership was growing. A letter from 'working people' demanded to know why Dubček, Smrkovský, Černík and Císař had not had the 'decency' to follow Josef Pavel and František Kriegel's examples by leaving their posts, or at least intervened to save Goldstücker, Hoffmeister and other popular figures. Černík, they concluded, was 'no better than Husák', while Svoboda, who had once stabbed Beneš in the back, was now 'betraying' the nation again, this time from Moscow.[129] The first serious signs of public discontent came in the shape of anti-Soviet demonstrations held on 28 October 1968 (Czechoslovak Independence Day and Nationalization Day) and again on 7 November (the anniversary of the Great October Revolution). There were student protests, most notably in the form of a three-day strike held from 18 to 20 November, which workers supported by issuing declarations of solidarity and bringing food to the striking students. Workers' councils were elected in various factories and state enterprises, and a group of economists proclaimed their continued commitment to full economic reform.[130] There was a further spate of demonstrations in December 1968 and January 1969, when the federalization of the country into distinct Czech and Slovak parts was being widely discussed.[131] Because the new constitutional arrangement for the federalization of the country meant that the old National Assembly, which was still headed by Smrkovský, was to be abolished, there was a widespread suspicion that the change would be used as an excuse to push Smrkovský, whom most Czechs wanted to take over the new Federal Assembly, from office. Although many individuals and organizations, including some important trade unions, protested and threatened action if Smrkovský were not given the post, the wind was taken out of their sails when Smrkovský broadcast a personal message to the nation to insist that, since there were already two Czechs (President Svoboda and Prime Minister Černík) in high office, but only one Slovak (First Secretary Dubček), the post should go to a Slovak.

Peter Colotka, thought to be a mild progressive, therefore became chairman of the new Federal Assembly from 1 January 1969.[132]

While a conservative group was forming to the Dubček leadership's right, a progressive group – composed mainly of intellectuals, students and some workers – was simultaneously forming to his left. Taking literally the clauses in the Moscow Protocol and their own leaders' statements that insisted that the Soviet Union would not interfere in Czechoslovakia's internal affairs and that the post-January reforms were to continue, young people and students proved particularly reluctant to adopt the spirit, rather than the letter, of the by then generally accepted need for 'Normalization' to enable the troops to be removed. Another group with the potential to exert pressure on the Dubček leadership was made up of recent émigrés, most notably Hájek, who as foreign minister had first brought the invasion to the UN Security Council's attention, and afterwards chose to leave Czechoslovakia permanently; and Ota Šik, the person most closely associated with the economic reforms in the Action Programme, who also defected. They were ultimately to be joined in exile by tens of thousands of people who either failed to return from their summer holidays at the end of August 1968 or else took advantage of the fact that there had not yet been a clampdown on travel abroad to leave the country as soon as possible after the invasion.

Luckily for Dubček, these émigrés, although united in their protests against the military intervention by the Warsaw Pact, continued, like most of the population at home, to regard Dubček as a national hero and so failed to form any kind of organized opposition group.[133] Largely because of the widespread belief in Dubček's personal integrity and the commitment of Svoboda, Dubček, Černík and Smrkovský to the Prague Spring reforms with which they were so closely associated in the public mind, in mid-September 1968 a public opinion poll found that they were still endorsed, respectively, by 97.8, 97.2, 90.4 and 90.1 per cent of all respondents, a resounding 94 per cent of whom also answered 'yes' when asked whether they still supported the endeavours of the KSČ to continue to implement the Action Programme.[134]

By the time the first signs of mass discontent with the Dubček leadership's form of Normalization made themselves felt, it was too late to try to turn back the clock. On 16 January 1969, Jan Palach, a student from the Philosophy (Arts) Faculty of Charles University in Prague captured the country's attention in a particularly vivid way, by standing outside the National Museum at the top of Wenceslas Square, pouring petrol over his head and setting himself alight. He died several days later, on Sunday, 19 January, of third-degree burns, having left a note that warned that more suicides would follow unless censorship was abolished, a general strike held, and Zprávy, the pro-invasion newssheet, taken out of circulation. The next day, President Svoboda went on television to give a special address to the nation in which he expressed sorrow at the loss of a young person of 'unblemished character' and 'good intentions' and reminded his listeners, 'You gave us your trust after January and in August', and ended with the engaging appeal: 'Without you, comrades and friends, neither Comrade Dubček nor I can or want to govern.'[135] Palach's funeral, which it was left to the students to organize, was held on 25 January 1969. The funeral procession, carefully filmed and monitored by the *StB*, went from outside Charles University's Arts Faculty, through the Old Town Square to Olšany cemetery. An estimated 100,000 people took part, with 200,000 lining the pavements, the vast majority of whom responded to official student appeals not to let the event be 'misused' for political purposes.[136] By 25 February, when another student, Jan Zajíc, followed Palach's example, also burning himself to death in Wenceslas Square, there was no corresponding public reaction. The leadership, by seeming to share the nation's view of the tragedies, managed to defuse any risk that they might otherwise have held for the regime.[137]

From the spring, there were rumours that the Soviet Union, disappointed with the slow pace of Normalization in Czechoslovakia, was waiting for popular protests to erupt at the annual May Day celebrations so that it could accuse the regime of being unable to control the population and impose firmer measures of its own. Whether or not this was *StB* disinformation, just such an occasion presented itself in late March, when Czechoslovakia won two world-championship ice-hockey matches against the Soviet Union. The first match (held in Stockholm on 21 March 1969) provoked widespread rejoicing in Czechoslovakia, together with some anti-Soviet chants and graffiti; the second (held on 28 March) caused a veritable explosion, in which there were demonstrations of joy in cities all over Czechoslovakia: in Prague tens or even hundreds of thousands of people, cheering and shouting, took to the streets. Apparently because piles of cobblestones had mysteriously been left in front of the Aeroflot building in Wenceslas Square, the building was smashed and set alight before riot police managed to disperse the mob. The government responded immediately by condemning the hooligans and apologizing formally to the Soviet Union, but it was too late.[138] On 31 March, Marshal Grechko and Deputy Foreign Minister Semenov unexpectedly arrived in Prague, where they handed Svoboda, Dubček and Černík an ultimatum from the Brezhnev leadership. Either they would immediately impose order and censorship and stop discussion about the leading role of the party, or the members of the Warsaw Pact would again be asked to intervene.[139] This time, the leadership took the threat seriously, and there were immediate reshuffles. In April, Dubček was replaced as first secretary of the *KSČ* by Gustáv Husák, making him the second Slovak to hold the highest position in the land. Dubček became chairman of the Federal Assembly, while Colotka became prime minister, Smrkovský was dropped from the Presidium altogether, and Sekera was replaced as editor of *Rudé právo* by Miroslav Moc, a hardliner.[140] In May, the Central Committee expelled Kriegel and five other prominent Dubček supporters, restaffing the vacancies with Husák cronies, while the *SNB* concerned itself with trying to hush up a provocative demonstration held in Plzeň on 5 May 1969, to commemorate the twenty-fourth anniversary of the city's liberation by US troops, at which pictures of T.G. Masaryk were held aloft, the Stars and Stripes pointedly waved, and officers from the *Veřejná bezpečnost* (*V.B.* or Public Security) actually pelted with stones.[141]

Members of the *StB* who had remained 'loyal' to the old guard, despite Minister of the Interior Pavel's attempts at reform, were now rewarded with increased powers and scope for monitoring ordinary citizens, including their former fellow employees. In the 1950s, internal *StB* rules had been put in place to restrict the period of surveillance to which a particular individual could be subjected to a maximum of ten periods of up to twenty-four hours each. Now the period of initial surveillance was lengthened to four months.[142] The Ministry of the Interior also came to an arrangement with the Ministry of Post and Telecommunications to enable selected post offices to be turned into special centres for the bugging of conversations, which were picked up by microphones hidden in – among other places – ashtrays, briefcases, books, cars and typewriters.[143] The same agreement also made provision for the interception, reading, resealing and delivery of private letters, which could be turned around within a couple of hours and were graded according to whether or not the *StB* wished the recipient to know that his or her post had been tampered with. In May 1969, a month for which records have survived, the volume of letters that could be dealt with in a single day was 170,000.[144] The only form of secret-police surveillance that decreased after 1969 was covert flat searches, of which 205 were carried out in 1966 but only 53 in 1970, despite the fact that the *StB* had at its disposal 1,128 illicitly copied varieties of the commonest house key.[145]

On 21 August 1969, the first anniversary of the Warsaw Pact invasion, a petition calling itself the Ten Point Manifesto was presented to the Federal Assembly, federal government, Czech National Council, Czech Lands Committee and *KSČ* Central Committee by a group that included Ludvík Vaculík and Václav Havel, the writers who had first attracted attention to themselves at the Fourth Congress of the Writers' Union in June 1967. Since the right to petition was explicitly guaranteed by the 1960 constitution, their action was perfectly legal; but the petition's content, which objected to censorship and voiced concern at the banning of the Society for Human Rights, was clearly provocative. Meanwhile, a far more radical society calling itself the New Left, led by Petr Uhl, pushed the line far enough for all its members to be picked up by the police. These rare pockets of continued protest and stubborn resistance were at the time unknown to most people, but they were to leave their mark on what was later dubbed the 'dissident movement' by outsiders (but the 'second culture' by insiders). More obvious to the ordinary person – party or non-party – who minded having the country occupied by Soviet troops was the shame of watching the Czechoslovak leadership, led by Husák, welcome the Soviet delegation, led by Brezhnev, to the Castle on 6 May 1970 to renew the Czechoslovak–Soviet Friendship Treaty for a further twenty years.[146]

The purges, which had initially seemed almost cosmetic, continued to spread. The Central Committee itself underwent three separate purges – in September 1969 and January and June 1970 – to make it ready for the official Fourteenth Party Congress, which was finally held in May 1971.[147] Suspected or disgraced members of the Presidium and higher echelons of the party were also removed in slow, discreet stages. Dubček himself, expelled from the Presidium, was sent to be ambassador to Turkey, until he was recalled to be expelled from the party altogether in June 1970 and sent to work for the Forestry Commission.[148] In January 1970, Černík and Sádovský were dropped from the Presidium to make room for Lenárt and Kapek; Piller, having been permitted to resign in February 1971, was replaced by Indra, while Hoffmann was brought on board in May 1971. Once the top leadership had been purged, it was the turn of the regions, districts and 'apparatuses'. In the Czech republic, nine regional chief secretaries and fifty-nine district chief secretaries were removed from their posts, and about a third of all regional functionaries were either expelled or forced to resign from the KSČ. The Federal Assembly was purged three times between October 1969 and March 1971; the Czech National Council five times; the Slovak National Council three times; the federal government four times; the Trades Union Council three times; the Union of Youth six times.[149] The newly federalized Ministry of the Interior, People's Militia and army were also purged. A few organizations, rather than be purged, were simply disbanded. Finally, in the next logical step, the entire rank and file of the Communist Party – some 1,650,000 people – as well as a large number of non-party public employees were individually screened by 70,217 individual screening groups made up of 235,270 interviewers. Milan Šimečka, a Slovak academic working in Brno, remembered his own expulsion from the Communist Party as 'undramatic and business-like'. Summoned to appear before the Party District Committee, he later recalled:

> I presented myself at a room where some fifteen gloomy and unfriendly men were already seated. I knew none of them, and none of them knew me, apparently. They handed me several pages of pointedly-chosen quotations from my articles

and papers. In glancing through the pages I immediately realized that nothing had been forged, everything was just as I had written it. And that was precisely the question they asked. I replied that the sentences, which had already been taken out of context and sounded so incredible to their ears, were indeed my own work. I realized that it was pointless to say any more; they liked me as little as I did them. . . . What was there left to talk about? The principles of textual criticism? It was all over in less than half an hour. I regret to this very day that I was unable to resist making a comment about the inconclusiveness of a whole lot of sentences taken out of context, and also that I asked them to leave me alone for an hour with Lenin's works so that I could supply them with material for his posthumous expulsion from the VKP(b). On my way out, I gave in my Party card to the secretary in the outer office.[150]

The lower screening groups were duly screened, in their turn, by the higher ones.[151] The astonishing feat of purging the entire Party, in which there was roughly one interviewer for every six people being interviewed, was conducted with the help of a questionnaire listing fourteen questions to elicit reactions to – among other topics of political sensitivity – the Action Programme, '2,000 Words', the entry of the Warsaw Pact troops, the death of Jan Palach, the ice-hockey matches, and the replacement of Dubček by Husák. Some interviews lasted as long as it took the member being screened to hand in his party card with a few well-chosen words; others must have been very lengthy, since the average interview lasted for about an hour.[152] By the time the dust had settled, 1,200,000 people held a Communist Party card,[153] which meant that the regime had given the seal of its formal political approval to roughly one in ten inhabitants of the socialist state. Czechoslovakia had been 'normalized'.

The Prague Spring, and especially the Warsaw Pact intervention which hastened its demise, had encouraged the *KSČ* and *KSS*, for the first time since 1948, to revive the language of Czech and Slovak nationalism to win widespread popularity and save the Czechoslovak Communist leadership from exile, disgrace or worse. The patriotic response throughout the country, which was dramatic, widespread and disciplined enough to succeed in preventing a conservative *coup d'état* and the establishment of a revolutionary tribunal, did indeed save the Dubček leadership, at least in the short term; but not the policies that had made it popular. In no time censorship, travel restrictions and strict one-party rule had been reimposed; the challenge of getting the post-invasion imagery that equated Brezhnev with Hitler and 1968–89 with 1938–39 out of people's heads was to prove much more difficult.

The Communist Party had come to power in postwar Czechoslovakia on the back of its skilful appropriation of pre-existing Czech and Slovak nationalism. Throughout the 1950s, when seeking to consolidate power and rid itself of internal enemies, it had leaned heavily on the Soviet Union, to whose Communist leaders it frequently appealed for advice and support. Now, in political crisis, it sought once again to rally the people to its side by making use of native patriotism and xenophobia, ascribing to itself the deepest Czech and Slovak values. In the short term, to make the Soviet Union – treated for decades with reverence as the socialist motherland – into a bogeyman comparable to Nazi Germany, audacious as it was, worked beautifully not only with the party faithful, but even with the mass of ordinary people. In the longer run, however, by making cooperation with the Soviet Union seem tantamount to national treason, it broke the link in many ordinary people's minds between socialism and Czech/Slovak nationalism, so making the next twenty years of socialism – felt as a 'foreign occupation' – especially difficult to bear.

CHAPTER 10

FROM RESENTMENT TO REVOLUTION

The policy known as 'Normalization' split the *KSČ* into what was in effect two Communist parties: the official Communist Party, consisting of those members who remained in power and were treated to all the usual rewards for obedience; and a kind of virtual or shadow Communist Party – made up of the purged, outlawed and exiled – whose disappointed, indignant and resentful members formed the core of the only visible dissent, at home or abroad, to protest aloud against the Husák regime.[1] As one of the most articulate of these expelled party members, Milan Šimečka, observed, it was all too easy to go with the flow. 'In order to 'integrate into the new society', as he put it, all the citizen needed to do was to come to terms with a few very basic notions:

> that there is only one party of government; that there is only one truth; that every-thing belongs to the State which is also the sole employer; that the individual's fate rests on the favour of the State; that the world is divided into friends and foes; that assent is rewarded, dissent penalized . . . that the State does not require the entire person, just that part that projects above the surface of public life; and that if this part accepts the sole truth then the individual may do what he or she likes in the private sphere.[2]

Zdeněk Mlynář, who left Czechoslovakia permanently for Austria after his own expulsion from the party, similarly explained to Westerners (who assumed that life under Communism was like something out of George Orwell's *1984*), 'People who live in such existing authoritarian systems do not actually have to love Big Brother and be convinced of his unmistakable genius: it is sufficient merely to behave in public as if that is how they felt.' But while it was undoubtedly preferable to live under a regime like that which prevailed in Czechoslovakia to being in 'a system that literally brainwashes the individual into loving Big Brother', the 'great drawback for people' was that the Czechoslovak regime was 'not fictional but real'.[3]

As early as June 1971, when the *KSČ* finally held its 'real' Fourteenth Party Congress to wipe out the memory of Vysočany, most Czechs had already made the transition from protest to acceptance of the new reality. Reports from the regular and secret police (*SNB* and *StB*), drawing on their vast network of informers, showed that only a very few people, such as the handful of actors at Prague's *Semafor* theatre, insisted that socialism was 'unacceptable' because of its inability 'to provide' or to 'guarantee civic freedoms' or were willing to say aloud that the *KSČ* had 'lost its nerve' and 'sold' Czechoslovakia 'to the Soviet Union'.[4] The number of people who were picked up by the police between January and May 1971 for speaking out of turn in restaurants, shop queues, railway stations, at work or even at home, and subsequently prosecuted for 'political offences' (under paragraphs 100, 102, 103, 104 and 198), showed the same pattern of steady decline.[5]

Silent conformity was not the same thing as active support for the party. An *StB* regional situation report from eastern Bohemia complained that the only students in Pardubice to show any interest in the *KSČ* Congress were those who were mugging up for their exams in Marxism-Leninism, while in the nearby city of Hradec Králové, a group of students who spent their time listening to American pop music refused to join the official organization for students, the Socialist Union of Youth (*Svaz socialistické mládeže* or *SSM*).[6] In private, members of the non-Communist parties of the National Front called the Communists 'despicable' and advised one another that the only thing to do was to wait for 'better times'. Expelled party members, meanwhile – including former *SNB* and *StB* officers – blamed their predicament on their superiors or complained that their dismissals had been 'unfair'.[7]

In Prague, where the secret police described the atmosphere as pervaded by a 'deep passivity', there were reported to be widespread fears among former members of the Union of Artists, the Academy of Sciences and the Social Democratic Party that 'a return to the 1950s' was imminent.[8] 'Anti-state people' in Moravia were predicting that Husák would be ousted as first secretary of the *KSČ* and Dubček, Smrkovský and Pavel put on trial. Actors and artists were longing for a return to the 'good old days' (*zlaté časy*) under Novotný.[9] Christians everywhere seemed anxious and pessimistic, Catholics were bracing themselves for a new flood of 'progressive' collaborator-priests, while deputies from the Czechoslovak People's Party complained that they were being 'forced' to support the *KSČ* against their will. The Jehovah's Witnesses, who were predicting the end of the world to be just around the corner, in 1975, added their voice to the general chorus of doom.[10]

Contempt for the Communist Party, although seldom voiced openly, was expressed through jokes, evasion and indifference. Non-party people evidently calculated, usually correctly, that if they kept their mouths shut, joined a minimum of state-approved organizations, appeared at the most important Communist rallies, displayed their flags and turned up to vote when asked to do so, they would be left alone to enjoy a moderately comfortable life. From Friday afternoons, cities were deserted as people flocked to the countryside to their privately owned *chatas* (weekend and holiday cottages, known in Russian as *dachas*), where – among family and friends – they could breathe more easily and express their real opinions, and where objects which they had pilfered from work or bought 'under the counter' (on the black market) could be put to good use. At the *chata* – as opposed to work, school or university – no one would use the term 'comrade' except as a joke; and the revolutionary greeting '*Čest práci!*' ('Honour to work!'), which had been *de rigueur* in the 1950s, was used only ironically, to raise a laugh.

While millions of citizens could be relied upon to turn out for elections and May Day parades and to join the Pioneers, *SSM* and other overtly Communist organizations, it became a matter of some concern to the regime that they failed to show enthusiasm for the task. The phenomenon of emotional withdrawal from official culture became so widespread that a special term was coined for it: 'inner emigration', meaning that even those who had not physically left the country nevertheless held the current regime in scorn, seeing it as something to be kept apart from their own values, priorities and understandings of how the world really functioned. This was not to say that most people were actually anti-socialist. Typically, their resentments were restricted to inchoate, largely apolitical expressions of disapproval: that their political leaders were 'idiots', 'corrupt', had 'ruined the country', 'sold out the nation' and so on. Disaffection seemed to be widespread; but, apart from a handful of reform Communists, a number of whom were living abroad in exile, no one seemed to have any better idea as to how things should be run.

Alienation from the values officially preached by the regime tended not to be expressed through coherent or organized political opposition, which would in any case only have led to an *StB* interrogation, but rather by dressing in certain ways, reading the sorts of books or listening to the kinds of music which, although not actually banned, were neither officially promoted nor considered to be 'socialist'. As in the West, listening to rock music, growing one's hair long, or rejecting the regulation jacket and tie or skirt for blue jeans and a T-shirt signalled 'anti-establishment' attitudes; but since the establishment in Czechoslovakia was socialist, these sorts of behaviour were officially considered 'unsocialist'. These were the years when the Jazz Section (*Jazzová sekce*) of the official Musicians' Union, while just about managing to stay on the right side of the law, let a number of daringly nonconformist or critical pieces slip through the net and be published under its auspices. It was also the quintessential age of *samizdat* ('self-published') literature (meaning the surreptitious circulation of works in typed-manuscript, rather than printed, form, in order to avoid official censorship requirements). Although technically legal, in practice the possession or dissemination of *samizdat* literature was usually the cause for – at the very least – *StB* questioning, if not outright persecution. Ivan (Magor) Jirous, a member of a distinctly anti-establishment rock group called the Primitives (later renamed the Plastic People of the Universe), coined the phrase 'second culture' to describe the phenomenon of non-approved music, plays and works of literature that were surreptitiously circulating in *samizdat* form in unspoken competition with the regime's own officially approved 'socialist' culture.[11]

By failing to provide a dignified way for even middle-of-the-road reform Communists to continue to participate in public life, the Husák leadership created potentially powerful enemies in the half a million party members who were either expelled, or else resigned, from the *KSČ* and the *KSS* and swelled the ranks of an already vocally critical émigré community. The unspoken tension between anxious rulers and sullen subjects created a spiral in which there was an inbuilt tendency for mutual mistrust steadily to worsen. The regime, aware of its unpopularity, came to see potentially subversive activity in even the most apparently innocuous deviations from political norms, and therefore continually to step up its levels of *StB* surveillance. As an ever-increasing proportion of the population became aware of being watched, filmed or bugged, or actually had the experience of being called in by the *StB* for a 'little chat' (whether to be reprimanded, invited to collaborate, or both), increasing numbers can be presumed to have become further alienated from the regime. This, in turn, reinforced the regime's impression that there were more and more potential enemies who needed to be monitored and watched, leading to the surveillance of still more citizens. As Václav Havel was repeatedly to point out to Western journalists over the next few years, people in Czechoslovakia did not choose to be what were called 'dissidents'; rather, as levels of repression steadily rose, it became increasingly likely that – simply by attempting to live normally – in one way or another they would inadvertently fall foul of the regime.[12]

In addition to the problem that the Husák regime brought upon itself by making its purges so widespread that it created a large number of malcontents, there were further reasons for the apparatus of the police state to continue to grow with steady increases throughout the 1970s and with a noticeable jump at the beginning of the 1980s. One of the unavoidable consequences of the Prague Spring and the subsequent Warsaw Pact reaction was that it brought Czechoslovakia to the centre of world attention. Not only had the invasion scandalized the Western democracies, which had been following the rapid escalation of the Prague Spring reforms with sympathy and interest; it also caused a split within the worldwide socialist movement, forcing ordinary Communist Party members all over the world to choose between officially regarding the Soviet Union as the truest exponent of Leninism, or else to conclude that, by failing to respect the sovereignty of a fellow socialist state, it had lost its moral authority to speak for the international Communist movement. The Soviet and Warsaw Pact intervention to end the Prague Spring experiment in reform socialism thus helped to create what came to be known as Eurocommunism, a current within the Italian, French and Spanish Communist parties which from the mid-1970s took up three main points from the *KSČ* Action Programme of April 1968: that the Soviet Union was not the only model for socialist change; that 'progressive forces' might work together for the 'democratic' and 'socialist renewal' of society; and that Communist parties must transform themselves or else risk losing their 'constituency and legitimacy'.[13]

The one Communist leadership in the world that could not afford to retreat even an inch from the official line as officially broadcast from Moscow in the summer of 1968 was, of course, the Czechoslovak one. The Husák leadership had justified its rise to power on two ideological pillars: the need to oppose reforms of the kind proposed during the Prague Spring; and moves towards an ever-closer 'friendship' (political, economic and diplomatic ties) with the Soviet Union. But just as Khrushchev had created problems for the *KSČ* and *KSS* leaderships in the mid-1950s with his denunciations of Stalin, twenty years later the Soviet Union again pulled the rug out from under the Czechoslovak Communist leadership. This time, pressure came in the form of the US–Soviet policy shift known as *détente*, which required the Soviet Union to make at least some concessions to improve its human-rights record in exchange for slowing down the nuclear-arms race.

Détente placed the Husák régime in an awkward position. On the one hand, Czechoslovakia was unexpectedly put under pressure by the Soviet Union not to incur accusations of outright brutality that might damage the international standing of the 'socialist camp'. At the same time, the *KSČ* and *KSS* needed to be ruthless to prevent the recurrence of anything that could be taken to resemble the 'chaos' and internal dissent brought about by the Prague Spring. To all appearances, Husák's immediate reaction, like that of Novotný and Dubček before him, was to consolidate his own position within the *KSČ* before allowing any 'softening' to bring Czechoslovakia into line with changed Soviet priorities. But Husák also had the benefit of his predecessors' experience. Unlike Novotný – who had paid for his inability to control his party – and Dubček – who had paid even more dearly for his inability to control his people – Husák knew where relaxing the party's hierarchical struc-tures or allowing compromise over the party's 'leading role' could lead. Unsurprisingly, given the tightrope the post-invasion regime needed to walk, the Husák leadership found it difficult to find the right balance and made some miscalculations and mistakes. Overall, however, the Husák regime proved canny enough to ensure that Czechoslovakia was one of the very last countries in the socialist camp to fall in the European anti-Communist revo-lutions of 1989–90, and that it remained hardline – yet without having to resort to all-out political terror – right up to the last minute. One of the ways that it did this – as Milan Šimečka argued in the critique of 'Normalization' that earned him a year in prison – was by taking what he called the path of 'civilized violence' as opposed to the 'old explicit forms of violence'. In the 1970s, unlike the 1950s, as he put it:

> No representative of the Czechoslovak intelligentsia really underwent third degree treatment. Nobody was forced to die of hunger or beg for a living. In prison, convicted academics would be treated according to the regulations. In certain cases, people were free to choose exile. Despite being banned, people could continue to occupy their flats and drive around in their cars. Banned authors could take the risk of publishing abroad. StB interrogations would take place during normal office hours. People would not be woken up at four in the morning. Interrogators would not taunt accused persons, nor rough them up. When bugging devices were installed in people's flats, it would be done without damage to the furniture. . . . Everyone had the chance to write a denunciation of themselves or their friends, which could win them a review of their case, albeit sceptical, and the chance of being accepted as a reformed sinner.[14]

On 29 May 1975, after months of intrigue within the *KSČ* and some tinkering with the constitution, Ludvík Svoboda, by then aged eighty, was finally persuaded to step down as president. He was replaced by Gustáv Husák, who followed Novotný's lead in choosing to retain his post as first secretary of the Czechoslovak Communist Party. Combining the two functions in one person consolidated Husák's power and kept his rivals at bay. In mid-April 1975, at the *KSČ* Fifteenth Party Congress and accompanied by a message that emphasized unity, continuity and loyalty to the Soviet Union, Husák was unanimously re-elected first secretary of the *KSČ*. The gesture put the formal seal on 'Normalization', the reversal of the post-January 1968 internal party reforms. Having secured his power base within the Presidium and made clear to everyone that the question of 'democratization', like that of loosening ties with the Soviet Union, would not be reappearing on the agenda, Husák was in a strong enough domestic position to begin taking cautiously controlled steps to follow the Soviet Union into *détente*, the gradual easing of Cold War tensions and rebuilding of trade relations with the West. The *KSČ* leadership therefore felt safe to follow the Soviet Union by taking part in an international conference held in Helsinki on 30 July–1 August 1975 and by signing, along with thirty-two other European countries, the Helsinki Final Act, a treaty that stated that all territorial changes that had come about at the end of the Second World War were henceforward to be considered as final, and that certain fundamental human rights would be respected by all signatories.

On 11 November 1975, the Czechoslovak Federal Assembly – as always, on the instructions of the *KSČ* leadership – ratified two United Nations international covenants (one on 'Civil and Political Rights', the other on 'Economic, Social and Cultural Rights'), which, although first signed in New York on 7 October 1968, had because of the Warsaw Pact invasion been left untouched as too politically explosive to handle. After finally being signed into law by President Husák and deposited with the UN secretary-general, the two covenants technically came into force in Czechoslovakia on 23 March 1976 and their contents were made known to the Czechoslovak public when they appeared in the relevant supplement to *Sbírka zákonů* (Collection of Laws and Ordinances) which could be bought by anyone for the modest price of 2 crowns 60.[15] At about the same time, the usual degrading farce of 'elections' was held, in which more than ten and a half million people (10, 617, 152 or 99.7 per cent of all registered voters) turned up, as usual, to cast their vote for the single list of party-approved National Front candidates to the Federal Assembly, Czech and Slovak National Councils and the National Committees, giving the usual absurd results of about 99 per cent of the vote in favour of the approved list.

It was the coincidence of these two formal political events, together with the announcement that 1977 was to be internationally celebrated as the 'Year of the Rights of Political Prisoners', that was later claimed to have provided the impetus for the creation of the most noteworthy group in 1970s Czechoslovakia self-consciously and publicly to oppose the repressive machinery of the Communist state, a task in which it continued right up to the regime's collapse in 1989–90. A small group of intellectuals living in Prague who had seen a copy of the bulletin of Laws and Ordinances containing ordinance 120 felt enough disgust with the regime to wish to challenge some of its hypocrisies openly. With the government having signed the Helsinki Final Act and passed the two UN covenants on human rights into Czechoslovak law, they believed that they had finally found a chink in the regime's armour. The result was the formation, in the first week of 1977, of a would-be human-rights watchdog and pressure group calling itself 'Charter 77'.

Charter 77 announced its existence in a cleverly worded 'Proclamation' penned on 1 January 1977, to which 242 Czech (and one Slovak) signatures had been appended by 6 January. The idea was that the document would be delivered in person as a petition to the Czechoslovak government and Federal Assembly, and that a further copy would be handed in to the Czechoslovak Press Agency.[16] Although the authors of the text were not given, three people were explicitly named as 'spokesmen' for Charter 77: the philosopher Jan Patočka, the playwright Václav Havel and the former foreign minister in the Dubček administration, Jiří Hájek.[17] The Proclamation announcing Charter 77 opened simply by stating that, as of 23 March 1976, two UN covenants had become binding on both the Czechoslovak state and all of its citizens. In Czechoslovakia, it stated, many of the human rights described in these binding documents existed 'regrettably, on paper only'. Tens of thousands of Czechoslovak citizens, the Proclamation asserted, were unable to work in their chosen professions or were subject to a kind of 'apartheid' simply because their opinions differed from the 'official' line. Hundreds of thousands more were not 'free from fear' because they risked losing their jobs if they expressed their 'real opinions'. Although Article 13 of the pact on Economic, Social and Cultural Rights declared education to be a 'right', Czechoslovak citizens could not voice their views without putting their children's ability to study at *gymnázium* or university at risk.[18] The right freely to disseminate and have access to information, whether in written, spoken or published form, the Proclamation continued, was prevented by both juridical and extrajuridical means and even – as in the current trials 'of young musicians' (the Plastic People of the Universe rock band) – treated as a criminal offence.[19] Not only was freedom of expression heavily curtailed, but there was no protection for ordinary citizens from the slurs made against them in official 'propaganda'. Freedom of religion was systematically and arbitrarily limited, and clergy lived with the 'constant threat' of being barred from carrying out their pastoral and religious duties if they fell out of favour with the state.[20] Even workers were prevented from forming independent trade unions or from going on strike to improve their working conditions.[21]

The suppression of all these human rights, according to Charter 77's damning analysis, was enforced by 'all institutions and organizations' through the ruling party's 'apparatus' from which there was, in practice, no protection through recourse to the constitution, laws or legal norms, since all were interpreted in the state's own interests.[22] The Ministry of the Interior, whose practices were secret and unregulated, offered a host of additional human-rights abuses. The secret police interfered with the right to privacy by tapping phones, bugging and searching flats, using informers, reading private mail, and other such underhand methods. They ensured that public organizations, employers, lawyers, judges and others discriminated against those who fell foul of the regime. They treated political prisoners in such a way as to undermine their human dignity and to destroy their health and moral character.[23] Those who complained openly about the suppression of these and other 'human rights' and 'democratic freedoms' were either ignored or else their protests were used as the basis for fresh interrogations, allegations and persecution.[24]

The Charter 77 Proclamation concluded, with Švejkian false naïveté, that, since it was the duty of all citizens to help enforce conformity to the law – including the United Nations guidelines on human rights which the Czechoslovak government had made legally binding – Charter 77 members intended to draw attention to, and document, cases of the infringement of human rights; put forward suggestions as to how human rights could be better protected; and volunteer their services as go-betweens in cases of alleged abuses. The Proclamation did not condemn 'socialism', 'the republic' or 'the Communist Party'; it also took care to remain within the letter of the law by presenting itself as a petition to the government (the right to petition was explicitly guaranteed by the 1960 Constitution), by attempting to deliver copies of the charter in person (thus making it difficult for the group to be accused of the usual charges of 'subversive', 'illicit', 'conspiratorial' or 'espionage' activity), by including the disclaimer that Charter 77 'does not form the basis for any oppositional political activity', and by describing itself not as an organization, but rather as 'a loose, informal and open community of people of various shades of opinion, faiths and professions, united by the will to strive individually and collectively for the respecting of civil and human rights in our own country and throughout the world'.[25] In order to defend these human rights, it further set up what it called a *Výbor na obranu nespravedlivě stíhaných* (Committee to Defend the Unjustly Persecuted), known by its acronym as *VONS*.

That Charter 77 hit its target, threatening to embarrass the regime on the world stage and to undermine the unofficial sources of its power, can be deduced from the dramatic response that its Proclamation provoked. The three men who attempted to deliver the petition to the Federal Assembly building on 6 January 1977 – Pavel Landovský, Ludvík Vaculík and Václav Havel – never reached their destination. Instead, they were chased into the Dejvice district of Prague, trapped under a railway underpass by a squad of police cars, arrested and taken to police headquarters in Bartolomějská Street, where Havel was interrogated all night before eventually being released. This action did not prevent a copy of the Proclamation of Charter 77 from being picked up by the West German press on the night of 6 January 1977. On the morning of 7 January, news of the 'launch' of Charter 77 by 'hundreds' of Czechoslovak 'dissidents' appeared as a news item, not only on Voice of America but also – through the Associated Press service – on tens of thousands of radio and television stations and in newspapers as prominent as *Le Monde, The Times* and the *Frankfurter Allgemeine Zeitung*, the last of which also printed the Charter 77 Proclamation in full.

The launch of Charter 77, although initially known only to a couple of hundred people in Czechoslovakia, became widely known in the West (including, of course, in Czechoslovak émigré circles, whose own writings were continually smuggled back). Presumably because of this foreign press attention, which showed that Charter 77 had contacts with the West, Patočka, Havel and Hájek were promptly rearrested soon after they had returned home from their first all-night interrogation, on 7 January 1977. After Charter 77 released its second document, on 8 January 1977, which protested at the police methods being used, the same pattern of being questioned for long sessions, released and then immediately rearrested was repeated for the rest of the week, while anonymous phone calls and threatening letters were added to the *StB*'s repertoire of ways to seek to intimidate Charter 77's 'spokesmen' into silence.[26] Since the news had already been picked up by Radio Free Europe, which broadcast to Czechoslovakia from Munich and could only be imperfectly jammed, on 12 January the *KSČ*'s *Rudé právo* and the *KSS*'s *Pravda* launched a joint press campaign in which prominent persons from all walks of life stepped forward to condemn the document (which virtually no one in Czechoslovakia had actually seen) while those who had signed Charter 77 were publicly named and shamed.

On 14 January 1977, Havel, identified by the authorities as the chief ring-leader, was charged under section 98 of the constitution with 'committing serious crimes against the basic principles of the Republic' and kept in solitary confinement at Ruzyně prison for over four months. Other signatories were placed under surveillance, subjected to house searches and repeatedly brought back for more questioning by the *StB*.[27] The campaign to isolate the 'Chartists' and arouse public indignation against them was crowned, on 28 January 1977, with a grand, televised ceremony held in the National Theatre in Prague, packed with prominent artists, actors, playwrights, film directors and representatives of five artists' unions. After being treated to vehement speeches about the treasonous, imperialist and capitalist wiles of the Chartists, or simply the importance of keeping Czechoslovakia socialist, the meeting concluded, rather in the spirit of an Evangelical revival, with all members invited to come forward to sign a declaration in favour of 'New Creative Works in the Name of Socialism and Peace'. The document, in itself perfectly anodyne, was nevertheless understood by everyone to be what it soon came to be called: the 'Anti-Charter'.[28]

Although he had already stuck his neck out by protesting against the Warsaw Pact invasion on public radio in 1968, and afterwards declined to accept the offer to become a secret-police informer,[29] it was Charter 77 that made Václav Havel a celebrity in the West, a 'dissident' to be classed in the same league as the Soviet Union's Solzhenitsyn. It was therefore important to the *StB* that Havel should be generally discredited. At first, attention was directed towards building resentment among other writers and actors, mainly through the use of *StB* plants, on the grounds that Havel's 'selfish' heroics had scuppered their own chances of getting ahead with their careers. The general public, meanwhile, was encouraged to vent its anti-intellectual resentments and anti-élitist instincts by widespread publicity that presented Havel as a spoiled bourgeois brat and a millionaire's son, while the party faithful were tempted to suspect him as an agent of the 'well-known CIA agent Pavel Tigrid' and an 'inveterate anti-socialist'.[30] Although some news of Charter 77's stated aims trickled through to Czechoslovakia via Radio Free Europe and Voice of America broadcasts, the Husák regime's tactic of discrediting Charter 77 and smearing the signatories to its Proclamation appears to have been over-whelmingly successful. Whereas by 1 February 1977 a total of 450 signatures, almost all from a narrow circle of Prague artists, academics, intellectuals and reform Communists – most of whom were also the Havels' personal friends – had been scraped together for Charter 77, the 'Anti-Charter' could already claim more than 7,500 signatures, including those of between 800 and 1,000 celebrities, among them household names such as the comedian Jan Werich and crooner Karel Gott.[31] Especially after a programme designed to discredit Havel was broadcast on Czechoslovak radio on 9 March 1977, doubts about his integrity were at the very least raised in the minds of people who did not know him personally, and in the end a good deal of the mud stuck, many of these rumours that were deliberately begun by the *StB* in the 1970s coming back to haunt him long after the fall of the Communist regime in 1989–90.[32]

Because he had been visited by the Dutch foreign minister, Jan Patočka, the principal founder of Charter 77, was taken in for a series of *StB* interro-gations, the last of which went on for ten hours until Patočka collapsed. On the next day, 13 March 1977, Patočka died of a brain haemorrhage. The Chartists – whose movement was becoming known in the West – blamed his death on *StB* brutality; the regime – which had the media at its disposal – blamed it on the ruthlessness of the Chartists, who it claimed had cynically pushed their friend into the limelight because they knew he had a heart condi-tion.[33] More and more celebrities were encouraged, tempted or pressured to come forward to condemn Charter 77. One of the more important was František Tomášek, who had been named a cardinal by Pope Paul VI in May 1976 and archbishop of Prague *in petto*, and was persuaded to sign a declara-tion stating that representatives of the Catholic Church had not signed Charter 77, which seemed to imply that there was something immoral about it. He was then allowed to take up his position as archbishop.[34] Even Havel, when eventually released from prison on 20 May 1977, went so far as to resign as a spokesman for Charter 77 and to promise 'not to take part in activ-ities which could be qualified as punishable by law'; but nevertheless doggedly insisted to the *StB* that he had not 'renounced his signature under Charter 77 or the moral obligation arising from it, namely to defend people who fall victim to unlawfulness'.[35] Official reports naturally went no further than to announce Havel's resignation, together with his self-critical admission of 'errors' and promises to stay out of the limelight.

Charter 77, of whose original spokesmen only Hájek now remained, did not accomplish any of its stated aims: to influence the Czechoslovak government to stand up for human rights; to alter its police methods; or to redraft or reapply its statutes and laws so as to bring them into line with the Helsinki Final Act. It did, however, give a sense of purpose to its signatories and provide a cause for Western civil liberties groups, Czechoslovaks in exile and Eurocommunists to support. From the regime's point of view, it was obvious that the most active and prominent members were the same old suspects – Ludvík Vaculík, Václav Havel, Zdeněk Mlynář and a few others – who, having stuck their necks out or made trouble for the party in the past, already had fat *StB* files and were untypical of the general population. From Charter 77's point of view, it was essential to keep the movement alive – even if only in skeletal form – and to keep to the same tactics of focusing narrowly on the human-rights question and staying scrupulously within the letter of the law. Only by doing so could the organization hope to keep such a highly disparate group of people together, since they ranged from maverick intellectuals like Václav Havel through reform Communists like Ludvík Vaculík, Zdeněk Mlynář, Petr Pithart, Eva Kantůrková, Jiří Hájek and Jiří Dienstbier to banned clergymen like Catholic priests Václav Malý and Josef Zvěřina and the Evangelical pastor Jan Šimsa.

After the first wave of anti-Charter attacks had begun to subside, internal debates about where Charter 77 should go next, together with analyses of what exactly was wrong with 'Normalized' Czechoslovakia, began to be discussed in special seminars and meetings, usually held in Charter 77 signatories' flats, the results then being circulated in *samizdat* form. One of the first widely influential *samizdat* political essays to emerge from these discussions was a short piece by Václav Benda, a Catholic layman and philosopher who, in 1979 and again in 1984, took his turn as one of Charter 77's rotating spokesmen. In this essay, 'The Parallel *Polis*' (May 1978), which found its way to Poland and other socialist countries, Benda argued that, in authoritarian societies, unofficial activity – from the circulation of unapproved poetry, music or literature to informal meetings and seminar discussions – represented more than what could simply be seen on the surface. Just as the (black-market) 'unofficial' economy underpinned the 'official' economy described in Five-Year Plans, so 'unofficial culture' – what rock musician Jirous had first dubbed the 'second culture' – represented a shadow world that was actually more authentic and meaningful than the one sponsored by the state. The time had come, Benda suggested, for Charter 77 to go one step further and begin to create 'parallel structures' to those offered by the state. Ultimately, Benda argued, there was no reason why *samizdat* culture, scientific and academic 'publications', private seminars and discussions, documents such as Charter 77 and the like could not turn the 'second culture' into a 'parallel *polis*' in which every form of official political, cultural and economic activity – from interpretations of the law to a 'parallel' foreign policy – might offer a real alternative to those policies simultaneously being pursued by the official government and ruling establishment.[36]

Inspired by Benda, Václav Havel wrote an essay of his own which was to have just as deep an effect on the thinking of small groups of intellectual 'dissidents', not only in Czechoslovakia, but also abroad. This was 'The Power of the Powerless', which offered what is still probably the best description in print of how the post-1968 regime in Czechoslovakia – as well as equally unpalatable regimes and bureaucracies elsewhere – was able to maintain power and control over ordinary people's lives. Perhaps the most striking image from the essay is that of a greengrocer who places in his shop window the slogan 'Workers of the world, unite!' 'Why,' Havel asks, 'does he do it? What is he trying to communicate to the world?' The poster, Havel goes on to explain, which was delivered to the greengrocer from the enterprise headquarters along with the onions and carrots, was placed in the window 'because it has been done that way for years, because everyone does it, and because that is the way it has to be'. If the greengrocer were to refuse to place the poster in his window, there could be trouble. He might be 'reproached for not having the proper "decoration" in his window; someone might even accuse him of disloyalty. He does it because these things must be done if one is to get along in life. It is one of the thousands of details that guarantees him a relatively tranquil life.'[37]

The greengrocer does not put up the sign 'Workers of the world, unite!' because he wishes the public to be acquainted with the ideal it expresses; but rather to communicate a quite different message: 'I am obedient and therefore have the right to be left in peace.' If the greengrocer had been instructed to display a different slogan, 'I am afraid and therefore unquestioningly obedient,' he would 'not be nearly as indifferent to its semantics, even though the statement would reflect the truth. The greengrocer would be embarrassed and ashamed to put such an unequivocal statement of his own degradation in a shop window.' To overcome this 'complication', the greengrocer's 'expression of loyalty' must take the form of

> a sign which, at least on its textual surface, indicates a level of disinterested conviction. It must allow the greengrocer to say, 'What's wrong with the workers of the world uniting?' Thus the sign helps the greengrocer to conceal from himself the low foundations of his obedience, at the same time concealing the low foundations of power.[38]

This, in a nutshell, was the purpose of ideology: to enable the greengrocer, like everyone else in what Havel termed 'post-totalitarian' society, to conceal his own craven behaviour even from himself, to ensure that he, like everyone else, added his own weight to the group pressure to conform, while simultaneously being able to maintain the illusion that he had preserved his own human dignity, morality and identity.

A world in which greengrocers voluntarily put up slogans to proclaim messages that are, in themselves, meaningless to both those who read them and those who display them, is one that Havel describes as 'living *within* a lie', i.e. a world in which everyone – from a greengrocer to the prime minister – is at once a victim and a perpetrator of the general climate of fearful conformity in which lies must be maintained at all costs. The 'real accomplice' in this involvement, Havel concludes, is not 'another person', but the 'post-totalitarian system itself' in which people are willing *en masse* to surrender 'higher values' in exchange for the 'trivializing temptations of modern civilization'. The unspoken contract between state and people, he seemed to be suggesting, was no longer one in which citizens entrusted their security to the state, but rather one in which citizens upheld and protected the state in return for material benefits. This was not a narrowly Czechoslovak, or even a specifically Communist, problem, but rather a world problem in which socialist Czechoslovakia offered 'a kind of warning' to the West and revealed its 'own latent tendencies'.[39]

In the summer of 1979, the Czechoslovak government was forced sharply to increase the price of oil and petrol, together with telephone and postal rates and the cost of children's clothing; at the same time it clamped down on hoarding and panic buying. When similarly ham-fisted measures in Poland led, in the spring of 1980, to the formation of the independent shipworkers' trade union in Gdańsk called 'Solidarity', the Czechoslovak regime redoubled its efforts to keep an eye on all unofficial organizations and groupings, including Charter 77; it also ordered all factory committees and managers to respond quickly and sensitively to any shop-floor complaints. In the light of the Polish crisis, two internal *StB* reforms – in 1980 and again in 1982 – were enacted to increase the state's ability to combat any organized 'illegal' activity before it had the chance to get off the ground. From 1980, surveillance of any individual could be automatically extended for a second four-month period; from 1982, the initial period of surveillance, again with the possibility of automatic extension, was extended to a full six months.[40] The tapping of phone conversations, originally restricted to an initial period of two months except in special cases, was similarly extended from 1982, again with the possibility of automatic renewal; while secret filming and photography, initially restricted to a four-month period, were now allowed for six months, with a further provision in 'special cases' for filming to be continued without any fixed time restriction.[41] Although evidence was destroyed by the Ministry of the Interior in December 1989, it seems highly probable that the number of intercepted private letters followed the same pattern of being increased in 1980 and again in 1982. At especially sensitive times, such as the twenty-first anniversary of the arrival of the Warsaw Pact troops, which fell in August 1989, three thousand letters a day were read by *StB* agents in Prague alone.[42]

Over the course of the 1980s, the *StB*'s increased police powers were used with special force to disrupt plays, lectures and seminars in private flats, and especially to seek to isolate Chartists and other known 'anti-state elements' from contact with the outside world. In order to counteract the bar on children of the politically disgraced to be allowed to study at university, members of Charter 77 established, as part of the 'second culture', what they called an 'underground university' to which scholars from the West – including some as distinguished as philosophers Jacques Derrida and Antony Kenny – were periodically invited to give papers or hold special seminars. Although the Chartists hoped that providing an alternative high-quality 'parallel' university would encourage more intellectuals to join, such meetings almost invariably ended in disruption, with the arrest of those who took part followed by the unceremonious deportation of the visiting scholars back to their country of origin. The inclusion of well-known Western academics nevertheless had the considerable advantage of keeping Charter 77 in the international headlines and so discouraging the authorities from behaving with such brutality as to risk provoking a diplomatic incident or irritating the Soviet Union.

In 1981, when the situation in Poland appeared to be spiralling out of control, the Czechoslovak authorities postponed further price rises, launched a press campaign against Solidarity and its leader, Lech Wałęsa, and cracked down on travel to or from Poland. At the Sixteenth *KSČ* Congress (6–11 April 1981), which Brezhnev attended, there was an obvious attempt to show Warsaw Pact solidarity against recent developments in Poland through a series of gestures ominously reminiscent of those that had preceded the arrival of the Warsaw Pact troops in Czechoslovakia twelve years before. Husák made the analogy plain by publicly comparing the situation in Poland to that of East Germany in 1953, Hungary in 1956 and Czechoslovakia in 1968.[43] On 7–8 May 1981, the Czechoslovak authorities rounded up more than forty activists – mainly Chartists, including Jiří Hájek – who were put on trial in July. This prompted protests from Amnesty International and from a group of American playwrights led by Arthur Miller. In September, when six of the most outspoken Czechoslovak Catholic priests were sentenced to prison terms of up to three years, there was more Western indignation. By the end of the year, the Chartists' cause was well enough known to the US Helsinki Watch Committee that it decided to feature photographs and short biographies of a number of Czechoslovak Chartists in its new calendar for 1982.

From the end of 1982, there was considerable jumpiness throughout the 'socialist camp' as one after another ageing leader of the Communist Party of the Soviet Union grew sick and eventually died. On 10 November 1982, Brezhnev died and was succeeded as general secretary by Yury Andropov. Andropov died just over a year later, on 9 February 1984, and was succeeded on 13 February by Konstantin Chernenko. Chernenko also lasted for only a year, dying on 10 March 1985, but was succeeded the next day, 11 March 1985, by a much younger, former KGB man who was not well known abroad: Mikhail Gorbachev. Gorbachev used the occasion of Chernenko's funeral to follow the usual practice of meeting with the leaders of the Warsaw Pact countries (Todor Zhivkov of Bulgaria, Nicolae Ceaușescu of Romania, Erich Honecker of the German Democratic Republic; János Kádár of Hungary, Wojciech Jaruzelski of Poland and Gustáv Husák of Czechoslovakia) to let them know what new directions the Soviet Union was planning to take. Gorbachev claims to have warned the six leaders of his intention to introduce some serious reforms and to change the balance of power within the socialist bloc so that individual Communist parties would have much more independence from Moscow. Years later, he recalled how the leaders had treated his remarks 'with polite curiosity and even condescending irony: "This isn't the first time a new Soviet leader has started out by criticizing his predecessors, but later everything falls into place." '[44]

It was the ceremony to commemorate the 1,100th anniversary of the death of St Methodius, which was held at Velehrad in Moravia on 7 July 1985, which first brought Catholic anti-regime feeling out into the open. In the presence not only of observant Catholics but also of a papal representative and Cardinal František Tomášek, a local Communist official was booed and whistled down when he tried to avoid any explicitly Christian vocabulary by introducing the ceremony as the 'peace festival of Velehrad'. 'From that moment,' one of the Slovak Catholic participants afterwards remembered, 'neither he nor the minister of culture . . . was allowed to say anything that the people didn't agree with. The faithful shouted "We want religious freedom! We want the Holy Father! Long Live the Church!" ' If only for a moment, 'the secret church came aboveground' in front of 'some 150,000 people'.[45] The Polish example, combined with the sense of safety in numbers, made the Catholic opposition in Slovakia bolder, leading to the formation of discussion and prayer groups and to a marked increase, over the course of the decade, in participation at pilgrimages to local Slovak shrines (at Levoča, Šaštín, Nitra, Ľutina, Mariánka, Staré Hory and Gaboltov), gestures that could be seen as primarily religious, anti-regime or Slovak nationalist, depending upon the outlook of both participants and onlookers.[46]

By 1986, Charter 77 members, who were watching with interest the resurgence of widespread dissidence in Poland, reform Communism in Hungary and the first indications of Gorbachev's new policies of *perestroika* (restructuring) and *glasnost* (transparency) in the Soviet Union, saw some grounds for optimism even in hardline Czechoslovakia, where the phenomenon of the 'second culture', although not overt political criticism, seemed to be spreading. Asked to give their opinion on the nature, meaning and possible purposes of 'independent society', 'independent civic initiatives' and the concept of a 'parallel *polis*', a number of Czechoslovak dissidents – mostly Chartists – put pen to paper to consider how far things had come since the creation of Charter 77 nine years earlier.[47] Embarrassed that the number of Czechoslovaks prepared to risk 'anti-state' statements or activities remained so small in comparison with Poland or Hungary, they explained that other indices of discontent with the regime – such as the shunning of official culture, circulation of illicit *samizdat* and even attendance at unofficial 'seminars' – were growing. Although, as Václav Benda put it, no one was suggesting that Charter 77 could ever start a revolution, he hinted that – should a serious political crisis arise – its input might 'not be insignificant' and its members might even be required to discharge their responsibility 'in something more than mere idle chatter and vague declarations'. While perfectly aware that there was not the slightest sign to suggest that the Communist regime in Czechoslovakia was likely to begin to crumble any time soon, Benda tried to encourage his readers with the thought that, while 'no systematic doctrine' existed that could liquidate 'totalitarian power from within, or replace it', it was in the very nature of totalitarianism that 'a single loose pebble can cause an avalanche, an accidental outburst of discontent in a factory, at a football match, in a village pub, is capable of shaking the foundations of the state'. The important thing, he stressed, 'is the chance factor: totalitarian power can successfully block any apparent adversary, but it is almost helpless against its own subjects who foolishly and infectiously start working to bring about the notion that they need not go on being mere subjects'.[48]

In Slovakia, things looked different. In contrast to traditional Czech nationalism, which had been overwhelmingly anticlerical since the late nineteenth century, traditional Slovak nationalism (which had come over the course of the twentieth century to be associated with the Catholic rather than the Lutheran Church), was instinctively averse to all forms of Bolshevism. This left Slovak Christians more receptive than Czechs to the example of Catholic dissent in neighbouring Poland and Hungary. Slovak Communists in the *KSS*, on the other hand, had less reason than their Czech comrades in the *KSČ* to feel resentful of the post-1968 regime: not only had a much smaller proportion of Slovak than Czech Communists been purged from the Communist Party, but party and state were being led by a man with sound Slovak nationalist credentials; the previously centralized country was now a federation of technically equal Czech and Slovak socialist republics; and the party was investing heavily in Slovakia to industrialize, modernize and raise its standards of living, education, housing and technical expertise.

A great deal of this careful work was undone by the Chernobyl disaster of April 1986, which shocked the Eastern bloc – which had to bear the direct consequences – even more than it shocked the West. In Slovakia, as in Poland, the Ukrainian nuclear disaster was all too close for comfort, and helped to energize a growing ecological movement that fell into the murky 'grey zone' that lay between officially approved and officially condemned activities. Mária Filková, the secretary of a permitted organization called the 'Slovak Union of Protectors of Nature and the Land', worked with architects, scientists and others to begin compiling data on pollution, insensitive demolition and other ecological *faux pas* which put the regime in a bad light. By presenting its findings to the censor in the form of an appendix of minutes (which ran to more than sixty pages) to one of its dreary meetings, the Union got *Bratislava nahlas* (Bratislava Out Loud), a document as sensational in Slovak dissident circles as Charter 77 was in Czech ones, published in one thousand approved, and a further three thousand unapproved, copies. With its damning indictments, not only of Bratislava's poor air and water quality, but also of its poor housing, inadequate social infrastructure, unsatisfactory safety record and the crass insensitivity of its urban planning, *Bratislava nahlas* hit the regime where it hurt. By offering what one observer has called 'perhaps the most comprehensive condemnation of developed socialism published anywhere in Central Europe', it made the Slovak ecological critique 'a touchstone for opposition for the next two years'.[49] Crucially, it was able to provide a cause around which secularists and religious, Communists and Catholics, students and mothers, could rally.

The effects of Gorbachev's experiments in *perestroika* and *glasnost* in the Soviet Union, together with his increasingly hands-off approach to the rest of the Warsaw Pact countries, did not really begin to make themselves felt in Czechoslovakia – as opposed to Poland or Hungary – until 1987 or even 1988, and then only patchily. The *KSČ*'s first reaction to having the pillars of its domestic power undermined by the Soviet Union was to bury its head in the sand, opting to take the Soviet version of *Pravda* out of circulation in Prague rather than raise the spectre of reform. By 1988, there had been some cadre changes, a loosening of the limits of what it was permissible to publish or say in public and, most dramatically, an end to the jamming of foreign broadcasts. When, in January 1989, the *KSČ* finally saw that it had no choice but officially to launch reform, its own version of restructuring (*přestavba*) chose to take things nearly – but not quite – as far as the Action Programme of 1968. The *KSČ* recommended some 'democratization' (i.e. decentralization) of economic decision-making within the party, together with the judicious use of elements of the market economy to improve international competitiveness and do more to meet domestic demand for consumer goods. The Husák regime also announced that it would be bringing out a new constitution, and set up a constitutional commission, under the leadership of Marián Čalfa, to come up with a draft. By the autumn of 1989, when the draft constitution was ready, it went so far as to omit any mention of either the 'leading role' of the Communist Party or of Marxist-Leninist ideology.[50]

While the *KSČ* was going back to reform socialism, something very like the Dubček Presidium's Socialism with a Human Face (but this time without the trust or support of the people), Catholic feeling, especially in Moravia and Slovakia, together with a growing sense of disgust at the ecological devastation caused by socialist planning, began to lead the way. In December 1987, on the first Sunday of Advent, a Moravian Catholic farmer named August Navrátil launched a petition to demand the release of the Church from state control, a free Catholic press, the creation of seminaries and lay societies, and the filling of empty bishoprics. Six weeks later, Cardinal Tomášek of Prague lent his support by declaring 'cowardice and fear' to be 'unworthy of a true Christian'. A year later, the petition had already been signed by nearly 200,000 people; in the end, it was signed by about 500,000 people, of whom some 300,000 were Slovak.[51] Ján Čarnogurský, a Slovak lawyer who had spent time in Poland, including after the election of Pope John Paul II and during the Solidarity years, was determined to find a way to combine popular Catholic and civil dissent in a single pressure group along the lines of the Catholic-Solidarity example in Poland. Marián Šťastný, a Slovak exile and vice-president of the World Congress of Slovaks who was living in Switzerland, smuggled him a letter (in a bar of chocolate) suggesting that a series of coordinated demonstrations be held at Czechoslovak embassies around the world on Friday, 25 March 1988 to demand civil rights, including the freedom to worship, for all Czechoslovak citizens. František Mikloško, a member of the secret (unofficial and unapproved) Church that met every Sunday in Bratislava, put it to the group, suggesting that they join in the protest by standing with other dissidents, in silence and holding lighted candles, for half an hour from 6 p.m. in Hviezdoslav Square in central Bratislava. The plan was agreed, and the forthcoming protest announced on Voice of America, Vatican Radio and elsewhere.[52]

The Slovak police were ready. Roads into Bratislava were blocked off, coaches turned back and cars refused permission to proceed. The obvious ringleaders or attractions – Mikloško, Čarnogurský and Bishop Ján Korec – were detained and taken in for questioning by the Slovak branch of the *StB*, the *ŠtB*. From 6 p.m., Hviezdoslav Square was cordoned off. At the appointed time, several thousand people who had been in the square before it was closed off, together with more who had been left outside, began lighting candles and singing a hymn. Mária Filková, the young ecologist who had been responsible for getting *Bratislava nahlas* published and circulated, was among them. Martin Šimečka – the son of Milan Šimečka, the searing critic of Husák's Normalization policy – cursed his 'bad luck' at having Catholic friends and wished he could stay at home rather than turn up for a demonstration which he glumly told himself was likely to consist of a 'few fanatics'. The half-hour that followed has been powerfully described, in Slovak by Ján

Šimulčík and in English by Padraic Kenney.[53] As an 'onslaught of police vans, water cannons and truncheon-wielding officers' sought to clear the square, 'the crowd fought only to stay on its feet and on the square for thirty minutes. This simple goal gave the demonstration a remarkable clarity.'[54] In front of Šimečka's astonished eyes, 'Karol Nagy was handing out copies of the law permitting freedom of assembly – until he was arrested and taken away'. In all, the police are thought to have arrested 141 people on or near the square, the vast majority of whom were under the age of forty. 'Dozens – it is diffi-cult to tell how many – were beaten. Yet the crowd remained in place, some singing hymns quietly, and even kept the candles lit, while the high-pressure hoses beat down. Some, at least, made it until 6:30, in quiet triumph.'[55]

While Catholics, ecologists and civil-rights dissidents were beginning to work together in Bratislava, in Prague it was mainly Charter 77 spokesmen and a few radically minded students and ecologists who took advantage of the slight relaxation in the regime's control over its citizens in the time-honoured way: by pushing at the previous boundaries of the permissible to locate where the new limits were to be found. Václav Benda's son, Marek, whose parents had told him that he was under no circumstances to join the *SSM* (Socialist Union of Youth), nevertheless managed to get into a technical school in Prague in 1988, where he took part in a number of demonstrations, including a week-long series of short-lived public demonstrations held in Wenceslas Square to commemorate the public suicide of Jan Palach, the Czech student who had set himself alight in Wenceslas Square in 1969.[56] In the more permissive atmos-phere of Prague in 1989, he was then accepted into the Mathematics and Physics (Science) Faculty at Charles University, where he promptly set about trying to petition the dean to allow independent (e.g. non-*SSM*) student repre-sentation. Although the petition got nowhere, Benda and his fellow students were not disciplined. By October 1989, Benda was occasionally meeting up with a handful of students, mainly *SSM*, from other Prague faculties, including the prestigious school of film and the performing arts *FAMU* (*Filmová akademie múzických umění*), and the Philosophy (Arts) Faculty of Charles University.

The idea of holding a student demonstration on 17 November 1989, inter-national student day and the fiftieth anniversary of the closure of the Czech universities by the Nazis after the death of medical student Jan Opletal, came up when Marek Benda spoke to a few friends at a pub in the Old Town Square on about 15 November 1989 (Slovak students independently held an uncontroversial demonstration in Bratislava on 16 November). The plan was that the students, who would be invited to bring flowers and candles, would meet up in the Albertov district of Prague, outside Charles University's Natural Sciences Faculty building. They would then march to the grave of the nineteenth-century poet Karel Hynek Mácha at Slavín in the Vyšehrad district of Prague, where they would lay their flowers and candles, listen to some speeches and then quietly disperse. Since the theme of the demonstration was 'anti-Fascist' and at least two of the principal organizers were leaders of the Communist *SSM*, the application to hold the demonstration – as Marek Benda's father and other dissident friends pointed out – would go through the relevant legal channels and undoubtedly be approved by the appropriate party functionaries as evidently pro-regime. By permitting some non-*SSM* members to speak, however, the boundaries of what was permissible would be slightly enlarged; and it would be possible to slip in a few well-chosen remarks about the current regime. At the pub in the Old Town Square, the four students were easily able to agree that the official speakers at Slavín would be Marek Benda, various *SSM* leaders, a veteran of the original 1939 student march and Martin Klíma, an 'independent' student leader. The question of how critical Klíma ought to be in his speech, however, became the subject of a long and heated debate.[57]

That the student march of 17 November 1989 should have turned out to be the 'pebble' that began the collapse of the Communist regime in Czechoslovakia was not predicted: certainly not by the student leaders who had organized it and taken particular care to ensure that it be legally approved. The first surprise was the turnout, which was much bigger than the organizers had expected. By 4 p.m. on the afternoon of 17 November 1989, something like fifteen thousand students, mostly from the *SSM*, were reported by the *StB* to have turned up in Albertov to take part in the officially sanctioned march. The fact that the crowd was so large led to unprecedented boldness and an increasingly excited sense that this demonstration was going to be different. Vít Novotný, a pharmacy student from Hradec Králové who had recently begun to feel ashamed of his political conformity, in part because of witnessing the boldness of the East Germans who had camped out in the West German embassy in Prague some four weeks before, found himself intoxicated by the daring of those around him, some of whom were sporting a lone Tricolour on their lapels, unaccompanied by any Soviet or Communist symbol, and shouting provocative slogans such as '*Svobodu!*' ('Freedom!').[58]

For the first part of what was turning out to be more than a straightforward commemoration of the martyrdom of Czech students in 1939 – the march from Albertov to Mácha's grave in Vyšehrad – everything went as planned. After the speeches had concluded, most of the demonstrators – some two-thirds – dispersed. However, a large block of people – perhaps as many as five thousand – did not go home, but instead continued to call out ever-more radical anti-regime slogans and chants. *StB* officers reported hearing 'We don't want Jakeš!', with reference to the same Miloš Jakeš who had voted to welcome the fraternal Warsaw Pact armies in 1968 and succeeded Gustáv Husák as first secretary of the *KSČ* in 1978, 'We want a different government!',

'Break the monopoly of the *KSČ*!', 'Free elections!', 'Liberate all political prisoners!', 'We want Charter 77!' and 'Long live Havel!'[59] Marek Benda, who was beginning to panic, tried to persuade the group to continue to march up Vyšehrad hill, away from the city centre; but fellow student leader Roman Růžička, together with a particularly aggressive blonde woman, shouted that he was betraying the students' cause, and that the demonstrators should head to Wenceslas Square. Benda gave up trying to prevent the flow of people, who proceeded down the hill and along the embankment of the River Vltava towards the city centre, excitedly shouting out slogans such as 'The Red Star has fallen!'[60]

Benda rushed home to tell his father what was going on before catching up with the march just as it reached the National Theatre and turned into *Národní třída* (National Avenue) on the way to Wenceslas Square. Ivan Havel, Václav Havel's brother, left the demonstration for the Bendas' house, where he reported what was going on to Radio Free Europe.[61] By 8 p.m., when the student march was about halfway up National Avenue, it was blocked by a wall of *SNB* police officers bearing riot shields and wearing white helmets, who prevented the protestors from either continuing forwards towards Wenceslas Square or from leaving the scene down the many side streets that feed into the avenue, but which had been blocked. Further units of special riot police, wearing distinctive red berets, were then introduced into the middle of the block of demonstrators, so that the march was cut in two, consisting of a forward section of about a thousand people, blocked in on all sides by walls of riot police, and a rear section, consisting of about two thousand people. With nowhere to go, the students proceeded to offer flowers to the police, sit down on the asphalt road, light candles, call out anti-Communist slogans, jingle their keys in unison and sing songs, among others 'We Shall Overcome', the Czechoslovak national anthem, and '*Ach, synku, synku*', the folk song said to have been T.G. Masaryk's favourite.[62]

A long stand-off followed, neither the police nor the students moving from their positions. At 8.45 p.m., Public Security officers and riot police called on the demonstrators to disperse. Since the students were blocked in on all sides and had nowhere to run to, panic began to set in. The special police units responded by beating the students in front of them with truncheons. In the ensuing confusion, some members of the crowd were so badly crushed that one student had a key press right into his leg, soaking his jeans with blood; others, afraid that they would be unable to breathe, threw themselves under parked cars.[63] In the end, the students were allowed to exit by means of a single, narrow route whose colonnade set it apart from the rest of the avenue (a modest plaque to the events of 17 November 1989 now marks the spot) and so to safety through the one side street that had been set aside as a controlled exit route. As students were funnelled through this covered passage, those who continued to call out slogans or insults, or who were dressed in what the police deemed to be a provocative way (such as wearing Western clothes or sporting the Tricolour), were taken aside and beaten before being either arrested or released, so that the enclosed space was covered in blood and most of the students who passed through it left in a state of shock. According to the official *StB* report that was afterwards compiled of the incident, 179 persons were arrested, 145 brought into formal police custody and 38 – one of whom turned out to be an undercover *SNB* officer and one a United States citizen – beaten seriously enough to require hospital treatment. By 9.15 p.m., 'order' had been restored and the march brought to an end.[64]

At first, the swift and brutal police response to the student march appeared to have had the desired result. Only a few hundred people returned to the site of National Avenue, or to Wenceslas Square, on the next day (Saturday) to take stock of what had happened. Behind closed doors, however, as students were beginning to recover from their shock, friends were consulting each other about how to react and what to do next. Among those who were already trying to organize a student strike to protest at the police brutality were the medical student from Charles University whose leg had been pierced by a key, who went knocking on doors in the high-rise student dormitory at Kajetánka in Prague to spread the news of what had happened and encourage students to come to a meeting set for Sunday, and students from the Theatrical Academy of Musical Arts (*Divadelní akademie múzických umění* or *DAMU*), who won the support and cooperation of a number of Prague theatres, thus linking more students with Czech dissident circles.[65]

On Saturday, 18 November, the day after the student march, a student leader told Marek Benda that one of the student demonstrators, a boy from the Mathematics and Physics Faculty called Martin Šmíd, had died as a result of his beating by the police. When Benda went to the Faculty to find out more, it turned out that there were three students named Martin Šmíd, only one of whom was in his own year, and who lived with his parents outside Prague. A group of students were dispatched to go to his house and tell his parents the bad news; but when they arrived back, late that night, it turned out that the only Martin Šmíd who had attended the march was – although badly shaken – alive and well.[66] As it later transpired, Martin Šmíd, the student whose reported death was to become the catalyst for the so-called 'November Events', which then turned into the 'Velvet Revolution', was not only alive and well, but also an undercover *StB* agent, one whose instructions and motives have yet to be clarified. But in the immediate aftermath of the student march of 17 November 1989, as rumours of a 'massacre' began to spread, it was the false rumour that an innocent young life had been taken that aroused increasingly uncompromising indignation, anger and outrage.

No doubt because the news carried highly charged collective political memories of other student demonstrations (February 1948, November 1939, October 1967) and other student 'martyrs' (Jan Opletal, Jan Palach), this turned out to be the 'pebble' that began the national 'avalanche' which overwhelmed the current regime.

On the morning of Sunday, 19 November, Marek Benda was picked up by the *StB*, who then proceeded to arrest everyone – about twenty-five people in all – who stopped by his house during the course of the day. Petr Uhl, a reform Communist and no friend to the Husák regime, leaked the story of Martin Šmíd's supposed death during a live interview with the BBC World Service that same day, and was then also taken in for questioning.[67] Václav Havel, alerted to what was happening, rushed back from his *chata* to be in Prague, where the action was. Meanwhile, *StB* headquarters in the city was picking up reports from its regional chiefs that leaflets announcing the news of Šmíd's death, together with an appeal to everyone to take part in a general strike on 27 November 1989, were circulating not only in Prague, but also in Brno, Liberec, Ústí nad Labem, Opočno and Strakonice.[68] In Most, there were further calls to demonstrate on 22 November against ecological problems; in Liberec, for demonstrators to meet outside the town hall on 21 November; in Brno, for citizens to meet on 20 November to light candles at *Náměstí svobody* (Freedom Square) in the city centre. In Bratislava, a first petition put together by Slovak actors and addressed to 'fellow Slovaks' began with the simple announcement: 'On 17 November 1939, Fascists killed student Opletal in Prague. On 17 November 1989, blood once again flowed in Prague.'[69] Marek Benda, on his way to be questioned at Pankrác, noted how even the *StB* seemed suddenly unsure of themselves, to the point where they let him stop to buy something to eat when he complained of feeling hungry. He was released, together with the other student leaders, that same night.[70]

It was not on Sunday, 19 November, as the *StB* had expected, but rather on Monday, 20 November that there was a sudden explosion of organized activity right across the state. Students from Prague were sent all over the country in pairs, bearing copies of an amateur video that showed the police brutality at the march of 17 November in order to spread the news of the beatings – and, in one case, the supposed death – of the students and so win support for the general strike. At Ústí nad Labem, schoolgirl Ilona Bílková remembered how the headmistress cancelled classes so that pupils could attend a special assembly to hear what the students from Prague had to say; when another pair of students from Prague turned up at the Pharmacy Faculty at Hradec Králové to 'tell us what to do', a local university student, who had already set up a strike committee, with some friends, felt that he already 'knew what to do'. Students all over the territory of the Czechoslovak Socialist Republic evidently felt much the same.[71]

Charter 77 and the other dissident groups that had not taken part in the demonstration in Prague on 17 November 1989 quickly jumped on the bandwagon, exploiting the momentary sense of student outrage and talk of holding a general strike to press for further, more specific expressions of 'No Confidence' in the regime. At a press conference at his flat, which had been planned earlier and for an entirely different reason, Václav Havel drew on his Charter 77 experience to declare himself the spokesman of a new group calling itself *Občanské fórum* (which can be translated into English either as Citizens' Forum or as Civic Forum, and will hereafter be referred to as 'Civic Forum'); in Bratislava, a group calling itself *Verejnost' proti násiliu* (Public against Violence) similarly announced its existence through a declaration that condemned not only the police brutality shown at the march, but the entire state of current Czechoslovak 'social and political life', which it characterized as politically 'deformed', economically 'diseased' and in a state of 'crisis'.[72]

Civic Forum followed directly in the footsteps of Charter 77 and *VONS* by declaring itself not to be a formal organization as such, but rather a loose collective of all those who insisted upon an explanation for the police 'massacre' of students at National Avenue on 17 November, and to which anyone who identified with these aims automatically belonged.[73] By the time the Czechoslovak authorities managed to produce a shaken, but alive and unharmed Martin Šmíd for the television cameras, it was too late. Not only did a large and active portion of the student population, Charter 77 and *VONS* immediately declare themselves a part of Civic Forum, but so did just about every recently created 'independent civic initiative'. In Slovakia, meanwhile, in addition to the solidarity shown by a spate of new student groups and coordinating committees at Comenius University in Bratislava, a group calling itself 'Independent Hungarian Initiative' announced to the world that it had come into existence on 18 November and that it was demanding a democratic constitution, free elections and the immediate release of political prisoners.[74]

By Tuesday, 21 November, the anti-regime pressure was already so intense that when Prime Minister Adamec met with Civic Forum, he promised a new government, and Miloš Jakeš, first secretary of the *KSČ*, went on television to declare that 'further socialist development would not be possible without reform'.[75] The next day, 22 November, Havel and Dubček addressed the first mass rally to take place in Bratislava, at SNP Square, symbolically joining together Czech and Slovak, dissident and reform Communist, a double act that they then repeated in Prague the next day (23 November), when prominent Slovak dissident Ján Čarnogurský was released from prison to take his place alongside the rest of a newly emerging anti-regime élite.[76] The public pairing of Havel and Dubček raised a last-minute hope among many devout Communists that the dream to which they had been clinging since 1968 – that a miraculous return to the Prague Spring, led by the very same leader, might actually be possible, the clock really turned back. Miloš Jakeš called together what turned out to be a last extraordinary meeting of the KSČ Central Committee to plead for party 'unity' so that it could effectively 'deliver' socialism to the whole country.[77] Journalists at Czechoslovak television, eager for a return to the good old days when censorship had been lifted, voted eagerly to cease following directives and to show 'objective' news reporting instead. Even a branch of the People's Militia proclaimed that it would 'not take steps' against 'working people' or 'working youth, including the student community', but instead work 'to build socialism in common and work towards perestroika'.[78]

An opinion poll taken on 23–24 November for the use of the Ministry of the Interior, based on a sample of 780 citizens (230 from Prague and 450 from elsewhere in the country), showed the government how badly it had miscalculated in its response to the student demonstration of 17 November: 79 per cent of those polled strongly objected to the security services' handling of the situation, arguing that no force whatsoever should have been used; a further 14 per cent argued that less force should have been used. Just 4 per cent thought that the use of force had been justified and 1 per cent that more force should have been used.[79] Public confidence in the political leadership was at a correspondingly dramatic low, with 88 per cent expressing the desire to see 'cadre changes', 85 per cent supporting continued demonstrations and strikes, and 81 per cent expressing the desire that official negotiations take place between the current leadership (Adamec and Mohorita) with 'the ranks of the opposition' (Dubček and Havel). The only good news for the government was that 84 per cent of those surveyed called for 'calm and circumspection', 85 per cent for more *přestavba* (*perestroika* or restructuring) and 45 per cent still believed in a 'socialist path' for Czechoslovakia. Tellingly, although a further 47 per cent wanted 'something between socialism and capitalism', only 3 per cent declared themselves to be in favour of capitalism.

On Friday, 24 November, exactly one week after the 17 November student demonstration, the KSČ decided to accelerate its policies of *glasnost* and *perestroika*. Among the 'seven suggestions' that were put to the Central Committee that day were: some relaxation of compulsory military service, tax cuts for students, and more personnel changes in the state and party apparatus. The party agreed that 'the Party must not be frightened of the truth, even if it is sometimes hard and unpleasant – it is absolutely necessary to tell the truth in the press, radio and television', and equally 'necessary' to 'publicize the video recordings of the police intervention of November 17 and, after the state prosecutor's investigation, to publish its results in the mass media'. It further declared that the party bureaucracy should be trimmed, and that units of the People's Militia should be used 'only in the event of a direct threat to the socialist system'.[80] The most notable cadre changes were the immediate removal of Jakeš, a figure of fun among students for his lack of education and poor speaking style who was also detested by reform Communists as a symbol of 'collaboration' with the 1968 invasion, and his replacement with Karel Urbánek; and Prime Minister Adamec's announcement of his intention to resign. Even the politically orthodox *SSM* declared its support for the student demonstrators of 17 November, condemned 'violent demonstrations, whether from one side or the other' and called for more 'perestroika and democratization of society'.[81]

After another mass rally in Wenceslas Square, at which Dubček and Havel again appeared together on the balcony of the Melantrich building (where the Social Democratic newspaper *Svobodné slovo* was published) and official Catholic support was shown through speeches and singing led by dissident priest Václav Malý and the archbishop of Prague, František Tomášek, all of which was by now being beamed around the world, the sensational announcement came that the entire Presidium of the Central Committee had resigned. The *KSČ* was by now clearly on the run. Not only was it battling to maintain internal order, but at the same time frantically trying to respond appropriately to a constant barrage of student, Civic Forum and public criticism, as expressed through a bewildering number of leaflets, posters, petitions, news reports – all of which were becoming more radical by the hour – as well as through the well-coordinated slogans that were being chanted at daily mass demonstrations all over the country.

On Saturday, 25 November, a crowd estimated at half a million gathered on Letná plain, the very spot where mass shows of staged support for the Communist regime were held every May Day, to chant that the changes in the government were not radical enough. A further seventy thousand demonstrators turned up at SNP Square in Bratislava to demand that Jakeš step down. Czechoslovak television, meanwhile, broadcast the whole of the canonization ceremony of Agnes of Bohemia. On 26 November, Public against Violence released its 'A Chance for Slovakia', the anti-regime movement's first list of concrete demands, which ranged from the transformation of the Slovak National Council into a functioning parliament of the Slovak nation and the separation of Church and state, to the abolition of the leading role of the Communist Party and the elimination of ideology from schools and culture. It also demanded a free press and a restoration of the rights to assembly, association and 'entrepreneurship'.[82] These shows of continuing No Confidence in the regime then led to a formal meeting between a delegation from the government and National Front, led by Adamec, and a delegation from Civic Forum, led by Havel. By now, it seemed, even Civic Forum had lost control of the mob and when Adamec began to talk about the need for discipline, an end to the strikes and the need for primarily economic rather than political change, he was booed off the stage. At this point, Václav Klaus, an economic forecaster from the 'grey zone' who was neither a party member nor a dissident, but – like anyone else who cared to claim the title – a member of Civic Forum, began to publicize his importance by putting together a petition called 'What We Want: Programmatic Principles of the Civic Forum'.[83]

By the time the general strike, planned as a nationwide two-hour stoppage (from noon to 2 p.m.) was held, on 27 November 1989, its success was virtually guaranteed. As if in a conscious re-creation of the strikes held by the students' pro-Communist grandparents in 1948 and pro-reform Communist parents in 1968, the newspapers advertised the strike on their front pages; just before noon, even the anchorman on Czechoslovak television announced that he was stopping broadcasting in order to take part. For the next two hours, Czechoslovak television simply showed footage of mass demonstrations taking place all over the country. In Wenceslas Square, the end of the two-hour strike was announced in front of a crowd of 200,000 and there were speeches to the assembled masses on Letná plain, where the emphasis was on free elections, a new constitution, the resignation of the Central Committee and even an end to Communism, though Dubček was still speaking of 'Socialism with a Human Face'.[84]

The general strike demonstrated that not even the army, People's Militia or 'the workers' were prepared to come to the regime's defence. On 28 November, against a background of triumphant news headlines that 'the entire republic' had taken part,[85] Prime Minister Adamec agreed that article 4, which guaranteed the 'leading role' of the Communist Party, be dropped from the constitution. When the offending article was voted out of existence the next day, it was widely taken to represent the formal end of Communist dictatorship in Czechoslovakia – although in fact the same suggestion had been included in the Communist leadership's own draft constitution ten months earlier. On 30 November, the KSČ agreed that free elections would have to follow, hoping against hope to be re-elected on a wave of popularity to return to the Prague Spring of 1968.

On 1 December 1989, the KSČ declared the 1968 Warsaw Pact invasion to have been 'wrong'. The next day, it announced both a new Action Programme and a new government. Even two weeks earlier, this last-ditch attempt to redress the wrongs of Normalization and rally support around reform Communism might still have been enough. Now it was too late. After Civic Forum's response, on 3 December, that the government still contained too many Communists, the inevitable mass demonstrations followed. On 7 December, Adamec resigned as prime minister, to be replaced by the Slovak Communist Marián Čalfa. Jakeš and Štěpán, who were by now beyond political redemption, were expelled from the party. In Bratislava, it was not long before there were calls to demolish the enormous statue of Klement Gottwald which had for decades been a symbol both of Prague centralism and of hard-line Communism. On 8 December, a new Government of National Understanding, to be led by Čalfa, was announced. President Husák resigned on 10 December. The only question now was whether Alexander Dubček – as the prime symbol of reform Communism – or Václav Havel – as the prime symbol of Charter 77 and anti-regime dissent – would be made the principal figurehead of the suddenly transformed state. On 28 December 1989, Havel was elected as the first non-Communist president of the Czechoslovak Socialist Republic and Dubček as chairman of the Federal Assembly. The anti-Communists had managed to wrest control of the revolution from the reform Communists. And the Czechs, once again, seemed to be eclipsing the Slovaks.

CHAPTER 11

THE END OF CZECHOSLOVAKIA

The unexpected collapse of the Communist regimes of Central and Eastern Europe at the end of 1989 was widely greeted in the West with joy, incredulity and self-congratulation. As if in a fairy tale, the spell that had put half of Europe to sleep for half a century was broken. The Cold War was 'over'. History had 'returned' or maybe even 'ended'. The Soviet political and economic system, unable to meet ordinary people's needs and desires, had apparently imploded, helpless in the face of 'people power'. Those who had preached the universal validity of liberal democracy and the free market as against state-sponsored socialism and one-party rule claimed to have been proved right. Poles, Hungarians, East Germans, Bulgarians, Romanians, Yugoslavs, Soviets and Czechoslovaks, who on their rare visits to the West had seemed like so many colourless *apparatchiks*, with their disapproval of everything Western and their wooden phrases about the superiority of socialism, suddenly behaved and spoke differently, making clear that the Soviet system had been a deeply resented foreign imposition and showing how they, too, wanted a share of freedom, sovereignty and consumerism. Czechoslovakia, like the other countries of East-Central Europe which had finally been liberated from Soviet bondage, was supposed to live happily ever after. Instead, it promptly fell apart.

In the three years between the overthrow of the old regime and the dissolution of the state, the Czechoslovak Socialist Republic rid itself of its most obvious, outward symbols of Communism by changing its name, removing statues, flags and red stars, and renaming streets, factories, and bus, tram and metro stops. Soviet troops, present in the country since 1968, were asked to leave; Soviet flags no longer twinned with Czechoslovak ones; and busts and portraits of Communist worthies were removed. But the Czechoslovak Communist Party was not abolished; and the removal of some symbols of the old regime, such as Soviet Tank Number 23, proved controversial, many arguing that, since a debt of gratitude for liberation from the Nazis was genuinely owed to Soviets, it ought to be left alone. In a brief period of time, the state's name was changed twice (in March and again in April 1990); there were two general elections to parliament (in June 1990 and 1992); and Václav Havel was twice re-elected President of the Republic by the senate. More profound changes were not so easy either to agree or to achieve. The 1960 constitution, as amended by the Federation Law of 1968, remained in place, to be reformed piecemeal rather than comprehensively overthrown. Similarly, the old legal system remained: although political prisoners were amnestied and the most offensive laws scrapped, there was no comprehensive restructuring of the juridical system that had underpinned Czechoslovak totalitarianism. Fundamental changes to the way the economy worked – feared by those with a stake in the old system but championed by the young as a panacea for all society's ills – opened up all sorts of new possibilities, but did not entirely succeed in removing wealth and property from the old Communist élite. Attempts to deal with the enormities of the previous regime's human-rights abuses could not seem anything but inadequate and led to some high-profile scandals. Jews who had fled abroad before 1948 were unable to get restitution; Gypsies who had lost everything during the war did not even try. The Catholic Church proved another difficult area: although the state immediately released religious prisoners and allowed vacant bishoprics to be filled and crumbling ecclesiastical buildings to be reopened, it remained reluctant to free the Church from state control or to return confiscated Church property.

The sheer scale of the problems, combined with the impossibly high expectations raised by the revolution and the reality of deeply ingrained social, economic and political habits, meant that 'transition' (as the process of changing from a totalitarian political system and command economy was widely termed) was never likely to be either smooth or wholly successful. As Václav Havel's brother explained to a foreign interviewer:

> We were going very fast into a transition, which is not 'a' transition, but a multiple of transitions. You have to change the economy on various scales. You have to change politics on various scales. You have to change public organization, or municipal activity in multiple scales. You have to change people's minds, their behaviour. You have to release the freedom of the press, the freedom of movement. And now all of those changes cannot be done at the same time. Some of them are fast. The freedom of the press was done in one day. Freedom of travel was done in a few days. It was just cancelling the exit permits which were obligatory, so whoever had passports could go. Immediately. To issue a new passport took maybe some days, some weeks maybe. But to change the economy, it cannot be done overnight. And now the fact that there were various speeds for these changes caused the transition period to seem not logical – it was neither totalitarian, nor democratic, nor something else. It has no name. It was just a mess. And what we enthusiasts, we optimists, thought is that mess [*sic*] would last two years at the most. And it lasted ten years, and still exists.[1]

The revolution of November and December 1989 had been able to bring together and coordinate the actions of millions of Czechs and Slovaks who hated the regime in large part because Civic Forum and Public against Violence did not require their members to hold any particular political, economic or religious views. In the Czechoslovak revolution, orthodox Catholics rubbed shoulders with reform Communists, ecologists with advocates of the free market, hippie rock musicians with former members of the KSČ Presidium. Beyond hatred of the regime, there was little to tie these disparate groups together. Although terms such as 'freedom' and 'democracy' sounded self-explanatory to enthusiastic Western onlookers, in practice 'democracy' could mean anything from Prague Spring-style reform Communism to proportional representation in multiparty elections, while 'freedom' could mean anything from the ability of an individual to travel without an exit permit to the right of 'the nation' to shake off central government or rid itself of unwanted foreigners. The obvious glue to hold such disparate views together was nationality, the mythical kinship based on shared language, culture and ethnicity that had fascinated Czech and Slovak political leaders for a century, but that was something quite different from civic loyalty as preached by Civic Forum and Public against Violence.[2]

Since 1968, the Czechoslovak Socialist Republic had been a federation of two socialist republics: the Czech Socialist Republic and the Slovak Socialist Republic, each with its own executive and administrative bodies which were in turn overseen by federal structures. Like the empty shell of the National Front, which had also been retained throughout, formal federalism had not made any real difference so long as the state-wide Communist Party dictated policy; but now that the KSČ had lost its power, it created an awkward duplication of administrative structures and put the Slovak republic – which made up roughly one-third of the state – in the position of being able to block legislation favoured by the Czech republic, which represented the remaining two-thirds. While the Czech republic was trying to work out how best to leave behind the Communist past, embrace the free market, and 'return' to what it liked to think of as its natural European home, in the Slovak republic there was anxiety about what the removal of state support might mean and as much interest in regulating relations between the two federal republics as in making the economic and political 'transition' to a post-Communist society.

The interim Government of National Understanding as set up on 10 December 1989 was composed of fifteen Czechs and six Slovaks; nine were from Civic Forum or Public against Violence or were independent; two from the People's Party; two from the Socialist Party; and eight from the Communist Party. The Federal Assembly, led by reform Communist Alexander Dubček, was rapidly purged (between December 1989 and January 1990) by the removal or resignation of about a hundred deputies, together with the appointment of dissidents and others in their place, while some Communists remained in parliament, but publicly renounced their ties to the *KSČ* or the *KSS*. By the end of February 1990, this left 138 deputies who were members of the Communist Party, 152 who were either independents or supporters of Civic Forum, 27 who belonged to the old non-Communist parties of the National Front (Czechoslovak People's Party, Czechoslovak Socialist Party, Slovak Freedom Party and Slovak Revival Party) and 33 deputies who were affiliated either to newly re-established small parties (such as the Social Democratic Party) or to newly created parties (such as the Christian Democratic Initiative, Christian Democratic Party, Green Party, and Hungarian Independent Initiative).[3]

The overwhelming majority of Czechoslovak citizens had no direct experience of either parliamentary democracy or the workings of the free market. The models of the non-Communist future that people carried in their heads were not only sketchy but utopian, often based on little more than crude inversions of the known evils associated with the Communist system, together with a smattering of pro-Western propaganda picked up from Voice of America or Radio Free Europe. 'The West', which tended to be seen as an undifferentiated mass (much as the 'Eastern bloc' was viewed in Western countries), was believed, almost as an article of faith, to be rich, modern and free. Little, if any, serious attention was paid to the price that Westerners typically paid for these benefits through job insecurity, lower welfare provision, longer working hours and higher crime rates, not to speak of the aggressive advertising and consumer kitsch that tend to accompany capitalism.

The gap between the popular image of Czechoslovakia as a misplaced 'Western' and intrinsically 'democratic' nation and the reality of its citizens' expectations, behaviour and political inexperience turned out to be considerably wider than anyone appears at first to have realized or expected. In a society where no one had much experience of how to compete for jobs, it was taken for granted that virtually everyone should be able to afford a second home, have a short working week, not be allowed to fall below a certain standard of comfort, and be able to remain indifferent to the quality of customer service or goods produced without risk either to pay or to job security. The practice of putting one's family first had become so entrenched that cheating on tax forms, bribing officials, stealing from work and making use of one's connections had all come to be considered perfectly natural ways of achieving what one wanted for oneself or others within the close circle of family and friends. Petty bureaucratic procedures, involving the production of appropriate documentation, form-filling and official rubber-stamping, were involved in almost every transaction, from a visit to the post office, visa department or registry of births, marriages and deaths, to taking out membership in a local public library, buying something from an electrical goods shop or even visiting a museum. The instinct to ensure that all visits and transactions be officially documented ran especially deep since such practices – entrenched since Habsburg times – had suited both the Communist and earlier authoritarian Czechoslovak regimes' desire to monitor citizens' behaviour and to mete out political rewards and punishments for virtually every public act. Other legacies of totalitarianism were the habits of keeping one's political opinions to oneself, of agreeing with whoever expressed the most trenchant or self-assured opinion and generally trying to keep out of the public eye. For Czechs, the prime public virtues held up for emulation were self-deprecation, gentleness, modesty and *slušnost* ('decency' or 'civility'), in practice meaning something like regular habits combined with good manners. According to public-opinion polls, Slovaks considered their own – rather more traditionally Catholic and rural – national virtues to be friendliness, hospitality, sincerity and humility.[4] Despite the reputation of both nations for hard work, this was no society in which an American-style emphasis on individuality, creativity, enterprise and self-publicity seemed likely to strike much of a chord.

Like everyone else, it took former dissidents time to learn the rules of politics and international relations and to discover that not everything was politically possible, and that not everything the Communists had done was necessarily so stupid or unusual after all. The new foreign minister, Jiří Dienstbier, for example, in January 1990 simply announced that Czechoslovakia would no longer trade in weapons. The statement was greeted with loud applause by those who hoped for a morally pure, distinctly different post-totalitarian future from the tarnished Communist past, but caused considerable astonishment to those countries that were awaiting their usual shipments of tanks and plastic explosives. It also led to an outcry from Slovakia, where most Czechoslovak armaments were made. The foreign minister's thoughtless announcement, meant to boost the new regime's moral authority, instead shook international confidence in Czechoslovakia and was taken in Slovakia as yet another good reason for the Slovak republic to pursue its own foreign policy, independently of the federal government in Prague. In March, the Slovak premier (former Slovak dissident and Christian Democrat Ján Čarnogurský) stated in public that Slovakia would prefer to meet the challenge of Central European integration as an autonomous entity, rather than through the mediation of the Prague government. This embarrassed and seemed to undermine the authority of the federal government at just the time when it most needed the world's confidence and goodwill. (Fifteen months later, the next Slovak prime minister – Vladimír Mečiar – was removed from office for holding secret arms talks with the Soviets, leading Havel to hail his ousting as a triumph for 'democracy'. The alarmingly demagogic Mečiar was swept back to victory in the June 1992 elections on a tide of Slovak nationalist feeling.)

Havel, who had long represented the authentic voice of one strand of Czech intellectual dissident culture, remained consistently liberal and democratic in his political pronouncements and public reactions after 1989. This made him seem a reliable and impressive figure on the world stage, gaining for Czechoslovakia – and in particular for the Czechs – immediate international recognition as one of the more 'advanced' nations of the former Eastern bloc whose natural home seemed clearly to lie in the West.[5] This fitted in neatly with stereotypes about the supposedly impeccable democratic credentials of the Czechs, as well as about the supposed political immaturity of the Slovaks, which were part of Czechs' perceptions of themselves, and which had been well publicized in the West in 1918, 1938 and again in 1968. But although Havel appears to have had genuinely liberal and democratic impulses – to say nothing of moral courage – in addition to an idiosyncratic brand of ambition, these aspects of his character made him neither typical of Czech nationalist discourse nor especially popular with the Czech electorate. His positions, admirable and even humbling as they often were, were highly untypical of all but a tiny dissident Czech élite, most of whom were soon to leave or be voted out of political office as unfit to represent the Czech nation. Only Havel – although curiously insensitive to Slovak sensibilities – had the combination of international savvy and political courage to apologize publicly to Germany for the postwar Sudeten German expulsions, to speak up for Gypsies, to realize that it was in his country's interests to support NATO even when it was bombing Serbs, or to insist on the inherent evil of the Communist system, even when it was dressed up in the more acceptable guise of reform Communism. The same internationalist attitudes that made him one of the most respected leaders of the post-Communist states abroad made him increasingly suspect at home. One part of his mission, to be sure, was effectively to lobby for the Czechoslovak state's interests abroad, especially in the USA, NATO and the European Union; but the other, the one that he began to seem to be neglecting, was to speak for 'the nation': the Czech nation.

In addition to being ignorant of how democracy, the law or the free market actually worked in liberal societies, Czechs and Slovaks were saddled with highly partial views of their own past or pasts. The short-lived First Czechoslovak Republic, although it had been marked by injustices and ended in disaster, was now rediscovered by Czechs as a Golden Age, a time when the state was claimed to have been held in international esteem, ranked tenth in the world economy and been closely tied to the West. Superimposed onto this glowing image were two other brief chapters of which Czechoslovakia's Czech citizens felt they could be proud: the postwar Third Czechoslovak Republic, now widely presented as a time when Czechoslovakia had offered a middle way between the twin extremes of the capitalist West and the Communist East; and the Prague Spring, whose 'Socialism with a Human

Face' had anticipated Gorbachev's conceptions of *glasnost* and *perestroika* by two decades. For many Slovaks, by contrast, it was the independent Slovak state under Tiso, which, for all its authoritarian faults, had allowed for the full expression of political Catholicism and delivered Slovaks the sovereignty they had been persistently denied by the Czechs; and the era of Normalization, which, although it had clamped down on religious freedom, at least brought Slovakia formal autonomy, modernization and serious investment from the central government.

Buoyed up on a wave of enthusiasm that everyone knew could not last, the new Government of National Understanding, led by Marián Čalfa (the Communist lawyer who in 1988 had been put in charge of drafting the constitution originally scheduled for 1990), needed to buy all the time it could if it was even to begin to satisfy the political, economic, moral, religious, ecological and nationalist expectations it had raised before the bubble of goodwill burst. The best way to do this was to keep the focus firmly on the widely detested past rather than on nebulous and divisive visions of the future. In a masterly speech given on 1 January 1990, as his first New Year's address as President of the Republic, Havel began arrestingly. 'For forty years,' he told his fellow citizens, 'you heard from my predecessors how the nation was flourishing, how many millions of tonnes of steel had been produced, how contented we all were, how much we trusted our government, and how many wonderful prospects lay ahead. I do not suppose,' he went on, 'that you placed me in this office so that I should also lie to you.' In the same apparently frank and open style, so refreshingly free of ideological clichés, he proceeded to damn the legacy of the Communist regime:

> Our country is not flourishing. Our huge creative and intellectual potential is not being used sensibly. Whole industries exist that produce things of no interest to anyone, while we lack the things that we actually need. The state that calls itself a workers' state humiliates and exploits workers. Our backward economy wastes energy, of which we have too little. The country that was once proud of its people's educational attainments now spends so little on education that it ranks seventy-second in the world. We have spoiled the land, rivers and forests that were bequeathed to us by our ancestors and now have the worst pollution in the whole of Europe. Life expectancy here is lower than in most European countries.[6]

And so on. Havel's speech was not only rhetorically brilliant; it was also politically canny. By stating from the very start that the country could not be in worse shape, it would have nowhere to go but up. Nor, unlike his political rival Václav Klaus, did Havel make the mistake of crusading for raw capitalism.

In a public-opinion poll taken in January 1990, 86 per cent of respondents declared themselves happy with recent political changes, 54 per cent declared themselves ready to take an active involvement in public affairs and an astonishingly high 38 per cent declared themselves to be willing to run for political office.[7] The carnival atmosphere created by the revolution, in which anyone who wished to could claim to belong to the new guard, had yet to evaporate. Havel's personal standing increased dramatically between late November 1989 (when only 10 per cent of those polled had named him as the politician they most trusted and 13 per cent named him as the politician they trusted least) to late January 1990 (by which point 60 per cent trusted him most and only 4 per cent least).[8] Everything was done to prolong the atmosphere of goodwill. Having already abolished the institution in Bratislava where the despised teachers of compulsory Marxism-Leninism classes were trained, on 1 January 1990 President Havel passed an amnesty law to release political and other prisoners jailed under the previous regime.[9] Within a couple of months, arrangements had been made for the removal from Czechoslovakia of all Soviet troops, which was accomplished by the end of March.[10]

For the whole of 1990, culminating in the Bill of Rights which came into effect in January 1991, the momentum was kept up through the reversal or abolition of one after another of the most resented political aspects of the Communist system. This helped to soften the blows of a steady decline in the standard of living, increases in crime, an influx of mainly German-speaking tourists, entrepreneurs and developers, disparities in the direction and pace of change taking between the two republics, and other features that were beginning to cause many people unease. The first step in the direction of change from a command to a market economy came in the form of the so-called 'small-scale privatization law' of October 1990 which provided for the restitution of some seventy thousand properties belonging to Czechoslovak citizens that had been confiscated or nationalized by the state between 1955 and 1961. The law seems to have succeeded in its aim of bringing most shops, pubs, small businesses and workshops into private hands relatively painlessly and quickly. It was the second round, the 'big privatization', which followed a year later (October 1991), in which property worth billions of Czechoslovak crowns – hotels, factories, estates, transport companies and the like – was sold off through a coupon system that was intended to enable citizens to become responsible shareholders with a sense of having a financial stake in society, but in practice led to some widespread swindles and backdoor dealings in which lucrative assets often ended up concentrated in the hands of so-called 'Mafia'.

Large-scale restitution of property confiscated by the state between Victorious February 1948 and 1955 was passed into law on 22 February 1991, after debates, bordering on a constitutional crisis, paralysed the Federal Assembly for a fortnight. It was no accident that what was euphemistically termed the 'period of unfreedom' came to be dated from February 1948 rather than May 1945. Had the earlier date been selected, millions of Germans and hundreds of thousands of Hungarians, Jews and others whose property had been confiscated by the state, either in 1938–39 or in 1945–48, would have been eligible to apply for restitution amounting to sums that, as President Havel warned, would be large enough to bankrupt the state and bring the Czechoslovak economy to a standstill. What also emerged from public debates on the subject, however, was the apparently widespread feeling that the postwar victimization and collective expulsion of Germans and Hungarians, as ordered by the Beneš decrees, had been both morally justified and – because undertaken by the 'democratic' government of the Third Republic – 'legal'. Parliamentary deputies similarly dragged their feet and made objections when it came to the restitution of property formerly belonging to the Catholic Church (the Protestant Hussite Church, which was poorer and also associated with Czech/Czechoslovak nationalism, aroused less controversy), not only to save money but also because of their anticlerical instincts. The federal government refused to go any further, when it finally signed an agreement with the Vatican in July 2002, than to promise to 'look for a solution'.[11]

Next came a series of fumbled attempts to deal with the problem of purging public institutions of accomplices in the crimes perpetrated by the old regime, including the especially delicate problem of how to deal with the intelligence services, border guards and secret police. According to Kieran Williams, the process got off to a bad start during the revolution of November–December 1989 because of Civic Forum's reluctance to demand that the Communists abandon control of the ministries of the Interior and Defence in case the move provoked Soviet intervention. There was then more fumbling to find an appropriate minister of the interior, precious weeks during which about a third of files relating to the *StB/ŠtB*'s 52,000 ongoing operations are estimated to have been destroyed.[12] Even worse was to come, when *StB* officers whom a special screening commission had judged fit to remain in service were nevertheless dismissed by Richard Sacher, the new, non-Communist minister of the interior, only to be re-employed and paid millions of crowns in compensation and back pay. Eventually, at the end of June 1990, Sacher was replaced by Ján Langoš, a Slovak computer engineer favoured by Havel. The removal of just 3,500 *StB/ŠtB* officers from government service was afterwards estimated to have cost the taxpayer in the region of 30 million crowns.[13]

A more difficult problem than how to rid the public sector of acknowledged state-security officers was what to do about the estimated hundreds of thousands of informers and secret agents of the former *StB/ŠtB*. In the end, the route taken was neither that of outright criminalization, as in East Germany, or of Truth and Reconciliation, as in South Africa, but rather an uncomfortable compromise between the two. 'Lustration' (*lustrace*), as the special screening process (uncomfortably reminiscent of the first stage of Normalization) was called, was initially intended to offer those unjustly accused of collaboration with the regime the opportunity to clear their names by having the accusations officially checked against the evidence contained in the *StB* archives. Its scope was widened after a law was passed, on 5 November 1991, in which various categories of people – *KSČ* functionaries; members of the People's Militia; *StB* agents, together with *StB* informers and candidate members – were prevented from holding public office for five years; people who wished to work in the state sector would have to present a certificate from the Ministry of the Interior affirming that they had no links with the secret police (the requirement was not extended to those wishing to work in the police force until 1992).[14] The system was open to absurd anomalies, leaving former first secretary of the *KSS* and *KSČ* Alexander Dubček legally entitled to preside over parliament, but not to run a local post office.[15] The underlying problem, as Muriel Blaive rightly points out, was one that no one much wanted to think about: the extent to which the Czechoslovak population as a whole was implicated in the establishment and maintenance of the Communist system. With one of the most heavily involved populations in the whole of the Communist world, it is hardly surprising that the institutional reaction to the uncomfortable past 'was to strongly condemn the old regime and to draw a thick line between the present and the past, so as not to have to deal with it anymore'.[16] As David Green has found in interviews with representatives of the 'silent' generation of Czechs who came to maturity under the Husák regime's Normalization and were neither protestors in 1968 nor revolutionaries in 1989, there is a marked tendency – even on the part of those who were themselves members of the *KSČ* – to blame the past on 'the Communists' in just the same uncritical way that current problems are blamed on an equally amorphous 'Mafia' (a term not used in Czech/Slovak to refer to any specific or organized criminal gang, but rather a blanket term embracing corrupt politicians, louche businessmen and other real or imagined wheeler-dealers).[17]

As the dust began to settle, it became clear that attempts at a purge had failed to enable society to move on, confident that those most compromised under the old regime had either changed their habits or been taken out of harm's way. While accusations of *StB* involvement continued to be slung at public figures, often by their political rivals, it seemed that *lustrace* certificates were not worth the paper they were printed on. While only about 7 per cent of applicants (12,917 people) in 1992 were judged by the Ministry of the Interior to have been compromised by their links with the former *StB*, given the patchy state of the *StB* archives and the murkiness of the categories of *StB* 'informer' and 'candidate', neither a negative nor a positive result could be taken as conclusive.

This led to the continuation of highly damaging accusations of *StB* involvement against those officially pronounced clean, and to hundreds of complaints and protests, in the press and in the courts, from those officially deemed to have been implicated.[18] On the other hand, professionals in all walks of life who had been thoroughly compromised by their involvement with the old regime – including people employed in such sensitive areas as the courts and the media – had competencies, together with authoritarian attitudes, that meant that they caused one kind of problem if they stayed, but another if they left. Martin Vadas, the news editor at Czechoslovak television from April to December 1992, later remembered how badly the *lustrace* law redounded on the quality of political reporting in the most sensitive period in Czech–Slovak relations, when the devolution of regional television to Slovakia (at the same time that private stations were first unleashed) resulted in dangerously uneven reporting of events in the two republics and opened the way for Czech, Slovak and Czechoslovak television either to miss the important stories through incompetence and lack of resources, or else to be hijacked for political purposes by powerful politicians like Vladimír Mečiar, the Slovak prime minister, who used his regular 'Ten Minutes with the Premier' broadcasts as a means of shaping public debate and maintaining power.[19]

The economic blows of 'transition' were felt much harder in Slovakia, which had industrialized heavily from 1968, than in the Czech republic, which had less to unlearn and was further cushioned – through deliberate government policy – from abrupt economic shocks for a good five years. In Slovakia, industrial production (given in 1990 prices) fell from 276.1 billion crowns in 1989 to 186.9 billion crowns in 1993, during which period agricultural production fell by a third and gross domestic product by 26 per cent. Real wages fell by 27 per cent and were accompanied by the shock not only of high inflation, but also of the first mass unemployment to have been suffered for decades. In 1990, 39,603 people were declared unemployed; in 1993, the figure had risen to ten times that number. By the end of the 1990s, unemployment figures for Slovakia had reached nearly half a million people, or one-fifth of the workforce, in a region where unemployment had not officially existed – or been legally permitted – for half a century.[20]

Most accounts of Czechoslovakia's 'Velvet Revolution' imply that the events of November–December 1989 were essentially a Czech phenomenon, in which the Slovaks – formally, and rather superficially – joined at the last minute, jumping on the revolutionary bandwagon in 1989 rather as they had in 1918, with all the work already done for them and freedom handed to them on a plate. Czech-centred accounts like these fail utterly to notice not only that Slovakia had its own (apparently deeper and more widespread) tradition of dissent from the Communist regime; but also that its revolutionary hopes, although they overlapped to some extent, were different, emphasizing religious freedom and national sovereignty where the Czechs' focused more sharply on civil rights and 'democracy' (whether of the reform socialist or Western parliamentary kind). It therefore came as a surprise to the Czechs and their friends that President Havel's proposal legally to remove the term 'socialist' from the state's name (to make it '*Československá republika*' instead of '*Československá socialistická republika*') quickly led to a proposal from the Slovak side to take advantage of the occasion to reintroduce the hyphen into the state's name, making it the Czecho-Slovak (*Česko-Slovenská*) rather than the Czechoslovak (*Československá*) republic.

The result, laughingly termed 'the hyphen war' by incredulous foreign observers, was a bitter dispute, including a three-week period during which, absurdly, the state's name was different in the federation's two republics. In the end, because the hyphenated name 'Czecho-Slovakia' was too painful a reminder to the Czechs of the Slovaks' and Ruthenians' 'betrayals' of 1938 and 1939, and the unhyphenated form 'Czechoslovakia' was too bitterly reminiscent to the Slovaks of Prague centralism and a string of broken promises by successive central governments, the state was formally renamed the Czech and Slovak Federative Republic (*Česká a Slovenská Federativní Republika* or *ČSFR*) and the socialist content removed, in separate Czech and Slovak laws, from the flags, emblems and official anthems of each of the republics of the federated state.[21] The differences in perceptions could not be so easily removed. In July, a memorial plaque to commemorate Jozef Tiso was unveiled, to the horror of Czech popular opinion but with the approval of the Christian Democratic Movement (*KDH*) in Slovakia, while an article in *Svobodné slovo*, the Czech(oslovak) Socialist Party daily caused equal offence in Slovakia by erroneously referring to Fr Andrej Hlinka (whom it had presumably mixed up with Fr Jozef Tiso) as a 'Fascist murderer'.

Between the summer of 1990 and the elections in June 1992, summit after summit between the Czech and Slovak governments was called to try to reach a consensus on a formulation for a new kind of federalization that would be deemed acceptable by both sides and so could be passed by the Federal Assembly. At the first meeting of the leaders of the Czech, Slovak and federal governments (held at Trenčianské Teplice on 8–9 August 1990), a proposal was drawn up suggesting that decision-making power be devolved to the republics, but that defence, foreign policy, border security and police powers, together with taxation and price controls, be retained by the federal government. After the proposal was rejected by representatives of the Slovak National Party, together with eight smaller parties, Czech prime minister Petr Pithart announced that the Trenčianské Teplice agreement was the only viable alternative to the disintegration of the state. At a celebration to commemorate Andrej Hlinka held a couple of weeks later and attended by about fifteen thousand people, speakers called on the Slovak National Council to declare

Slovak sovereignty and shouted 'Down with Czechoslovak federation!' and 'Long live the Slovak state!' Demonstrations followed in Bratislava to demand that Slovak be made the official language in Slovakia. On 25 October 1990, the Slovak parliament adopted a new law to do just that, with the right for minorities (only in areas where they formed at least 20 per cent of the population) to use their own language in an official capacity. In a television address on 28 October 1990 to mark the seventy-second anniversary of the founding of the Czechoslovak state, President Havel pleaded with Czechs to put aside their condescending attitude towards the Slovaks and appealed to the Slovaks to avoid nationalist demagoguery. The Trenčianské Teplice proposal was twice returned to the negotiating table, barely amended, before being approved by republican bodies on both sides in November, and finally by the Federal Assembly on 12 December 1990.[22] Agreement on devolution seemed finally to have been reached.

The next round of difficulties arose over the need to draft three separate constitutions (federal, Czech and Slovak). As Allison Stanger explains, article 1 of the 1968 Law on Federation opens with the claim that Czechoslovakia's two constituent nations, each of which possesses sovereignty (*suverenita*), have joined together of their own will, but fails to explain how this kind of *suverenita* relates to *svrchovanost* (e.g. 'sovereignty' in international affairs).[23] This left the way open for Mečiar to argue that Slovakia had the right to negotiate its own treaties and enter independently into international negotiations with foreign powers, and for Čarnogurský to maintain that the two republics must conclude a treaty (*smlouva*) to codify Slovak–Czech equality before embarking on the question of federal competencies. The Czech side, unwilling to countenance any radical break with the legal past on the grounds that this would be potentially dangerous for future constitutional developments, insisted that there was no need to clarify the meaning of 'sovereignty' and that only internationally recognized bodies could enter into treaty agreements. The Slovak side, mistrustful of Czech promises, refused to budge until its national 'sovereignty' was assured. The result was a complete impasse.

By March 1991, things were starting to get ugly. Thousands of Slovaks, whose anti-regime revolution – aimed at the federal government in Prague as well as at Communist rule – was still in full swing, kept up the momentum by repeatedly turning up in SNP Square in Bratislava to reject Prague and call for independence; while calls for a referendum on the continuation of the state were being heard from every quarter, Czech as well as Slovak. On 13 March, between five and ten thousand people turned up to a ceremony to consecrate a cross on Tiso's grave in Bratislava in honour of the fifty-second anniversary of the founding of the first Slovak state. When Havel unexpectedly appeared at the rally, he was shouted at and even attacked. Later that day, the president made a television address to the Slovak people in which he pleaded with them not to seek independence by unconstitutional means, but also declared that he would respect any outcome of a Slovak referendum on the question. After a parliamentary crisis in April, Mečiar was replaced as Slovak prime minister by Čarnogurský and Public against Violence formally split into two: a new faction, led by Mečiar and calling itself Movement for a Democratic Slovakia (*Hnutie za demokratické Slovensko* or *HZDS*), and the remainder, which now represented a substantially weakened rump Public against Violence. By September, everyone was speculating openly about the division of the state and calling for a referendum on the issue; petitions were being circulated and signed on both sides; a movement for Moravian autonomy also seemed to be gaining ground. On 3 November 1991, in a last-ditch attempt to avoid a split, President Havel held a meeting with the Czech and Slovak leaders at his summer house at Hrádeček at which a number of constitutional amendments were proposed. All were blocked by the Slovak nationalist side, which saw no good reason to give up its only trump card: the ability to block any unwanted piece of Czech-sponsored Czechoslovak legislation.[24] In the end, after two failed attempts to agree on even the terms of a dissolution of the state, on 25 November 1992 the Federal Assembly agreed that the constitution should be amended to separate the Czech and Slovak republics into completely independent states.[25]

On 31 December 1992, Czechoslovakia ceased to exist. The next day, 1 January 1993, two new states – the Czech Republic and the Slovak Republic – took their place on the third 'new' map of Europe to have appeared in a century. The Czech Republic, which claimed in the preamble to its constitution to be 'reconstituting' an 'independent Czech state', drew its line of descent from the medieval Kingdom of Bohemia down to the twentieth-century Czechoslovak Republic without so much as mentioning the Habsburg Empire, let alone the Holy Roman Empire. It kept the old Czechoslovak flag and other national and state symbols, although explicitly forbidden to do so by law; retained the Castle as its official seat of state power and Prague as its state capital; and kept 28 October 1918 as 'Independence Day'. Slovakia revived the double-barred cross, advertised itself as a Christian country, and kept its Hungarian and Gypsy populations at a distance, even in the preamble to its own constitution, by defining the Slovak people as heirs to the Great Moravian Empire of the ninth century who – together with 'members of national minorities and ethnic groups living in the Slovak Republic' – wished to 'implement democratic forms of government' and promote 'spiritual, cultural and economic prosperity'.[26]

Czechoslovakia's peaceful separation into independent Czech and Slovak states was widely hailed in the West as an example of Czech political maturity, a 'Velvet Divorce' to match its 'Velvet Revolution', in contrast with the mess left by the bloody disintegration of Yugoslavia and the chaos unfolding in the former republics of the Soviet Union. Spokesmen for the Czechs made the most of the contrast, suggesting that the legality and peacefulness of the separation proved the Czechs to be mature, confident and responsible enough as a nation to allow the younger, more impetuous Slovaks to go. Slovaks, on the other hand, argued that the Czechs had deliberately left them in the lurch to speed up their own transition to capitalism and curry favour with the West, leaving Slovakia with no option but to plump for independence by refusing all viable alternative forms of sovereignty. Although neither the Czech nor the Slovak populations wanted to take responsibility for ending the state, let alone stand accused of petty nationalism or ethnic chauvinism, prominent spokesmen for both sides seemed relieved to have had the decision taken out of their hands. The split was therefore described, on both sides, as undesirable but 'inevitable', as if it had been predestined, a natural development in the course of the 'life' of the Czech and the Slovak nations.

As Abby Innes has pointed out, the flattering notion of a 'Velvet Divorce' to follow a 'Velvet Revolution' underestimates the depth of the authoritarian Communist legacy, which made it possible for such a radical act to be passed, without a referendum, and apparently against the wishes of a majority in both republics.[27] At home in Czechoslovakia, the decision to end the state was widely blamed on the 'arrogance' and high-handedness of the two politicians – the Slovak Vladimír Mečiar and the Czech Václav Klaus – who brokered the deal, securing their own political positions in the process. It has since become a question of almost obsessive interest to scholars to seek to solve the paradox of how, as Carol Leff has put it, it could have come about that a democratic state could have 'disintegrated even though a majority of its citizens favoured its continuance'.[28] In fact, the 'Velvet Divorce' followed quite logically both from the course of the Velvet Revolution – which had really been two revolutions, one Czech and one Slovak – and, more profoundly, from Czech–Slovak tensions which had dogged Czecho-Slovakia/Czechoslovakia from its inception and meant that, while most Czechs were able to identify with the state, a majority of Slovaks considered their nationality to be Slovak, not Czechoslovak. Had the state remained in one piece – as might easily have happened – it is unlikely that this problem would have gone away any more than the widespread fear of Germans and Hungarians, suspicion of Jews or contempt for Gypsies went away.

In an established democracy, divisions and conflicts within society are supposed to be a healthy sign, a sign of normality. This fundamental feature of democracy was in tension not only with Communist practice, but also with traditional understandings of both Czech and Slovak nationalism, which were largely predicated upon a unified and united 'us' existing in permanent opposition to an alien and oppressive 'them'. Under the surface, the new leaders who emerged after the fall of Communism were far more deeply shaped by a combination of long-standing authoritarian conventions, Communist discourse and nationalist conceptions than they themselves appear to have realized or liked to admit. As Abby Innes has observed, with characteristic wit, even Václav Klaus, the self-styled apostle of Milton Friedman and follower of Ronald Reagan and Margaret Thatcher, although he never aspired to the sort of control that the Communist Party had exercised, might nevertheless be understood as a 'vanguardist of the market, a Lenin for the bourgeoisie' in the sense that his Civic Democratic Party insisted upon the 'scientific and absolute validity of one ideology – and only one': a form of capitalism that was at once 'vanguardist' and 'historically determined'.[29]

The end of the Cold War may have seemed at first like the happy ending to a fairy tale, in which the ice melted away; but not everything that had been put away in cold storage in 1945 was especially attractive to rediscover. With a sharply reduced fear of the police, together with free reporting, came a sharp rise in published statistics of disagreeable features of life such as unemployment, homelessness and crime. In Bohemia, there were racially motivated attacks by Czech skinheads: not only against Gypsies, who began to pour out of Czechoslovakia to escape poverty, unemployment and both institutional and popular racism; but also against Vietnamese, who, despite their reputation for working hard and leading blameless lives, appeared to have been entirely segregated and excluded from Czech life.[30] In Slovakia, meanwhile, demonstrations held on 14 March 1993 to commemorate the founding of the first independent – and thoroughly Fascist – Slovak state were accompanied by the chanting of anti-Hungarian and anti-Jewish, as well as anti-Czech, slogans.

Czechoslovakia/Czecho-Slovakia had been brought into existence in 1918 because self-appointed spokesmen for a mystical entity calling itself the 'Czech' (and, later, the 'Czecho-Slovak') nation had spent the First World War exploiting fears and fanning hatred of an equally vaguely defined group known as 'the Germans'. This was how the postwar replacement of the Habsburg Empire with a series of independent nation-states, including one named for the Czechs of Austria and the Slovaks of Hungary, had been legitimized. Czechoslovakia's founding fathers had nevertheless insisted, for economic and strategic reasons, upon the inclusion of large and hostile German and Hungarian populations within the state's borders. It was the potentially destabilizing presence of these official minorities that was used to justify the Prague government's rigid centralism, Czech favouritism and sweeping laws for 'the protection of the republic'. Not only Germans and Magyars, but also Slovaks, Poles and Rusyns/Ukrainians came to feel unfairly excluded from power, which they attributed above all to petty Czech chauvinism. After Europe was brought to the brink of war by the Czechoslovak crisis of 1938, even Czechoslovakia's closest allies temporarily washed their hands of the state, although they were to help it back on its feet – despite the

taint of domestic Fascism – at the end of the Second World War, even permitting it forcibly to expel its German and exchange its Hungarian populations.

Czechoslovakia was unique among the states of the postwar Eastern bloc in
having actively courted the closest possible alliance with the Soviet Union,
together with strongly socialist policies, even before May 1945. In the immediate postwar period, it was the only European state to vote the Communists
into power and to turn its own political system from an (albeit imperfectly)
democratic to a frankly authoritarian national-socialist one. After fifteen years
marred by state-sponsored ethnic cleansing, class warfare, religious persecution
and political purges, it won the dubious honour of being considered second
only to the Soviet Union in its 'socialist' achievements. After a brief appearance
on the world stage in 1968 as the embodiment of humane socialism, within a
couple of years Czechoslovakia had been so thoroughly 'Normalized' that
it remained one of the most hardline, authoritarian European states for the
next twenty years, not daring to throw off Communism until all its immediate
neighbours had safely done so first.

Czechoslovakia was to be remembered for none of these things. Instead,
thanks partly to the fact that two of its founding fathers had been brilliant
propagandists and partly to the talent and energy of many of its political
émigrés, but also because it suited France, Britain and the United States – first
for strategic interwar, and later for global Cold War, reasons – to portray it in
the best possible light, its history was presented much more selectively and
charitably. Czechoslovakia was not officially remembered as an aggressor
but rather as a victim country; not as a perpetrator but rather as a martyr
to state-sponsored racism, ethnic intolerance and political repression. Even
its most hateful episodes – the terrorizing of vulnerable minorities during the
late 1930s and throughout the 1940s; the persecutions and hate campaigns
of the 1950s; the petty viciousness of Normalization policy in the 1970s and
1980s – were downplayed, ignored or blamed on the unseen hand of other,
stronger powers. The state nevertheless took the credit for its better
moments – such as during the First Republic or the Prague Spring – naturally
wishing to believe that these, and these alone, were characteristic of the Czech
and Slovak nations. Even episodes that could not plausibly be blamed on
outsiders – postwar Czech and Slovak retribution and the establishment of
socialism; the adoption of Gestapo methods in punishing ethnic Germans and
Hungarians; the incitement of widespread anti-Semitism during the 1950s –
were excused, implicitly or explicitly, as being justified by the supposed collective 'guilt' of 'national enemies' of the righteous Czech and Slovak nations.

Flattering and self-serving national self-images are hardly unique to citizens of the former Czechoslovak state. But Czechoslovakia's particularly
stormy political history meant that it never had the opportunity to take stock
of itself with anything approaching detachment. Almost the whole period of

the First Republic had been dominated by the need to justify and defend the state's existence; thereafter it had been in the shadow of either Nazi Germany or the Communist Soviet Union, and ruled by the authoritarian domestic regimes that favoured them. The story of this state, like that of twentieth-century Europe as a whole, is one badly marred by the eternal problem of man's inhumanity to man: but on a new scale, involving masses of ordinary people rather than a narrow political élite. It was fuelled by a nationalism heady enough to attract even the apolitical and malleable enough to fit itself to every newly fashionable ideology, whether democratic or authoritarian, Communist, socialist or Fascist.

In the post-1993 Czech and Slovak successor states, the 'return to Europe', as the euphemism for closer integration with the Western powers is usually known, has seemed astonishingly smooth, at least on the surface. Only occasionally have Westerners been disturbed to hear news items such as the building of a wall by Ústí nad Labem City Council to divide Gypsies from Czechs or wondered what to make of the steady exodus of Gypsies from Slovakia, together with repeated complaints by ethnic Hungarians of state-sponsored discrimination. Formerly grey and crumbling Baroque façades are now painted in jaunty colours, towns are dotted with cafés and tourist centres, and roads filled with cars – most of which are no longer rusty Škodas. Red stars, Communist Party banners, Soviet flags and portraits of Gottwald and Lenin have long gone. Gleaming shopping centres sell every imaginable consumer good, and supermarkets stock every variety of fruit and vegetable, in or out of season. The homeless and unemployed, invisible under Communism, are back; graffiti, no longer monitored or removed by the secret police, is everywhere. The Velvet revolutionaries, now middle-aged, have been busy travelling the world, building their careers and raising their children. A first generation of voters who know no other political system than democracy, have never had reason to fear informers, secret police or border guards, and can live and work anywhere in the European Union, has just come of age. The Communist Party, although back on the political map, does not feel like a threat. Nationalism, not Communism, is the unreformed, unrepentant force in the region. A particularly Habsburg way of conceiving of national identity – as tied to language and culture even more than to race or religion – ended twice in the creation, and twice in the destruction, of a state called Czechoslovakia. It also led its peoples into authoritarianism, demagoguery and caused millions unnecessary suffering. It is time to abandon the Whig interpretation of Czechoslovak history.

NOTES

CHAPTER 1: BEFORE CZECHOSLOVAKIA

1. It is incorrect to refer collectively to Bohemia, Moravia and Silesia as the historic 'Czech' (as opposed to 'Bohemian') lands, since they were linguistically German (in the cases of Bohemia and Moravia) and Polish (in the case of Silesia) as well as Czech. The error arises from the ease with which the Czech adjective *český*, which can mean either 'Bohemian' or 'Czech', is mistranslated into English.
2. The expression 'Cisleithania', literally meaning 'on this side of the River Leitha' (i.e. on the Austrian side of the border with Hungary), refers to those lands in the Habsburg Empire that were represented in the Vienna *Reichsrat* or parliament.
3. The unofficial geographical term 'Felvidék', derived from the Hungarian for 'uplands' or 'highlands' (*Felső-Magyarország*), refers, strictly speaking, not only to the territory of modern-day Slovakia (for which it is sometimes given as an alternative), but also includes a small section of Subcarpathian Ruthenia, together with the territory of the modern Hungarian counties of Nógrád, Heves and Borsod-Abaúj-Zemplén.
4. See especially J. King, *Budweisers into Czechs and Germans: A Local History of Bohemian Politics, 1848–1948* (Princeton, N.J., 2002); T. Zahra, 'Reclaiming Children for the Nation: Germanization, National Ascription and Democracy in the Bohemian Lands, 1900–1945', *Central European History* 37 (2004), pp. 499–540; E. Glassheim, *Noble Nationalists: The Transformation of the Bohemian Aristocracy* (Cambridge, Mass., 2005); P. Judson, *Guardians of the Nation: Activists on the Language Frontiers of Imperial Austria* (Cambridge, Mass., 2006); T.M. Kelly, *Without Remorse: Czech National Socialism in Late-Habsburg Austria* (Boulder, Colo., 2006) and C. Bryant, *Prague in Black: Nazi Rule and Czech Nationalism* (Cambridge, Mass., 2007).
5. For excellent, balanced accounts of Bohemian medieval heresies (including several varieties of Hussitism) which avoid the usual nationalist distortions, see especially H. Kaminsky, 'John (Jan) Hus', in J.R. Strayer, ed., *Dictionary of the Middle Ages*, 13 vols (New York, 1982–89), vol. 6 (1985), pp. 365–68 and M. Lambert, *Medieval Heresy: Popular Movements from the Gregorian Reform to the Reformation*, 3rd edn (Oxford, 2002), pp. 333–82. My thanks to Peter Biller for bringing both scholars' work to my attention.
6. Robert Seton-Watson, a Hungarian specialist who was sympathetic to Slovak nationalist grievances, agreed that the number of 'nationally conscious' Slovaks on the eve of the First World War was between 750 and 1,000 people in total. R. Seton-Watson, *The New Slovakia* (Prague, 1924), p. 14.
7. See Chapter 3 of this work for an explanation of why these alternative phrasings of the language question in successive Habsburg/Czechoslovak censuses mattered.
8. In 1646, sixty-three Orthodox priests met in Užhorod (*Uzhhorod, Ungvár, Uzhgorod*), the future provincial capital of Subcarpathian Ruthenia, in what came to be known as the Union of Užhorod, to swear allegiance to the Pope. In so doing, they joined their congregations to a compromise Church, known by outsiders as the Uniate Church and by its adherents as the Greek Catholic Church, which had first been formed, through the Union of Brest-Litovsk (1596), by Orthodox priests from Galicia and Belarus. This Uniate or Greek Catholic Church kept the Slavonic rite and most Orthodox traditions, including the right of priests to marry, but differed in recognizing the bishop of Rome (the Pope), rather than the patriarch of Constantinople, as its head.
9. Because Greater Moravia ended by conforming to the rites of the Western Church, Slovakia and Moravia – like Bohemia – were left with the Western Church and the Latin script and later fell under the umbrella of the Church of Rome, whereas Subcarpathian Ruthenia, which never belonged to the Greater Moravian Empire, retained an Eastern Christian (subsequently Greek Catholic or Uniate) rite, together with a version of the Cyrillic, rather than the Latin, script. A thousand years later, this was to

leave Subcarpathian Ruthenia open to claims that it 'naturally' belonged to the Orthodox world of the Ukrainians and Russians, whereas Slovakia, Moravia and Bohemia were held to belong to the Catholic world of the Habsburgs.

10. The current fashion in scholarly works published in English is to replace the generic term 'Gypsy', considered by some to sound pejorative, with the more technical-sounding Roma (*Romové*), meaning a speaker of the Romany language (and thus, in Central European logic, a member of the Romany 'nation'). The term *Roma* is not, however, an adequate substitute for the term 'Gypsy', since it excludes non-Romany-speaking Gypsies, who are probably in the majority, and who are in any case subject to the same discrimination as those who speak only Romany. The familiar English term 'Gypsy', derived from 'Egyptian', is also inaccurate, but at least points to racial, rather than behavioural or linguistic, distinctiveness as being what defines the people it describes. It is perhaps worth pointing out that Central European Gypsies, who are in no way related to the so-called 'Travellers' of the British Isles, are not nomadic and do not necessarily speak or understand Romany. They stand out because their skin colour makes them look physically different from local Whites.

11. The Bohemian/Moravian Brethren were originally inspired by the writings of the religious reformer Petr Chelčický (*c.* 1390–1460). The Brethren gradually lost their radical puritan edge and social peculiarities over the course of the fifteenth and sixteenth centuries (rather as the English Quakers did over the course of the nineteenth century), making them at once more theologically respectable and socially influential. See the excellent summary in Lambert, *Medieval Heresy*, pp. 412–13.

12. C. Macartney, *Hungary and her Successors: The Treaty of Trianon and its Consequences* (London, New York and Toronto, 1973), p. 209; A.J.P. Taylor, *The Habsburg Monarchy 1809–1918* (London, 1948; 1990 edn), p. 17; P.R. Magocsi, *The Rusyns of Slovakia* (New York, 1993), pp. 22–23.

13. Other such societies included the Moravian-Silesian Society for the Promotion of Agriculture, Natural Science and 'Knowledge of the Fatherland' (*vlastivěda*), which set up an equivalent 'Land Museum' in Brno (*Brünn*), the regional capital of Moravia, in 1817. In Hungary, the Lutheran school at Pozsony brought out a five-volume *Description of Hungary* (written in Latin); while a Slovak Learned Society of the 1780s to 1820s, which published mainly theological and devotional works in Slav/Slovak, also brought out some practical guides in the vernacular, books with titles like *Pilný domácí a poľný hospodár* (The Diligent Householder and Farmer) or *Zelinkár* (The Herbalist). See A. Stich, '*Rané obrození*' in J. Lehár, A. Stich, J. Janáčková, *et al.*, *Česká literatura od počátků k dnešku* (Prague, 1997, 1998), pp. 152–53; D. Sayer, *Coasts of Bohemia: A Czech History* (Princeton, N. J., 1998), pp. 53–55; L. Vykoupil, *Slovník českých dějin* (Brno, 2000), p. 369; E. Mannová, ed., *A Concise History of Slovakia* (Bratislava, 2000), p. 183; L. Kontler, *A History of Hungary* (Houndmills, Basingstoke, 2002), p. 208.

14. This was apparently to distinguish it from alternative conceptions of a National Rebirth, *Risorgimento* or National Revival. See V. Macura, 'Problems and Paradoxes of the National Revival' in M. Teich, ed., *Bohemia in History* (Cambridge, 1998), pp. 182–97.

15. R.B. Pynsent, *Questions of Identity: Czech and Slovak Ideas of Nationality and Personality* (Budapest, 1994), p. 52.

16. Mannová, *Concise History of Slovakia*, pp. 179, 184.

17. G. Oddo, *Slovakia and its People* (New York, 1960), pp. 100, 110; J. Kirschbaum, *A History of Slovakia* (New York, 1995), p. 100; Bartl *et al.*, *Slovak History: Chronology and Lexicon* (Bratislava and Wauconda, Ill., 2002), pp. 96–97; Kontler, *History of Hungary*, p. 244.

18. C. Nolte, 'Choosing Czech Identity in Nineteenth-Century Prague: The Case of Jindřich Fügner', *Nationalities Papers* 24:1 (1996), p. 54.

19. It was only when Tomáš Vlastimil Masaryk married that he exchanged his adopted middle name for 'Garrigue', which was his American wife Charlotte's maiden name. He appears to have been flexible about how to present his own name throughout his life: as a young man who was helped into a German *Gymnasium* (élite secondary school) by a German police officer from Brno (who subsequently also helped him to get a university place in Vienna), he changed the spelling of his (Slovak) surname 'Masárik' to 'Masaryk'; in his *The New Europe: The Slav Viewpoint*, a pamphlet published in London and circulated in the USA in 1918, he signed himself 'Thomas' rather than 'Tomáš'. In the Czech and Slovak traditions, he is usually referred to as 'T.G. Masaryk'.

20. Y. Jelinek, *The Parish Republic: Hlinka's Slovak People's Party 1939–1945* (New York and London, 1976), p. 7.

21. See L. Holý, *The Little Czech and the Great Czech Nation* (Cambridge, 1996), pp. 49–50. I would suggest that the importance that Herder also placed on 'blood' was largely absent in Habsburg, as opposed to Prussian, understandings of 'the nation', but the importance of language correspondingly heightened.

22. Oddo, *Slovakia and its People*, pp. 126–28; Kirschbaum, *A History of Slovakia*, pp. 132–34; Mannová, *Concise History of Slovakia*, p. 209.

23. Magocsi, *The Rusyns of Slovakia*, p. 43; Macartney, *Hungary and her Successors*, p. 208.

24. Nolte, 'Choosing Czech Identity in Nineteenth-Century Prague', p. 52.

25. K. Döge, 'Dvořák, Antonín' in S. Sadie, ed., *The New Grove Dictionary of Music and Musicians*, 29 vols, 2nd edn, vol. 7 (London, 2001), pp. 779–80.
26. A. Němcová, 'Smetana, Bedřich' in Sadie, ed., *The New Grove Dictionary of Music and Musicians*, vol. 23, pp. 541–42.
27. R.F. Nyrop, ed., *Czechoslovakia: A Country Study* (Washington, D.C., 1982), p. 24; D. Perman, *Shaping of the Czechoslovak State: Diplomatic History of the Boundaries of Czechoslovakia, 1914–1920* (Leiden, 1962), p. 12.
28. As cited in Magocsi, *Rusyns of Slovakia*, p. 48.
29. Kirschbaum, *A History of Slovakia*, p. 137.
30. Glassheim, *Noble Nationalists*, p. 8.
31. K. Bahm, 'The Inconveniences of Nationality: German Bohemians, the Disintegration of the Habsburg Monarchy, and the Attempt to Create a "Sudeten German" Identity', *Nationalities Papers* 27:3 (1999), p. 387.
32. K. Cordell, ed., *The Politics of Ethnicity in Central Europe* (London, 2000), ms. edn, chapter 4, 'Silesia and the Dawning of the Modern Age', f. 19.
33. J. Havránek, 'Fascism in Czechoslovakia' in P. Sugar, ed., *Native Fascism in the Successor States 1918–1945* (Santa Barbara, Cal., 1971), pp. 52–53.
34. See Kelly, *Without Remorse*, p. 5.
35. Bahm, 'The Inconveniences of Nationality', p. 402, note 30.
36. Magocsi, *Rusyns of Slovakia*, pp. 51–53.
37. M. Sheppard, *Czechoslovakian Year* (London, 1938), p. 258.
38. Mannová, *Concise History of Slovakia*, p. 191; Macartney, *Hungary and her Successors*, p. 202; Magocsi, *Rusyns of Slovakia*, p. 59.

CHAPTER 2: THE INVENTION OF A STATE

1. J.F.N. Bradley, *The Czechoslovak Legion in Russia, 1914–1920* (Boulder, Colo., 1991), p. 27.
2. J. Kalvoda, *The Genesis of Czechoslovakia* (Boulder, Colo., 1986), p. 70; G.C. Ference, *Chronology of Twentieth-Century Eastern European History* (Detroit, Washington, D.C. and London, 1994), pp. 103–4.
3. Slightly different translations of the text of the memorandum (20 August 1914) are given in Kalvoda, *Genesis of Czechoslovakia*, pp. 60–61 and in Bradley, *Czechoslovak Legion in Russia*, p. 17.
4. See, for example, the morning edition of 1 August 1914, which boasted itself as 'a new edition following two confiscations', or a special supplement printed on 8 August 1914, which declared itself to be a 'new, post-confiscation edition'. *Čas* 28:213 (1 August 1914) and *Čas* 28:227 (8 August 1914).
5. The first *cause célèbre* was Masaryk's attempt, in 1886, to expose as fraudulent two purportedly ancient manuscripts which, if genuine, would have helped to make the case for a Czech national consciousness and cultural achievement stretching back to well before any embryonic German national consciousness. The second, and more internationally famous, case (which blew up just five years after the Dreyfus Affair in France) concerned his involvement in the Hilsner case of 1899, in which a Jewish vagrant was accused of the murder of a girl, Anežka Hrůzová, for alleged ritual purposes, and which brought to the surface a deep well of popular anti-Semitism throughout the Habsburg Empire. Years later, as president, Masaryk confided to his close associate Karel Čapek his view that 'during the war I saw how useful the affair had been to me: the Press of the world is largely managed or financed by Jews; they knew me from the Hilsner case, and repaid me for what I had done for them by writing favourably about our cause – or at least not unfavourably. That helped us a great deal politically.' K. Čapek, *President Masaryk Tells his Story* (London, 1934), p. 189.
6. R.W. Seton-Watson, *Masaryk in England* (Cambridge, 1943), pp. 33–35; T.G. Masaryk, *Světová revoluce za války a ve válce 1914–1918*, 3rd edn, vol. 2 (Prague, 1938 [1925]), p. 6.
7. K. Pacner, *Československo ve zvláštních službách: Pohledy do historie československých výzvědných služeb 1914–1989*, vol. 1 (Prague, 2002), p. 33.
8. Z. Zeman and A. Klimek, *The Life of Edvard Beneš 1884–1948: Czechoslovakia in Peace and War* (Oxford, 1997), p. 20.
9. His *Le problème autrichien et la question tchèque* (The Austrian Problem and the Czech Question) concluded, like Masaryk, that the only solution to the Czech Question lay in reforms to the Habsburg Empire.
10. This is a brief précis of the arguments and information given in Zeman and Klimek, *Life of Beneš*, pp. 10–13.
11. E. Beneš, *Světová válka a naše revoluce*, vol. 1 (Prague, 1935), p. 18; K. Čapek, *Hovory s T.G. Masarykem* (Prague, 1969), p. 129.
12. These included Jan Herben, Cyril Dušek and Přemysl Šámal. See J. Herben, *Proti proudu* (Prague, 1997 [1935]), p. 105.
13. Beneš, *Světová válka*, vol. 1, pp. 51, 19–20.

14. *Masarykův ústav AV ČR* (Masaryk Institute of the Czech Republic Academy of Sciences), TGM-R (*Osobní sekretariát*), box 350 (untitled letters received by TGM's private secretary, 1911–19), Maximilian Kirschman to Thomas G. Masaryk, President (10 August 1917).
15. The letters had been secretly copied by the minister of the interior's butler, a Czech whose brother was in Masaryk's Realist Party. Beneš, *Světová válka*, vol. 1, pp. 19–20.
16. Masaryk, *Světová revoluce*, vol. 2, pp. 26–27.
17. Seton-Watson, *Masaryk in England*, pp. 38–39.
18. Ibid., p. 44.
19. 'Memorandum on Conversations with Masaryk (October 1914)', as reproduced in ibid., pp. 44–45.
20. Beneš, *Světová válka*, vol. 1, p. 37; Pacner, *Československo ve zvláštních službách*, vol. 1, p. 38.
21. Herben, *Proti proudu*, p. 101.
22. Beneš, *Světová válka*, vol. 1, pp. 43–44.
23. As cited in Z. Zeman, *The Masaryks: The Making of Czechoslovakia* (London, 1990), p. 81.
24. C. Parrott, *The Bad Bohemian: A Life of Jaroslav Hašek* (London, 1978), pp. 159–60, 166; Masaryk, *Světová revoluce*, vol. 2, p. 56.
25. See Bradley, *The Czechoslovak Legion*, pp. 27–31 on why this may not have been as 'patriotic' as it was afterwards portrayed.
26. Seton-Watson, *Masaryk in England*, p. 63; Beneš, *Světová válka*, vol. 1, p. 70.
27. D. Perman, *The Shaping of the Czechoslovak State: Diplomatic History of the Boundaries of Czechoslovakia, 1914–1920* (Leiden, 1962), pp. 16–17, 21.
28. Beneš, *Světová válka*, vol. 1, pp. 48, 50.
29. J. Kalvoda, *The Genesis of Czechoslovakia* (Boulder, Colo., 1986), pp. 50, 148.
30. Masaryk, *Světová revoluce*, vol. 2, p. 130.
31. Seton-Watson, *Masaryk in England*, pp. 57, 71.
32. He had received his last cache of secret documents from the minister of the interior's Czech butler just weeks before. Kalvoda, *Genesis of Czechoslovakia*, p. 85; Pacner, *Československo ve zvláštních službách*, vol. 1, p. 47.
33. The American equivalent, set up a few months later, was called the 'Slav Press Bureau'.
34. Masaryk, *Světová revoluce*, vol. 2, p. 91.
35. J. Kalvoda, *Genesis of Czechoslovakia*, p. 83; J. Bartl, V. Čičaj, M. Kohútová, R. Letz *et al.*, *Slovak History: Chronology and Lexicon*, tr. D.P. Daniel (Bratislava and Waucona, Ill., 2002), pp. 205–6.
36. Beneš, *Světová válka*, vol. 1, pp. 95–96.
37. Ibid., p. 101.
38. As cited in Kalvoda, *Genesis of Czechoslovakia*, p. 86.
39. Beneš, *Světová válka*, vol. 1, p. 109.
40. Kalvoda, *Genesis of Czechoslovakia*, p. 89.
41. Beneš, *Světová válka*, vol. 1, p. 117 and note.
42. Masaryk, *Světová revoluce*, vol. 2, p. 92.
43. Kalvoda, *Genesis of Czechoslovakia*, pp. 99–102.
44. Zeman, *The Masaryks*, p. 82; V.S. Mamatey, 'The Establishment of the Republic' in V.S. Mamatey and R. Luža, eds, *A History of the Czechoslovak Republic 1918–1948* (Princeton, N.J., 1973), p. 15.
45. E. Beneš, *My War Memoirs*, tr. P. Selver (London, 1928), p. 228. See also Masaryk, *Světová revoluce*, vol. 2, p. 142.
46. As cited in Kalvoda, *Genesis of Czechoslovakia*, p. 157.
47. Ibid., p. 158.
48. Ibid., p. 251; Zeman and Klimek, *The Life of Edvard Beneš*, p. 28.
49. As cited in Perman, *The Shaping of the Czechoslovak State*, p. 55, note 32.
50. R. Lansing, *The Peace Negotiations: A Personal Narrative* (London, 1921), p. 87.
51. From a note of 20 December 1918 as cited in ibid., p. 86.
52. Lansing, *The Peace Negotiations*, p. 87.
53. D. El Mallakh, *The Slovak Autonomy Movement, 1935–1939: A Study in Unrelenting Nationalism* (Boulder, Colo., 1979), p. 27.
54. Perman, *The Shaping of the Czechoslovak State*, pp. 31–32.
55. 'Česko-Slovenská dohoda, uzavrená v Pittsburgu, Pa., dňa 30. mája 1918', as reproduced in Ústav mezinárodních vztahů, *Vznik Československa 1918: Dokumenty československé zahraniční politiky* (Prague, 1994), p. 123.
56. P. Magocsi, *The Shaping of a National Identity: Subcarpathian Rus', 1848–1948* (Cambridge, Mass., 1978), pp. 79–80.
57. Ibid., p. 82.
58. Masaryk to Frank Polk, acting secretary of state (20 July 1918), as cited in Perman, *Shaping of the Czechoslovak State*, p. 43; Kalvoda, *Genesis of Czechoslovakia*, p. 370.

59. *Vznik Československa 1918: Dokumenty*, pp. 164–66; p. 54; Perman, *Shaping of the Czechoslovak State*, pp. 35–37; Beneš, *Světová válka*, vol. 2, p. 214, note.
60. Frazier to Lansing (2 July 1918), as cited in Perman, *Shaping of the Czechoslovak State*, p. 38.
61. As reproduced in *Vznik Československa 1918: Dokumenty*, pp. 163–64.
62. Perman, *Shaping of the Czechoslovak State*, pp. 38–39.
63. 'Declaration' attached to a letter from Beneš to Masaryk (11 August 1918), reproduced in *Vznik Československa 1918: Dokumenty*, p. 201.
64. See Perman, *Shaping of the Czechoslovak State*, pp. 42–43 and '*Déclaration du gouvernement des États-Unis*' (2 September 1918), as reproduced in *Vznik Československa 1918: Dokumenty*, p. 104.
65. '*Avant-project d'un accord à intervenir entre le gouvernement français et le conseil national tchécoslovaque*' (before 10 September 1918), as reproduced in *Vznik Československa 1918: Dokumenty*, pp. 252–54.
66. The text is reproduced in full as Document 145 in *Vznik Československa 1918: Dokumenty*, pp. 305–7. A table of diplomatic recognitions is given in an appendix to T.G. Masaryk, *The Making of a State: Memories and Observations 1914–1918*, tr. H. Wickham Steed (New York, 1927), pp. 498–509.
67. Masarykův ústav Akademie věd ČR, *Declaration of Independence of the Czechoslovak Nation by its Provisional Government* (Prague, 1998), *passim*.
68. Lansing to the minister of Sweden (18 October 1918), as cited in Beneš, *My War Memoirs*, pp. 437–38.
69. F. Peroutka, *Budování státu*, vol. 1 (Prague, 1991), p. 53.
70. As cited in Bahm, 'The Inconveniences of Nationality', pp. 385–86.
71. Mamatey, 'The Establishment of the Republic', pp. 24–25.
72. Peroutka, *Budování státu*, vol. 1, p. 60.
73. 'Declaration of Common Aims of the Mid-European Nations', as reproduced in *Vznik Československa 1918: Dokumenty*, pp. 330–32; Perman, *Shaping of the Czechoslovak State*, p. 26; Magocsi, *Shaping of a National Identity*, p. 84.
74. J. Rokoský, '*Antonín Švehla a 28. říjen 1918*' in [A. Švehla], *Hovory s Antonín Švehlou (a o něm)*, ed. K. Čapek (Prague, 2001), p. 44; F. Soukup, *28. říjen 1918*, vol. 2 (Prague, 1928), pp. 987–88; Masaryk, *Světová revoluce*, vol. 2, p. 473.
75. Rokoský, '*Antonín Švehla a 28. říjen 1918*', pp. 46–47.
76. Soukup, *28. říjen 1918*, vol. 2, pp. 993–94, 1004.
77. Beneš, *Světová válka*, vol. 2, pp. 429–31.
78. Soukup, *28. říjen 1918*, vol. 2, pp. 1020–21; Peroutka, *Budování státu*, vol. 1, p. 84.
79. Masaryk, *The Making of a State*, pp. 434, 391, 396; Beneš, *My War Memoirs*, pp. 454–55; Soukup, *28. říjen 1918*, vol. 2, pp. 1000–1.
80. Soukup, *28. říjen 1918*, vol. 2, pp. 1092, 1094.
81. 'Declaration of the Slovak Nation', as given in English translation in Bartl *et al.*, *Slovak History: Chronology and Lexicon*, p. 219.
82. See I. Nurmi, *Slovakia: A Playground for Nationalism and National Identity* (Helsinki, 1999), p. 52 and El Mallakh, *The Slovak Autonomy Movement*, pp. 34–35, 46, 48.
83. Perman, *Shaping of the Czechoslovak State*, p. 69.
84. Beneš, *My War Memoirs*, p. 460.
85. Magocsi, *The Rusyns of Slovakia*, p. 61 and Magocsi, *Shaping of a National Identity*, pp. 86–87.
86. This brief synopsis is based on Perman, *Shaping of the Czechoslovak State*, pp. 65–71.
87. Bahm, 'The Inconveniences of Nationality', p. 389.
88. Nurmi, *Slovakia: A Playground for Nationalism*, p. 52, note.
89. Mamatey, 'Establishment of the Republic', pp. 30–31.
90. Bahm, 'The Inconveniences of Nationality', p. 389.
91. J.B. Heisler and J.E. Mellon, *Under the Carpathians: Home of a Forgotten People* (London, 1946), p. 55.
92. M. Sheppard, *Czechoslovakian Year* (London, 1938), p. 244.
93. Magocsi, *Rusyns of Slovakia*, p. 63.
94. Perman, *Shaping of the Czechoslovak State*, p. 104.

CHAPTER 3: A TROUBLED DEMOCRACY

1. C. Paces, ' "The Czech Nation Must Be Catholic!" An Alternative Version of Czech Nationalism during the First Republic', *Nationalities Papers* 27: 3 (1999), pp. 407, 416–22.
2. M. Feinberg, *Elusive Equality: Gender, Citizenship, and the Limits of Democracy in Czechoslovakia, 1918–1950* (Pittsburgh, 2006), p. 7.
3. See G. Capoccia, 'Legislative Responses against Extremism. The "Protection of Democracy" in the First Czechoslovak Republic (1920–1938)', *East European Politics and Societies* 16: 3 (2002), pp. 691–738.

4. One of the most influential was probably J. Korbel, *Twentieth-Century Czechoslovakia: The Meanings of its History* (New York, 1977), from which this example is taken. Josef Korbel, future US Secretary of State Madeleine Albright's father, also supervised future US Secretary of State Condoleeza Rice's interesting PhD thesis on the Czechoslovak army, which was afterwards published as C. Rice, *The Soviet Union and the Czechoslovak Army, 1948–1983* (Princeton, N.J., 1984).

5. For English translations of the party's hilarious hustings speeches, as held in various Prague pubs, see C. Parrott, *The Bad Bohemian: A Life of Jaroslav Hašek* (London, 1978), pp. 109–20. My grateful thanks to Peter Biller for first introducing me to this aspect of Hašek's life.

6. See e.g. Sheppard, *Czechoslovakian Year*, pp. 254–68; Heisler and Mellon, *Under the Carpathians*; M. Winch, *Republic for a Day: An Eye-Witness Account of the Carpatho-Ukraine Incident* (London, 1939); R. Marel, *La Ruthénie Subcarpathique (Podkarpatska Rus)* (Paris, 1935).

7. As cited in H. Arendt, *The Origins of Totalitarianism* (San Diego, New York and London, 1973 [1966 edn]), p. 270, note 5.

8. Law 64, '*Zákon o mimořádných přechodných ustanoveních na Slovensku*' (10 December 1918), *Sbírka zákonů a nařízení státu československého* (Prague, 1918), pp. 55–56.

9. Population figures for the city in 1910 record, out of a total of 65,867, an overwhelming majority of Germans (32,104), followed by 18,744 Magyars and 9,004 Slovaks. Not until 1930 did Slovaks (34,836) for the first time outnumber Germans (32,801); the number of Magyars remained virtually unchanged (18,890).

10. Paces, ' "The Czech Nation Must Be Catholic!" ', pp. 408–9, 414.

11. Laws 61 '*Zákon, jímž zrušují se šlechtictví, řády a tituly*' (11 December 1918); 63 '*Zákon o podpoře nezaměstnaných*' (10 December 1918); 91 '*Zákon o 8 hodinné době pracovní*' (19 December 1918), *Sbírka zákonů a nařízení státu československého* (Prague, 1918), pp. 50, 51, 81.

12. Law 30 (10 January 1919), *Sbírka zákonů a nařízení státu československého* (Prague, 1919), p. 30.

13. Glassheim, *Noble Nationalists*, p. 81.

14. Law 84, '*Zákon ze dne 25. února jímž se ministr financí zmocňuje, aby provedl nařízením okolkování bankovek a soupis jmění za účelem uložení majetkové dávky*' (25 February 1919), *Sbírka zákonů a nařízení státu československého* (Prague, 1919), pp. 101–3.

15. Law 30, '*Cestování do území ČSR*' (20 January 1919), ibid., p. 30.

16. As reproduced in English translation in J. Bruegel, *Czechoslovakia before Munich: The German Minority Problem and British Appeasement Policy* (Cambridge, 1973), p. 19.

17. Ibid., p. 20.

18. H. Nicolson, *Peacemaking 1919* (London, 1933 [1945]), pp. xviii–xix.

19. From C. Seymour, ed., *Intimate Papers of Colonel House*, vol. 4, p. 275, as cited in Perman, *Shaping of the Czechoslovak State*, p. 122.

20. As cited in A. Sharp, *The Versailles Settlement: Peacemaking in Paris, 1919* (Houndmills, Basingstoke, 1991), pp. 26–7.

21. H. Nicolson, *Peacemaking 1919* (London, 1933 [1945]), p. 92.

22. E. Beneš, 'Note on the Régime of Nationalities in the Czecho-Slovak Republic' (Paris, 20 May 1919), as reproduced in full in E. Wiskemann, *Czechs and Germans: A Study of the Struggle in the Historic Provinces of Bohemia and Moravia*, 2nd edn (London, 1967), pp. 92–93.

23. D. Lloyd George, *Memoirs of the Peace Conference*, vol. 2 (New Haven, 1939), pp. 587, 605.

24. E. Dillon, as cited in P. Milyukov, 'Edvard Beneš', *Slavonic and East European Review* 17 (January 1939), p. 307.

25. As cited in Zeman and Klimek, *Life of Edvard Beneš*, p. 40.

26. Extracts from Beneš's speech to the peace conference (5 February 1919), as cited in Lloyd George, *Memoirs of the Peace Conference*, vol. 2, pp. 605–8.

27. Bahm, 'The Inconveniences of Nationality', pp. 389–90.

28. As cited in Perman, *Shaping of the Czechoslovak State*, p. 24.

29. Zeman and Klimek, *Life of Edvard Beneš*, p. 45.

30. Ibid., pp. 37–38.

31. As cited in ibid., p. 38.

32. Oddo, *Slovakia and its People*, pp. 191–92; M. Schwitzer, *Slovakia: The Path to Nationhood* (Bratislava and London, 2002), p. 92; Kirschbaum, *A History of f Slovakia*, p. 163.

33. Magocsi, *The Rusyns of Slovakia*, pp. 65–66.

34. For a brief summary, see Kontler, *A History of Hungary*, pp. 332–39.

35. Perman, *The Shaping of the Czechoslovak State*, pp. 225–26; Schwitzer, *Slovakia: The Path to Nationhood*, pp. 92–93; W. Wallace, *Czechoslovakia* (London and Tonbridge, 1977), p. 158, 134.

36. El Mallakh, *The Slovak Autonomy Movement*, p. 32; J. Felak, '*At the Price of the Republic*': Hlinka's Slovak People's Party, 1929–1938* (Pittsburgh and London, 1994), pp. 27, 111. The full text of the

memorandum is reproduced in J.A. Mikus, *Slovakia: A Political History, 1918–1950* (Milwaulkee, Wis., 1963), pp. 331–40.

37. Felak, '*At the Price of the Republic*', pp. 23–24.
38. As cited e.g. in Perman, *Shaping of the Czechoslovak State*, p. 247 and note 86.
39. They enumerated these as the counties of: Szepes/Spiš; Sáros/Šariš; Zemplén/Zemplín/Zemplyn; Abauj/Abaúj; Borsod/Borsód; Ung/Užh/Uzh; Ugocsa/Ungosca, Bereg; Máramoros/Marmaroš. See V. Shandor, *Carpatho-Ukraine in the Twentieth Century: A Political and Legal History* (Cambridge, Mass., 1997), p. 6.
40. Magocsi, *The Rusyns of Slovakia*, p. 72.
41. 'Justinian', 'Carpathian Ruthenia', *Eastern Europe* 5: 4 (June 1921), pp. 231–34.
42. Sharp, *The Versailles Settlement*, p. 151; J. Rothschild, *East Central Europe between the Two World Wars* (Seattle and London, 1992 [1974]), p. 85.
43. As cited in Perman, *Shaping of the Czechoslovak State*, p. 150 and Lloyd George, *Memoirs of the Peace Conference*, vol. 2, p. 612, respectively.
44. As cited in P. Milyukov, 'Edward Beneš', *Slavonic Review* (January 1939), p. 316.
45. 'Nationalities Living in the Territories of Czechoslovakia', from *Manuel statistique de la république tchécoslavique* (Prague, 1925), vol. 2, pp. 362–63; *Statistická příručka Republiky československé* (Prague, 1928), vol. 3, p. 275, as reproduced in V.L. Beneš, 'Czechoslovak Democracy and its Problems 1918–1920' in V.S. Mamatey and R. Luža, eds, *A History of the Czechoslovak Republic 1918–1948* (Princeton, N.J., 1973), p. 40. See also figures from *Statistická ročenka Republiky československé 1934* (Prague, 1934), p. 11, as cited in P.R. Magocsi, *Historical Atlas of East Central Europe*, vol. 1 (Seattle and London, 1993), p. 133.
46. Magocsi, *The Rusyns of Slovakia*, pp. 73–74.
47. H. Kohn, 'Before 1918 in the Historic Lands' in Society for the History of Czechoslovak Jews, *The Jews of Czechoslovakia: Historical Studies and Surveys*, vol. 1 (New York, 1968), pp. 18–19. In Slovakia, according to the 1921 census, out of a total population of 3,000,870, about 21.6 per cent were classified as 'Magyar', 4.6 per cent (145,844) as 'German'; but only 88,970 as 'Ruthene' (Rusyn/Ruthenian/Ukrainian) and 73,628 as 'Jewish'.
48. Feinberg, *Elusive Equality*, p. 7.
49. Articles 113, 116 and 117, 'The Constitutional Charter of the Czechoslovak Republic', as reproduced in *Selected Constitutions of the World* (Dublin, 1922), pp. 164, 165.
50. Article 106, ibid., pp. 164, 163.
51. Article 58, ibid., p. 156.
52. Article 54, ibid., p. 154.
53. Article 126, ibid., p. 166.
54. Article 120, ibid., p. 165.
55. Articles 22, 65, 73 and 98, ibid., pp. 148, 158, 159, 162. Public oaths of loyalty to the state, to be taken by all government bureaucrats, including public transport workers, had been made obligatory in 1919. See laws 74, 154, 178 and 179 in *Sbírka zákonů a nařízení státu československého* (Prague, 1919), pp. 76, 197, and 229.
56. Beneš, 'Democracy and its Problems', p. 97.
57. Law 542 (15 September 1920), *Sbírka zákonů a nařízení státu československého* (Prague, 1920), p. 1355. F.L. Cross and E.A. Livingstone, eds, *The Oxford Dictionary of the Christian Church*, 3rd edn (Oxford, 1997), pp. 444–45.
58. V. Bystrov and J. Pergler, '*Kořeny StB v rakouském mocnářství*', *Lidové noviny* (13 August 1993), p. 16.
59. Article 128, 'Constitutional Charter', *Selected Constitutions of the World*, p. 166.
60. Article 134, ibid., p. 167.
61. Article 132, ibid.
62. Article 131, ibid.
63. Article 113, ibid., p. 165.
64. Article 128, ibid., p. 167.
65. Article 131, ibid.
66. P. Augusta and F. Honzák, *Československo 1918–1938* (Prague, 1992), p. 7; Law 252 (30 March 1920), *Sbírka zákonů* (Prague, 1920), pp. 540–41; J. Oulík and P. Sedláček, '*Nadpřirozený lev a modrý klín*', *Literární noviny* 43 (21 October 2002), p. 15.
67. Law 266 (14 March 1920), *Sbírka zákonů a nařízení státu československého* (Prague, 1920), p. 595.
68. Law 252 (30 March 1920), ibid., pp. 540–41.
69. A. Dušek, ed., *Příručka pro sběratele československých známek a celin* (Prague, 1988), p. 50.
70. V. Novotný and V. Šimek, *Československé mince 1918–1993. Mince české a slovenské republiky 1993–1994* (Hodonín, 1994), pp. 13–14; Augusta and Honzák, *Československo 1918–1938*, p. 13.

71. Dušek, ed., *Příručka pro sběratele československých známek a celin*, pp. 76–77.
72. Ibid., p. 83.
73. See e.g. Capoccia, 'Legislative Responses against Extremism.', pp. 707–8.
74. See the excellent précis in Z. Suda, *Zealots and Rebels: A History of the Ruling Communist Party of Czechoslovakia* (Stanford, Cal., 1980), pp. 23–37.
75. Wallace, *Czechoslovakia*, p. 177.
76. Felak, *'At the Price of the Republic'*, p. 32; El Mallakh, *The Slovak Autonomy Movement*, pp. 51–52.
77. Capoccia, 'Legislative Responses against Extremism', pp. 709–10.
78. Felak, *'At the Price of the Republic'*, pp. 30–31; El Mallakh, *The Slovak Autonomy Movement*, pp. 51–52 and Appendix D, pp. 210–15.
79. Beneš, 'Democracy and its Problems', p. 72.
80. Ibid. Membership in the Slovak People's Party rose from a negligible 2,115 in 1918 to 11,983 by 1920, 17,958 by 1925 and 22,467 by 1930. Felak, *'At the Price of the Republic'*, p. 30.
81. Felak, *'At the Price of the Republic'*, p. 36; El Mallakh, *The Slovak Autonomy Movement*, pp. 54–55; Jelinek, *The Parish Republic*, pp. 10–11.
82. Photograph entitled 'Slovaks in Diplomacy' in R.W. Seton-Watson, ed., *Slovakia Then and Now: A Political Survey* (London, 1931), between pp. 32 and 33.
83. Zeman and Klimek, *Life of Edvard Beneš*, p. 59.
84. E. Wiskemann, *The Europe I Saw* (London and Glasgow, 1968), p. 76.
85. F. Moravec, *Master of Spies: The Memoirs of General Frantisek Moravec*, ed. H. Disher (London, 1975), p. 42.
86. El Mallakh, *The Slovak Autonomy Movement*, p. 58; Felak, *'At the Price of the Republic'*, p. 109.
87. El Mallakh, *The Slovak Autonomy Movement*, pp. 58–60; Felak, *'At the Price of the Republic'*, pp. 87–88.
88. From *Bulletin of International News*, vol. 13, p. 747, as cited in P.M.H. Bell, *The Origins of the Second World War in Europe*, 2nd edn (London and New York, 1997), p. 258.
89. Capoccia, 'Legislative Responses against Extremism', p. 717.
90. Ibid.
91. M. Campbell, 'Keepers of Order? Strategic Legality in the 1935 Czechoslovak General Elections', *Nationalities Papers* 31:3 (September 2003), p. 297.
92. Ibid., p. 296.
93. This fascinating episode is succinctly explained in Zeman and Klimek, *Life of Edvard Beneš*, pp. 103–16 and also in Felak, *'At the Price of the Republic'*, pp. 152–55.
94. Felak, *'At the Price of the Republic'*, p. 166.
95. Among those named in police reports of a small counter-demonstration were two noteworthy future Communists: Vladimír Clementis, who rose to become foreign minister before being executed as a traitor; and Gustáv Husák, who, after narrowly surviving his own political trial, was to outlive most of his political rivals as head of the Czechoslovak Communist Party and President of the Socialist Republic until his death in 1991. See El Mallakh, *The Slovak Autonomy Movement*, pp. 83–84 and *'Gustáv Husák'* in M. Churaň *et al.*, *Kdo byl kdo v našich dějinách ve 20. století*, vol. 1 (Prague, 1998), p. 257.
96. Capoccia, 'Legislative Responses against Extremism', pp. 728–9.
97. Anon., 'The German Minority in Czechoslovakia', *Slavonic and East European Review* (1936), 295–300.
98. As discussed in Chapter 2, the predominantly German-speaking regions of the Bohemian Crown Lands had in late 1918 sought inclusion in Austria-Germany as the autonomous territories of Deutschböhmen (in northern Bohemia, along the German frontier), Sudetenland (in Silesia and northern Moravia, adjoining Germany), Böhmerwaldgau (in south-western Bohemia, facing Bavaria) and Deutschsüdmähren (in southern Moravia adjoining Austria). In the late 1920s and throughout the 1930s, the terms 'Sudeten' and 'Carpathian' Germans came to be applied, respectively, to the German-speakers of the Bohemian Crown Lands and of the formerly Hungarian territories of Slovakia and Subcarpathian Ruthenia (to distinguish them from the German-speakers of neighbouring Austria, Germany and Poland).
99. *Hansard's Parliamentary Debates*, 5th series, vol. 326 (5 July 1937); *The Times* (15 July 1938), p. 5.
100. From the Runciman Report (21 September 1938), as reproduced in J. Wheeler-Bennet, *Munich: Prologue to Tragedy* (London, 1963), p. 453.
101. Bell, *Origins of the Second World War*, p. 271.
102. Radio broadcast of 27 September 1938, as reported in *The Times* (28 September 1938).
103. This summary draws heavily on the painstakingly researched reconstruction in T. Telford, *Munich: The Price of Peace* (Garden City, N.Y., 1979), pp. 29–33.
104. 'Sketch Map Based on the Map Annexed to the Agreement Signed at Munich on September 29, 1938' in H. Ripka, *Munich: Before and After*, tr. I. Šindelková and E.P. Young (New York, 1969 [London, 1939]), p. 222.

105. 'Agreement Reached on September 29, 1938, between Germany, the United Kingdom, France and Italy', as reproduced in full in Telford, *Munich*, pp. 50–53.
106. Telford, *Munich*, pp. 49, 55.
107. Zeman and Klimek, *Life of Edvard Beneš*, p. 54.
108. T. Procházka, *The Second Republic: The Disintegration of Post-Munich Czechoslovakia (October 1938–March 1939)* (New York, 1981), p. 10.
109. P. Drtina, *Československo můj osud* (Toronto, 1982), part 1, book 1, p. 180.
110. Telford, *Munich*, p. 55.
111. From 23 September 1938, during the mobilization scare and in expectation of imminent war, *Lidové noviny* began to issue separate Prague versions of the Brno-based newspaper, which were explicitly called *Pražské Lidové noviny* between 27 September and 2 October 1938. See *Lidové noviny* (23 September 1938), vol. 1/46, no. 232/480 and *Pražské Lidové noviny* (27 September 1938–2 October 1938), vol. 1, nos 1–8.
112. This paragraph closely shadows Zeman and Klímek's findings as published in their *Life of Edvard Beneš*, pp. 135–37, together with those of Procházka in his *The Second Republic*, pp. 9–12.
113. Telford, *Munich*, pp. 55–56.
114. Zeman and Klimek, *Life of Edvard Beneš*, p. 137.
115. Procházka, *The Second Republic*, pp. 15, 21–22.
116. Sir Neville Henderson, as cited in ibid., p. 18.
117. 'Preface'; 'Personal Notes on the Munich Crisis, written in early October 1938', in G. Kennan, *From Prague after Munich: Diplomatic Papers 1938–1940* (Princeton, N.J., 1968), pp. vi, 3–4. The fine detail of the implementation of the Munich Agreement on the ground is well summarized in Procházka, *The Second Republic*, pp. 16–30.
118. 'President Beneš's Farewell Broadcast to the Czechoslovak Nation on October 5th, 1938', as translated in full into English and reproduced as an appendix to *Memoirs of Dr Eduard Beneš: From Munich to New War and New Victory*, tr. G. Lias (Boston, 1954), pp. 292–93.
119. Ibid., p. 294.
120. Ibid., p. 293.
121. Ibid., p. 294.
122. Ibid., p. 295.
123. Anon., *Dejiny štátu práva na území Československa v období kapitalizmu 1848–1945*, vol. 2 (Bratislava, 1973), p. 432. At his trial for treason in 1947, Tiso was to remind the court that he, just like the other Slovak ministers, had been legally appointed by the Czechoslovak prime minister. See J. Tiso, *Dr. Jozef Tiso o sebe (Obhajobná reč pred tzv. Národným súdom v Bratislave dňa 17. a 18. marca 1947)* (Passaic, N.J., 1952), p. 170.
124. F. Vnuk, 'Slovakia's Six Eventful Months (October 1938–March 1939)', *Slovak Studies*, 4 (1964), p. 27.

CHAPTER 4: THE FASCIST APPEAL

1. 'Manifesto of the Slovak People's Party (Issued at Žilina on October 6, 1938)', as reproduced in full as Appendix I in Vnuk, 'Slovakia's Six Eventful Months', p. 32, and also as Appendix N in El Mallakh, *The Slovak Autonomy Movement*, p. 233.
2. Pavol Teplanský became minister for the economy and Ján Lichner minister for transport and posts.
3. As cited in Magocsi, *The Shaping of a National Identity*, p. 237.
4. Ibid.; Ripka, *Munich*, p. 242; Shandor, *Carpatho-Ukraine in the Twentieth Century*, p. 70. .
5. These were Laws 299, '*Ústavný zákon o autonómii slovenskej krajiny*', and 328 and 329, '*Ústavní zákon ze dne 22. listopadu 1938 o autonomii Podkarpatské Rusi*', *Sbírka zákonů a nařízení státu česko-slovenského, ročník 1938, částka 109* (Prague, 1938), pp. 1161–64, 1199–1204.
6. Jelinek, *The Parish Republic*, p. 19.
7. 'Report on Conditions in Slovakia, written in January 1939', in Kennan, *From Prague after Munich*, p. 19.
8. Bartl *et al., Slovak History: Chronology and Lexicon*, p. 137; Vnuk, 'Slovakia's Six Eventful Months', p. 30; Schwitzer, *Slovakia*, p. 109.
9. Suda, *Zealots and Rebels*, p. 160.
10. Vnuk, 'Slovakia's Six Eventful Months', p. 80; Jelinek, *The Parish Republic*, p. 20.
11. J. Lettrich, *History of Modern Slovakia* (London, 1956), p. 115; Jelinek, *The Parish Republic*, pp. 19–20.
12. See Decrees 220 and 311, *Sbírka zákonů a nařízení* (Prague, 1939); Lettrich, *History of Modern Slovakia*, pp. 149–50.
13. Jelinek, *The Parish Republic*, p. 19.
14. From a speech given in Užhorod/Uzhhorod on 12 October 1938, as cited in Magocsi, *The Shaping of a National Identity*, p. 238.

15. Ibid., p. 238; Shandor, *Carpatho-Ukraine in the Twentieth Century*, p. 75.
16. Ibid.
17. Magocsi, *The Rusyns of Slovakia*, pp. 89–90; Magocsi, *The Shaping of a National Identity*, p. 238; Procházka, *The Second Republic*, p. 66.
18. Shandor, *Carpatho-Ukraine in the Twentieth Century*, p. 125, note 1.
19. As cited in Procházka, *The Second Republic*, p. 28.
20. Vnuk, 'Slovakia's Six Eventful Months', pp. 33–34, 38.
21. 'Composition of the International Commission', addendum to 'Agreement Reached on September 29, 1938, between Germany, the United Kingdom, France and Italy', as reproduced in Telford, *Munich*, p. 53.
22. Mannová, *A Concise History of Slovakia*, p. 257.
23. Jelinek, *The Parish Republic*, p. 23.
24. J. Tiso, radio broadcast 'We Have Become a Sacrifice to Injustice' (2 November 1938), as reproduced in C. Murin, ed., *Remembrances and Testimony (Dr. Jozef Tiso and the Slovak Republic 1939–45)*, tr. V. Cincík (Montreal, 1992), p. 244.
25. Lettrich, *History of Modern Slovakia*, p. 175.
26. E. Levy, *Just One More Dance: A Story of Degradation and Fear, Faith and Compassion from a Survivor of the Nazi Death Camps* (Edinburgh and London, 1998), pp. 17, 24, 43–47.
27. Lettrich, *History of Modern Slovakia*, p. 116.
28. Heisler and Mellon, *Under the Carpathians*, pp. 104–5.
29. Procházka, *The Second Republic*, p. 67.
30. The agreement was passed as Law 300, '*Smlouva mezi Československou [sic] republikou a Německou říší o otázkách státního občanství a opce*', *Sbírka zákonů a nařízení státu česko-slovenského* (Prague, 1938), pp. 1165–70, 1171.
31. K. Weisskopf, *The Agony of Czechoslovakia '38/'68* (London, 1968), pp. 140–41.
32. Shandor, *Carpatho-Ukraine*, pp. 108–9; D. Kelly, *The Czech Fascist Movement 1922–1942* (New York, 1995), pp. 147–48.
33. As cited in Zeman and Klimek, *Life of Edvard Beneš*, p. 141.
34. Ibid., pp. 143–46; C. MacDonald, *The Killing of SS Obergruppenführer Reinhard Heydrich* (London, 1989; 1990), p. 56.
35. Suda, *Zealots and Rebels*, pp. 161–62.
36. P. Milyukov, 'Edvard Beneš', *Slavonic and East European Review*, 17 (January 1939), p. 297.
37. Procházka, *The Second Republic*, pp. 56–57.
38. See e.g. D.C. Newton to Lord Halifax (8 December 1938), as reproduced in B. Vago, *The Shadow of the Swastika: The Rise of Fascism and Anti-Semitism in the Danube Basin, 1936–1939* (London, 1975), p. 362.
39. Excerpts from a personal letter (8 December 1938), as cited in Kennan, *From Prague after Munich*, pp. 7, 9.
40. Kelly, *The Czech Fascist Movement*, pp. 142–46; Procházka, *The Second Republic*, pp. 57–58.
41. B.C. Newton to Lord Halifax, 'Annual Report for 1938' (14 January 1939), as reproduced in Vago, *The Shadow of the Swastika*, p. 368.
42. *Kronika Českých zemí* (Prague, 1999), p. 695.
43. Shandor, *Carpatho-Ukraine*, p. 102.
44. V. Mastny, *The Czechs under Nazi Rule: The Failure of National Resistance, 1939–1942* (New York, 1971), p. 23; Kelly, *The Czech Fascist Movement*, p. 143.
45. Excerpts from a personal letter (8 December 1938), as cited in Kennan, *From Prague after Munich*, p. 8.
46. 'Dr F. Chvalkovský, the New Minister of Foreign Affairs', *Central European Observer* 16 (16 December 1938), p. 391, as cited in Kelly, *The Czech Fascist Movement*, p. 143.
47. Conversations with Hitler and Ribbentrop (13–14 October 1938), as cited in Mastny, *Czechs under Nazi Rule*, p. 21.
48. Law 330, '*Ústavný zákon o zmocnení ku zmenám ústavnej listiny a ústavných zákonov republiky Česko-Slovenskej a o mimoriadnej moci nariad'ovacej*', *Sbírka zákonů a nařízení státu česko-slovenského* (Prague, 1938), pp. 1205–6.
49. Procházka, *The Second Republic*, p. 58.
50. Law 355, '*Vládní nařízení o politických stranách*' (23 December 1938), *Sbírka zákonů a nařízení státu česko-slovenského* (Prague, 1938), p. 1249, was further supplemented by Decree 4 (13 January 1939), *Sbírka zákonů a nařízení* (Prague, 1939), p. 9. See also E. Táborský, *Czechoslovak Democracy at Work* (London, 1945), pp. 146–47.
51. Lettrich, *History of Modern Slovakia*, p. 119.
52. Jelinek, *The Parish Republic*, p. 25.
53. 'Report on Conditions in Slovakia (January 1939)', cited in Kennan, *From Prague after Munich*, p. 16.

54. Excerpts from a personal letter (8 December 1938), in ibid., p. 9.

55. Procházka, *The Second Republic*, p. 59.

56. Telegram from B.C. Newton to the British Foreign Office (22 October 1938), in Vago, *Shadow of the Swastika*, p. 335.

57. As cited in Procházka, *The Second Republic*, p. 55.

58. 'Record of a Conversation between Count Rat Kinsky and R.J. Stopford' (14 November 1938) and J.K. Roberts, 'Foreign Office Memorandum Concerning the Position of Jews in Czechoslovakia since Munich' (4 January 1939), in Vago, *Shadow of the Swastika*, pp. 350, 374. See also J.M. Troutbeck to Lord Halifax (Prague, November 15, 1938), 'Minutes by R.M. Makins' (November 24, 1938) and 'Copy of a Letter from R.M. Makins to S.D. Waley (Foreign Office, November 26, 1938)', as reproduced in ibid., pp. 351, 352, 353.

59. 'Foreign Office Memorandum (by J.K. Roberts) Concerning the Position of Jews in Czechoslovakia since Munich' (4 January 1939), in ibid., p. 374.

60. Decrees 14, '*Vládní nařízení ze dne 27. ledna 1939, jímž se doplňují předpisy o pobytu cizinců, pokud jsou emigranty*', and 15, '*Vládní nařízení ze dne 27. ledna 1939 o přezkoumání česko-slovenského státního občanství některých osob*', *Sbírka zákonů a nařízení státu česko-slovenského* (Prague, 1939), pp. 39–42. J.M. Troutbeck to Lord Halifax (9 February 1939), in Vago, *Shadow of the Swastika*, pp. 387–88.

61. *Slovák* (3 February 1939) and speeches (27 January 1939 and 22 February 1939), as cited in Tiso, *Dr. Jozef Tiso o sebe*, pp. 315–17; 'Report on Conditions in Slovakia, written in January 1939' in Kennan, *From Prague after Munich*, pp. 23–24.

62. A. Voloshyn, as cited in *Karpato-Ukrajinská Svoboda* (Prague, 20 January 1939), as cited in Shandor, *Carpatho-Ukraine*, p. 111.

63. Shandor, *Carpatho-Ukraine*, p. 79.

64. See e.g. R.B. Pynsent, 'The Literary Representation of the Czechoslovak "Legions" in Russia', in M. Cornwall and R.J.W. Evans, eds, *Czechoslovakia in a Nationalist and Fascist Europe 1918–1948* (Oxford, 2007), pp. 63–64. On postwar Czech anti-Semitism, see Jana Svobodová, *Zdroje a projevy antisemitismu v českých zemích 1948–1992: Studie* (Prague, 1994).

65. Kelly similarly found that, 'central as anti-Semitism was to the [late-nineteenth-century Czech] National Socialist party's activities, when the moment suited them party leaders made distinctions between "Czech-Jews" who were good and loyal members of the nation and "Jew-Germans" who were enemies of the nation'. Kelly, *Without Remorse*, p. 5.

66. O. Grünfeld, *The Survivor's Path* (Prague, 1995), pp. 13, 15, 17.

67. E. Stein, *Czecho-Slovakia: Ethnic Conflict, Constitutional Fissure, Negotiated Breakup* (Ann Arbor, Mich., 1997; 2000), p. 31.

68. G. Kennan, 'Excerpts from a Despatch of February 17, 1939, from George F. Kennan (as secretary of legation at Prague) to the Department of State, on the Jewish problem in The New Czechoslovakia' in Kennan, *From Prague after Munich*, pp. 47–49.

69. L. Benda, *Židé v našem hospodářství* (Prague, 1939), pp. 34, 27–31, 32–33, 38, 39.

70. As cited in J. Havránek, 'Fascism in Czechoslovakia' in Sugar, ed., *Native Fascism in the Successor States 1918–1945*, p. 49.

71. The currently fashionable term *Roma* was rarely used at the time. It is in any case misleading, since the Gypsy population of Czecho-Slovakia included German-(*Sinti*), Czech-, Slovak- and Hungarian-as well as Romany-speakers.

72. Decrees 72, '*Vládní nařízení o kárných táborech*' (2 March 1939), and 188, '*Vládní nařízení, kterým se mění vl. nař. č. 72/1939 Sb. o kárných pracovních táborech*' (28 April 1939), *Sbírka zákonů a nařízení státu česko-slovenského* (Prague, 1939), pp. 368, 619; B. Kenety, 'The "Devouring": A Look at the Romani Holocaust', http://www.romove.cz (27 January 2005); '*Deportace českých Romů do Osvětimi*', http://www.holocaust.cz/cz2/history/rom/czech/czrom5 (15 November 2001).

73. 'Report on Conditions in Ruthenia, written March 1939', in Kennan, *From Prague after Munich*, p. 65.

74. Shandor, *Carpatho-Ukraine*, p. 128 and p. 160, note 4; 'Report on Conditions in Ruthenia', in Kennan, *From Prague after Munich*, pp. 65–66.

75. Procházka, *The Second Republic*, p. 66.

76. Vnuk, 'Slovakia's Six Eventful Months', p. 90 and note 27.

77. Tiso, as cited in his 'Report to the Slovak Parliament' (14 March 1939) as reproduced in Murin, *Remembrances and Testimony*, p. 236.

78. Bartl *et al.*, *Slovak History*, p. 138; Vnuk, 'Slovakia's Six Eventful Months', p. 90; Jelinek, *The Parish Republic*, p. 27.

79. As cited in Ripka, *Munich*, p. 362.

80. G. Luciani, '*La Tchécoslovaquie après Munich*', *Le Temps* (2 March 1939), as cited in Procházka, *The Second Republic*, p. 63.

81. G. Kennan, 'Excerpts from Despatch of March 9, 1939, from Minister Carr to the Department of State, on Slovak-Czech relations' (portion drafted by George F. Kennan); 'Despatch on Slovak-Czech Relations (9 March 1939)' and 'Report on Conditions in Ruthenia' in Kennan, *From Prague after Munich*, pp. 75 and 69; Vnuk, 'Slovakia's Six Eventful Months', p. 106.

82. 'Despatch on Slovak-Czech Relations', as cited in Kennan, *From Prague after Munich*, pp. 78–79; Ripka, *Munich*, pp. 363–64.

83. G. Kennan, 'Personal Notes, dated 21 March 1939, on the March Crisis and the Final Occupation of Prague by the Germans' in Kennan, *From Prague after Munich*, pp. 81–82; Bell, *The Second World War in Europe*, p. 281; Mastny, *The Czechs under Nazi Rule*, p. 34.

84. Ripka, *Munich*, pp. 366–67.

85. Vnuk, 'Slovakia's Six Eventful Months', pp. 109–10; Ripka, *Munich*, p. 366.

86. Bartl *et al.*, *Slovak History*, p. 138; Lettrich, *History of Modern Slovakia*, pp. 124–26; Ripka, *Munich*, pp. 368–69.

87. N. Henderson, *Failure of a Mission: Berlin 1937–1939* (London, 1941 [1940]), p. 202; Mastny, *Czechs under Nazi Rule*, pp. 35–36.

88. Henderson, *Failure of a Mission*, p. 202; 'Personal Notes (21 March 1939)', in Kennan, *From Prague after Munich*, p. 81.

89. As cited in Vnuk, 'Slovakia's Six Eventful Months', p. 138.

90. Vnuk, 'Slovakia's Six Eventful Months', p. 115.

91. Tiso, *Jozef Tiso o sebe*, p. 186; J. Tiso, 'Dr. Tiso's Report to the Slovak Parliament' (14 March 1939), as reproduced in Murin, *Remembrances and Testimony*, pp. 233–39.

92. J. Kirschbaum, 'Facts and Events behind the Scenes of Slovakia's Declaration of Independence', *Slovakia* 9 (March 1959), p. 3, as cited in Jelinek, *The Parish Republic*, p. 30.

93. Vnuk, 'Slovakia's Six Eventful Months', p. 118; Tiso, 'Dr. Tiso's Report to the Slovak Parliament' (14 March 1939), as reproduced in Murin, *Remembrances and Testimony*, p. 238.

94. Winch, *Republic for a Day*, pp. 280–81.

95. '*Vládne nariadenie zo dňa 15. marca 1939 o priechodnom opatrení pôdy roľníkom-utečencom cestou nútenej krátkodobej árendy*' (15 March 1939); '*Vládne nariadenie zo dňa 18. marca 1939 o zriadení Penzijného ústavu súkromných úradníkov v Bratislave*'; '*Vyhláška ministra financií zo dňa 24. marca 1939, ktorou sa uverejňuje opatrenie Národnej banky Česko-Slovenskej, filiálky v Bratislave . . . o platebnom styku medzi Slovenským štátom a Nemeckou ríšou*', *Slovenský zákonník* (Bratislava, 1939), pp. 3, 15, 21–22.

96. Winch, *Republic for a Day*, pp. 281, 282–83.

97. Henderson, *Failure of a Mission*, pp. 207–8.

98. See his excellent television documentary *The Nazis: A Warning from History* (1997) as well as his many published works on the topic.

99. A. Hitler, 13 January 1942, as reported in *Hitler's Table Talk, 1941–1944*, tr. N. Cameron and R.H. Stevens, ed. H. Trevor-Roper (London, 2000 [1953]), p. 204; Mastny, *Czechs under Nazi Rule*, p. 51.

100. Mastny, *Czechs under Nazi Rule*, p. 41.

101. Ibid., pp. 45, 41.

102. G. Kennan, 'Excerpts from a Personal Letter of 30 March 1939', in Kennan, *From Prague after Munich*, p. 104.

103. As cited in Weisskopf, *The Agony of Czechoslovakia '38/'68*, p. 140.

104. Kennan, 'Personal Notes, dated March 21, 1939 . . .', in Kennan, *From Prague after Munich*, p. 87.

105. Henderson, *Failure of a Mission*, p. 206.

106. Mastny, *Czechs under Nazi Rule*, pp. 47–49.

107. *Lidové noviny*, vol. 47, no. 137 (16 March 1939), morning edition, p. 1.

108. E.V. Erdely, *Germany's First European Protectorate: The Fate of the Czechs and Slovaks* (London, 1941), p. 34.

CHAPTER 5: A REPUBLIC AND A PROTECTORATE

1. The full text of the agreement, which was written in German and Slovak and signed on 23 March 1939, was not included in the usual bulletin of Slovak law until 23 September 1940. See *Slovenský zákonník*, Law 226, '*Zmluva o ochrannom pomere medzi Nemeckou ríšou a Slovenským štátom/Vertrag über das Schutzverhältnis zwischen dem Deutschen Reich und dem Slowakischen Staat*' (23 September 1940), (Bratislava, 1940), pp. 363–64. An English translation of the full text can be found as the 'German-Slovak Treaty' (23 March 1939), reproduced in 'Report, written about May 1, 1939 on Conditions in Slovakia', in Kennan, *From Prague after Munich*, pp. 140–42.

2. Tiso was made president on 27 October 1939, at which point Vojtech Tuka took over as prime minister. Karol Sidor later claimed that the pope warned Tiso in July 1939, and several times

afterwards, that as a priest he ought not to accept the office of president of the Slovak state. K. Sidor, *Šesť rokov pri Vatikáne* (Scranton, Pa., 1947), pp. 61–63, 69, 84, 273–74.

3. See also Slovak Law 166, '*Zákon zo dňa 4. júla 1940 o Hlinkovej garde a Hlinkovej mládeži*' (6 July 1940); *Slovenský Zákonník* (Bratislava, 1940), pp. 253–56.

4. Ernest Druffel (25 March 1939), as cited in Vnuk, 'Slovakia's Six Eventful Months', p. 154.

5. Speech (16 March 1939), as cited in Tiso, *Dr Tiso o sebe*, p. 318.

6. This was Decree 32, '*Vládne nariadenie zo dňa 24. marca 1939 o zaisťovacom uväznení nepriateľov Slovenského štátu*' ('Government Decree of 24 March 1939 concerning the Detention of Enemies of the Slovak State'). An English translation appears as Document 20 in the appendix to a history of Slovakia written by one of the camp's first inmates. See Lettrich, *History of Modern Slovakia*, pp. 300–1.

7. Lettrich, *History of Modern Slovakia*, pp. 144–45. See also '*Prezídium ministerstva vnútra v Bratislave-Ústredňa štátnej bezpečnosti*', '*Rozvrh práce pre rok 1942*' (2 January 1942), ff. 1–9, as consulted at www.upn.gov.sk.

8. Paragraphs 1, 6, 7, 58 and 95 from Law 185, '*Ústavný zákon zo dňa 21. júla 1939 o ústave Slovenskej republiky*' (31 July 1939), *Slovenský zákonník* (Bratislava, 1939), pp. 375, 380, 185.

9. Novotný and Šimek, *Československé mince 1918–1993*, pp. 30, 32.

10. '*Slovensko nebolo fašistické*' in Tiso, *Tiso o sebe*, pp. 190–91.

11. Law 63, '*Vládne nariadenie zo dňa 18. apríla 1939 o vymedzení pojmu žida a usmernení počtu židov v niektorých slobodných povolaniach*' (20 April 1939), *Slovenský zákonník* (Bratislava, 1939), pp. 77–79.

12. Despatch on the new law limiting the rights and activities of Jews in Slovakia (10 May 1939), in Kennan, *From Prague after Munich*, pp. 149–56.

13. Law 36, '*Vládne nariadenie zo dňa 30. marca 1939 o zákaze výroby bohoslužobných a náboženských predmetov kresťanských nekresťanmi a obchode týmito*' (31 March 1939), *Slovenský zákonník* (Bratislava, 1939), p. 35. The law referred to 'non-Christians' in its title, but to 'Jews' in the text.

14. Laws 63, 74, 145, 147, 184, 150, 197 in *Slovenský zákonník* (Bratislava, 1939), pp. 77–79; 17 (26 April 1939), pp. 88–89; 32–44 (June–August 1939), pp. 288–301.

15. J. Gjuričová, *Na okraji: Romové jako objekt státní politiky* (Prague, 1999), p. 13.

16. Paragraphs 76, 87, 34, 42 and 53, Law 185, '*Ústavný zákon zo dňa 21. júla 1939 o ústave Slovenskej republiky*' (31 July 1939), *Slovenský zákonník* (Bratislava, 1939), pp. 382, 383, 378, 379, 380.

17. Paragraphs 88 and 90, Law 185 '*Ústavný zákon zo dňa 21. júla 1939 o ústave Slovenskej republiky*', ibid., p. 383.

18. Paragraphs 60 and 62, Law 185 '*Ústavný zákon zo dňa 21. júla 1939 o ústave Slovenskej republiky*', ibid., pp. 380–81.

19. Article 1, *Erlaß des Führers und Reichskanzlers über das Protektorat Böhmen und Mähren von 16. März 1939/Výnos Vůdce a říšského kancléře ze dne 16. března 1939 o Protektorátu Čechy a Morava*, *Sbírka zákonů a nařízení* (Prague, 1939), p. 373 (German version); p. 375 (Czech version).

20. C. Bryant, *Prague in Black: Nazi Rule and Czech Nationalism* (Cambridge, Mass., 2007), p. 52.

21. Articles 3 and 5, *Erlaß des Führers und Reichskanzlers*, pp. 373–74 (German version); p. 375 (Czech version).

22. This paragraph is heavily indebted to Bryant, *Prague in Black*, pp. 45–50.

23. 'Report of 29 March 1939 on the New Regime in Bohemia and Moravia', in Kennan, *From Prague after Munich*, pp. 99–101; 'Adolf Hrubý', *Kdo byl kdo v našich dějinách ve 20. století* (Prague, 1998), vol. 1, p. 246; *Kronika Českých zemí* (Prague, 1999), p. 697.

24. As cited in King, *Budweisers into Czechs and Germans*, p. 179.

25. 'Letter of May 11, 1939, from Consul General Linnell to the Chargé d'Affaires at Berlin, concerning the Political Situation in Bohemia', in Kennan, *From Prague after Munich*, pp. 157–58; Bryant, *Prague in Black*, p. 45.

26. R. Luža, *The Transfer of the Sudeten Germans* (New York, 1964), pp. 214–15.

27. 'Letter of May 11, 1939, from Consul General Linnell to the Chargé d'Affaires at Berlin, concerning the Political Situation in Bohemia', in Kennan, *From Prague after Munich*, pp. 157–59.

28. See e.g. A. Hitler, *Mein Kampf*, tr. R. Manheim (London, 1992 [1943]), pp. 99, 110, 118.

29. Luža, *The Transfer of the Sudeten Germans*, p. 205, note 1.

30. I. Linnell, 'Despatch of 6 June 1939, from Consul General Linnell to the Department of State, concerning the Situation in Bohemia and Moravia', in Kennan, *From Prague after Munich*, p. 182.

31. C. Nečas, *The Holocaust of Czech Roma*, tr. Šimon Pellar (Prague, 1999), p. 41.

32. These were Decrees 14, '*Vládní nařízení ze dne 27. ledna 1939, jímž se doplňují předpisy o pobytu cizinců, pokud jsou emigranty*', and 15, '*Vládní nařízení ze dne 27. ledna 1939 o přezkoumání česko-slovenského státního občanství některých osob*', *Sbírka zákonů a nařízení státu česko-slovenského* (Prague, 1939), pp. 39–42.

33. Government Decree 136, '*Vládní nařízení ze dne 4. července o právním postavení židů ve veřejném životě*' (4 June 1939), as published in *Sbírka zákonů a nařízení Protektorátu Čechy a Morava* (Prague, 1940), paragraphs 1a and b (24 April 1940), p. 337.

34. Linnell, 'Despatch of July 3, 1939, from Consul General Linnell to the Department of State, on General Conditions in Bohemia and Moravia', in Kennan, *From Prague after Munich*, p. 189.

35. The fine detail and chronology of the legal restrictions to which Jews in the Protectorate were subjected have been carefully traced and published as H. Petrův, *Právní postavení židů v Protektorátu Čechy a Morava*, 2 vols (Prague, 2000; 2007). The surviving diary of a young Jewish boy, growing up in the eastern Bohemian town of Hradec Králové until his family's transportation in 1942, first to Theresienstadt and then to Auschwitz, gives a good sense of the noose tightening. See J. Münzer, *Dospívání nad propastí: Deník Jiřího Münzera* (Prague, 2002).

36. Linnell, 'Despatch of August 19, 1939, from Consul General Linnell to the Department of State, on the General Trend of Developments in Bohemia and Moravia', in Kennan, *From Prague after Munich*, p. 220.

37. S. Grant Duff, *A German Protectorate: The Czechs under Nazi Rule* (London, 1942), p. 84; Linnell, 'Despatch of June 6, 1939 . . .', in Kennan, *From Prague after Munich*, p. 181.

38. Linnell, 'Despatch of August 19, 1939 . . .', in Kennan, *From Prague after Munich*, p. 224.

39. As cited in Zeman and Klimek, *Life of Edvard Beneš*, p. 149.

40. E. Beneš, *Paměti: Od Mnichova k nové válce a k novému vítězství*, 3rd edn (Prague, 1948), p. 116.

41. Luža, *The Transfer of the Sudeten Germans*, pp. 226–27.

42. Zeman and Klimek, *Life of Edvard Beneš*, pp. 155–60.

43. N. Davies, *Europe at War, 1939–1945: No Simple Victory* (Basingstoke, 2006), pp. 306–7.

44. Suda, *Zealots and Rebels*, pp. 161–62.

45. *Benešův Archiv*, 2SV, box 36, as cited in Zeman and Klimek, *Life of Edvard Beneš*, p. 160.

46. Law 222 (18 September 1939), in *Sbírka zákonů a nařízení* (Prague, 1939), pp. 717–19.

47. Decrees 242, '*Vládní nařízení ze dne 27. září 1939 o chování v silniční dopravě (dopravní řád silniční – d.ř.s.)*', and 243, '*Vládní nařízení ze dne 27. září 1939 o připuštění osob a vozidel k dopravě na silnicích (řád o připuštění k silniční dopravě – ř.p.s.d.)*', *Sbírka zákonů a nařízení*, (Prague, 1939), pp. 767–804, 804–27.

48. Laws 211, 212, 213, 214 (29 September 1939), *Sbírka zákonů a nařízení* (Prague, 1939), pp. 686–702; Law 225, ibid., pp. 723–31.

49. Grant Duff, *A German Protectorate*, pp. 241–42.

50. Lettrich, *History of Modern Slovakia*, p. 161; Mastny, *The Czechs under Nazi Rule*, p. 108.

51. Mastny, *The Czechs under Nazi Rule*, p. 111; Grant Duff, *A German Protectorate*, pp. 87–88.

52. J. Masaryk, '*Svátek svobody*' (28 October 1939), in J. Masaryk, *Volá Londýn* (Prague, 1948), p. 17.

53. Mastny, *The Czechs under Nazi Rule*, p. 111; Grant Duff, *A German Protectorate*, pp. 87–89; Kennan, 'Report, written October 1940, on a Year and a Half of the Protectorate of Bohemia and Moravia', in Kennan, *From Prague after Munich*, p. 233; Luža, *The Transfer of the Sudeten Germans*, p. 206, note 8.

54. Letter to R.W. Seton-Watson (24 January 1940), in J. Rychlík, T. Marzik and M. Bielik, *R.W. Seton-Watson and his Relations with the Czechs and Slovaks: Documents, 1906–1951*, vol. 1 (Martin, 1995), p. 577.

55. Luža, *The Transfer of the Sudeten Germans*, p. 215.

56. As cited in Mastny, *The Czechs under Nazi Rule*, p. 121.

57. As cited in Bryant, *Prague in Black*, pp. 220–21.

58. See Law 20: '*Branný zákon Slovenskej republiky zo dňa 18. januára 1940*' (31 January 1940) *Slovenský zákonník* (Bratislava, 1940), pp. 21ff. Decree 40, '*Nariadenie o odškodnení židov, prepustených zo štátnych a verejných služieb*' (1 March 1940) *Slovenský zákonník* (Bratislava, 1940); Law 113, '*Zákon zo dňa 25. apríla 1940 o židovských podnikoch a o židoch zamestnaných v podnikoch*' (17 May 1940) *Slovenský zákonník* (Bratislava, 1940), *čiastka* 22 (17 May 1940), pp. 163–70.

59. Law 130, '*Nariadenie s mocou zákona zo dňa 29. mája 1940 o dočasnej úprave pracovnej povinnosti Židov a Cigánov*', and Decree 127, '*Vyhláška ministerstva národnej obrany zo dňa 22. mája 1940*' (10 June 1940) *Slovenský zákonník* (Bratislava, 1940), pp. 206, 201–2.

60. '*Pamät' národa*' (Bratislava, 2005), p. 12; M. Husová, 'Uncovering the Past', *Transactions Online* issue no. 01/31/2006 as accessed at http://www.ceeol.com/aspx/issuedetails.aspx?issueid=accb6193-786b-4bd7-ba8b-82e (30 January 2006).

61. J. Masaryk, '*Uznání československého národního výboru britskou vládou – československá armáda ve Velké Británii*' (22 December 1939) in Masaryk, *Volá Londýn*, pp. 20–21; Zeman and Klimek, *Life of Edvard Beneš*, pp. 162–65.

62. Speech to the British Royal Society (22 January 1940), as cited in M. Cornwall, 'Dr Edvard Beneš and Czechoslovakia's German Minority, 1918–1943' in J. Morison, ed., *The Czech and Slovak Experience* (New York, 1992), p. 188.

63. K. Wallace, 'Edvard Beneš and the Sudeten German Expulsions, 1938–1945' (unpublished University of Strathclyde undergraduate dissertation, 1999), ff. 21, 22.

64. Bryant, *Prague in Black*, p. 102.

65. Ibid., pp. 76–77.

66. As cited in ibid., p. 117.

67. Grant Duff, *A German Protectorate*, pp. 198–99.

68. Constitutional Law 210, *'Ústavný zákon zo dňa 3. septembra 1940 ktorým sa vláda splnomocňuje, aby činila opatrenia vo veciach arizácie'* (3 September 1940), *Slovenský zákonník* (11 September 1940), p. 343; Decree 271, *'Nariadenie o židovských viazaných účtoch a úschovách'* (18 October 1940), *Slovenský zákonník*, (24 October 1940), p. 428.

69. Kennan, 'Report on a Year and a Half of the Protectorate of Bohemia and Moravia (October 1940)', in Kennan, *From Prague After Munich*, pp. 227, 237.

70. Ibid., pp. 237–38.

71. From a speech of 25 May 1940, as cited in Lettrich, *History of Modern Slovakia*, p. 153.

72. D. Kováč, *Dějiny Slovenska*, tr. E. Charous (Prague, 1998; 2002), p. 222.

73. For the details, see Suda, *Zealots and Rebels*, pp. 164–65.

74. B. Frommer, *National Cleansing: Retribution against Nazi Collaborators in Postwar Czechoslovakia* (Cambridge, 2005), p. 137.

75. Bryant, *Prague in Black*, pp. 84–86.

76. Kováč, *Dějiny Slovenska*, p. 220.

77. MacDonald, *The Killing*, p. 71.

78. At the end of July 1940, Royal Air Force (RAF) squadron 311 was formed in Suffolk out of Czech Air Force personnel who had been serving in France; another Czech contingent, squadron 313, was created at Catterick in May 1941.

79. MacDonald, p. 94.

80. Zeman and Klimek, *Life of Edvard Beneš*, pp. 178, 180.

81. B. Dmytryshyn, 'The Legal Framework for the Sovietization of Czechoslovakia 1941–1945', *Nationalities Papers* 25:2 (1997), p. 257.

82. Zeman and Klimek, *Life of Edvard Beneš*, p. 181.

83. Decree 198, *'Nariadenie zo dňa 9. septembra 1941 o právnom postavení Židov'* (10 September 1941), *Slovenský zákonník* (Bratislava, 1941), pp. 643–84; Mannová, *Concise History of Slovakia*, p. 264; H. Petrův, *Právní postavení židů v Protektorátu Čechy a Morava*, 2 vols (Prague, 2000; 2007), p. 162 and note 204; Lettrich, *History of Modern Slovakia*, p. 179.

84. Speech (2 October 1941), as summarized in Mastny, *The Czechs under Nazi Rule*, pp. 185–86.

85. Speech (4 February 1942), as cited in ibid., p. 193.

86. Bryant, *Prague in Black*, p. 143.

87. Moravec, *Master of Spies*, p. 209.

88. Mastny, *The Czechs under Nazi Rule*, p. 189.

89. MacDonald, *The Killing*, p. 121.

90. Bryant, *Prague in Black*, p. 149.

91. M. Clarke, 'Prisoner of Paradise', BBC Four, *Storyville* series, ed. Nick Fraser, 2003.

92. The text of this report, also known as the 'Vrba Report' and 'The Auschwitz Protocols', together with an account of how the two Slovak Jews – Rudolf Vrba and Alfred Wetzler – made their escape, may be found in Vrba, *I Escaped from Auschwitz*.

93. Schwitzer, *Slovakia*, p. 120

94. Ibid., p. 121.

95. Ibid., pp. 121–22.

96. Bryant, *Prague in Black*, pp. 160–61.

97. Ibid., p. 5; King, *Budweisers into Czechs and Germans*, pp. 179–82.

98. Moravec, *Master of Spies*, p. 210.

99. See MacDonald, *The Killing*.

100. The message is kept on permanent display as part of the *Národní památník obětí heydrichiády* (National Monument to the Victims of the Heydrich Reprisals) held in the crypt of the Orthodox church of SS Cyril and Methodius in Prague.

101. Reports differ as to the exact time and causes of death. See MacDonald, *The Killing*, p. 181 and notes to permanent exhibition in the crypt of the church of SS Cyril and Methodius, Prague.

102. See J. Čvančara, *Heydrich* (České Budějovice, 2004), p. 86; notes to permanent exhibition in the crypt of the church of SS Cyril and Methodius, Prague; report signed by R.H. Bruce Lockhart (undated) attached to 'Most Secret Memo from D/CD(O) to C.D. re: meeting between MX and Colonel Moravec' (30 December 1942), HS 4/1 58385, unpaginated [f.1], Public Record Office, Kew; Moravec, *Master of Spies*, p. 211; E. Beneš, *Paměti: Od Mnichova k nové válce a k novému vítězství* (Prague, 1948), *passim*.

103. Luža, *The Transfer of the Sudeten Germans*, pp. 210–11.

104. MacDonald, *The Killing*, pp. 178–79.

105. Ibid., pp. 178–81.

106. Ibid., pp. 180–81.

107. Reports differ in slight details. The most accurate seems to be that to be found in Čvančara, *Heydrich*, p. 205.

108. MacDonald, *The Killing*, p. 189.
109. Luža, *The Transfer of the Sudeten Germans*, p. 210, note 27.
110. Ibid., p. 211
111. Fučík became the foremost symbol of specifically Czech Communist martyrdom after the war. The published version of his *Notes from the Gallows*, every bit as well known in postwar Czechoslovakia as *The Diary of Anne Frank* was in the West, ended with the famous words: '*Lidé, měl jsem Vás rád. Bděte!*' or 'People, I have loved you. Be vigilant!' J. Fučík, *Reportáž psaná na oprátce* (Most, 1994), pp. 43–48, 184. See also G. Fučíková, *Julius Fučík ve fotografii* (Prague, 1977), p. 7.
112. Davies, *Europe at War, 1939–1945*, p. 172.
113. Bryant, *Prague in Black*, p. 182.
114. As cited in Frommer, *National Cleansing*, pp. 69–70.
115. The full text of the treaty, in English translation, may be found in Beneš, *Memoirs of Dr. Eduard Beneš*, pp. 255–57. See also ibid., p. 287, note 5.
116. As cited in Dmytryshyn, 'The Legal Framework for the Sovietization of Czechoslovakia 1941–1945', p. 259.
117. Lettrich, *History of Modern Slovakia*, p. 198. The text of the Christmas Agreement may be found as Appendix VI in J. Mikus, *Slovakia: A Political History 1918–1955* (Milwaulkee, 1963), pp. 346–47 and as Document 26 in Lettrich, *History of Modern Slovakia*, pp. 303–5.
118. As cited in Lettrich, *History of Modern Slovakia*, p. 304.
119. 'Declaration of the Slovak National Council in Banská Bystrica, September 1, 1944', as reproduced in ibid., p. 305.
120. 'Agreement on the Founding of an Underground Slovak National Council Announced at Christmas, 1943', as reproduced in ibid., p. 306.
121. Public Record Office, Kew, 'The Slovak Rising: Report on a Discussion with General Golian at Tri Duby, Slovakia, on October 7th, 1944', HS 4/1 (23 October 1944), ff. 4–5.
122. Lettrich, *History of Modern Slovakia*, pp. 210, 223–24.
123. Mannová, *A Concise History of Slovakia*, pp. 268–71.
124. Decree 18/1944, as cited in Frommer, *National Cleansing*, p. 46. The reader may recall that National Committees had been used during the Czecho-Slovak revolution of 1918–20 and again (exclusively in Slovakia) during the Second Czecho-Slovak Republic.
125. Public Record Office, Kew, Top Secret report no. 4 from Northern Department re: 'Czechoslovakia: the Russians in Ruthenia' (12 January 1945), HS 4/11, f. 1.
126. *Masarykův ústav AV ČR, Benešův archiv*, EB II, 350, *Koš* 1/1, '*čs. Vládní fronty. Programové dokumenty vlády Národní fronty. Návrhy březen 1945*', K. Gottwald, '*Návrh programu nové československé vlády národní fronty Čechů a Slováků*' (Moscow, 21 March 1945), f. 13; Z. Fierlinger *et al.*, *Košický vládní program: Program nové československé vlády Národní fronty Čechů a Slováků* (Prague, 1974 [Košice, 1945]), p. 17.
127. As cited in B. Abrams, 'The Politics of Retribution: The Trial of Jozef Tiso', *East European Politics and Societies* 10:2 (1996), p. 270.
128. As cited in Lettrich, *History of Modern Slovakia*, p. 226.
129. Fierlinger *et al.*, *Košický vládní program*, paragraph viii, p. 19.
130. Ibid., paragraph viii, pp. 19, 33.
131. E. Steiner, *The Slovak Dilemma* (Cambridge, 1974), pp. 78–79.
132. 'The Relation between the Czechs and Slovaks Stated in the Program of the First Government of the National Front of the Czechs and the Slovaks, Promulgated in Košice April 5, 1945', as translated into English and reproduced in full as Document 41 in Lettrich, *History of Modern Slovakia* (London, 1956), p. 317.
133. Ibid., pp. 317–18.
134. Ibid., p. 318.
135. M. Otáhal, 'Czechoslovakia behind the Iron Curtain' in M. Teich, ed., *Bohemia in History* (Cambridge, 1998), p. 309.
136. As cited in Frommer, *National Cleansing*, p. 51.
137. Luža, *The Transfer of the Sudeten Germans*, 259–60.
138. Public Record Office, Kew, Report re: 'The Czech Rising: History of Events 30th April–9th May 1945' (16 May 1945), HS 4/7, f. 4.

CHAPTER 6: FROM NATIONAL CLEANSING TO COMMUNIST DICTATORSHIP

1. King, *Budweisers into Czechs and Germans*, p. 191.
2. Public Record Office, Kew, Report re: 'The Czech Rising: History of Events 30th April–9th May 1945' (16 May 1945), HS 4/7, f. 8 (internal pagination, 3).

3. Although the exact figures can never be known, somewhere between 66 and 89 per cent of the Jewish population of Bohemia-Moravia and between 78 and 83 per cent of the Jewish population of Slovakia had not survived the persecution that began at the hands of the Slovak and Czech authorities and usually ended in German-run concentration and death camps. These percentages are based on official figures of 118,310 Jews living in the Protectorate and 88,950 in Slovakia as of March 1939, with recorded losses, by the end of the war, of 78,150 Czech Jews and between 68,000 and 71,000 Slovak Jews. I. Gutman, ed., *The Encyclopedia of the Holocaust*, 4 vols (New York, 1990). As discussed in Chapter 4 of this work, the criteria for categorizing someone as a Jew, which never followed Jewish law, were initially different in Bohemia-Moravia and in Slovakia. Over time, as discussed in Chapter 5, legal definitions in both polities were brought into closer conformity with the Nazi German model.

4. E. Benda, 'From Prague to Theresienstadt and Back', in *And Life Is Changed Forever: Holocaust Childhoods Remembered*, ed. M. Glassner and R. Krell (Detroit, Mich., 2006), p. 266.

5. See e.g. H.M. Kovály, *Under a Cruel Star: A Life in Prague 1941–1968* (Cambridge, Mass., 1986), p. 47; Benda, 'From Prague to Theresienstadt', pp. 266–67; interview with Sr Anna Magdaléna Schwarzová in J. Štern, documentary series '*Ztracená duše národa*', no. 6, '*Ztráta víry*', directed by Olga Sommerová (Česká televize/Vision, 2001).

6. E. Benda [*née* Blochová], unpublished reminiscences, 1939–48, f. 40.

7. The figure of 5 per cent comes from Kenety, 'The "Devouring"' and the figure of 12 per cent from G. Lewy, *The Persecution of the Gypsies* (Oxford, 2000), p. 190.

8. Antonín Novotný spent 1941–45 at Mauthausen concentration (later, extermination) camp; Antonín Zápotocký, who had already served time during the 1920s, was jailed for the whole of the period 1939–45, first in Czech prisons (Pankrác and Drážďany) and then in Sachsenhausen-Oranienburg concentration camp.

9. J. Korbel, *Twentieth-Century Czechoslovakia: The Meanings of its History* (New York, 1977), p. 223; V. Kusin, *The Intellectual Origins of the Prague Spring* (Cambridge, 1971), p. 4.

10. G. Wightman and A.H. Brown, 'Changes in the Levels of Membership and Social Composition of the Communist Party of Czechoslovakia, 1945–73', *Soviet Studies* 27:3 (July 1975), pp. 396–97.

11. Ibid., p. 397.

12. M. Blaive, 'The Czechs and their Communism, Past and Present', *Inquiries into Past and Present*, ed. D. Gard, I. Main, M. Oliver and J. Wood (Vienna, 2005), as consulted (01/01/2009) online at http://www.iwm.at/index.php?option=com_content&task=viw&id=293&Itemid=276, p. 3. J. Spurný, 'Jeden za všechny ...', *Respekt* 9 (9 May 1990) and *Lidové noviny* (27 September 1997), as cited in K. Williams and D. Deletant, *Security Intelligence Services in New Democracies: The Czech Republic, Slovakia and Romania* (Houndmills, Basingstoke, 2001), note 28, p. 50; Steiner, *The Slovak Dilemma*, p. 80.

13. For a fascinating discussion of the importance of the postwar age structure in Czechoslovakia, see B. Abrams, *The Struggle for the Soul of the Nation* (Lanham, Md., 2004 [2005]), pp. 32–34.

14. Z. Mlynář, *Night Frost in Prague: The End of Humane Socialism*, tr. P. Wilson (London, 1980), p. 3.

15. Suda, *Zealots and Rebels*, p. 233; Blaive, 'The Czechs and their Communism, Past and Present', p. 3.

16. Kovály, *Under a Cruel Star*, pp. 46–47.

17. Ibid., p. 53.

18. R. Kavan, *Love and Freedom* (London, 1985; 1988), p. 38.

19. Decree 1 (14 May 1945), *Úřední list* 26 (Prague, 15 May 1945), pp. v–vi.

20. These were Decrees 109–21, 124–28, 131–33, 135, 137–38, 143 (27 October 1945), *Sbírka zákonů a nařízení* (Prague, 1945), pp. 255–342.

21. *Úřední list* 26 (Prague, 15 May 1945), *passim*; *Sbírka zákonů a nařízení* (Prague, 1945), *passim*.

22. *Úřední list* 26 (Prague, 15 May 1945), p. v.

23. Frommer, *National Cleansing*, p. 55 and note 78.

24. N. Martin, *Prague Winter* (London, 1990), p. 215.

25. Kavan, *Love and Freedom*, p. 12.

26. See Chapter 4 of this work for the prewar techniques that were used to expel Jews (especially German Jews) from Bohemia-Moravia, and Czechs, Jews and Gypsies from Slovakia.

27. As cited in Frommer, *National Cleansing*, p. 42.

28. No. 9, '*Dekret presidenta republiky o neplatnosti některých majetkově-právních jednání z doby nesvobody a o národ. správě majetkových hodnot Němců, Maďarů, zrádců a kolaborantů a některých organisací a ústavů*' (19 May 1945), *Sbírka zákonů a nařízení* (Prague, 1945), p. 13.

29. Frommer, *National Cleansing*, p. 63.

30. As cited in ibid., pp. 51–52.

31. Ibid., p. 50.

32. From a speech of 1 July 1945, as cited in Glassheim, *Noble Nationalists*, p. 211.

33. No. 186, '*Zmluva medzi Československou republikou a Zväzom sovietskych socialistických republík o Zakarpatskej Ukrajine*' (29 June 1945), and no. 2, '*Ústavný zákon o Zakarpatskej Ukrajine a úprave štátnych hraníc so Sväzom sovietskych socialistických republík*' (22 November 1945), *Sbírka zákonů a nařízení* (Prague, 1945), pp. 1175 and 121. The population figures are from Lettrich, *History of Modern Slovakia*, p. 230.

34. Decree 33/1945, Collection of Decrees of the Slovak National Council, amended by Decree 57/1946 (14 May 1946), as cited in Lettrich, *History of Modern Slovakia*, p. 243. The equivalent Czech retribution law, commonly known as the Great Decree (Decree 16/1945), was not to be signed into law until 19 June and not finally made public, together with another decree (no. 17) which established a National Court in Prague, until 9 July 1945. Frommer, *National Cleansing*, p. 77.

35. Bartl *et al.*, *Slovak History*, p. 257.

36. The government passed the order (17 May 1945) to give Germans the same starvation rations that Jews had received; the restriction remained in force until April 1947. Special rations were given to children and to 'heavy manual workers' and, in September 1946, 'German specialists and their families' became entitled to the same rations as Czechs. Luža, *The Transfer of the Sudeten Germans*, p. 269, note 11.

37. Martin, *Prague Winter*, pp. 218–19.

38. Luža, *The Transfer of the Sudeten Germans*, pp. 269–70.

39. '*Kdy zahájí činnost Lidové soudy?*', *Mladá fronta* (15 June 1945), p. 1 and '*Co je vlastně KVNB*', *Mladá fronta* (22 June 1945), p. 2 as cited in Frommer, *National Cleansing*, p. 53.

40. Frommer, *National Cleansing*, pp. 56–57.

41. This was on 16 June 1945. Luža, *The Transfer of the Sudeten Germans*, p. 273, note 31.

42. No. 12, '*Dekret presidenta republiky o konfiskaci a urychleném rozdělení zemědělského majetku Němců, Maďarů, jakož i zrádců a nepřátel českého a slovenského národa*' (21 June 1945), *Sbírka zákonů a nařízení* (Prague, 1945), p. 17.

43. Luža, *The Transfer of the Sudeten Germans*, p. 275.

44. Accounts of the infamous incident vary considerably. A serious history written by local Czechs estimates the number of dead at between 80 and 100; Sudeten German societies, calling it the 'Sudeten Lidice', have put the figure much higher, at well over 400. See K. Kaiserová and V. Kaiser, eds, *Dějiny města Ústí nad Labem* (Ústí nad Labem, 1995), p. 227.

45. No. 28, '*Dekret presidenta republiky o osídlení zemědělské půdy Němců, Maďarů a jiných nepřátel státu českými, slovenskými a jinými slovanskými zemědělci*' (20 July 1945), *Sbírka zákonů a nařízení* (Prague, 1945), pp. 47–48.

46. J. Sejna, *We Will Bury You* (London, 1982), pp. 16–18.

47. See also I. Lukes, 'The Birth of a Police State: The Czechoslovak Ministry of the Interior, 1945–48', *Intelligence and National Security* 11: 1 (1996), pp. 79–86. Williams and Deletant, *Security Intelligence Services*, p. 27.

48. No. 16, '*Dekret presidenta republiky o potrestání nacistických zločinců, zrádců a jejich pomahačů a o mimořádných lidových soudech*' (19 June 1945), *Sbírka zákonů a nařízení* (Prague, 1945), p. 25.

49. Frommer, *National Cleansing*, p. 97.

50. Figures taken from Frommer, *National Cleansing*, p. 34. A much earlier collection of documents edited by Theodore Schieder put the figures at approximately 700,000 expelled, 300,000 fled and 30,000 killed or died in concentration camps in 1945. See T. Schieder, ed., *Documents on the Expulsion of the Germans from Eastern-Central-Europe*, vol. 4 (Bonn, Federal Ministry for Expellees, Refugees, and War Victims, 1960), p. 127. Tomáš Staněk, the foremost historian of the immediate postwar wave of persecutions, suggests that in August 1945 there were more than 69,000 prisoners, including 8,275 persons classified as Czechs, being held against their will in Bohemia alone; while Benjamin Frommer, the first to bring the full horror of the 'transfer' to the attention of an English-speaking readership, has found a Ministry of the Interior report citing 221 internment camps in Bohemia and Moravia alone by November 1945. Staněk, *Tábory*, p. 46; Frommer, *National Cleansing*, pp. 53–54.

51. Frommer, *National Cleansing*, pp. 121, 113. In May 1946, a year after liberation, things were still so bad that the authorities in Mariánské Lázně (*Marienbad*) felt obliged to complain to the minister of justice, Prokop Drtina, that the constant stream of public executions was scaring off tourists, who came to the spa town to relax. Frommer, *National Cleansing*, p. 100.

52. Lettrich, *History of Modern Slovakia*, p. 243.

53. Abrams, 'The Politics of Retribution', p. 244.

54. Frommer, *National Cleansing*, p. 321.

55. No. 33, '*Ústavní dekret presidenta republiky o úpravě československého státního občanství osob národnosti německé a maďarské*' (2 August 1945), *Sbírka zákonů a nařízení* (Prague, 1945), pp. 57–58. The earlier Czecho-Slovak law (Law 15), which was decreed on 27 January 1939, some seven weeks before the Nazi occupation of 15 March 1939, is discussed in Chapter 4 of this work. After detailed consideration of the claims and counter-claims made by spokesmen for the ethnic Czechs and ethnic Germans,

Radomír Luža put the figure at about 3,400,400, i.e. approximately 100,000 fewer than being claimed by some Sudeten German scholars. Luža, *The Transfer of the Sudeten Germans*, p. 300.

56. Frommer, *National Cleansing*, p. 90.

57. *Masarykův ústav AV ČR, Benešův archiv*, EB III, '*Transfery obyvatelstva (odsun Němců, repatriace čs. občanů*'), 44, P44/3, Nosek and Kučera to Beneš (15 November 1946), ff. 1–4.

58. *Masarykův ústav AV ČR, Benešův archiv*, EB III, '*Transfery obyvatelstva (odsun Němců, repatriace čs. občanů*'), 44, P44/2, Ministerstvo vnitra, '*Směrnice k provádění soustavného odsunu (transferu) Němců z území Československé republiky*', ff. 1–2.

59. Ibid., ff. 4–5.

60. Ibid., f. 6.

61. V. Gollancz, *Our Threatened Values* (London, 1946), p. 97, as cited in K. Wallace, 'Edvard Beneš and the Expulsion of the Sudeten Germans, 1938–1945' (University of Strathclyde unpublished undergraduate dissertation, 1999), f. 1.

62. *Archiv Ministerstva vnitra České republiky*, Regional *SNB* reports (Pardubice 1945–46), 304-182-3, f. 14, Confidential report from regional *SNB* chief in Pardubice to the *SNB* central office in Prague (15 July 1946).

63. The most prominent German and Czech war criminals escaped justice altogether: Konrad Henlein killed himself in his prison camp at Plzeň on 10 May 1945; Emil Hácha died in the prison hospital at Pankrác on 27 June 1945 and – on orders from the Ministry of the Interior – was buried in an unmarked grave at Vinohrady cemetery in Prague. Even Konstantin von Neurath, although eventually brought before the international military tribunal at Nuremberg and found guilty of crimes against humanity, was sentenced to just fifteen years; as things turned out, he was released, on medical grounds, in 1954. See 'Moravec, Emanuel', 'Hácha, Emil', 'Frank, Karl Hermann', in Churaň *et al.*, *Kdo byl kdo v našich dějinách ve 20. století*, vol. 1, pp. 460, 160, 190; 'Neurath, Konstantin von', in ibid., vol. 2, p. 22.

64. Frommer, *National Cleansing*, pp. 233–34.

65. The motto *Arbeit macht frei*, originally taken from Hegel but made infamous through its use at Auschwitz and other SS-run forced-labour and extermination camps, was translated into Czech as *Prací ke svobodě*. See photographs and notes from the permanent exhibition at the museum Památník Vojna u Příbrami (pobočka Hornického muzea Příbram), Lešetice 43, Milín.

66. *Masarykův ústav AV ČR, Benešův archiv*, EB III, '*Transfery obyvatelstva (odsun Němců, repatriace čs. občanů*'), 44, P44/3, Nosek and Kučera to Beneš (15 November 1946), ff. 1–4.

67. *Masarykův ústav AV ČR, Benešův archiv*, EB III, '*Slovensko 1945*', 60, '*Výmena obyvateľstva medzi Československom a Maďarskom a repatriovanie Slovákov z Juhoslávie [sic], Rumunska a Bulharska*', ff. 1–35.

68. *Masarykův ústav AV ČR, Benešův archiv*, EB III, '*Slovensko 1945*', 60, P60/1, '*Návrhy*' (13 September 1947) and covering letter from the head of the Re-Slovakization Commission in Bratislava to V. Clementis c/o Ministry of Foreign Affairs in Prague, ff. 1–8.

69. Mannová, *A Concise History of Slovakia*, p. 276.

70. Steiner, *The Slovak Dilemma*, pp. 94–95.

71. Other formerly Hungarian towns were renamed 'Hviezdoslavovo' and 'Bernolákovo' after Slovak national heroes. Ibid., p. 96.

72. Ibid., p. 97.

73. Luža, *The Transfer of the Sudeten Germans*, pp. 271–72.

74. See, for example, the evocative 'before' and 'after' photographs of Sudeten German landscapes collected for the Forestry Commission by '*Antikomplex a kolektiv*' in *Proměny sudetské krajiny* (Nakladatelství Českého lesa, n.p., 2006).

75. On distortions in the first Czechoslovak census, see Chapter 3 of this work. Information on the 1950 census is taken from C.S. Leff, *National Conflict in Czechoslovakia: The Making and Remaking of a State, 1918–1987* (Princeton, N.J., 1988), p. 93.

76. K. Kaplan, *The Short March: The Communist Takeover in Czechoslovakia 1945–1948* (New York, 1987 [1981]), p. 56 and note 3, pp. 63–64.

77. Abrams, 'The Politics of Retribution', pp. 263–64. See also V. Prečan, *Slovenský katolicismus pred Februárom 1948* (Bratislava, 1961), *passim*.

78. Abrams, 'The Politics of Retribution', pp. 263–65; Lettrich, *History of Modern Slovakia*, p. 244.

79. Kaplan, *The Short March*, p. 56 and note, pp. 63–64.

80. Beneš, *Memoirs of Dr Eduard Beneš*, pp. 284–85.

81. Kaplan, *The Short March*, p. 57.

82. K. Kaplan, 'Czechoslovakia's February 1948' in N. Stone and E. Strouhal, eds, *Czechoslovakia: Crossroads and Crises, 1918–1988* (Houndmills, Basingstoke, 1989), p. 150.

83. H. Pollitt, *In Memory of Joseph Stalin and Klement Gottwald* (London, n.d. [1953]), p. 15.

84. Kaplan, 'Czechoslovakia's February 1948', p. 150.

85. Mannová, *Concise History of Slovakia*, p. 275.
86. Steiner, *The Slovak Dilemma*, p. 81.
87. Lettrich, *History of Modern Slovakia*, p. 241.
88. Kaplan, *The Short March*, p. 59.
89. Abrams, 'The Politics of Retribution', pp. 267, 269.
90. As cited in ibid., p. 271.
91. Ibid., pp. 272–73.
92. Lettrich, *History of Modern Slovakia*, p. 245.
93. Steiner, *The Slovak Dilemma*, p. 81.
94. Abrams, 'The Politics of Retribution', p. 279.
95. Ibid., p. 276.
96. Lettrich, *History of Modern Slovakia*, p. 247.
97. Ibid., p. 249; Bartl *et al.*, *Slovak History*, p. 1947; J. Bloomfield, *Passive Revolution: Politics and the Czechoslovak Working Class 1945–1948* (New York, 1979), p. 191.
98. Steiner, *The Slovak Dilemma*, p. 85.
99. Kaplan, 'Czechoslovakia's February 1948', p. 158; Mannová, *Concise History of Slovakia*, p. 277; Bartl *et al.*, *Slovak History*, p. 1947; Steiner, *The Slovak Dilemma*, p. 87.
100. As cited in Lettrich, *History of Modern Slovakia*, p. 253.
101. V. Kusin, *The Intellectual Origins of the Prague Spring: The Development of Reformist Ideas in Czechoslovakia* (Cambridge, 1971), p. 11.
102. J.-P. Rageau, *Prague 48: Le rideau de fer s'est abattu* (Bruxelles, 1981), p. 45.
103. Lettrich, *History of Modern Slovakia*, pp. 259–60.
104. Bartl *et al.*, *Slovak History*, p. 1948.
105. Rageau, *Prague 48*, p. 48.
106. Kusin, *Intellectual Origins of the Prague Spring*, p. 11.
107. The comrade who had to be removed from the photograph, leaving behind only his fur hat, was Vladimír Clementis, who, as will be seen in the next chapter, was framed in the Slánský political show trial and executed in 1953. See also discussion of the photograph in the opening passages of Milan Kundera's *The Book of Laughter and Forgetting*, tr. A. Asher (London, 1996 [1978]), p. 3. The famous photograph of Gottwald reading out a speech from the balcony of the Kinský palace overlooking the Old Town Square actually took place, as can be confirmed by a glance at contemporary newspaper reports, on 21 February. The victory speech of 25 February, which contains the famous opening words 'I have just returned from the Castle . . .', was given in Wenceslas Square, again according to the newspaper reports of the day. That Gottwald was audibly drunk can be confirmed by listening to any recording of his speech, such as the one available as part of the permanent display at the Technical Museum in Prague; it has also been confirmed to me privately by a former Communist Party member old enough to remember hearing the speech, and who was also able to confirm that the famous 'balcony speech' is actually a conflation of two separate speeches given on different days.
108. '*Nová Gottwaldova vláda jmenována*' and '*Lid čistí republiku od sabotérů, zrádců a nespolehlivých živlů*', *Rudé právo* 48 (26 February 1948), p. 1.
109. Mannová, *Concise History of Slovakia*, p. 277.
110. Kavan, *Love and Freedom*, p. 44.
111. P. Kettner and I. Jedlička, *Proč zemřel Jan Masaryk?* (Prague, 1990 [1968]), pp. 12, 14–15. Kavan reported to his wife that, when he had seen Masaryk on the night of 9 March 1948, the foreign minister had been depressed and was already in bed, flushed and in low spirits about political developments and fearing for his own sanity. There could have been no question of a premeditated suicide, however, since Masaryk had asked Kavan to return in the morning to pick up a letter for the ambassador in London. The heap of cigarette ends found in his ashtrays in the morning suggested to Kavan yet another sleepless night, the stress of which Masaryk could no longer bear. Kavan, *Love and Freedom*, pp. 45–46.
112. For a brief summary of the latter two cases, see M. Myant, 'New Research on February 1948 in Czechoslovakia', *Europe-Asia Studies* 60:10 (December 2008), p. 1711.
113. See e.g. M. Zeman, '*Jan Masaryk jak ho jsme znali*', special supplement to *Svět v obrazech* (March 1948); Anon., *Na půl žerdi: Jan Masaryk odešel*, Zrcadlo doby reportážní knižnice, no. 13 (Prague, n.d. [1948]), unpaginated.
114. See e.g. C. Sterling, *The Masaryk Case: The Murder of Democracy in Czechoslovakia* (New York, 1969).

CHAPTER 7: BUILDING THE SOCIALIST STATE

1. Law 75, '*Zákon o volbách do Národního shromáždění*' (16 April 1948), *Sbírka zákonů a nařízení* (Prague, 1948), pp. 762–80.

2. Laws 114, 115, 118, 119, 120, 121, 137 and 138 were all passed on 28 April 1948. See *Sbírka zákonů a nařízení* (Prague, 1948), pp. 933–1046.

3. As explained in D. Miller, *Forging Political Compromise: Antonín Švehla and the Czechoslovak Republican Party 1918–1933* (Pittsburgh, Pa., 1999), pp. 19–20.

4. Law 150, '*Prohlášení, Ústava Československé republiky*' (9 June 1948), *Sbírka zákonů a nařízení* (Prague, 1948), p. 1085.

5. Fundamental Article 2, ibid., p. 1087.

6. Fundamental Articles 6 and 7, ibid., p. 1087.

7. Fundamental Articles 1, 2, 8, 9, ibid., p. 1087.

8. See K. Schelle, '*Rok 1918 a národní výbory*', *Správní právo* 16:7 (Prague, Ministerstvo vnitra, 1983), pp. 400–415.

9. The jingle (which rhymes in Czech) ran: '*Tluče bubeníček, tluče na buben/ národ půjde k volbám, bude slavný den/ Tluče bubeníček, tluče na buben/ kdo dá bílý lístek/ jde z národa ven*' and translates awkwardly into English as: 'The little drummer boy is beating his drum / the nation is going to vote, it's going to be a big day/ the little drummer boy is beating his drum;/ anyone who uses the blank ballot/ is excluding himself from the nation.' J. Zábrana, *Celý život*, vol. 1 (Prague, 1993), pp. 16, 29.

10. Benda, unpublished reminiscences, f. 44.

11. An additional 3.56 per cent of votes in the Czech lands and 1.11 per cent in Slovakia were disqualified as spoiled. *Československé dějiny v datech* (Prague, 1987), p. 633.

12. See e.g. Kovály, *Under a Cruel Star*, pp. 89–90; Šlingová, *Truth Will Prevail* (London, 1968), pp. 45–46.

13. Steiner, *The Slovak Dilemma*, p. 93.

14. As cited in ibid., p. 91.

15. Suda, *Zealots and Rebels*, p. 230; Leff, *National Conflict in Czechoslovakia*, p. 100.

16. *AMV* 305-487-1, ff. 1–4 (24 March 1948); 305-374-2, Hřebík, ff. 1–223, 321–24 '*JUDr Ant. Hřebík, starosta ČOS*' (received 12 April 1948), ff. 189–96.

17. *AMV* 305-487-1, ff. 1–4 (24 March 1948); 321–4, unsigned report '*Posl. dr. Hřebík*' (14 April 1948), ff. 4; 9.

18. A. Dušek *et al.*, *Příručka pro sběratele československých známek a celin* (Prague, 1988), p. 105.

19. *AMV* 305-374-3 '*Sokolský slet*', Oblastní úřadovna Státní bezpečnosti Praha oddělení B/3 (2 July 1948), ff. 1–138, 5.

20. *AMV* 305-374-3, Ústřední národní výbor hl. města Prahy, secret memo (2 July 1948), ff. 26–28, 43–44.

21. '*Ať to slyší svět/Beneš musí zpět*' and '*Každý Sokol dobře ví/že jen Pravda zvítězí*'.

22. See e.g. the poster '*Zátopkovské hnutí: Cesta k zvýšení politické a sportovní úrovně sportovců a tělocvikářů*' on permanent display at the Muzeum komunismu (Museum of Communism), Na Příkopě 10, Prague, Czech Republic.

23. Although carefully watched by the *StB*, the Zátopeks' links with 'reactionary agents' abroad were kept strictly confidential; the rest of the group associated with Ingr were tried in secret at Pankrác in August 1950. Interview with Jiří Hovorka (23 February 2003), tape 2, ff. 6–7; Churaň *et al.*, *Kdo byl kdo v našich dějinách ve 20. století*, vol. 1, p. 268.

24. This was *Lví silou* (Prague, Družstvo Máj, 1948), as cited in C. Nolte, *The Sokol in the Czech Lands to 1914: Training for the Nation* (Houndmills, Basingstoke, 2002), p. 236, note 7.

25. Dušek *et al.*, *Příručka pro sběratele československých známek a celin*, p. 121.

26. Zábrana, *Celý život*, p. 53.

27. Ibid., pp. 56–59.

28. *AMV* 305-210-2, *StB* regional reports from Opava (30 September 1948), f. 2; Tábor (4 October 1948), f. 2; Uherské Hradiště (3 October 1948), f. 2; Ostrava (29 September 1948), f. 5; Český Těšín (30 September 1948), ff. 3–4. A full list of the 24 *StB* regions is given in *AMV* 305-210-1 (minister of the interior directive dated 20 October 1948).

29. *AMV* 310-61-2, '*Informace pro pana ministra: Studentské demonstrace dne 25.ii.1948 v Praze*', ff. 3–11.

30. Interview with Josef Lesák in documentary series '*Ztracená duše národa*' directed by J. Štern, no. 5, '*Ztráta odpovědnosti*', Česká televize/Vision, 2001. The *StB* archives include Lubomír Hanák's written confession to having been arrested while attempting to cross the border with Josef Lesák on 4 May 1948. See AMV 305-108-8. Hanák was later claimed by the *StB* to have been a '*Gestapo konfident*'; see 305-108-8z.

31. AMV V-6301/MV vol. 1, '*Rozsudek jménem republiky*' (8 June 1950), ff. 1–50.

32. H. Čápová, '*Kat Milady Horákové žije*', *Respekt* 14:9 (24 February–2 March 2003), p. 6.

33. Suda, *Zealots and Rebels*, p. 232.

34. J. Korec, *The Night of the Barbarians: Memoirs of the Communist Persecution of the Slovak Cardinal* (Wauconda, Ill., 2002), pp. 55–56.

35. K. Kaplan, *Stát a církev v Československu v letech 1948–1953* (Brno, 1993), p. 23, note; pp. 27–28; R. Ströbinger and K. Nešvera, *Stalo se v Adventu: 'čihošťský zázrak'* (Prague, 1990), p. 133, note 2.

36. Seven years later, on 8 February 1955, Plojhar formally entered the *StB* books as a secret agent. Ministerstvo vnitra, *Zveřejnění evidenčních pokladů a seznamu personálních spisů*, vol. 5 (Prague, 2002), p. 2233.

37. Kaplan, *Stát a církev*, pp. 39–40; Ströbinger and Nešvera, *Stalo se v Adventu*, p. 134, note 4.

38. G. Ference, ed., *Chronology of Twentieth-Century Eastern European History* (Washington, D.C., 1994), pp. 125–26.

39. See, for example, A. Svoboda, A. Tučková and V. Svobodová, *Spiknutí proti republice* (Prague, 1949), *passim*.

40. Law no. 217, '*Zákon, kterým se zřizuje Státní úřad pro věci církevní*' (14 October 1949), *Sbírka zákonů a nařízení*, (Prague, 1949), p. 639.

41. J. Kalous, *Instruktážní skupina StB v lednu a únoru 1950* (Prague, 2001), p. 11.

42. The novel was first published in 1972 as *Mirákl: politická detektivka*, by Sixty-Eight Publishers in Toronto, where Škvorecký had been living in exile from his native Czechoslovakia since 1969. In 1991, it was published in English, in a characteristically brilliant translation by Paul Wilson, as J. Skvorecky, *The Miracle Game* (New York and Toronto, 1991).

43. Kalous, *Instruktážní skupina StB*, p. 13.

44. Ibid., pp. 13–14.

45. Archive footage as shown in J. Štern, documentary series '*Ztracená duše národa*', no. 6, '*Ztráta víry*', Česká televize/Vision, 2001, directed by Olga Sommerová.

46. Kaplan, *Stát a církev*, p. 135.

47. Korec, *The Night of f the Barbarians*, pp. 4, 12–13.

48. *AMV* H-718/1, '*Akce "K" Evidence klášterů': 'Celková potřeba'*, f. 293; '*Akce "K"*' (č.j. A-21283/50651-1950), f. 2; Kalous, *Instruktážní skupina*, pp. 14–15; interview with Fr Oto Mádr in Štern, '*Ztracená duše národa*', no. 6, '*Ztráta víry*'; Kaplan, *Stát a církev*, pp. 120–21.

49. Kaplan, *Stát a církev*, p. 185; Ströbinger and Nešvera, *Stalo se v Adventu* pp. 137–38, note 15.

50. Kovály, *Under a Cruel Star*, p. 94; Šlingová, *Truth Will Prevail*, pp. 74–75.

51. Suda, *Zealots and Rebels*, p. 234.

52. This was Julius Fučík; see Chapter 5 for details.

53. Kovály, *Under a Cruel Star*, pp. 98–99.

54. *Československý filmový týdeník* (weekly ten-minute newsreels as shown between January 1952 and August 1953)

55. Examples of political cartoons and posters on permanent display at the Museum of Communism, Prague.

56. See, for example, *AMV* 305-210-2, '*Měsíční situační zpráva za měsíc září*' (monthly situation reports for September 1948) as reported from regional *StB* and *SNB* headquarters in Kolín (5 October 1948), Tábor (4 October 1948) and Český Těšín (1 October 1948), unpaginated.

57. On the first Colorado beetle scare, see Decrees 40, '*Vládní nařízení o opatřeních proti zavlečení mandelinky bramborové*' (25 February 1939), and 45, '*Vládní nařízení proti mandelince bramborové*' (24 February 1939), *Sbírka zákonů a nařízení* (Prague, 1939), pp. 119 and 243. See also the fascinating and well-informed article on the history and political uses of the Colorado beetle by P. Formánková, '*Kampaň proti "americkému brouku" a její politické souvislosti*', *Studie a články: paměť a dějiny* (January 2008), pp. 22–38.

58. *Akce B* (1951), a ninety-minute feature film directed by Josef Mach and starring Josef Bek, Rudolf Deyl Jr, Jiří Sovák, Mikuláš Huba and Svatopluk Čech.

59. *Bylo to v Máji* (1950), an eighty-minute feature film directed by Martin Frič and Václav Berdych, starring Jaroslav Marvan, Ella Nollová, Jana Dítětová, Miloš Vavruška and Ota Motyčka.

60. Interview with Raimund Musil in Štern, '*Ztracená duše národa*', no. 2, '*Ztráta tradice*'.

61. J. Bílek, *Pomocné technické prapory: o jedné z forem zneužití armády k politické perzekuci* (Prague, 2002), p. 21.

62. Ibid., Appendices 3 and 2, pp. 186–87 and 181–85.

63. Ibid., p. 24.

64. Ibid., pp. 92–101.

65. *Hořké vzpomínání. Z dopisů a vzpomínek chlapců pétépáků*, vol. 1 (Prague, 1996), p. 121.

66. F. Lewis, *The Red Pawn: The Life of Noel Field* (Garden City, N.Y., 1965), pp. 85, 96–98, 117–19, 110–15, 135, 185–87; B. Barth, '*Wer war Noel Field? Die unbekannte Schluesselfigur der osteuropaeischen Schauprozesse*' in A. Leo and P. Reif-Spirek, eds, *Vielstimmiges Schweign: Neue Studien zum DDR-Antifaschismus*, tr. J. Schwarzmantel (Berlin, 2001).

67. Lewis, *Red Pawn*, pp. 197, 9, 199, 201–3, 9–10.

68. J. Pelikán, ed., *The Czechoslovak Political Trials, 1950–1954* (London, 1971), p. 73.

69. Ibid., p. 74; Šlingová, *Truth Will Prevail*, p. 75; Kavan, *Love and Freedom*, p. 110, note.

70. E. Loebl, *Sentenced and Tried: The Stalinist Purges in Czechoslovakia* (London, 1969), pp. 9–10.

71. Ibid., pp. 10–15.

72. Ibid., p. 18; K. Kaplan, ed., *StB o sobě: výpověď vyšetřovatele Bohumila Doubka* (Prague, 2002), p. 137.

73. Šlingová, *Truth Will Prevail*, pp. 51–52, 54–55, A. London, *L'Aveu: Dans l'engrenage du procès de Prague* (Saint-Armand, 1968), pp. 15, 17–18, 20, 39–40, 282–83; J. Slánská, *Report on my Husband* (London, 1969), pp. 150–53; Kavan, *Love and Freedom*, pp. 76–77, 80–81, 85–90, 165–70; Kovály, *Under a Cruel Star*, pp. 105–25.

74. Pelikán, *Czechoslovak Political Trials*, pp. 75–77, 80.

75. Ibid., p. 78.

76. Ibid., pp. 82–85.

77. Steiner, *The Slovak Dilemma*, pp. 100–1.

78. K. Kaplan, *Report on the Murder of the General Secretary*, tr. Karel Kovanda (Columbus, Ohio, 1990), p. 107.

79. Pelikán, *Czechoslovak Political Trials*, pp. 93–98.

80. Ibid., p. 101.

81. Igor Lukeš, 'Operace "Velký metař" ' (paper presented to the conference 'Politické procesy 50. let a Případ Slánský', held at Pankrác prison, Prague, 14–16 April 2003).

82. Slánská, *Report on my Husband*, pp. 133, 136–37, 16; Pelikán, *Czechoslovak Political Trials*, pp. 101, 104, 106–7, 109.

83. Pelikán, *Czechoslovak Political Trials*, p. 112.

84. H. Schling, 'Constructing the Enemy: Anti-Semitism, Dehumanisation and Physical Metamorphosis in Czechoslovak Communist Party Caricature of the Slánský Trials of 1952' (unpublished undergraduate dissertation, Wadham College, Oxford, 2008), f. 29.

85. Kovály, *Under a Cruel Star*, p. 103.

86. *Proces s vedením protistátního spikleneckého centra v čele s Rudolfem Slánským* (Prague, 1953), p. 8.

87. As cited and discussed in Steiner, *The Slovak Dilemma*, p. 100.

88. Frejka's son published a famous letter in the press that denounced his own father. London's French Communist wife, although she later smuggled out his account of how his 'confession' had been obtained, initially believed the verdict and published a condemnation of her husband. Kavan's wife, Rosemary, confused at hearing her husband admit to crimes that she knew he had not committed, could detect nothing suspicious in his voice or behaviour during his recitation as a 'witness' until he began to answer one question before it had been put to him by the prosecutor. This single slip, though broadcast live on radio, was easily edited out, since the precaution had been taken of taping the many rehearsals for the final trial. Kavan, *Love and Freedom*, p. 106.

89. Schling, 'Constructing the Enemy'.

90. *Proces s vedením protistátního spikleneckého centra.*

91. *Československý filmový týdeník*, no. 11 (March 1953), directed by E. Kaněra.

92. Z. Jirásek and J. Šůla, *Velká peněžní loupež v Československu 1953 aneb 50:1* (Prague 1992).

93. *Československý filmový týdeník*, no. 12 (May 1953).

94. Mlynář, *Night Frost in Prague*, p. 27; A. Dubček, *Hope Dies Last: The Autobiography of Alexander Dubcek*, tr. J. Hochman (New York, Tokyo, London, 1993), p. 71.

95. See '*Sletové cvičiště* as shown on *Orientační plán sídel hlav. města Prahy* (Prague, Český zemský svaz ku povznesení návštěvy cizinců v Čechách [July 1920]).

96. Z. Hojda and J. Pokorný, *Pomníky a zapomníky*, 2nd edn (Prague, 1997), pp. 205–18.

97. V. Kostka, 'Czechoslovakia' in J. Riordan, ed., *Sport under Communism* (London, 1978), p. 62; J. Hronek et al., *Czechoslovakia: A Handbook of Facts and Figures* (Prague, 1964), insert opposite p. 153.

98. Mlynář, *Night Frost in Prague*, p. 27; Dubček, *Hope Dies Last*, p. 72.

99. At the state-wide party conference in the spring of 1956, for example, the *KSČ* voted to 'support the new line in Moscow' and resolved that 'several ideological and political theses of Stalinism were no longer valid', but then, at the plenary session of the party Central Committee in June 1956, roundly condemned 'revisionism'. See Kusin, *The Intellectual Origins of the Prague Spring*, pp. 19–20, 23–25.

100. J. Matthews, 'Majales: The Abortive Student Revolt in Czechoslovakia in 1956', Woodrow Wilson International Center for Scholars, Cold War International History Project, Working Paper no. 24 (Washington, D.C., 1998), p. 14.

101. Ibid., p. 14.

102. *Mladá fronta* (28 April 1956), as cited in Matthews, 'Majales', p. 14.

103. Matthews, 'Majales', p. 18.

104. Mlynář, *Night Frost in Prague*, p. 49.

105. Article 1, Fundamental Articles of the Constitution of Socialist Czechoslovakia, as reproduced in *Czechoslovakia*, p. 24.

106. Law 113, *Sbírka zákonů* 44 (14 July 1960), pp. 337–44.
107. Article 4, Fundamental Articles, *Handbook of Facts and Figures*, p. 25.
108. Article 12, ibid., p. 26.
109. Article 16, ibid., p. 27.
110. Article 14, ibid., p. 27.
111. Ibid.

CHAPTER 8: THE BRATISLAVA AND PRAGUE SPRINGS

Much of this chapter has already appeared in print as M. Heimann, 'The Scheming *Apparatchik* of the Prague Spring', *Europe-Asia Studies*, 60:10 (December 2008), pp. 1719–36.

1. *Sbratření* (Brotherhood) was begun by Karel Pokorný in 1945 and completed in 1950, to great critical acclaim. The image was later included on a Czechoslovak postage stamp. The original statue can be seen in the permanent exhibition of Czech art at the Národní galerie, Veletržní palác; a copy still stands along the walkway to Prague's central railway station (*Hlavní nádraží*).
2. L. Mot'ka and authors' collective, *Touring Czechoslovakia* (Prague, 1962), pp. 18–19.
3. Steiner, *The Slovak Dilemma*, p. 113.
4. Dubček, *Hope Dies Last*, pp. 98, 83.
5. A. Novotný, speech to the Central Committee of the *KSČ* (15 November 1961), as published in *Rudé právo* (21 November 1961) and reproduced in full (in English translation) in Slánská, *Report on My Husband*, p. 57.
6. Ibid., p. 58.
7. G. Deitch, *For the Love of Prague*, 2nd edn (Příbram, 1998 [1995]), p. 24, note.
8. '*Takoví jsme byli*', 1962, Česká televize, 1996.
9. Photo from 1949 and also of protestors in 1968 gathered on the empty plinth in L. Bielik, *August 1968* (Bratislava, 2008), p. 21. It was apparently removed by demonstrators in early 1990.
10. Mlynář, *Night Frost in Prague*, p. 58. Jan Šejna claims to have found 'some files on Khrushchev's conversations and behaviour during his visits to Czechoslovakia' in addition to 'a large amount of foreign currency' in Barák's private safe. Sejna, *We Will Bury You*, p. 88.
11. Mlynář, *Night Frost in Prague*, pp. 68–69.
12. *Státní ústřední archiv v Praze, Archiv ÚV KSČ* (hereafter cited as *ÚV KSČ*), fond 00/12, box sv. 1, '*XII. Sjezd KSČ (1962), a.j. 10 'Informační zpráva o některých zvláštních a negativních připomínkách a názorech z diskuse k návrhu stanov KSČ*, příloha iv), f. 1.
13. Kaplan, *Report on the Murder of the General Secretary*, pp. xvi–xvii; Dubček, *Hope Dies Last*, p. 86; Steiner, *Slovak Dilemma*, p. 115.
14. Dubček, *Hope Dies Last*, p. 89; Bartl *et al.*, *Slovak History*, p. 155.
15. Steiner, *Slovak Dilemma*, p. 119.
16. Dubček, *Hope Dies Last*, pp. 90–91.
17. Steiner, *Slovak Dilemma*, p. 121.
18. Kaplan, *Report on the Murder of the General Secretary*, p. xv.
19. Mlynář, *Night Frost in Prague*, pp. 68–69.
20. K. Williams, *The Prague Spring and its Aftermath: Czechoslovak Politics 1968–1970* (Cambridge, 1997), p. 22.
21. H.G. Skilling, *Czechoslovakia's Interrupted Revolution* (Princeton, N.J., 1976), p. 120.
22. Kusin, *The Intellectual Origins of the Prague Spring*, p. 60, note 1.
23. Deitch, *For the Love of Prague*, pp. 93, 146.
24. Mlynář, *Night Frost in Prague*, p. 61.
25. Ibid., p. 62.
26. K. Kaplan, '*Všechno jste prohráli!*' (*Co prozrazují archivy o IV. sjezdu Svazu československých spisovatelů 1967*) (Prague, 1997), pp. 36, 39.
27. Ibid., pp. 37, 40–41, 50.
28. So Kaplan has found, ibid., p. 55. The only references to Havel in the official lists of *StB* informers issued by the Ministry of the Interior in 2002 are from 1955, 1956, 1978 and 1984, but he was being closely monitored from at least as early as 1965. See Ministerstvo vnitra, *Zveřejnění evidenčních podkladů a seznamu personálních spisů*, vol. 2 (Prague, 2002), pp. 804–5.
29. Mlynář, *Night Frost in Prague*, p. 70; Dubček, *Hope Dies Last*, pp. 100–1; 'Moravus', 'Shawcross's Dubcek – A Different Dubcek', *Survey* 17 (1971), pp. 4, 81, 207–8.
30. Williams, *The Prague Spring and its Aftermath*, p. 54; J. Navrátil, ed., *The Prague Spring 1968: A National Security Archive Documents Reader* (Budapest, 1998), p. 44, note 15; 'Moravus', 'Shawcross's Dubcek', p. 208.

31. Sejna, *We Will Bury You*, p. 92.
32. Dubček, *Hope Dies Last*, p. 94.
33. Steiner, *Slovak Dilemma*, pp. 113–15, 120, 122–23.
34. Kusin, *The Intellectual Origins of the Prague Spring*, p. 70.
35. Dubček, *Hope Dies Last*, pp. 106–7, 7.
36. P. Pithart, *Osmašedesátý* (Prague, 1990), pp. 109–10; Dubček, *Hope Dies Last*, pp. 114–15. The rumour continues to be routinely reproduced in histories of Slovakia and Czechoslovakia.
37. *AMV*, A 2/2-1019 (counter-intelligence reports from the Ministry of the Interior to President Novotný dated 5 November 1965; 12 November 1965; 19 November 1965; 29 November 1965; 4 December 1965; 20 December 1965; 29 December 1965, microfiche; Dubček, *Hope Dies Last*, p. 106.
38. V. Mencl and F. Ouředník, 'What Happened in January' (1968) in R. Remington, ed., *Winter in Prague: Documents on Czechoslovak Communism in Crisis* (Cambridge, Mass., 1969), p. 24.
39. *ÚV KSČ, Fond* 00/13 (*XIII. Sjezd KSČ 1966*), sv. 5, ar.j. 56 '*Diskuse*', '*Dubček, A.*', ff. 9, 5.
40. Ibid., ff. 5, 4–5, 12, 10.
41. Ibid., f. 10.
42. Dubček, *Hope Dies Last*, p. 112.
43. L. Vaculík, 'Speech to the Fourth Writers' Congress of the Czechoslovak Communist Party' (1967) in Remington, *Winter in Prague*, p. 7.
44. Navrátil, *The Prague Spring 1968*, pp. 11–12.
45. Williams, *The Prague Spring and its Aftermath*, p. 55; Dubček, *Hope Dies Last*, p. 113.
46. Mencl and Ouředník, 'What Happened in January', p. 24.
47. Dubček, *Hope Dies Last*, pp. 115–16.
48. Mencl and Ouředník, 'What Happened in January', p. 19.
49. 'Strahov 1967' (broadcast 8 January 2003) in J. Večeřa, director, '*Osudové okamžiky*' (Česká televize, 2003).
50. Kieran Williams found that the VB (*Veřejná bezpečnost* or 'Public Security') were keeping an especially close watch on students because of the unprecedented numbers (some six thousand) who had been allowed to travel to the West in the previous year. Williams, *The Prague Spring and its Aftermath*, p. 56.
51. *AMV* A2/3-2133, '*Písemnosti ke strahovským událostem*'; '*Zpráva o událostech, které proběhly 31.10.1967, vypracovaná na základě svědectví přímých účastníků*', f. 144 (internal pagination, ff. 1–2); '*Zpráva tiskového tajemníka vlády o studentské demonstraci v Praze na Strahově dne 31.10*', ff. 66–70 (internal pagination, ff. 1–5); interview with Pavel Dvořák, Pavel Janda and others in '*Strahov 1967*' (2003), J. Večeřa, J. director, '*Osudové okamžiky*' (Česká televize, 2003).
52. Dubček, *Hope Dies Last*, pp. 116–17.
53. Ibid., pp. 118–21; M. Jakeš, *Dva roky generálním tajemníkem* (Prague, 1996), p. 37.
54. Mlynář, *Night Frost in Prague*, p. 71; Dubček, *Hope Dies Last*, p. 122; Skilling, *Czechoslovakia's Interrupted Revolution*, p. 179.
55. *AMV* microfiche A/213-2327 '*Jan Šejna – mimoriadna informácia*', ff. 1–8; A 9-796-1, '*kniha jednacího protokolu založena v arch. ve Spiš. Podhradě*'; A9-796-2 '*Záznam*' (24 September 1969); A/3-237 '*Jan Šejna*', ff. 1–12. See also Dubček, *Hope Dies Last*, pp. 123–25 and Šejna's own account in *We Will Bury You*.
56. Navrátil, *The Prague Spring 1968*, p. 35.
57. Dubček, *Hope Dies Last*, p. 41.
58. Šamalík, as cited in Skilling, *Czechoslovakia's Interrupted Revolution*, p. 183.
59. J. Smrkovský, '*Jak nyní dál: Nad závěry lednového pléna ÚV KSČ*', *Rudé právo* (9 February 1968), p. 2.
60. Dubček, *Hope Dies Last*, p. 138.
61. Williams, *The Prague Spring and its Aftermath*, p. 68.
62. *AMV* microfiche A/24-963, '*Sekretariát MV plk. Demjana, Správa pasů a víz*' (5 March 1968), unpaginated; A/3-237, '*Informace pro vládu k případu trestné činnosti Jana Šejny a Jaroslava Moravce*' (11 March 1968), ff. 1–67.
63. Dubček, *Hope Dies Last*, p. 139; Mlynář, *Night Frost in Prague*, p. 102.
64. Remington, *Winter in Prague*, p. 54.
65. Dubček, *Hope Dies Last*, p. 125.
66. Mlynář, *Night Frost in Prague*, pp. 104–5.
67. Law 231, '*Zákon na ochranu lidové republiky*' (6 October 1948), *Sbírka zákonů Republiky československé* (Prague, 1948), pp. 1461–72.
68. 'Dresden Communiqué' (25 March 1968), as translated into English and reproduced in Remington, *Winter in Prague*, p. 57.
69. Dubček, *Hope Dies Last*, p. 141.
70. Ibid., pp. 141–42.

71. Speech by Nicolae Ceauşescu to the Bucharest Party Aktiv (26 April 1968); speech by Kurt Hager on 'The Philosophical Teaching of Karl Marx and its Current Meaning' (26 March 1968); V. Havel, 'On the Subject of Opposition', *Literární listy* (4 April 1968), as reproduced in Remington, *Winter in Prague*, pp. 58–60, 61–62, 64–65.
72. 'The Action Programme of the Communist Party of Czechoslovakia adopted at the plenary session of the Central Committee of Czechoslovakia on April 5th 1968', as given in English translation in P. Ello, ed., *Czechoslovakia's Blueprint for Freedom* (Washington, D.C., 1968), pp. 89–178.
73. Ibid., pp. 91–93.
74. Ibid., p. 97.
75. Ibid., pp. 98–99.
76. Ibid., pp. 102–3.
77. Ibid., p. 103.
78. Ibid., pp. 104–5.
79. Ibid., p. 106.
80. Ibid., p. 109.
81. Ibid., p. 110.
82. Ibid., pp. 110–11.
83. Ibid., pp. 112–13.
84. As cited in J. Pelikán, ed., *The Secret Vysočany Congress: Proceedings and Documents of the Extraordinary Fourteenth Congress of the Communist Party of Czechoslovakia, 22 August 1968*, tr. G. Theiner and D. Viney (Vienna, 1969), p. 2.
85. I. Sviták, 'With your Head against the Wall' (20 March 1968), published in *Student* 15 (10 April 1968) and reproduced in Remington, ed., *Winter in Prague*, p. 74.
86. Dubček, *Hope Dies Last*, p. 150.
87. M. Dowling, *Czechoslovakia* (London and New York, 2002), p. 111.
88. A. Indra in *Pravda* (30 April 1968), as cited in Remington, *Winter in Prague*, p. 158, note 5.
89. See *AV ÚV KSČ, fond* 02/1, P70/68 čj. P4174, as cited in K. Williams, 'Czechoslovakia 1968', *Slavonic and East European Review* 74:1 (January 1996), p. 83, note 4.
90. Ibid., p. 83.
91. L. Vaculík, '2,000 Words to Workers, Farmers, Scientists, Artists and Everyone', as reproduced in English translation in Remington, *Winter in Prague*, pp. 196–202.
92. I. Alexandrov, 'Attack on the Socialist Foundations of Czechoslovakia', *Pravda* (11 July 1968), in Remington, *Winter in Prague*, p. 204.
93. The full text of this letter to the *KSČ* Central Committee (hereafter cited as the 'Warsaw Letter') is given in English translation as 'To the Czechoslovak Communist Party Central Committee' (15 July 1968) in Remington, *Winter in Prague*, pp. 225–31.
94. Ibid., p. 225.
95. Ibid., p. 226.
96. Ibid., pp. 225, 227, 229–30.
97. The full text, in English translation (hereafter cited as 'Czechoslovak Reply to the Warsaw Letter'), may be found as 'Czechoslovak Reply to the Warsaw Letter' (18 July 1968) in Remington, *Winter in Prague*, pp. 234–43.
98. Ibid., p. 243.
99. Ibid., pp. 235–36.
100. Ibid., pp. 238, 241.
101. Ibid., pp. 240–41.
102. A. Dubček, 'Manifest Victory for the Sovereignty Principle' (19 July 1968), as reproduced in English translation in Remington, *Winter in Prague*, pp. 244–48.
103. 'Concerning the Point of View of the CCP Central Committee' (22 July 1968), as reproduced in English translation in Remington, *Winter in Prague*, pp. 249–52.
104. L. Svoboda, 'The ČSSR Is Not Going to Commit Suicide' (27 July 1968), as reproduced in English translation in Remington, *Winter in Prague*, pp. 252–53.
105. See 'Joint Communiqué on Meeting of Politburo of CPSU Central Committee and Presidium of CCP Central Committee' (2 August 1968) and 'Statement of Communist and Workers' Parties of Socialist Countries' (4 August 1968), as reproduced in English translation in Remington, *Winter in Prague*, pp. 255, 256–61.
106. Dubček, *Hope Dies Last*, pp. 167–71.
107. See 'KSČ Draft Statutes' (10 August 1968), as reproduced in Remington, *Winter in Prague*, pp. 264–87.

CHAPTER 9: BACK TO NORMAL

1. One Warsaw Pact country – the People's Republic of Romania – refused to take part, but only so that the first secretary of its own Communist Party could exploit the crisis to cement his position at home as unchallenged leader in a distinctly Stalinist mould. See K. Adamson, 'Nicolae Ceauşescu, the Romanian Communist Party and 1968: The Deployment of Prague Spring Symbolism in the Service of National Stalinism' (unpublished talk presented to the 'Remembering 1948 and 1968' conference held at the University of Glasgow, 4 April 2008).
2. Williams, *The Prague Spring and its Aftermath*, p. 121.
3. This was the famous *Sedm pražských dnů 21.–27. srpen 1968: Dokumentace*, or 'Czech Black Book', which was brought out as a riposte to the Press Group of Soviet Journalists' 'White Book': *On Events in Czechoslovakia: Facts, Documents, Press Reports and Eye-Witness Accounts* (Moscow, 1968).
4. 'Report by Defence Minister Martin Dzúr Regarding his Activities on the Night of August 20–21 August 1968' (9 June 1970), as reproduced in English translation in J. Navrátil, ed., *The Prague Spring 1968: A National Security Archive Documents Reader*, tr. M. Kramer, J. Moss, R. Tosek (Prague, 1998), p. 412; Institute of History of the Czechoslovak Academy of Sciences, *The Czech Black Book*, ed. R. Littell (London, 1969), pp. 9, 16; Mlynář, *Night Frost in Prague*, p. 146; Dubček, *Hope Dies Last*, p. 178; Williams, *The Prague Spring and its Aftermath*, p. 131.
5. Top-secret telegram to Stepan Chervonenko, Soviet ambassador in Prague, with a message for President Svoboda (19 August 1968), as reproduced in English translation in Navrátil, ed., *The Prague Spring 1968*, p. 408.
6. Chervonenko, report to Moscow on conversation with Ludvík Svoboda (21 August 1968), as reproduced in English translation in Navrátil, ed., *The Prague Spring 1968*, p. 408.
7. Mlynář, *Night Frost in Prague*, p. 146.
8. Ibid., pp. 146, 203.
9. Dubček, *Hope Dies Last*, p. 178.
10. Mlynář, *Night Frost in Prague*, pp. 147, 150.
11. Report by Defence Minister Dzúr (9 June 1970), as reproduced in Navrátil, ed., *The Prague Spring 1968*, p. 412; Mlynář, *Night Frost in Prague*, p. 146; Dubček, *Hope Dies Last*, p. 178; Williams, *The Prague Spring*, p. 131.
12. *Sedm pražských dnů*, pp. 16–17.
13. Mlynář, *Night Frost in Prague*, p. 150; *Sedm pražských dnů*, p. 19.
14. Mlynář, *Night Frost in Prague*, pp. 150–51.
15. Dubček, *Hope Dies Last*, p. 181.
16. *Sedm pražských dnů*, p. 19.
17. Ibid., pp. 19, 25, 26; Mlynář, *Night Frost in Prague*, p. 176.
18. *Sedm pražských dnů*, pp. 25–26.
19. An account of Černík's arrest was also given to the Vysočany congress on 22 August, see Pelikán, *The Secret Vysočany Congress*, pp. 66–68.
20. Mlynář, *Night Frost in Prague*, p. 179; Dubček, *Hope Dies Last*, p. 182.
21. Mlynář, *Night Frost in Prague*, p. 177.
22. *Sedm pražských dnů*, pp. 28, 29; Mlynář, *Night Frost in Prague*, p. 176.
23. *Sedm pražských dnů*, p. 33.
24. Ibid., p. 35.
25. Ibid., pp. 36–37.
26. Mlynář, *Night Frost in Prague*, p. 176; Navrátil, ed., *The Prague Spring 1968*, p. 415, note 121.
27. *Sedm pražských dnů*, pp. 38–9. 117; Mlynář, *Night Frost in Prague*, p. 176.
28. *Sedm pražských dnů*, p. 40.
29. Ibid., pp. 33–34.
30. Ibid., pp. 39–40; Williams, *The Prague Spring*, p. 130.
31. Navrátil, ed., *The Prague Spring 1968*, p. xxxv; Williams, *The Prague Spring*, p. 131.
32. Navrátil, ed., *The Prague Spring 1968*, p. xxxv.
33. Dubček, *Hope Dies Last*, p. 183; Mlynář, *Night Frost in Prague*, pp. 183, 179; Navrátil, ed., *The Prague Spring 1968*, pp. 418–19; p. 421, note 132.
34. Mlynář, *Night Frost in Prague*, p. 180; Dubček, *Hope Dies Last*, p. 182.
35. *Sedm pražských dnů*, p. 45.
36. Dubček, *Hope Dies Last*, pp. 183–85.
37. *Sedm pražských dnů*, p. 52.
38. Ibid., pp. 54, 57.
39. Ibid., pp. 57–62.
40. Ibid., pp. 61–62.

41. Ibid., p. 64.
42. Navrátil, ed., *The Prague Spring 1968*, p. xxxv.
43. Williams, *The Prague Spring*, pp. 135–36.
44. Ibid., pp. 135–37.
45. Ibid., pp. 136–37.
46. Ibid.
47. Dubček, *Hope Dies Last*, pp. 184–85.
48. V. Kusin, *From Dubček to Charter 77: A Study of 'Normalisation' in Czechoslovakia 1968–1978* (Edinburgh, 1978), p. 27.
49. Mlynář, *Night Frost in Prague*, pp. 201–2.
50. Ibid., p. 203.
51. Williams, *The Prague Spring*, pp. 124–25; Mlynář, *Night Frost in Prague*, p. 187.
52. Ibid., pp. 125–26.
53. Ibid., p. 84.
54. Ibid., p. 126.
55. Ibid., p. 127; Mlynář, *Night Frost in Prague*, p. 203.
56. Williams, *The Prague Spring*, p. 129.
57. Ibid.
58. Williams, *The Prague Spring*, p. 129; Mlynář, *Night Frost in Prague*, pp. 207–8.
59. Williams, *The Prague Spring*, pp. 131–32; Mlynář, *Night Frost in Prague*, p. 200.
60. Williams, *The Prague Spring*, p. 134.
61. 'Transcript of a Tape Recording of the Proceedings of the Extraordinary Fourteenth Congress on 22 August 1968', as reproduced in Pelikán, *The Secret Vysočany Congress*, pp. 19–20.
62. Mlynář, *Night Frost in Prague*, p. 188.
63. Ibid., pp. 188–89.
64. Ibid., p. 188.
65. Mlynář, *Night Frost in Prague*, pp. 188–89.
66. Ibid., p. 190.
67. Ibid., pp. 191–94; Pelikán, *The Secret Vysočany Congress*, pp. 30–33, 34–49, 63–65, 79–82.
68. *Sedm pražských dnů*, pp. 89–91; Mlynář, *Night Frost in Prague*, p. 206; Pelikán, *The Secret Vysočany Congress*, pp. 32–33, 92–94.
69. 'Proclamation Adopted at the Opening of the Congress', as reproduced in Pelikán, *The Secret Vysočany Congress*, p. 88.
70. Ibid., p. 89.
71. Mlynář, *Night Frost in Prague*, p. 194.
72. Ibid., pp. 194–96.
73. Ibid., p. 196.
74. *Sedm pražských dnů*, p. 142.
75. Williams, *The Prague Spring*, p. 137.
76. Dubček, *Hope Dies Last*, pp. 188–89; Williams, *The Prague Spring*, pp. 135–37; Mlynář, *Night Frost in Prague*, p. 197.
77. *Sedm pražských dnů*, p. 143.
78. Dubček, *Hope Dies Last*, pp. 187, 190.
79. Ibid., pp, 190–91.
80. Ibid., p. 191.
81. Ibid., p. 199.
82. *Sedm pražských dnů*, p. 177.
83. Ibid., p. 210.
84. Ibid., p. 212.
85. Dubček, *Hope Dies Last*, p. 202.
86. Ibid., pp. 202–3.
87. Kusin, *From Dubček to Charter 77*, p. 24.
88. *Sedm pražských dnů,*. pp. 178–79.
89. Kusin, *From Dubček to Charter 77*, p. 25.
90. Ibid., p. 28.
91. Dubček, *Hope Dies Last*, pp. 203–4.
92. Ibid., pp. 204–5.
93. Mlynář, *Night Frost in Prague*, pp. 211, 236.
94. Ibid., pp. 219–20, 211–12.
95. Ibid., pp. 214–15.

96. Ibid., pp. 217–18.
97. Ibid., pp. 227–28.
98. Ibid., pp. 233–37.
99. This summary is based on the eyewitness account of the meeting as given in Mlynář, *Night Frost in Prague*, pp. 236–44.
100. 'The Moscow Protocol', as reproduced in Remington, *Winter in Prague*, p. 379.
101. Ibid., p. 379.
102. Ibid.
103. Ibid., pp. 379–80.
104. Ibid., pp. 381–82.
105. Mlynář, *Night Frost in Prague*, pp. 244–45, 246.
106. Dubček, *Hope Dies Last*, p. 214; Mlynář, *Night Frost in Prague*, p. 246.
107. Mlynář, *Night Frost in Prague*, p. 246; Dubček, *Hope Dies Last*, p. 216.
108. *Sedm pražských dnů*, p. 279.
109. Speech by Gustáv Husák at the Extraordinary Fourteenth Congress of the *KSS*, as reproduced in English translation in Navrátil, ed., *The Prague Spring 1968*, p. 487.
110. *Sedm pražských dnů*, p. 280.
111. Ibid., pp. 298–99.
112. Ibid., pp. 299–300.
113. Williams, *The Prague Spring*, pp. 145–46.
114. *Sedm pražských dnů*, pp. 322–32.
115. *AMV* A 34–2650, '*Ohlasy na vstup vojsk VS*' (letters received in August–September 1968).
116. *Sedm pražských dnů*, p. 303.
117. Mlynář, *Night Frost in Prague*, pp. 246–47.
118. See e.g. Josef Smrkovský's address to the people after his return from Moscow, 29 August 1968, in Navrátil, *The Prague Spring*, p. 489 and note.
119. *AMV* A 34–2649, '*Výzvy-letáky-rezoluce*' (August 1968) and A 34–2650, '*Ohlasy na vstup vojsk VS*' (August and September 1968).
120. Kusin, *From Dubček to Charter 77*, p. 43.
121. Ibid., pp. 44–45.
122. Ibid., p. 76.
123. Ibid., pp. 53–54.
124. Bilateral treaty on the 'Temporary Presence of Soviet Forces on Czechoslovak Territory' (16 October 1968), as reproduced in Navrátil, ed., *The Prague Spring 1968*, pp. 533–34.
125. Laws 66–85, '*Ústavní zákon o československé federaci*', *Sbírka zákonů Československé socialistické republiky*, vol. 143 (Prague, 1968).
126. Law 143, '*Ústavní zákon zedne 27. října 1968 o československé federaci*', *Sbírka zákonů Československé socialistické republiky, ročník* 1968, *částka* 41 (4 November 1968), pp. 381–403.
127. On how token federalization gradually narrowed, see the informed and insightful article by Petr Pithart, published as Chapter 11, 'Towards a Shared Freedom, 1968–89', in J. Musil, ed., *The End of Czechoslovakia* (Budapest, 1995), pp. 201–22.
128. Kusin, *From Dubček to Charter 77*, pp. 56–58.
129. *AMV* A34 2650, '*Pracující lid*' to '*Soudruh Dubček, Smrkovský, Černík, Císař a spol*' (14 September 1968), unpaginated.
130. Kusin, *From Dubček to Charter 77*, p. 49.
131. Ibid., p. 58.
132. Ibid., p. 53.
133. Ibid., pp. 46–48.
134. J. Piekalkiewitz, *Public Opinion Polling in Czechoslovakia 1968–69* (New York, 1972), as cited in Kusin, *From Dubček to Charter 77*, p. 46.
135. L. Svoboda, broadcast to the nation (20 January 1969), *Rudé právo* (21 January 1969), p. 1.
136. See e.g. *AMV* cb 17/09, '*Nedopusťte zneužití pohřbu Jana Palacha*' (undated poster signed by the Action Committee of Prague Students).
137. *AMV* cb 16/08, '*Zpráva o pokusu sebevraždy upálením studenta Jana Palacha*' (19 January 1969), ff. 1–20; cb 16/01, '*Podezření z pokusu sebevraždy upálením studenta železniční školy v Šumperku – Jana Zajíce – hlášení*' (25 February 1969); 16/05, '*Protokol o výslechu svědka*' (26 February 1969); cb 16/09, '*Výpis z hlášení Městské správy veřejné bezpečnosti/vyšetřovací oddělení*' (19 January 1969).
138. Kusin, *From Dubček to Charter 77*, pp. 62–63.
139. Ibid., p. 63.
140. Ibid., p. 70.

141. *AMV* A 2/3–2401, '*Priebeh demonštrácie dňa 5.5.1969 v Plzni*', ff. 3–4.

142. D. Povolný, *Operativní technika v rukou StB* (Prague, 2001), pp. 10, 11.

143. Ibid., pp. 20–21.

144. Ibid., p. 59.

145. Ibid., p. 43.

146. *AMV* A 34/3884, '*Ohlasy k uzavření spojenecké smlouvy mezi ČSSR a SSSR*' (May 1970).

147. Kusin, *From Dubček to Charter 77*, pp. 71–72.

148. Ibid., pp. 72–73.

149. Ibid., pp. 73–75.

150. M. Šimečka, *The Restoration of Order: The Normalization of Czechoslovakia 1969–1976*, tr. A.G. Brain (London, 1984), p. 44.

151. Kusin, *From Dubček to Charter 77*, pp. 79, 81.

152. Ibid., p. 81.

153. Ibid., p. 88.

CHAPTER 10: FROM RESENTMENT TO REVOLUTION

1. Outraged exposés of 'Normalized' Czechoslovakia are too numerous to cite, but the two most influential nonfiction works are probably M. Šimečka, *The Restoration of Order: The Normalization of Czechoslovakia 1969–1976* (London, 1984) which was originally published in Bratislava in 1984 as *Obnovenie poriadku/Obnovení pořádku*; and Z. Mlynář, *Night Frost in Prague: The End of Humane Socialism*, tr. P. Wilson (London, 1980), which was originally published in West Germany in 1978 as *Nachtfrost*. Milan Kundera and Josef Škvorecký's many novels of the 1970s and 1980s, which were published in France and in Canada, their respective countries of exile, treated the same themes in fictional form and became well known in the West.

2. Šimečka, *The Restoration of Order*, p. 8.

3. Z. Mlynář, preface to Šimečka, *The Restoration of Order*, pp. 8–9.

4. *AMV* A34/3886, '*Názory čs. občanů na XIV. sjezd KSČ*', Hradec Králové regional *SNB* report to *II. správa FMV* (17 June 1971), ff. 108, 11.

5. *AMV* A34/3886, '*Názory čs. občanů na XIV. sjezd KSČ*' (1 June 1971), ff. 17–18.

6. *AMV* A34/3886, '*Názory čs. občanů na XIV. sjezd KSČ*', Hradec Králové regional *SNB* report to *II. správa FMV* (17 June 1971), ff. 109–10.

7. Ibid., ff. 113, 112, 105.

8. *AMV* A34/3886, *O. Pilát (1. odbor II. správy FMV)* to *Analytický odbor II. správy FMV*, f. 30.

9. *AMV* A34/3886, *A. Burda (StB Brno)* to *II. správa FMV*.

10. *AMV* A34/3886, '*Názory čs. občanů na XIV. sjezd KSČ*', *V. Šubrt, II. správa FMV 3. odbor* to *FMV* headquarters (22 June 1971), f. 42; Hradec Králové regional *SNB* report to *II. správa FMV* (17 June 1971), ff. 111–12, 122, 119.

11. H. Skilling and P. Wilson, eds, *Civic Freedom in Central Europe: Voices from Czechoslovakia* (Basingstoke, 1991), p. 6.

12. V. Havel, 'The Power of the Powerless' in J. Vladislav, ed., *Václav Havel or Living in Truth: Twenty-Two Essays* (London and Boston, 1986), p. 83.

13. I. McLean, ed., *Oxford Concise Dictionary of Politics* (Oxford, 1996), p. 164.

14. Šimečka, *The Restoration of Order* pp. 78–79.

15. Ordinance 120, '*Vyhláška ministra zahraničních věcí ze dne 10. května 1976 o Mezinárodním paktu o občanských a politických právech a Mezinárodním paktu o hospodářských, sociálních a kulturních právech*', *Sbírka zákonů Československé socialistické republiky* (Prague, 1976), pp. 570–83.

16. The full text of this initial Proclamation, together with the periodic reports issued by Charter 77 between 1977 and 1989, were simultaneously published in Prague and Bratislava in 1990 as V. Prečan, ed., *Charta 77 1977–1989. Od morální k demokratické revoluci: Dokumentace* (Prague and Bratislava, 1990).

17. See V. Havel, '*Jak se rodila Charta 77*' in ibid., pp. 17–18. According to a Czech television documentary made in 1996, Václav Havel wrote the first draft, Zdeněk Mlynář criticized and redrafted sections, and the novelist Pavel Kohout came up with the name 'Charter 77'. '*Charta 77: Začátky*', Česká televize 2 (Prague, 1996), as cited in J. Keane, *Václav Havel: A Political Tragedy in Six Acts* (London, 1999), p. 246, note.

18. '*Prohlášení Charty 77*' (1 January 1977), in Prečan, ed., *Charta 77*, p. 9.

19. Ibid., pp. 9–10.

20. Ibid., p. 10.

21. Ibid,. p. 11.

22. Ibid., p. 10.

23. Ibid., p. 11.
24. Ibid., pp. 11–12.
25. Ibid., p. 12.
26. Keane, *Václav Havel*, pp. 243, 254.
27. Kusin, *From Dubček to Charter 77*, p. 315.
28. Anon., *Anti-charta* (Prague, Revolver Revue, 2002), *passim*.
29. *Zveřejnění evidenčních podkladů a seznamu personálních spisů*, vol. 2 (Prague, 2003), p. 805.
30. See, for example, *Rudé právo* (12 January 1977); *Pravda* (12 January 1977); *Práce* (11 March 1977).
31. '*Anotovaný seznam dokumentů Charty 77 za léta 1977–1989*', in Prečan, *Charta 77*, p. 384; Kusin, *Dubček to Charter 77*, p. 315; Keane, *Václav Havel*, p. 248. See also Anon., *Anti-charta, passim*, which brings together newspaper clippings, documents and photographs of the regime's 'Anti-Charter' campaign of 1977.
32. R. Řezáč, '*Kdo je Václav Havel?*', Czechoslovak radio (9 March 1977), as cited in Keane, *Václav Havel*, p. 250. See also the film-length documentary (on general release and available on DVD) '*Občan Havel: scény z prezidentské kuchyně*', dir. Pavel Koutecký and Miroslav Janek (Film & Sociologie, Negativ, Michael Wolkowitz, FTV, Studio KF, 2008).
33. Kusin, *Dubček to Charter 77*, p. 313.
34. Keane, *Václav Havel*, p. 249; G. Ference, ed., *Chronology of Twentieth-Century Eastern European History* (Detroit, 1994), p. 144.
35. Kusin, *Dubček to Charter 77*, pp. 315–16.
36. V. Benda, 'The Parallel "*Polis*" ' in H. Skilling and P. Wilson, eds, *Civic Freedom in Central Europe: Voices from Czechoslovakia* (Houndmills, Basingstoke, 1991), pp. 35–37, 40.
37. V. Havel, 'The Power of the Powerless' in J. Vladislav, ed., *Václav Havel or Living in Truth: Twenty-Two Essays* (London and Boston, 1986), p. 41.
38. Ibid., p. 42.
39. Ibid., pp. 53–54.
40. D. Povolný, *Operativní technika v rukou StB* (Prague, 2001), p. 12.
41. Ibid., pp. 25, 33.
42. Ibid., p. 59.
43. Ference, *Chronology*, p. 146.
44. M. Gorbachev, *Memoirs* (London, 1997 [1995]), p. 624.
45. J. Žatkuliak *et al.*, *November 1989 a Slovensko: Chronológia a dokumenty (1985–1990)* (Bratislava, 1999), p. 19; P. Kenney, *A Carnival of Revolution: Central Europe 1989* (Princeton, N.J. and Oxford, 2002), p. 36.
46. Korec, *The Night of the Barbarians*, p. 452; Kenney, *Carnival of Revolution*, p. 36.
47. Their responses were later published in Skilling and Wilson, eds, *Civic Freedom in Central Europe*, pp. 42–128.
48. Benda, untitled essay in ibid., pp. 54, 53.
49. Kenney, *Carnival of Revolution*, pp. 83–84.
50. A. Stanger, 'The Price of Velvet' in M. Kraus and A. Stanger, eds and trs, *Irreconcilable Differences? Explaining Czechoslovakia's Dissolution* (Lanham, Md, 2000), p. 140.
51. Kenney, *Carnival of Revolution*, p. 37.
52. Ibid., p. 215.
53. See J. Simulčik, *Čas svitania: Sviečková manifestácia 25. marec 1988* (Prešov, 1998).
54. Kenney, *Carnival of Revolution*, pp. 215–16.
55. Ibid., pp. 216–17; Korec, *The Night of the Barbarians*, pp. 452–53.
56. M. Otáhal, interview with Marek Benda (May and October 1977), as published in M. Otáhal and M. Vaněk, *Sto studentských revolucí* (Prague, 1999), pp. 210–16; J. Obrman, 'The Wastage of Talent', Radio Free Europe Situation Report 19 (30 December 1987), pp. 31–34.
57. Interview with Marek Benda in Otáhal and Vaněk, *Sto studentských revolucí*, pp. 216–17.
58. Unpublished interview with a university student at the Pharmaceutical Faculty of Charles University in Hradec Králové about the 'Velvet Revolution' of 1989 (29 October 1998), as cited in S. Skinner, 'How Distinctly Czech Was the Velvet Revolution of 1989?' (unpublished University of Strathclyde Independent Study Project, 1999), f. 3.
59. *Denní situační zprávy StB z listopadu a prosince 1989* (Prague, 2000), p. 34.
60. Interview with Vít Novotný.
61. Interview with Ivan Havel in M. Long, *Making History: Czech Voices of Dissent and the Revolution of 1989* (Lanham, Md, 2005), p. 29.
62. *Denní situační zprávy StB*, p. 34.
63. M. Vaněk interview with Jan Bubeník (September and December 1998) in Otáhal and Vaněk, *Sto studentských revolucí* p. 237.

64. *Denní situační zprávy StB*, p. 34.
65. Interviews with Bubeník and Benda in Otáhal and Vaněk, *Sto studentských revolucí*, pp. 237, 219.
66. Interview with Benda in ibid., p. 221.
67. V. Bartuška, *Polojasno* (Prague, 1990), p. 225; Benda in Otáhal and Vaněk, *Sto studentských revolucí*, p. 220.
68. *Denní situační zprávy StB*, p. 35.
69. As reproduced in Žatkuliak *et al.*, *November 1989 a Slovensko*, p. 324.
70. Interview with Benda in Otáhal and Vaněk, *Sto studentských revolucí*, p. 220.
71. M. Heimann, unpublished interview with Ilona Bílková (17 June 1999) and with Vít Novotný (August and September 1999); Skinner, unpublished interview with Vít Novotný (29 October 1998).
72. *'Prvé vyhlásenie občianskeho hnutia Verejnost' proti násiliu'*, as reproduced in Žatkuliak *et al.*, *November 1989 a Slovensko*, p. 325; interview with Ivan Havel in Long, *Making History*, p. 30. See also F. Gál, *Z prvej ruky* (Bratislava, 1991).
73. A photocopy of the original Proclamation, together with many other documents from the revolution, may be consulted in the appendices to J. Bradley, *Czechoslovakia's Velvet Revolution: A Political Analysis* (Boulder, Colo., 1992). A selection also appears, in English translation, in B. Wheaton and Z. Kavan, *The Velvet Revolution: Czechoslovakia 1988–1991* (Boulder, Colo., San Francisco and Oxford, 1992).
74. Žatkuliak *et al.*, *November 1989 a Slovensko*, p. 326.
75. *'Projev M. Jakeše v Čs. televizi'*, *Svobodné slovo* (22 November 1989), p. 1.
76. Žatkuliak *et al.*, *November 1989 a Slovensko*, p. 67.
77. *Poslední hurá: Stenografický záznam z mimořádných zasedání ÚV KSČ 24. a 26. listopadu 1989* (Prague, 1992), p. 4.
78. S. Humphreys, 'A Comparative Chronology of Revolution, 1988–1990', in G. Prins, ed., *Spring in Winter: The 1989 Revolutions* (Manchester, 1990), p. 229; 'Proclamation of the Meeting of the People's Militia in Kolben-Daněk, Sokolovo, held on November 23, 1989', as reproduced, in English translation, in Wheaton and Kavan, *The Velvet Revolution*, pp. 212–13.
79. *AMV* uncatalogued, *Ústav pro výzkum veřejného mínění při FSÚ*.
80. The full text is reproduced, in English translation, in Wheaton and Kavan, *The Velvet Revolution*, pp. 212–13.
81. The full text is reproduced, in English translation, in ibid., pp. 209–10.
82. Bartl *et al.*, *Slovak History*, p. 168; A. Innes, *Czechoslovakia: The Short Goodbye* (New Haven, Conn. and London, 2001), p. 49.
83. T.G. Ash, *The Magic Lantern: The Revolution of '89 Witnessed in Warsaw, Budapest, Berlin and Prague* (New York, 1990), pp. 101–3.
84. Žatkuliak *et al.*, *November 1989 a Slovensko*, p. 71.
85. *'Stávky se zúčastnila celá naše republika'*, *Svobodné slovo* (28 November 1989), p. 1.

CHAPTER 11: THE END OF CZECHOSLOVAKIA

1. Interview with Ivan Havel by Michael Long in Long, *Making History*, p. 34.
2. See the brilliant book-length essay on this theme: L. Holy, *The Little Czech and the Great Czech Nation: National Identity and the Post-Communist Social Transformation* (Cambridge, 1996), *passim*.
3. S. Wolchik, *Czechoslovakia in Transition: Politics, Economics and Society* (London and New York, 1991), pp. 70–71, 91.
4. According to a public-opinion poll taken in January 1992, as cited in S. Fisher, *Political Change in Post-Communist Slovakia and Croatia: From Nationalist to Europeanist* (New York, 2006), p. 14.
5. See e.g. Ash, *The Magic Lantern*, pp. 79, 89, 121, 126, 130.
6. *'Projev k občanům na Nový rok'* (1 January 1990), in V. Prečan, ed., *Václav Havel: Projevy (leden–červen 1990)* (Prague, 1990), p. 11.
7. Wolchik, *Czechoslovakia in Transition*, pp. 115–17.
8. Ibid., p. 67.
9. *'Rozkaz prezidenta Československé socialistické republiky ze dne 29. prosince 1989. Změny ve vojenském školství'* (2 January 1990), *Sbírka zákonů Československé socialistické republiky* (Prague, 1990), p. 3 and *'Rozhodnutí prezidenta Československé socialistické republiky o amnestii ze dne 1. ledna 1990'*, ibid., pp. 1–2.
10. No. 71, *'Sdělení federálního ministerstva zahraničních věcí: Dohoda mezi vládou Československé socialistické republiky a vládou Svazu sovětských socialistických republik o odchodu sovětských vojsk z území Československé socialistické republiky'* (26 February 1990), *Sbírka zákonů Československé socialistické republiky* (Prague, 1990), pp. 319–20.
11. See E. Galway, 'Restitution: The Case of the Roman Catholic Church in the Czech Republic' (unpublished M.Res dissertation, Department of Central and East European Studies, University of Glasgow, 2002), ff. 13–16, 46.

12. Williams and Deletant, *Security Intelligence Services in the New Democracies*, pp. 55–56.
13. Ibid., p. 61.
14. No. 451, '*Zákon, kterým se stanoví některé další předpoklady pro výkon některých funkcí ve státních orgánech a organizacích České a Slovenské Federativní Republiky*' (5 November 1991), *Sbírka zákonů České a Slovenské Federativní Republiky* (Prague, 1991), pp. 2106–2110.
15. Blaive, 'The Czechs and their Communism, Past and Present', p. 6.
16. Ibid., p. 7.
17. See D. Green, 'Memories and Perceptions of Czechoslovakia's 1989 Revolution' (unpublished MRes thesis in Russian, Central and East European Studies, University of Glasgow, 2008).
18. Some of their stories, whose aim was to show how misleading the public slur of collaboration could be, were gathered together and published as Z. Salivarová-Škvorecká, ed., *Dopisy lidí ze seznamu* (Toronto, 1993).
19. M. Vadas, 'Notes on the Role of Television in Czechoslovakia's Dissolution', in Kraus and Stanger, eds and trs, *Irreconcilable Differences?*, pp. 270–72, 279.
20. Mannová, *A Concise History of Slovakia*, p. 297.
21. No. 50, '*Ústavný zákon Slovenskej národnej rady z 1. marca 1990 o názve, štátnom znaku, štátnej pečati a o štátnej hymne Slovenskej republiky*' (1 March 1990) and no. 53, '*Ústavní zákon České národní rady ze dne 6. března 1990 o změně názvu České socialistické republiky*' (6 March 1990), *Sbírka zákonů Československé socialistické republiky* (Prague, 1990), pp. 241, 250.
22. 'Narrative Chronology of the Czech-Slovak Conflict, 1990–1992' in Kraus and Stanger, *Irreconcilable Differences?*, pp. 310–12.
23. Stanger, 'The Price of Velvet' in ibid., p. 144.
24. Ibid., pp. 146–50.
25. See Laws 460, '*Ústava Slovenskej republiky*' (1 October 1992), *Sbírka zákonů České a Slovenské Federativní Republiky* (Prague 1992), p. 241 and 13 (6 March 1990), pp. 2659–80; 542, '*Ústavní zákon o zániku České a Slovenské Federativní Republiky*', *Sbírka zákonů České a Slovenské Federativní Republiky*, r. 1992, č. 110 (8 December 1992), pp. 3253–4, 1, '*Ústava České republiky*', *Sbírka zákonů České republiky*, r. 1993, č. 1 (28 December 1992), pp. 1–16.
26. This English version is from the approved translation published as National Council of the Slovak Republic, *The Constitution of the Slovak Republic* (Press Agency of the Slovak Republic, Pressfoto, 1993), p. 15.
27. Innes, *Czechoslovakia*, pp. xii, 73.
28. C.S. Leff, *The Czech and Slovak Republics: Nation versus State* (Boulder, Colo., 1997), p. 128.
29. Innes, *Czechoslovakia*, pp. 174–75.
30. See e.g. '*Odsouzení rasových útoků*', *Lidové noviny* (10 May 1990), p. 1.

BIBLIOGRAPHY

MANUSCRIPT SOURCES

Archiv Ministerstva vnitra České republiky (AMV) **(Archive of the Czech Ministry of the Interior)**

Fond 304 (boxes 176, 178, 182, 185, 186) monthly regional *SNB* situation reports for 1945, 1946, 1947, 1948 and 1949; 374 files re: Sokol (1948); summary of 'ordinary' and 'revolutionary' activities in Pardubice district (May–June 1945); weekly *SNB* reports from Pardubice District Headquarters for 1946

Fond 305 (boxes 108, 210, 365, 374) *StB* situation reports for 1948 from: Prague; České Budějovice; Česká Lípa; Hradec Králové; Jičín; Karlovy Vary; Klatovy; Kolín; Liberec; Mladá Boleslav; Most; Pardubice; Písek; Plzeň; Tábor; Ústí nad Labem; Brno; Olomouc; Uherské Hradiště; Jihlava; Znojmo; Ostrava; Opava; Český Těšín (*hereafter cited as* 'regional *StB* situation reports'); 231 re: Junák

Fond 310 (box 61) re: government crisis and 'anti-state' activity in February 1948

A 2/1–155, 175, 178, 382, 591, 670, 1647 State security (*MNB*) instructions to all regional districts in the Czechoslovak Republic, 29 June 1951; surveillance of private correspondence and undercover surveys of public opinion 1954; notes and papers from Ministry of the Interior meetings in 1954; regional reports from Slovak Ministry of the Interior; report re: '*Akcia "B"*' (30 July 1953); report on the Slovak security and political situation during elections to the Slovak National Council in October 1954

A 2/2 1019 re: counter-intelligence reports for the attention of President Novotný in 1965

A 24/767 re: Czechoslovak public opinion on the current situation; files re: Jan Šejna 1966 and 1967

A 10 203 re: attack on Aeroflot building in Prague 1969

A 213–2133 re: Strahov student demonstration in 1967

A 213–2401 re: demonstration in Plzeň 1969

A 213–2285 re: USSR-ČSR relations in 1969

A 34/2647 (1968); 2648 (1968); 2649 (1968); 2650 (1968); 2654 (1968); 2656 (1968); 2658 (1968); 2660 (1968–1969); 3884 (1970); 3885 (1970); 3886 (1971) *StB* regional situation and special reports before and after Warsaw Pact invasion of August 1968; reports sent from other socialist countries; reports by foreign diplomats; hate mail sent to the *KSČ* leadership by Czechoslovak citizens; posters, leaflets and resolutions collected by the Ministry of the Interior during and after 21–27 August 1968

A 34/1 Ministry of the Interior public opinion survey (1989)

CD 16 re: suicide of Jan Zajíc 1969; CD 17 re: suicide and funeral of Jan Palach 1969

Uncatalogued materials

StB regional reports re: state-wide reactions to the meeting between Reagan and Gorbachev in December 1987; unpublished booklets in Czech and in Slovak for internal Ministry of the Interior use re: Czechoslovak public opinion (especially youth) about the international situation in 1987

H 718 1–4 documentation re: '*Akce "K"* ' 1950
V-4042/MV, ff. 257–64
V-33766–014 interrogations of witnesses and signatories to Charter 77
V-6301/MV papers concerning the Milada Horáková trial
11868 Ministry of Foreign Affairs report re: Czechoslovak participation in meetings of volunteers from the International Brigades in Spain, 30 October 1945

Masarykův ústav AV ČR (Masaryk Institute of the Czech Academy of Sciences)
Benešův archiv (Beneš Archive)
EB II, boxes 190 re: wartime activities and propaganda; 310 re: wartime activities and propaganda; 238 papers from the office of the president; 345 re: wartime exile; P 40 re: state-Church relations 1945–48
EB III, boxes 44 re: postwar population transfers; 60 re: Slovakia 1945–47; 350 re: Košice political programme and National Front government

Masarykův archiv (Masaryk Archive)
TGM Kor I T.G. Masaryk's correspondence 1914
TGM R presidential secretary's correspondence
JGM I Jan Masaryk's correspondence

Státní ústřední archiv v Praze (State Central Archive in Prague)
ÚV KSČ (Czechoslovak Communist Party Central Committee Archive)
Fond 00/09 '*IX. Sjezd KSČ (1949)*'; 00/12 '*XII. Sjezd KSČ (1962)*'; 00/13 '*XIII. Sjezd KSČ (1966)*'; 02/4 '*Informace pro sekretariát ÚV KSČ*'

Úřad říšského protektora (Reich Protectorate Archive)
I 3e: box 13 (*Památková péče*)
Dodatky (supplemental materials) I: Boxes 26, 27, 28
PMV: box 92

Public Record Office, Kew
HS 4/1; 4/7; 4/11; 4/16; 4/44; 4/56; 4/68; 4/78; 4/79; 4/82 SOE papers, reports, telegrams re: negotiations with President Beneš 1942 and operations in Czechoslovakia, 1944–45, including reports on Czech Brigade and SOE recruiting 1943; Slovak National Uprising 1944; post-operational report of Wolfram team 1944; lists of alleged Gestapo agents and informers in Moravia, 1944; top-secret report on Soviet activity in Czechoslovakia, January 1945; report of Prague Uprising May 1945.
FO 371/4681 letters from Germans in Silesia routed through George Bell

NEWSPAPERS AND MAGAZINES

Čas (1914)
Český zápas (1945)
Czechoslovak Life (1951; 1952)
Hlas revoluce: List československé obce legionářské (1948)
Katolické noviny (1968)
Lidové noviny (1938; 1939; 1948; 1988; 1989; 1990)
Literární noviny (1990)
Národní osvobození (1948)
Národní politika (1918)
Pravda (1968)
Právo živnostníků (1948)
Pražské Lidové noviny (1938)
Rudé právo (1948; 1989; 1990)
Slovák (1939; 1943; 1944; 1945)

Student (1968)
Svobodné slovo (1989)
Zemědělské noviny (1967; 1974; 1977; 1980; 1981)
Zprávy Státního úřadu statistického Republiky československé (1920; 1921)

UNPUBLISHED INTERVIEWS AND PRIVATE FAMILY PAPERS

Interviews by Mary Heimann with: Ilona Bílková (17 June 1999; 27 June 1999); Jan Čulík (19 June 2000); Jiří Hovorka and Mariana Hovorková (23 February 2003); Matúš Minárik (21 May 2000); Vít Novotný (August 1999; 3 September 1999; 8 September 1999); Marcela Reslová (13 May 2000)

Eva Benda papers. Duplicates of family photographs and documents re: transportations from Prague to various concentration camps; reminiscences of imprisonment in Terezín/ Theresienstadt, Auschwitz and Oederan concentration camps (1944–45) and postwar Prague (1945–48)

Květa Bihellerová papers. 'My Century and My Many Lives' (1993; unpublished reminiscences of František Munk [b. 1901]); 'Leaving Praha: Some Details' (1997; written by Misha Munk); untitled autobiographical and political reminiscences written in 2003 by Květa Prášilová-Bihellerová (1915–2008); '*Zpráva o půlroční činnosti třicetičlenné skupiny československých uprchlíků žijících za II. světové války (1939–1945) ve Velké Británii a o "The Derby Czechoslovak arts group", kterou vytvořili*' (2000; unpublished reminiscences, photographs, newspaper clippings and other records of experiences as part of a group of Czechoslovak refugees in Britain during the Second World War and of 'The Derby Czechoslovak Arts Group' which they formed)

Mariana Kloudová papers. Documents and family papers re: exclusion, registration and deportation of Jews in Prague (1943–44); documents, family papers and newspaper clippings re: state trial in Prague of the International Standard Electric Corporation trial in October 1951

PUBLISHED PRIMARY SOURCES

Andrew, C. and O. Gordievsky, *KGB: The Inside Story of its Foreign Operations from Lenin to Gorbachev*. New York: HarperCollins, 1990

Anon., *The Action Programme of the Czechoslovak Communist Party*. Nottingham: Bertrand Russell Peace Foundation, n.d. [1968]

Anon., *Československý státník Klement Gottwald*, 2nd edn. Prague: Ministry of Information, 1947

Anon., 'The Constitutional Charter of the Czechoslovak Republic [1920]', *Select Constitutions of the World*. Dublin: Eason, 1922, 145–67

Anon., *Czechoslovakia: A Handbook of Facts and Figures*, 2nd edn. Prague: Orbis, 1964

Anon., *Czechoslovakia's Blueprint for Freedom. Dubček's Statements: The Original and Official Documents Leading to the Conflict of August 1968*, ed. P. Ello. Washington, D.C.: Acropolis Books, 1968

Anon., *Denní situační zprávy StB z listopadu a prosince 1989*, vol. 6, 3 parts. Prague: MVČR, 2000

Anon., *Dr Edvard Beneš ve fotografii: Historie velkého života*, 8th edn. Prague: Orbis, 1947

Anon., 'The German Minority in Czechoslovakia', *Slavonic and East European Review* (1936), 295–300

Anon., *Hořké vzpomínání. Z dopisů a vzpomínek chlapců pétépáků*, ed. A. Drobílek *et al.*, vol. 1. Prague: Academia, 1996

Anon., *Jan Masaryk jak jsme ho znali*, 2nd edn. Prague: Ministry of Information, 1948

Anon., *Kronika sametové revoluce*. Prague: Československá tisková kancelář, n.d.

Anon., *Masaryk ve fotografii: Historie velkého života*. Prague: Orbis-Čin, 1937

Anon., *Na půl žerdi: Jan Masaryk odešel*. Prague: Svoboda, n.d. [1948]

Anon., *On Events in Czechoslovakia: Facts, Documents, Press Reports and Eye-Witness Accounts*, tr. from the original Russian. Moscow: Press Group of Soviet Journalists, 1968

Anon., *Poslední hurá: tajné stenografické záznamy z posledních zasedání ÚV KSČ v listopadu 1989*. Prague: Cesty, 1992

Anon., *Proces s vedením protistátního spikleneckého centra v čele s Rudolfem Slánským*. Prague: Ministerstvo spravedlnosti, 1953

Anon., *Prohlášení nezávislosti československého národa zatímní vládou československou (Declaration of Independence of the Czechoslovak Nation by its Provisional Government)*. Prague: Patriae, 1998 (1918)

Anon., *Sbierka nariadení Slovenskej národnej rady*. Košice: WIKO, 1945

Anon., *Sbírka zákonů a nařízení*. Prague: Tiskárna Protektorátu Čechy a Morava, 1939

Anon., *Sbírka zákonů a nařízení Protektorátu Čechy a Morava*. Prague: Tiskárna Protektorátu Čechy a Morava, 1940–44

Anon., *Sbírka zákonů a nařízení státu československého*. Prague: Státní tiskárna, 1918–38

Anon., *Sbírka zákonů a nařízení státu česko-slovenského*. Prague: Státní tiskárna, 1938

Anon., *Sbírka zákonů a nařízení státu československého*. Prague: Státní tiskárna, 1945–59

Anon., *Sbírka zákonů Československé socialistické republiky*. Prague: Knihtisk, 1960–66; Statistické a evidenční vydavatelství tiskopisů, 1966–89

Anon., *Sbírka zákonů České a Slovenské Federativní Republiky*. Prague: Statistické a evidenční vydavatelství tiskopisů, 1990–92

Anon., *Sbírka zákonů České republiky*. Prague: Statistické a evidenční vydavatelství tiskopisů, 1993

Anon., *Slovenský zákonník*. Bratislava: Vláda Slovenské republiky a Sněm Slovenské republiky (podle podpisu), 1939–45

Anon., *Students in Czechoslovakia: Life and Work of the Young Intelligentsia*. Prague: National Union of Czechoslovak Students, 1949

Anon., *Švehla ve fotografii*. Prague: Orbis, 1938

Anon., *Thomas G. Masaryk, President of the Czechoslovak Republic*. London: Eyre & Spottiswoode, 1923

Anon., *The Treatment of Minorities in Czechoslovakia and Hungary*. Prague: Orbis, 1927

Anon., *Úradný vestník*. Košice: Úrad Predsedníctva Slovenskej národnej rady, 1945

Anon., *Vznik samostatného Československého státu v roce 1918: svědectví a dokumenty*. Prague: Melantrich, 1988

Anon., *What Happened in Czechoslovakia? An Account of the Government Crisis in February 1948*. Prague: Orbis, 1948

Antalová, I., ed., *Verejnosť proti násiliu 1989–1991: svedectvá a dokumenty*. Bratislava: Nadácia Milana Šimečku, 1998

Ash, T.G., *The Magic Lantern: The Revolution of '89 Witnessed in Warsaw, Budapest, Berlin and Prague*. New York: Vintage Books, 1990; 1993

Augusta, P. and F. Honzák, *Československo 1918–1938*. Prague: Albatros, 1992

Bartuška, V., *Polojasno*. Prague: Ex Libris, 1990

Benda, E., 'From Prague to Theresienstadt and Back', in M. Glassner and R. Krell, eds, *And Life Is Changed Forever*. Detroit: Wayne State University Press, 2006

Benda, L., *Židé v našem hospodářství*. Svaz Čechů židů, 1939

Benda, M. *et al.*, eds, *Studenti psali revoluci*. Prague: Univerzum, 1990

Benda, V., 'The Parallel "Polis" ' in H.G. Skilling and P. Wilson, eds, *Civic Freedom in Central Europe: Voices from Czechoslovakia*. Basingstoke and London: Macmillan, 1991

[Beneš, E.], *Dekrety prezidenta republiky 1940–1945*, 2 vols, ed. K. Jech and K. Kaplan. Prague: Ústav pro soudobé dějiny AV ČR, 1995

Beneš, E., *Demokracie dnes a zítra*, 3rd edn. Prague: Čin, 1946

Beneš, E., *Mnichovské dny: Paměti*. Prague: Svoboda, 1968

Beneš, E., *Paměti. Od Mnichova k nové válce a k novému vítězství*, 3rd edn. Prague: Orbis, 1948, tr. into English as *Memoirs of Dr Eduard Beneš: From Munich to New War and New Victory*, tr. G. Elias. Boston: Houghton Mifflin, 1953 [1947])

Beneš, E., *Šest let exilu a druhé světové války: Řeči, projevy a dokumenty z r. 1938–45*. Prague: Orbis, 1946

Beneš, E., *Světová válka a naše revoluce: vzpomínky a úvahy z bojů za svobodu národa*, 2 vols, 6th edn. Prague: Orbis and Čin, 1935, tr. into English as *My War Memoirs*, tr. P. Selver. London: George Allen & Unwin, 1928

[Beneš, E.], 'U.S.S.R. and France – Germany and Hungary. Two Speeches by President Beneš', *Central European Observer* (15 May 1942)

Bil'ak, V., *Paměti Vasila Bil'aka*, 2 vols. Prague: Agentura Cesty, 1991

Brod, T. *et al., Proč jsme v listopadu vyšli do ulic*. Brno: Doplněk, 1999

Brook, S., *The Double Eagle: Vienna, Budapest and Prague*. London: Hamish Hamilton, 1988

Buriánek, F. ed., *Svědectví: příběhy českých studentů z akce 17. listopad*. Prague: Mladá Fronta, 1979

Čápová, H., '*Kat Milady Horákové žije*', *Respekt* 14:9 (24 February–2 March 2003), 6

'Committee to Defend Czechoslovak Socialists', *Voices of Czechoslovak Socialists*. Whitstable, Kent: 1976

De Colonna, B., *Czecho-Slovakia Within*. London: Thornton Butterworth, 1938

Deitch, G., *For the Love of Prague*, 2nd edn. Příbram: PBTisk, 1998 [1995]

Deutscher, T., Z. Bluh-Sling and K. Coates, *Political Prisoners in Czechoslovakia and the USSR*. Nottingham: Bertrand Russell Peace Foundation, n.d. [1975]

[Doubek, B.], *StB o sobě: výpověď vyšetřovatele Bohumila Doubka*, ed. K. Kaplan. Prague: Úřad dokumentace a vyšetřování zločinů komunismu, 2002

Doubek, B., *StB o sobě: výpověď vyšetřovatele Bohumila Doubka*, ed. K. Kaplan. Prague: Úřad dokumentace a vyšetřování zločinů komunismu, 2002

Drtina, P., *Československo můj osud*, 2 vols. Toronto: Sixty-Eight Publishers, 1982

Dubček, A., *Hope Dies Last: The Autobiography of Alexander Dubček*, ed. and tr. J. Hochman. New York, Tokyo and London: Kodansha International, 1993

Dušek, A., *Příručka pro sběratele československých známek a celin*, 1st edn. Prague: Svoboda, 1988

Ello, P., ed., *Czechoslovakia's Blueprint for Freedom*. Washington, D.C.: Acropolis Books, 1968

Erdely, E.V., *Germany's First European Protectorate: The Fate of the Czechs and Slovaks*. London: Robert Hale, 1941

Fermor, P. Leigh, *A Time of Gifts*. London: John Murray, 1977

Fierlinger, Z. *et al., Košický vládní program: Program nové československé vlády Národní fronty Čechů a Slováků*. Prague: Svoboda, 1974 (Košice, 1945)

Frolik, J., *The Frolik Defection: The Memoirs of an Intelligence Agent*. London: Leo Cooper, 1975

Frolík, J., '*Ještě k nástinu organizačního vývoje státobezpečnostních složek sboru národní bezpečnosti v letech 1948–1989*', *Sborník archivních prací* 2 (2002), 371–519

Frolík, J., '*Nástin organizačního vývoje státobezpečnostních složek Sboru národní bezpečnosti v letech 1948–1989*', *Sborník archivních prací* 2 (1991), 447–508

Fučík, J., *Reportáž psaná na oprátce*. Most: Orego, 1994

Fučíková, *G. Julius Fučík ve fotografii*. Prague: Novinář, 1977

Gál, F., *Z prvej ruky*. Bratislava: Archa, 1991

Gorbachev, M., *Memoirs*. London: Bantam Books, 1997 [1995]

Gottwald, K., *Kupředu, zpátky ni krok!*, 5th enlarged edn. Prague: Orbis, 1949

Gottwald, K., *O otázkách války a obrany vlasti*. Prague: Naše vojsko, 1953

Gottwald, K., *Spisy*, vols 14 and 15. Prague: Rudé právo, 1958; 1961

Grant Duff, S., *A German Protectorate: The Czechs under Nazi Rule*. London: Macmillan, 1942

Grant Duff, S., *The Parting of Ways: A Personal Account of the Thirties*. London: Peter Owen, 1982

Granville Baker, B., *From a Terrace in Prague*. London: George Allen & Unwin, 1923

Grünfeld, O., *The Survivor's Path*. Prague: Aislaby Press, 1995

Hájek, J.S., *Wilsonovská legenda v dějinách ČSR*. Prague: Státní nakladatelství politické literatury, 1953

Hašek, J., *The Good Soldier Švejk*, tr. C. Parrott. London: Penguin Books, 1973

Hašek, J., *The Red Commissar: Including Further Adventures of the Good Soldier Švejk and Other Stories*, tr. C. Parrott. London: Heinemann, 1981

Havel, V., *Dálkový výslech*. Prague: Melantrich, 1989

Havel, V., 'The Power of the Powerless' (1978) in *Václav Havel or Living in Truth: Twenty-Two Essays*, ed. J. Vladislav. London and Boston: Faber and Faber, 1986

Havel, V., *Prosím stručně: Rozhovor s Karlem Hvížďalou, poznámky, dokumenty*. České Budějovice: Gallery, 2006

Havel, V., *Summer Meditations*, tr. P. Wilson. New York: Vintage Books, 1993 (1992)

Havel, V., *Václav Havel: Projevy (leden–červen 1990)*, ed. V. Prečan. Prague: Vyšehrad, 1990

Heisler, J.B. and J.E. Mellon, *Under the Carpathians: Home of a Forgotten People*. London: Lindsay Drummond, 1946

Henderson, A., *Eyewitness in Czecho-Slovakia*. London: George G. Harrap, 1939

Henderson, N., *Failure of a Mission: Berlin 1937–1939*. London: Hodder & Stoughton, 1941 (1940)

Herben, J., *Proti proudu*. Prague: Česká expedice/Riopress, 1997 [1935]

Hesse, F., *Hitler and the English*, tr. F.A. Voight. London: Allan Wingate, 1954

Hitchcock, E.B., *'I Built a Temple for Peace': The Life of Eduard Beneš*. New York and London: Harper, 1940

Hitler, A., *Hitler's Table Talk, 1941–1944*, tr. N. Cameron and R.H. Stevens, ed. H. Trevor-Roper. London: Phoenix Press, 2000 (Weidenfeld & Nicolson, 1953)

Hodža, M., *Federation in Central Europe: Reflections and Reminiscences*. London: Jarrolds, 1942

Hoffman, E., *Exit into History: A Journey through the New Eastern Europe*. London: Heinemann, 1993

Hrabal, B., *I Served the King of England*, tr. P. Wilson. London: Picador, 1989

Hromadka, J.L., *Thoughts of a Czech Pastor*, tr. M. Page and B. Page. London: SCM Press, 1970

Institute of Marxism-Leninism [of the Central Committees of the *KSČ* and *KSS*], *An Outline of the History of the Communist Party of Czechoslovakia*. Prague: Orbis, 1980

Jakeš, M., *Dva roky generálním tajemníkem*. Prague: AZ Servis, 1996

James, H.A. and J.P. Musil, *Prague, My Love: An Unusual Guide Book to the Hidden Corners of Prague*. Prague: Crossroads of Prague, 1992

Jandík, S., *T.G.M. v Lánech*. Prague: Za Svobodu, 1946

Jesina, C., ed., *The Birth of Czechoslovakia*. Washington, D.C.: Czechoslovak National Council of America, 1968

Josten, J., *Oh, my Country*. London: Latimer House, 1949

'Justinian', 'Carpathian Ruthenia', *Eastern Europe* 5:4 (June 1921), 228–36

Kavan, R., *Love and Freedom*. London: Grafton Books, 1985

Kavka, F., *An Outline of Czechoslovak History*. Prague: Orbis, 1960

Kennan, G., *From Prague after Munich: Diplomatic Papers 1938–1940*. Princeton, N.J.: Princeton University Press, 1968

Kennan, G., *Memoirs 1925–1950*. Boston: Little, Brown, 1967

Kerner, R.J., ed., *Czechoslovakia: Twenty Years of Independence*. Berkeley and Los Angeles: University of California Press, 1940

Kettner, P. and I. Jedlička, *Proč zemřel Jan Masaryk?* Prague: Horizont, 1990 [1968]

Kirschbaum, J., 'Facts and Events behind the Scenes of Slovakia's Declaration of Independence', *Slovakia* 9:4 (1959), 1–7

Kirschbaum, J., 'The Politics of Hlinka's Slovak People's Party in the Slovak Republic', *Slovakia* 1:1 (1951), 43–49

Klaus, V., *Rebirth of a Country Five Years After: Collection of Speeches of the Prime Minister of the Czech Republic*. Prague: Ringier ČR, 1994

Klaus, V., *Renaissance: The Rebirth of Liberty in the Heart of Europe*. Washington, D.C.: Cato Institute, 1997

Klaus, V., *Rok první: 2003: projevy, články, eseje*. Prague: Knižní klub, 2004

Klíma, I., *The Spirit of Prague and Other Essays*, tr. P. Wilson. London: Granta Books, 1994

Kobak, A., *Joe's War: My Father Decoded*. London: Virago, 2004

Korec, J.C. Cardinal, *The Night of the Barbarians: Memoirs of the Communist Persecution of the Slovak Cardinal*, tr. P. Siska *et al.* Wauconda, Ill.: Bolchazy-Carducci Publishers, 2002

Kovály, H.M., *Under a Cruel Star: A Life in Prague 1941–1968*, tr. F. Epstein and H. Epstein. Cambridge, Mass.: Plunkett Lake Press, 1986

[Kramář, K.], *Paměti Dr. Karla Kramáře*, ed. K. Hoch. Prague: Pražské Akciové Tiskárny, n.d.

Kramář, K., *Řeči a projevy předsedy prvé vlády československé*. Prague: Politický klub Československé národní demokracie, 1935

Krejčí, A., *T.G. Masaryk a Sokol*. Prague: Československá obec sokolská, 1947

Krofta, K., *A Short History of Czechoslovakia*, tr. W. Beardmore. London: Williams & Norgate, 1935

Kryl, K., *Znamení doby*, ed. J. Šulc. Prague: Mladá Fronta, 1996

Lansing, R., *The Peace Negotiations: A Personal Narrative*. London: Constable, 1921

Lettrich, J., *History of Modern Slovakia*. London: Atlantic Press, 1956

Levy, A., *Rowboat to Prague*. New York: Orion Press/Grossman Publishers, 1972

Levy, E., *Just One More Dance: A Story of Degradation and Fear, Faith and Compassion from a Survivor of the Nazi Death Camps*. Edinburgh and London: Mainstream Publishing, 1998

Lewis, F., *The Red Pawn: The Life of Noel Field*. Garden City, N.Y.: Doubleday, 1965

Littell, R., ed., *The Czech Black Book*. London: Pall Mall, 1969

Lloyd George, D., *Memoirs of the Peace Conference*, vol. 2. New Haven, Conn.: Yale University Press, 1939

Lochman, J., *Church in a Marxist Society: A Czechoslovak View*. New York: Harper & Row, 1970

Lockhart, R.H. Bruce, 'The Second Exile of Eduard Beneš', *Slavonic and East European Review* 28 (1949–50), 39–59

Loebl, E., *Sentenced and Tried: The Stalinist Purges in Czechoslovakia*, tr. M. Michael. London: Elek Books, 1969

London, A., *L'Aveu: Dans l'engrenage du procès de Prague*. Saint-Armand: Folio, 1968

Long, M., ed., *Making History: Czech Voices of Dissent and the Revolution of 1989*, Lanham, Md.: Rowman & Littlefield, 2005

Marco, J., *Soudruh Agresor*. Prague: Mladá Fronta, 1990

Marel, R., *La Ruthénie Subcarpathique (Podkarpatska Rus)*. Paris: Paul Hartmann, 1935

Margolius, I., *Reflections of Prague*. Chichester, West Sussex: John Wiley & Sons, 2006

Martin, N., *Prague Winter*. London: Peter Halban, 1990

Masaryk, T.G., *The Lectures of T.G. Masaryk at the University of Chicago Summer 1902*, ed. D.B. Shillinglaw. London: Associated University Presses, 1978

Masaryk, T.G., *The New Europe: The Slav Standpoint*. London: Eyre & Spottiswoode, 1918

[Masaryk, T.G.], *President Masaryk Tells his Story*, ed. K. Čapek, tr. D. Round Heim. London: George Allen & Unwin, 1934

Masaryk, T.G., *Světová revoluce za války a ve válce 1914–1918*, 2 vols. Prague: Čin, 1938 (1925). (Published in English as *The Making of a State: Memories and Observations, 1914–1918*, tr. H. Wickham Steed. New York: Frederick A. Stokes, 1927)

[Masaryk, T.G.], *Talks with T.G. Masaryk*, ed. K. Čapek, tr. D. Round Heim. North Haven, Conn.: Catbird Press, 1995

Masaryk, J., *Volá Londýn*. Prague and London: Lincolns-Prager, 1948

Masaryková, C., *Listy do vězení*, ed. A. Masaryková. Prague: Vladimír Žikeš, 1948

Masarykův ústav Akademie věd ČR, *Declaration of Independence of the Czechoslovak Nation by its Provisional Government: Prohlášení nezávislosti československého národa zatímní vládou československou*. Prague: Patriae, 1998

Milyukov, P., 'Edward Beneš', *Slavonic and East European Review* 17:50 (1939), 297–328

Ministerstvo vnitra, *Zveřejnění evidenčních podkladů a seznamu personálních spisů*, 12 vols. Prague: Ministerstvo vnitra, 2002

Mlynář, Z., *Night Frost in Prague: The End of Humane Socialism*, tr. P. Wilson. London: C. Hurst, 1980

Moravec, F. and H. Disher, *Master of Spies: The Memoirs of General Frantisek Moravec*. London, Sydney and Toronto: The Bodley Head, 1975

Morrell, S., *I Saw the Crucifixion*. London: Peter Davies, n.d. [1938]

Mothersole, J., *Czechoslovakia: The Land of an Unconquerable Ideal*. London: John Lane/The Bodley Head, 1926

Mot'ka, L. and Authors' Collective, *Touring Czechoslovakia*. Prague: Sportovní a turistické nakladatelství, 1962

Münzer, J., *Dospívání nad propastí: deník Jiřího Münzera*. Prague: Radioservis, 2002

Murín, C., *Remembrances and Testimony (Dr. Jozef Tiso and the Slovak Republic 1939–1945)*, tr. V. Cincík. Montreal: RealTime Publishing, 1992

Navrátil, J., ed., *The Prague Spring 1968: A National Security Archive Documents Reader*. Budapest: Central European Press, 1998

Nicolson, H., *Peacemaking 1919*. London: Constable, 1933 (1945 edn)

Nosek, V., *Independent Bohemia: An Account of the Czecho-Slovak Struggle for Liberty*. London and Toronto: J.M. Dent, 1918

Novotný, V. and V. Šimek, *Československé mince 1918–1993. Mince české a slovenské republiky 1993–1994*. Hodonín: OB a ZP servis, 1994

Obrman, J., 'The Wastage of Talent', *Radio Free Europe Situation Report* 19 (30 December 1987), 31–34

Otáhal, M. and Z. Sládek, *Deset pražských dnů: 17.–27. listopad 1989*. Prague: Academia, 1990

Otáhal, M. and M. Vaněk, *Sto studentských revolucí*. Prague: Lidové noviny, 1999

Pelikán, J. ed., *The Czechoslovak Political Trials, 1950–1954: The Suppressed Report of the Dubček Government's Commission of Inquiry, 1968*, various translators. London: Macdonald, 1970

Pelikán, J. ed., *The Secret Vysočany Congress: Proceedings and Documents of the Extraordinary Fourteenth Congress of the Communist Party of Czechoslovakia, 22 August 1968*, tr. G. Theiner and D. Viney. London: Allen Lane/The Penguin Press, 1969

Piekalkiewitz, J., *Public Opinion Polling in Czechoslovakia 1968–69*. New York and London: Praeger, 1972

Pithart, P., *Osmašedesátý*. Prague: Rozmluvy, 1990

Pollitt, H., *In Memory of Joseph Stalin and Klement Gottwald*. London: Communist Party/Farleigh Press, n.d. [1953]

Prečan, V., ed., *Charta 77 1977–1989. Od morální k demokratické revoluci: Dokumentace*. Prague and Bratislava: Scheinfeld-Schwarzenberg and Archa, 1990

Prečan, V., ed., *Prague-Washington-Prague: Reports from the United States Embassy in Czechoslovakia, November–December 1989*. Prague: Václav Havel Library, 2004

Price, C., ed., *Eastern Europe: A Monthly Survey of the Affairs of Central Eastern and South Eastern Europe. Incorporating The Balkan Review* 5:4–5 (June–July 1921). London: Rolls House Publishing

Prins, G., ed., *Spring in Winter: The 1989 Revolutions*. Manchester: Manchester University Press, 1990

Rašín, A., *Paměti Dra Aloise Rašína*. Prague: n.p., 1929

Rašla, A. and E. Žabkay, *Proces s dr. J. Tisom: Spomienky*. Bratislava: Tatrapress, 1990

Remington, R.A., ed., *Winter in Prague: Documents on Czechoslovak Communism in Crisis*. Cambridge, Mass.: MIT Press, 1969

Ripka, H., *Munich: Before and After*, tr. I. Šindelková and E. Young. London: Victor Gollancz, 1939

Ripka, H., 'The Possibilities of Central European Federation', *Central European Observer* (1 November 1940)

Ripka, H., *The Soviet-Czechoslovak Treaty: Speech Delivered before the State Council on the 15th December, 1943*. London: Czechoslovak Ministry of Foreign Affairs, 1943

Ripka, H., 'West and East', *European Observer*, 18:15 (25 July 1941), 1–2, 189–90

Robson, E., *A Wayfarer in Czecho-Slovakia*. London: Methuen, 1925

Rychlík, J., T. Marzik and M. Bielik, eds, *R.W. Seton-Watson and his Relations with the Czechs and Slovaks: Documents 1906–1951*, 2 vols. Martin: T.G. Masaryka/Matica Slovenská, 1995

Salivarová-Škvorecká, Z., ed., *Osočení: dopisy lidí ze seznamu*. Toronto: Sixty-Eight Publishers, 1993

Šejna, J., *We Will Bury You*. London: Sidgwick & Jackson, 1982

Seton-Watson, R., *Masaryk in England*. Cambridge and New York: Cambridge University Press and Macmillan, 1945

Seton-Watson, R., *The New Slovakia*. Prague: Borový, 1924

Shandor, V., *Carpatho-Ukraine in the Twentieth Century: A Political and Legal History*. Cambridge, Mass.: Ukrainian Research Institute, 1997

Sheppard, M., *Czechoslovakian Year [1936]*. London: Skeffington, 1938

Sidor, K., *Moje poznámky k historickým dňom*, ed. F. Vnuk. Middleton, Penn.: Cleveland and Rome, n.p., 1971

Sidor, K., *Šesť rokov pri Vatikáne*. Scranton, Pa.: Obrana Press, 1947

Šimečka, M., *Konec nehybnosti*. Prague: Lidové noviny, 1990

Šimečka, M., *Letters from Prison*, tr. G. Turner. Prague: Twisted Spoon Press, 2002

Šimečka, M., *The Restoration of Order: The Normalization of Czechoslovakia 1969–1976*, tr. A.G. Brain. London: Verso, 1984

Skilling, H.G. and P. Wilson, eds, *Civic Freedom in Central Europe: Voices from Czechoslovakia*. Basingstoke and London: Macmillan, 1991

Slánská, J., *Report on my Husband*, tr. E. Pargeter. London: Hutchinson, 1969

Šlingová, M., *Truth Will Prevail*. London: Merlin Press, 1968

Smrkovský, J., 'Jak nyní dál: Nad závěry lednového pléna ÚV KSČ', *Rudé právo* (9 February 1968), 2

Soukup, F., *28. říjen 1918*, 2 vols. Prague: Orbis, 1928

Sterling, C., *The Masaryk Case*. New York: Harper & Row, 1969

Stokes, G., ed., *From Stalinism to Pluralism: A Documentary History of Eastern Europe since 1945*, 2nd edn. New York and Oxford: Oxford University Press, 1996

Stransky, J., *East Wind over Prague*. London: World Affairs Book Club, 1950

[Švehla, A.], *Hovory s Antonín Švehlou (a o něm)*, ed. K. Čapek. Prague: Votobia, 2001.

Svoboda, A., *Prague*. Prague: Olympia, 1964 [1968 edn]

Svoboda, A., A. Tučková and V. Svobodová, *Spiknutí proti republice*. Prague: Melantrich, 1949

Táborský, E., *Czechoslovak Democracy at Work*. London: George Allen & Unwin, 1945

Tigrid, P., *Why Dubcek Fell*, tr. P. Tigrid and L. Lawrence. London: Macdonald, 1971 [1969]

Tiso, J., *Dr. Jozef Tiso o sebe (Obhajobná reč pred tzv. Národným súdom v Bratislave dňa 17. a 18. marca 1947)*. Passaic, N.J.: Nákladom a tlačou Slovenského Katolíckeho Sokola, 1952

Urban, G., *Radio Free Europe and the Pursuit of Democracy: My War within the Cold War*. New Haven, Conn. and London: Yale University Press, 1997

Ústav mezinárodních vztahů, *Vznik Československa 1918: Dokumenty československé zahraniční politiky*. Prague: Ústav mezinárodních vztahů, 1994

Vaculík, L., 'Naše slovenská otázka', *Literární noviny* (3 May 1990), 1

Vago, B., *The Shadow of the Swastika: The Rise of Fascism and Anti-Semitism in the Danube Basin, 1936–1939*. London: Institute of Jewish Affairs, 1975

Vaňek, M. and P. Urbášek, eds, *Vítězové? Poražení? Politické elity a disent v období tzv. normalizace*, 2 vols. Prague: Prostor, 2005

Voska, E. and W. Irwin, *Spy and Counterspy*. New York: Doubleday, Doran, 1940

Vrba, R., *I Escaped from Auschwitz*. London: Robson Books, 2006 [2002]

Wanklyn, H., *Czechoslovakia*. London: George Philip, 1954

Weil, J., *Život s hvězdou*. Prague: Mladá Fronta, 1964

Weisskopf, K., *The Agony of Czechoslovakia '38/'68*. London: Elek, 1968

Wheaton, B. and Z. Kavan, *The Velvet Revolution: Czechoslovakia 1988–1991*. Boulder, Colo., San Francisco and Oxford: Westview Press, 1992

Winch, M., *Republic for a Day: An Eye-Witness Account of the Carpatho-Ukraine Incident*. London: Robert Hale, 1939

Wiskemann, E., *The Europe I Saw*. London: Collins, 1968

Zábrana, J., *Celý život*, 2nd edn, vol. 1. Prague: Torst, 1993

Žatkuliak, J. et al., *November 1989 a Slovensko: Chronológia a dokumenty (1985–1990)*. Bratislava: Nadácia Milana Šimečku, 1999

Zeman, M., 'Jan Masaryk jak ho jsme znal', special supplement to *Svět v obrazech* (March 1948)

SECONDARY WORKS

Abrams, B., 'The Politics of Retribution: The Trial of Jozef Tiso', *East European Politics and Societies* 10:2 (1996), 255–92

Abrams, B., *The Struggle for the Soul of the Nation: Czech Culture and the Rise of Communism*. Lanham, Md.: Rowman & Littlefield, 2004 [paperback edn, 2005]

Adamson, K., 'Nicolae Ceauşescu, The Romanian Communist Party and 1968' (unpublished talk presented to the 'Remembering 1948 and 1968' conference held at the University of Glasgow, 4 April 2008)

Agnew, H., *The Czechs and the Lands of the Bohemian Crown*. Stanford, Cal.: Hoover Institution Press, 2004

Anon., *Československé dějiny v datech*, 2nd edn. Prague: Svoboda, 1987

Anon., *Dejiny štátu a práva na území Československa v období kapitalizmu 1848–1945*, 2 vols. Bratislava: Slovenská akadémie vied, 1973

Anon., '*Deportace českých Romů do Osvětimi*', http://www.holocaust.cz/cz2/history/rom/czech/czrom5 (15 November 2001)

Anon., *Julius Fučík ve fotografii*. Prague: Vydavatelství Novinář, 1977

Anon., *Kronika Českých zemí*. Prague: Fortuna Print, 1999

Anon., *Proměny sudetské krajiny*. [N.p.]: Nakladatelství Českého lesa, 2006.

Arendt, H., *The Origins of Totalitarianism*. San Diego, New York and London: Harcourt Brace, 1973

Bahm, K.F., 'The Inconveniences of Nationality: German Bohemians, the Disintegration of the Habsburg Monarchy, and the Attempt to Create a "Sudeten German" Identity', *Nationalities Papers* 27:3 (1999), 375–405

Barth, B., '*Wer war Noel Field? Die unbekannte Schluesselfigur der osteuropaeischen Schauprozesse*', in A. Leo and P. Reif-Spirek, eds, *Vielstimmiges Schweign: Neue Studien zum DDR-Antifaschismus*, tr. J. Schwarzmantel. Berlin: Metropol Verlag, 2001

Bartl, J., V. Čičaj, M. Kohútová *et al.*, *Slovak History: Chronology and Lexicon*, tr. D. Daniel. Bratislava and Wauconda, Ill.: Slovenské Pedagogické Nakladateľstvo and Bolchazy-Carducci Publishers, 2002

Bartuška, V., *Polojasno: Pátrání po vinících 17. listopadu 1989*. Prague: Ex Libris, 1990

Bell, P., *Origins of the Second World War*, 2nd edn. London and New York: Longman, 1997 [1986].

Berend, I., *Decades of Crisis: Central and Eastern Europe before World War II*. Berkeley: University of California Press, 1998

Bielik, L., *August 1968*. Bratislava: O.K.O., 2008

Bílek, J., *Pomocné technické prapory: o jedné z forem zneužití armády k politické perzekuci*. Prague: Úřad dokumentace a vyšetřování zločinů komunismu, 2002

Blaive, M., 'The Czechs and their Communism, Past and Present', *Inquiries into Past and Present*, ed. D. Gard, I. Main, M. Oliver and J. Wood. Vienna: Institut für die Wissenschaften vom Menschen, 2005

Bloomfield, J., *Passive Revolution: Politics and the Czechoslovak Working Class 1945–1948*. New York: St. Martin's Press, 1979

Břachová, V., '*Destrukce důstojnického sboru čs. armády po únoru 1948*', *Studie a články* 3 (Prague, 1993), 109–26

Bradley, J.F.N., *Czechoslovakia: A Short History*. Edinburgh: Edinburgh University Press, 1971

Bradley, J.F.N., *Czechoslovakia's Velvet Revolution: A Political Analysis*. Boulder, Colo.: Columbia University Press, 1992

Bradley, J.F.N., *The Czechoslovak Legion in Russia, 1914–1920*. Boulder, Colo.: East European Monographs, 1991

Brown, S., 'Prelude to a Divorce? The Prague Spring as a Dress Rehearsal for Czechoslovakia's "Velvet Divorce" ', *Europe-Asia Studies* 60:10 (December 2008), 1783–1804

Bruegel, J., *Czechoslovakia before Munich: The German Minority Problem and British Appeasement Policy*. Cambridge: Cambridge University Press, 1973

Bryant, C., *Prague in Black: Nazi Rule and Czech Nationalism*. Cambridge, Mass.: Harvard University Press, 2007

Bystrov, V. and J. Pergler, '*Kořeny StB v rakouském mocnářství*', *Lidové noviny* (13 August 1993), 16

Campbell, M., 'Keepers of Order? Strategic Legality in the 1935 Czechoslovak General Elections', *Nationalities Papers* 31:3 (September 2003), 295–308

Capoccia, G., 'Legislative Responses against Extremism. The "Protection of Democracy" in the First Czechoslovak Republic (1920–1938)', *East European Politics and Societies* 16:3 (2002), 691–738

Churaň, M. *et al.*, *Kdo byl kdo v našich dějinách ve 20. století*, 2 vols. Prague: Libri, 1998

Cohen, G., *The Politics of Ethnic Survival: Germans in Prague, 1861–1914*, 2nd edn. West Lafayette, Ind.: Purdue University Press, 2006

Cohen, S.J., *Politics without a Past: The Absence of History in Postcommunist Nationalism*. Durham, N.C. and London: Duke University Press, 1999

Conway, M., *Catholic Politics in Europe: 1918–1945*. London: Routledge, 1997

Cordell, K., *The Politics of Ethnicity in Central Europe*. London: Macmillan, 2000

Cornwall, M. and R. Evans, eds, *Czechoslovakia in a Nationalist and Fascist Europe 1918–1948*. Oxford: Oxford University Press, 2007

Cornwall, M., *The Undermining of Austria-Hungary: The Battle for Hearts and Minds*. Houndmills, Basingstoke: Macmillan Press, 2000

Crampton, R.J., *Eastern Europe in the Twentieth Century – and After*, 2nd edn. London and New York: Routledge, 1994; 1997

Crane, R.F., *A French Conscience in Prague: Louis Eugène Faucher and the Abandonment of Czechoslovakia*. Boulder, Colo.: East European Monographs, 1996

Čulík, J., *Jací jsme: česká společnost v hraném filmu devadesátých a nultých let*. Brno: Host, 2007

Čvančara, J., *Heydrich*. České Budějovice: Gallery, 2004

Davies, N., *Europe: A History*. London: Pimlico, 1997 (1996)

Davies, N., *Europe at War: No Simple Victory*. Basingstoke: Macmillan, 2006

Dawisha, K., *Eastern Europe Gorbachev and Reform: The Great Challenge*, 2nd edn. Cambridge: Cambridge University Press, 1988; 1990

Dawisha, K., *The Kremlin and the Prague Spring*. Berkeley: University of California Press, 1984

Demetz, P., *Prague in Black and Gold: Scenes in the Life of a European City*. New York: Hill & Wang, 1997

Dmytryshyn, B., 'The Legal Framework for the Sovietization of Czechoslovakia 1941–1945', *Nationalities Papers* 25:2 (1997), 255–68

Döge, K., 'Dvořák, Antonín', in S. Sadie, ed., *The New Grove Dictionary of Music and Musicians*, 29 vols, 2nd edn. London: Macmillan Publishers, 2001, vol. 7, 777–814

Dowling, M., *Czechoslovakia*. London: Arnold, 2002

El Mallakh, D.H., *The Slovak Autonomy Movement 1935–1939: A Study in Unrelenting Nationalism*. New York: Columbia University Press, 1979

Evans, R.J.W., *The Making of the Habsburg Monarchy 1550–1700: An Interpretation*. Oxford: Clarendon Press, 1979

Fawn, R., *The Czech Republic: A Nation of Velvet*. Amsterdam: Harwood Academic, 2000

Feinberg, M., *Elusive Equality: Gender, Citizenship and the Limits of Democracy in Czechoslovakia, 1918–1950*. Pittsburgh, Pa.: University of Pittsburgh Press, 2006

Felak, J., 'At the Price of the Republic': Hlinka's Slovak People's Party, 1929–1938*. Pittsburgh, Penn. and London: University of Pittsburgh Press, 1994

Ference, G.C., ed., *Chronology of 20th-Century Eastern European History*. Detroit, Washington, D.C. and London: Gale Research, 1994

Fiala, P. ed., *Politický extremismus a radikalismus v České republice*. Brno: Masarykova univerzita, 1998

Fisher, S., *Political Change in Post-Communist Slovakia and Croatia: From Nationalist to Europeanist*. New York: Palgrave Macmillan, 2006

Formánková, P., 'Kampaň proti "americkému brouku" a její politické souvislosti', *Studie a články: paměť a dějiny* 1 (2008), 22–38

Frommer, B., *National Cleansing: Retribution against Nazi Collaborators in Postwar Czechoslovakia*. Cambridge: Cambridge University Press, 2005

Galandauer, J., *Vznik Československé republiky 1918: Programy, projekty, předpoklady*. Prague: Svoboda, 1988

Galway, E., 'Restitution: The Case of the Roman Catholic Church in the Czech Republic' (unpublished University of Glasgow MA dissertation, 2002)

Gjuričová, J., *Na okraj: Romové jako objekt státní politiky*. Prague: Ministerstvo vnitra, 1999

Glaser, K., *Czecho-Slovakia: A Critical History*. Caldwell, Id.: The Caxton Printers, 1961

Glassheim, E., *Noble Nationalists: The Transformation of the Bohemian Aristocracy*. Cambridge, Mass.: Harvard University Press, 2005

Golan, G., *Reform Rule in Czechoslovakia: The Dubček Era 1968–1969*. Cambridge: Cambridge University Press, 1973

Green, D., 'Memories and Perceptions of Czechoslovakia's 1989 Revolution' (unpublished MRes thesis in Russian, Central and East European Studies, University of Glasgow, 2008)

Grzymala-Busse, A., 'Reform Efforts in the Czech and Slovak Communist Parties and their Successors, 1988–1993', *East European Politics and Societies* 12 (Fall 1998), 442–71

Guy, W., ed., *Between Past and Future: The Roma of Central and Eastern Europe*. Hatfield, Herts.: University of Hertfordshire Press, 2001

Havlík, T. and J. Fenyk, '*Trestná činnost příslušníků některých represivních orgánů v 50. letech*', *Prokuratura* 3–4 (Prague, 1992), 5–74

Havránek, J., 'Fascism in Czechoslovakia' in P. Sugar, ed., *Native Fascism in the Successor States 1918–1945*. Santa Barbara, Cal.: ABC-Clio Press, 1971, 47–55

Heimann, M., 'The Scheming *Apparatchik* of the Prague Spring', *Europe-Asia Studies* 60:10 (December 2008), 1717–34

Hermann, A.H., *A History of the Czechs*. London: Allen Lane/Penguin Books, 1975

Hochman, J., *Historical Dictionary of the Czech State*. Lanham, Md. and London: The Scarecrow Press, 1998

Hojda, Z. and J. Pokorný, *Pomníky a zapomníky*, 2nd edn. Prague: Litomyšl, 1997

Holy, L., *The Little Czech and the Great Czech Nation: National Identity and the Post-Communist Social Transformation*. Cambridge: Cambridge University Press, 1996

Hruby, P., *Fools and Heroes: The Changing Role of Communist Intellectuals in Czechoslovakia*. Oxford: Pergamon Press, 1980

Innes, A., *Czechoslovakia: The Short Goodbye*. New Haven, Conn. and London: Yale University Press, 2001

Jelinek, Y., *The Parish Republic: Hlinka's Slovak People's Party 1939–1945*. Boulder, Colo.: East European Quarterly, 1976

Jirásek, Z. and J. Šůla, *Velká peněžní loupež v Československu 1953 aneb 50:1*. Prague: Svítaní, 1992

Judson, P., *Guardians of the Nation: Activists on the Language Frontier of Imperial Austria*. Cambridge, Mass.: Harvard University Press, 2006

Judson, P. and M. Rozenblit, eds, *Constructing Nationalities in East Central Europe*. New York and Oxford: Berghahn Books, 2005

Kaiserová, K. and V. Kaiser, eds, *Dějiny města Ústí nad Labem*. Ústí nad Labem: Město Ústí nad Labem, 1995

Kalous, J., *Instruktážní skupina StB v lednu a únoru 1950*. Prague: Úřad dokumentace a vyšetřování zločinů komunismu, 2001

Kalous, J., '*Represe důstojnického sboru československé armády po roce 1945*', *Výchova k evropskému demokratickému občanství. Výchova v přerodu společnosti ČR z postkomunistické v demokratickou* (Prague, 1998), 144–54

Kalvoda, J., *The Genesis of Czechoslovakia*. Boulder, Colo.: East European Monographs, 1986

Kaminsky, H., 'John (Jan) Hus' and 'Hussites', in J.R. Strayer, ed., *Dictionary of the Middle Ages*, 13 vols (New York, 1982–89), vol. 6 (1985), 364–69 and 371–78

Kaplan, K., '*Cenzura 1945–1953*', *Sešity* 22 (1994), 8–17

Kaplan, K., 'Czechoslovakia's February 1948' in N. Stone and E. Strouhal, eds, *Czechoslovakia: Crossroads and Crises, 1918–1988*. Houndmills, Basingstoke: Macmillan, 1989

Kaplan, K., *Report on the Murder of the General Secretary*, tr. K. Kovanda. Columbus: Ohio State University Press, 1990

Kaplan, K., *The Short March: The Communist Takeover in Czechoslovakia, 1945–1948*, tr. from the German (1981) as *Der kurze Marsch. Kommunistische Machtübernahme in der Tschechoslowakei 1945–1948*. London: C. Hurst, 1987

Kaplan, K., *Stát a církev v Československu v letech 1948–1953*. Brno: Doplněk, 1993

Kaplan, K., '*Všechno jste prohráli!*' (*Co prozrazují archivy o IV. sjezdu Svazu československých spisovatelů 1967*). Prague: Ivo Železný, 1997

Keane, J., *Václav Havel: A Political Tragedy in Six Acts*. London: Bloomsbury, 1999

Kelly, D., *The Czech Fascist Movement 1922–1942*. Boulder, Colo.: East European Monographs, 1995

Kelly, T.M., *Without Remorse: Czech National Socialism in Late-Habsburg Austria*. Boulder, Colo.: East European Monographs, 2006

Kendrick, D., *Historical Dictionary of the Gypsies (Romanies)*. Lanham, Md.: Scarecrow Press, 1998

Kenety, B., 'The "Devouring": A Look at the Romani Holocaust', http://www.romove.cz (27 January 2005)

Kenney, P., *A Carnival of Revolution: Central Europe 1989*. Princeton, N.J. and Oxford: Princeton University Press, 2002

Kershaw, I., *The 'Hitler Myth': Image and Reality in the Third Reich*. Oxford: Clarendon Press, 1987

King, J., *Budweisers into Czechs and Germans*. Princeton, N.J.: Princeton University Press, 2002

Kirschbaum, J., 'Facts and Events behind the Scenes of Slovakia's Declaration of Independence', *Slovakia* 9:4 (1959), 1–7

Kirschbaum, J., 'The Politics of Hlinka's Slovak People's Party in the Slovak Republic', *Slovakia* 1:1 (1951), 43–49

Kirschbaum, S., *A History of Slovakia: The Struggle for Survival*. New York: St. Martin's/Griffin, 1995

Klimek, A., *Boj o hrad*. Prague: Panevropa, 1996

Kohn, H., 'Before 1918 in the Historic Lands' in Society for the History of Czechoslovak Jews, *The Jews of Czechoslovakia: Historical Studies and Surveys*, vol. 1. New York: Jewish Publication Society, 1968

Kontler, L., *A History of Hungary*. Houndmills, Basingstoke: Palgrave Macmillan, 2002

Kopecek, H., '*Zusammenarbeit* and *spoluprace*: Sudeten German-Czech Cooperation in Interwar Czechoslovakia', *Nationalities Papers* 24:1 (1996), 63–78

Korbel, J., *Twentieth-Century Czechoslovakia: The Meanings of its History*. New York: Columbia University Press, 1977

Kostka, V., 'Czechoslovakia' in J. Riordan, ed., *Sport under Communism*. London: C. Hurst, 1978

Ková č, D., *Dějiny Slovenska*. Prague: Lidové noviny, 1998

Kraus, M. and A. Stanger, eds and trs, *Irreconcilable Differences? Explaining Czechoslovakia's Dissolution*. Lanham, Md.: Rowman & Littlefield, 2000

Krejčí, J., *Czechoslovakia at the Crossroads of European History*. London and New York: I.B. Tauris, 1990

Krejčí, J., *Social Change and Stratification in Postwar Czechoslovakia*. London: Macmillan, 1972

Krygier, M., 'Ten Traps for Young Players in Times of Transition', *Budapest Papers on Democratic Transition*, no. 239. Budapest: Hungarian Center for Democracy Studies Foundation, 1999

Kučera, R., *Omyly české transformace (politické analýzy z let 1993–1998)*. Prague: Institut pro středoevropskou kulturu a politiku, n.d.

Kundera, M., *The Book of Laughter and Forgetting*, tr. A. Asher. London: Faber and Faber, 1996

Kural, V., Z. Radvanovský *et al., 'Sudety' pod hákovým křížem*. Ústí nad Labem: Albis International, 2002

Kusin, V., *From Dubček to Charter 77: A Study of 'Normalisation' in Czechoslovakia 1968–1978*. Edinburgh: Q Press, 1978

Kusin, V., *The Intellectual Origins of the Prague Spring: The Development of Reformist Ideas in Czechoslovakia*. Cambridge: Cambridge University Press, 1971

Lambert, M., *Medieval Heresy: Popular Movements from the Gregorian Reform to the Reformation*, 3rd edn. Oxford: Blackwell Publishing, 2002

Leff, C.S., *The Czech and Slovak Republics: Nation versus State*. Boulder, Colo.: Westview Press, 1997

Leff, C.S., *National Conflict in Czechoslovakia: The Making and Remaking of a State, 1918–1987*. Princeton, N.J.: Princeton University Press, 1988

Legters, L., *Eastern Europe: Transformation and Revolution, 1945–1991. Documents and Analyses*. Lexington, Mass.: D.C. Heath, 1992

Lehár, J., A. Stich, J. Janáčková and J. Holý, *Česká literatura od počátků k dnešku*, 5 vols. Prague: Lidové noviny, 1996–98

Lešanovský, K., *Se štítem a na štítě: Nezradili skautský slib*. Prague: Úřad dokumentace a vyšetřování zločinů komunismu, 2002

Lewis, F., *The Red Pawn: The Life of Noel Field*. Garden City, N.Y.: Doubleday, 1965

Lewy, G., *The Nazi Persecution of the Gypsies*. Oxford: Oxford University Press, 2000

Lukes, I., 'The Birth of a Police State: The Czechoslovak Ministry of Interior, 1945–48', *Intelligence and National Security* 11:1 (1996), 79–86

Luža, R., *The Transfer of the Sudeten Germans: A Study of Czech-German Relations, 1933–1962.* New York: New York University Press, 1964

Macartney, C., *Hungary and her Successors: The Treaty of Trianon and its Consequences.* London, New York and Toronto: Oxford University Press, 1937

MacDonald, C., *The Killing of SS Obergruppenführer Reinhard Heydrich.* London: Macmillan, 1989; 1990

Macura, V., 'Problems and Paradoxes of the National Revival' in M. Teich, ed., *Bohemia in History.* Cambridge: Cambridge University Press, 1998

Magocsi, P., *Historical Atlas of East Central Europe*, vol. 1. Seattle and London: University of Washington Press, 1995 [1993]

Magocsi, P., *The Rusyns of Slovakia: An Historical Survey.* New York: Columbia University Press, 1993

Magocsi, P., *The Shaping of a National Identity: Subcarpathian Rus' 1848–1948.* Cambridge, Mass.: Harvard University Press, 1978

Mamatey, V. and R. Luža, eds, *A History of the Czechoslovak Republic 1918–1948.* Princeton, N.J.: Princeton University Press, 1973

Mannová, E., ed., *A Concise History of Slovakia.* Bratislava: Historický ústav Slovenskej akadémie vied, 2000

Mason, J., 'Slovakia's Long Road to Democracy', *History Today* 18 (September 1998), 6–9

Mastny, V., *The Czechs under Nazi Rule: The Failure of National Resistance, 1939–1942.* New York: Columbia University Press, 1971

Matthews, J.P.C., *Majales: The Abortive Student Revolt in Czechoslovakia in 1956*, Woodrow Wilson International Center for Scholars, Cold War International History Project, Working Paper no. 24 (1998)

Mikuš, J.A., *Slovakia: A Political History, 1918–1950.* Milwaulkee, Wis.: Marquette University Press, 1963

Miller, D., *Forging Political Compromise: Antonín Švehla and the Czechoslovak Republican Party 1918–1933.* Pittsburgh, Penn.: University of Pittsburgh Press, 1999

Milyukov, P., 'Edward Beneš', *Slavonic and East European Review* 17 (January 1939), 297–328

Ministerstvo vnitra České republiky, *Securitas imperii. Sborník k problematice bezpečnostních služeb*, 9 vols. Prague: MVČR, 1994

Ministerstvo vnitra České republiky, *Zveřejnění evidenčních podkladů a seznamu personálních spisů*, 12 vols. Prague: Ministerstvo vnitra, 2003

Morison, J., ed., *The Czech and Slovak Experience: Selected Papers from the Fourth World Congress for Soviet and East European Studies, Harrogate 1990.* New York: St. Martin's Press, 1992

Musil, J., ed., *The End of Czechoslovakia*, 2nd edn. Budapest, London and New York: Central European University Press, 1997 [1995]

Myant, M., *The Czechoslovak Economy, 1948–1988.* Cambridge: Cambridge University Press, 1989

Myant, M., 'New Research on February 1948 in Czechoslovakia', *Europe-Asia Studies* 60:10 (December 2008), 1697–1715

Namier, L., *Diplomatic Prelude 1938–1939.* London: Macmillan, 1948

Navrátil, J., ed., *The Prague Spring 1968: A National Security Archive Documents Reader.* Budapest: Central European University Press, 1998

Nečas, C., *The Holocaust of the Czech Roma*, tr. Š. Pellar. Prague: Prostor, 1999

Němcová, A., 'Smetana, Bedřich' in S. Sadie, ed., *The New Grove Dictionary of Music and Musicians*, 29 vols, 2nd edn. London: Macmillan Publishers Ltd, 2001, vol. 23, 537–59

Nolte, C., 'Choosing Czech Identity in Nineteenth-Century Prague: The Case of Jindřich Fügner', *Nationalities Papers* 24:1 (1996), 51–62

Nolte, C., *The Sokol in the Czech Lands to 1914: Training for the Nation.* Houndmills, Basingstoke: Palgrave Macmillan, 2002

Nurmi, I., *Slovakia: A Playground for Nationalism and National Identity.* Helsinki: Suomen Historiallinen Seura, 1999

Nyrop, R. ed., *Czechoslovakia: A Country Study*. Washington, D.C.: U.S. Government Printing Office, 1982

Oddo, G., *Slovakia and its People*. New York: Robert Speller, 1960

Olivová, V., *The Doomed Democracy: Czechoslovakia in a Disrupted Europe 1914–38*, tr. G. Theiner. London: Sidgwick & Jackson, 1972

Otáhal, M., 'Czechoslovakia behind the Iron Curtain' in M. Teich, ed., *Bohemia in History*. Cambridge: Cambridge University Press, 1998

Oulík, J. and P. Sedláček, '*Nadpřirozený lev a modrý klín*', *Literární noviny* 43 (21 October 2002), 15

Paces, C., ' "The Czech Nation Must Be Catholic!" An Alternative Version of Czech Nationalism During the First Republic', *Nationalities Papers* 27:3 (1999), 407–28

Pacner, K., *Československo ve zvláštních službách: Pohledy do historie československých výzvědných služeb 1914–1989*, vol. 1. Prague: Themis, 2002

Parrott, C., *The Bad Bohemian: A Life of Jaroslav Hašek, Creator of the Good Soldier Švejk*. London, Sydney and Toronto: The Bodley Head, 1978

Parrott, C., *The Serpent and the Nightingale*. London: Faber and Faber, 1977

Pasák, T., *Emil Hácha (1938–1945)*. Prague: Rybka, 1996; 2007

Patočka, J., *Dvě studie o Masarykovi*. Toronto: Sixty-Eight Publishers, 1980

Perman, D., *The Shaping of the Czechoslovak State: Diplomatic History of the Boundaries of Czechoslovakia, 1914–1920*. Leiden: E.J. Brill, 1962

Peroutka, F., *Budování státu, 1918–1922*, 4 vols, 3rd edn. Brno-Horní: Spektrum, 1991

Péter, L. and R.B. Pynsent, eds, *Intellectuals and the Future in the Habsburg Monarchy 1890–1914*. Houndmills, Basingstoke: Macmillan, 1988

Petrův, H., *Právní postavení židů v Protektorátu Čechy a Morava*, 2 vols. Prague: Sefer, 2000; 2007

Pithart, P., 'The Break-Up of Czechoslovakia', *Scottish Affairs* 8 (Summer 1994), 20–24

Pithart, P., 'Towards a Shared Freedom, 1968–89' in J. Musil, ed., *The End of Czechoslovakia*. Budapest: Central European University Press, 1995

Poche, E., *Prahou krok za krokem*. Prague: Panorama, 1985

Polišenský, J., *Britain and Czechoslovakia: A Study in Contacts*, 2nd edn. Prague: Orbis, 1968

Povolný, D., *Operativní technika v rukou StB*. Prague: Úřad dokumentace a vyšetřování zločinů komunismu, 2001

Powell, R., 'Jan Masaryk', *Slavonic Review* 28 (1949–50), 332–41

Prečan, V., 'Dimensions of the Czechoslovak Crisis of 1967–1970', *Europe-Asia Studies* 60:10 (December 2008), 1659–76

Prečan, V., *Slovenský katolicizmus pred februárom*. Bratislava: Osveta, 1961

Procházka, T., *The Second Republic: The Disintegration of Post-Munich Czechoslovakia (October 1938–March 1939)*. Boulder, Colo.: East European Monographs, 1981

Pynsent, R.B., *Questions of Identity: Czech and Slovak Ideas of Nationality and Personality*. Budapest, London and New York: Central European University Press, 1994

Rageau, J.-P., *Prague 48: Le Rideau de fer s'est abattu*. Bruxelles: Éditions Complexe, 1981

Renner, H., *A History of Czechoslovakia since 1945*, tr. E. Hurst-Buist. London and New York: Routledge, 1989

Rice, C., *The Soviet Union and the Czechoslovak Army, 1948–1983*. Princeton, N.J.: Princeton University Press, 1984

Riordan, J., ed., *Sport under Communism: The U.S.S.R., Czechoslovakia, the G.D.R., China, Cuba*. London: C. Hurst, 1978

Robbins, K. *Appeasement*, 2nd edn. Oxford: Blackwell, 1997

Rothschild, J., *East Central Europe between the Two World Wars*. Seattle and London: University of Washington Press, 1992 [1974]

Rothschild, J., *Return to Diversity: A Political History of East Central Europe since World War II*, 2nd edn. New York and Oxford: Oxford University Press, 1993

Rupnik, J., *The Other Europe*. New York: Pantheon Books, 1988; 1989

Rychlík, J., '*Proces s Jozefem Tisem v roce 1947*', *Časopis český historický* 96, 3 (1998), 574–601

Sayer, D., *The Coasts of Bohemia: A Czech History*. Princeton, N.J.: Princeton University Press, 1998

Schelle, K., 'Rok 1918 a národní výbory', Správní právo, 16:7 (Prague, Ministerstvo vnitra, 1983), 400–15

Schling, H., 'Constructing the Enemy: Anti-Semitism, Dehumanisation and Physical Metamorphosis in Czechoslovak Communist Party Caricature of the Slánský Trials of 1952' (unpublished University of Oxford undergraduate dissertation, 2008)

Schwitzer, M., Slovakia: The Path to Nationhood. London and Bratislava: M.K. Schwitzer, 2002

Šedivý, I., Češi, České země a Velká válka 1914–1918. Prague: Lidové noviny, 2001

Seton-Watson, R., A History of the Czechs and Slovaks. London, New York and Melbourne: Hutchinson, 1943

Sharp, A., The Versailles Settlement: Peacemaking in Paris, 1919. Houndmills, Basingstoke and London: Macmillan, 1991

Shawcross, W., Dubcek: Dubcek and Czechoslovakia 1918–1990. London: Hogarth Press, 1990 [1970]

Šimulčík, J., Čas svitania: Sviečková manifestácia 25. marec 1988. Prešov: Vydavateľstvo Michala Vaška, 1998

Skilling, H.G., Charter 77 and Human Rights in Czechoslovakia. London: George Allen & Unwin, 1981

Skilling, H.G., ed., Czechoslovakia 1918–88: Seventy Years from Independence. Basingstoke: Macmillan, 1991

Skilling, H.G., Czechoslovakia's Interrupted Revolution. Princeton, N.J.: Princeton University Press, 1976

Skilling, H.G., Samizdat and an Independent Society in Central and Eastern Europe. Houndmills, Basingstoke and London: Macmillan, 1989

Skinner, S., 'How Distinctly Czech was the Velvet Revolution of 1989?' (University of Strathclyde unpublished Independent Study Project, 1999)

Smelser, R., 'The Expulsion of the Sudeten Germans: 1945–1952', Nationalities Papers 24:1 (1996), 79–92

Smelser, R., The Sudeten Problem: Volkstumspolitik and the Formulation of Nazi Foreign Policy, 1933–1938. Folkestone, Kent: Dawson, 1975

Society for the History of Czechoslovak Jews, The Jews of Czechoslovakia, vol. 2. Philadelphia and New York: The Jewish Publication Society of America and the Society for the History of Czechoslovak Jews, 1971

Sperber, J., The European Revolutions, 1848–1851. Cambridge: Cambridge University Press, 1994

Staněk, T., Perzekuce 1945. Prague: Institut pro středoevropskou kulturu a politiku, 1996

Staněk, T., Tábory v českých zemích 1945–1948. Ostrava: Tilia, 1996

Stein, E., Czecho/Slovakia: Ethnic Conflict, Constitutional Fissure, Negotiated Breakup. Ann Arbor: University of Michigan Press, 1997; 2000

Steiner, E., The Slovak Dilemma. Cambridge: University of Cambridge Press, 1973

Stich, A., 'Rané obrození' in J. Lehár, A. Stich, J. Janáčková and J. Holý, Česká literatura od počátků k dnešku. Prague: Lidové noviny, 1997, 1998

Stone, N. and E. Strouhal, eds, Czechoslovakia: Crossroads and Crises, 1918–88. Houndmills, Basingstoke and London: Macmillan, 1989

Ströbinger, R. and K. Nešvera, Stalo se v Adventu: 'čihošťský zázrak'. Prague: Vyšehrad, 1990

Stronge, H., 'The Czechoslovak Army and the Munich Crisis: A Personal Memorandum' in B. Bond and I. Roy, eds, War and Society. London: Croom Helm, 1975

Suda, Z., The Czechoslovak Socialist Republic. Baltimore, Md.: The Johns Hopkins University Press, 1969

Suda, Z., Zealots and Rebels: A History of the Ruling Communist Party of Czechoslovakia. Stanford, Cal.: Hoover Institution Press, 1980

Sugar, P., ed., Native Fascism in the Successor States 1918–1945. Santa Barbara, Cal.: ABC-Clio, 1971

Sugar, P. and I. Lederer, Nationalism in Eastern Europe. Seattle and Washington: University of Washington Press, 1971 [1969]

Suk, J., *Labyrintem revoluce: aktéři, zápletky a křižovatky jedné politické krize (od listopadu 1989 do června 1990)*. Prague: Prostor, 2003

Szomolanyi, S., 'Was the Dissolution of Czechoslovakia Inevitable?', *Scottish Affairs* 8 (Summer 1994), 31–43

Taylor, A.J.P., *The Habsburg Monarchy 1809–1918*. London: Penguin Books, 1948 [1990 edn]

Taylor, T., *Munich: The Price of Peace*. Garden City, New York: Doubleday, 1979

Teich, M., ed., *Bohemia in History*. Cambridge: Cambridge University Press, 1998

Teichova, A., *An Economic Background to Munich: International Business and Czechoslovakia 1918–1938*. Cambridge: Cambridge University Press, 1974

Tomek, P., *Dvě studie o československém vězeňství 1948–1989*. Úřad dokumentace a vyšetřování zločinů komunismu, 2000

Ullmann, W., *The United States in Prague, 1945–1948*. Boulder, Colo.: East European Quarterly, 1978

Unowsky, D., *The Pomp and Politics of Patriotism: Imperial Celebrations in Habsburg Austria, 1848–1916*. West Lafayette, Ind.: Purdue University Press, 2005

Unterberger, B., *The United States, Revolutionary Russia and the Rise of Czechoslovakia*. College Station: Texas A & M University, 2000 (1989)

Urban, O., *České a slovenské dějiny do roku 1918*. Prague: Svoboda, 1991

Urban, O., *Petite histoire des pays tchèques*, tr. M. Braud. Paris: Institut d'Etudes Slaves, 1996

Valdez, J., *Internationalism and the Ideology of Soviet Influence in Eastern Europe*. Cambridge: Cambridge University Press, 1993

Vaněk, M., ed., *Mocní? a bezmocní? Politické elity a disent v období tzv. normalizace*. Prague: Prostor, 2006

Vnuk, F., 'Slovakia's Six Eventful Months (October 1938–March 1939)', *Slovak Studies* 4 (Rome and Bratislava, 1964), 7–164

Vykoupil, L., *Slovník českých dějin*. Brno: Georgetown, 1994

Wallace, K., 'Edvard Beneš and the Sudeten German Expulsions, 1938–1945' (University of Strathclyde unpublished Independent Study Project, 1999)

Wallace, W., *Czechoslovakia*. London and Tonbridge: Ernest Benn, 1976

Wheeler-Bennett, J., *Munich: Prologue to Tragedy*. London: Macmillan, 1963

Wightman, G. and A.H. Brown, 'Changes in the Levels of Membership and Social Composition of the Communist Party of Czechoslovakia, 1945–73', *Soviet Studies* 27:3 (July 1975), 396–417

Williams, K., *The Prague Spring and its Aftermath: Czechoslovak Politics 1968–1970*. Cambridge: Cambridge University Press, 1997

Williams, K. and D. Deletant, *Security Intelligence in New Democracies: The Czech Republic, Slovakia and Romania*. Houndmills, Basingstoke: Palgrave, 2001

Wilson, F., *Aftermath: France, Germany, Austria, Yugoslavia 1945 and 1946*. Harmondsworth: Penguin Books, 1947

Wingfield, N., 'The Battle of Zborov and the Politics of Commemoration in Czechoslovakia', *East European Politics and Societies* 17:4 (Fall 2003), 654–81

Wingfield, N., 'Czech-Sudeten German Relations in Light of the "Velvet Revolution": Post-Communist Interpretations', *Nationalities Papers* 24:1 (1996), 93–106

Wiskemann, E., *Czechs and Germans: A Study of the Struggle in the Historic Provinces of Bohemia and Moravia*. London, New York, Toronto: Oxford University Press, 1938

Wojatsek, C., *From Trianon to the First Vienna Arbitral Award: The Hungarian Minority in the First Czechoslovak Republic 1918–1938*. Montréal: Institut des civilisations comparées/Institute of Comparative Civilizations, 1980

Wolchik, S., *Czechoslovakia in Transition: Politics, Economics and Society*. London and New York: Pinter, 1991

Zacek, J., 'Czechoslovak Fascisms' in P. Sugar, ed., *Native Fascism in the Successor States 1918–1945*. Santa Barbara, Cal.: ABC-Clio Press, 1971, 56–62

Zahra, T., 'Reclaiming Children for the Nation: Germanization, National Ascription, and Democracy in the Bohemian Lands, 1900–1945', *Central European History* 37:4 (2004), 501–43

Žatkuliak, J., ed., *November 1989 a Slovensko: Chronológia a dokumenty (1985–1990)*. Bratislava: Nadácia Milana Šimečku a Historický ústav SAV, 1999.

Zeman, Z. and A. Klimek, *The Life of Edvard Beneš 1884–1948: Czechoslovakia in Peace and War*. Oxford: Clarendon Press, 1997

Zeman, Z., *The Masaryks: The Making of Czechoslovakia*. London: I.B. Tauris, 1990 [1976]

Zinner, P., *Communist Strategy and Tactics in Czechoslovakia, 1918–48*. London and Dunmow: Pall Mall Press, 1963

INDEX

NOTE: The names for the various incarnations of the state of Czechoslovakia are given as individual index headings along with the relevant dates. They are listed at the entry for Czechoslovakia.